ALSO BY VERA STRAVINSKY
Fantastic Cities and Other Paintings

ALSO BY ROBERT CRAFT
Current Convictions

BY THE SAME AUTHORS
Stravinsky: The American Period (in preparation)

STRA

VINSKY

in pictures
and documents

by
VERA STRAVINSKY
and
ROBERT CRAFT

SIMON AND SCHUSTER   NEW YORK

Copyright © 1978 by Vera Stravinsky, Trapezoid, Inc., and Robert Craft
All rights reserved
including the right of reproduction
in whole or in part in any form
Published by Simon & Schuster
A Division of Gulf & Western Corporation
Simon & Schuster Building
Rockefeller Center
1230 Avenue of the Americas
New York, New York 10020
Designed by Edith Fowler
Manufactured in the United States of America

1   2   3   4   5   6   7   8   9   10

Library of Congress Cataloging in Publication Data

Stravinsky, Vera.
    Stravinsky in pictures and documents.

    Bibliography: p.
    Includes index.
    1.   Stravinskiĭ, Igor Fedorovich, 1882–1971.
    2.   Composers—Biography. I. Craft, Robert, joint author.
    I.   Title.
    L410.S932S787   780'.92'4 [B]   78-15375

    ISBN 0-671-24382-9

Acknowledgments

The authors are grateful to photographers known and unknown, among the former, Henri Cartier-Bresson, Ernst Haas, Gjon Mili, Arnold Newman, Wolf Koenig, and Lord Snowdon; to Mrs. Helen Wright, who has given freely of her time and knowledge of photography; to Edwin Allen for his research, and for generously sharing his vast knowledge of Stravinsky's world; to Richard Buckle, for exchanging biographical data about Diaghilev; to Robert Fizdale and Arthur Gold, for information concerning Misia Sert; to Robert Silvers, Barbara Epstein, Elbert Lenrow, Lawrence Morton, and Phyllis Crawford for correcting parts of the text and for helpful suggestions; to Richard Burgi for translating Stravinsky's poem on Plate 31; to Arnold Arnstein for his copies of musical excerpts; to Martin Garbus and Helene Kaplan for their valuable advice; to Susan Dorlen, Donna Wright, Patricia Crain, and Kristin Crawford for typing the manuscript; and to Alice Mayhew, Edith Fowler, Sophie Sorkin, and the entire production department of Simon and Schuster, whose talents and belief in the book brought it to fulfillment.

The authors also wish thank the editors of the following publications for permission to use material that, in different form, originally appeared in their periodicals: *The New York Review of Books, The Times Literary Supplement, Encounter, Dance* magazine, *Ballet Review, The Saturday Review, The Musical Quarterly,* and *Tempo.*

The publishers of Stravinsky's music have kindly given their permission to reproduce passages from original manuscripts of *Petrushka, The Nightingale, Three Japanese Lyrics, Le Sacre du Printemps, Three Pieces for String Quartet, Symphonies of Wind Instruments, Oedipus Rex, Apollo, Capriccio, Symphony of Psalms, Duo Concertant, The Rake's Progress, Septet, Agon, Abraham and Isaac, Variations, Introitus, Requiem Canticles,* "Wunden Trägst Du . . ." and an unfinished orchestra piece (Boosey & Hawkes, Ltd., London); *The Firebird, Pribaoutki, Berceuses du Chat, Renard, Histoire du Soldat,* and *Les Noces* (J. & W. Chester, Ltd., London); and *Jeu de Cartes, Symphony in C,* and *Symphony in Three Movements* (B. Schott's Söhne, Mainz).

To the memory of Igor Stravinsky

He was one of those few whose history is the history of their own time, who are a part of the consciousness of an age which cannot be understood without them.

—T. S. Eliot on W. B. Yeats

Contents

Preface

This portrait of Stravinsky in pictures and documents comprises an album of vignettes rather than a full-scale biography. Nevertheless, the photographs represent every period of Stravinsky's life and are a very moving record of his growth, maturity, and aging. It hardly needs to be said that the life that passes before the reader from picture to picture is one of the richest, most productive, and most exciting of this century. But nearly eighty-nine years, more than sixty of which were lived in the public arena, engendered a mountain of factual material. Stravinsky kept copies of his own letters, and saved most letters written to him, as well as countless references in publications. He also preserved hundreds of photographs of himself, often adding the word "I" under pictures that could not conceivably be mistaken for anyone else. (The ego was Wagnerian, the reader might say, or, as the next century will say, Stravinskyan; but this is part of the man.) The information from the pictures has been collated with that from other documents in an attempt to present as broad a view as is possible as background for the letters, diaries, memoirs of friends and other observers.

Countless snapshots and portraits by professional photographers reveal that Igor Stravinsky was extraordinarily photogenic. Therefore, one of the principal problems in compiling this book was to select from the abundance of pictures of the man. Another was the difficulty in choosing music for illustration, since almost all of his compositions seem equally representative. Not all could be included, of course, and sketches for such major works as the Octet, Concerto in E-flat, and *A Sermon, a Narrative, and a Prayer* are regrettably absent from the text.

Although Stravinsky's name is associated more widely with his creations for the stage than with his concert music, the book contains comparatively few pictures relating to his life in the theater. Because the visual aspects of his ballets and operas are already familiar from books of set and costume designs and from photographic histories of the scenic and choreographic arts, here he is shown more often with friends than with prima donnas and ballerinas. Rather than offering another panorama of peripheral artwork, this volume presents reproductions of the composer's manuscripts, many of them in color. Considered as calligraphic specimens, they are unsurpassed. In fact, when Stravinsky gave the holograph score of *Apollon Musagète* to the Library of Congress, in 1928, the manuscript was returned to him with a note requesting "the original, not a copy." ·

The reason for including only three views of Stravinsky conducting is that film reels of him leading orchestras are readily available [1] and, by their nature, incomparably more satisfactory in this regard than still photographs. Also, though concertizing and recording consumed a large part of his time, these were secondary occupations. Not that it is possible to describe the primary one, composing, but the manuscripts assembled here seem to give some sense of the presence of the composer.

Stravinsky was an amateur photographer,[2] and of the thousand and more photos which he took before 1940, he captioned, mounted, and filed a great many himself. Yet the score or more in the present volume have been included less for their merits as photography than for the importance of the subjects: Rimsky-Korsakov, Debussy, Diaghilev, Nijinsky, Ravel, and others. After 1940, as well as before, Stravinsky remained a connoisseur of the photographer's art, and throughout his life he kept scrapbooks of pictures of the people, plants, and especially animals that he had clipped from magazines and newspapers.

Like Stravinsky's life and works, the book naturally divides into three periods: the Russian and Swiss years, the two decades in France, and the three in America. The arrangement by subject is not strictly chronological, the narrative sometimes digressing, and taking the story further in time than the general narrative, in order to encompass in their entirety the chronicles of the creation of such works as *Le Sacre du Printemps*, and of such subjects as Stravinsky's relationships with the Rimsky-Korsakovs and with Debussy.

Throughout his life, Stravinsky used both the Old and New Style Russian calendars, but inconsistently, and frequently without specification. Every effort has been made to determine the New Style dates, though in many cases these are unverifiable. Except when otherwise noted, all dates in this book are New Style, the authors having made the required transpositions; but errors are unavoidable.

In the spelling of ordinary Russian words, let alone of Russian names, it seems best to admit defeat. "Koussevitzky" is as firmly established in America as "Kussevitzky" in England. But the assumption is erroneous that English and American readers will pronounce the French "j"—in "Nijinsky," for example—and such a supposition should be opposed, at least in cases where these orthographies have not already been consecrated by usage. To the present writer, too, it seems unnatural to spell Stravinsky's patronymic "Feodorovich," instead of, as he pronounced it, the four-syllable "Fyodorovich."

Stravinsky favored the Russian titles for some of his works— *Zhar-Ptitza, Vesna Sviasschennaya, Solovey, Svadebka*—but the reader would scarcely have time to become familiar with them in this book. Of the second and fourth of these compositions Stravinsky preferred the French titles (*Le Sacre du Printemps, Les Noces*) to the English, and of the other two (*The Firebird, The Nightingale*), the English to thè French. He also objected to the use of the French spelling of *Pétrouchka* in English-speaking countries, especially since many Americans had fallen into the habit of pronouncing the name with a hard "ch."

Russian is the original language of the excerpts from most of Stravinsky's letters in Part One, but many of his interviews during the same period were conducted in French, a fact not mentioned by newspapers quoting him. In Parts Two and Three, the language of the original letters and documents is noted where it is not obvious. Translations from the Russian were made by Mrs. Vera Stravinsky, Mr. Henry Cooper, Mr. and Mrs. Franklin Reeve, Mr. Edwin Allen, Mrs. Lucia Davidova. Miss Kristin Crawford made the translations from the Spanish, the present writer those from the French and Italian. Limitations of space confined the bibliography to the most important of those publications, in Russian and English only, which have appeared since Stravinsky's death and which required commentary and the corrections of errors that might otherwise have become accepted as historical fact.

The biographer of a man as complex as Stravinsky has many courses from which to choose. At present, when so much remains to be learned and the assembling of the purely factual context has barely begun, the most feasible method seemed to be that of indicating some of Stravinsky's immense variety rather than of pursuing any one aspect of the man or of his life. This accounts for the very limited amount of detail concerning the music, but, in any case, the book is intended not for specialists but for general readers. It reflects this author's feelings about Stravinsky seven years after his death.

R.C.
July 1978

1. The best of these were made by the CBC in Toronto (in 1962, 1963, 1967), CBS in New York (1965), Eurovision in Hamburg (1965), and—the finest of all films of Stravinsky conducting—by the BBC in Festival Hall, London, September 1965. But many of Stravinsky's concert performances all over the world were televised and preserved, beginning with his first telecast on January 14, 1954, WGN Chicago, and including an appearance on Television Bogotá, August 11, 1960. Moreover, a great number of films of him conducting have been made by orchestra players from as early as 1935 (by Philip Kahgan, a violist in the Los Angeles Philharmonic; Stravinsky wrote in his diary, Sunday, June 26, 1960: "Dinner at Phil Kaghan [sic] . . . we saw old films Kaghan made . . . In 1935, myself, Schoenberg, Klemperer. How far away!!") to as late as 1966, when the tuba player in the New York Philharmonic (Sam Butterfield) photographed Stravinsky rehearsing the *Symphony of Psalms*.

2. "Wherever he goes he takes his camera. When friends persuaded him to go and see Niagara Falls . . . he snapped scores of pictures." (*Newsweek*, January 23, 1937)

Part One

IN RUSSIA
AND SWITZERLAND,
1882-1920

Travels in
Germany,
France,
Italy,
England,
Austria-Hungary,
Spain

In later life, Igor Stravinsky described his youth as obsessed by music, with the outstanding events of his early years being private musical discoveries and the concerts and operas that he attended. But his childhood associates, especially the female cousins with whom he spent each summer from age fourteen in the Ukrainian village of Ustilug, may not have been aware of this, let alone of his musical gifts. His piano playing was not sufficiently precocious to warrant parental aspirations of a virtuoso's career for him, nor did his early compositions bear substantial evidence of originality. In short, and no matter what his cousins and others might have thought of him, Stravinsky at twenty seems to have been something of a dilettante, at least when compared to his contemporaries Prokofiev and Glazunov, who were established composers while still in their teens.

The only early letters by Stravinsky that have been published to date (1978) refer less frequently to practicing the piano than to painting, and to acting in amateur theatricals, which was one of his greatest pleasures. The following excerpts are from letters to his parents written in Ustilug during his seventeenth and nineteenth years:

... This is the schedule of our day: after morning tea all three of us, Katia,[1] Olga Dmitrievna,[2] and I look for a suitable spot where we can sketch. Gury[3] and Vera Dmitrievna[4] learn their parts for the play on the tennis court. Sofiya Dmitrievna[5] and Olga Ivanovna[6] hull raspberries, which grow here in great abundance. Then we have breakfast. After that, if it doesn't rain, the three of us again set out to sketch, but until yesterday it has drizzled steadily since our arrival. . . .

I have made a sketch of a sunset . . . and now would like to have the opportunity to see a number of good pictures so that I can become even more dissatisfied with my own work. Only in such circumstances can I be certain of making progress. . . .

We play the piano a lot. I am not reading much. All the same, I've finished [Tolstoy's] *Resurrection* and have derived the highest pleasure from this brilliant work by Lev Nikolayevich. The most recent numbers are the most striking. I do not know if they have reached you and whether you are reading them. If so, give me your impressions. Probably the same as mine. [I have also read] Guyau's *The Problems of Contemporary Aesthetics*,[7] which contains some interesting discussions.

Today, we—Dmitri Andreyevich and all the young people—are going to Vladimir-Volynsk to buy props for the theater. The production will probably take place in a week. The plays are [Hartmann's] *Seize Your Chance While You May* and [Chekhov's] *The Bear*, in both of which I have important parts. I know them—how could I not—but cannot predict how successful the performances are going to be. [Letter of July 21, 1899, from Ustilug]

The first paragraph of this letter might have been by Chekhov, to be read by a character in a story or a play. But Stravinsky's remark about wanting to see good pictures in order to become dissatisfied with his own work is so characteristic that he could have uttered it at any time throughout his life. All of his life, too, Stravinsky complained that he had been handicapped in his youth by his isolation from an intellectually stimulating environment. In his mind, the unique advantage of his early years was the wide traveling he had enjoyed, both in Russia—he especially cherished his trips on the Volga—and in Germany and Switzerland. By almost any other person's standards, of course, he would be considered unusually privileged, but Stravinsky did not think so, and, even in his seventies, would blame his intellectual and artistic "shortcomings" on his repressive family and its lack of interest in new ideas.

Other letters to his parents, written that summer and the next, describe more theatrical activity. Two of these communications, from Ustilug, in July 1900 and July 1901 respectively, reveal further aspects of Stravinsky's personality. The second, a meticulous accounting of expenditures on a journey, is typical of his carefulness about money and of the kind of bookkeeping he habitually practiced. (See Illustration, page 458.) It seems probable that his parents demanded this; hence that "stinginess," even with his music, of which he liked to boast, may have been a family trait. Here is the nineteen-year-old artist's description of travel in Russia in terms of rubles and kopeks, rather than of inspiring sunsets for future sketching:

With all my care and economy . . . the journey cost 26 rubles and 45 kopeks; ticket: 8 rubles and 70 kopeks; baggage: 1 ruble and 30 kopeks; journey by horse: 5 rubles and 70 kopeks (and 20 kopeks for tea); transport of basket from Kovel to Ustilug: 4 rubles and 50 kopeks (and this was by private arrangement—if it.had gone by post, the cost would have been 3 rubles). . . . Now the minor expenses: porters: 1 ruble and 60 kopeks; refreshments at the station: 1 ruble and 95 kopeks; at Kovel: 30 kopeks between the station and the carriage. The porters were comparatively expensive, 50 kopeks to each of the other three, at Proskurov,[8] Zhmerinka,[9] and Kazatin. . . . The cost for the short stretch of 18 versts from Turizhisk to Kovel was 1 ruble and 50 kopeks. But enough of all this. . . .[10] [Letter of July 30, 1901]

The other letter shows Stravinsky's response to kindness as well as his sensitivity about his size—for he was a head shorter than his younger brother, and the reference to the "superior height" of others is physical, as well as to the attitude *"de haut en bas"*:

Meeting with kindness in another, you become doubly attached to that person, drawing closer and understanding him more easily. . . . I see this all the time in the case of Katenka [11] and am moved by it. Unfortunately I do not find it in Mila,[12] but, since people's characters are so different, I will not reproach her for that. I cannot abide it when others look down on me from their superior height. Something of that condescension is in Milochka, in her constant light irony about everything I say. . . . As to myself, I do not waste any time—I sketch, I read, I play. [Letter of July 27, 1901]

In 1901, Stravinsky received his certificate of admission to study law at St. Petersburg University, thus following in the footsteps of his father, who had pursued a law degree at the University of Kiev. Also in 1901, Stravinsky appeared for the first time in public as a pianist, in the role of accompanist in a recital. His father died the next year. Some months before his death, and by this time possibly with intimations that his son might have talent as a composer, Fyodor Stravinsky had entrusted him to Rimsky-Korsakov, although the young man was not ready to become a regular pupil.

The acquaintance with Rimsky-Korsakov immediately gained Stravinsky admission to a circle of musicians, writers, and intelligentsia for whose society he had been longing. This group was a nucleus of liberalism, and the newcomer became an ardent disciple in this as in everything else—a fact worth mentioning only because, later in life, Stravinsky recalled his political inclinations of the time somewhat differently.

. . . We couldn't live quietly where the revolutionary ferment is strongest. Meetings and clashes are everywhere there, and the ship crews strike almost daily. . . . It is impossible to live in such a boiling pot unless one is indifferent to the life around one, and unless one looks upon the great Russian Revolution with hatred. As you know, we are of the opposite conviction. [Letter of July 1906]

A letter of March 1908 to the composer and critic G. H. Timofeyev is the equivalent of a *Who's Who* entry and provides a brief autobiography of Stravinsky's early years as well as verification of the remarkable accuracy of the composer's memory in his seventies, for his much later "Conversation" books contain substantially the same information:

I was born in Oranienbaum [13] on June 18, 1882. At the age of nine I began to take piano lessons from A. P. Snyetkova, the daughter of the violinist in the Maryinsky Theater orchestra. At eleven I entered St.

Petersburg School No. 27, where I was a poor student as well as an ill-behaved one. I remained there until the end of the fifth grade, then entered the Gurevich School. Here I completed my intermediate education. I then went to St. Petersburg University for a total of eight semesters.

Hoping to make a pianist of me, my parents did not stint on the cost of teachers but gave me the opportunity to study with the very best ones, such as L. A. Kashperova, from whom I took lessons for two years. But I was attracted to composition before that and have always had a lively interest in the musical classics. I did a large amount of sight-reading, which helped my development. The lack of education in theory became an ever greater obstacle, however, and though I improvised endlessly and enjoyed it immensely, I was unable to write down what I played. I ascribed this to my lack of theoretical knowledge. Until I began to take lessons in harmony from Akimenko, you might say that I ripened in ignorance. But I soon switched from him to K. V. Kalafati, with whom I studied harmony and counterpoint.

In my University years I became friendly with the Rimsky-Korsakov family and then advanced very rapidly. I composed many comic songs, especially to the words of *Koz'ma Prutkov*,[14] and in 1903–1904 wrote a large—four-movement—Piano Sonata in F-sharp minor,[15] incorporating many suggestions by Rimsky-Korsakov. It was performed at his home by [Nicolas] Richter, the pianist to whom it is dedicated. In 1906 I composed a Suite, *The Faun and the Shepherdess*, and in the summer of the same year composed a song, *Spring*, to words by Gorodyetsky. This winter I wrote the Pastorale,[16] a song without words, and now I am finishing the *Scherzo Fantastique*, for orchestra.[17]

Stravinsky does not mention the earliest of his surviving compositions, the *Scherzo* for piano and *Storm Cloud*, a romance for voice and piano on Pushkin's text; both works were composed in 1902.

Writing to Vladimir Vladimirovitch Derzhanovsky,[18] after *The Firebird* and *Petrushka* had formed Stravinsky's critical perspectives, he professed to be

. . . not at all ashamed of the Symphony. . . . It is my first opus. It has a few nice passages, but the rest of it crudely follows the Glazunov-Tchaikovsky style, and the instrumentation is official. The piece is interesting not in itself but as a document to show once more how *not* to compose. . . .

In this, the habit of self-criticism is again revealed as one of Stravinsky's predominant qualities. But the Symphony and all of the other early works together are hardly a cornucopia from a composer of genius in his mid-twenties. On the contrary, his pre-*Firebird* creations are surprisingly plodding, evincing little more than an acquisition of competence in other composers' idioms. His leap from academic anonymity into *The Firebird* is extraordinarily sudden, and his own voice is at times clearer in his words than in his music, as, for example, in this pharmaceutical metaphor in a letter to Rimsky-Korsakov:

The harmony in "Bees"[19] will be fierce, like a toothache, but should immediately alternate with agreeable harmony, like cocaine.

If the foregoing inventory of compositions had been drafted a year and a half later, it would have contained the *Chant Funèbre* for Rimsky-Korsakov (d. 1908), as well as four piano *Etudes*, and *Fireworks*, the score that captured the attention of Diaghilev, though precisely when the impresario first heard it has not been established. It had been performed three times privately before Siloti's [20] concert of January 22, 1910—on a program, incidentally, that included the Schumann Cello Concerto played by Pablo Casals. Apropos the conductor for that night, Stravinsky was later to write, "It seems that Siloti intends to specialize in the failure of our compositions," a comment that expressed the composer's lifelong feelings about most orchestra-directing *maestri*.

From the vantage point of today, the true landmarks of this century's music appeared in the years immediately before World War I. A note dated April 4, 1913, to G. P. Jurgenson,[21] Stravinsky's Moscow publisher, bears witness to the young composer's musical leadership even before *Le Sacre du Printemps* had been performed:

Esteemed Grigory Petrovich! . . . a concert is planned for May—probably toward the end, New Style—for which I have been asked to give *Zvezdoliki*.[22] I am therefore turning to you with the request to hasten the printing of the score as well as to copy the parts. You can check these against the manuscript, and we will make the corrections at rehearsals. . . . This concert is very important. It . . . will be dedicated to contemporary music, the newest trends of various nations. From Germany, Schoenberg; from France, Debussy; from England, Cyril Scott; [23] from Hungary, Bartók; from Russia, I.

Thus, within two years, and on the strength of *The Firebird* and *Petrushka* alone, Stravinsky gained recognition as one of the foremost composers in Europe. He was the youngest of these five, and, most important of all to him, the representative Russian.

Surely this acclaim explains the ill-concealed envy of Stravinsky's colleagues in St. Petersburg. When the *Firebird* Suite was first performed there,[24] no member of the Rimsky-Korsakov family wrote to him about the event. Stravinsky had wanted them to come to the Paris premiere and was deeply disappointed when they did not.[25] It may have been naïve on his part not to have anticipated their reactions to his success, but the recognition of his genius was as much of a surprise to him as it was to his friends. He regarded *The Firebird* as a phenomenon only accidentally related to himself, and he genuinely wanted to share its beauties and discoveries with them. "I take no pride in my artistic talents," he later told one of his biographers, Domenico di Paoli; "they are God-given and I see absolutely no reason to become puffed up over something that one has received." [26] But Stravinsky's letters to the Rimsky-Korsakovs are psychologically revealing, demonstrating as they do that the young musician turned to them as to a substitute family.

In Berlin, June 30, 1910, en route to Russia after the first performances of *The Firebird*, Stravinsky wrote to Rimsky-Korsakov's widow [27]—at 3:43 A.M., which indicates how deeply the matter was on his mind:

> I greatly regret that you and Andrey did not witness my success. *The Firebird* was more acclaimed than any other ballet this season.... Write to me in Ustilug. I will be happy to have even a small letter from you.

But the Ballets Russes performed works by Rimsky-Korsakov and by his son-in-law, Maximilien Osseyevich Steinberg,[28] whose wife, Nadyezhda, rightly seems to have regarded Stravinsky as a threat to her husband. Surely Stravinsky might have foreseen that the success of *The Firebird* would not be considered a matter for rejoicing by his teacher's widow and son, and might have remembered, too, that when "Joseph dreamed a dream, and . . . told it to his brethren . . . they hated him yet the more."

Four months later, after the St. Petersburg performance of the *Firebird* Suite, the rift became irreparable. Stravinsky wrote to Andrey Rimsky-Korsakov:

> ... Mama said that you would tell me the details. I waited and waited until I lost patience. But apart from the indiscriminate name-calling in the newspapers, I know nothing. Siloti also writes nothing, and my soul is much oppressed. No word from anyone! Surely I had a right to expect a letter from you. I have only just received a tiny postcard from Steinberg—from which I learned nothing new, only that for some reason or other Siloti wanted to cut the Dance from the Suite and that Steinberg would not let him, for which I am very grateful. But nothing about his or anyone else's reactions, nothing at all about the effect of my new piece on the archpriests of Russian music. No one writes anything, from which I conclude that my *Firebird* made either a very small impression or a negative one on all of you, as well as on the public. ... [Letter of November 20, 1910]

But *The Firebird* made a very powerful impression, of course, and Andrey and Steinberg certainly understood that the pupil not only had absorbed his master's idiom, but had also outstripped him in the direction of the new. *The Firebird*, though less essentially new than it must have seemed in 1910, was as outwardly iconoclastic and modern—in "Kastchei's Dance," for instance—as the music of any contemporary except Schoenberg, whose truly new works had not yet been performed. In a single stroke, the young composer had exhausted his teacher's world and given birth to a new one. Yet apparently Stravinsky still expected to be congratulated by the family of the man he had superseded!

In short, Stravinsky was remarkably slow in realizing that his compatriots, and especially the fellow students of Rimsky-Korsakov, would forgive him everything but his success. Even after *Le Sacre du Printemps,* when he had become a composer of world stature as well as, to a majority of the younger generation, the most exciting creative musician alive, this indifference and even hostility in St. Petersburg continued to torment him. From the Rimsky-Korsakovs he desperately wanted the approbation that a child seeks from his own family above all others. His rejection by his adopted family was an extremely painful experience that cast a shadow on the next few years of life.

Several weeks after the premiere of the *Sacre,* Stravinsky wrote to Steinberg from Paris:

I am gradually recovering from this hellish disease of typhus, walking like a fly on two legs. If everything goes according to plan, I will leave for Ustilug on Friday [July 11]. Nijinsky's choreography is incomparable and, with a few exceptions, everything was as I wanted it. But we must wait a long time before the public becomes accustomed to our language. Of the value of what we have already done, I am convinced, and this gives me the strength for further work. From the heart I wish you the same liveliness of the creative spirit, for I love you. [Letter of July 3, 1913]

The same liveliness of the creative spirit? But how many people have ever had that? Stravinsky's "I love you" must have seemed to poor Steinberg like a bear hug. And, in a second letter, Stravinsky advises him to

. . . play the *Sacre* in spite of everything. I am certain that in time you will begin to feel it, the creation of it having brought me countless happy hours. I consider you to be a sensitive person. Approach it, then, with a pure heart. Yes, and it isn't all that difficult. [Letter of July 29, 1913]

But when the *Sacre* was played in St. Petersburg (by Kussevitzky) the following winter, many of Stravinsky's former friends joined the attack, as one of Stravinsky's letters, written shortly afterward, reveals. The addressee is Reynaldo Hahn,[29] the occasion the acknowledgment of some remarks of Hahn's in the *Journal de l'Université*—

I have had the good fortune to spend long and frequent moments in the presence of the young and already illustrious composer Stravinsky, whose orchestral genius is prodigious

—as well as Hahn's letter in which the article was enclosed:

My dear friend, I thank you sincerely for your telegram, and I wish for this year the continuing development of your young glory. I enclose an article of mine that mentions your fascinating personality. You have had in me an admirer "from the first hour," and do not think me a flatterer: I am too pedantic and, I dare say, too meticulous in my feelings to burst without restraint, as some do, or to resign myself hypocritically, like some others. I simply avow my admirations and my true preferences, and I honor whoever is to be honored. I admire you and esteem you very highly: you are a great musician.

Stravinsky's answer shows how troubled he was by the Russian reception of *Le Sacre*:

My dear friend, It is a long time since I received your packet (*Journaux* [sic] *de l'Université des Annales*) with your friendly lines, and a long time that I have put off replying. But that proves nothing. You have touched me more profoundly than I am able to say. I never really knew what you thought of me (without grimaces [30]), and your letter has greatly encouraged me, especially now, when I need it, the very thought of your words giving me confidence and comfort. My *Sacre* has just been played in concerts in Moscow and Petersburg, and in both of these capitals of my dear country it was the same song: much booing, little applause, and the most unfair and vicious critics. The latter are of no importance, but what did upset me was that my best friends turned their backs on me and joined my enemies.

Your letter was all the more important to me because I was aware that, in the past, you did not like me, or the music of the *Sacre*.[31] Yet you never denied the artistic honesty of my work, and by that road you will some day recognize the value of my music. You are one of the most intelligent artists I know. I shake your hand in all confidence. Your cordially devoted Igor Stravinsky. [Letter of March 13, 1914, from "Leysin sur Aigle"]

With his first three ballets, Stravinsky became the most glittering star in the brilliant constellation of Serge Diaghilev's pre-1914 Ballets Russes, whose glory is now attested to by only a few unfaded survivors, supreme among them these Stravinsky masterpieces. The composer was an outspoken critic of his associates—designers, choreographers, dancers—but an educated one, schooled in the art of the ballet and endowed with a keen sense of décors. The following letter may be his only general and on-the-spot appraisal (rather than reminiscence) of the Diaghilev of the early years. Addressed to Vladimir Rimsky-Korsakov,[32] it answers criticisms of Diaghilev's production of Rimsky-Korsakov's *Sadko*:

. . . On the whole I am far from agreeing with Diaghilev's acquiescence in the matter of cuts, just as I do not agree with Napravnik's.[33] This year Kauts [34] (so I believe his name is written) made an absolutely brilliant cut in the Tartar pogrom scene in *Kitezh*, and intended to make another one, which it seems you were able to prevent. But none of these people—Kauts, Napravnik—has suffered the insults that Diaghilev has had to endure,[35] Diaghilev, who, in the end, achieves immeasurably higher and artistically more valuable results than all of the others. I can testify disinterestedly to this, though please do not assume on this account that I spend my time with Diaghilev in enamored yea-saying. Quite the contrary: no day goes by when I do not criticize, argue, disagree with him.

But that is one thing. An awareness of the significance of the created work is quite another. And here we come to precisely what you have placed in doubt. I refer to ballet. You say that you are not an enemy of ballet but later call it the "lowest sort" of scenic art. . . . Let me tell you that I am at the opposite extreme. I am interested in and love the ballet more than anything else. . . . And I believe that if some

Michelangelo were alive today—so it occurred to me, looking at the frescoes in the Sistine Chapel [36]—the only thing that his genius would admit and recognize is choreography. And this is now coming to life again. Undoubtedly he would have dismissed everything else that takes place on the stage today as a cheap spectacle, for the only form of theater art that makes its cornerstone the problems of beauty and nothing more is the ballet, just as the only goal that Michelangelo pursued was the beauty of the perceived.

Not until I had actually worked in choreography did I realize this, as well as the necessity and value of what I am doing. I refer not only to my music but to the work in its entirety, for I am the author of the *Petrushka* libretto, which I wrote with as much love as your father did his operas. . . . You say that ballet is lower than opera, but in my view all art is the same. There are no lower or higher arts but only different kinds of art, and unions of art, one strengthening and complementing the other.

Still I can understand someone opposing these unions of drama with music (opera) or choreography with music (ballet). And what is to be done with such a person? He loves pure art: if music, then music, if movement, then movement. But I cannot understand you, my dear, for you yourself love, or until now used to love, the plastic arts. I understand your father, Nikolai Andreyevich, who admitted that he had no feeling for them. And what can one do in that case? If someone does not feel, he does not feel. But then why did his creativity pour out in the form of operas and even ballets, in which music is deliberately united with these other arts? I believe that this was due not so much to a lack of love or understanding of the other arts as to a lack of familiarity with them. . . . [Letter of July 21, 1911]

On the evidence of his letters, Stravinsky shared his artistic confidences more closely with Alexander Benois [37] than with anyone else in Diaghilev's entourage—though he may have been personally more intimate with Léon Bakst,[38] whose companionship Stravinsky enjoyed and whose flashy dress the composer seems to have emulated, at least at the time of Jacques-Émile Blanche's portrait. Stravinsky would open his imagination to Benois as he would do to no one else:

Obviously life has rules about which we have no understanding and from which the artist's gaze, always directed to the beyond, sometimes manages to snatch something or other. . . . Still, there is no tearing oneself away. You can stand before the keyhole, pressed to the door; you see very little, but no one can drag you away. . . . Argutinsky [39] is in Petersburg. Greet him from me. [Letter of February 15, 1912]

Benois's décors for *Petrushka* were the most enduring of any early Stravinsky ballet, and the same artist's sets and costumes for *Le Baiser de la Fée* were among the most attractive of any of Stravinsky's later stage works. All this is recognized, but not the extent to which Benois was an artistic chaperon to the composer,[40] who occasionally bowed to the older man's taste and judgments, sometimes with important consequences.[41] Stravinsky wrote to Vladimir Rimsky-Korsakov:

. . . you try in vain to tear me out of the sphere of Benois's influence.

He is an extraordinarily subtle, clearsighted, and sensitive person, in music as well as in the plastic arts: indeed, of all the artists I have managed to see and meet, he is the most sensitive about music, which he understands as well as a professional musician. . . . [Letter of July 21, 1911]

But the two men quarreled in later life, partly because of a disagreement concerning the authorship of the title and libretto of *Petrushka*. The memoirs of each make short shrift of the other.

Although domiciled on the shores of Lake Geneva during the war, Stravinsky identified with the struggle of the Russian people, and his isolation from them made him more conscious than ever of his own Russian-ness. He immersed himself in their folk literature and—contrary to his own statements on the subject in later years—in their folk music,[42] as is revealed in a letter to his mother in Petrograd, February 23, 1916, in which he asks her to send phonograph recordings and reminds her that he already owns Linevaya's *Great Russian Songs and Folk Harmonizations*. The major compositions of this period, *Renard* and *Les Noces*, as well as the songs and female choruses,[43] form the summit of Russian music—except that these masterpieces of a super-sophisticated primitive are unique, descending from neither the Tchaikovsky nor the Rimsky-Korsakov side of Stravinsky's heredity. If any other composer comes to mind, it is Mussorgsky,[44] at least in spirit and subject—the song of a pilgrim in a snowstorm,[45] the birds and animals with whom Stravinsky felt such rapport.

World War I disrupted Stravinsky's life and changed the course of his art, for he lost not only his home and his country but also the sources of commissions to compose and perform new ballets. In 1917, by which time he had a tubercular wife and four children to support, his income from Russia had ceased, and performance fees, greatly diminished in number because of the war, were the composer's chief means of sustenance. Not Diaghilev but a Swiss industrialist, Werner Reinhart, paid for *Les Noces* and *Histoire du Soldat*, while *Renard* was commissioned by the sewing-machine heiress, the Princesse Edmond de Polignac, née Winnaretta Singer.[46] The reduced ensembles of these three scores, as well as corresponding changes in every dimension of Stravinsky's art, were partly the result of wartime conditions, but here it must suffice to say that the war years were a period of experimentation for him. He composed ragtime; imitated popular styles in tiny dances (polkas, waltzes, a tango, a galop, a pasodoble); flirted with mechanical instruments and with mechanistic rhythmic devices (such as changing tempi through the relationship of the sesquialtera, as at ⟨81⟩[47] in *Renard*); explored the musical possibilities of his native language— shifting the accents, isolating and stretching the syllables, combining verbal and instrumental sounds—in ways that pointed to the musical direction of later years.

What was Igor Stravinsky "like" just before the war, by which time his music had begun to be performed all over Europe? To judge from his letters, so different from those to Cocteau and other French friends of the time, he was generous and unsparing of himself; exuberant and high-spirited; incapable of sustained melancholy; choleric (as one would expect in so passionate a nature); unselfconscious; deeply ironic; [48] fanatic in all matters concerning the arts:

One must not let one Gauguin, not one Cézanne or any of the other whales out of Russia. . . . [Letter to Benois, February 15, 1912]

In sum, this Stravinsky would seem to be almost exactly the opposite of the one who was later celebrated for his hauteur and icy wit. The change could be due to the radical differences in his circumstances during and after the war, to the evolution of his music, and to the consequences of his new musical philosophy. Nevertheless, the sympathetic interest shown in the letters of his Russian period for the music of Strauss and Scriabin [49] is in striking contrast to the judgments of a decade later. In February 1913, after hearing two performances of Elektra in London, Stravinsky wrote to Steinberg:

I am completely ecstatic. It is Strauss's best composition. Let them talk about the vulgarisms that are always present in Strauss—to which my reply is that the more deeply one goes into German works of art, the more one sees that all of them suffer from that. . . . Strauss's Elektra is a marvelous thing! [50] [Letter of March 2, 1913]

In October of the same year, Stravinsky again wrote to Steinberg:

I traveled here [Clarens] from Russia with Scriabin,[51] whose father is the Russian Consul in Lausanne. Moreover, I visited the composer in Lausanne as well. We spoke of many interesting things, and he played excerpts for me from his new sonatas. I like them; one must have a look at them in their entirety. [Letter of October 12, 1913]

All too soon after this, Stravinsky was writing to Prokofiev:

How terrible is Scriabin's death! I cannot get over it! Seeking details of this awful event, I looked in the Russian newspapers, Rech and Petrograd. Instead of what I wanted to know, I came upon an ocean of the usual journalistic stupidities, such as the article by Karatygin [52] about odd-numbered overtones—as his "to Scriabin's Memory" is titled—and other trash. Indeed, I, with all my severe criticism of Scriabin, paid him more respect than Karatygin did with his overtones.[53] [Letter of May 12, 1915]

By the end of 1913, Stravinsky had begun to realize that other people might find his music difficult to understand. Before his mother first heard Le Sacre du Printemps—in St. Petersburg, conducted by Kussevitzky—her son warned her: "Do not be afraid if they whistle at Le Sacre. That is in the order of things" (letter of December 20, 1913). Stravinsky is much less tolerant when the incomprehension is that of a journalist, but even then the composer is annoyed primarily by bad style:

Svetlov praises everything indiscriminately, but the way he writes reminds me of the messy student compositions of second-graders.

After *Le Sacre*, Stravinsky became aware of the most important fact about his own development as a composer: that he would never repeat himself. He wrote to Benois:

I cannot ... compose what they want from me, which would be to repeat myself. ... *That* is the way that people write themselves out. [Letter of October 3, 1913].

And Stravinsky had understood this truth even earlier, in the case of Mikhail Fokine. Here the composer writes to his mother from Monte Carlo:

Mamachka, Mamussia ... Diaghilev and Nijinsky are mad about my new child, *Le Sacre du Printemps*. The unpleasant part is that it will have to be done by Fokine, whom I consider to be an exhausted artist, one who traveled his road quickly, and who writes himself out with each new work (i.e., *Narcissus*, *Sadko*, *Spectre de la Rose*, *Petrushka*), and all of them are immeasurably inferior and weaker. *Schéhérazade* was an inspired spectacle. ... New forms must be created, and the evil, the greedy, and the gifted Fokine [54] has not even dreamed of them. At the beginning of his career he appeared to be extraordinarily progressive, but the more I knew of his work, the more I saw of him, the more clearly I understood that in essence he was not new at all. There is no salvation in *habilité*. Genius is needed, not *habilité*..... [Letter of March 17, 1912]

As for Stravinsky seen through the eyes of others, it should be obvious to the reader that at this period only Russians *could* have known him, and that his Swiss friends, Ramuz,[55] Cingria,[56] Ansermet,[57] Auberjonois,[58] at least in their earlier associations with the composer, had only an incomplete understanding of him. Here is a glimpse of him by a Lake Geneva neighbor, C. Stanley Wise. In answer to Wise's question as to whether Nijinsky had been consulted about the choreography of *Le Sacre du Printemps*, Stravinsky said: "Surely not. It would be impossible for two persons to compose a work." But Wise also noted that

Unless one is intelligently interested and inquires about Stravinsky's work, it is possible to pass hours with him and know nothing of what he is doing.

Stravinsky's Russian letters should be read in conjunction with one of his compatriots' portraits of him. The most perspicacious of these is Vaslav Nijinsky's description of his final encounter with the composer, in mid-February 1916, a few weeks before the dancer left to join Diaghilev's company in New York. A rumor had been spread that Nijinsky did not make the trip with the others because Stravinsky was detaining him in Switzerland. Actually Nijinsky had reached Berne c. February 10, from Vienna, where he had been interned—apparently the Comtesse Greffuhle had arranged for his release through Franz Josef himself—but the dancer's military status was unclear, and a danger existed that he might be arrested at the French frontier. Although Stravinsky cabled to Diaghilev on March 17 that the Russian government, through its Embassy in Berne, had declared Nijinsky "non-mobilizable," a cable arrived on the 23rd from Diaghilev, in Pittsburgh, saying that the Metropolitan Opera was charging him with a plot to have Stravinsky keep Nijinsky in Switzerland. "*Trouve prétentions Nijinsky absolument absurdes*," the message said, but it also begged Stravinsky to accompany Nijinsky to Bordeaux. On the same day, Stravinsky answered that Nijinsky was already en route.[59]

Nijinsky's picture of Stravinsky is not flattering, yet Stravinsky can hardly be blamed for refusing the responsibility of caring for Nijinsky's infant daughter during her father's foreign tour. And the reader must bear in mind that by this date the composer was alarmed at the symptoms of Nijinsky's mental instability. But Nijinsky *did* know Stravinsky:

Stravinsky smells things out. He is not my friend, but at the bottom of his heart he loves me. . . . Diaghilev loves Massine but not me, and that is awkward for Stravinsky. Stravinsky forces his wife to carry out all of his caprices. . . . His wife loves him. I feel that he does not love her as much, but he does love the children. He loves his children strangely, however, and shows his love for them by making them paint. . . . He is like an emperor, and his children and wife are the servants [60] and soldiers. Stravinsky reminds me of Tsar Paul, but he will not be strangled because he is cleverer than the Tsar was. Diaghilev wanted to strangle him many times, but Stravinsky is too sly. Diaghilev cannot exist without Stravinsky, nor Stravinsky without Diaghilev.

After my liberation from Hungary, I went to Morges to see Stravinsky and to ask him, being certain that my wish would not be refused, if he and his wife would take my child while I was in America. He had many children, and I felt that my Kyra [61] would be safe with them. I asked Stravinsky to take my Kyra, and though his wife almost wept, Stravinsky said that he was very sorry, but that he could not assume responsibility for the child. I thanked him and did not say anything else. Looking at his wife sadly, I felt the same answer. Being a woman, she knew what it means to drag a child from train to steamer, from place to place, and she was sorry for me. She did not agree with her husband, but because he spoke so quickly and decisively, he made her understand that he did not wish to keep my daughter. I told him that I would pay all of Kyra's expenses, but he did not agree with this either.

Stravinsky saw me off at the station, and I gave him my hand very coldly. I did not like him then and wanted to show him, but he did not feel it because he kissed me. I had a nasty feeling. [*The Diaries of Vaslav Nijinsky* (University of California Press, 1971)]

One other letter to a friend in Russia should be quoted here, though it was written in 1932, after fifteen years of near-silence in Stravinsky's communications with his native country.[62] Since during Stalin's time Stravinsky almost never wrote to anyone there, including his brother and nieces, the date is as surprising as is the subject, Mussorgsky, who would seem to be far from Stravinsky's thoughts by this time. In fact Mussorgsky is rarely mentioned in connection with Stravinsky, partly because of Stravinsky's public partisanship on behalf of Tchaikovsky, whom the French abominated in about the same measure as they venerated the composer of *Boris*. But Diaghilev needed Stravinsky's endorsement of *The Sleeping Beauty*, not of *Khovanshchina*.[63] Thus Stravinsky's true feelings about Mussorgsky may have been recorded only once, in the excerpt quoted below. The letter is addressed to Vladimir Napravnik, son of the conductor Eduard Napravnik, who had led the first performance of *Boris*—as well as that of the *Symphonie Pathétique*, in a concert after Tchaikovsky's death that the nine-year-old Stravinsky had attended.

In 1925, Vladimir Napravnik went from the U.S.S.R. to visit Stravinsky in Nice. Now, seven years later, this younger Napravnik was seeking Stravinsky's blessing for the elder Napravnik's performances of *Boris* in Rimsky-Korsakov's version rather than in the original. This Stravinsky was unwilling to give:

I knew your father's severely conservative manner and tastes. They were an insuperable barrier in his attempts to evaluate the innovativeness of his contemporaries, the Group of Five [*Pyatyorka*], and, particularly, of the greatest of them, Mussorgsky. Your father's, as well as Tchaikovsky's, negative opinion of Mussorgsky is a secret to no one. But from whom *could* one conceal the fact that the milieu in which Mussorgsky's powers developed was wholly alien to the attitudes and tastes of the official musical world of that time? Even Rimsky-Korsakov, who was thought to be closer to Mussorgsky than the others, actually understood very little about him. But how could Rimsky-Korsakov, from his academic point of view, value the authentic musical discoveries of his friend? In truth, Rimsky-Korsakov could see no more in them than a kind of tongue-tiedness, the result of an inadequate musical education and an incomplete compositional technique. . . . And I speak of Mussorgsky's *Boris*, not Rimsky-Korsakov's pseudo-*Boris*. . . .[64]

Mussorgsky's triumphant letter to your father after the first performance of *Boris* in 1873—about which you write—does not change the matter, in my view. The letter is an altogether natural gesture of thanks on the part of Mussorgsky. . . . But from that to making your father a propagandist of Mussorgsky is quite a leap. . . . Do not condemn my severe straight-forwardness and inability to fulfill your request. . . . [Letter of November 15, 1932]

Stravinsky was absorbed in Mussorgsky's music immediately after completing *Le Sacre du Printemps* and, in April 1913, orchestrated Chaklovity's aria [65] and the concluding chorus of *Khovanshchina*.[66] (In addition, Stravinsky seems to have planned to orchestrate Mussorgsky's *Marriage*.[67]) Two months later, Diaghilev produced the opera in Paris, giving three performances, which a severe case of typhus prevented Stravinsky from hearing. It was well received, in spite of the opera's supposed musical ankyloglossia and real dramaturgical weaknesses, but, at the premiere, as a practical joke, Diaghilev substituted the Rimsky-Korsakov version of the concluding chorus for the Stravinsky version. The Stravinsky version had been announced, and the wily impresario, knowing that the press would denounce it, was successful in catching the reviewers red-handed.

Stravinsky's interest in Mussorgksy, therefore, was at its apogee just before the composition of the second and third acts of The Nightingale. The cortège in Stravinsky's third act was obviously inspired by Mussorgsky's Coronation Scene, Stravinsky's Emperor of China by Mussorgsky's usurper of the Russian crown—vocally speaking, at least. But even this does not explain Stravinsky's strong feelings for Mussorgsky some twenty calendar years [68] after The Nightingale, and eons beyond it in musical development. The latter seems to prove that, no matter how powerfully Stravinsky's uprooting from Russia affected his work, the enforced separation in no way diminished his Russian identity.

1877. Ivan Ivanovich Skorokhodov, Stravinsky's father's maternal grandfather. The photograph was taken in his 111th year. He died in 1879.

1868, 1872. The composer's paternal grandparents, Ignatsy Ignatievich Stravinsky and Alexandra Ivanovna Skorokhodova, were married June 3, 1834. The photograph of Alexandra Ivanovna was taken in Vitebsk in 1868, that of Ignatsy Ignatievich in St. Petersburg in 1872. He died in Tiflis, May 29, 1893, and is buried in the Roman Catholic cemetery there.

C. 1850. Kirill Kholodovsky. Medallion portrait.

March 24, 1880. Kiev. The composer's maternal grandmother, Marya Kholodovskaya (née Furman).

Igor Fyodorovich ("Ghima") Stravinsky was born in Khudyntzev Cottage, 137 Shveitzarksy (Switzerland) Street (now Uprising Street), Oranienbaum (now Lomonosov), at noon, June 5 (now June 18), 1882. A few hours after birth, he was baptized by a prelate of the Russian Orthodox Church. A ukase of His Imperial Majesty Alexander III confirms that the infant's father was Fyodor, whose father was Ignace, and that the mother was the daughter of Kirill Kholodovsky. The formal baptismal ceremony took place in the Nikolsky Sobor, St. Petersburg, on July 11, and was witnessed by Igor's godfather and paternal uncle, Alexander, a lieutenant colonel, and by Igor's paternal aunt, Olga Dymaievskaya, "épouse de noble."

In a program note for a performance of the "Lullaby" from *The Firebird* by the Orchestra of the Society of Saint Cecilia, Bordeaux, February 8, 1914, Florent Schmitt [69] wrote that Stravinsky's given name was in honor of "his godfather, Borodin." Although the composer of *Prince Igor* had no connection with Stravinsky, this joke has persisted as fact in some publications.

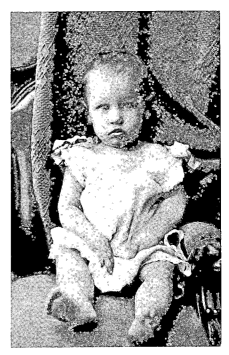

September 17, 1883. St. Petersburg. Igor at fifteen months. Photograph by F. de Mezer.

June 23, 1872. St. Petersburg. The composer's maternal grandparents, Kirill Grigorievich Kholodovsky and Marya Romanovna Furman.

1866. Anna Kirillovna Kholodovskaya. The composer's mother, aged twelve.

December 26, 1874. Kiev. Fyodor and Anna Stravinsky, married six months and eighteen days.

Igor accompanied his parents on their trips to Germany partly because, having had a German governess, he could translate for them. He never lost his command of German and in later life was reluctant to use it only when in the presence of such a writer as Thomas Mann, whom Stravinsky first met after playing his Piano Concerto at a concert in Zürich, November 6, 1928. In *The Story of a Novel*, Mann wrote:

I remembered how Stravinsky, years ago in Zürich, confessed to me that he admired Tchaikovsky (I had asked him about it).[70]

Again, Mann described an evening with Stravinsky in Los Angeles:

. . . a conversation with Stravinsky at a party in our house sticks in my memory with remarkable clarity. We talked about Gide—Stravinsky expressed his ideas in German, French, and English—then about literary "confessions" as a product of the different cultural spheres: the Greek Orthodox, the Latin Catholic, and the Protestant. In Stravinsky's opinion, Tolstoy was essentially German and Protestant. . . .[71]

February 27, 1886. St. Petersburg. Igor, aged three and a half. In the summer of this year, the child was taken to Pavlovka, in the Samara district, to the estate of his uncle Alexander Yelachich, the husband of Anna Stravinsky's sister Sofiya.

"1895, July 8, 8:30 A.M., at the Elizabeth Spa, Homburg," Fyodor Stravinsky wrote on the back of this photograph. Igor's parents are to his right, and he is identified by the arrow.

March 13, 1894. St. Petersburg. The Stravinsky family at home, 66 Krukov (now Griboyedova) Canal. The marriage between Fyodor Ignatievich Stravinsky and Anna Kirillovna Kholodovskaya took place in Kiev, June 5, 1874. On their twenty-first wedding anniversary, less than a year after this picture was taken, Fyodor wrote that he hoped his children would have lives as rich and happy as he had had as a consequence of marrying their mother. Igor is at the lower left with his eldest brother, Roman, behind him. Yury is standing in the center, and Gury, the youngest of the four sons, stands to the right.

Roman Stravinsky died in 1897, and, not long after that, Fyodor fell ill with cancer. Alluding to this, the seventeen-year-old Igor wrote to his parents from Ustilug, July 19, 1899:

If only God would allow our family to be free of these detestable illnesses, at least for a short time. . . . It seems that fate has allowed us a limited portion of happiness and now wishes to snatch even that away. . . . What our unhappy family has experienced!

The statement is crucial, for Stravinsky's whole life was darkened by illness and death. His father died three years after this letter, and, six years after that, the young Stravinsky was shocked by the sudden demise of Rimsky-Korsakov. Igor's younger brother died while still in his early thirties, and, later, Stravinsky's wife succumbed at fifty-eight to tuberculosis, which also killed his elder daughter at the age of thirty. Stravinsky himself was constantly ill with lung diseases, and dangerously ill several times with pneumonia, Spanish influenza, typhus, grippe, and tuberculosis.

The effect of suffering and grief on Stravinsky's artistic beliefs was that he determined to keep his art and his life as nearly separate as possible instead of seeking an outlet for his feelings in music. His philosophy was defined by T. S. Eliot's aphorism:

The more perfect the artist, the more completely separate in him will be the man who suffers and the mind which creates.

1897. Homburg-vor-der-Höhe. While walking with his father this summer, the fifteen-year-old Stravinsky caught a glimpse of Clara Schumann.

A lengthy study of Stravinsky in Ustilug, "Dom Strawinskiego W Uscilugu," by Pawel Hostowiec, was published in *Kultura*, Paris, November 1949. The following excerpt is from another essay, this one by the Polish musicologist G. Stempowski:

When I visited Ustilug in 1939, I was able, with the help of the mayor, to obtain some facts about the place from the city archives. These date back to the middle of the last century, when the territory belonged to the Lubomirski family, whose castle there was destroyed. Since 1945 the Bug River has defined the border between the Soviet Union and the New Republic of Poland, and in 1946 a bridge was erected at Ustilug.
   In 1906, after Stravinsky married Catherine Nossenko, the young couple built a country house called "Old Farm," still known by that name. Stravinsky had no connection with the inhabitants of the city—which was thriving in 1939—except through his father-in-law, Dr. Gabril Nossenko, and Dr. Nossenko's wife, who founded a hospital there. But it was generally known that a composer lived at the "Old Farm," and that he would leave his house and take quick walks in the park for

C. 1898. Ustilug. Four white bonnets in a tarantass (a calash without springs). Catherine [Ekaterina] Nossenko, the composer's first cousin and first wife, holds the whip. Before her marriage, she had studied singing and drawing in Paris. After the marriage, she became her husband's principal copyist. Dr. Beliankin is standing in the doorway.

a quarter of an hour at a time. . . . Stravinsky showed part of *The Firebird* to the Regent of the Ustilug Territory. The "Lullaby" is typical of Volhynian folk music—from the north, around Kovel, rather than from Ustilug. . . . I found an old choir singer, born in that region, and living in a moss-covered hut, who knew all of the songs of the territory. [From *DU*, December 1950]

Dr. Gabril Nossenko, husband of Stravinsky's mother's sister Marya, purchased an estate at Ustilug in 1890. Since the doctor's wife was tubercular, he wanted her, as well as his daughters, Liudmilla and Catherine, to live in the country. In the mid-1890s, Igor and Gury Stravinsky spent their summers there, while their older brothers, Roman and Yury, lived with their parents at Pechisky, an estate owned by the doctor's wife near Yarmolintsy in Podoly Province. Fyodor and Anna Stravinsky and their sons lived at Pechisky in the early 1890s, before the Ustilug period; after the death of Roman, in 1897, his parents continued to visit the grave of this oldest and apparently favorite son, which was on the Pechisky estate. At one time, Yury also stayed there with his parents, as a letter from Igor to them, July 27, 1901, reveals:

I'm pleased for you and for Yury, dear Papa and Mama, that he is coming to spend two weeks with you in Pechisky. I understand your desire for him to stay longer, and I will do nothing to hasten his departure for Ustilug.

Two letters from Stravinsky's Ustilug gardener and caretaker, G. Kozlovsky, dated January 16, 1914, and February 6, 1914, indicate the size of the composer's estate there. It had orchards and vegetable gardens, potato and oat fields, hothouses containing

Map of the Western Ukraine. Ustilug, Lat. 50.51 N. and Long. 24.10 E., is at the eastern extremity of the bulge formed by the River Bug's two crossings of the 24th longitude south of the 51st parallel. The city of Vladimir-Volynsk is approximately 12 kilometers east of Ustilug; Kovel, the main terminus, is 50 kilometers further northeast. The region is one of forests, rivers, and wheatfields.

banana plants; Kozlovsky asks for money for seeds, and for fifty cartloads of manure. In the letter of January 16, he informs the composer that

a horse was sold to Pan Lutinsky for sixty rubles. Also, Kruchky [Stravinsky's dog] had a large litter, but we were obliged to drown all except one pup.

Stravinsky had other business interests in the Ukraine, the management of which he entrusted to his brother-in-law, Grigory Beliankin. The following note from Beliankin is typical:

I send a procuration; if you are in agreement, make a copy and send it to me. . . . The mill will cost 25,000 rubles but will earn 15,000 yearly. . . . Bakst has been exiled from Petersburg on 24 hours notice, as a Jew. . . . Gania [Beliankin's epileptic son] is better. Today I go to Ustilug.

And here are excerpts from two of Stravinsky's letters to the Agricultural Bank of Kiev:

Ustilug, September 20, 1912: Honorable Fyodor Fyodorovich: When Grigory Pavlovich was in Rovno, he told Matusevich that point 3 cannot be conceded under any conditions. I have just received Grigory Pavlovich's letter about the matter, and I sent a telegram to him, "TRI Stravinsky" [Latin letters in the orginal], because he had an agreement with Matusevich about this Cabbalistic number. I fervently ask you to finish with that affair as soon as possible, since poor Yarotsky telegraphs to me almost daily; but I cannot help him without you. I ask you to compose the final draft for the mortgage, excluding the numbers that you have already shown to me, 2 and 4. But, I repeat, the number 3 must be in the mortgage. I am sorry, but I cannot come; and, for this reason, you must use your power-of-attorney to do everything. Igor Stravinsky.

Stravinsky could not come because he was composing the last part of the *Sacre*. The second letter is dated February 9, 1914, Leysin:

Since September 9, 1912, I have held a mortgage on the property of M. B. Yarotsky in the town of Rovno.[72] I therefore request that the directors of the bank notify me if the interest has not been paid, and if the property is being threatened by sale, and I respectfully ask to be informed each time that the percentage is not paid. Following my instructions, a copy of the mortgage has already been sent to the bank from the village of Ustilug in Martynenko. From the landed proprietor, Igor Fyodorovich Stravinsky.

Until the Russian Revolution, Stravinsky continued to receive money from the Azov-Don Commercial Bank in Petrograd, through the Federal Bank in Zürich—400 francs, for example, on June 27, 1916.

In 1902, Rimsky-Korsakov was living at Neckargemünd, and it was at this time that Igor deepened his acquaintance with the

C. 1899. St. Petersburg. With Gury, in the cadet uniforms of the Gurevich School. Igor is at the right (smaller than his younger brother!). Both young men were to become law students.

composer. Twenty-six years later, Stravinsky said that his father had given him a letter of introduction to Rimsky-Korsakov,

who had seen me in the *coulisses* of the theater, but without paying much attention to me. During our meeting in Germany he examined the compositions that I had brought and advised me to continue the study of music and composition. [*Journal de Genève*, November 14, 1928]

Frau Marie Wilhelm, the Stravinskys' landlady in Bad Wildungen, wrote to the composer, May 17, 1952:

Lieber Professor Stravinsky. Thank you for your New Year's card from New York. I was so happy, so happy. I never forgot the wonderful weeks with you and Gury in 1902, when you were here with your parents for the cure. You went from here to Berlin. Did your dear parents die in Russia? Did Ghima [73] also become an artist? Do you have children and a family? Will you come again to Wildungen (by airplane)? I am very proud of your friendship and have followed all of your great triumphs. From my heart I wish you "*Dieu vous garde*," and to be, as you were before, full of humor. My dear *amie* Florence Kunz died, otherwise I would come to New York. One of my sons is a doctor, the other a jeweler. We speak English and French. . . .
Please, dear Professor Igor Stravinsky, send your photograph, please, please, for a memory. Marie Wilhelm. [Translated from the German by V.A.S.]

Frau Wilhelm wrote again on November 14, 1958, this time adding the nobiliary particle to the composer's name:

Dear Mr. Igor von Stravinsky: It was in 1902 that you were living in my house, "Johanna," with your brother Gury (Ghima) and your parents. Your father told me he was at the Imperial Opera in St. Petersburg, and

C. 1898. 66 Krukov Canal. Igor in his room. Note the icon of Berlioz among those of the masters.

C. 1900. 66 Krukov Canal. Fyodor Stravinsky at his desk. Like his most famous son, Fyodor Stravinsky was passionately interested in literature. He knew Turgenev personally. [According to an interview with Igor Stravinsky in *Die Stunde*, Vienna, March 17, 1926]

he showed a gold watch to me, a present from the Tsar. Your dear mother was a charming lady. You were 17 years old and called me "sister." You cooked scrambled eggs in my kitchen for yourself and for Gury, and your mother laughed about it. . . . Once Gury sat in the windowsill, both legs outside, and took pictures of Wildungen, while I held him by his jacket. I was 22 years old and married. . . . Now I am over 70. . . . Please give me a small sign of *your* life. Maybe one day you will come here. Greetings, Frau Marie Wilhelm. [Translated from the German by V.A.S.]

Fyodor Stravinsky was born June 20, 1843, in Novy Dvor. Although endowed with acting talent and an exceptional bass voice, he studied law rather than music, entering Novorossisky University in Odessa in the autumn of 1865, transferring, the following year, to Vladimir University in Kiev, and matriculating four years later at the Nezhin Lyceum. On September 23, 1869, he arrived in St. Petersburg. He became a pupil of Everardi[74] at the St. Petersburg Conservatory and, after three years of study, was engaged at the Kiev Opera. On April 30, 1876, Fyodor made his debut in the Maryinsky Theater, St. Petersburg, as Mephistopheles in Gounod's *Faust*.

Between this event and his retirement from the theater a quarter of a century later, Fyodor sang sixty-six roles. More than half were in Russian operas little known in the West, but he was also celebrated for his Leporello, his Sparafucile, his Pistol, his Kaspar, and other characters in operas of Bellini, Donizetti, Verdi, and Wagner that his composer son was to remember all of his life. The Maryinsky renewed Fyodor's contract every three years with a substantial increase in salary. On April 5, 1891, he was awarded the Order of St. Stanislas, and, in 1898, the same

Order, Third Degree. In 1892, Fyodor was asked to contribute to an autograph album of "Russian and French Celebrities," to be sold for the benefit of the victims of a famine in Russia, and published by the magazine *La Vie Russe*. He quoted Pushkin and some music from the Tavern Scene in *Boris*, in a handwriting remarkably like that of his composer son, and wrote half of an introductory letter in French, half in Russian, an idea that might also have occurred to his son.

Like Igor Stravinsky, Fyodor was an actor onstage, an introvert in private. His diary contains numerous avowals of the happiness he found in his marriage. But the entry on his fifty-second birthday, June 20, 1895, questions if he is too old and whether "it may be time to conclude this stupid, futile, senseless life in a spiritless society." Otherwise his diary is largely a record of business transactions and anniversaries. Thus, on April 18, 1888, he signed a new contract with the Imperial Theater and on May 12, 1891, yet another contract, this one for 8,000 rubles a year for three years (until September 1, 1894). One entry, October 23, 1897, records a visit to the Treasury Department to receive his first pension after twenty years in the Imperial Opera. But, marking his twenty-fourth wedding anniversary, June 5, 1898, he utters a cry of despair, exclaiming that everything in his life has collapsed with the death of his son Roman.

A bookish man, like his composer son after him, Fyodor Stravinsky tabulated every acquisition and loss in his library. At Christmas 1887, for example, he noted the gift to his wife of some seventeenth-century tomes by Pierre Lacroix. Fyodor also mentions an operation performed on him by Dr. Eugene Pavlov, March 22, 1888, but does not name the ailment. On October 28, 1902, Fyodor Stravinsky returned from Bad Wildungen to St. Petersburg, where he died at home, December 4, of a sarcoma of the throat.

A quarter of a century later, Igor Stravinsky told an interviewer for the *Journal de Genève*:

1912. 66 Krukov Canal. The winter view from the Stravinsky apartment, in a painting by the composer's sister-in-law, Elena Nikolayevna, wife of Yury. The dome is that of a synagogue; the large entranceway, to the left, part of a food market. By an extraordinary coincidence, this picture was included in the same exhibition, *Art in the Crimea*, in Yalta, in 1918, in which Vera de Bosset Sudeikina (later Mrs. Igor Stravinsky) first displayed one of *her* paintings, "Flower Bouquet" (No. 242 in the exhibition catalogue), and twenty silhouettes (Nos. 222–41).

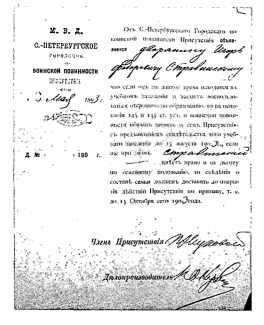

November 10, 1903. This student deferment from military service allowed Stravinsky to continue his schooling.

...I spent my childhood on the stage of the opera, where my love of music was born. My father's career as a singer did not help me very much, for he wanted me to avoid an artist's life, knowing its difficulties. Neither my piano playing [75] nor my essays in composition convinced him that these aptitudes were sufficiently promising to enable me to earn my living in music. [November 14, 1928]

Yury Stravinsky and his wife did not play a prominent role in Igor's life, and, in fact, never saw him after 1912. Yury died shortly before the siege of Leningrad (1941), but the news did not reach Igor until half a year later, by way of Dmitri Borodin,[76] who had heard it in turn from a brother-in-law of one of the Rimsky-Korsakovs.

In November 1946, Elena, Yury's widow, sent the details of his death to Stravinsky: Yury had telephoned from his office one day, said that he felt very ill, and, a few moments later, lost consciousness, the cause of death apparently being a stroke. The letter says that Yury had written extensively, "not only about his science of engineering but also about the architecture of Leningrad." Elena Nikolayevna added:

I live with Xenia and her thirteen-year-old daughter. We have two rooms in the apartment of Napravnik—where everybody died during the blockade—and these rooms are better than those in the apartment at No. 66. Tanya lives separately, with her husband and eighteen-year-old son. ... Xenia married a second time, three months ago.

C. 1904. The first page of a volume of Georgian folk songs copied by Stravinsky.

The English title page of the same, added in July 1949. Stravinsky made several attempts to imitate the rigidly vertical Georgian script but could not change the natural slant of his handwriting.

Stravinsky answered this on February 17, 1947, expressing great sorrow, chiefly, it seems, about the loss of his father's library. Tanya came to France in 1925, and Stravinsky saw Xenia in Russia in 1962 and in Evian in 1970.

The young composer had spent the summer of 1903 with his Aunt and Uncle Yelachich in Pavlovka and had begun a Piano Sonata there. See Part I, note 15, and the caption for photo, page 36. Since even the name Yelachich did not appear in Stravinsky's *Autobiography* (1935), the identification of "Uncle Alexander Yelachich" in later memoirs as a source of encouragement and an influence on the future composer's youthful musical development was a surprise. When a full biography of Stravinsky is written, the role of his Yelachich inlaws must be explored. At the end of World War II, Stravinsky's cousin Elizabeth Yelachich wrote to him from China, saying that she had continued to visit his mother and family in St. Petersburg until the Revolution:

I was especially fond of your brother Gury. . . . My husband was musical and used to play parts of *Petrushka* and *The Nightingale* on the piano. During the Revolution we fled to China, where my husband died. Both of my daughters married Frenchmen and live in Paris, but my son is here, and when I saw him, he was working for the Americans (Ford). Conditions here are extremely difficult, and often I live at near-starvation level. . . . The brother of Serge lives in Yugoslavia but does

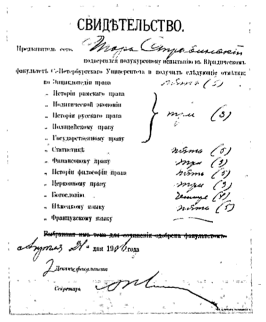

May 4, 1906. Certificate from the University of St. Petersburg. Three is a passing grade, five the highest possible mark.

Statistics	5
History of Financial Law	5
Encyclopedia of Law	5
German	5
French	5
Geology	4
State Law	3
Police Law	3
History of Russian Law	3
History of Roman Law	3
Financial Law	3
Church Law	3

May 11, 1906. Certificate. "The bearer, Igor Fyodorovich Stravinsky, Russian Orthodox religion, son of a nobleman, born June 5 [17], 1882, is accepted as a student of the Imperial St. Petersburg University School of Jurisprudence, August 1901, having received his diploma from the Gurevich School. He will attend the following courses. . . ." The subjects are those listed to the right.

July 1905. Ustilug. With Catherine Nossenko.

1906. St. Petersburg. The newlyweds, with samovar.

not answer me. No one will help me. I am sorry to bother you but drowning people must clutch at straws. . . .

This letter was brought to the United States by Lieutenant A. Van Keller of the United States Army, a resident of 1136 Fifth Avenue, New York City, and sent to Stravinsky through an intermediary. Stravinsky's cousin Alexis Yelachich, a philologist living in Belgrade, came to see the composer at Echarvines in the summer of 1928 to invite him to conduct *Petrushka* at the Zagreb Opera and a concert in Belgrade. Writing to his Paris representative, Robert Lyon, February 1, 1926, Stravinsky inquires about "my nephew, George Yelachich, 15, rue Beaujolais, Paris." Then, in Hollywood, on August 17, 1969, the composer received a visit from Michel Yelachich of Paris, with whom, one year later, Stravinsky's niece Xenia was to stay before visiting her uncle in Evian.

It would seem that Katia and I have grounds for reveling in dreams of parenthood. At least everything looks that way. Since we are keeping it a secret, we ask you to tell *no one* about it. . . . Then, Mama, another circumstance which you should keep to yourself is that life in two rooms with aunt Sofiya [77] would be very burdensome for us, Milochka [78] having long ago decided to leave. In the first place we disagree in our views, and this makes me extraordinarily uneasy in auntie's company. As you know, our contact with people is almost the sole interest . . . at this historic moment in Russian life, and it is unbearable when you hear not a word about this. The situation was literally that way while we were in Kiev, for which reason we went to Ustilug as quickly as possible.
   Then still a second thing. Music evidently upsets auntie, and consequently life together with her would be an insufferable burden on all of us. If Milochka were with us, then the place would be bigger, the inconvenience could be dealt with, and the first condition would disappear. But, like ourselves, Mila has decided that to continue in the current state of affairs would be impossible. Well, Mama, I have to finish, since they are sending the letters to the post office. . . . perhaps you are writing to us about Yury,[79] and we will read your letter today. . . . [Igor in Ustilug, to his mother, July 1906]

Stravinsky composed the *Scherzo Fantastique* during the latter half of 1907. A decade later, the music became known in the ballet *Les Abeilles*, first performed at the Paris Académie de Musique de l'Opéra, January 10, 1917, and repeated on January 18 and 27 and February 4, 17, and 18, with choreography by Léo Staats. The conductor was Gabriel Grovlez,[80] who also made the piano reduction of the score; one of his letters to Stravinsky (December 28, 1916) reveals that the composer had agreed to conduct the gala performance but canceled because of ill health—and in fact Stravinsky was ill during most of December 1916. The role of the "Queen Bee" was danced by Mlle Zambelli, that of "a drone" by Mlle Schwartz, and that of "An Amiable Bee" by Mlle Barbier. According to Pierre Lalo:

The music of M. Stravinsky's *divertissement* is combined with a scenario probably borrowed from a chapter, "The Nuptial Flight," in Mau-

Until he became a conductor, in the 1920s, Stravinsky wore either a pince-nez or a monocle.*

* In Picasso's full-face drawing of the composer, he is wearing not a monocle but half of a pair of broken spectacles—as he explained to Rolf Liebermann in a television interview, March 1965.

rice Maeterlinck's celebrated book, the *Life of the Bee*. Here the poet's conception is transformed into a ballet. The scene represents the interior of a beehive penetrated by the steamy sunlight of a beautiful summer day. The honey bees are at work, coming and going to and from the narrow entrance of the hive. Suddenly the Queen Bee appears. The suitors have been waiting for her in the nearest cells. They appear one by one, the drones who lovingly sidle up to her and try to encircle her, the most humble among them rubbing against her. ... The Queen seems to undress herself. The deceived male tries to follow and caress her at the same time that he carries out the nuptial flight. At the moment of his triumph, the drone must die. He falls, is immediately rejected, quickly forgotten outside of the hive, and the work inside is resumed. [*Feuilleton du Temps*, January 27, 1917]

On January 31, 1917, Stravinsky received a letter from Robert Montfort [81] in Paris:

I was present a fortnight ago at the performance of *Les Abeilles*. Next to me sat our old master, Camille Saint-Saëns, who left immediately afterward. I hope that this detail will not leave you indifferent, and that it will let you know of the interest that musicians have in your work.

Stravinsky also received a letter from Maurice Maeterlinck, on the envelope of which the composer later wrote:

Letter from M. Maeterlinck and his ridiculous statements concerning the subject of *"Les Abeilles,"* a classical ballet without subject composed on the music of my *Scherzo Fantastique*.

Stravinsky told an interviewer for *Comoedia* (January 31, 1920):

my master, Rimsky-Korsakov, was tall and severe, a man with eyeglasses and a redingote. He had a profound respect for the classical rules of musical composition, and he did not always approve of what I was doing.

In March 1944, at the request of the United States Office of War Information, Stravinsky, "with deepest emotion," prepared a statement for Rimsky-Korsakov's centenary, to be broadcast in Russia:

... not only in a tribute to his genius but gratefully for his loving, unforgettable, fatherly guidance in the very inception of my creative musical life: To the master and man whom I love, I bow. [March 15]

Yet Stravinsky's comments about Rimsky-Korsakov's music were scathing. For example, he wrote to Ansermet, July 14, 1932: "I have just heard your performance of *Dubinochka*, which is strangely German and as academic as a Russian revolutionary song."

The following letters from Stravinsky to Rimsky-Korsakov were sent from Ustilug in the summer of 1907. The first, dated July 1, is concerned with publishing, a subject that occupies one of the largest parts of Stravinsky's correspondence as a whole:

1908. St. Petersburg. Rimsky-Korsakov at home, photographed by Stravinsky.

Dear Nikolai Andreyevich, I want to write to you about my life, my
studies, and my first failure. . . . Three weeks ago I received a letter
from young Zimmerman,[82] who excused himself for having made me
wait so long for an answer. The reason he gave was that his father
already has too large a backlog of orchestra pieces awaiting publication
. . . and cannot use my . . . manuscript.[83] . . . A week later my unfortunate manuscript was returned to me. . . . I would have written an angry
answer but decided to cool off instead, and, in a few days, before the
Suite [84] was also returned, I wrote a tactful one suggesting that they
purchase the whole work, the orchestra score as well as the piano,
though it was understood that only the piano score would be published. As for the orchestra score, that could be printed, I said, only
when they did not have so much orchestra material on hand. . . . Since
Siloti asks me about all of this, I'll tell him, for . . . he has promised not
to recommend anyone's compositions to Zimmerman again. . . .

    I am hard at work on the instrumentation of the symphony and the
composition of the *Fantastic Scherzo*, "Bees," about which I will have
more to say later. Besides this, I have completed a Romance [85] which I
began in St. Petersburg and played for you there (the one with the
sound of bells). I am thinking of composing two more songs to words
by the same author.[86] Many things in the symphony have had to be

done over completely. . . . But I hope to finish the first part in about two weeks. The fourth part is still unfinished, and I will bring it along when I come to Petersburg—if I'm alive and well and everything is all right. . . . As for . . . "Bees," the idea of this Scherzo came to me in Petersburg, as you know, but I did not have a subject. Just now Katya and I have read Maeterlinck's *Life of the Bees,* a partly artistic, partly philosophical book that pleased me, as they say, to my toes. For the complete program of the music, I thought at first about selecting a few quotations from the book, but now I see that this is impossible because the language of science and the language of *belles-lettres* are too closely interwoven. I have decided, therefore, that during the composition I would follow a definite program but not use quotations in my headings, simply "Bees (from Maeterlinck), A Fantastic Scherzo." When we are together I will show you what I have chosen for the program. I can't write all this in a letter.

As you see, Nikolai Andreyevich, the construction of our house does not disturb me at all. In fact it even helps, willy-nilly forcing me away from my studio so that I always start work with fresh energy. As for the desire you expressed to Mama that we should have bad weather more often, I must say that this has turned out to be positively sinister. Except for the past five days, constant rain.

I conclude with congratulations on your brilliant success in your works and on your part in them. I bow humbly and send you my heartfelt regards. With sincere affection, Igor Stravinsky.

Stravinsky's second letter to his teacher, dated July 23, concludes with the same elaborate courtesy (not rendered in full in these translations):

Dear Nikolai Andreyevich! I am deliriously happy to have your letters and happy to be assured once again of your interest in me and my work. The awareness that you are always concerned about my compositions has an amazingly encouraging effect on me and makes me feel like working still more industriously and zealously; perhaps this will sound stilted to you, and you will say "Can't he speak more plainly?" But, believe me, I will never be able to find words of true gratitude that would express it.

I am spending my time usefully, orchestrating and correcting what seems bad from the beginning of the first part of the symphony, as well as collecting material for "Bees," which will be giving me a lot of bother. I have taken your comments on the program into account.

I am enjoying Beethoven's symphonies, which I play four-hands with Katia in the evening. I have many thoughts about Beethoven, but I will tell them to you this winter.

Please do not hold it against me, but I am curious to know how *Le Coq d'Or* is progressing. . . . I am following your advice [87] and sneezing at Zimmerman.

Stravinsky wrote to his teacher again, in August:

Dear Nikolai Andreyevich: Yesterday I received your letter with the most *fantastically joyous news for me.* I am in raptures. In my thoughts I bow humbly to my benefactors, and to you, Nikolai Andreyevich, dear friend, *most humbly.*

By August 15 I will write to N. V. Artsybashev [88] with a detailed title for my Suite, and I'll also say that you have informed me that it

has been scheduled for performance. It seems that this is how I understood you. Am I correct?

You write about how much you have composed of *Le Coq d'Or*, remarking that "One slows down in old age." Well, if I in my youth could work as fast as you do in your old age, that wouldn't be so bad. I'm delighted that *Le Coq d'Or* is moving so quickly to completion.

I embrace you in my thoughts, dear Nikolai Andreyevich, and send my regards to your family. Devoted and grateful to you until the grave. Igor Stravinsky.

By the next summer, the composer of *Schéhérazade* was in his grave, and his pupil had written a *Chant Funèbre*. Its performance is the subject of the next two letters to Rimsky-Korsakov's widow:

Dear close-to-my-heart Nadyezhda Nikolayevna, perhaps you have no time for letters and will be annoyed that I am distracting your attention with this one. But I cannot refrain from informing you that I have composed, and already orchestrated, a piece commemorating the death of our dear, immortal Nikolai Andreyevich.

I do not know how to get the piece performed, and this thought disturbs me. It will be very painful for me if it isn't given at even one concert dedicated to the memory of Nikolai Andreyevich. I have just written to Siloti asking for advice, and I await his answer with impatience, this being my tribute to the memory of Nikolai Andreyevich— the tribute of his student whom he loved. You will certainly understand me and my wishes, dear Nadyezhda Nikolayevna.

I send everyone my regards, and I kiss your hand affectionately. With all my soul and thoughts, your Igor Stravinsky. [Ustilug, August 1908]

1908. At Rimsky-Korsakov's, 28 Sagorodny. Igor Stravinsky, Nikolai Rimsky-Korsakov, Nadyezhda Rimsky-Korsakov Steinberg, Maximilien Steinberg, Catherine Stravinsky. In 1976, this house was converted into a state museum. A letter from Paul Collaer, June 7, 1924, Stravinsky's first biographer, reveals that the young composer visited Rimsky-Korsakov here every day toward the end of his life.

Nadyezhda Nikolayevna, if you only knew how I share your grief, how I feel the loss of the eternally dear and beloved Nikolai Andreyevich.

You write that you wish to have my piece performed, just as I do. ... If this would only come to pass. But Siloti has now answered that he does not consider it feasible to perform two mourning pieces in one concert. ... He advises me to try Glazunov, or Count Sheremetyev,[89] and that if nothing works out then, to write letters to the provinces so that it is performed there. But, Nadyezhda Nikolayevna, is one last thing possible? I must, at any cost, and even if it hurts, have it performed in Petersburg. I must take part in honoring Nikolai Andreyevich's memory, and I feel this with all the strength in my soul! A few days ago I telegraphed in detail to Volodya,[90] asking him to speak to Count Sheremetyev, or to his conductor, Vladimirov.[91] I prepaid the answer in order not to cause him any trouble and at the same time to have the verdict as soon as possible. But as yet I have received no reply, and I sent a second telegram today.

I have not approached Glazunov, feeling, as I do, that he would not pay the necessary attention to my letter or to my work. He is indifferent to me, and it is because of this that I unwillingly bring myself to turn to you. I would be grateful to you, Nadyezhda Nikolayevna, if you would write to him about this. If it is your wish, I think he would fulfill your request, which would oblige me infinitely. If *you* want him to, I think he will perform the piece. ... [Ustilug, August 11, 1908]

The *Chant Funèbre* was conducted by Felix Blumenfeld in the Grand Hall of the St. Petersburg Conservatory, February 13, 1909, after which concert the score and parts were lost. Stravinsky's next letter to Nadyezhda Nikolayevna, June 16, 1909, also sent from Ustilug, refers to the publication of Rimsky-Korsakov's *Chronicle* and to a malicious review of it:

... the anniversary of dear Nikolai Andreyevich's death is approaching. *Gospodi*, I cannot tell you how, these days, I've been reliving last year's loss. It is as if my communion with Nikolai Andreyevich had not ceased but that it exists even now. It is particularly painful for me now, too, because of my thoughts about the *Chronicle*, as well as about what is in the *Musical Gazette*. This fiction is terrible. ... Nevertheless, I still want to read about him, and, above all, to read him. We will discuss the *Chronicle* when we see each other in the fall. Meanwhile I will limit myself to expressing my complete delight with this truly amazing book. (I must admit that, having read the whole book straight through and without looking ahead,[92] I definitely retract what I told you in the spring. ...)

I am reading reviews, and not even reviews but simply a useless retelling of passages from the *Chronicle* (which, moreover, are incomplete). I have read Ivanov,[93] and the appallingly evil and foolish piece by Valter.[94] The proverb that your family often repeats about the evil fool is truly correct: "Better to be *n'importe quoi* than to be an evil fool." This fits Valter exactly. It is better not to know a line of music, not to know how to write grammatical Russian, than to be an evil fool. But enough about such people. They're getting too much attention as it is, and their caliber is so poor!

When did you move to Lyubensk? Long ago? Are you planning to go abroad with Andrey? We have not forgotten Andrey's promise to come to Ustilug. As for myself, I'm hard at work on *The Nightingale*. We have read about the great success of *Pskovityanka* in Paris. Tcherepnine, who had promised to let me know how my instrumentations of Chopin came out,[95] has not written a word, so I know nothing.... Your devoted and loving Stravinsky. P.S. I received a letter from Max. I'll write to him shortly.

On June 30, 1910, Stravinsky wrote to his teacher's widow from Berlin, en route to Ustilug after the triumph of *The Firebird* in Paris:

Dear Nadyezhda Nikolayevna, I do not know whether this letter will reach you in Lyubensk, but they will forward it. I hasten to inform you that I have been to the notary, Flammand-Duval (24, rue La Fayette), who asks you to provide him at once with the addresses of all the co-heirs, and to specify which of them will be in Paris in person. Those who come to Paris will sign a general attestation there; the other attestations will be sent for signatures, after which you will receive the money.... Flammand-Duval took the documents that you sent to me. ...I am writing from Berlin on my way to Ustilug, from whence I will go to Brittany for two months and then to Nice for the winter. Meanwhile, write to me in Ustilug. I'll be happy to receive even a small letter from you. Your Igor Stravinsky.

The most important sentence from this letter (quoted above, on page 24) expresses Stravinsky's regrets that Andrey and his mother did not come to Paris for the *Firebird* premiere. Writing to Andrey from Paris, November 20, 1910, Stravinsky went directly to this sore point, but he quickly wrote again, and this and all of his subsequent letters show that he hoped to keep the friendship alive:

Dear Friend! I have just returned from a rehearsal for Hasselmans's [96] concert tomorrow: he is playing my *Fireworks*.[97] But I must return to Beaulieu-sur-Mer, having purchased my ticket. I went to the rehearsal incognito, accompanied by a Parisian friend. At the end I wanted to make Hasselmans's acquaintance and to thank him for a marvelous performance. In fact I heard my music for the first time in a really good one, all difficulties overcome, all my intentions realized and everything sounding fine. Hasselmans was so surprised and embarrassed that he did not know what to do....I thanked him warmly, as I said, but indicated one place that ought to be played differently. The orchestra heartily applauded me.... *Fireworks* will also be given by Pierné at the Concerts Colonne.... Everyone here is amazed and greatly upset by the reception—according to the newspapers—of my *Firebird* in St. Petersburg.

It was fortunate that Stravinsky did not stay for the performance of *Fireworks,* if Florent Schmitt's report in *La France* is true:

... a remarkable work by Igor Stravinsky was not heard because of the turbulence and hostility of the Parisian audience....

Fireworks attained a certain popularity in a dance version by Loïe Fuller, in Paris in May 1914, though Stravinsky thought that she was crazy.

Stravinsky's next letter, sent from Beaulieu-sur-Mer, December 16, 1910, after a trip to St. Petersburg, asks Andrey to forward the originals of two popular songs that were to be used in *Petrushka*,[98] though Stravinsky was not yet ready to reveal anything about this new work:

Friend, I beg you to send immediately two street (or factory?) songs. That is, please send, on a slip of paper, the following. The first starts thus:

and the second thus

I don't swear to my accuracy, and I do not remember these songs, but I do recall that you and Volodya sang them for Gurych's [99] sake. It seems that the first is also sung to the words "Toward evening in a rainy autumn. . . ."

If you do this, you are a friend, and I'll always pray for you. But for God's sake, do it without delay and keep it a secret. When you send the songs, I'll tell you what I'm composing and details about my work in general. Your Igor Stravinsky.

Stravinsky was in mid-*Petrushka* when he wrote again, January 20, 1911, from Beaulieu-sur-Mer:

Read this letter only when you have the time—no rush, it's the merest drivel. I often think of you and regret that contact with you is possible only on a sheet of paper, though better that way than no way at all. But why don't you write? Believe me, even the smallest letter would give me joy. I write, assuming that my letters are welcome and agreeable to you, though I have become lazy myself about writing, probably because I am now obliged to keep an extensive correspondence. . . . I'm a bit tired of work at the moment, and, by way of relaxation, am imagining you with me (which cannot happen, as the deceased Gurevich [100] used to say). . . .

Gnessen [101] is clever and subtle but also *rotten*. His opinions suffer from the same corrupt one-sidedness as do all of those well-known opinions about the styles of Roerich,[102] Bilibin,[103] Stelletsky,[104] when they were compared to Repin,[105] the Perovs,[106] the Pryanishnikovs,[107] the Ryabushkins,[108] *et al.* I highly esteem this last, but on that account must Roerich, Bilibin, and Stelletsky become for me *less* Russian? I hope that this parallel clarifies my meaning. By the same token, why must *my* compositions be approached with the measure of the Conservatory? So that I can be beaten on the skull with it, of course. Well, let them beat! Soon you'll be talking that way, too.[109]

So, having begun with a toast to your health, I should probably end with one to your eternal rest. Forgive me, yours with all my heart, Igor Stravinsky.

The composer wrote again from Beaulieu-sur-Mer on March 7, 1911:

Dear Andrey, please forgive me for not having thanked you yet for Anichkov's [110] book. Tell me how much it cost. I am grateful to you for the errand, and I embrace you heartily. Tell Max Steinberg that I received his kind postcard the other day but am without means of answering, for fear of infecting him and his darling Mitya with the whooping cough of my elder children.[111] Whooping cough is a protracted and repulsive business, and we are in quarantine, unable even to see the Beliankins. If you want details, you can get them from Mama.

Tell Max that I have not forgotten him, and, on the contrary, am thirsting to know what he is doing. I heartily shake his hand but cannot embrace him because I have a cough and a head cold. . . . I am waiting for a "homage" from him, for which I thank him in advance. If he is not afraid of receiving a letter from me, then let him write a few words, for I have things to write to him. . . . Our *Firebird* has been sold to Jurgenson on rather profitable terms. He is printing everything, moreover, orchestra score, vocal score, piano score, and paying 1,500 gold rubles. Did you give the Pastorale to Nadyezhda, and did Max get my piano Etudes from Gury?

Stravinsky's next letter is postmarked Warsaw, August 21, 1911, two months after the premiere of *Petrushka*:

Dear Andrey, No sooner did I get your letter than I weighed anchor and sailed off to Diaghilev in Karlsbad. Now I am going to see Benois in Lugano, after which I will return to Ustilug. On September 15 we go to Clarens for the winter. You know, dear, that Switzerland is better for me as well as for the family. I have to grow strong spiritually but in the Fatherland would become completely neuraesthenic. Your letter is marvelous, but I object to it, nonetheless, and will do so when I am back in Ustilug, from whence I intend to write to you a good deal. God! What a pity we are not together! I'm convinced we would get along well. And how! Your friend, Igor. P.S. I have sent *The Firebird* to you. *Petrushka* sends you no regards, for you have forgotten him.

In 1912, the feud became open, and when Jurgenson, the publisher of *The Firebird*, wished to acquire Stravinsky's Symphony in E-flat, and the composer asked Nadyezhda Steinberg to lend it to him (the manuscript being in the possession of the Rimsky-Korsakov family), she answered rudely and did not comply with the request until he sent a second letter. Meanwhile, Stravinsky wrote to Andrey on October 7, 1911:

Dear beloved and excellent Andrey, I'm writing to you, as you see, from Warsaw, on my way to Switzerland. I have been meaning to answer for a long time, as you know, and most likely you have been waiting for my answer to your letter (no less excellent than yourself). But, strange as it seems, I am not going to answer that letter of yours. Why? Better to answer with actions than with words! Now is the time to say that you ought to read *The Dance* by George Fuchs (in the *Vial of Passions*, St. Petersburg, published by Venok, 1910). Please send to me—in Clarens, Switzerland, Maison "Les Tilleuls"—the *News of Western Literature* (same publisher). I will be patient only when you read the Fuchs article and spell out your opinion to me on paper, affirmed by your signature and witnessed by the local police.

You ask, what can be better and more beautiful than the development of artistic forms that already exist? I answer, only one thing: the creation of new forms. Insofar as I see, *you* abide by the first. But since I do not see you, I will not swear that you agree, or have already agreed, with the second—not with words and mind (of which no one ever has as much as he needs) but with feelings, which we possess to the degree that we need them.[112] Yes or no? Give Siloti the finger.[113]

Stravinsky was composing the *"Glorification de l'Elue" (Le Sacre du Printemps)* when he wrote again, March 7, 1912:

Dear friend: I have just received *Apollo*, with the addendum (Chronicle No. 3), and have read Levinson's criticism of Svetlov's book, *Contemporary Ballet*. Though far from agreeing with Levinson's views, as expressed in his articles in the last numbers of *Apollo* last year, I must declare him unconditionally correct in his condemnation of the contents of Svetlov's book—which do not correspond at all to its external appearance. To add to Levinson's review, it remains to be said that Svetlov's text is nothing more than an article from the *Petersburg News*, handsomely published.

Here is the real problem: We have many powerful enemies who have much truth on their side, and who rejoice in our artistic failures. But instead of understanding this, and instead of seeing our shortcomings and failures himself and thereby disarming the enemy, Svetlov praises everything indiscriminately.... It may amaze you that I am writing to you at all, but I know that although the subject is personally alien to you, you are objective and will understand.

Gospodi! It is two years since we have seen each other and exchanged feelings and thoughts. I would love to see you. And how much we have to talk about. I am living (with the family, of course) away from everything that seethes and rumbles, but I follow it all intensely.... Unchangingly yours, Igor Stravinsky. In a tavern, where I drank two glasses of Munich [beer] to your health. My address: Clarens, Maison "Les Tilleuls."

Stravinsky wrote from Clarens again on November 5, during the composition of the *"Danse Sacrale"*:

Dear one, if you will seek out Levitsky [114] for me as you promised, that will be wonderful. Mama has already found the entire series of *Old Years* for 1907; and for only 70 rubles. What do you say to that? Lucky? I bought Japanese paper in Berlin. Will you come there? We will be there for a month, from the 20th of November to the 20th of December.

Between this letter and Stravinsky's final one, Andrey had attacked both *Petrushka* and *Le Sacre du Printemps* [115] in his critical reviews. But perhaps this is understandable in view of comments such as the following, from *Russian Newspaper*, February 1, 1913:

Stravinsky was the pupil of Rimsky-Korsakov, and we cannot imagine him without Rimsky-Korsakov. We see the influence of ideas, the attraction of fantasy, or Russian tales, and technical influence—especially in the orchestration. Like Rimsky-Korsakov, Stravinsky tries to exploit the best of each instrument. But Stravinsky's orchestral palette, particularly in Petrushka, is much richer than that of Rimsky-Korsakov. Stravinsky even uses the piano,[116] and so effectively. . . .

He also knows Debussy and Ravel, of course, but is deeply talented, original, and still very young. . . . We expect many more new and formidably original scores from this thirty-one-year-old composer. . . .

The final breakdown of the friendship is clearly attributable to Stravinsky's participation in the new version of Mussorgsky's Khovanshchina. A letter from Maximilien Steinberg reveals how this news was received in Russia:

Dear Igor: I wrote to your address in Clarens (which Gury gave to me). Thanks for your letter.[117] Petrushka was very well played here. I am enraptured by the sonority.[118] I hope that you will not be offended by my frank opinion: Petrushka should be performed only with staging. The beginning of the Fourth Tableau and the Dance of the Coachmen sound very well. As for the Wetnurses, the conductor took it too fast for my taste. And why, at the appearance of the bear, did the tuba play an octave lower? Is it intended to be that way? . . . Now something else. Did you know from the Russian Newspaper that Diaghilev will produce Khovanshchina? It would be good if you could give some explanation in the Russian Newspaper or in the Russian Report (where Andrey writes). Address a letter to my name and I will print it immediately. I do not believe the ridiculous gossip that you would correct the orchestration of Nikolai Andreyevich. This is very important, and I ask you to do it. I do not write about myself; Diaghilev will tell you. [St. Petersburg, January 28, 1913]

Stravinsky received a letter from Andrey, January 31, 1914, announcing his marriage and saying that "our artistic differences do not affect my friendship for you, but perhaps this confession already comes too late. . . ." Stravinsky answered from Lausanne, February 16, 1914:

Dear Andrey, I sincerely congratulate you and your wife, and I wish you long and great happiness in your life together. I say this to you with all my heart because I believe in your sincerity. Also, our friendship should not be an illusion, and this could happen in spite of ourselves because of our different ways in art, or because we so rarely see each other. Your poisonous blasts against my creations, and your protests against my "anti-artistic" activity—and this after your letter, in which I have no cause to doubt your sincerity—all this should not affect our friendship. I am unable to write more, my mind being occupied with other things. My wife had a temperature after the birth of Milène. The doctor says it is tuberculosis with pleurisy. A difficult time for me.

Stravinsky and Andrey met once again, in June 1914, in London, where Andrey had come to see Le Coq d'Or [119] and Nuit de Mai, but could not avoid seeing The Nightingale as well. A postcard dated June 20, 1914, to Stravinsky, in London, from his wife, in Salvan, refers to the composer's "fascinating" account of his meeting and conversation with Andrey. In 1915, in the magazine *Apollo,* Andrey remarked of Stravinsky's subject matter that he had "begun with fairy tales and progressed to primitivism." This is true, but fairy tales were to remain a part of Stravinsky's imaginative world *(Le Baiser de la Fée),* as was primitivism, though under the larger concept of ritual, both secular *(Les Noces)* and sacred (the Mass). And to these he was to add moral fables *(Histoire du Soldat, The Rake's Progress),* myths *(Oedipus Rex, Perséphone),* and, finally, biblical drama *(The Flood, Abraham and Isaac).*

The Firebird

Last year a young man composed for his debut a ballet, The Firebird. . . . Well, this work was an exquisite and original piece. . . .
—Debussy, Excelsior, March 9, 1911

Stravinsky wrote to G. G. Païchadze, March 29, 1929:

So far as my rights to *The Firebird* are concerned, no one has ever raised the question because the subject is a folk tale; Fokine is merely the composer of the dances of the choreography that Diaghilev uses. On the other hand, the libretto of the ballet was composed by everyone, myself included, and in the same measure as Diaghilev and Fokine, Golovine and Benois and Bakst.

Perhaps the most striking feature of *The Firebird* is the orchestral color, and it is safe to assert that, since Wagner, no composer had developed a more individual sense of color than Stravinsky. . . . It will be years before the mandarins and textbooks catch up to him. . . . His vitality is amazing, and to use the recent words of a famous French critic, "How are we to analyze the irresistible attraction of work so outrageous, so deliberately aggressive, so rich in individuality, so contrary to those of our tastes which appear the most respectable? One does not analyze, one submits." [From the *Christian Science Monitor,* October 8, 1913, on a performance of the *Firebird* Suite in London]

The above review is of the first suite, which employs the same orchestra as the ballet. The idea of arranging *The Firebird* for smaller orchestra occurred to Stravinsky as early as 1914. On July 24 of that year, he wrote to Jurgenson, the publisher of the original ballet:

In April 1915 I plan to conduct parts of *The Firebird* (the "Berceuse" and "Finale") with the *Scherzo Fantastique,* in Queen's Hall, London. These *Firebird* movements have not yet been performed in concert, and I have had no time to re-orchestrate the music, being terribly busy. Now I am more free and will do it. Therefore I ask you to send the orchestra score of the "Berceuse," as well as the orchestra score of the whole ballet. I will arrange both pieces for a smaller orchestra (as I already did for the "Berceuse"). Too many orchestras do not have enough good musicians.
　　Now to other things. I have already orchestrated the Verlaine songs, and I ask you to buy these versions. I want 200 rubles for each one. As for the "Finale" of *The Firebird,* I give it to you, together with the "Berceuse." . . . I heard *The Firebird* in London, a tremendous success.

I live in Salvan (Valais), Switzerland, Pension Bel-Air. It would be nice if you would come there this summer.

Stravinsky did re-orchestrate the "Finale" in spite of the war and the cancellation of the London concert. (The manuscript score of this movement, dated March 31, 1915, was sold at auction in Monaco in November 1975.) In 1918, he began a complete revision of the *Firebird* Suite. As he wrote to Otto Kling: [120]

I have spent six months (October, November, December 1918, and January, February, March 1919) composing [the new *Firebird*]. . . . [Letter of August 17, 1920]

A fortnight earlier, Stravinsky had written to Kling justifying the publication of this version, the rights to the original having belonged to the Russian publisher Jurgenson:

The new regime in Russia has entirely altered the concept of private property, material and intellectual. . . . I am as much a victim as Jurgenson.

All the same, Stravinsky did not inform Jurgenson of the existence of a new version of the *Firebird* Suite, and that it had been sold to an English publisher. The composer had last heard from Jurgenson on May 27, 1918, by way of a telegraphed message (sent from Moscow on May 20) to the effect that Emil Cooper wished to conduct *The Firebird* in June 1918 in the Moscow Grand Theater. Stravinsky telegraphed a reply stipulating a fee in Swiss francs payable in Zürich, which seems to have been impossible for the Soviets. On June 25, 1922, Jurgenson wrote from Moscow inquiring about the English edition of the Suite; and since Jurgenson had continued to publish and distribute through its Leipzig office, later selling to a German publisher, Robert Forberg, Stravinsky became involved in a decade of litigation over the rights to the music, which Schott finally purchased from Forberg.[121] It is worth remarking, however, that when recording the *Firebird* Suite (Paris, November 8, 9, and 10, 1928), Stravinsky used the original, Jurgenson, version.

Nor did Stravinsky introduce his new version of the Finale when he conducted *The Firebird* (the complete ballet) at the Paris Opéra for a Red Cross benefit performance by the Ballets Russes, Wednesday, December 29, 1915 at 3:30 P.M.[122] This program opened with the national anthems of the Allies—the King and Queen of England and the President of the Republic were present—continued with *Schéhérazade, The Firebird, Soleil de Nuit* (from Rimsky-Korsakov's *The Snowmaiden*), a *Pas de Deux*, and the *Polovtsian Dances*. In a letter to Siloti, February 11, 1916, from Paris, Stravinsky describes his performances of *The Firebird* as "a colossal success." [123]

In May 1929, Aeolian released *The Firebird* played by Stravinsky on "audio-graphic" Duo-Art pianola rolls. The left-hand side of each roll contained a running commentary on the development of the themes, the instrumentation, and other technical

Spring 1910. St. Petersburg. On Nevsky Prospect, at the time of the composition of *The Firebird.* "The Nevsky Prospect consists of a vast expanse for the circulation of the public (not of air, to be sure); the houses, which line it and shape its frontiers, are what give it substance. In the evening, the Nevsky Prospect is lighted by electricity. By day the Prospect needs no illumination. The Nevsky Prospect is rectilinear. . . . The wet slippery prospect was intersected by another wet prospect at a ninety-degree angle. . . . Precisely the same kind of houses rose here, and the same kind of gray human streams flowed by, and the same greenish hell of fog hovered in the air. Parallel with the running prospect was another running prospect with the same row of boxes, the same system of numeration, and the same clouds. . . . There is an infinity about the running prospects, and an infinity about the running intersecting shadows. Petersburg, as a whole, represents a sum to infinity of the prospect, elevated to the nth degree. Beyond Petersburg, there is nothing." [Andrey Biely, *St. Petersburg* (1913)]

1910. First page of the Finale of *The Firebird*, original version, also used for the 1919 Suite.

aspects of the music, while the right-hand side contained a minute description of the action of the ballet. Program notes could hardly be made more explicit, information and music being perfectly synchronized; and, in this case, the program revealed that, originally, almost every measure of the ballet had been tied to a stage episode. Sometimes the composer is startlingly literary, as when he says that in *The Firebird* he had

not yet completely broken with all the devices covered by the term Music Drama. I was still rather susceptible to the system of musical characterization of different people or of different dramatic situations. And this system shows itself in the introduction of processes belonging to the order of what is called Leitmotiv. . . . All that is concerned with the evil genius Kastchei, all that belongs to his kingdom—the enchanted garden, the ogres and monsters of all kinds who are his subjects, and, in general, all that is magical and mysterious, marvelous or supernatural—is characterized in the music by what might be termed a Leit-harmony. . . .

In contrast with the magical chromatic music, the mortal element (the prince and the princess) is allied with characteristically Russian music of a diatonic type.[124]

After explaining that the melodic intervals of an upward augmented fourth and a downward minor second "serve to form the basis of the benevolent . . . apparitions of the Firebird," Stravinsky terms the "interrupting thirds" of Kastchei "spiteful"—which is remarkable coming from a composer who, not many years later, was to contend that "music is powerless to express anything at all."

One aspect of *The Firebird* about which Stravinsky has nothing to say is that of his folk-music sources, but this was a subject that he always refused to discuss. In *The Firebird* he incorporates longer folk melodies and scarcely modifies them—such as the following two from Rimsky-Korsakov's *100 Russian Folk Songs* (Op. 24), numbers 79 and 21 respectively.

Stravinsky and Debussy

Stravinsky's debt to Debussy began while Stravinsky was still a student of Rimsky-Korsakov,[125] and it ranges from imitation (the Prelude to *The Nightingale*) to the expansion and intensification of harmonic, melodic, and orchestral idioms (*Le Sacre du Printemps* [126]). Stravinsky told Janet Flanner that he "started [*Petrushka*] in a comfortable garret in Switzerland before a signed photograph of Debussy" (the *New Yorker*, January 5, 1935). Stravinsky confided his thoughts about Debussy at this time to the margins of the chapter on the French composer in Paul Landormy's *Histoire de la Musique* (Paris, 1910).

The *Symphonies of Wind Instruments*, one of Stravinsky's most powerful works, was composed in memory of Debussy. The astral cantata *Zvezdoliki*, for male chorus and orchestra, one of the Russian composer's most curious works, was dedicated (1911) to the living French master. A postcard to Florent Schmitt, signed "July 21, 1911, Ustilug," contains the first ref-

June 1910 and 1911. Paris. With Debussy, in his home at 80, avenue du Bois de Boulogne. Photograph by Erik Satie (1910).

Debussy at his desk, with his daughter Emma-Claude ("Chou-Chou"), and in the garden with his wife. Photographs by Stravinsky.

erence to the short cantata, whose intervallic motto, a major second up and a fourth down, lies at the center of Stravinsky's music. In the same postcard, Stravinsky says that he is "playing only Debussy and Scriabin."

Probably realizing that *Zvezdoliki* could not be commercially profitable, Jurgenson was slow to publish it, and only a few copies were printed. One of his letters to Stravinsky, November 27, 1913, explains that "only three copies were sent because the printing was small." Another letter, December 22, 1913, announces that an additional copy is being mailed, that the printing of the Symphony in E-flat is almost complete, that Stravinsky should "try to get money from Diaghilev for *The Firebird*, since the contract has almost expired," and that "I will tell Scriabin about your wish" (whatever that may have been). A project to perform *Zvezdoliki* in Paris in May 1912 [127] seemed likely as late as April 8, when Stravinsky wrote to the conductor Pierre Sechiari (who later became the conductor of the Marseille Orchestra and who directed a performance of Stravinsky's Piano Concerto with the composer as soloist):

I will come to Paris in May . . . and will be happy to hear my work—it is not large, a cantata for male voices and orchestra—under your direction. . . .

But this came to nothing. On October 13, 1912, Sechiari wrote to Stravinsky: "I have received your manuscript, but the chorus [parts are] too difficult. . . ." On November 28, Sechiari wrote again saying that the piece would require seventy rehearsals and even then would not be given a good performance. He returned the score to Maurice Delage, who wrote to Stravinsky, November 7, 1912, asking whether to keep or to return the manuscript of the piano reduction. Ravel, seeing the score in Clarens several months later, reported to Mme Alfredo Casella:

I assured Stravinsky that, thanks to Inghelbrecht,[128] our choruses in France have already been ruined and would not be able to sing what he has composed lately, which is most difficult (and very short, hardly 5 minutes) but excellent for an orchestral concert. [Letter of April 2, 1913]

On the twenty-fifth anniversary of Debussy's death, Stravinsky recorded a verbal tribute for broadcast in Occupied France. Later, in an interview in Montreal, he acknowledged Debussy as "my father in music" (and Ravel as "my uncle"). Stravinsky, in his final years, listened to more of Debussy's music, and with more pleasure, than at any other time since the first decade of the century. On July 29, 1968, Mrs. Stravinsky wrote to the Radiodiffusion Télévision Belge extending the hope that "in Switzerland or in France, in the autumn," her husband might grant a requested interview about Debussy:

Debussy has been much in Stravinsky's thoughts lately, and he has been listening to a great deal of Debussy's music on our gramophone.

The interview did not take place, but, in November 1968, the composer of the *Sacre* visited the birthplace of the composer of *Pelléas*, in St. Germain-en-Laye.

As for Debussy on Stravinsky, the first and last recorded impressions were confided to Robert Godet.[129] Debussy's first letter to Godet is dated June 1911:

Near you in Switzerland is a young Russian who has an instinctive genius for color and rhythm. I am sure that both he and his music will give you infinite pleasure. And what a mind he has! His music is full of feeling for the orchestra, conceived directly for the orchestral canvas [*C'est fait en pleine pâte orchestrale*], and it is concerned only with conveying an emotional intensity. He is afraid of nothing, nor is he pretentious. It is music that is childlike and untamed. Yet the layout [*la mise en place*] and the co-ordination of ideas is extremely delicate. If you have an opportunity to meet him, do not hesitate.

Debussy's final impression is dated January 4, 1916:

I have just seen Stravinsky.[130] He says "my *Firebird*, my *Sacre*," just as a child would say "my top, my hoop," and that is just what he is: a spoiled child who wears tumultuous cravats [131] and kisses the hand of a lady while stepping on her feet; when he is an old man he will be insupportable. That is to say, he will support no music whatever. But at this moment he is something unheard of! He professes friendship for me because I have helped him to mount a ladder, from the top of which he hurls grenades, some failing to go off.[132]

Debussy's letters to Stravinsky are well known [133] but must be quoted in part if only because the French master's criticism of *Petrushka* is the most perceptive ever published:

Thanks to you I have passed an enjoyable Easter vacation in the company of *Petrushka*, the terrible Moor, and the delicious Ballerina. I can imagine that you spent incomparable moments with the three puppets. ... I do not know many things of greater value than the passage you call "*Tour de passe-passe*." ... There is in it a kind of sonorous magic, a mysterious transformation of mechanical souls, which become human by a spell, and of which, until now, you seem to be the unique inventor. Finally, there is an orchestral infallibility that I have found only in *Parsifal*. You will understand what I mean, of course, and though it is certain that you will go much further than *Petrushka*, you can be proud already of the achievement of this work. [April 1912]

Debussy was less wholeheartedly devoted to *Le Sacre du Printemps*, and the two men were less candid with each other after the premiere of the *Sacre* had eclipsed that of Debussy's *Jeux*, performed earlier in the same month. More than half a year before, Debussy had written to Stravinsky:

... As soon as I have a good proof copy of *Jeux* I will send it to you. ... I would love to have your opinion of this "badinage in three parts." Speaking of *Jeux*, you were surprised that I chose this title, to which your preferred *The Park*. I beg you to believe that *Jeux* is better, first because it is more appropriate, and then because it more nearly invokes the "horrors" that occur among these characters. . . . When are you coming to Paris so that one may at last play good music? Very affectionately from us three to you and to your wife. Your old friend, Claude Debussy. [November 5, 1912]

On January 1, 1913, the two composers celebrated their friendship and the beginning of the new year with an exchange of telegrams. Six months later, after the *Sacre* and Stravinsky's bout with typhus, Debussy wrote to him in Ustilug expressing "the hope that you have recovered; take care, music needs you." But the letter after that, dated November 9, 1913, raises storm warnings:

Dear Stravinsky, It is natural that people who are a little embarrassed by your growing mastery have not neglected to spread discordant rumors; if you're not already dead, it is not their fault. I have never believed in a rumor—is it necessary to tell you this? No! Also, it is not necessary to tell you of the joy I have had to see my name associated with a very beautiful thing that will be more beautiful still with the passage of time. For me, who descend the other slope of the hill but keep an intense passion for music, it is a special satisfaction to tell you how much you have enlarged the boundaries of the permissible in the empire of sound. Forgive me for using such pompous words, but they exactly express my thought. . . .

Debussy wrote again on November 17:

Dear Stravinsky, Kussevitzky has telegraphed that I am expected in Moscow on December 3. Since the St. Petersburg concert is on the 10th, you can see that I will not have time for anything else. . . . If you have nothing better to do, I advise you to go to Moscow. It is a marvelous city, and you probably do not know it very well. You will meet there Claude Debussy, French musician, who loves you very much. . . .

When Sabaneyev, a critic for *Muzyka* (Moscow), attacked Debussy during his 1913 Russian tour, Stravinsky complained to the editor, Derzhanovsky:

It is impossible not to notice that Sabaneyev's evaluation of Claude Debussy's work is openly biased and indeed of an unheard-of one-sidedness. Yet these charming lines appear in *Muzyka*, that passionate defender of the French musician who has just arrived in Moscow. You seem to think that a complete and multi-faceted evaluation of one artistic phenomenon, Scriabin, guarantees the same kind of evaluation of another phenomenon, Debussy. . . . Either the same issue of your magazine should have included articles expressing other opinions, or you should have mentioned that the publication of this article was the personal responsibility of its author, since *Muzyka* is essentially in disagreement with him. But nothing of the sort was done, and now it is not Sabaneyev who will answer for this scandalous article but you, Vladimir Vladimirovich. . . . Laloy [134] and Calvocoressi,[135] both of whom speak Russian *and* read *Muzyka*, will tell Debussy and . . . what will he think of you? . . . After all, I explained the whole situation to Debussy when he was preparing to go to Moscow. . . . Be assured that I am not hiding a stone behind *my* back. [December 26, 1913]

On October 14, 1915, Debussy wrote to Robert Godet:

Just now we may wonder into whose arms music may fall. The young Russian school offers us hers. But in my opinion they have become as un-Russian as possible. Stravinsky himself is leaning dangerously in the direction of Schoenberg, but nevertheless remains the most wonderful orchestral technician of our time.

Ten days later, on October 24, 1915, Debussy wrote to Stravinsky, answering a letter of his dated October 11:

Dear Stravinsky, you are a great artist. Be with all your strength a great Russian artist. It is so wonderful to be of one's country, to be attached to one's soil like the humblest of peasants! . . . It is very difficult to know when we will see each other, and so we have only the weak resource of words. . . .

But the composers saw each other at least once more. Writing from Morges to Diaghilev, in Rome, November 21, 1916, Stravinsky says:

I have just come from Paris. . . . I saw both Ravel and Debussy at a Concerts Colonne rehearsal for the *Rapsodie Espagnole* and *Saint Sébastien*. Debussy is better now and very much thinner. . . . Except for one or two pieces, I do not care for *Saint Sébastien*, but I greatly admire Ravel's *Rapsodie*.

Petrushka

Petrushka must be called a masterpiece, one of the most unexpected, most impulsive, most buoyant and lively that I know. . . . The music is by Igor Stravinsky; this name, that we have come to know through The Firebird, *we will never forget now.*
—*Jacques Rivière,*
La Nouvelle Revue Française,
September 1911

In early accounts of the origins of *Petrushka*,[136] Stravinsky does not mention a puppet but a kind of Svengali:

My first idea for *Petrushka* was to compose a *Konzertstück*, a sort of combat between the piano and the orchestra. This became the Second Tableau. . . . In that first vision I saw a man in evening dress, with long hair, the musician or the poet of romantic tradition. He placed several heteroclite objects on the keyboard and rolled them up and down. At this the orchestra exploded with the most vehement protestations—hammer blows, in fact. . . .

I was not attracted by any folklore element in *Petrushka*, always being tempted, in the life of things, by something very different from that. [*Les Nouvelles Littéraires*, December 8, 1928]

In 1931, an article by Herbert Fleischer, "*Stravinskys Weltbild*," published in the *Berliner Tageblatt* (September 16), concluded with the statement:

In the final music of *Petrushka*, human existence is ridiculed through the shadow of a puppet . . . this mechanical victory. . . .

Here Stravinsky penciled in the margin: "But it is exactly the contrary." And writing to Nigel Gosling of the London *Observer*, May 2, 1958, the composer stated that

The "ghost" at the end is the real Petrushka . . . the character in the [preceding] play only à doll. The "ghost's" gesture is . . . not so much one of triumph as a nose-thumbing to the magician.

The critical commentary surrounding *Petrushka* is vast and too well known for quotation here. One article that should be mentioned, however, is that by Jacques Dalcroze in *La Tribune de Genève*, February 8, 1917, in which the inventor of eurhythmics remarks that "the question of the moment in the salons of Geneva is 'Aimez-vous Petrushka?' " When Ansermet first performed excerpts from the ballet, Geneva, Saturday, January 20, 1915, Dalcroze wrote to Stravinsky the same night:

Cher ami, I leave the theater bursting with joy and pride that such a human being as you exists. What an abundance in expressing popular feeling, what an acuteness of sensation in the primitive and eternal, and in nuances, intensities, dynamism. All this proves that, even after centuries, music is capable of renewing itself and developing, through genius—yours. . . .

Writing about *Petrushka* in London, October 1928, for the pianola version of the music, Stravinsky says:

For me the piece had the character of a burlesque for piano and orchestra, each with an equal role. . . . But I was not satisfied with the title "Pièce Burlesque" . . . the real subject was the droll, ugly, sentimental, shifting personage who was always in an explosion of revolt . . . a sort of guignol called Pierrot in France, Kasperle in Germany, and Petrushka in Russia. . . . I began to meditate an entire poem in the form of choreographic scenes . . . of the mysterious life of Petrushka, his birth, his death, his double existence—which is the key to the enigma, a key not possessed by the one who believes that he has given him life, the Magician.

Stravinsky's most vivid statement about *Petrushka* is found in a letter to Andrey Rimsky-Korsakov written shortly after the composer's return to Beaulieu-sur-Mer from discussions with Diaghilev, Fokine, Nijinsky, and Benois in St. Petersburg, in December 1910. The letter is also powerful proof that life, not art, was the source of the composer's inspiration:

. . . My last visit to Petersburg did me much good, and the final scene is shaping up excitingly . . . quick tempos, concertinas, major keys . . . smells of Russian food—*shchi*—and of sweat and glistening leather boots. Oh what excitement! What, in comparison, is Monte Carlo, where it is forbidden even to smoke in the Salle de Jeu? All of these considerations of Gnessen about "reflexes" in Russian music, to the effect that they are present in my composition: all are pure nonsense. [Letter of January 20, 1911]

The correspondence between Stravinsky and Benois in the winter of 1910–11 offers an intimate view of a collaboration between masters of two different arts. Benois's letters were published long ago, but Stravinsky's appear here for the first time in English:

November 3, 1910. Clarens. If the St. Petersburg meeting about *Petrushka* is to take place, I will participate in it, at least by letter. . . . It is my very strong desire that *Petrushka* end with the Magician, who, after the Moor has killed Petrushka, would arrive on the stage, gathering up all three—Petrushka, the Moor, and the Ballerina—and leave with an elegant and mincing bow, exactly the way he came out in the first scene. I have composed the Shrovetide Carnival in Scene One before the Magician's trick, as well as the Russian Dance after it. But I have not yet begun the trick itself. I am waiting for it from you, so fulfill your obligation and send it, otherwise it will hold up the composition of the ballet. . . . Since *Petrushka* is the title, it seems to me that there should be more of Petrushka in the action. But his part, in both quantity and quality, is no greater than that of the Moor or of the Ballerina. I think we should concentrate to a greater extent on Petrushka. Don't you agree?

The "trick" is the *Tour de Passe-passe*, which Debussy singled out as one of the most impressive episodes in the score. Stravinsky thought so as well and, no matter how much cutting he submitted to elsewhere in the opus, never omitted these pages. Another letter makes clear that in the early years he did not sanction *any* cutting for concert performances, or, in other words, any *Petrushka* Suite, though he allowed Kussevitzky to perform excerpts in concert form as early as 1912, and, in April 1917, conducted a "*Petrushka* Suite" himself in Rome. In the Société des Auteurs agreement for the *Petrushka* Suite, February 9, 1921, Stravinsky estimates the duration of the excerpts from the ballet as twenty minutes but does not describe the contents. He first outlined these in a letter, October 18, 1928, to the Concert Society, Zürich:

The following fragments comprise what is called the Suite from *Petrushka*: 1) The *Tour de Passe-passe* and the Russian Dance; 2) the entire Second Tableau; 3) the Fourth Tableau until No. 125, at which point the music goes to the concert ending.

Twenty years later, he instructed Boosey & Hawkes that the so-called Suite consisted of either

the whole First Tableau, ending with the fifth measure after $\boxed{90}$ (marked "for ending"), or the Second, beginning at $\boxed{58}$ (the rehearsal numbers are those of the new version) and going to the same ending, then resuming at $\boxed{93}$ and continuing until $\boxed{119}$. The Suite switches from the last measure of page 164 to the concert ending.[137] [Letter of March 21, 1948]

January 15, 1911. Monte Carlo. Dear Alexander Nikolayevich Benois, I hasten to inform you of a change. But have no fears. I have recomposed the street organ in the first act, and with repetitions, but the beginning remains a humorous strum ("*naigrysh*"). Also, where a change had been proposed, during the overlapping of the two organs, I have inserted a musical snuffbox which plays once *during the motif of the two organs*

and a second time parallel with it.

The second change is in Scene Four, after the entry of the Wetnurses. It now seems to me that the Coachmen must enter alone, without "ladies." . . . Excuse the disorder of this letter. I have drunk a lot of Pilsen [Pilsner].

Beaulieu-sur-Mer. January 26, 1911: Dear Alexander Nikolayevich . . . I have just composed the Wetnurses, the Bear, the dashing young Merchant, and the Coachmen—almost, that is; a few trifles remain. In the fourth scene, only the "Mummers," the "drama," the "Cripples," and the "revelry" remain to be done. The lack of time frightens and unnerves me—a feeling very familiar from *The Firebird*, which is no concern of yours or of Diaghilev's, but what cruelty! Yesterday I sent the four-hand score of the second scene, "Petrushenka." I do not have time to make copies of these things and am mailing the original manuscripts. If they are to be copied in St. Petersburg, *then I want to know how many times and who has the copies.*

You write to me about the whistles and the "gong" (actually a tam-tam), which warn of various happenings and horrors. I myself had such a thought, but it has already been realized in part by the introduction of the drum beating (before the trick, Petrushka and the Moor). And actually we have only one event, the trick! A whistle or a blow on the tam-tam could be used to prepare for this, but it turns out to be superfluous because the two blockheads warn of it with the drums. Then there are no more events—for us, that is, but not for those who do the warning.

I am extremely interested in your work and burning with impatience to see your designs. I envy your speed of production. As for the gypsy girls with the "young rogue," the music is already composed, and one may no longer speak of gypsy motifs, especially since my young rogue plays the *garmoshka:* somewhere in his little one-and-a-half-minute number he squeezes an accordion in his hands. In general the form of this dance turned out to be rather interesting. After the bear dances something awkward, imitating—to the tuba—the peasant who is playing the pipes and leading him on a rope (or whatever), the animal is led across the stage and disappears; all of this lasts one minute. Little by little a carousel begins to sound, at one point seeming to quiet down, then beginning to play again. The Merchant does not dance to the carousel at all but crawls out of the tavern on his own, and only then . . . dances to some kind of music which is wafted out with the steam of the cabbage soup from the tavern. He squeezes the accordion, again dances "to the tavern," and once again to the *garmoshka.* At this point the carousel starts up, and the Merchant passes, as in the beginning, with his theme.

Beaulieu-sur-Mer. February 3, 1911: Dear Alexander Nikolayevich! Yesterday a brilliant thought came to me, and perhaps a most common one—namely, to do away with the drum before the entrance of Petrushka (second act) and before the Moor (third act). Here is the reason. The drum beat invites the on-stage listeners attending the fair (*bologanny*) to a spectacle, but does not invite the public sitting in a Monte Carlo or Paris theater. The drum could have a place and would be very nice, but is not appropriate in the context, for it distracts the listener in the audience, especially since a drum beat is used in the first act to attract the fair crowd to the spectacle of the Trick. Petrushka's actions and the Moor's, on the other hand, are not a presentation for the stage crowd but are for us. Consequently, the drum is inappropriate here.

Beaulieu-sur-Mer. February 15, 1911: Dear Alexander Nikolayevich! I received your postcard. Unfortunately you do not agree with me. This greatly complicates the matter, for I see that Petrushka won't catch his breath after the "trio." But wait! After all, Petrushka doesn't do anything in particular (in my view), beginning his mournful dance only after his cry out of the window. It is a different matter if the change of decors troubles you; that is really unpleasant, particularly for me. I have a minimum of time as it is, and you ask me to compose another minute of music. (60 seconds, you write, so that it doesn't look quite so bad.) Well, there's the essence of the problem, and it is very serious. I do not see, and I do not know of, any more appropriate introduction into the mood of the scene than the drum roll. . . . While I was composing the Petrushka scene and had not yet thought that three scenes would sprout from his little apartment, then I imagined him giving a performance on the Champs de Mars. Now it turns out the other way around, that *no one sees* all of this; it is his personal experience for which no one has time. . . . Only the drum roll did not come to mind, and that was obvious!

Sonia Botkina wrote to Stravinsky November 13, 1923, from her home, 48, avenue Victor Hugo, but he seems not to have answered. She attended his performance of *Threni* in Paris, November 14, 1958, and wrote to him afterward:

April 16, 1911. Beausoleil. Riviera Palace Hotel. The women with the large hats on the edges of the group are the Botkin sisters, Lydia and Sonia. Standing, from the left, are Pavel ("Pavka") Koribut-Kubitovich (Diaghilev's cousin), Tamara Karsavina, Nijinsky, Stravinsky, Benois, Diaghilev. Photograph by Nikolai Besobrasov.

Dear Igor Fyodorovich, I came to your concert with Dr. Pierre Chekov, but we could not reach you. I regret it. We have not seen each other for so many years, and I so much wanted to know about you and your family, whom we knew and loved for such a long time. All of my sisters have died, as you probably know. L. S. Chekov died six years ago, and your godson, Alexis Chekov, was killed in the War (1944). . . . Write even two words if you are still in Paris. My telephone is Balzac 76–76. With all my heart, Sonia Botkina (Mme S. de Konne, 66, rue Pierre Charron, Paris, November 15, 1958)

But Stravinsky did not like intrusions from the past and did not call.
  Stravinsky and Alexandre Benois were friends until 1929:

After my return from Weimar, I saw Benois, who had just arrived from Petersburg. . . . though he belongs to another generation than mine, and though he must return to his job as the director of the Hermitage, I conceived some vague projects of collaboration with him. For I am strongly convinced that his work will be presented to the public a thousand times better than that of any other painter, including those whom I admire much more than I admire him. [Stravinsky to Ansermet, September 9, 1923]

In June 1929, Stravinsky sought Benois's permission to make a sound film of *Petrushka*, and attempted to change the agreement of the Société des Auteurs, according to which Benois, as co-author of the scenario, received royalties from purely musical, as well as from staged, performances. In Paris, on June 21, Stravinsky drafted a statement for an attorney, J. Raulet:

. . . In 1911 Benois played an important role in advising Fokine on the staging and choreography, and because of that I named Benois co-author. But this was not really true: My *scènes burlesques* in four tableaux are entirely composed by me.

On July 4, Raulet gave his opinion that Stravinsky would not succeed in his purpose, and that he should try to get Benois's acquiescence in the matter of the film by direct personal request. On July 14, Stravinsky wrote to Païchadze:

. . . inform Benois by letter that you wish . . . to use *Petrushka* in its original form, that is, in a filming of its scenic-ballet production . . . and that you . . . would like to know in what way he, as co-author of the libretto, would want to be recompensed, with a single sum or in the usual division with me (that is, one sixth). . . . Probably he will choose, as always, to be in the same portion with me. . . . But I am not so much afraid of this as of a demand by him to take part in the adaptation of *Petrushka* for filming . . . [though] we will even agree to that, in order not to shit up the transaction. . . .

  The next year the Russian émigré newspaper *News* published (March 21, 1930) some remarks by Benois attributing the origins of *Petrushka* to Stravinsky's memories of his childhood. The composer vigorously underscored these comments and wrote in the margin that they were "lies and nonsense." But on

April 1911. Rome. Stravinsky composing *Petrushka*, drawing by Alexander Benois. Benois and Stravinsky were living at the Albergo Italia, near the Quattro Fontane, and Stravinsky's room overlooked the Barberini Gardens. The drawing was made in the basement of the Teatro Costanzi. On Thursday, June 1, the Ballets Russes left Rome for Paris, and, on the 13th, *Petrushka* was performed at the Théâtre du Châtelet.

November 20, 1920. Petrograd. A poster for a performance of *Petrushka* at the Maryinsky Theater, conducted by Emil Cooper.*

* 1877–1960. Cooper conducted the performance of *Così fan tutte* that Stravinsky heard in Central City, Colorado, in July 1948, and that had an influence on *The Rake's Progress*.

hearing of Benois's death, Stravinsky wrote to his Paris friend Pierre Suvchinsky on March 10, 1960:

This death has filled me with emotion, not only because of many recollections both good and bad, the latter associated with my last visit to see Benois thirty years ago.

Despite the harsh criticisms of *Petrushka* by Andrey Rimsky-Korsakov, the Russian press of 1912 was not unanimously unfavorable, and the ballet was revived in Petrograd shortly after World War I. The following excerpt from a St. Petersburg newspaper is in connection with the first concert performance of the "Suite":

The fragments from *Petrushka*, the ballet by Stravinsky, comprised Kussevitzky's seventh concert. After them everything was pale, simply filling out the program. Last summer we heard the refined and fragrant music of *The Firebird*. Now *Petrushka*. How quickly the remarkable talent of this young composer is developing. It overflows with new freshness and brilliance and grows not by years but by hours. The music is stunning, unexpected, kaleidoscopic. It can even knock out a listener. . . . [*Russian Morning*, February 12, 1912]

"Akahito," No. I of the *Three Japanese Lyrics*, is dedicated to Maurice Delage, and, to judge from the intimacy of the correspondence, he would seem to have been Stravinsky's closest French friend. October 14, 1912, Stravinsky wrote to him from Ustilug:

. . . Here, far from the tumult of the Grande Saison of the Ballets Russes, all is calm and intimate. . . . There are two Parises—one that gives me fame and money and whose temptations eat away at my vitals almost without my being aware of it. The other is Maurice. . . .

Delage's answer (October 23) is no less intimate, reminding Stravinsky of the

fifteen adorable days that we spent together in Paris *à deux*, and the admirable pear that we shared one night after taking Argutinsky home.

This same letter informs Stravinsky that Ravel has returned to St. Jean de Luz:

always the *blagueur*, he has done nothing there. . . . I hope to be the first to welcome you in Switzerland after Berlin.

Delage *was* the first, and he stayed in Clarens with the Stravinsky family when the composer went to Budapest at the beginning of January 1913. Delage wrote to Stravinsky in the Hungarian city at this time:

I hope you have now regained all of your good humor in the arms of that fiend, Diaghilev.

Two months earlier, Delage had helped Stravinsky with bureaucratic formalities in connection with his membership in the Société des Auteurs:

You must establish by birth certificate that you are a legal Russian subject. . . . If necessary I will go to see Argutinsky. [Letter of November 7, 1912]

But Delage criticized Stravinsky's neoclassic music and, in consequence, the two did not see each other between *Les Noces* (1923) and the Concerto in E-flat (1938). Manuel Rosenthal then effected a reconciliation, persuading Stravinsky to attend a dinner at Ida Rubinstein's at which Delage was present.

Stravinsky and Ravel

Stravinsky's friendship with Ravel was on a different basis from that with Debussy, partly because of the absence of competition between the two younger composers, who were *copains* both in and out of music. The following note, Ravel to Stravinsky, January 1913, indicates the tone of the relationship:

Vieux, many good wishes from the three of us. These are late in being sent because I have not finished correcting the proofs of *Daphnis*—in which I have found things to make Astruc's hair stand on end. I have had news of you from Delage, who had gone about looking into the *Sacres* [sic] *du Printemps* for the antidote that his own harmonies required. . . . When one thinks that M. D'Indy, whose *Ferval* I heard the other day, is in good health, there is no justice! . . . I am told that Nijinsky wants to hear no more talk about dancing, so I can see that M. Poincaré had better get busy with some choreography.

A year and a half later, Stravinsky wrote to Benois:

I love Ravel very much, not sentimentally but actually . . . he is one of those artists who give me great pleasure. . . . What Ravel *says*, well, one ought never to judge people on that basis. [Letter of July 14, 1914]

Stravinsky and Ravel remained on amicable terms until the latter's death, though at the time of *Mavra*, which, predictably, Ravel did not like, the friendship had to endure a period in the desert. Stravinsky, for his part, did not like *any* of Ravel's later music, and when Blair Fairchild [138] described the French composer's piano concerto to Stravinsky (letter of December 31, 1931) as a "*mélange* of Saint-Saëns and Gershwin," the remark was intended to gratify. On October 18, 1928, Stravinsky and Ravel were co-conductors of the inaugural concert for the new

December 1910. Charles Maurice Delage* in Stravinsky's apartment in Beaulieu-sur-Mer.

* Composer (1879–1961).

Salle Pleyel, leading, respectively, the *Firebird* Suite and *La Valse*. Ten years later, on the morning of Ravel's death, Stravinsky read the following phrases ("*insignifiantes*," he later described them) over the telephone to the *Journal de Paris*, which had asked for an obituary:

The death of Ravel did not come as a surprise to me. I had known for some time that the seriousness of his illness was causing the gravest concern to those close to him. I also knew that the type of illness would put an abrupt end to his musical productivity.

He was my friend for a long time. I knew him when I made my debut in Paris with *The Firebird*, and it was then, I remember, that he played some fragments for me from his wonderful *Daphnis*, which he was composing at the time.

France loses one of her greatest musicians, one whose value is recognized throughout the world. He now belongs to history, assured of a place of glory in the domain of music, a place that he conquered with courage and unfaltering conviction. [December 29, 1937]

Five days later, writing to Samuel Dushkin (January 4, 1938), Stravinsky said that

I went so see [Ravel] before the body was placed in the coffin. He lay on a table that was draped in black, a white turban around his head (which had been shaved for the trepanation of the cranium), dressed in a black suit, and wearing white gloves. His arms seemed as long as his body. The wrinkles were black in his very pale face, but this had an expression of great majesty. I went to the interment—a lugubrious experience, these civil burials where everything is banned except protocol. . . .

April 1913. Clarens. Ravel, and Ravel and his mother.

Le Sacre du Printemps:
A Chronology

The first text, below, a translation of the libretto in Stravinsky's hand, differs from the two surviving Roerich versions, one of them (2) in a letter to Diaghilev "at the Theater" (in Paris probably during the spring season of 1912), the other (3) in a letter to Diaghilev, published by Serge Lifar,[139] undated but not earlier than February or March 1913, since Roerich mentions Nijinsky's choreography [140] for the next-to-last dance in Part One.

1

Vesna Sviasschennaya is a musical-choreographic work. It represents pagan Russia and is unified by a single idea: the mystery and great surge of the creative power of Spring. The piece has no plot, but the choreographic succession is as follows:

FIRST PART: THE KISS OF THE EARTH

The spring celebration. It takes place in the hills. The pipers pipe and young men tell fortunes. The old woman enters. She knows the mystery of nature and how to predict the future. Young girls with painted faces come in from the river in single file. They dance the spring dance. Games start.[141] The Spring Khorovod. The people divide into two groups, opposing each other. The holy procession of the wise old men. The oldest and wisest interrupts the spring games, which come to a stop. The people pause trembling before the great action. The old men bless the spring earth. *The Kiss of the Earth.* The people dance passionately on the earth, sanctifying it and becoming one with it.

SECOND PART: THE GREAT SACRIFICE

At night the virgins hold mysterious games, walking in circles. One of the virgins is consecrated as the victim and is twice pointed to by fate, being caught twice in the perpetual circle. The virgins honor her, the chosen one, with a marital dance. They invoke the ancestors and entrust the chosen one to the old wise men. She sacrifices herself in the presence of the old men in the great holy dance, the great sacrifice.

2

I. THE KISS OF THE EARTH

> *Yarilo begins his adoration of the earth.*
> *The earth starts to bloom, a golden bloom.*
> *Divination with twigs.*
> *The people dance for joy.*
> *They pick flowers and bow to the red sun.*
> *The oldest and wisest is led to kiss the rich soil.*
> *The people stomp on the earth with great gladness.*

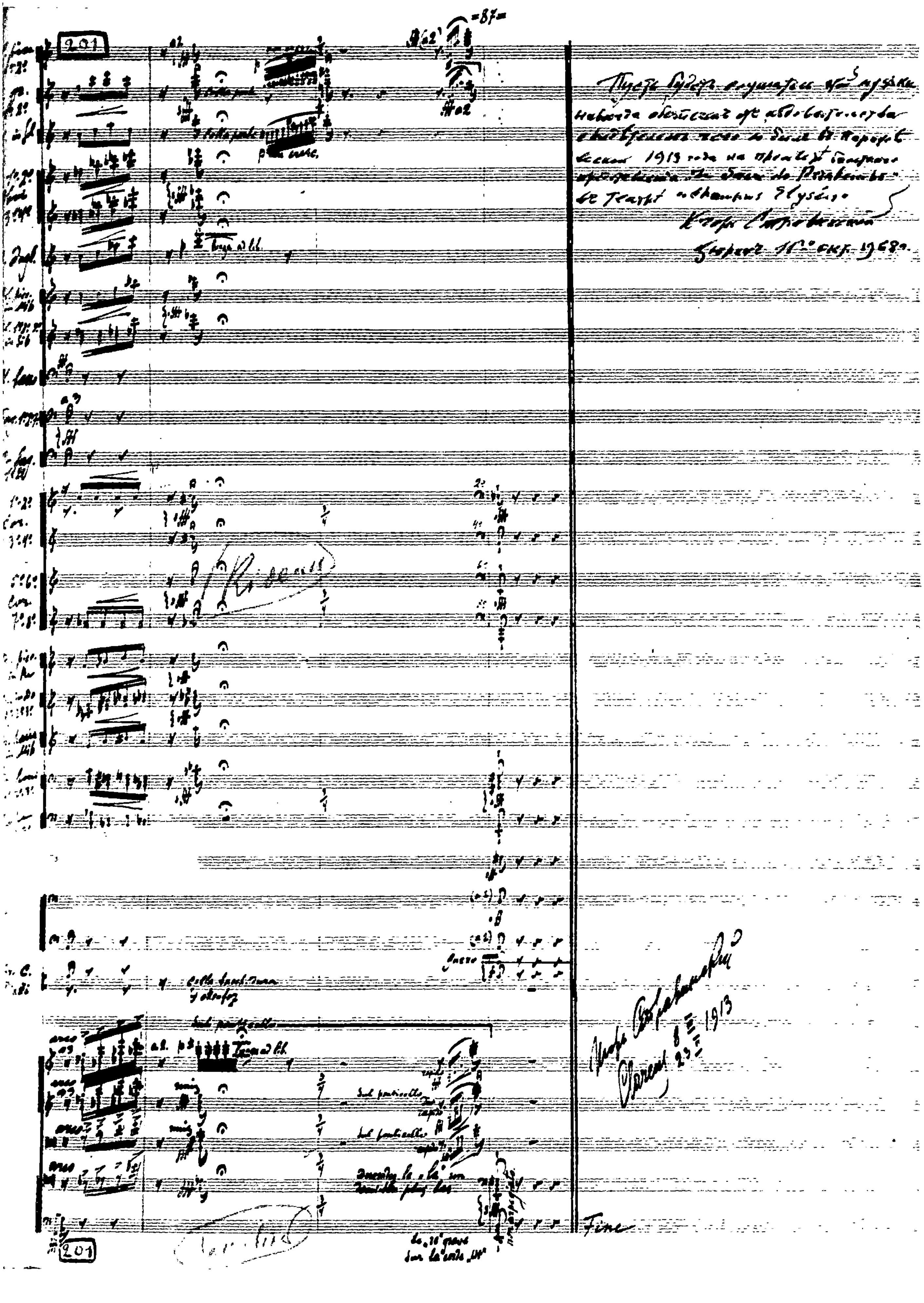
201
Fine
201

II. THE GREAT OFFERING

(THE SACRIFICIAL VICTIM)

Day and night the stones are always in the hills. The maidens hold secret games there. They glorify the victim. They call the oldest and wisest as witness to the victim. They give the victim to the beautiful Yarilo.

3

In the ballet . . . [as] conceived by myself [Roerich] and Stravinsky, my object was to present a number of pictures of earthly joy and celestial triumph, as understood by the Slavs. . . . My intention is that the first set should transport us to the foot of a sacred hill, in a lush plain, where Slavonic tribes are gathered together to celebrate the spring rites. In this scene there is an old witch, who predicts the future, a marriage by abduction, round dances. Then comes the most solemn moment. The wisest ancient is brought from the village to imprint his sacred kiss on the new-flowering earth. During this rite the crowd is seized with a mystic terror, and this our excellent Nijinsky has stylized for us extremely well.

   After this uprush of terrestrial joy, the second scene sets a celestial majesty before us. Young virgins dance in circles on the sacred hill, amid enchanted rocks; then they choose the victim they intend to honor. In a moment she will dance her last dance, before the old men clad in bearskins, to show that the bear was man's ancestor. Then the greybeards dedicate the victim to the god Yarilo.

1910

End of March. "My first thought about my new choreodrama, *Vesna Sviasschennaya (Le Sacre du Printemps, Frühling der Heilige),* came to me in the spring of 1910 as I was finishing *The Firebird.* I wanted to compose the libretto with N. K. Roerich because who else could help, who else knows the secret of our ancestors' close feeling for the earth? . . ." (To N. F. Findeizen,[142] December 15, 1912, from Clarens)

July 2. Ustilug. Writes to Nicolas Roerich: "Naturally the success of *The Firebird* has encouraged Diaghilev for future projects,[143] and sooner or later we will have to tell him about 'The Great Sacrifice.'"

OPPOSITE:
March 1913. The final page, full score, of *Le Sacre du Printemps.* The composer's words in the upper right corner, added in October 1968, read, in part: "May whoever listens to this music never experience the mockery to which it was subjected and of which I was the witness in the Théâtre des Champs-Elysées, Paris, Spring 1913."

December 1912. Nicolas Roerich, photographed in 1910, at the time of Stravinsky's first discussions with him about *Le Sacre du Printemps.*

1910. The libretto in Stravinsky's hand.

1911. Draft of the beginning.

1912. First draft of the music from measure 2 of ⟦147⟧ to ⟦149⟧. The heading, in Russian, says "Dance, the Sacrifice." The indications for pizzicato were retained in the first full score but then eliminated.

1913. A page with Stravinsky's indications for the choreography.

August 9. La Baule (Brittany). To Roerich: "I have started work (sketches on 'The Great Sacrifice'). Have you done anything for it yet?"

November 3. Clarens. To Benois: "Have Diaghilev and Fokine made up—that is, agreed on terms? This is very important, for if they have, then 'The Great Sacrifice' will be Diaghilev's, if not, then Telyakovsky's,[144] which is hardly good news. . . ."

November 16. To Benois: "I cannot come to Petersburg on the 20th of November for the conferences about the new ballet on which Diaghilev and I have decided. I also do not know whether or not Roerich is angry with me, but for some reason he has not written. There is no point in getting angry, in any case, for I do

1926. Revised full score of the beginning of the "Danse Sacrale."

not intend to postpone 'The Great Victim' indefinitely and will compose it as soon as I have completed *Petrushka*. Also, I could never finish 'The Great Victim' ('*Velekaya Zhertva*') by April, the time-limit that Diaghilev has imposed on me." (Stravinsky did go to St. Petersburg, where Benois wrote that: "Igor played [*Petrushka*] to me in my little dark blue drawing room: . . . what I now heard surpassed my expectations. . . .")

Stravinsky met Florent Schmitt in 1910, at the time of *The Firebird*, the music of which so impressed the French composer that he renamed his house "*Villa l'Oiseau de Feu*." Stravinsky's letters to Schmitt, in the Bibliothèque Nationale in Paris, extravagantly praise his ballet *La Tragédie de Salomé*, the decors for which were created by Serge Sudeikin, the future husband of Stravinsky's wife-to-be of twenty-seven years later. In August 1969, Richard Buckle, the ballet critic and future author of *Nijinsky* and *Diaghilev*, wrote to Stravinsky, asking if he still had the same high opinion of *Salomé*, and "whether Diaghilev had decided to mount it, or was he persuaded?" Stravinsky replied that the decision was indeed a political one, Schmitt being an important critic, and added: "It's terrible music." The tie between Stravinsky and Schmitt was broken during the 1914–18 war, partly because of Stravinsky's growing friendship with Erik Satie, who wrote to Stravinsky: "*Il s'appelle Schmitt pour nous épater.*" In 1934, Schmitt was elected to the French Academy over Stravinsky. The two men saw each other for the last time on October 14, 1957, at a reception in the home (2, avenue d'Iéna) of United States Ambassador Houghton.

June 1912. St.-Cloud. With Florent Schmitt at his home.

1911

July 13. Ustilug. To Benois: "I will set out for Talashkino, where, in a few days, Roerich will come from abroad."

July 15. To Roerich: "Dear Nikolai Konstantinovich, it is imperative that we see each other and decide about every detail—especially every question of staging—concerning our 'child.' I expect to start composing in the fall, and, health permitting, to finish in the spring. Another reason why we must meet now is that I will not spend the winter this year in St. Petersburg, but probably in Switzerland, going from there to Paris. Please write immediately on your arrival in Talashkino, telling me the best means of conveyance from Smolyensk. If it is not too far, could some horses be sent to fetch me? Remember that my train from Warsaw arrives very early, I think at 5 o'clock in the morning. Waiting to hear from you . . . Igor Stravinsky. P.S.: Is it possible that you will be in Smolyensk yourself, and that the Talashkino trip will not be necessary?"

Stravinsky's description of this journey vividly suggests the rural Russian nineteenth-century setting in which this representative twentieth-century masterpiece was begun: "In July I traveled to the Princess Tenisheva's country estate near Smolyensk, to plan the scenario of Le Sacre du Printemps with Roerich. He was on good terms with the Princess, and he wanted me to see her collection of Russian ethnic art. I went from Ustilug to Brest-Litovsk, and, discovering that I would have to wait two days for the next passenger train to Smolyensk, I bribed the conductor of a freight train to let me ride in a cattle car. There I was alone with a bull, leashed by a single rope. He glowered and slavered, and I barricaded myself behind my small suitcase. Arriving in Smolyensk, I must have looked peculiar as I left that *corrida* carrying an expensive, or at least not tramp-like, bag, and brushing my clothes and hat, but I must also have looked relieved. The Princess Tenisheva placed a guest house at my disposal, and, after two days with Roerich, the plan of action and the titles of the dances were composed. . . . Our name for the ballet at this time was Vesna Sviasschennaya—'Sacred Spring,' or 'Holy Spring.' The French title, Le Sacre du Printemps, was Bakst's, but, in English, 'The Coronation of Spring' is closer to my original meaning than 'The Rite of Spring.' " [145]

August 8. Karlsbad. Stravinsky visits Diaghilev, after receiving 100 kronen from him for the trip,[146] and Le Sacre du Printemps is commissioned. (Writing in 1912, Stravinsky dates the Karlsbad trip "July 1911"—i.e., according to the Old Style Russian calendar.) The composer then goes to Warsaw, Lugano (to see Benois), Berlin (to deliver the corrected proofs for the first two scenes of Petrushka to the Russischer Musik Verlag), and returns to Ustilug.

August 20. Ustilug. To Schmitt: "I have just returned from Karlsbad and Lugano . . ."

September 26. Clarens. To Roerich: "I have already begun to compose, and, in a state of passion and excitement, have sketched the Introduction for '*dudki*' [147] as well as the 'Divination with Twigs.' The music is coming out very fresh and new. The picture of the old woman in a squirrel fur sticks in my mind. She is constantly before my eyes as I compose the 'Divination with Twigs.' [148] I see her running in front of the group, sometimes stopping it and interrupting the rhythmic flow. I am convinced that the action must be danced, not pantomimed, and for this reason I have connected the 'Dance of the Maidens' and the 'Divination with Twigs,' a smooth jointure with which I am very pleased."

November 4. Clarens. Writes to Debussy.

November 19. Paris. Receives "479 Fr. 80 Centimes" from Diaghilev, part of the honorarium for the Sacre.

November 21. Clarens. To Benois, in St. Petersburg: ". . . I have just been to Paris twice. The first trip was voluntary, a rest after strenuous composing. I stayed at Delage's and had barely arrived back here when Diaghilev summoned me by telegram. He had come from London for two days. I went for one day. I was at Mme Edwards's,[149] and I played there what I had composed of the Sacre du Printemps. Everyone liked it very much."

January 2. Clarens. To Benois, in St. Petersburg: "... I have worked very hard and almost completed the first tableau of *Le Sacre du Printemps*, the orchestration as well as the music; only the ending, 'The Dance of the Earth,' remains to be done. If you see Roerich, tell him that I composed very well."

January 7. Completes Part One.

February 19. Vienna. Attends the premiere performance of the Ballets Russes.

March 1. Clarens. Begins "The Chosen One." [150]

March 2. Works on the Introduction to Part Two.

March 3. Works on the music at $\boxed{96}$.

March 4. Composes the link from $\boxed{97}$ to $\boxed{99}$ and the "Ritual of the Old Man."

March 5. Composes the four measures preceding $\boxed{96}$.

March 6. Composes part of "The Chosen One."

March 7. Composes part of the Introduction to Part Two. Writes to Andrey Rimsky-Korsakov from Montreux: "... You probably know that I am working on the piece that I conceived after *The Firebird*. The Russian name is still not definite, but the French is *Les Sacres* [sic] *du Printemps*. I have finished the entire first part (with instrumentation) and am now composing the second. Our season in Paris begins May 10 (New Style), and my new work will probably be performed at the end of it. My God, what happiness it will be for me when I hear it. It seems as if I am indulging in a bit of self-praise. But if you hear it, then you will understand what you and I have to talk about. It is as if twenty and not two years had passed since *The Firebird* was composed."

March 8. Continues work on the Introduction to Part Two.

March 10. Writes "The very beginning of the second tableau."

March 11. Writes the Khorovod melody at $\boxed{99}$.

March 16. Receives a check from Diaghilev "for 300" [rubles? Swiss francs? French francs?] to come to Monte Carlo to play the *Sacre*.

March 17. Monte Carlo. To his mother: "Diaghilev summoned me here to get acquainted with my music. . . . He and Nijinsky were wild about it. . . . Today or tomorrow I'll leave for home. . . . Yesterday I won 15 francs and Diaghilev 220. The son of a bitch . . ."

March 19. Clarens. To Roerich: "A week ago I completed the first tableau, orchestration as well as music. It is regrettable that we planned both tableaux to be equal in length. The first will rep-

March 17, 1911. Monte Carlo. Nijinsky, photographed by Stravinsky.

resent almost three-fourths of the whole, and, the tempi being
all madly fast, this has meant an immense amount of writing.
But it seems to me that I have penetrated the secret of the rhythm
of spring, and that musicians will feel it."

March 26. To Benois: "*Le Sacre* will not be performed this year.
Fokine is too busy with other ballets, especially Ravel's *Daphnis
et Chloë.*"

March 27. Writes to Nicolas Gustavovich Struve, acknowledging
the receipt of two copies of *Petrushka*, but complaining about
misprints ("Did nobody look at it?") and asking "Why always
the problem with *Zvezdoliki?*"

March 29. Writes to Diaghilev at the Riviera Palace, Monte Carlo: "I received a letter from Schmitt. . . . Truhanova [the dancer] gives two concerts. . . ."

March 31. Writes to Dalençon (11, rue de la Turbée, Monaco): "When are the orchestra rehearsals for *Petrushka*?"

March 31: Writes to Struve: "I received the 6-page erratum, but I still do not know if this is appended to the scores in the Russian edition. You have not answered this and other questions. And now, alas, I have found a mistake in the erratum."

April 4. Writes to Pierre Monteux [151] in Monaco, asking him to return the *Petrushka* parts that were used for the performances the year before, in exchange for new parts being sent by the Editions Russes.

April 7. Writes to Maximilien Steinberg. Writes to Struve: "First of all, happy Easter. . . . I am sending the piano score of *Petrushka*, which should be proofread again—as I do continually, always finding many mistakes. . . . I am in a hurry to finish for Paris by the 15th or 20th. . . . I will ask Diaghilev to announce in the programs that *Petrushka* has been published. . . . I wrote to Benois about the drawing of the Magician. . . . I live between Berlin, Vienna, Budapest and Monte Carlo. . . . Where is Serge Alexandrovich [Kussevitsky]? It is very important for me to know. Will he come to Paris, and will I be able to see him?"

April 9. Telegraphs to Diaghilev asking for money for the *Petrushka* parts.

April 10. Writes to Jurgenson: "Now I have the whole *Firebird*. . . . It is very handsomely printed."

April 11. Writes to Dmitri Calvocoressi: "*Très cher ami*, I am, as you already know, a *sale cochon*, but I must say that I have not had any news of you for a long time. . . . I leave Clarens for Monte Carlo, where my ballets will be played. When will you return to your charming capital? . . . Have you succumbed to the influence of Steinberg, who plunges ever more relentlessly into academicism? To judge from his recent letters, he understands nothing in my later compositions. . . . *Avec amitié . . . je ne vous oublie . . . et mes hommages à Madame Calvocoressi. Je vous attends à Monte Carlo et je vous verrai à Paris, n'est-ce pas? 'Le Sacre' est bientôt fini.* I will play it for my friends, among whom you are one of the first."

April 11. Diaghilev pays another installment on the *Sacre*.

April 12. Writes to Struve: "Yesterday I sent a sheet of errata. Perhaps you can print it again, since there are two particularly annoying mistakes."

April 13 or 14. To Monte Carlo, Beausoleil, Olympia Hôtel.

April 18. Monte Carlo. Attends performance of *Petrushka*.

April 19. Writes to his mother: "*Petrushka* was an enormous, deafening success. It will be performed here three more times; then they are going to put on *The Firebird.*"

April 20 (c.). "One day in 1912 . . . Diaghilev summoned me to a tiny rehearsal room in a Monte Carlo theater where the Ballet was at that time appearing. . . . With only Diaghilev and myself for an audience, Stravinsky sat down to play a piano reduction of the entire score [of the *Sacre*]. Before he got very far, I was convinced he was raving mad. . . . The very walls resounded as Stravinsky pounded away, occasionally stamping his feet and jumping up and down. . . ." (Monteux) [152]

May 2 (c.). Returns to Clarens, via Genoa.

May 16 (c.). Goes to Paris.

May 29. Théâtre du Châtelet. Attends the first performance of the ballet *L'Après-midi d'un Faune.*

June 1. Louis Laloy, editor of *La Grande Revue,* writes: "I remind you of our hope that you will come Sunday, 17 bis, rue des Capucines, Bellevue. We will be *en famille.* It will be a great honor for my home. You can come by taxi, train, or even a boat. M. and Mme Debussy will also be there."

June 8. Théâtre du Châtelet. Attends the premiere of *Daphnis et Chloë,* in a loge with Ravel and his mother and brother, Schmitt, and Delage.

June 9. Bellevue. "One bright afternoon in the spring of 1913 [sic],[153] I was walking about in my garden with Debussy. We were expecting Stravinsky. As soon as he saw us, the Russian musician ran with his arms outstretched to embrace the French master, who, over his shoulder, gave me an amused but compassionate look. Stravinsky had brought an arrangement for four hands of his work, *Le Sacre du Printemps.* Debussy agreed to play the bass. Stravinsky asked if he could remove his collar. His sight was not improved by his glasses, and, pointing his nose to the keyboard, and sometimes humming a part that had been omitted from the arrangement, he led into a welter of sound the supple, agile hands of his friend. Debussy followed without a hitch and seemed to make light of the difficulty.[154] When they had finished, there was no question of embracing, nor even of compliments. We were dumbfounded, overwhelmed by this hurricane which had come from the depths of the ages, and which had taken life by the roots." (Laloy)

June 18. Ustilug. Writes to V. V. Derzhanovsky: "Your letter of May 15 to Clarens has only just reached me. I was in Paris, and though the letter was forwarded there, it lay about at Ravel's for ten days."

July 7. London. Diaghilev telegraphs to Stravinsky in Ustilug: "*Félicites grand succès Oiseau de feu, amitiés.*"

August 20. Bayreuth. Hears *Parsifal,* having traveled to Bayreuth

June 1912. Ustilug. In a boat on the Bug River during a flood, with a cap and "Charley's Aunt" blazer.* A month later, Stravinsky wrote to Schmitt that "*Les Sacres*" [sic] will be in two parts, and that the choreography is of the utmost importance.

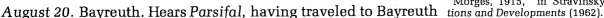

* This photograph is incorrectly captioned "Morges, 1915," in Stravinsky's *Expositions and Developments* (1962).

August 25, 1912. Isola Bella, Lago Maggiore. Nijinsky photographed by Stravinsky.

by way of Vienna and Nuremberg. (In an interview in the Nuremberg *8 Uhr-Blatt*, December 3, 1930, Stravinsky revealed that he had been in the city eighteen years before, "hurrying from Vienna to Bayreuth to hear Hans Richter's last performances of *Meistersinger*." As a boy in St. Petersburg, Stravinsky had translated for Richter in his rehearsals with the Russian orchestra.)

August 21. Goes with Diaghilev to Lugano to see Benois.

August 24. Lugano. Stravinsky plays the *Sacre* for Diaghilev, Nijinsky, Benois.

August 26 (?). Stravinsky and Nijinsky go from Stresa to Venice.

September 6. Stravinsky returns to Ustilug.

September 8. Santa Lisabetta, Lido, Venice. Diaghilev telegraphs to Stravinsky in Ustilug: "Maeterlinck has made a proposition and I consider his participation desirable."

September 9. Diaghilev telegraphs to Stravinsky: "Telegraph to me at the Hôtel Crillon, Paris."

September 14. Paris. An associate of Astruc [155] writes to Diaghilev, in Venice, saying that the Société des Auteurs has agreed to give four-sixths of the authors' rights for *Petrushka* to Stravinsky.

September 17. Ustilug. Writes to his bank in Kiev: "Grigory Beliankin wants a mortgage. I do not agree, but I see that you want me to explain it to him."

September 22. Venice. Diaghilev telegraphs to Stravinsky, in Us-

tilug, asking him to attend a conference with Maeterlinck "on Monday in Paris, Hôtel Crillon." (Diaghilev is in Paris on September 25.).

October 3. Paris. Diaghilev telegraphs to Mme Maeterlinck, Abbaye de Wandrille, Seine Inférieure, asking her to send a hired car to meet his train in Rouen at 10:00 A.M. the next day.

October 19. Ustilug. Completes piano score of "Akahito" *(Three Japanese Lyrics).*

October 23. Paris. Delage writes: "Thank you, friend, for your

September 2 (?). Venice. Nijinsky, Diaghilev, and Misia Sert (part of her hat is visible on Diaghilev's right), photographed by Stravinsky on the porch of the Grand Hotel, where, in a salon on the ground floor, Stravinsky played *Le Sacre* (completed through [99] at this date) for his colleagues. On this occasion, during the *"Danses des Adolescentes,"* the impresario asked the composer, "When will it stop?", a scene that Stravinsky re-enacted in 1965 for television.

delicious long letter [from Ustilug]. . . . I would like to hope that I am the first to welcome you back in Switzerland. Impossible to write to you in Berlin, having received your letter only last evening."

October 27. Cologne. Monteux begins rehearsing for the November opening of the Ballets Russes season.

November 2. Clarens. To Schmitt: "I have nearly finished the instrumentation of the first part of the Sacres [sic]."

November 5. Paris. Debussy to Stravinsky: "Our reading at the piano of Le Sacre du Printemps is always in my mind. It haunts me like a beautiful dream, and I try in vain to reinvoke the terrific impression. That is why I wait for the stage performance like a greedy child impatient for promised sweets."

November 11. Munich. The Hotel Vier Jahreszeiten. Diaghilev telegraphs: "Have you completed Sacre? Please come to Berlin on November 20." A telegram from Astruc informs Stravinsky that Diaghilev arrived in Munich on November 8.

November 12. Paris. La France publishes an article by Schmitt: ". . . In a faraway pavilion of Auteuil,[156] which from henceforth will remind me of the most magnificent of temples, M. Igor Stravinsky played Les Sacres [sic] du Printemps for my friends. I will speak to you of its importance to all music which will be played throughout the world, for the piece tells of freedom, newness, and the richness of life."

November 16. Berlin. Monteux telegraphs: "Beginning rehearsals piano and dancers Monday. Performance Tuesday. Come Wednesday. Amitiés."

November 17. Clarens. Hôtel du Châtelard. Completes the sketch score, "with an unbearable toothache."

November 21. Berlin. Adlon Hotel. Attends the Ballets Russes performance of The Firebird and is congratulated afterward by Richard Strauss. The Berliner Tageblatt, December 5, 1912, quotes Strauss in answer to a question about Stravinsky's music: "Es interessiert einen immer seine Nachfolger zu hören."

November 22. Supervises a piano rehearsal of the Sacre with dancers: "Hearing the way his music was being played, he blazed up, pushed aside the fat German pianist, nicknamed 'Kolossal' by Diaghilev, and proceeded to play twice as fast as we had been doing and twice as fast as we could possibly dance. He stamped his feet on the floor and banged his fist on the piano and sang and shouted. . . ." [157]

November 23. St. Petersburg. Roerich writes to Stravinsky at the Adlon Hotel: "I have just sent twenty-four costumes and two books with designs. I want to come at the end of December, but where? I have changed the first act, and it is better now. Greetings to Diaghilev. Please write about everything. . . . Your sincerely devoted N.R."

1912. Berlin. Handbill for the season of the Ballets Russes.

December 4. Attends a performance of *Petrushka* with Arnold Schoenberg. ("I really liked *Petrushka*, parts of it very much indeed," Schoenberg wrote, February 24, 1928.)

December 8. (Sunday). Twelve noon. Choralion-Saal, Bellevue-strasse 4. Stravinsky, in row five, seat five, hears the "*Lieder* [sic] *des Pierrot Lunaire*," conducted by Schoenberg. (The work is given with two intermissions.)

December 11. Clarens. Sends a photograph of himself to his mother.

December 13. Writes to Debussy. Receives a letter from Gabriel Astruc's secretary promising that competent pianists will be assigned for the dance rehearsals of the *Sacre*.

December 14. To Roerich: "I have just returned from Berlin and received your costume designs for our 'Spring!' I am pleased that they were sent to me first so that I could see them—they are a real miracle, and I only hope that the realization of them will be good!—but I regret the delay before Nijinsky receives them, which is the reason that my telegram said, 'Send to Nijinsky.' I am forwarding them to him today.... Nijinsky started his staging of the 'Spring' only yesterday, Friday, and he begged me to stay longer. I had to leave but promised that if he couldn't manage without my help, I would come to him (for the third time!). ... How I hope that Nijinsky has time enough to stage the 'Spring.' It is very complex, and I feel that it must be done as nothing has ever been done before!"

December 15. To N. F. Findeizen: "In a few meetings with Roerich we worked out the libretto, which, roughly, takes the following form:

> *First Part. The Kiss of the Earth*. This contains the ancient Slavic dances, 'The Joy of Spring.' The orchestral introduction is a swarm of spring pipes *(dudki)*.
>
> Later, after the curtain rises, fortune-telling *(gadonia)*, dance games *(Ignye Khorovodnye)*, the game of abduction, the dance game of the city with the city, all of which is interrupted by the procession of the 'Eldest-Wisest,' the elder who kisses the earth. The first part ends with the wild dancing-out *(vysplyasyvanie)* on the earth, of the people drunk with spring.
>
> *Part Two*. The secret night games of the young maidens on the sacred hill. One of them is condemned by fate to be sacrificed. She enters a stone labyrinth, and the other maidens celebrate her in a wild, martial dance. The elders come, and the chosen one, left alone with them, dances her last Sacred Dance, *The Great Victim*, which is the title of the *Second Part*. The elders are the witnesses of her last dance, which ends with the death of the condemned.

I wanted the whole of the composition to give the feeling of closeness between men and earth, the community of their lives with the earth, and I sought to do this in lapidary rhythms. The whole thing must be put on in dance *(tantsevel'no)* from beginning to end. I give not one measure for pantomime. Nijinsky directs it with passionate zeal, forgetting himself."

December 17 (?). St. Petersburg. Roerich writes to Stravinsky in Clarens: "My dear, thank you for your letter, but it is strange that Diaghilev does not write to tell me where he wants me to come at the end of December. Please ask for the reason; I must know in time. The difference in the first act is that I have eliminated the trees—a definite improvement. . . . I wish you and your wife good holidays. Yours, N.R."

December 18. Paris. Delage writes: "Is the *Sacre* finished now? How I envy you! It always seems to me that you must work in a state of joy." Berlin. Diaghilev telegraphs: "Rehearsals have not yet begun. We have no designs, and no need of arrangements for pianola." Serge Grigoriev [158] writes: "Nijinsky has not started the rehearsals of our new ballet; he is waiting for the drawings of the costumes. . . . I sent two programs, for November 21 and December 4. *The Firebird* was performed nine times in Berlin, *Petrushka* seven times. We are not going to Brussels; the stage is small and the orchestra bad. Instead, we will be in Budapest from December 23 to January 6 and will give *The Firebird,* and in Vienna from January 8 to 16. *L'Après-midi d'un Faune* had a huge success, and we repeated it at both the first and second performances."

December 26. Clarens. Writes to V. G. Karatygin [159] about Schoenberg.

December 27. Budapest. The Royal Opera. The Ballets Russes performs *The Firebird, Les Sylphides,* and *Carnaval.* (Béla Bartók evidently attended this *Firebird,* since he refers to the "1912 performances." [160])

1913

January 2. Budapest. Diaghilev telegraphs to Stravinsky in Clarens: "Unless you come here immediately for fifteen days, the *Sacre* will not take place. Roerich's presence is superfluous. His designs have not yet been received. . . ." Stravinsky telegraphs to Diaghilev: "Can arrive Sunday evening impossible to have ticket before Saturday. If you leave Budapest Monday, I prefer to come directly to Vienna."

January 3. Budapest. Diaghilev telegraphs: "Leave for Petersburg Sunday morning must see you before."

January 4. Budapest. Hotel Hungaria. Attends a performance of *The Firebird* at the Royal Theater and blames Monteux for the poor quality. The same night Monteux, in the Hotel Europa, sends a note to Stravinsky: ". . . I was so stunned by the reproaches that you addressed to me a while ago that I tendered my resignation to M. Diaghilev. You hold me responsible for playing *The Firebird* under bad conditions, but what could I do with a contract that obliges me to conduct every performance? . . . My admiration and devotion, however, are unshaken. . . ."

January 10. Paris. Delage writes: "*Ça va le 'Sacre'? Que fait Nijinsky? J'ai vu les costumes de Roerich. Ils sont splendides.*"

January 15. Vienna. Hofoper. Attends performance of *Petrushka.*

January 16. Returns to Clarens.

January 17. Vienna. Diaghilev telegraphs: "Second *Petrushka* great success four curtain calls ask Florent Schmitt telegraph me 22 quai anglais Petersburg."

January 20. Paris. Schmitt writes: ". . . do not be discouraged by the treatment of *Petrushka* in Vienna, my dear Igor. You are young. You will live to see your universal triumph. . . . Meanwhile, all of us here anxiously await the *Sacres* [sic]. . . ."

January 21. Schmitt writes: "I dined yesterday with Ravel, Grovlez, Aubert,[161] Casella,[162] Vuillermoz.[163] . . . We discussed the next program of the SMI,[164] agreeing on *Pierrot Lunaire* and the quartet of Bela Bartock [165] [sic]. . . . Later, I was with the pianist Lazare-Lévy [166] and Dumesnil.[167] I tried to argue the necessity of a Bayreuth 'Strawinskysque.' They are not completely convinced but will be after the *Sacres* [sic]." *La France* publishes Schmitt's prediction: "The generation of the year 2000, closed to Berlioz or Mussorgsky, will belatedly exalt . . . 'des *Sacres* [sic] du Printemps,' and the Farnésiens of music will enrich the Austro-Balkan soil in order to harvest the cigar ashes of Arnold Schoenberg."

January 22. Stravinsky writes to Schmitt: "I am happy that I was able to interest you in Schoenberg and to influence you to play his prodigious *Pierrot Lunaire*. . . . Certainly you will not like it, but, to me, for my part, I am convinced that it will be accepted in time. Schoenberg is a remarkable artist. I feel it."

January 25. Leipzig. Hotel Hauffe. Nijinsky writes to Stravinsky: "Dear Igor, I have been able to make five rehearsals since our departure from Vienna. This is not very many, of course, considering how much remains to be done, but with the burden of work that we have, and with these tiring moves from town to town, where we stay only two or three days, it was not possible to do more. I squeezed as much out of these rehearsals as I could, and if I am able to continue this way, I will possibly have enough time for everything—without damaging my health and at the same time dancing well at the performances. We have composed almost everything through the games and dances in the ring, and the game of abduction. I am very pleased with the way everything has turned out. If the work continues like this, Igor, the result will be something great. I know what *Le Sacre du Printemps* will be when everything is as we both want it: new, and, for an ordinary viewer, a jolting impression and emotional experience. For some it will open new horizons flooded with different rays of sun. People will see new and different colors and different lines. All different, new and beautiful. I go to Dresden today, where it will be impossible to rehearse since we are only there for one day. From Dresden we go to London. Address: Savoy Hotel. So, goodbye until we see each other. A bow to your wife. I kiss your hand. Vaslav."

January 26. Monte Carlo. Attends performance of *Parsifal*.

January 28. Arrives in London. Savoy Hotel.

February 2. St. Petersburg. Diaghilev telegraphs: "Ask Florent Schmitt come Monday at seven Hôtel Crillon. Can you come Tuesday London premiere *Petrushka.*"

February 4. Royal Opera House. 8:30 P.M. Attends English premiere of *Petrushka.* (On February 7, Prokofiev writes from London to Miaskovsky:[168] "Petrushka is very interesting, but the music is a bit too descriptive at the liveliest moments on the stage. There Stravinsky does not compose music but illustrations.")

February 7. Royal Opera House. 8:45 P.M. Attends performance of *Elektra.*

February 11. Royal Opera House. 8:30 P.M. Attends performance of *Petrushka.*

February 12. Dines with Cyril Scott and Edwin Evans.[169] "Please bring something with you, the delicious Japanese poems, perhaps, or a scene from the *Sacre.*" (From Evans's invitation.)

February 13. 2:45 P.M. Attends performance of *Elektra.* 8:30 P.M. Attends performance of *The Firebird.*

February 13. The *Daily Mail* publishes an interview with Stravinsky: "My new ballet 'The Crowning of Spring' has no plot. It is a series of ceremonies in ancient Russia. . . ." (In the same interview: "The Viennese are barbarians. . . . They chased Schoenberg away to Berlin. Now Schoenberg is one of the greatest creative spirits of our day. . . . There is little that interests me in the music of the past. Bach is too remote. He is always said to be like a cathedral. Well, I am outside and cannot say what, if anything, is going on inside. . . . Thought so soon grows old-fashioned, but emotion remains the same. I confess to remaining faithful to the fresh feeling and joy of life in Schubert's music. . . . I dislike opera. Music can be married to gesture or to words but not to both without bigamy. What operas have been written since *Parsifal?* Only two that count, *Elektra* and *Pelléas.* . . . *Petrushka* was performed at St. Petersburg the same day as here, and I see the newspapers are now all comparing my work with the smashing of crockery.")

February 15. The *Pall Mall Gazette* publishes an interview with Nijinsky: ". . . I am working hard on . . . *Sacre du Printemps.* . . . It is really the soul of nature expressed by movement to music. It is the life of the stones and the trees. There are no human beings in it. It is only the incarnation of Nature . . . and of human nature. It will be danced only by the corps de ballet, for it is a thing of concrete masses, not of individual effects."

February 16. The *London Budget* publishes an interview with Stravinsky: "Vaslav Nijinsky has worked out the story, and we are calling it *Le Sacre du Printemps,* which might be translated as 'The Innocence of Spring.'" The same newspaper mentions

February 10. London. Photographed on New Bond Street.

that "a soft, tiny beard rims [Stravinsky's] chin," though none is visible in any of the photographs of him at the time, which might be due to the extreme lightness of his reddish hair. The *Budget* also states that "The music of *Petrushka* has been greeted by the highest praise of the London audiences and critics, and the young composer of this extraordinary music stands before Europe as one of the most important figures in his profession. A small pale man is Monsieur Stravinsky . . . If modesty mantles the form of greatness, then this Russian is great. . . ."

February 22. London. Monteux writes to Stravinsky in Clarens: "Should the orchestra score conform to Nijinsky's two-hand score or the other way around? . . . The day you left, Nijinsky showed me some passages in the piano score that are not in agreement with the orchestra score, and he said that the orchestra score is correct. . . . I cannot make changes, and, of course, no one but you can touch the orchestra. . . ."

March 1 (?). London. Savoy Hotel. Delage writes: "*Mon cher petit* . . . I spent the evening with Evans . . . stopped by at Monteux's, who was absent, but left the pages of the *Sacre* with him."

March 3. London. Diaghilev telegraphs: "Can you come to Paris Sunday for one day."

March 5. Monteux writes: "I leave London Saturday morning and will be most obliged to you if you will send the score of *Le Sacre* as soon as possible. I plan to begin studying it in the first days of the following week. . . ."

March 11. Avignon. Schmitt sends regrets that he cannot come to Clarens: "I would have been so pleased to hear a little more of *Sacres* [sic]."

March 19. Inscribes four-hand score to Roerich.

March 23. St. Petersburg. Diaghilev telegraphs: "Send Roerich's design books immediately."

March 24. Beausoleil. Nijinsky telegraphs: "Finished first part send immediately piano score sacred dance. Watza."

March 29. Clarens. Adds eleven measures ([86] to [87]).

March 30. Paris. Monteux writes about the rehearsals of Part One: "After my first telegram you will have understood that since I am not yet rehearsing in the hall of the theater, I cannot say what *Le Sacre* will be like when the orchestra is in the pit. But to compare it to *The Firebird* and *Petrushka*, which I have rehearsed in the same hall, *Le Sacre* sounds at least as good. . . . The passages . . . which will possibly need some modification are the following: at [38], measure 5, the horns and violas playing the melody are scarcely audible unless the rest of the orchestra plays *pianissimo*. At [35], measures 3 and 4, it is impossible to hear a single note of the flute above the horns and trumpets 'ff,' and the violins 'ff,' since only the first flute plays the theme during all of this noise. At ☐41☐, measures 1 and 2, the sonority of the tubas is weak despite 'ff,' the seventh and eighth horns do not sound at all in the low register, and the trombones are very loud in comparison with the first six horns. I have added the fourth horn to the seventh and eighth but without attaining an equilibrium for the four groups. One hears: 1. mf; 2. nothing; 3. ff; 4. f. At ☐65☐, measure 3, the first horns, with the theme, are barely heard. They play 'f' but are muted. . . .

"I had two rehearsals for *The Firebird*, strings and winds separately, the same for *Petrushka*, then a full rehearsal for each work. For the *Sacre*, I have had two string rehearsals, three wind rehearsals, and two full rehearsals. Yesterday I finally rehearsed all three works. What a pity that you could not be here, above all that you could not be present for the explosion of *Le Sacre*. I thought of you constantly and regretted your absence, but I know that you are very busy. Now it will be for the month of May. . . . Please give my *amitiés* to Ravel."

Not the least astonishing feature of this letter is the absence of any reference to the music's difficulties; moreover, the number of rehearsals would be considered modest even today, for an orchestra playing the *Sacre* for the first time but inevitably familiar with the music. Most remarkable of all is Monteux's diagnosis of the weak places in the instrumentation and the directness with which he discusses them in his letter, as if to say, "This is my *métier*, not esthetic judgments." But since he is also the first to be hearing the actual sound of the music, and since some comment of a general kind is incumbent on him, he saves for last that single-barreled but never bettered word "explosion."

Stravinsky's reaction is no less amazing. Solely on the authority of this letter, he rewrote the first of the four problem passages, transferring the horn-and-viola music to trumpets and three solo cellos, a change that required rebalancing in every other part as well. (The holograph full score—Sacher Collection, Basel—preserves both the canceled and the revised versions.) To remedy the second problem passage, Stravinsky added another flute to the solo part, as well as an oboe, a piccolo clarinet, and, during the final rehearsals in May, a piccolo trumpet playing an octave lower. In the third troublesome place, he joined two more horns to the three that Monteux could not hear, but without overcoming a weakness that still exists except when artificially corrected by recording engineers. The fourth fault was eliminated simply by dispensing with the mutes.

Stravinsky's absence from these rehearsals remains a mystery. True, he had finished an added section of the *Sacre* only a day or two before receiving the letter, and he and Ravel were working against a deadline to complete their arrangements of parts of *Khovanshchina*. Yet ordinarily Stravinsky was ready to travel almost anywhere to assist at rehearsals of his music, and he had already interrupted work on the *Sacre* several times to come to Nijinsky's aid. Why, then, did the composer not go to Paris to attend at least one orchestra rehearsal of what he knew to be his most important creation? Could his absence have had an emotional cause, a fear of the first contact with the actuality of the music? Did he want it to be experienced first by an intermediary, a trusted conductor like "The Little King"—as the composer, borrowing from the comic strip, used to call Monteux? Admittedly, this was unlike Stravinsky. But so was the *Sacre* unlike anything that he (or anyone else) had ever wrought.

April 2. Paris. Monteux writes: "I received another score from your publisher this morning, but the last twenty measures are missing. . . . I am taking the orchestra parts with me to Monte Carlo in case you wish to make changes."

April 4. St. Petersburg. Diaghilev telegraphs: "Ask you to come to the Riviera Palace Monte Carlo with final chorus [*Khovanshchina*] leaving [here] this evening."

April 15. Monte Carlo. Théâtre du Casino. Monteux writes asking for the score with the corrections in order to copy them into the parts. He acknowledges the receipt of the additional music (86 to 87), from the Russischer Musik Verlag in Berlin: "*Petrushka passe demain; l'orchestre le joue comme le reste, sans aucune flamme. Ce sont les gens pourris par toute la musique d'amateurs qu'ils jouent toute l'année. . . .*"

April 21. Beausoleil. Diaghilev telegraphs: "You will be paid in installments from St. Petersburg for Chaklovity aria and chorus. . . ."

April 27. Monte Carlo. Diaghilev telegraphs: "Chorus received you can take the money tomorrow."

April 28. Diaghilev telegraphs program to Astruc in Paris, with the *Sacre* scheduled for May 29, June 2, 4, 6, 13, and 21.

May 1. Paris. Hôtel Crillon. Diaghilev telegraphs: "When do you plan to come?"

May 3. Lausanne. Stravinsky writes to Maximilien Steinberg in St. Petersburg: "Dear one, order a tromba piccolo in Ré [170]; if a timpani piccolo cannot be had, that is only half a problem, but the tromba is essential, *contre-tout*; it isn't to be found in Paris, nor is there any way to procure one. A further request. Obtain mutes from Zimmerman, two for the tubas, and three for the trombones (whether bronze or leather does not matter) and have them sent immediately to the head of the Russian Ballet—*Direction des Ballets Russes, chez G. Astruc et Cie, Pavillon de Hannover, Rue Louis le Grand, Paris.* Your I. Stravinsky."

May 5. Paris. Ravel writes: "Be assured, the acoustics of the Théâtre des Champs-Elysées are perfect, to the extent that one is able to perceive the finesse of Berlioz's harmonies. . . . The rooms are reserved for May 13."

May 7. Paris. Léon Bernstein of L'Action Littéraire, the "agency for Russian Theater," writes to Stravinsky in Clarens saying that 3,325 francs have been collected from *The Firebird*. Bernstein wonders whether the money should be sent to Stravinsky in Switzerland or held for him until he arrives in Paris.

May 9. Paris. Delage writes: "*On va bientôt le voir, comme vous m'écrivez de Clarens. . . .*"

May 12. Lugano. Benois writes: "I wanted so much to come to the premiere of the *Sacre,* but I am half ill and simply cannot think of the Paris trip. You will understand me."

N.D.: Lugano. Benois writes: "In the name of all saints, please answer . . . Bernstein about the percentages. . . . If you do not answer immediately, all of these people will bombard me with questions."

May 13. Stravinsky arrives in Paris, Hôtel Splendide, and directs a piano rehearsal with Nijinsky. Stravinsky also attends the rehearsals, and, on May 15, the first performance, of *Jeux.* On the 15th, Debussy sends a "*pneu*" to Stravinsky: "If you have seen Nijinsky, if he has signed the papers for the royalty agreement of *Jeux,* please give them to my chauffeur. It is urgent that they be at the Société des Auteurs by five o'clock. Thank you, your old friend Debussy."

(May 16. St. Petersburg. Stepan Stepanovich Mitussov writes asking Stravinsky to recommend the singer Alexandra Vassilievna Saknovskaya to Diaghilev.)

May 18. Afternoon. Théâtre des Champs-Elysées. The first rehearsal of *Le Sacre du Printemps* with the dancers on the stage.

May 21. Paris. Maurice Fanet writes that the Tribunal has not agreed to the provisional settlement. Fanet asks Stravinsky to go to see the opposition lawyer M. Bomet on one of the following mornings to discuss a settlement.[171]

May 26–7. Théâtre des Champs-Elysées. Rehearsals with the full orchestra.

May 27 (?). Monteux leaves a note for Stravinsky at the Splendide: "I stopped by to work with you, but, since you were out, I will go to the library at the Théâtre to make the changes which you made yesterday in the parts. Are you free this evening? Perhaps we can work together after dinner."

May 27 (?). Frederick Delius writes: "I cannot attend the dress rehearsal but will attend the performance."

May 28. 8:30 P.M. The dress rehearsal. Debussy and Ravel are present.

May 29. Extract from a Paris newspaper (unidentified): "*Le Sacre du Printemps* will be presented this evening in the Théâtre des Champs-Elysées. It is the most astonishing creation that I have ever witnessed by the admirable troupe of M. Serge Diaghilev. . . ."

"*Montjoie! No. 8, Organ de l'impérialisme artistique français*" publishes "*Ce que j'ai voulu exprimé dans 'Le Sacre du*

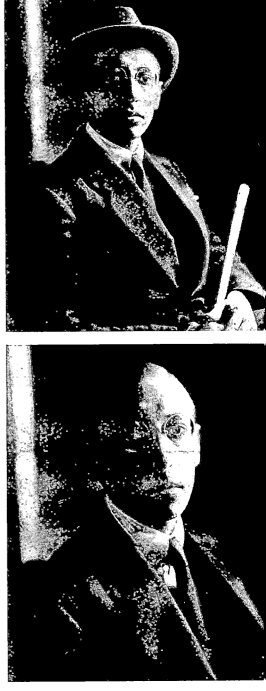

May 1913. Paris. Photographs by Gershel.

Printemps,' par Igor Stravinsky," with a facsimile of the first page of the full score of *Spring Rounds* inscribed "A Riccioto [sic] *Canudo en toute sympathie artistique, son ami Igor Stravinsky.*" [172]

The premiere of *Le Sacre du Printemps*. Stravinsky is in seat 111 at the start of the performance. The bassoonist is Abdon Laus. The program contains the following "argument" of the ballet:

> 1er *tableau: l'adoration de la Terre. Printemps. La Terre est couverte de fleurs. La Terre est couverte d'herbe. Une grande joie règne sur la Terre. Les Hommes se livrent à la danse et interrogent l'avenir selon les rites. L'Aïeul de tous les sages prend part lui-même à la glorification du Printemps. On l'amène pour l'unir à la Terre abondante et superbe. Chacun piétine la Terre avec extase.*
>
> 2e *tableau: Le Sacrifice. Après le jour, après minuit. Sur les collines sont les pierres consacrées. Les adolescentes mènent les jeux mythiques et cherchent la grande voie. On glorifie, on acclame Celle qui fut désignée pour être livrée au dieu. On appelle les Aïeux, témoins vénérés. Et les sages aïeux des hommes contemplent le sacrifice. C'est ainsi qu'on sacrifie à Idrilo le magnifique, le flamboyant.*

May 30. A Paris newspaper reports that when someone shouted: *"Taissez-vous les grues du XVIe,"* Schmitt's voice was recognized in the answer: *"Ils sont mûrs pour l'annexion."* [173]

May 31. Debussy sends a *pneumatique* inviting Stravinsky to dinner and not mentioning the performance.

Comoedia publishes an account of the premiere by Louis Vuillemin: "... people sang, whistled, applauded, shouted ironic bravos even before the curtain rose." Vuillemin attributes this to the exchange of controversial opinions all over Paris from people who attended the rehearsals, and he says that "Every critic in Paris was invited to the dress rehearsal on May 28. At the performance, by the end of the prelude, one had stopped listening to the music and attention was directed to the choreography, which was ugly or indifferent ... interesting, perhaps, from time to time. ..."

May 31. Khovanshchina is performed.

June 3. Afternoon. Théâtre des Champs-Elysées, backstage. Stravinsky gives an interview to Henri Postel du Mas of *Gil Blas*. At dinner, eats oysters (in an R-less month), then, feeling ill, calls a doctor (Oppenheim), who diagnoses typhus. Enters the Villa Borghese, *maison de santé*, 29, boulevard Victor Hugo, Neuilly-sur-Seine.

June 4. "In all fairness, I must say that the composer was not greatly upset and did not fulminate too violently against his detractors when we interviewed him yesterday. Stravinsky is small in stature but looks tall because he holds his forehead high, thus dominating his interlocutor. 'I quite understand that my music could not be immediately accepted. But the lack of good will on the part of the audience is unjustifiable. It seems to me that it should have waited to express its disappointment until the end of the performance. This would have been courteous and honest. I gave them something new, and I fully expected that those who had applauded *Petrushka* and *The Firebird* would be somewhat dismayed. But I also expected an understanding attitude. I have acted in good faith; my previous works . . . were a guarantee of my sincerity and should have proved that I had no intention of making fun of the public. During the premiere, when the commotion made it impossible for the dancers to hear the music, we were disturbed, not so much because of our own pride, but because we feared that we would not be able to go on.' " *(Gil Blas)*

La France publishes Schmitt's review of the premiere: ". . . The genius of Igor Stravinsky could not have received more striking confirmation than in the incomprehension and vicious hostility of the crowd. . . . With a logic, with an infallibility, human stupidity demands its rights."

Second performance of the *Sacre*, on a program between *Les Sylphides* and *Schéhérazade*. "The unexpected tranquility of the audience which had come because of real interest and to try to penetrate the music of Stravinsky and the choreography of Nijinsky . . . The first tableau was heard in a calm and almost complete silence. . . . From the beginning of the second tableau, the '*chahut*' began. . . . When the hall lights were turned on and relative calm was established, only a few spectators in the upper balconies continued their manifestations. . . ." (G. Linor)

June 5. 12:30 A.M. Georges Jean-Aubry, leaving the theater after the second performance, writes: "It took place in an atmosphere of near-calm. I heard with regret from Ravel that you were ill." [174]

Mme Debussy writes to Mme Stravinsky offering the use of the Debussy automobile.

8:30 P.M. Théâtre des Champs-Elysées. Second performance of *Khovanshchina* with the Stravinsky and Ravel additions.

June 6. Ravel writes: "At any rate, the whole work was heard [on June 4]."

June 6. The third performance. G. Linor reports that this was "much calmer, though some whistles were heard before the music began and some protestations at the beginning of the Second Tableau. Vigorous applause followed the final curtain, nor was there any significant counter manifestation."

June 9. Moscow. Derzhanovsky writes: "I do not understand what the newspapers are writing about *Sacre* and *Khovanshchina,* but they are not writing about the music."

June 13. Paris. Misia Edwards writes to Mme Stravinsky at the Villa Borghese asking for news of "*votre cher malade.*"

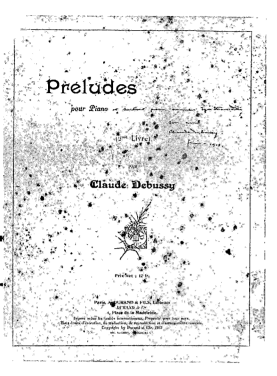

June 15. Cover of Debussy's *Préludes* (2ième livre) pour Piano "et surtout pour amuser Igor Strawinsky, son ami Claude Debussy. Juin 1913."

June 14. Arcueil. Erik Satie writes: *"Mon cher ami, j'apprends que vous êtes malade d'un embarras d'estomac qui vous désoblige un peu. Ce n'est rien, n'est-ce pas? Je compte venir vous consoler, dans deux ou trois jours. Amicalement."*

June 16 (?). Receives a visit from Giacomo Puccini. (After hearing one of the *Sacre* performances, Puccini had written to Tito Ricordi: "Sheer cacophony but strange and not without a certain talent.")

June 23. Debussy to André Caplet, Covent Garden: *"Je vous réserve le lecture du 'Sacre du Printemps' qui ne peut pas vous laisser indifférent."*

June 30. Paris. Jeanès (the painter) writes: "I had hoped to see you and to tell you of the intense emotion that your *Sacre* aroused in me, but, hearing that you are ill, I want to write to you. It seems to me that you have expressed one of the elementary forces of Man. . . . In the few brief moments that I have been near you—at Debussy's—I wanted to speak to you about your work, but you were always occupied with other matters. . . . [The *Sacre*] was one of the greatest emotional experiences of my life."

July 1. London. Drury Lane. First performance in England of the Stravinsky-and-Ravel *Khovanshchina*.

July 3. Paris. Writes to Steinberg in St. Petersburg: "I am very satisfied with 'Holy Spring' in the orchestra and was happy, truly happy, to hear the long-awaited orchestra performance. The presentations went very stormily. Fights actually occurred. Nijinsky's choreography was incomparable. With the exception of a few places, everything is as I wanted it. One must wait a long time before the public becomes accustomed to our language, but of the value of what we have done I am certain, and this gives me the strength for further work. . . ."

July 4. Excelsior publishes a statement by Stravinsky to the effect that he will not collaborate with Canudo in *"Bloc en Glace."*

July 4. Edvard Benedictus writes: "Yesterday I saw Ravel, who said that your wife had left for Lausanne. . . . I wrote to Dr. Oppenheim."

July 6. Visit from M. D. Calvocoressi, to whom Stravinsky gives the sketchbook containing his arrangement of the *Khovanshchina* finale.

July 7. London. Monteux writes to Stravinsky in Ustilug: "Rhené Baton [175] [*sic*] rehearses the strings for Part One while I rehearse the winds for Part Two, and vice versa. . . . Baton will have time for six rehearsals between my performance and his. . . ."

July 8 (?). Paris. Stravinsky returns to Clarens.

July 10 (?). London. Hotel Cecil, Strand. Misia Edwards writes the orchestra rebelled against the *Sacre* during rehearsal, and that Monteux lost his temper. (See Appendix B.)

July 11. The Stravinskys leave for Ustilug, via Berlin.

July 11. London. Theater Royal, Drury Lane. The *Sacre* is performed for the first time in England, conducted by Monteux. Edwin Evans, music critic of the *Pall Mall Gazette*, gives a pre-curtain lecture. "Evans came out on the curtained stage and tried to calm us with [an] erudite little speech. . . . No one listened to him, though no one spoke, just a ferment of restless rustling and dry coughing could be heard through the house in the darkness. . . . Evans hurriedly faltered into silence and bowed himself off stage." (*Music At Midnight*, by Muriel Draper, Harper & Brothers, 1929)

July 11. London. Misia Edwards cables to Stravinsky in the Russischer Hof, Berlin: "Complete success of *Sacre* spoiled by your letter to Monteux unjustly wounding Serge." (See Appendix B.)

July 12. Berlin. Russischer Hof. Stravinsky cables to Diaghilev in London: "Sorry to have caused trouble but did not understand your diplomatic position. Cable to Ustilug."

July 13–14. En route to Ustilug.

July 15. Paris. Hôtel Meurice. Misia Edwards writes to Stravinsky in Ustilug describing the scene in which Monteux read his letter from Stravinsky forbidding any cuts.

July 18. Le *Sacre* is performed for the second time in England, conducted by Rhené-Baton. *Le Spectre de la Rose* is also on the program.

July 20. (Sunday). London. M. D. Calvocoressi sends newspaper clippings and a note: "Cher Igor: On my knees I beg your pardon. . . . I send these things to calm a little your understandable impatience. . . . Greetings to your mother as well as your wife." (Original in French)

July 24. Le *Sacre* is performed for the third time in England, conducted by Rhené-Baton.

July 25. Oxford. Calvocoressi writes: "*Le Sacre* was far better received in London than in Paris."

July 27. London. *The Times* reviews the ballet: ". . . Even the colors of the dresses are to some extent reflected in the orchestration—as, for instance, in the first scene, when a group of maidens in vivid scarlet huddles together to the accompaniment of closely-written chords on the trumpets. Movements, too, are mirrored in an equally realistic way when, a little later on, the dancers thin out into a straggling line, while the orchestra dwindles to a trill on the flutes; then a little tune begins in the woodwinds two octaves apart, and two groups of three people detach themselves from either end of the line to begin a little dance that exactly suits the music. The same thing is seen equally clearly in the dance of the Chosen Maiden in the second scene, though as this is a solo dance the effect is less striking and more obvious. As regards gesture, the convention employed seems to be a treble one. First we have purely ritual movements of a primitive kind, such as leaping on the earth and looking toward the sun; then imitative or realistic gestures, seen when all the dancers shiver with terror at the entry of the old seer; [176] and lastly movements of a purely emotional value, neither ritual nor imitative. . . . What is really of chief interest in the dancing is the employment of rhythmical counterpoint in the choral movements. There are many instances, from the curious mouse-like shufflings of the old woman in the first scene, against the rapid steps of maidens in the last. But the most remarkable of all is to be found at the close of the first scene, where figures in scarlet run wildly round the stage in a great circle, while the shifting masses within are ceaselessly splitting up into tiny groups revolving in eccentric axes. It is here that M. Nijinsky joins hands with M. Jacques Dalcroze; and it is in this direction that his theories on ballet are capable of indefinite expansion. . . . The third and last performance was received with scarcely a sign of opposition."

July 31. Dieppe. Monteux writes: "The *Sacre* went very well with the admirable London orchestra, nor did we have many rehearsals (only seven). The London public was much better behaved than the Parisian, and the whole work was heard from beginning to end. The success was considerable—six or seven curtain calls. I greatly regretted that you were not there."

August 1. Maurice Fanet, the lawyer, writes to Stravinsky in Ustilug saying that M. Alzieu has finally signed the "acquiescence." (See source note 171)

August 3. London. Serge Grigoriev writes: "The *Sacre* was given a total of seven times."

August 25. Ustilug. Writes to Derzhanovsky: "I've certainly caused enough trouble with my telegram to [Nicolas] Miaskovsky . . . but I have so much to do that I cannot cope with the correcting part of it alone. Therefore I decided to appeal to Miaskovsky, being aware of his ability to find his way quickly in other people's scores. I would much like to get to know him personally and to speak to him about this, for I would like to entrust to him not only this task, which I now have in mind, but several others as well. . . ." In mid-July, Stravinsky had sent an orchestra score of the *Sacre* Part One to Miaskovsky to ask him to read it for corrections, writing in the upper left-hand corner of the first page of the music: "Nicolas Yacovlevich Miaskovsky, please, I beg you to return this manuscript not later than August 14, Old Style [August 27], and do not show it to anyone, only, exceptionally, to Vladimir Vladimirovich Derzhanovsky, Igor Stravinsky." On the lower margin of the page, Stravinsky wrote, at a later date: "This score is a copy made from my other one before changing it." (In fact the first page of the score does not contain any tempo changes at all.) The manuscript now belongs to the heirs of the late André Meyer, Paris. In Berlin, September 23, 1913, Stravinsky purchased two sets of pieces by Miaskovsky. In Brussels, in January 1924, Stravinsky told an interviewer: "Russia today has two musicians of very great talent, Prokofiev and Miaskovsky. The large public still ignores them, but that is no reflection on their merit." (Unidentified Brussels newspaper)

October 3. Clarens. Writes to Benois: "This last child, the *Sacre*, does not give me a moment's rest. There is some incredible gnashing surrounding it. Seriozha [177] tells me of the very hard-to-accept betrayal by people who used to regard my previous works with great enthusiasm, or, if not that, at least with unshakable sympathy. Well, I say—or rather, I think—so it *must* be. But why has Seriozha himself wavered toward the *Sacre*? He used to listen to it at rehearsals with exclamations of 'divine,' and he even said, which one actually might have taken as a compliment, that the music should have been put aside after it was composed until the public was ready for it. . . . Quite simply I fear that he is under evil influences, which are not so much morally as materially strong. To tell the truth, in summing up my impressions about his relationship to the *Sacre*, I have come to the conclusion that he is not encouraging me in this direction. In effect, I have been deprived of the one and truest support in the propagation of my artistic ideas. . . . But enough of the *Sacre*."

1914

January 26. Lausanne. Writes to Struve in Berlin: "I have just come back from Paris, where I met with Monteux concerning his forthcoming concert performances of *Petrushka* and *Le Sacre*."

February 14–17. St. Petersburg. Benois writes: "It is already a week that I have been living with the sounds of the *Sacre* in my ears. It started in Moscow and continues now in St. Petersburg. I am longing to hear it again . . . [though] I am still completely bewildered by it. Nor do I know if Kussevitzky conducted it correctly. . . . That the Rimsky-Korsakov clan hissed it violently is a consolation. . . . Perhaps the ending is too abrupt. People who saw the stage performance say that it is even more noticeable there. . . ."

March 30. A.M. Conducts part of his Symphony in E-flat at Ansermet's rehearsal of the piece in the Kursaal de Montreux, then leaves on the 2:00 P.M. train for Paris.

April 4. Paris. Salle du Casino. Attends Monteux's dress rehearsal for the first concert performance of the *Sacre* outside of Russia.

April 5. (Sunday) 2:30 P.M. Attends the performance of the *Sacre* (at the end of a program consisting of Schmitt's *Salomé*, a Mozart violin concerto played by Georges Enesco, a *Nocturne* by Jean Huré, and Bach's Cantata No. 32), afterward is borne from the hall on the shoulders of the crowd and carried in triumph through the Place de la Trinité.

April 6. Comoedia publishes a review by Vuillermoz: "The crowd that invaded the Casino de Paris stopped all traffic in the Rue de Clichy and upset strollers in the Place de la Trinité. . . .

December 14. Zürich. Stravinsky, photographed by Ernest Ansermet. On this trip to Zürich, the composer heard Mahler's Eighth Symphony, and, on December 15, back in Clarens, wrote to Delage: "What can I say about the music of this German 'Kolossal Werk,' with its 800 performers, 600 in the chorus and some 200 in the orchestra? . . . Imagine that during two hours you are made to understand that two times two is four." Stravinsky dated the photograph himself.

After the last chord there was delirium. The mass of spectators, in a fever of adoration, screamed the name of the author, and the entire audience began to look for him. An exaltation, never to be forgotten, reigned in the hall, and the applause went on until everyone was dizzy. The reparation is complete. Paris is rehabilitated. For Igor Stravinsky, the homage of unlimited adoration."

Three Japanese Lyrics

On June 16, 1913, Miaskovsky wrote to Prokofiev:

It is bad that the Russians again play at being innocent and print the "holy nonsense" of Stravinsky (that is not my opinion; I think that it is poorly composed, sometimes wild, sometimes not bad) . . . The Japanese romances . . . could be sung with the correct accent only by moving them one eighth to the left. All this is very amusing, but the music is printed only because big profits are expected from the work—which will not come. [Stravinsky] contradicts every principle, and condescendingly.

In fact the sketches for "Akahito" (completed in Ustilug, October 19, 1912) show that Stravinsky used conventional prosody (one eighth-note "to the left") in the first draft.

On July 12, 1913, Derzhanovsky wrote to Stravinsky in Paris:

The music of the *Japanese Lyrics* is enchanting, marvelous, but what is the meaning of this constant and stubborn disharmony between musical meter and text? Some of the accents are at the eighth, some at the

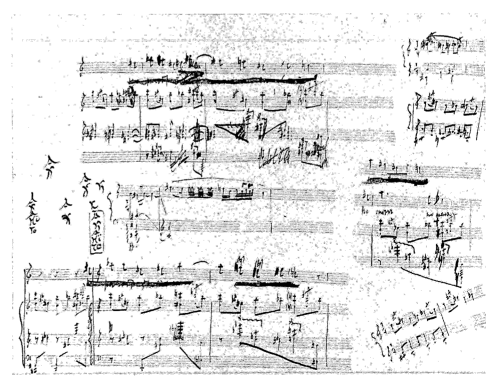

October 1912. Note the imitation of Japanese calligraphy in Stravinsky's drawing of the title (middle of the page, left side) of the sketches for "Akahito," the first of the *Three Japanese Lyrics*. The music in measure 2, middle staff, seems to be an early idea for the concluding figure of "Tsaraiuki," the third of the *Lyrics*. Stravinsky's first sketches for the instrumentation of "Akahito" — two violins, two violas, cello, piano, piccolo, flute — are on the reverse of this sheet and were written at the same time, October 1912.

quarter. I see the intention in the modulations, in which you are always so subtle, but what is your intention in the text?

Stravinsky's answer seems to have been lost, but, in any case, Derzhanovsky wrote to him again later in July, in Ustilug:

I have read your explanation of the *Japanese Lyrics* with great interest and can now defend your direction. Your idea is simple, subtle, complex, theoretical. . . .

Derzhanovsky did not understand Stravinsky's "idea," however, and wrote again on September 24:

Why does the musical meter not correspond to the meter of the texts? If it's your secret, tell it to me.

The origins of the *Lyrics* were visual as well as verbal. Delage wrote to Stravinsky, October 23, 1912: "I have your Japanese prints in a drawer waiting for you." And the following excerpt from a Tokyo newspaper forty-seven years later sheds more light on Stravinsky's inspiration for the work:

Stravinsky said that he had an "old contact" with Japan through his composition on old Japanese "Waka" poems. In 1913 he produced three pieces on a Russian version of the old Japanese poems. . . . The maestro, who had been interested in Japanese wood-block prints at the time, was deeply impressed by a "nature of two dimensions," characteristic of these prints. . . . His "two-dimensional" music met with severe criticism from contemporaries, he said, but critics at that time were idiots. . . . Asked to name works of his own that he would like to recommend, he replied: "I would like to recommend all of my works." . . . He explained that the best works are those "which are felt in the heart and ears, as is the case with an expectant mother." "Are you now expecting a baby?" came a question. "Yes, I am, but I am interrupted by this visit to Japan. And may I now interrupt you and take my lunch?" [*Mainichi*, Tokyo, reporting on a press conference, April 7, 1959]

The *Japanese Lyrics* were first performed in the Salle Erard, Paris, Wednesday, January 14, 1914, at 9:00 P.M., together with Fauré's C-minor String Quartet, some pieces by Delage and Schmitt, and the premiere of Ravel's *Trois Poèmes de Stéphane Mallarmé*. Satie's *Chapitres Tournés en Tous Sens*, also heard for the first time, was "side-splitting," according to a note in Delage's hand on the program that he sent to Stravinsky—who was in Lausanne for his wife's accouchement. Delage also wrote, on the night of the concert, "Do you agree that the second of your songs is the most magnificent?" and went on to say that the audience gave the opus "a splendid success; there were some protests, naturally, but do not, on that account, catch typhus."
A month before the concert, Delage wrote to Stravinsky:

Do you want the three Japanese melodies sung in Russian? . . . I have just returned from London . . . impossible to obtain ten minutes with Rudyard Kipling, even after being invited by his agent. [December 9, 1913]

On January 6, Delage described his difficulties in engaging a Russian singer:

I spent eight days trying to find a singer, Andrieff being in St. Petersburg, Allchersky in Marseille. . . . Finally it has been settled with Nikitina, who has a very high register. . . . The worst of this is that I have had to work with her at the piano. . . . But it will go. . . . You absolutely must hear this concert of "the latest things" . . . better, at worst, than listening to Mahler. . . . But I fear that the little Hôtel Civry is no longer sumptuous enough for Prince Igor. . . .

One or two nights after the first performance, Nikitina sang the Lyrics again at a semi-private gathering, with Alfredo Casella at the piano, replacing the instrumental nonet.

The Nightingale

Stravinsky left for Paris on the night train, January 19, and was met at the station the next morning by Delage, who, after helping to install his friend in the Hôtel Crillon, bought soap and a toothbrush for him to replace those Stravinsky left in Lausanne. He wrote to his wife on the 21st:

Delage telephoned about my arrival. Seriozha and Bakst were waiting for me in the vestibule of the hotel. Diaghilev talked until 3 A.M. Tonight I will play The Nightingale at Misia's, and I will send a telegram about my impressions. . . . Petrushka will not be performed in Paris but in Berlin, Cologne, Leipzig. . . . One good idea came to Diaghilev, to have the Nightingale's aria sung in French. Diaghilev does not go to Moscow directly but first to Berlin.

Stravinsky spent the 20th with Delage. On the evening of the 21st, he dined with Diaghilev at the home of Mme Edwards. (In later years, Stravinsky used to talk about her baccarat table, eventually sold to the Baroness d'Erlanger,[178] who installed it in her Venetian palace.) After dinner, Stravinsky played the first two acts of The Nightingale for the impresario and his hostess, who remarked on the stylistic differences between the earlier and later acts but said that this did not seem disturbing.[179] Diaghilev told Stravinsky that The Nightingale would be presented at the end of the Paris season and at the beginning of the London one, and Diaghilev confessed that he had not actually heard the Japanese Lyrics but had been told about "the brilliance" of the work.

On January 21, Stravinsky dined alone with Debussy—Diaghilev, who was also invited, having already left for Berlin and Moscow.[180] It was on this occasion that Stravinsky noticed a transformation in the French master, who "looked very pale, has lost weight and seemed oppressed in his soul (tormented in spirit). Something has happened to him. He talked at length about Russia. He liked The Nightingale." (Stravinsky to his wife,

January 22) The next day Delage and Cocteau came at 7:00 P.M. and accompanied Stravinsky to *La Nouvelle Revue [Française]*, where he played Acts I and II of *The Nightingale* [181] for Ravel, Jacques Rivière, Jacques Copeau, Gallimard, Monteux, and others. Apropos of this evening, Jacques Rivière wrote:

Editions de la Nouvelle Revue Française, 35 and 37, rue Madame, Paris. February 4, 1914. My dear Stravinsky, I am rather late in telling you how grateful I am. But I have been near you in my thoughts all these days as I have started to put on paper some ideas about *The Nightingale*. You were very kind to have sent these two cards to Gallimard and to me. They gave us great pleasure. . . . Believe me, my dear Stravinsky . . . Jacques Rivière.

But Stravinsky had already returned to Lausanne, where he wrote to Struve, his publisher in Berlin:

I have just come back from Paris. . . . *The Japanese Songs* had a noisy success, and Madame Nikitina sang them beautifully. . . . A new theater has been formed in Paris, the "Vieux-Colombier." I have been asked by them to compose a dance suite. I agreed in principle, and you will receive a letter from M. Cocteau. [Letter of January 26]

Cocteau's role in Stravinsky's life became prominent during his visit to Paris in January 1914, and, in the weeks following, Cocteau was to become a positive nuisance. That this was not for the first time is revealed in a letter, Cocteau to Stravinsky, not dated but marked "1913" by the composer, and definitely pre-1914, since Cocteau does not use the familiar "*tu*":

Mon cher Igor, what you call "arrogance" should correspond to what I call "lucid pride"—without which you would not know my tender *élan* toward your work. Enthusiasm is one of the highest manifestations of pride. And the stronger it is, the more it proves the instinctive value that we place on our judgments. For the rest, a just pride is the noblest of all forms of honesty. And I detest falseness. Your friend, Jean Cocteau.

Delage wrote to Stravinsky in Clarens, February 5, 1914, proposing to come there for a period of work, but, when Stravinsky moved to Leysin, Delage said that this eyrie was too remote for him. Cocteau came to Leysin on March 7, and offered to collaborate with Stravinsky. Francis Steegmuller tells this story with great skill in his *Cocteau*, providing excellent translations of the correspondence of both men, showing, for example, Stravinsky's frankness:

Vieux maniaque: What a peculiar idea to go to Aïgle. Go instead to Villeneuve . . . to the Hôtel Byron. You will be comfortable there and, for comparatively modest rates, you will find everything you need: rooms, hot and cold water; lukewarm women, boys aged 8 to 13. . . . [Letter of February 27, 1914]

On February 28, Stravinsky asks Cocteau to postpone his trip for a few days, saying that

1914. Leysin, annex of the Grand Hotel. With Turkish coffee-maker. *The Nightingale* was completed here, and the first of the Three Pieces for String Quartet. On November 4, 1915, Stravinsky's sister-in-law Liudmilla Beliankin wrote to his wife from Odessa: "[I picture] Ghima at his Swiss table, bent over his manuscript . . . or over a cup of Turkish coffee, then starting a little conversation that could be endless. Now I see him pacing from corner to corner and talking, talking. . . . Better not to think about it. How sad not to be together. . . . Grisha is in Moscow. . . ."

the weather is frightful, with fogs so thick that it is impossible to tell a goat from the housekeeper of the sanitarium. . . .

But Cocteau came, only a day or two after Stravinsky had returned from a trip to Berlin to see his publisher, and not to Aïgle or to Villeneuve, but to Leysin, accompanied, moreover, by Paul Thévenaz,[182] who painted a portrait of Stravinsky that was exhibited a month later in Lausanne. The purpose of the visit was to induce Stravinsky to compose the music for "David," a ballet. But, since this project was never realized, a full account of the exchanges of letters and telegrams, and of the injured feelings that resulted, would consume too large a part of this condensed anthological "life." Also, Stravinsky was never interested in "David," and he was in a great hurry to finish the third act of *The Nightingale*.

Two years later, Cocteau confessed to Misia that his relationship with Stravinsky had been

heavy and full of misunderstandings. . . . You know of my love for and dedication to Igor, of my sadness for a blot on the beautiful snows of Leysin, and perhaps of my project for a book about him. . . . I came up against Igor unaware that I was moving toward Satie, but Satie is coming, and perhaps he can reconcile things between Igor and me. [Letter of July 14, 1916]

To Stravinsky himself, Cocteau wrote:

I do not recall ever having approached the annex of the Leysin hotel without experiencing Nietzsche's emotion at the entrance of Triebschen. [Undated letter]

And, on August 11, 1916:

Dear Igor, I am taking advantage of a furlough to write to you. If I were free, I would join you in Switzerland, and we would again find our close contact. As I was telling my old friend Errazuriz,[183] "I have been put at odds with Stravinsky, I am entangled with Stravinsky," which is both less and more serious. . . . Gide took me to hear your little chamber pieces.[184] The first of them upsets and haunts me, like certain phrases in the Bible. . . . The second and third bring to mind Rimbaud's "*cauchemar des chinoises*" and "*après le déluge.*" Forgive me if I compare the incomparable. . . . We are working together for Serge (Satie and I) and . . . our piece [*Parade*] will be ready in October. . . . Goodbye, dear Igor—the idiots and the blind can't change anything in my heart. It remains intact.

After *Le Sacre du Printemps*, Stravinsky had lost interest in the opera that he had begun before *The Firebird*. He rejected the suggestion of the Moscow Svobody (Free) Theater that he complete the work, but, during March 1913, changed his mind, and, on the 31st of the month, telegraphed to A. A. Sanine,[185] the theater's principal director, stating conditions for the acceptance of a commission. These were a three-year exclusivity for Moscow, since Diaghilev wanted to produce the opera in Paris, in

1909. A page from the first act of *The Nightingale*, full score. Resuming work on the opera in 1913, Stravinsky rewrote this act, which explains why the instrumentation and the rhythmic figuration are more elaborate here than in the corresponding passage in the published version.

return for an advance of 3,000 rubles and two further payments of 3,500 rubles each, after the completion of the second and third acts. When the terms were not accepted, Stravinsky agreed to a smaller sum, which, he said, had to be paid at once or he would compose a ballet for Diaghilev.[186] The voluminous correspondence concerning the Moscow performance that was never to take place is summarized in a letter from Stravinsky, in Leysin, February 21, 1914, to Alexander Siloti, in the Hotel Bristol, Vienna.

Nicolas Struve wrote that you had asked him about the possibility of conducting *The Nightingale* next season in the Maryinsky Theater. I prefer to discuss the matter with you personally, and certainly it would be quicker that way. But first of all I must tell you about the situation with the work itself. The piano score of the first and second acts is already engraved and is being printed. Also, the French translation has been completed, and the orchestra parts to Act I have been extracted. I am composing and orchestrating Act III now, and I hope to send it to the publisher in a month. My obligations are as follows: the Moscow Free Theater commissioned me to finish the opera—of which Act I was composed and orchestrated just before *The Firebird*. I confess that I accepted the commission reluctantly, not having thought about the opera for such a long time and having other ideas in mind. But the financial side of the transaction made it unrefusable, and, accordingly, I finished the opera, adding two acts. I had an advance of 2,000 rubles, and the Free Theater must now pay me 10,000 more, which they promised to do soon, in installments. Diaghilev has purchased exclusivity from the publisher for Paris and London. That is all I can say. . . .

My impression is that the Free Theater will probably close, since even now the contract between the Theater and the publisher has not been signed. If Telyakovsky wishes to assume responsibility for *The Nightingale* from the Free Theater, I will immediately write to the director of the Free Theater to ask why they have not signed the contract; and if I do not receive a satisfactory answer, I will write to Struve instructing him to break off relations with the Free Theater and to give the material to the Imperial Theater.

Struve is demanding a minimum of ten performances, five in Moscow and five in St. Petersburg. Also, I must frankly say that, as for sending the piano score to Telyakovsky, if I do not play it myself and someone else does, they will say "nonsense," as the late Nikolai Andreyevich [187] used to say about Debussy and Strauss: "Nonsense *fortissimo*." It would be preferable if I could play the piece for Telyakovsky myself when he comes to Paris, which he does every spring. He has never come to *any* of my performances, incidentally, so if he is afraid of making acquaintance with the music, it would be good if we saw each other in person. I would be so happy to play the *Nightingale* for *you*, to see you and to gossip with you, and you are the only one for whom I could play it with pleasure.

But, despite Stravinsky's claims to have put the opera out of mind, the first of the following letters reveals that he had planned to return to the opera after *Petrushka* and before *Le Sacre*:

Stravinsky to Benois. July 13, 1911. Ustilug. Plans are maturing for me for a joint work with you which, if all is well, I hope to realize by 1913.

I refer to Andersen's *Nightingale*, one third of which—and it seems that you have already heard this—is composed. Write to me whether the prospect pleases you and whether you have objections. It is an opera toward which we both started to grow equally, but working with you might rehabilitate me in relation to the piece. In any case, I shall continue the *Nightingale* that I have begun. It is devilish good fun to compose such *Chinoiserie*. Think about it, dear, it will be a great joy for me. . . . In two months, it will already be necessary to have completed the second scene of *The Nightingale*, and then take up the "Great Victim."

Stravinsky to Benois. March 31, 1913. Clarens. Dear Friend! You cannot imagine how happy I am that you are taking part in *The Nightingale*. Dear, kind friend, how much fun it will be to work together. Where and when will we see each other? Your presence is essential to me at the beginning of my work, if only for a short time. The libretto must be continued according to the original plan that we agreed on with S. S. Mitussov [188] (don't repeat this, for he's keeping his name a secret). Try to see him and tell him that he will have to come to me in Ustilug at the beginning of June (Russian Style), and that I will pay for his work.

Stravinsky to Benois. August 12, 1913. Ustilug. I received your warm, kind letter while I was recuperating at the *Maison de Santé* in Paris. I stayed there for quite a while but am now thoroughly recovered from the painful and lengthy illness. All that, thank God, has now receded into the realm of "pleasant memories." On the one hand, I received much sympathy from people I am not particularly used to believing; and, on the other, I was assured of the good, fraternal feelings of Seriozha. But on the "third" hand, I became convinced of the complete indifference of my ballet and opera colleagues—which did not upset me very much, for I was not expecting anything from them. But forgive me for spending so much time on things that are probably of no interest to you. I shall write of something else—of *The Nightingale* and of your letter to me. . . .

Stepan Stepanovich was with me about four weeks ago, and we wrote the second-act libretto, which has turned out quite well. I am composing, and can say that I am now getting into the work. . . . The Japanese delegation, consisting of three fat, dark, Japanese tenors in sewn golden gowns, is having an effect on me. Their address to the Emperor turned out to be terrible. The music for the mechanical nightingale is already composed, and the beginning of the Nightingale's Song. The beginning is very interesting. All the conversations, and the crowds cleaning the porcelain palace for the holiday, must take place behind a lowered transparent tulle curtain *(Tyluli),* and with Chinese shadows. There will be exclamations of "Lamplighters! Lamplighters! Lively now!" Then: "Let them hang a little bell on each flower," and "Oh, that's utterly Chinese," I consider this a happy find, with the *faux-chinois* scale that I use—or rather, *fausse-chinoise*—and with which it blends in a broad way. These conversations are interspersed with questions about the Nightingale. They establish a very lively and bold character at the beginning of this fantastic act. I have tried, and so has Mitussov, to avoid everything that might have given food for dramatic *"cabotinage"* by the artists and singers.

Benois to Stravinsky. September 1913. St. Petersburg. Dear Igor Fyodorovich, dear friend, how sad that we are living so far apart. It seems to me that we could do great things together, but nothing will happen this way. All the others are dispersed, too, Serge being the Devil knows where. After discussing the Bach ballet with me in Baden, he was to have come to me in Lugano and to have brought Ravel with him. But I have heard nothing from him, and, since he has disappeared without a word, I am inclined to believe those charming gossipmongers, whose news has probably reached you as well, and who say that Vaslav married a Hungarian millionairess, and that Serge, in his grief, has sold the company to an impresario. Have you news of our dissolute genius Serge? Valechka,[189] who went to Paris—cursing his fate, poor fellow—also knows nothing.

In addition to staging the Goldoni, I must start to prepare *The Possessed* [190] for the spring season, and all this besides writing my *History of Painting*. I am passionately interested in *The Nightingale*. When do you think it will be ready? I do not give up hope of doing it myself, and it would be a creative aphrodisiac for me. I believe that Roerich [191] could achieve something miraculous with it, but some details he would probably not do, and just these details interest me enormously.

My dear friend, write again soon. I promise to answer without delay, and if you want some information, I will be glad to help you. . . .

In Warsaw, on September 21, 1913, Stravinsky obtained the necessary exit visas, and the next day, with his wife, three children, and nurse Sofiya Dmitrievna, left Russia at Alexandrov, the border station, en route from their summer home in Ustilug to their winter one in Clarens. While in Ustilug, Stravinsky completed the mechanical Nightingale's music, August 14, and, three weeks later, the true Nightingale's aria that precedes this *japonaiserie*. During the stopover in Warsaw, Stepan Mitussov came to see him and to discuss final questions about the opera.

Stravinsky to Benois. October 3, 1913. Clarens. The day before yesterday and yesterday Seriozha and I spent together: he stopped here on his way from Venice to Paris. . . . I knew nothing of Nijinsky's marriage, for I have not been reading the newspapers lately: I learned about it only from Seriozha.[192]

Benois to Stravinsky. October 11, 1913. St. Petersburg. Dear Igor Fyodorovich, I found your letter only on my return from Moscow. The news about Nijinsky's marriage was a thunderbolt. When did it happen? None of our friends is here in the city at the moment, and I know of no one who can give me any information about it, since I do not want to talk to a stranger like Svetlov.[193] When I saw Serge and Vaslav, almost on the eve of Vaslav's departure for Argentina, there was no hint about the coming event. Nijinsky was absorbed in studying Bach with us, preparing the Bach ballet. Can it be possible that he had no idea of it at that time? Be kind and tell me one thing: was it a complete surprise for Serge, or was he prepared for it? How deep was the shock? Obviously their affair was coming to an end, and I doubt that he was really heartbroken, but if he did suffer, I hope it was not too terrible for him. I can imagine that, as head of the company, he must be completely bewildered. But why can't Nijinsky be both a ballet master and a Hungarian millionaire? [194] The whole story is so fantastic that I sometimes think I have read it in a dream and am insane to believe it.

I am sorry to be unable to fill your request completely, but the two theaters are now rivals, and all connections between them have been broken. The talk that I hear about it has been contradictory, and I do not know what to believe. Some people say that everything in the Free Theater is perfect: that there is plenty of money; that each invention is more amusing and ingenious than the one before; that two of the subscription nights are already sold out (this, it seems, is true), etc., etc. ... Some people are delighted by Marzhdanov,[195] but others say he is impossible, etc., etc. Personally, I think that *The Nightingale* will be staged, but that this will take at least two years; and still, I would not promise even this absolutely. I also think they will make a mix of it, some interesting things and much *merde*. The Moscow public will swallow it all, of course, good and bad alike, since Moscow knows no better and will devour anything. But I am very impatient for the opening; a venture as naïve as this must at least result in something refreshing.

I am longing for *The Nightingale*, especially after seeing Mitussov, who gave me his impressions after Warsaw.

Benois to Stravinsky. January 14, 1914. St. Petersburg. Dear Igor Fyodorovich, I am just leaving for Moscow, and I write in a hurry. For the last two hours I have looked everywhere in vain for your letter containing the description of the sets and the enumeration of the characters. Just now, when I could start to study the libretto, this delay. I beg you, send a second copy immediately, and also a detailed libretto. I beg you not to insist on the colors. I have my own ideas, and I think the result will be good. The hall in the castle will be pink with dark blue and black. But, my God, where is the music? Is it possible that I will have to work without this main source of inspiration and without your personal promptings?

Goodness, the train!!! I embrace you cordially, Your Alexander Benois.

P.S. Write to me c/o Moscow Art Theater, Kammergersky Drive. Come!

Benois to Stravinsky. February 15, 1914. Moscow. Dear Igor Fyodorovich, Although your so-obstinate silence shows that you do not wish to talk to me, I am obliged to bother you to clarify a few points. But I flatter myself that the real reason for your silence is not a change of your feelings toward me, but rather circumstances that have enveloped you as much as they have me.

The hall of the Emperor will be white with blue. On the other hand, there will be much pink and green in the costumes. What keeps me from finishing the sketch of this setting—as well as of the set in this tableau in general—is the problem of what to do with the procession. You wanted a palanquin and you wanted the Emperor to be 'inserted' in the throne.[196] A marvelous idea! But how do you visualize the following combination: the throne is carried by a whole crowd of people, including eight small children, then placed on a scaffold? After that, the Emperor appears, surrounded closely by dignitaries who hold five parasols above *Him!* You wanted a palanquin, but every procession has one. This is new.

In general, I am constructing the procession as follows:
seven female dancers dressed in gold; seven female dancers dressed in silver; one male dancer and one female dancer very luxuriously costumed, and, with them, three dancers, monsters, two white boys with swords, five black boys with

swords, all of this party participating in a symbolic pantomime.

After this comes the Court (the chorus is already on the stage):

first appear two white-costumed mandarins; then two gray-
costumed mandarins; then a totally black Grand Master of the
Court; then the Chief Chamberlain with the Nightingale.

Then comes the throne, and, finally, His Majesty, heretofore invisible because of the parasols hiding him. The procession closes with two guards who take a standing position at
the foot of the throne. (The same kind of guards can walk in
front, or already be on the stage in the beginning.)

Do you see now what I mean? But perhaps you want something quite
different. The final word is with you, but, for God's sake, send me this
word immediately, or everything will go to hell. I shall not start the
definitive work until I have your exact instructions.

Perhaps an even more important question concerns the last act.
How do you see it yourself? But, first of all, I beg you to send the details
of the staging immediately, and the libretto itself, which I ask you to
mark with the basic tempi. This is supremely important (the music will
explain what I fail to understand in the text). I would prefer to have the
piano score, but probably it is far from finished.

How can we see each other to discuss all this? I wanted to come to
Berlin for a meeting, but this is now impossible. Think only how many
days will be wasted, and, just now, when every hour is precious. Is it
absolutely impossible for you to come here?

Concerning the decor of the third act, I imagine it like this: in
front, a kind of antechamber separated from the bedroom by a big
curtain (covering the whole stage: red, yellow, gold, and black). This
curtain is first drawn back, and we see a majestic bedroom at night and
in moonlight. The curtains are then closed, and, at the end, again
opened for us to see, a Sacrum Cubiculum in all of its splendor (many
windows, a gigantic bed, etc.). What do you think of it? Perhaps you
have conceived it quite differently? I implore you to answer.

I kiss Catherina Gavrilovna's hand and wish with all my heart
happiness for the newborn baby,[197] the mother, and the happy father.
I am burning with impatience to embrace you. One of these days, I
expect to hear Kussevitzky conduct *Le Sacre du Printemps.* . . .

P.S. Write to St. Petersburg, 31, Admirals' Canal, and, on the envelope: "In case of absence please forward the letter immediately." But
the best thing to do, my dear, would be to answer the main points by
telegram. If you are in agreement with all: *"Approuve tout"*; if not,
then in a few words: *"Empereur en palanquin"*; *"Trône en scène,"* or
something of this kind. For God's sake, hurry with an answer.

Benois to Stravinsky. February 14–17. St. Petersburg. Dear Igor Fyodorovich, I am in a great rush, for which reason I will limit myself to
business and avoid speaking about my artistic feelings.

My dear, what about the following combination: in the beginning,
a huge bedroom with a few windows flooded by moonlight; ghosts
(Serge does not want ghosts, but why not have them sitting on the bed
or showing their ugly mugs through the curtain of the bed—I do not
yet know myself exactly how to do it); a bed with a canopy; a catafalque
through which Death leaves (not through the window; the catafalque
must melt in front of you—is such a trick possible?). Day breaks during
the Nightingale's Song, and, with the bird's last notes, the couriers,
thinking the Emperor dead, ceremoniously close the curtains; the courtiers walk onstage, single file.

The next scene, the Court, is in front of the stage curtain, so that when the curtain goes up, the bedroom can be flooded by sunlight for the Emperor's "*Bonjour à tous.*" . . . Do not listen to that monster Serge, who has a mania for cutting, and who will cut until nothing is left. I await your confirmation of the plans, or any changes that have to be made.

The set for the second tableau is already done, and whether it is good or bad, I cannot say because I have no time to look at it again.

Anna Karlovna [198] had a sore throat and could not be present at the *Sacre.* . . .

P.S. My family all praise the *Nightingale* sets, but how can one believe one's family?

P.P.S. I know nothing about the Free Theater beyond what has been written in the newspapers. I hear, however, that Marzhdanov found another imbecile willing to give money, and that he wants to ruin this new one by introducing dramatic action spectacles.

Sanine will stay with Suhodolsky and probably stage operettas. Since my return from Moscow, where I did the decors and sets for Goldoni's *Tavern Keeper*, I am so deep in *The Nightingale*, I have no time to read or to learn anything. . . .

Stravinsky to Benois. February 20, 1914. Leysin. My dear friend, charming Alexander Nikolayevich! . . . I am in ecstasy with your ideas and projects, which are much superior to mine, above all that procession in which the palanquin is carried without the Emperor, while— just as you yourself drew it—he himself *walks* in. . . . You will see on the very last page of the notes: 1.) top of p. 59, "a few servants triumphantly bring the Emperor in a canopy." Here I will ask you to leave out the Chinese Emperor himself under the umbrellas. Later, where they place him in the canopy on a rise in the middle of the stage, especially prepared for this event, at the words: "The servants raise the canopy with the Chinese Emperor . . ." this should remain as follows: the Emperor will be taken directly from under the umbrellas into the palanquin! The role of the Emperor is almost purely choreographic. He has little to sing, and when he does open his mouth, the spoken part is accompanied with slow and expressive gestures (weighty ones—the rascal knows himself). As for the beginning of this act, I have noted that the so-called entr'acte, or introduction to the second act, must be performed with the curtain closed. Seriozha objected very much, but I insisted. I want something like Chinese shadows here— moving and colored, like a magic lantern. Don't be afraid of this *mauvais goût;* you can make it work wonderfully on the *tyluli.* . . .

Now about the third act. . . . First of all, I have not finished it yet and am in the midst of a spell of strenuous composition. But I would like to speak with you more factually and concretely about this act, for it seems to me, too, that it is the riskiest. If the other acts contain a minimum of movement, then here there isn't even that, until the Emperor's sunny, golden "Hello," at the end. . . . Now, when does the curtain rise, and when does the antechamber appear to the spectator? But before answering these essential questions, I ought to give the scenario of the third act to you, at least in brief. The Fisherman's song, which begins and ends it, is followed by a short orchestral introduction that connects directly with the chorus of the ghosts. Before your letter came, I had thought of raising the curtain here, to the last measures of this alto chorus. . . . Don't take me for an idiot, though that is not far from the truth. . . . Here, after the Nightingale vanishes, the courtiers appear immediately in the antechamber and gaze into the bedroom, from which the Emperor departs in all his majesty and says "Hello" before the astounded Chinese rogues. . . . But when should the main curtain go up? When should the screens, which separate the antechamber bedroom, be moved? The one thing that I know is that the main curtain ought to be raised . . . during the ghosts' chorus, when it is dark on the stage, and when Death begins to talk to the Nightingale. It is essential that Death flies out of the window before everyone's eyes. But then what? Write to me, dear. I have now come to the Nightingale's *Tanki*, having composed everything ending with the first conversation between Death and the Nightingale. The music for *Tanki* is the same.

Stravinsky to Benois. March 9, 1914. Leysin. Dear friend, regarding the third act, perhaps you are right, and it is necessary that the "ugly mugs" show themselves: I'm planning it that way. At the very beginning of their chorus, the curtain slowly begins to rise. (You have my sketch of this music.) After singing the first couplet, they should "Remember" (with the accent); then the "ugly mugs" can pop up, and then again hide. The same thing during the second couplet. Here the Nightingale begins to sing, and again the "ugly mugs" hide. At this point, the curtain is all the way up. I agree about Death disappearing without the flight out of the window, but let's think about how to do this at the Opéra! I am delighted by your idea of having the "ugly mugs" draw the curtain, since this would give the impression of padding an event whose whole effect is in its brevity. . . . In general, I'm a bit worried about this act. . . .

The opera was completed by March 28, on which date Stravinsky wrote to Ansermet asking him to arrange for the last pages to be copied and telling him that Liudmilla Beliankin would bring them to him.

The first performance of *The Nightingale*, May 26, 1914, at the Paris Opéra, was very widely reviewed, doubtless for the reason, as one critic wrote,

that the noise surrounding *Le Sacre du Printemps* the year before, and the triumph with which that work was received in concert performance this year, elevated the premiere of *The Nightingale* to the stature of a great event.

"As almost always happens in such cases," the same writer added, "the event did not quite match the expectations"; and he went on to say that, at the premiere, Stravinsky, not being quite assured of a third curtain call, came on stage somewhat prematurely. Some reviews mentioned signs of hastiness in the orchestral preparation, which would account for the following "open letter" from Stravinsky to Monteux:

Mon cher Monteux, after the second performance of *The Nightingale* I felt the need of thanking you warmly for your interpretation of my work. You and the orchestra of the Opéra truly surpassed yourselves in the rapid study of this score, which I have had the honor to present to the public on the stage of the Académie Nationale de Musique. Your intelligent devotion to the possible has truly touched me, and I ask you to convey my profoundest thanks to the valiant players. . . . [*Gil Blas,* May 30, 1914]

Emile Vuillermoz dismissed the orchestral performance as "mediocre" (*Comoedia*, May 28), but Ravel complimented the orchestra on its "prodigious effort," Monteux on his "*exécution honorable.*" Ravel remarked, too, that *The Nightingale* was given "only five rehearsals, while Strauss's *Joseph*, which is much less difficult, had three times that number" (*Comoedia Illustré*, June 5).

Reynaldo Hahn was ecstatic:

I do not believe that a more fascinating realization has ever been achieved in the theater, or a more perfect accord between music and staging. The music . . . suggests the barbaric and sensual China of legend, with an intensity bordering on the neuropathological. . . . The music of *The Nightingale* is of a perfect logic, adapted to the subject with a delicacy and discernment that are truly extraordinary. . . .

Colette [199] was so taken with the work that she sent the scenario of a ballet to Stravinsky, with the note: "*Le Rossignol me manque terriblement.*"

Ravel and Bartók detected the influence of Schoenberg. Ravel wrote:

To musicians, the most striking features of the score are its new audacities. Indeed, the musical conception is found only in embryo in the earlier works by the composer of the *Sacre.* . . . I would like to speak of the total contrapuntal freedom, of the bold independence of the themes, the rhythms, the harmonies, which, in combination, and thanks to one of the rarest musical sensibilities, form so seductive a whole. Stravinsky's newest creation approaches the last manner of Arnold Schoenberg, who is harder and more austere as well as—let us use the word—more cerebral. [*Comoedia Illustré*, June 5, 1914]

Here is Bartók, six years later:

Schoenberg's works, because of the abolition of tonality principles, exerted a more or less great influence on some of our younger, nay, even more mature composers. . . . I use the word "influence" in its best sense; that is, it is to be understood not as a servile counterfeiting but as a process similar to that in Stravinsky's work (especially in *The Nightingale*). Stravinsky's personality lost nothing under Schoenberg's influence; on the contrary, it developed, so to speak, in a still more unrestrained way. . . .[200]

Stravinsky attended the London premiere of *The Nightingale* at the Theater Royal, Drury Lane, on June 18, 1914.[201] Osbert Sitwell described him acknowledging the applause:

I was excited to see the great Russian composer, the master of the epoch, walk before the curtain. Slight of frame, pale, about thirty years of age, with an air both worldly and abstracted and a little angry, he bowed with solemnity to an audience that little comprehended the nature of the great musician to whom they were doing an honor, of the often eschatological import of his work. [From *Great Morning!* (Boston: Little, Brown, 1947)]

Anyone who has known Stravinsky will recognize the truth of

the observation about his anger and solemnity. Stravinsky described the same occasion himself, in a letter to Alexander Siloti, July 17, 1914, saying that, at the London premiere of *The Nightingale,* he was touched by the audience's warm reception. Apparently this was the only performance that Stravinsky attended.

On July 27,[202] 1914, he wrote to Benois:

I have received a letter from Evans and a telegram from [Diaghilev] that *The Nightingale* is quite successful and that (Evans writes this), in the sense of the *mise-en-scène,* it is much better than the first time. I would like to believe it.[203]

On June 23, Strauss's *The Legend of Joseph* was performed, and the two composers saw each other more than once. (According to an invoice from the Russischer Musik Verlag, June 10, 1914, Stravinsky had had the vocal score of his opera sent to Strauss in Garmisch.) Also, Stravinsky attended a concert in which Strauss conducted the original, chamber-music version of the *Siegfried Idyll.*

Prokofiev heard *The Nightingale* in London (and was introduced to Diaghilev by Walter Nouvel). This young composer wrote to Miaskovsky on June 25: " 'Svadba' [*Les Noces*] will be given in the coming Diaghilev season." Miaskovsky answered on August 19 that he had expected to hear more about *The Nightingale,* but "bought the score and found it poor and even indecently composed. [Stravinsky] has no power of invention. . . ." Prokofiev replied to this on August 26:

I heard *The Nightingale* only once, and that is insufficient. I think there are too many deliberate aggrandizements [dissonances?]. No one needs them, and they impoverish the composition. In comparison with the music of *Petrushka,* the humor is pale and the whole is less lively. . . . But European orchestra players are more progressive than ours and they are devoted to this music, which they have learned in detail.

The following glimpse of Stravinsky during his London sojourn is by Artur Rubinstein:

[I] saw *Petrushka* [204] again one night. . . . After a few curtain calls, a little man appeared to take a bow. A prolonged ovation greeted him; it was Igor Stravinsky. . . . I . . . rushed . . . backstage. Stravinsky was still on the stage, taking more bows. . . . With the last curtain call, Stravinsky turned around, ready to leave, when [a] man pointed a finger at me and said, "This is Rubinstein." The composer stopped, waiting for what I had to say.

"I have studied your *Sacre du Printemps,*" I said shyly, in Russian. . . . When I stopped talking, he hesitated for a second: "I am occupied all day tomorrow . . . but if you care to come at nine o'clock in the morning, you will find me at breakfast and we could talk for half an hour. I am staying at the Hotel Cecil on the Strand." . . .

It was almost noon [the next day] when he suggested . . . : "Let us sneak in on Richard Strauss's new ballet; they are rehearsing it just now. Diaghilev ruined himself on the decors and costumes by Sert; I want to see if it was worth it." . . . Strauss himself was conducting that last rehearsal. . . . Stravinsky pinched my arm at some salient moments and criticized the music in unprintable terms. . . . Out in the street, he said: "It's time for lunch. Do you know of a good place where we could eat?"

I was expected to lunch at Edith Grove with Paul, Zosia,[205] Karol,[206] and Jaroszynski. "Would you like to join me . . . ?" The idea pleased him. . . . Stravinsky sensed immediately the charm of the place, but at the sight of the concert grand he made some denigrating remarks about the piano. . . . "The piano is an instrument of percussion and nothing else," he said. Karol argued: "I don't agree with you. The greatest composers have written for the piano masterpieces which demand a singing tone."

"They were all wrong," said the Russian composer. "I am sure that a new music will be written treating it in the right way."

Karol, to win his point, became personal: "If you had heard Artur play your *Firebird* or *Petrushka* you would have changed your opinion about the piano."

"Is Rubinstein a pianist?" asked the astonished Stravinsky. Everybody laughed, taking it as a joke, but I suddenly realized that I had neglected to tell him. [Artur Rubinstein, *My Young Years* (New York: Knopf, 1973)]

Almost two years later, Stravinsky wrote to Siloti, who was then expecting to conduct the opera in Petrograd:

I hope to make some corrections before the performance at the Maryinsky: the guitar part, which is written an octave higher than it sounds, must be played by a virtuoso or not played at all, and the mandolin part must be doubled. The celesta in the fifth measure of $\boxed{119}$, Act III, is to be played by only one instrument, not two, but I think that I corrected this in London. . . . [Paris, February 11, 1916]

As early as September 1916, in San Sebastian, Diaghilev and Stravinsky discussed the possibility of extracting a ballet from *The Nightingale*, or, rather, from its last two acts, since these possessed a homogeneity of style that the opera lacked.

Diaghilev, in Rome, telegraphed to Stravinsky on November 3: "Money [for *Le Chant du Rossignol*] sent beg you come immediately to Rome very urgent business." The composer obtained an Italian visa in Lausanne on November 6, entered Italy at Iselle on the 7th, and was in Rome the next day, bringing with him a marked score showing his plan for the transformation of the opera. When he returned to Morges, via Paris (his French visa was procured in Rome on the 13th and his Italian exit visa on the 14th), the sum of 910 Swiss francs had been deposited in his account (on November 20) from Diaghilev's bank in Russia; Stravinsky wrote on the receipt: "Half of the commission for *The Nightingale* arrangement—minus 90 francs." Diaghilev also sent the following very remarkable letter of agreement:

1. Compose *The Song of the Nightingale*, cutting the measures on p. 49. 2. P. 51: cancel first three measures on last line. [Stravinsky deleted only the last seven notes.] 3. P. 60: cancel the first five measures. 4. P. 62: from the last measure on the page go back to p. 40, which you will have to recompose, and repeat until p. 49. 5. P. 59: after measure 1, go to measure 4 on p. 67, canceling pp. 63–66 and the first measures on p.

67. 6. On p. 67 transpose the last four lines. 7. Cancel p. 70 and measures 1–4 on p. 71; the next six measures on p. 71 must be recomposed. [Stravinsky added six measures of introduction before the six measures on p. 71, which he did not recompose.] 8. Cancel pp. 78 and 79. 9. P. 80: the first three measures should be recomposed, keeping the tremolo in the accompaniment. Measures 7 and 8 should be canceled. [Stravinsky recomposed and transposed the first three measures, but retained measures 7 and 8.] 10. P. 82: compose a good accompaniment, measures 3–8. [Stravinsky continued the accompaniment from the previous passage and transposed all of the music a minor second lower.] 11. P. 83: cancel measures 5 and 6 and change 7, 8, and 9. [Stravinsky canceled all five measures.] 12. P. 93: measures 3 and 4 should overlap.

The Nightingale's arias must be shortened, otherwise the choreography will be boring. Do not be sulky with me. I am a man of the theater and not, thank God, a composer.

Stravinsky finished the new score on April 4, 1917, but the work was not performed until two and a half years later, on December 6, 1919, and then not as a ballet but as a "tone poem" for orchestra. On this occasion, the audience—in Victoria Hall, Geneva—reacted violently, Le Sacre du Printemps not yet having been heard in Switzerland. In a letter to his London publisher written the day before the concert, Stravinsky said that he was "enchanted with the work," and that Ansermet had allotted six rehearsals for it. Writing again the day after the concert, the composer said that the music had provoked a tumult. The Frankfurter Zeitung noted that the counter-protestations in his favor were led by cries of "Vive Stravinsky, Vive Dada"—Geneva having been host, at the time, to the First International Congress of Dada.[207]

The storm over The Song of the Nightingale filled the newspapers and journals with debates. La Semaine Littéraire, December 20, 1919, published a two-column attack by one Joseph Lauber, a three-column "letter" answering him by Ansermet,[208] and a cartoon of Stravinsky flinging a harmony manual on a nightingale that is standing at his feet and singing to him. Stravinsky underscored and surrounded with interrogation marks Lauber's observation that

If the Bolsheviks seek to destroy the perfect chord of human harmony, [Stravinsky] tries to destroy the perfect chord in music: there is not a single one in his work.

The editor of La Suisse Musicale asked Stravinsky to explain his score, and though he refused, his letter is an artistic manifesto, one that contrasts startlingly with the Stravinsky of a few years later:

I have always believed that a composer can legitimately convince his public only through his music, and not through his music accompanied by explanations. . . . It is useless to try to force the time that the public takes to become accustomed to a new language, a new means of expression. This process . . . can in no case be replaced by explanations. . . . It is impossible to help the ear by means of guides. . . . The ear itself must be accessible to fresh sensations. [Morges, December 11, 1919]

The Song of the Nightingale was received with anger in Geneva, and with laughter in Lausanne, where Ansermet conducted it on December 29. A month later, on February 2, 1920, it was mounted as a ballet at the Paris Opéra, with decors by Matisse and choreography by Massine. In an interview in Comoedia, January 31, 1920, Stravinsky remarked about Diaghilev that "We understood each other from the first day," which was true, and that "we are bound by friendship and have always worked together," which was not. Stravinsky continued:

What I like above all in M. Diaghilev is that he is a man of the avant-garde, a creator always looking for the new . . . above all, an anti-bourgeois. By that I do not mean that he is a Bolshevik of art; bolshevism is another kind of bourgeoisie—in reverse, as it were, but with its own rules and conventions about what is done or what is not done.

In the same interview, Stravinsky testified that the Nightingale ballet "was prepared in close collaboration," but this would seem to be contradicted by a letter from Diaghilev to the composer shortly before the performance:

Massine, Depero, and myself were a minute late at the station, but you were not. I regret not having embraced you, and I wait for a word from you. The idea of composing new songs for The Nightingale, for the choreography, delights Massine, and he has no more fears about the ballet. We are certain to receive new masterpieces from you.

But Stravinsky did not compose new music to replace the Nightingale's—or the flute's—cadenza, and Diaghilev wrote again from Rome:

Did you receive my note sent in care of the Russian Consul in Lausanne? What did you do in Paris, and what did the old Polignac say, and what is the date of her spectacle? . . . Goncharova [209] and Larionov [210] came here to talk about The Nightingale. They are ecstatic about the music but in doubt about the choreography. Not enough music for choreographic movement, they say, because the Nightingale's songs are not for dancing.[211] I continue to wait for the new passages you promised to compose for me.

Louis Laloy's review of the ballet discusses the transformation from the original opera:

The score of The Nightingale is in three acts. . . . In The Song of the Nightingale here it all is again, but condensed, concentrated and uniquely translated, the song and the word replaced by movements of the ensemble and the gestures of individual characters. The two nightingales are no longer singers but dancers, and the episodes follow one another without transition or explanation. The music has achieved the solidity of a symphony.

The ironic dialogue of the search for the Nightingale, which formed the first act, has been eliminated, and the Fisherman's song has been given to the orchestra, the trumpet turning it into a kind of pre-lude. . . . The Bird makes its appearance with a melody that charms the courtiers and that eventually conquers Death. Mme Karsavina, draped in a translucent white garment embroidered with shivering bands, en-ters with this song. . . . M. Idzikovsky is the Mechanical Nightingale, confined in a varnished carapace; it is with the most amusing appear-ance of stupidity that this clever dancer opens his beak, jumps awk-wardly, and lifts his short wings—all following the gestures of his attentive showman.

The conquering of Death is represented by a struggle in which the supple grace of Mme Karsavina is opposed to the furious contortions of Mme Sokolova—that unforgettable Kikimora of the *Contes Russes*—dressed in a red costume adorned with a skeletal neckpiece. Death is finally strangled, and I confess that the brutality of this ending pleased me less than the willing departure of Death to her flowering cemetery in the first version of *The Nightingale*, which is also closer to the original Andersen story.

The most remarkable aspect of this version is the composition of the ensembles. M. Massine is not only a ballet master who choreo-graphs steps and formations, he is also a painter who executes a series of moving tableaux in space. M. Henri Matisse has furnished decors of elegant simplicity and costumes whose brilliant colors lend themselves to the most divine combinations. M. Massine is thus able to exercise his inspiration without directly copying the style of the Orient; instead, he can imply the most daring essence of that style. He has achieved some admirable effects. . . . The despotism, for example, is expressed by backs bowing low whenever the Emperor passes. . . . In the funeral cortège [the people] divide into two groups, knotting and unknotting their arms, of which they seem to possess several, like Hindu divinities. By its lines and attitudes, the extraordinary tableau which concludes the work seems to suggest a Chinese porcelain. . . . [*Comoedia*, Febru-ary 4, 1920]

The ballet was revived in 1925, this time with choreography by George Balanchine, and, in the part of the Nightingale, the twelve-year-old Alicia Markova, whose costume was made not by Marie Muelle (see the following letter from Henri Matisse to Stravinsky), but by Vera Sudeikina:

Nice, 1, Place Charles Félix, May 28, 1925. My dear friend, I have your letter in front of me—forgive me for not having replied sooner. I couldn't. I am very pleased about the revival of *The Nightingale*. But I hope that the stage will not be too small because of the proportions of the pillars—that the friezes will be visible—and that you will not elim-inate the major props which are an indispensable part of the decors. As for the costume of the young female dancer, I don't see the need for any great alteration. I hope that Karsavina's is still around, and that we are still inspired by it. It must be white, in any case, and the feathers formed by white silk petals bordered with a thin black thread, but probably larger. I hope that you will employ Marie Muelle, or her father, who will do it very well. . . . This costume had a happy effect of crystalline lightness, like the song of a bird and the sound of the flute. I don't foresee any other problems—it is important to keep the hips from being too heavy, although a young girl of twelve often has no hips at all—

As for the costume of the mechanical nightingale, the one that I

July 4, 1914. Moscow. Handbill for a concert of Stravinsky's music in Sokolniki Park, Nikolai Malko conducting the Serge Kussevitzky Orchestra, with Gury Stravinsky as baritone soloist.

made can serve as a reasonably good example. The colors should remain as they are. Replace the stiff lining by a slightly padded, supple costume; the feet, I think, should remain the same Chinese rose color—but smaller. (That depends on the turns, and it will be necessary to modify them according to the mobility of the dancer.) The same for the headpiece, which, I hope, still exists. I will return to Paris on about the 5th of June and will be able to see you then if you think it will be useful. In the meantime, dear friend, tireless worker, I wish you all the best. Henri Matisse.

The first of the Three Pieces for String Quartet was composed in Leysin on April 26, 1914, the second in Salvan on July 2—inspired by the clown Little Tich, whom Stravinsky had seen in London a fortnight before. On June 19, Alfred Pochon [212] wrote to Stravinsky, saying that, according to a Paris rumor, the composer had written a "Scherzo" for string quartet, which the Flonzaleys would like to play. Thus, as occurred so often in Stravinsky's life, the commissioning of the work—negotiated by Ernest Ansermet, to whom Stravinsky dedicated the opus and gave the manuscript—was ex post facto. In this case, the Flonzaley request diverted the composer from a plan to write an album of five Kammermusik pieces (letter to his Berlin publisher, July 26, 1914). The third of the Three Pieces was composed in Salvan on the 25th and 26th of July. On August 4, Pochon wrote to Ansermet asking for the music, since the players were about to leave for their American tour. In Chicago, November 8, 1915, the quartet gave what Pochon believed to be the world premiere, but a note from Alfredo Casella to Stravinsky, April 30, 1915, says that the Pieces "will be played in Paris on May 19." [213] A letter to Stravinsky from Ansermet's friend Templeton Strong, January 25, 1915, would have suggested that the opus was performed in Geneva at a still earlier date—at a "musicale" organized by a violinist, Hildebrandt—except that Ansermet warned Stravinsky (letter of January 23) that his attendance at this event would be expected.

In the summer of 1919, the Flonzaleys offered another commission to Stravinsky, which he accepted in September. Pochon wrote from New York, this time stipulating European as well as American exclusivity, and requesting the original manuscript. Stravinsky wanted to write a quintet, with a second viola, but Pochon suggested that the G string of the second violin be tuned to F. Stravinsky wrote from Morges, February 25, 1920, asking to be paid in advance the $500 which he was to receive for the piece. The sum was sent from New York on April 6. The Concertino was performed by the Flonzaleys, for the first time anywhere, in New York, November 23, 1920.

In 1934, Stravinsky told Janet Flanner that he began Les Noces in London in June 1914 (and that, while he was composing it during the war, he and his family subsisted to some extent on a diet of local—Swiss—chestnuts). In the London Observer, July 4, 1921, A. H. Fox Strangways remarked that the music of Les Noces

June 1914. Stravinsky's notation of (as his handwriting says) "The bells of St. Paul's in London. Astonishingly beautiful counterpoint such as I have never heard before in my life."

is likely to come from under the dome of St. Paul's. Stravinsky was there one Sunday morning, and when the bells from Wren's churches began their chorus he was greatly moved, and began busily noting down the cross rhythms they made, as one gained upon the other. . . .

In 1920, Béla Bartók wrote:

How is this influence of the completely tonal folk music compatible with the atonal trend? Reference to one, especially characteristic example is sufficient: Stravinsky's *Pribaoutki*. The vocal part consists of

June 1914.* Sketch for "Uncle Armand," originally the second song in *Pribaoutki;* Stravinsky completed the full score in Salvan, August 18, 1914. "Natashka," originally the first of the four songs, had been scored in Salvan, August 13, 1914. "The Colonel," the third of the group, was finished in full score in Salvan, August 29, 1914, and the fourth and final song, "The Old Man and the Hare," was completed September 29, 1914, in the Villa "La Pervenche," Clarens, which Stravinsky had rented from Ernest Ansermet. In view of Stravinsky's later changes in the "Con Moto" section of this fourth song, it should be mentioned that, in all of his copies of the printed score first received from the publishers, he added the metronome at this point, indicating that the pulsation should remain the same throughout the piece.

* The date is mistakenly given as July 1914 in *Themes and Conclusions* (London: Faber and Faber, 1972).

1914 and 1918. Final page of the Three Pieces for String Quartet, in the composer's reduction (1914) for piano four-hands, and in the revised (1918) quartet score.

motives which—though perhaps not borrowed from Russian folk music—throughout are imitations of Russian folk-music motives. The characteristic brevity of these motives, all of them taken into consideration separately, is absolutely tonal, a circumstance that makes possible a kind of instrumental accompaniment composed of a sequence of underlying, more or less atonal tone-patches very characteristic of the temper of the motives. . . . *Pribaoutki* No. 4 (consists of three sections):

I. Persistent repetitions of the motive which is comprised of two measures in A minor:

with the underlying *ostinato* accompaniment

II. Persistent repetitions of the motive which is comprised of two measures in D minor

with an underlying *ostinato* accompaniment

III = I with the end measure:

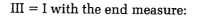

One should consider this chord as well as those in I, II above as unresolved chords tending toward ⟨♪⟩ ; the unresolved

chord ⟨♪⟩ in II may be thought of as tending toward

⟨♪⟩ Analyses of this kind do not make much sense, however,

since the composition maintains—despite all that atonality—a domineering ⟨♪⟩ which gives a solid base to the whole.[214]

But the objections to this analysis are that the voice and the instruments are parts of one and the same harmonic structure; that much of the instrumental music consists of "tonal" echoes of the vocal line; that the "unresolved chords" are combinations of "tonal" ones; and that the drone-note G-sharp, though harmonically remote from "the A on which the whole piece is based," nevertheless emphasizes the A. In short, it is difficult to agree that the piece contains any atonal tendency.

In Vevey, on September 24, 1914, Stravinsky told Romain Rolland about *Pribaoutki*, which, according to Rolland, the composer described as

Dicts, a form of very old Russian popular poetry, consisting of a succession of words which have almost no sense, and which are connected by association of images and sounds: ". . . [I like] to make sudden contrasts in music between the portrayal of one subject and another completely different and unexpected subject." [Rolland, *Journal des Années des Guerres, 1914–1919* (Paris, Albin Michel, 1952)]

June 1914. Sketches for "Uncle Armand" and "The Colonel."

The text of *Pribaoutki* (and that of *Berceuses du Chat*) attracted Louis Aragon, who, according to a letter from the publisher, J. & W. Chester, December 3, 1919, requested permission to reprint them.

Serge Prokofiev heard the first American performance of *Pribaoutki*, in Aeolian Hall, New York, December 9, 1919, and the next day sent his impressions of the work to Stravinsky:

Dear Stravinsky, I tell you the following with pleasure. Yesterday your *Pribaoutki* was performed for the first time in America. Vera Janacopoulos sang, a very talented artist.[215] Her approach was most loving, and she sang them beautifully, except, perhaps, "Uncle Armand," which is too low for her voice. The success was very great, and all four songs were repeated. Many people in the audience laughed, but gaily, not indignantly. I sat with Fokine, and we shouted "bravo" as loudly as we could. The instrumentalists played very well and performed their tasks with interest. Only the violinist and bassist may have been angry about it. The flutist,[216] who had already played the *Japanese Lyrics*, was so sure of himself that no difficulties could frighten him. I went to the rehearsals and tried to explain what was not clear. Personally, I like most of all "Uncle Armand," in which the oboe and clarinet are like the gurgle of an emptying bottle: you express drunkenness through your clarinet with the skill of a *real* drunkard; the whole of "Natashka," but above all the last five bars with the delightful gurgling of the winds; "The Colonel," entirely, but especially the oboe twitters and the climax on the words *"pala propala,"* etc.; many things in the last song, but especially the coda: the clarinet's G and A-natural and the English horn's A-flat are most excellent and most insolent.

I send my cordial greetings and best wishes. I shall be truly happy to hear from you. Yours, S. Prokofiev

Between July 3 and 13, 1914, Stravinsky made a trip to Ustilug to salvage some personal possessions, and to Kiev—where he stayed at 28 Annenskaya Street, the home of his father-in-law—to procure books of Russian folk poetry.[217] One of these was a volume of wedding songs published three years before as a supplement to *Pyesni sobrannye, P.I. Kireyevskim*—"Songs Collected by P.[eter] V.[asilievich] Kireyevsky." [218] The songs in this volume served as the main source of the libretto of *Les Noces*—indeed, as the only source apart from three lines in Tereshchenko's *Byt Russkago Naroda* (1848 edition, Vol. II, p. 332), used at 〔93〕 and apart from Stravinsky himself, since the unidentified lines, the neologisms, and the many amendments and modifications of the Kireyevsky originals could only be by the composer.[219] At one time, Stravinsky also planned to use a line (Song 229, p. 331) that he had marked in his father's bound volumes of the 1838 edition of Sakharov's *Pyesni Russkago Naroda*, but the composer finally changed his mind. One of the *Noces* songs, from the vicinity of Mikhailovskoe, *"Yagoda s yagodoi zakatilosya!"* ("A berry with a berry tumbled down!"), was transcribed by Pushkin and given by him to Kireyevsky. When Pushkin contributed his collection of folk songs to Kireyevsky, the great poet wrote: "One day as a pastime try to discover which ones are sung by the people and which I wrote myself."

(*Works*, Vol. III [Moscow, 1957], p. 536) Stravinsky was always delighted by the thought that the *Noces* libretto might include an original line by Pushkin.

On a train returning from Russia, Stravinsky reread *Koz'ma Prutkov* [220] and decided to compose music for an episode from it and to postpone *Les Noces*. Back in Switzerland, he wrote to Alexander Benois, seeking his advice and collaboration:

Dear Shura, . . . I have already come back from Kiev and do not want to go anywhere anymore, but only to sit and produce music. On the way to Russia, where I bought a number of interesting books (and about two dozen Moscow scarves; my God, what scarves: they surpass even yours in *Petrushka*—sorry, do not be angry), I also picked up *Koz'ma Prutkov*, of which, it seems to me, you do not think too highly, for some reason or other, or do not know very well. Oh, Shura, dear fellow, what I have found there! God himself, I do believe, is showing us where we must work. And, for God's sake, read it quickly—it's only a few pages—the last piece in the book, "The Affinity of all Worldly Powers," is a mystery in eleven scenes. From this moment on, I cannot find any peace with myself. I think only about this, I dream only of it. Dear one, have compassion!!! I am sending you this volume now and ask that you send it back to me as soon as possible. But tell no one of my idea. After you and I have talked it over, then perhaps we'll tell someone, although it's best to keep silent. . . . [Letter of July 27,[221] 1914, from Salvan]

In fact Stravinsky sketched music, very different from that of his other works of the time, for at least three episodes in *Koz'ma Prutkov*: "The Great Poet," in which he used a popular Russian tune, "The Night Hours," and "The Valley." He also composed examples in musical notation of trochaics, dactyls, and anapests, and even planned the instrumentation, which was remarkable in that it required nineteen woodwinds (including flute in G, two English horns, two contra-bassoons) but no brass except horns, and no strings except two solo cellos and six basses. Benois answered on August 7,[222] 1914, from St.-Jean-de-Luz, Hôtel de la Porte:

My dear friend, your letter puzzles me so much that I have gone about composing answers to it for the last five days, but without being able to manage a single one. I really do not like *Koz'ma Prutkov*; or, rather, I do not understand the gigantic importance that it assumes in Russian literature and in Russian life. *Koz'ma Prutkov* is funny, foolish, clever, and from time to time extremely talented, but the book never shows a really strong sense of humor, or the real art of laughter of Gogol and Dostoievsky. At any rate, I do not see real wit in *Prutkov's* too long and naïve—in the bad sense—parody salad. So, in my opinion, it is not worthwhile spending time on *Prutkov*, and I think it would be better to forget this "manual for Russian schoolboys," this copybook for our *Satirikon* and *Budilnik*.[223] Laughter, today, must be different, funnier and more terrible.

Nevertheless, I read the book from the first page to the last, and I thank you for it, because it gave me great pleasure. But your rapture over it perplexed me, and I wished with all my heart to feel the same. Alas, this did not happen, and I was left feeling like a cold fish. I decided to be frank and to tell you the truth, but my truth is not absolute, and I would be unhappy if my opinion were to disconcert you. Perhaps you find something where I see only emptiness. If so, start to work. Though I hold my opinion, I am certain that *Koz'ma Prutkov* as seen by Stravinsky will start to live a new and wonderful life. Also, I am certain that, listening to your music, and I believe in every note of it, I shall be able to catch your feelings and create something worthy of your music—or, at least, something that will not spoil it. But perhaps you should choose another painter—Sudeikin, for instance, who is underrated and who, more swiftly than I, will find response in his soul to what Jemchushnikov and Alexei Tolstoy fabricated.[224] My dear, I am very worried about the impression that this "cold-water" letter will make on you and your muse, but cold water is not so bad if it comes at the proper time and if you have a towel handy. If my douche was mistimed, and if you catch cold, please forgive me. . . .

Stravinsky promptly abandoned *Prutkov* and devoted himself to *Les Noces*.

For six months in 1915, Diaghilev and some members of his company lived in the Villa Belle Rive, at Ouchy. In August, in Milan, he met with Gatti-Casazza,[225] Henry Russell, and William Guard, all three representing the Metropolitan Opera Company in New York, to plan the 1916 American tour of the Ballets Russes. About two weeks after the Milan meetings, Guard came to the Belle Rive to continue negotiations with Diaghilev. One day,

with afternoon tea-time, arrived on a bicycle from Morges a young man of about 30 years of age, keen of eye, prominent of feature, nervous in movement, quick in observation, rapid in speech. The newcomer was Igor Stravinsky. . . . Two hours passed before we knew it, during which

1914. Draft of Stravinsky's letter to Bertha ("Bilibusch") Essert, his German *nanya*, who was living with his mother and younger brother in St. Petersburg at the time, inviting this elderly family retainer to come to live with him and his wife and children in Clarens. "Bertuschka" Essert was born in Königsberg in 1845 and died in Morges, April 28, 1917. The other side of the paper contains a sketch for *Les Noces*.

November 4 (Old Style), 1912. Bakst and Stravinsky, cartoon from a Russian newspaper, *Theatralny Izdonyi.* The captions are: "Painter Bakst, composer Igor Stravinsky," and, in parenthesis, "Letters About the Ballet."

Художникъ Бакстъ   Композиторъ Игорь Стравинскій

(Къ статьѣ «Письма о балетѣ»).

M. Stravinsky did most of the talking, which ranged all the way from his new ballets, which are either in embryo or in development, Russian art in general, and music and literature in particular. Stravinsky, as I said, did most of the talking (and a brilliant talker he is, so that none objected). . . . [William J. Guard, *New York Times,* January 9, 1916]

None of these Russian artists—and another was Jawlensky, who lived in nearby St. Prex—was more deeply concerned than Stravinsky with the fate of the mother country in the war, as well as with Russian political developments generally. Romain Rolland recorded a three-hour visit with Stravinsky in the garden of the

August 1915. Ouchy. The Villa Belle Rive, with Massine, Goncharova, Larionov, and Bakst.

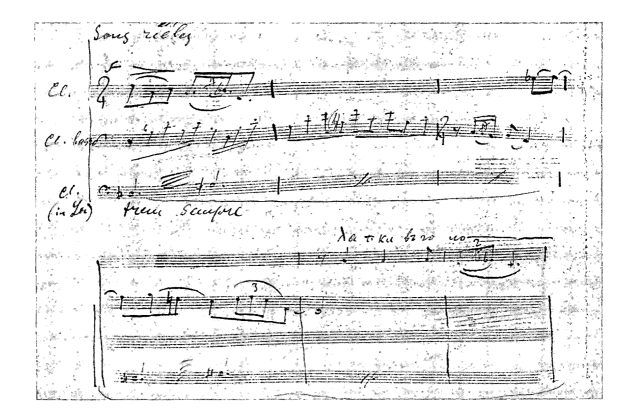

September 11, 1915. Draft of "On the Hearth" (Berceuses du Chat).

Hotel Mooser at Vevey, on September 26, 1914, when the war was young and the passions of both men were high, Rolland's *Au-dessus de la Mêlée* having been published only three days earlier:

Stravinsky ... is very intelligent and simple in his manner; he speaks fluently, though he sometimes has to seek French words; and everything he says is original and carefully thought out. ... In art, as in everything, Stravinsky loves only Spring, new life. ... [*Op. cit.*]

The first performance of the *Berceuses du Chat* (*Cat Lullabies*) and of *Pribaoutki* (with instruments: both song cycles had already been given in London and Paris with piano accompaniment) took place in Vienna, June 6, 1919, under the auspices of Arnold Schoenberg's Society for Private Performances. On June 8, Anton von Webern wrote to Alban Berg:

The last concert was entirely sold out. The Stravinsky was wonderful. These songs are marvelous, and this music moves me wholly and beyond belief. I love it and the lullabies are indescribably touching. How those clarinets sound! And *Pribaoutki.* Ah, my dear friend, it is something really glorious.

In June 1915, Stravinsky moved from Clarens to Morges, an attractive, shuttered town, even today the least spoiled of any on the shores of Lake Geneva. Stravinsky had three homes here, first the Villa les Sapins, on a hillside on the eastern outskirts of the city, with views of the lake and of Lausanne; the Villa les

Sapins is walled, like the adjoining Chemin Bellevue. His second Morges home, the Villa Rogivue (January 1916 to May 1917), is closer to the lake and on flat ground. The third, to which he moved on May 8, 1917, is the Maison Bornand, Place St. Louis. A church stands on this same Place, and over its central lintel is the inscription in marble letters, *"A la Gloire de Dieu,"* dated 1772. Thus almost every day for three years Stravinsky saw the phrase that was to become his dedicatory formula in the *Symphony of Psalms* and the Symphony in C.

On November 12, 1912, the Princesse Edmond de Polignac wrote to Stravinsky offering 3,000 francs for a short work requiring thirty to thirty-six players. A week later, the Princesse wrote again saying that in October she had been in Ouchy with Lady Ripon,[226] and that they had looked for Stravinsky in Clarens without success. The letter also stipulates that the new work should be completed by April 8, 1913. On December 4 and 6, 1912, Polignac sent lists of the instruments that could be placed at his disposal, and Stravinsky agreed to write a fifteen-minute concerto. On April 7, she wrote to ask when he expected to finish the promised work, but *Renard*, the comic masterpiece he eventually composed, was not begun until 1915, and not completed until August 1916.

In 1917, Stravinsky sold the manuscript of the piano score of *Renard*, together with copies of *Pribaoutki*, *Berceuses du Chat*, and the Eight Easy Pieces, bound with pages of manuscript, to Princesse Violette Murat. He asked his wife to write the letter offering the music for sale and explaining that the money was to be used to have the score engraved. The correspondence concerning this transaction lasted from January to May 20, when Mme Murat acknowledged the receipt of the *Renard* score. Following Mme Murat's instructions to him in a letter, July 2, 1917, Stravinsky sent the *Pribaoutki* and *Berceuses* to her, July 12, 1917, via the Countess de Segonzac, who was staying at the Beau Rivage in Ouchy. At one point, Mme Murat wrote saying that she had not seen the Princesse de Polignac in six months and did not want any "ennuis" with her concerning the purchase.

The Princesse de Polignac has described a dinner with the Stravinskys in the Villa Rogivue, February 5 (or 6), 1916: [227]

I can never forget the delight of that evening at Morges: the table brilliantly lighted with colored candles, and covered with fruit, flowers, and desserts of every hue. The supper was a wonderful example of Russian cuisine, carefully prepared by Madame Stravinsky and composed of every sort of sweet, making it a feast always to be remembered. ["Memoirs of the Princesse de Polignac," *Horizon*, August 1945]

At this dinner Stravinsky negotiated a commission for Larionov to execute the designs—according to a letter from Goncharova, in Paris, to Stravinsky, February 25, in which she says, "I have already completed certain things for *Les Noces*." Another letter from her the month before reveals that at the end of December 1915 or the beginning of January 1916 the composer had introduced the two painters to the Princesse de Polignac at a lunch in the Russian Embassy in Paris, and that, since then, the Princesse had twice invited them for dinner, once with Violette Murat and once with Argutinsky and Stelletsky, on the later occasion playing the organ for her guests.

Stravinsky's first notations for *Renard* antedate his contract, signed January 4, 1916, with the Princesse de Polignac. Some of the principal themes (in measures 64, 82–3, 85, 145, and 159) are found in a sketchbook preceding the first version of the song "The Bear" (from the *Three Tales for Children*; although the final manuscript version of this song—a whole tone lower than the draft in the sketchbook—is dated January 12, 1916, the original was probably composed in November 1915). These early sketches for *Renard* reveal that Stravinsky had a larger ensemble in mind than the one he was ultimately to employ, the first notations using two clarinets (one of them a bass), two bassoons, trombone, harp, and piano. The cimbalom flourish in measure 270 was originally composed without orchestral specification, and the instrument appears for the first time in a sketch for the music at measure 291, where Stravinsky writes "C.B. pizz.," then adds, "or cimbalom?" Still on the subject of the evolution of the instrumentation, it should be mentioned that at one point the bass and cello parts in the accompaniment figure at measure 67 were reversed, the E-harmonic being assigned to the former, the G-harmonic to the latter, while the two-note response was scored for a violin playing ponticello.

The notebook containing the beginnings of the libretto, with sketches for the music, is stamped "Morges" but not dated. Stravinsky began by copying verses from Afanasiev, rewriting them, abbreviating or lengthening them, using an entire passage but changing a word or two, and adding stage directions. The notebook contains instructions to himself, such as "See p. 81, *Tales*," and "See volume 1, p. 32," a reference to the text for the Rooster's lines when caught by the Fox. The libretto notebook also includes the composer's stage directions, from which it becomes clear that the Rooster lives with an old man. He plays the guzla to help the captured fowl by charming the Fox, who says "Go and see who is singing this beautiful song" (i.e., the duet of the Cat and the Goat). Stravinsky also seems to have thought of beginning *Renard* with a spoken prologue: "How the Fox made mischief, stealing a chicken, and behaved vainly, with his tail up, until the Devil removed him to an oat field." The next-to-last sketch in the libretto notebook, marked "beginning" by Stravinsky, contains the music for the first seduction of the Rooster by the Fox disguised as a nun, and the very last sketch is for the music at measure 7 followed by the music at measure 1. In the notebook, the first conversation between the Rooster and the Fox reads:

Fox: Come down and confess your sins.
Rooster: I did not observe Lent and did not pray.
Fox: I neither ate nor drank and came especially to confess you.
Rooster: But I did not fast and I did not pray.

Renard was composed in sections and out of sequence, in the general order end to beginning, the March, like the overtures to *Pulcinella* and *Mavra*, being written last. The first section completed was the final duet (though originally scored for only one voice and considerably shorter than in its final form) beginning at measure 533. This draft is dated "January 16, 1916," and titled "*Pribaoutki: Gospodi Pomilui*," which suggests a religious satire that was later diluted or bowdlerized, as was the case with the earthier language of the first libretto; for example, the Cat and the Goat tell the Fox, in measures 156–7: "You know, Yermak farted when he fasted and you will do the same." The first text in the libretto notebook is for measure 385, and the verses, copied from Afanasiev, are followed immediately by notations for the music. A notation for the screams at measure 505 follows, then several measures for the music and words at measures 271 and 306, then sketches for the section beginning at measure 385 and for the vocal part and some accompaniment at measure 421. The music exists in a complete draft through measure 447.

In the first proof of the title page of the score, dated 1917, the composition is described as an

HISTOIRE BURLESQUE CHANTÉE ET JOUÉE

Faite pour la Scène
D'Après des Contes Populaires Russes
Musique et Texte d'Igor Stravinsky

But, since the score was not published until after the Russian Revolution, Stravinsky omitted the reference to the Russian origins of the libretto. In the autumn of 1916, C. F. Ramuz translated the text into French—a "petite traduction," as he called it on the flyleaf of a notebook dedicating his work to Stravinsky's wife. On November 12, 1916, Ramuz wrote on a calling card, which he sent to Stravinsky:

Received from Madame Stravinsky (on behalf of Madame de Polignac) 500 fr. for the translation of Renard.

Ramuz was sometimes credited in programs as the librettist, nevertheless, and, as late as February 26, 1959, Stravinsky wrote to Paul Pittion, Conservatoire de Grenoble, emphasizing that the libretto of Renard is not by Ramuz, and that in fact he, Stravinsky, helped Ramuz with the translation.

Writing to Stravinsky from Madrid, August 12, 1916, Ernest Ansermet says that he

journeyed from Paris to San Sebastian with Diaghilev, who said that "my only reproach to Igor is in having given time to Renard that he should have saved for Les Noces."

Diaghilev asked Stravinsky to join him in San Sebastian, in a telegram dated July 21, to which Stravinsky replied on the 26th, asking for money and saying that he first had to finish his work for Polignac. On August 3, Diaghilev telegraphed that the money was coming from Moscow. At the beginning of September, Stravinsky was in San Sebastian, and he accompanied Diaghilev from there to Bordeaux, from whence the Ballets Russes sailed on the S.S. Lafayette to New York for a second American tour. Diaghilev returned to the Spanish city, where he heard Arbos conduct the Firebird Suite in the Casino on September 20, then went to Rome. Stravinsky returned to Morges, via Paris, where he received his exit visa on the 12th and re-entered Switzerland on the 14th. He wrote to his mother on the 11th:

... please do one favor for me: tell the St. Petersburg Stock Exchange News that I have finished a small one-act play, composed for the Princesse de Polignac, and called "The Tale of the Fox, Cock, Cat, and Ram." It is for an ensemble of sixteen instrumentalists and four male voices (two basses and two tenors, all solo). According to my contract, Polignac has acquired the rights to the "Tale" for several years, but since Russia does not enter into her plans for staging, Russian theaters, with my permission, may put the piece on. It is played by ballet dancers or marionettes, the musicians and singers being in the orchestra pit. I want the Russian theaters to know about this and am therefore asking you to inform the newspapers of it, exactly in the way I have written to you so that they do not add anything of their own. Love, your Ghima.

But Renard had to wait until 1922 for its first performance. It was given six times in the spring of that year, according to Stravinsky's account book of his payment of the translator's share of the performance fees to Ramuz.

The next year Stravinsky planned to

arrange a rather large fragment from *Renard* for concert performances. This version will include changes in the number of voices—two instead of four—which should greatly facilitate and encourage performers. I believe that this project could be profitable for your company, and, if the idea attracts you, please think about it. As for myself, I will make the arrangement in any case, since the work interests me very much. I would like to know whether you wish to consider it as a commission or to purchase it when the task is finished. I am going to Weimar in a few days to hear the *Soldat*. . . . [Letter to O. M. Kling, August 6, 1923]

Stravinsky wrote again to Kling from Biarritz, September 1, 1923:

Returning to the question of the concert excerpt from *Renard*, I will give you all of the details when I have the full score, which is in your hands, and which you need for the engraving.

When the Ballets Russes landed in Cadiz after the American tour, Diaghilev telegraphed to Stravinsky, May 17: "Come to Madrid immediately. We begin the season on Tuesday." Stravinsky left Switzerland for Lyons and Paris on the 19th, Paris for Madrid on the 20th. On the 23rd, in the Hotel Ritz, he heard a concert of songs, including three by Falla. Then began one of the most exciting months of his life. He visited Toledo and the Escorial, saw two *corridas* in the Plaza de Toros, the eighth and the tenth of the season (and saw Paco Madrid gored), and had a

May 1916. Madrid. Hotel Ritz. Seated, L. to R.: Massine, Conrado del Campo, Ansermet, Diaghilev, Miguel Salvador, Stravinsky, Manuel de Falla, Adolph Bolm. Adolfo Salazar is standing between Stravinsky and Falla.

romance with Lydia Lopokova [228]—"Lopushka," in Stravinsky's letters to her—who danced the title part in *Firebird* on May 25. Here is a calendar of the following weeks, ending with his visit to the French Consul in Madrid on June 20 and his arrival at Morges on the 22nd:

May 25. Attends performance of the Ballets Russes at the Teatro Real.

May 27. El Liberal states that Stravinsky orchestrated *Les Sylphides* with the help of Liadov and Glazunov.

May 28. After a performance of *The Firebird,* a tremendous success, Stravinsky is called to the stage to bow.

May 29. (Monday). *El Mundo* publishes a statement that "Stravinsky conducted the rehearsals, Ansermet the performances. Fernandez Arbos had presented fragments of *Firebird* in April, which had left the public somewhat disoriented and bewildered. . . . The scenic apparatus is crucial." *La Correspondencia de España* says that "The dilettantes of Madrid had already heard fragments of the *Firebird* [under] Arbos. . . . But last night the public applauded [the work] with delirious enthusiasm." *España Annuera* reports: "Last night . . . the second of nine performances, the *Firebird* was the most interesting work, and the audience was enchanted by it. Tomorrow will be the third of the series." *Acción* reports that "Last night the *Firebird* had a tremendous success. . . . Stravinsky took a bow from the 'scenic box.' . . . The entire royal family was present." According to *ABC:* "The royal family was in its gala box. . . . The influence of Stravinsky, the most modern, innovative, and probably revolutionary of contemporary Russian composers, can be detected on more than a few of our own composers. . . . Recently, Stravinsky's *Fireworks* and fragments of *The Firebird* were heard in our symphony concerts, but the ballet spectacle is visually seducing first, then aurally." *La Tribuna* states: "When *The Firebird* was performed [by Arbos] no one understood it. But last night it pleased even those most surprised by the audacities of this extremely modern composer. He is gifted with a great descriptive talent, and a potential of originality unequaled in contemporary musical art, reaching heights unsurpassed even by Richard Strauss. Stravinsky is an eccentric by conservative criteria, a genius by those who seek the progressive. Today Stravinsky is ahead of his time, tomorrow he will be a classic. That is the eternal law. . . . The Grand Opéra of Paris required fourteen rehearsals, the Royal Orchestra of Madrid only four. . . . The audience applauded so loudly that Stravinsky had to receive the ovation. Stravinsky was called to the King's loge."

May 30. Third performance of *The Firebird.* Stravinsky is introduced to Eugenia Errazuriz.

May 31. Fourth performance of *The Firebird.* In the afternoon, Artur Rubinstein plays *The Firebird, Carnaval,* and other pieces at the home of the Duchess of Montellanos, for an audience that includes the Queen.

June 3. Teatro Real. Stravinsky attends *The Firebird* and is received by the King and Queen.

June 6. Madrid premiere of *Petrushka,* between *Les Sylphides* and *Thamar.* The *Herald* reports: "The ultimate triumph was that of the music of Stravinsky."

June 7. El Imparcial: "Stravinsky obtained an extremely noisy success and was recalled by ovations from the audience."

June 9. Attends performance of *Petrushka.*

While in Madrid, Stravinsky became a close friend of Manuel de Falla and played *Les Noces* for him, as a letter from Falla, July 7, reveals: "I do not forget your *Noces Villageoises.* What a profound impression." [229] And Stravinsky became a friend of the wealthy Chilean Eugenia Errazuriz; a note from her to him in the Hotel Ritz, Madrid, asks if he has received the tobacco she sent and invites him to visit her at her Paris address, 60, avenue Montaigne. In effect she commissioned both the *Etude for Pianola,* which is dedicated to her, and the *Piano-Rag-Music.* [230] In the 1920s, she gave him a handsome Cartier wristwatch that he wore all of his life. [231]

Stravinsky was strongly attracted to Spain, and between his first and last trips there, in 1915 and 1955, he visited Seville, Granada, Cordoba, San Sebastian, La Coruña, and—many times—Barcelona and Madrid. It was in the capital, April 18, 1921, [232] that he first conducted the complete *Petrushka*—at a Ballets Russes spectacle and in the presence of King Alfonso XIII. At this time, too, Stravinsky wrote the following paragraphs for *Comoedia:*

It is very natural that we want to be inspired by, and, if I may say so, to take with us a bit of Spain. The question is, what can be transported? Certain wines must be consumed where they are made. Others, those which can stand the trip, we bring with us.

Affinities and resemblances can be remarked between Spanish music, especially that of Andalusia, and the music of Russia, no doubt through their common Oriental origins. Certain Andalusian songs remind me of Russian ones, and I enjoy these atavistic memories. Musically speaking, the Andalusians are not at all Latin, their rhythms being of Oriental inheritance. Rhythm and meter are different, of course, and so far as meter is concerned, four is always four. But rhythm poses a different question: what comprises four? Is it three plus one or two plus two?

One characteristic of this popular art is its extreme precision. A quarter-tone is a real quarter-tone. Nor does the rhythm change: it is *not* improvised, even among the whirling dervishes. This popular art is a very logical and very coldly calculated one, I would like to say a classical art, an art of composition. [*Comoedia,* May 15, 1921]

In 1917, Stravinsky asked his friend Lord Berners to procure some recordings of Spanish music, and a letter from him to Stravinsky, June 6, 1917, says that the records should be en route from Madrid.

Les Noces

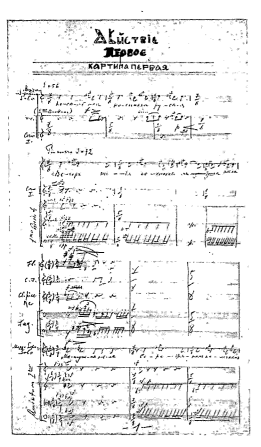

1914. *Les Noces*. First page of one of the first sketch scores. Note the 7/8 meter and the specifications for mezzo-soprano and double string quintet.

Les Noces ranks high in the by-no-means-crowded company of indisputable contemporary masterpieces.[233] But it presents cultural and linguistic barriers, unless audiences hear it simply as a piece of "pure music," ignoring the full implications of the work as a dramatic spectacle. *Les Noces* was intended for the stage, however, and the drama is Stravinsky's: he is responsible for the choice of subject, the form of its realization, the selection, ordonnance, and editing of the texts. In fact, *Les Noces* and the much slighter *Renard* are his only theatrical works to combine music with a text of his own in his mother tongue; the only works in which ritual, symbol, and meaning on every level are part of his direct cultural heritage. Of all of his creations, too, *Les Noces* is the one that underwent the most extensive metamorphosis, not only occupying his mind during the longest period, but, in aggregate, requiring the most time to compose. If a later Russia had recognized this masterpiece, it would have awarded him a Stakhanovite medal for his industry alone.

The reasons for the long gestation of *Les Noces* are twofold: first, that Stravinsky several times put it aside to work on other compositions, each of which left him greatly changed; second, that he was creating something entirely new in both music—the heterophonic vocal-instrumental style of the piece—and in theatrical combination and genre, an amalgam of ballet and dramatic cantata that he himself was unable to describe. "Russian Choreographic Scenes," the subtitle on the final score, does not even mention that the subject is a village wedding, and that the scenes are four: at the bride's (the ritual plaiting of her tresses); at the groom's (the ritual curling of his locks); the departure of the bride for the church; the wedding feast.

A study of the *Noces* sketches reveals that "in the beginning was the word"; in the very act of copying the text, Stravinsky added musical notations—unpitched rhythmic values, melodic or motivic fragments, intervals or chords that had occurred to him in conjunction with the words. He is at the opposite extreme in this from, say, Janáček, who, so he claimed, discovered

the musical motives and tempos adopted to demonstrating [the emotions] by declaiming a text aloud and then observing the inflections in my voice.

In short, Stravinsky's inspiration in his vocal works originated in the sounds and rhythms of syllables and words, though sometimes a poem's structure suggested its musical form and content (rhythm and melody). From the *Noces* sketches it is also clear that musical rhythms and stresses were far more frequently inspired by the text than imposed upon it, Stravinsky's claims to the contrary.[234] Obviously *Les Noces* should be sung only in

Medallion portrait on wood, of Stravinsky's* maternal great-grandfather, Roman Furman. The painter and year are unknown, but the time, to judge from the subject's apparent age (he was born in 1784), is probably in the 1840s. An iconographer might be able to provide a more precise date from the decorations and orders, and from the length of the dundrearies.

1957. This draft of one of Stravinsky's "Conversations" reveals more of his true feelings about the Rimsky-Korsakov family than does the published version of the same text. The typescript was dictated by Stravinsky; then the emendations in red ink were made by the present writer; then Stravinsky edited the text, changing the "and heard," for example, to "to hear."

* The name is often spelled with a "w" in Germany and France, partly because the composer's publishers were based in those countries, where "w" is sounded like the English "v," which is the correct pronunciation of this consonant. On December 26, 1941, Stravinsky wrote to Alfred Frankenstein, program annotator for the San Francisco Symphony, saying that although "w" does not exist in the Russian language, his father had replaced the "v" with a "w" because of the German pronunciation of the "v," which sounds like "f." On September 15, 1952, Erwin Stein, Schoenberg's former pupil and Stravinsky's editor at Boosey & Hawkes from 1947 to 1958, persuaded the composer to accept the "w" as a standardized spelling, but this caused such difficulties with passports, visas, and bank checks that he changed back to "v" a few years later.

1894. Gold watch with medallion portrait of the Tsar, presented to Fyodor Stravinsky in 1894 by Tsar Alexander III.

- 2 -

saying "there is nothing after death, death is the end, period." I then had the temerity ~~also~~ to suggest that perhaps ~~nothingxafterxdeat~~ this was also merely one point of view, but was made to feel for some time thereafter that I should have kept my ~~piece~~ peace.

I thought I had found friends in Rimsky's sons, three young gentlemen who, in provincial St. Petersburg were beacons of enlightenment. Andrei, a man three years my ~~senior~~ senior and a 'cellist of some ability was especially kind to me, though this kindness lasted only while his father was alive; when I had gone to Paris in 1910 and my name had come back to Russia he, and in fact the entire Rimsky-Korsakov family ~~suddenly~~ turned against me. He reviewed _Petroushka_ for a Russian newspaper dismissing it as "Russian vodka with French perfumes." Vladimir, his brother, was a competent violinist. I owe to him my first knowledge of violin fingering ~~problems~~. ~~Rimsky's daughters did not appeal to me at all, however, and I especially disliked Sophie.~~ ~~Incidentally~~ My last contact with the Rimsky-Korsakov family was through her husband Maximilian Steinberg who had come to Paris in 1924 ~~to hear~~ me play my _Piano Concerto_ ~~you may~~ imagine his response to that work when I tell you that the best he could do even for my _Fireworks_ was to shrug his shoulders. After hearing the _Concerto_ he wanted to lecture me on my whole mistaken career, and returned to Russia thoroughly annoyed when I refused to see him. ~~I was not fond of Mme. Rimsky-Korsakov either, as I have said elsewhere. She was an avowed enemy of Diaghilev too, but while she attacked his production of Sheherazade she was delighted at the same time to receive very handsome royalties from it.~~

PLATE 1

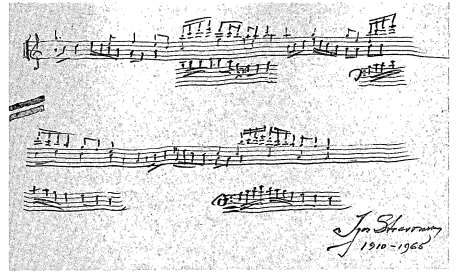

Two melodies from *Petrushka*, counterpointed in 1965.

1911. Benois's designs for *Petrushka*:
LEFT: The curtain.
BELOW: The first tableau with the spire of the Admiralty (not in the original design).
OPPOSITE ABOVE: The third tableau.
OPPOSITE BELOW: The fourth tableau.

PLATE 2

PLATE 3

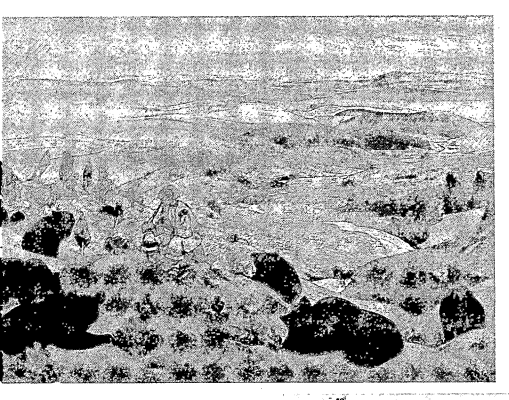

December 1912. Landscape study for the *Sacre* by Roerich.

June 1922. Revisions in the first miniature score of *Le Sacre*.

PLATE 4

December 1912. Sketches for "Mazat-sumi," second of the *Three Japanese Lyrics*. Stravinsky's Russian script says, "The spring begins here" — i.e., with this chord, which, in the next draft, he transposed an octave lower and transferred to the beginning of the song. In this first sketch, he did not compose a part for the voice but wrote the text at the end, adding the vocal line later. He completed the composition of "Mazatsumi" on December 18, and of "Tsaraiuki" on December 26, orchestrating both pieces the following month.

August 1975. Morges. "QUAI IGOR STRAVINSKY." Photograph by Vera Stravinsky.

PLATE 5

PLATE 6

1914. Cover for *Les Noces*, painted by Stravinsky. The words, in Old Russian orthography, are:
"Svadebka (Les Noces)
Songs and Dances
Composition."

1914. Draft of an epigraph, in Old Russian, "For the First Tableau" of *Les Noces*, the frame painted by Stravinsky:
"Before Act One"
"Two rivers flow together
Two matchmakers come together
They think about how to undo the flaxen braid
How to braid the flaxen hair."

1917. *Les Noces*. Sketch for the beginning of the fourth tableau.

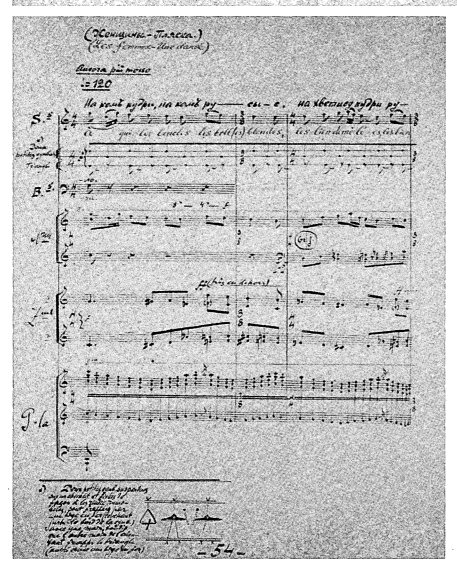

1917. *Les Noces*. Sketch for the beginning of the fourth tableau.

1919. Page from the pianola, cimbalom, harmonium, percussion score of *Les Noces*. The text and diagram beneath the music instruct the player to suspend the triangle and two cymbals, and to use a metal stick.

PLATE 7

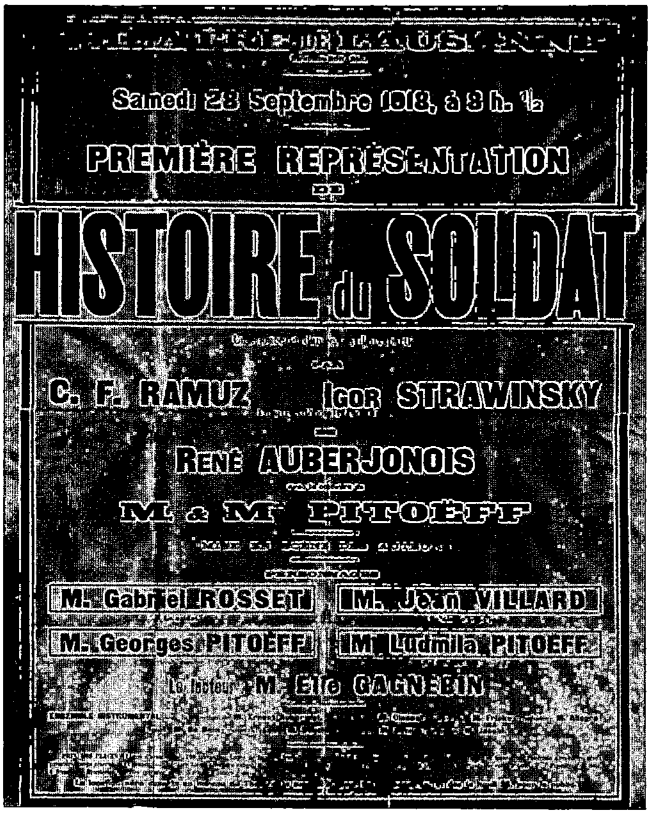

The name of Ernest Ansermet, who conducted the first performance of *Histoire du Soldat*, is in very small type at the bottom of the *affiche*.

ABOVE LEFT:
1972. Plaque on the Maison Bornand, stating that in this house Stravinsky composed "*L'Histoire du Soldat.*"

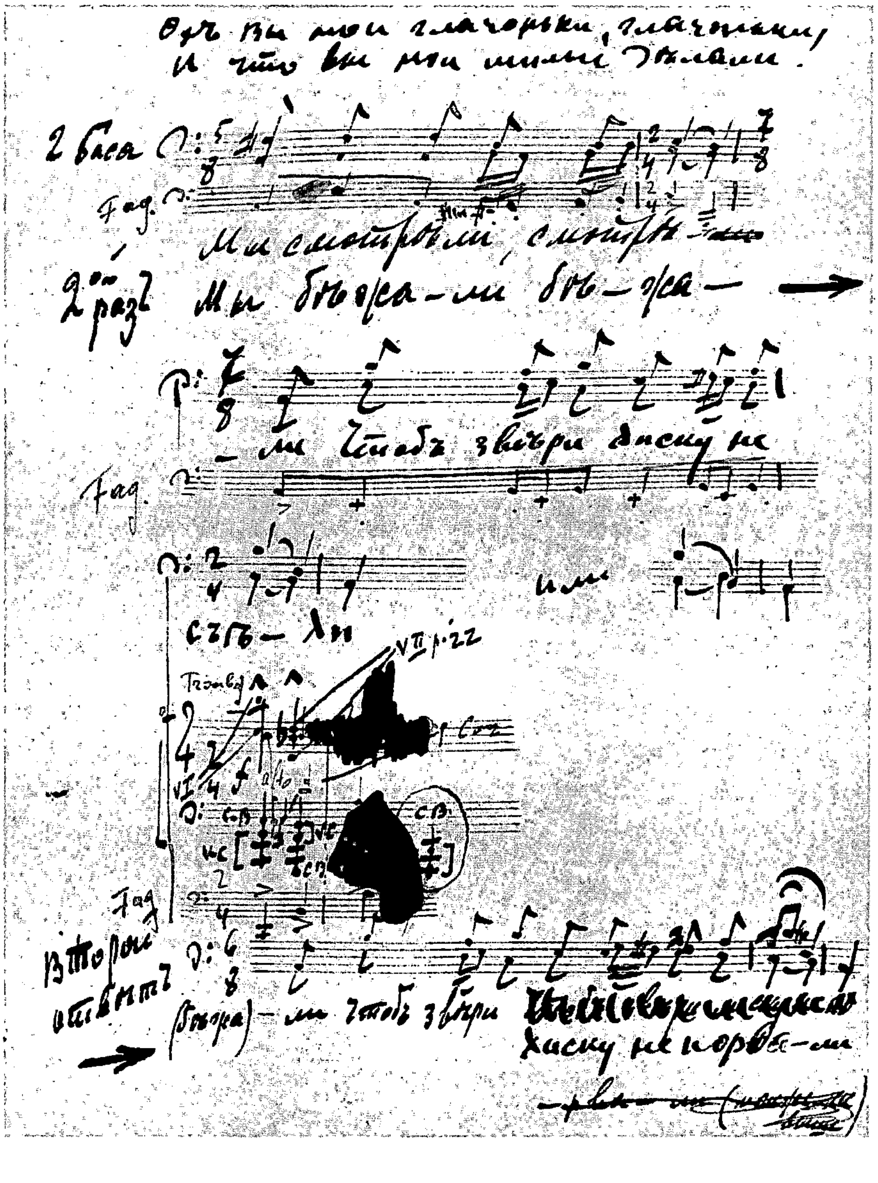

1915. Sketch for *Renard*.

PLATE 8

Russian, both because the sounds of the words are part of the music, and because their rhythms are inseparable from the musical design; a translation that satisfied the quantitative and accentual formulas of the original could not retain any approximation of its literal sense. For this reason, Stravinsky, who would sometimes sacrifice sense for sound's sake, abandoned an English translation on which he had labored for a recording of the work in the fall of 1959. Thirty years earlier, he had written to the Concerts Catalonia, which had invited him to conduct *Les Noces*:

...I do not like to hear *Les Noces* in French: too different from the prosody of the original. [Letter of November 15, 1929] . . . In my view the French translation . . . does not render the character of the rhythmic accentuation which constitutes the basis of the Russian chant of this work. [Letter of August 1930]

The earliest musical notations to spring directly from the texts occur in the Fourth Tableau, which was the last to be composed. But, in more than one instance, notations found on the same sketch page are widely separated in the final composition. Chronology can be determined not only from those drafts in which improvements are evinced from one writing to another, but also by graphic analysis, Stravinsky's Russian script generally being cursive in the preliminary versions, "printed" in the later ones.

Stravinsky selected, colligated, and edited the libretto from Kireyevsky's collection of songs. The first text was much longer than the final one, for the composer had originally planned to dramatize the complete wedding ritual and not to begin with the plaiting of the bride's hair, the point at which the final score starts. His first draft of the scenario is as follows:

LES NOCES: *Fantasy in Three Acts and Five Scenes*

Act I
The Inspection

Act II
    Scene 1
    The Bargain
        a. At the Bride's
        b. At the Groom's (An Incantation Against Sorcery—see
           page 49 [in Kireyevsky])
    Scene 2
        a. Devichnik (The Bride's Party)
           [Dyevishnik—Maiden's Day, the day before the wedding]
        b. The Girls Take Her to the Bath.
    Scene 3
    In the Bride's House Before the Departure for the Church

Act III
The Beautiful Table

Stravinsky soon scrapped this comprehensive scenario and abandoned the preliminary matchmaking scenes of the Devichnik and the ritual dunking [235] of the bride. The final version reduces this plan to four scenes—Act II, Scene 1, a and b, Scene 3, and Act III—and changes the content of Act II, Scene 1, b, abandoning the Incantation in favor of more barbering. The reduction in size, moreover, was accompanied by a drastic change in genre. Whether or not *Les Noces* was closer to opera than to the "ballet cantata" it finally became, Stravinsky appears to have begun with operatic musical characterizations, fitting out the *druzhka* (best man), for instance, with a hunting-horn fanfare— in his secondary role as master of ceremonies, the *druzhka* blew a horn—which, transformed beyond recognition except for rhythm, became the music of the bass voice at $\boxed{53}$.[236]

In the final form of the work, this and other roles of the kind, such as the *skomorokh* (busker), have been eliminated and replaced by voices that are loosely identified with the stage characters. Thus the bride and groom may seem to be sung by, respectively, soprano and tenor; yet no direct identification exists, and the same two voices also "speak" for the bride and her mother (see $\boxed{21}$). Even the groom's final love song is impersonated for him by the bass.

The change in genre also led to greater abstraction in the stage movement, so that not much is actually depicted, enacted, or even narrated, a collage of verse being substituted for narration. As for the stage action, the choreography was conceived as an extension of music; gesture and movement were to be stylized according to the rhythmic patterns of the music and not in imitation of popular or ethnographic dances.

As in *Le Sacre du Printemps*, Stravinsky began with stage pictures in mind, even depending on them. But after completing the score, he gradually pared away the stage directions until no picture existed, only music. Many of his original stage directions are direct quotations from Kireyevsky. The following excerpts from the composer's sketches were intended for the final score, though only one of them appears there even in part. They begin with an epigraph from Kireyevsky that Stravinsky appended to an early draft of the full score:

> Two rivers flow together
> Two matchmakers come together
> They think about the ash-blond braid,
> How will we unplait this ash-blond braid?
> How will we part the braid in two? [237]

First Tableau

The father and mother meet the bride with an icon, when she comes home from the bath. After the blessing, the bridesmaids seat the bride on a bench at the table and place a dish before her, next to which they place a comb. Each bridesmaid approaches the bride, takes a comb from the table, combs her tresses, replaces the comb on the table, and leaves some money in a dish. [Kireyevsky, page 241]

Second Tableau

The groom's train prepares for departure. . . .
The groom's train departs slowly, in their carts.

Third Tableau

The bride's cart, glittering with icons and mirrors, enters from the same side of the stage as in the First Tableau. The characters (the same as in the First Tableau) are dressed in sparkling clothes.

Fourth Tableau

The backdrop is raised, revealing a large room in a Russian *izba*. It is almost entirely filled by a table, around which many people are seated. They eat and drink. A door is open at the back, showing a large bed covered by an enormous eiderdown.

In the wedding parlor stands a wooden table, on which is a *karavay* [very large loaf of bread] with various wondrous decorations: figurines of a man, a little bird, *et cetera*. This *karavay* is surrounded by other, smaller *karavays*, and by honey cakes, cookies, sweetmeats. The mead is strong. The newlyweds eat the *karavay* first, for it signifies the marital union.

Les Noces ends with the following song, during which the *druzhka* and the *svaha* [female matchmaker] lead the young couple to bed. When the *druzhka* and *svaha* have put them to bed and left them, the parents of Khvétis and Nastasia close the door, place four chairs in front of it, and sit on them. The act is over. The curtain falls slowly. The music continues throughout. At the very end, a solo voice [tenor] sings, in a too sweet, or oily, voice, drawing out the words:

> Uzh i dushka, zhonushka Nastas'ushka,
> Pozhivem my s toboyu khoroshenichka,
> Shtoby liudi nam zavidovali.[238]

Stravinsky also wrote a program note about the staging, at the time that he was correcting the second proofs of the piano score:

THE VILLAGE WEDDING

Russian Scenes in 2 Parts with songs and music

The protagonists of the piece are ballet dancers, and the singers (chorus and soloists) are in the orchestra pit. The director is asked to follow this strictly, as well as all indications in the score as to the changing of scenery and entrances. On the other hand, he may exercise complete freedom with regard to the stage composition, which does not affect the drama, and which in no way interferes with the faithful rendering of the Russian costumes. The author himself is inspired with complete freedom.

The decor of the first three tableaux consists of a simple backdrop, which must evoke, at the same time, the interior of an *izba* and a village street. At the beginning of the Second Part, this drop is raised without interrupting the action.

The word "*Svat*," being untranslatable, has been retained in the French version. In the Russian countryside, the "*Svat*" is the person charged, in some official capacity, with conducting the marriage service, in other words, a male matchmaker. He is, naturally, one of the most important guests at the wedding ceremony.

Stravinsky was never more profoundly "reminded of Russian songs" than while composing *Les Noces*, and it is no exaggeration to say that most of its melodic material is closely related to folk or to church music. What cannot be said for certain is how much was actually modeled and how much was "innate"— a combination of memory and of a phenomenal stylistic intuition. Musicologists have triumphantly traced the phrase at two measures before 3 :

to

which comes from Rimsky-Korsakov's *Polnoe Sobranoe Sochinenii* (1871). But Stravinsky's sketches reveal that he began with an E-minor triad and even further from Rimsky-Korsakov's example than from his own final version. In an interview in *L'Etoile Belge*, May 22, 1930, Stravinsky said that

Obviously some composers have found their best inspiration in folk music. In my opinion, popular music has nothing to gain by being taken out of its frame. It is not suitable as a pretext for demonstrations of orchestral effects and complications. It loses its charm by being *déracinée*. One risks adulterating it and rendering it monotonous. . . .

Béla Bartók observed that

Stravinsky never mentions the source of his themes. Neither in his titles nor in footnotes does he ever allude to whether a theme of his is his own invention or whether it is taken over from folk music. . . . Stravinsky apparently takes this course deliberately. He wants to demonstrate that it does not matter a jot whether a composer invents his own themes or uses themes from elsewhere. He has a right to use musical material taken from all sources. What he has judged suitable for his purpose has become through this very use his mental property. . . . In maintaining that the question of the origin of a theme is completely unimportant from the artist's point of view, Stravinsky is right. The question of origins can only be interesting from the point of view of musical documentation.

Lacking any data, I am unable to tell which themes of Stravinsky's in his so-called "Russian" period are his own inventions and which are borrowed from folk music. This much is certain, that if among the thematic material of Stravinsky's there are some of his own invention (and who can doubt that there are), these are the most faithful and clever imitations of folk songs. It is also notable that during his "Russian" period, from *Le Sacre du Printemps* onward, he seldom uses melodies of a closed form consisting of three or four lines, but short motives of two or three measures, and repeats them "*à la ostinato.*" These short recurring primitive motives are very characteristic of Russian music of a certain category. This type of construction occurs in some of our old music for wind instruments and also in Arab peasant dances.

This primitive construction of the thematic material may partly account for the strange mosaic-like character of Stravinsky's work during his early period. The steady repetition of primitive motives creates an air of strange feverish excitement even in the sort of folk music where it occurs. The effect is increased a hundredfold if a master of Stravinsky's supreme skill and his precise knowledge of dynamic effects employs these rapidly chasing sets of motives . . . With *Petrushka*, a new element enters as a basis: Russian peasant music. This element is retained in a still more perfected style in *Le Sacre du Printemps*, more or less, perhaps in *The Nightingale*, also, and, finally, as the highest accomplishment, in *Les Noces.*

Now, almost all the motives . . . seem to be Russian peasant-music motives or their excellent imitations. And the harmonies into which they are inserted are marvelously suitable for the creation of a kind of apotheosis of the Russian rural music. But, despite the quite incredible novelty displayed throughout, the aforementioned bases as original starting points remain recognizable. Even the origins of the rough-grained, brittle, and jerky musical structure, backed by ostinatos, which is so completely different from any structural proceeding of the past, may be sought in the short-breathed Russian peasant-motives. For these, as we have seen, consist of four, two, or even one bar.[239]

It is possible to follow Stravinsky as he transforms received material, the music at $\boxed{50}$–$\boxed{53}$ being derived entirely—and the music after $\boxed{53}$ partly—from the Fifth Tone of the Quamennyi Chant,[240] which is sung at the beginning of the Sunday Dogmatik in the Russian Orthodox Service. Here is a fragment of the chant:

After several intermediate stages, including experiments with triplet notation (a symbol for the Trinity at least as old as Philippe de Vitry), Stravinsky altered this to

Another fragment of the chant

Stravinsky merely transposes and extends to

while still another phrase

he converts to

This last became the duet for the priest-like basses at $\boxed{50}$, which is as close as Stravinsky ever came to a representation of the Orthodox service on the stage. (Following the Church rule, the singers are unaccompanied,[241] and they are the only instance of this in *Les Noces*.) Yet the entire Second Tableau with its basso ostinato (C, A, C-sharp, A) at the end, imitating a great church bell, is "ecclesiastical" music.

Les Noces may have been inspired by a Jewish wedding that Stravinsky and Cocteau saw in Leysin, March 1914 (Cocteau's letter to the composer, August 11, 1916), and by hearing the bells of St. Paul's, London, in June 1914. On July 13, Diaghilev telegraphed from London to Stravinsky in Salvan, "I hope that *Noces* is on its way," and, on July 26:

Do you have anything for me to hear from *Les Noces*? If so, I can come to Lausanne for a short visit.

But at this date Stravinsky was still working on the libretto and filling his sketchbooks with *chastushkas* (folk rhymes). On September 5, Diaghilev telegraphed from Cernobbio:

Have rented villa with piano in Florence September 15 October 15. Will be delighted if you and your wife can come for a time reply Hotel Cavour Milan.

Stravinsky answered that he had no money and was returning to Clarens "next week," but Diaghilev telegraphed on the 21st, from Milan:

Necessary to see you, must come absolutely. I will take care of the expenses of the trip reply Florence 4 viale Torricelli.

"Beg you to come here if possible," Stravinsky answered, "if not, will come Florence send 200 francs."

Diaghilev sent the money on September 28 and a telegram ("Come quickly"), and, the next day, another telegram asking Stravinsky to bring all of his music as well as all of the French music that he had, including *Saint Sébastien*. The Florence trip cannot have taken more than ten days, since, by October 13, Diaghilev was again telegraphing the composer in Clarens, saying that Meštrović was waiting for them in Rome. This indicates that the purpose of the Florentine meeting was to try to convince Stravinsky to compose music for a stage work based on the Russian Liturgy, Meštrović already having been invited to provide the decors. Stravinsky opposed the idea from the start, but he seems not to have refused categorically at this time, since Diaghilev continued to write and telegraph from Rome (November 1 and 25, 1914), discussing the project and mentioning Meštrović.

By November 1914, Stravinsky had drafted some, probably most, of the First Tableau of *Les Noces*; in fact, the only date in the sketches is for the music at 21, composed that month, though the date actually refers to a succession of intervals on the same page that Stravinsky's then seven-year-old elder son had sung (whistled? hummed?), and that his father, with the immemorial pride of the parent in the prodigies of his offspring, had written down. (The absence of dates in *Les Noces* is especially remarkable because of Stravinsky's general obsession with them, the Piano Sonata, for instance, a comparatively brief work, containing approximately sixty.) On November 15, Stravinsky composed a Polka [242] for piano, music oddly remote from *Les Noces* and arguably the composer's first "neoclassic" work.

At the beginning of January 1915, Stravinsky moved to the Hôtel Victoria in Château-d'Oex, where Diaghilev bombarded him with telegrams asking him to come to Rome.[243] One night in the funicular to Clarens, his fellow passengers were two inebriated peasants, one of whom sang a tipsy tune while the other interjected an accompaniment of hiccoughs. In imitation of this debauched duet, Stravinsky composed a hocket, of which he made capital use in the Fourth Tableau, increasing the suggestion of drunkenness appropriate to the wedding feast by shifting the music from thesis to arsis, and then, in a brilliant unifying stroke, identifying the hocket rhythm with the motif of the Groom, Khvétis Pamfilievich, which dominates the ending of the work. What Stravinsky actually heard in the funicular was doubtless very different from the constructions it inspired in *Les Noces*, but the incident is typical: Stravinsky was in the habit of noting down the *music* in the rhythms and intervals of machinery, in street noises, in hurdy-gurdies and carousels—as well as in troubadours, intoxicated or otherwise, such as these Swiss.

On another excursion (January 28), this time to Geneva, Stravinsky dined with Ansermet in Maxim's Restaurant, where the composer happened to hear a cimbalom—which may not have provoked him quite so far as to say "Eureka," although that is what he thought. The original subtitle of *Les Noces* was

Songs and dances on Russian folk themes, for voices, woodwinds, brass, percussion, plucked and bowed instruments.

The plucked instruments were to have included balalaikas, guzlas,[244] and guitars, but these were replaced in the first drafts by a harpsichord and a string quintet playing pizzicato. Though the cimbalom is not plucked but hammered with wood or padded sticks, the instrument provided exactly the articulation Stravinsky required, as well as a harder and more resonant sound than the jangly balalaika of his native land. The cimbalom is a large dulcimer,[245] the biblical instrument, pictured on the Nineveh tablets, uncertainly evoked in *Ulysses* ("Like no voice of strings or reeds or whatdoyoucallthem dulcimers"), and partly described by Pepys: "Here among the Fidlers I first saw a dulcimore played on, with sticks, and is very pretty" (*Diary*, May 23, 1662).

That night in Geneva, the player [246] favored the composer—not knowing that it was the composer—with a demonstration of the instrument, and as a result Stravinsky purchased one for himself and had it sent to Château d'Oex, where he added a part for it to the orchestra of *Les Noces*. He taught himself to play the cimbalom, moreover, drawing a chart of its thirty-five strings and notating the fifty-three pitches [247] at the places where they are produced on the actual strings. At first, he designated the instrument in his manuscripts by its Russian name, *tympanon*, the name employed by Pantaléon Hebenstreit, its master maker and master player—its Stradivarius as well as its Paganini—whose patron had been Louis XIV. (A *tympanon* made by Pantaléon in 1705 survives among the effects of his descendant Sascha Votichenko, who died in Scottsdale, Arizona, in 1971—surely one of the odder cultural properties to have turned up in that state since London Bridge.) In the next five years, the cimbalom was never far from Stravinsky's instrumental palette, but he abandoned it after that because too few players could read and play his music.[248]

Ansermet had given *Petrushka* in Geneva, January 23, 1915, and with such success [249] that he repeated it February 6. After that, and after several postponements that had exasperated Diaghilev to the point of telegraphing Stravinsky in Château d'Oex: "*Suis révolté sans limites*" (January 16), he went to Rome to hear Casella conduct *Petrushka* at the Augusteo on February 14, a sensational success, after which Marinetti shouted from his loge, "*Abasso Wagner, viva Stravinsky.*" On the afternoon of February 13, Stravinsky played excerpts from his music, including parts of the *Sacre* four-hands with Casella, in a salon of the Grand Hotel, for an audience that included Rodin, Meštrović, Balla, Boccioni, Respighi. Stravinsky left Rome for Switzerland on the 17th, and, on the 18th, while his train was in Milan, wrote to his mother:

I embrace you and Grusha and send uncounted kisses from Italy, where I have spent ten excellent days. I was at Diaghilev's in Rome. They put on my *Petrushka* at the Augusteum with smashing success. I took innumerable bows from the box. Our Ambassador Krupyensky was present, and I was introduced to him and spoke with him during the entire intermission. After that, lengthy demonstrations continued in the corridors. All of the Italian Futurists were at hand and greeted me noisily. Marinetti came especially from Milan.

While in Rome, Stravinsky unveiled *Les Noces* privately for Diaghilev, as his letter of March 8 to the composer in Château d'Oex makes clear. Diaghilev was to hear further installments of *Les Noces* in the Hotel Continentale, Milan, at the beginning of April,[250] and still more of it in Clarens at the end of April.[251] From then to the end of the year, Stravinsky's only creative digressions from *Noces* were the composition of a tiny song, "The Bear," of some sketches for *Renard*, and of that miniature masterpiece of musical catnip, the *Berceuses du Chat*, the first phrase of which so resembles the first phrase of the soprano in *Les Noces* that the one could have suggested the other—and perhaps did, notations for both works being found on the same page. At Christmas 1915,[252] Stravinsky played *Les Noces*, with Massine as his page-turner, for Diaghilev and some others (including J. E. Blanche, who describes the scene in his *Cahiers d'un Artiste*) at Misia Sert's Quai Voltaire apartment. Then, on January 4, 1916, in ever more straitened circumstances because of the war, Stravinsky accepted the commission to compose *Renard*, a happy supervention, even though it caused *Les Noces* to be shelved for seven more months. After that time, interruptions were constant and included the excerpting and reorchestrating of a symphonic poem from *The Nightingale*, the composition of several short pieces, four changes of residence, frequent travels (two trips to Spain in 1916, and quite regular visits to Paris, Milan, and Rome), and answering endless questions relating to the performance and publication of ever more famous past works as well as *pourparlers* concerning commissions for future ones.

Nevertheless, in Rome, in April 1917,[253] Stravinsky was able to play at least three-fourths of *Les Noces* for Diaghilev, and, a month later, the New York *Herald* (May 30) quoted the composer as "expecting to finish *Les Noces Villageoises* this summer." In the latter part of July, Diaghilev visited Stravinsky in Les Diablerets, and, in a train that the impresario took to Italy, and in which the composer accompanied him as far as Aïgle, an agreement commissioning *Les Noces* was finally signed. On August 23, the Aeolian Company, Ltd., London, sent an estimate for the pianolization of *Noces* via Gerald Tyrwhitt (Lord Berners) at the British Embassy in Rome: the first three tableaux, at 4, 7–8, and 4 minutes respectively, could be "cut" on one roll, the fourth tableau, at 10 minutes, on another roll. Tyrwhitt forwarded this information to Stravinsky, who had not yet completed the sketch score. If work on the end of *Les Noces* proceeded at a slower pace, this may be attributable in some measure to three shocks: the death, April 28, of his beloved childhood *nanya*, Bertha Essert; the sudden demise of his brother Gury;[254] and the apprehension of the coming end of the Russia that Stravinsky knew.

Stravinsky welcomed the Revolution during its first convulsions, telegraphing to his mother and older brother at 66 Krukov Canal, Petrograd, May 24, 1917: *"Toutes mes pensées avec vous dans ces inoubliables jours de bonheur qui traverse[nt] notre chère Russie libérée...."* But the composer soon became an anti-Bolshevik and quickly foresaw the consequences to himself of the sundering from Russia, realizing that his voluntary exile was over and that the involuntary one had begun. The lament in the epithalamium at the end of *Les Noces* is as much for the loss of Holy Mother Russia as for that of the virginity of the stage bride, Nastasia Timofeyevna.

Les Noces was completed in sketch score, with much of the Fourth Tableau fully orchestrated, on October 11, 1917. In a letter to Otto Kling, November 19, 1918, Stravinsky refers to this score as if it were complete, but that is because he was trying to obtain a contract for its publication. The instruments required are 3 flutes (including piccolo), 3 oboes (including English horn), 3 clarinets (including E-flat and bass), 2 bassoons, 4 horns, 4 trumpets, 2 keyed bugles (flügelhorns), 3 trombones, a baritone horn in B-flat, a bass tuba, 3 solo violins, 2 solo violas, 2 solo cellos, 1 solo bass, 1 harp, 1 harpsichord, 1 piano, 1 cimbalom, timpani, bass drum, tambourine, triangle, drum without snare. The manuscript is in the Rychenberg-Stiftung, Winterthur.

The differences, musical as distinguished from instrumental, between the 1917 and the final, 1923, scores are most apparent in the Second Tableau, where the two versions vary extensively in meter. But listeners are also struck by changes in the distribution of the vocal parts; by overlappings (cf. [46]); by the absence of a pause at [55]; by the different position of the notes of the basso ostinato between [59] and [60]; by the startlingly beautiful chord, reminiscent of *Le Sacre du Printemps*, in the measure before [59]. The 1917 score does not provide any transition to the scene of the lamenting mothers (Third Tableau), and the Coda (Fourth Tableau) is considerably abbreviated, not to say weak and ineffective, compared to the final version, though Stravinsky did not expand the ending until after the first performance.[255] In other places in the Fourth Tableau, the 1917 score is superior, the changing groups of instruments offering richer means for characterization and for contrasts of color and dynamics than the four-piano orchestra that Stravinsky finally adopted.[256]

The ten years of work on the instrumentation of *Les Noces* offer a study in the processes of growth and refinement, a musical embryology, in fact, since these changes also affected the substance: the comparison of the sketches can illuminate at least a part of the composer's mind. He returned to the scoring in 1919, completing the first two tableaux in minutest detail, except that he did not take the time to write out literal repetitions. In a letter dated April 6, 1919, to Nicolas Struve of the temporarily defunct *Editions Russes de Musique*, the composer refers to *Les Noces* as

a cantata or oratorio, or I do not know what, for four soloists and an instrumental ensemble that I am in too great a hurry to describe.

But this ensemble, for which the music is fully scored to the end of the Second Tableau, is described in a letter of July 23, 1919, to Ansermet, who, a month before, in London, had negotiated a contract with Diaghilev, on Stravinsky's behalf, for the first performances:

I do not know what to do with the *Noces*. It is ridiculous to stage this *"divertissement"* (for it is not a ballet) without decors—although the decors would not represent anything, being there simply to decorate and not to represent anything—and with pianola, harmonium, 2 cimbaloms, percussion, singers, and conductor on the stage, together with the dancers.

The addition of the percussion was a legacy of *Histoire du Soldat,* composed the year before; together with the pianola and cimbaloms, the percussion shows Stravinsky well on the way to the *martellato* ensemble of the final score. Ansermet knew about the cimbaloms and had told Diaghilev about this exotic band.[257] Writing to Stravinsky on July 18, 1919, Ansermet quotes Diaghilev—"Can't Igor make a version without chorus? The Opéra chorus rehearses only three hours a week"—and pictures the impresario at table holding forth on the novelty of the instrumentation of *Les Noces:*

An audience hanging on his every word, Diaghilev says, with an *air fin:* "Our avant-garde painters continue to paint on canvases, as other painters do, nor do they feel compelled to demolish the theater in order to achieve something new. *Mais ce brave Stravinsky,* under the pretext of simplifying *my* task, does not employ the orchestra that we already have but asks for four musicians, one of whom can only be found in Honolulu, another in Budapest, and the other two God knows where!"

Stravinsky wrote to Otto Kling again on November 23:

... as for the *Noces,* you must put in the contract that it is to be described on *affiches* and in programs not as a ballet but as a *divertissement.* Here is the complete title to the work: "Les Noces (village scenes): *divertissement* in two parts with soloists and chorus and an ensemble of several instruments."

The contract, which describes the piece as a *"Divertissement avec Choeurs,"* was signed on December 7, 1919. But *Pulcinella,* the Concertino for String Quartet, the *Symphonies of Wind Instruments, Mavra,* and numerous smaller pieces were composed before Stravinsky could return to and complete the instrumentation. On March 3, 1921, Kling wrote to Stravinsky:

If I have understood M. Ansermet, the accompaniment will consist of four pianolas (two of them replacing cimbaloms), a harmonium and the percussion.

Then, on May 23, Kling wrote again:

I have heard that you have now decided to abandon the idea of a mechanical accompaniment [for *Les Noces*].

Stravinsky's answer, on May 26, reveals that he had surrendered before the problem of synchronizing live instrumentalists with the machinery of the pianola (though a letter from Ansermet reveals that the composer had commissioned Pleyel to construct a mechanical cimbalom on the principle of the pianola):

As for the *Noces,* I am in effect completely reworking the instrumentation for a new ensemble of winds, percussion, and one or two parts for piano. I think that this new ensemble will suit us as well as the former version which included mechanical instruments, something that could create all kinds of difficulties for you.

Winds or percussion, "sounding brass, or a tinkling cymbal"? Apart from the winds, Stravinsky was nearing the final stage of one of the most original ensembles in all music, a percussion orchestra, which is in the category of the actual orchestra of a Russian peasant wedding, at which, to drive away evil spirits, such instruments as pots and pans—as well as drums, tambourines, and cymbals—were bashed, clapped together, rattled, and rung throughout the ceremony and celebration.

Typesetting the Russian text created new and unforeseen difficulties and delays. On August 29, 1921, Stravinsky, in Biarritz, advised his publisher that

the [proof] page which you sent to me is good . . . but I ask you to draw the attention of your proofreaders to the Russian text. Literally not a single word is comprehensible. It is an agglomeration of letters with no sense. You must have a proofreader who knows Russian. Unfortunately I will not have the time to rewrite the whole Russian text in the proofs; and, anyway, it is perfectly clearly written in the manuscript that you have. Try to find a Russian proofreader; at the moment so many Russians are without work.[258]

On October 3, Stravinsky informed a London newspaper that *The Village Wedding* was finished. He meant the two-hand piano score, the final proofs of which did not reach him for another seven months, during which time he composed the one-act opera *Mavra*. He was so late in completing the full score of *Les Noces*, in fact, and the preparation of the parts and correction of the score was done in such haste, that the materials are full of errors to the present day. Stravinsky sent his manuscript to a well-known firm of music copyists in Paris, R. & J. Jakob. But the final pages of the score did not reach Paris (Stravinsky was living in the Hôtel des Princes in Monte Carlo) until Wednesday, May 9, 1923. Here is a timetable of the completion, performance, and publication of *Les Noces*:

1921

August 30. London. J. & W. Chester sends a specimen page of the engraved vocal score.

November 22. Paris. Hôtel Continental. Stravinsky writes to Ansermet: "Diaghilev is here! A folly! I have to finish the instrumentation of *Noces* for the May/June season in Paris. I have an atelier at Pleyel where I will install myself for this work."

1922

January 25. Chester acknowledges the receipt of the first 64 pages of the manuscript of the vocal score and apologizes for errors in the Russian text.

February 6. Chester acknowledges receipt of pages 65–86 of the manuscript.

February 13. Chester receives the remainder of the ms.

February 14. Chester sends second proofs of the first 89 pages.

February 25. Chester sends second proofs of the remainder of the score.

April 18. Telegraphs to Ansermet: "The new instrumentation of *Noces* consists of four pianos and percussion only."

April 21. Chester sends the title pages to Stravinsky, now in Monte Carlo.

April 23. Paris. Diaghilev telegraphs: ". . . Fear we must sacrifice *Noces* and mount it for new theater in the autumn Stop Are you sure Bronia [Nijinska] will be ready. . . ."

April 24. London. Otto Kling writes: ". . . Diaghilev visited us and we heard with much regret that *Les Noces* has been abandoned for the present. We understand the great difficulty of the work and the necessity of long and careful preparation. . . ."

April 25. H. Kling writes acknowledging the receipt of Stravinsky's corrections. O. Kling writes: ". . . The obstacle is not on my part but on Diaghilev's. . . . You have not yet delivered the orchestra score, due by contract since August 1, 1920. . . ."

May 6. Chester complains about the thirty special copies of the vocal scores that have been prepared in great haste and at great expense.

May 10. Monte Carlo. Stravinsky writes to O. Kling: ". . . you know that if I am late, the reason is that I have a new concept of the instrumentation, which will reduce performance problems and costs. . . ."

May 16. London. Chester writes, acknowledging corrected proofs.

1923

January 8. O. Kling writes: ". . . We continue to await the good news that the ballet will be performed. . . . The printers have worked day and night on Diaghilev's urgent request to prepare the thirty scores. . . . We also await the instrumental accompaniment. . . ."

February 28. Purchases old editions of Pushkin's *Pique Dame* and *The Stone Guest,* from the Editions Povolozky, 13, rue Bonaparte.

March 26. Chester acknowledges the receipt of the first 32 pages of the instrumental score.

March 28. H. Kling writes: "Is there a question of presenting *Les Noces* soon?"

April 9. O. Kling writes asking Stravinsky to send his full score to Mr. Gaston Roy, J. & W. Chester's copyist, at Romainville.

May 2. Chester writes: "It is regrettable . . . that Mr. Diaghilev has taken the *Noces* affair to his lawyer, thus obliging us to demand that you return the manuscript. . . ." (Diaghilev's lawyer had asked J. & W. Chester for the orchestra parts.) On November 7, 1923, Diaghilev filed a claim against J. & W. Chester for 300,000 francs damages, claiming that his three-year exclusivity for *Les Noces* from 1920 had been lost, since the material was delivered only in May 1923. (On June 26, 1924, it was decided that Diaghilev's exclusivity was to be extended to May 17, 1926.)

May 6. Monte Carlo. Hôtel des Princes. Stravinsky writes to Chester saying that the full score, "finished yesterday," has been sent to the copyist in Paris.

May 9. London. Chester writes apropos the cover and title.

May 14. Chester writes that Stravinsky's copyist in Paris must give his copy of the score to M. Roy.

May 24. Paris. Stravinsky writes to Chester that the score is ready.

May 26. Stravinsky writes to Chester complaining about mistakes in Roy's copies of the piano parts.

May 29. Stravinsky receives five copies of the vocal score.

On June 4, 1923, *Comoedia* published an advance notice of *Les Noces* by Louis Laloy,[259] who said that Stravinsky had played the score for him a year ago, and "If *Le Sacre du Printemps* was the music of the Earth, then *Noces* is the music of Man." The first performances took place on June 13, 14, 15, 16, 18, 19, 20, 21, at the Théâtre de la Gaieté-Lyrique in Paris. On July 1, a party to celebrate the event was given by Gerald Murphy in a restaurant on a Seine *péniche:*

The first person to arrive was Stravinsky, who dashed into the *salle à manger* to inspect, and even to rearrange the distribution of the place cards. He was apparently satisfied with his own seating . . . on the right hand of the Princesse de Polignac. . . . At one point . . . Ansermet and . . . Diaghilev's secretary had [taken] down the enormous laurel wreath, bearing the inscription *"Les Noces—Hommages"* . . . and were holding it for Stravinsky, who ran the length of the room and leaped nimbly through the center. . . .[260]

Diaghilev offered *Les Noces* again the following year, with Stravinsky conducting the gala, at the Théâtre des Champs-Elysées, May 26, 1924, and the work was acclaimed even more positively than it had been in 1923 (Stravinsky's letter to J. & W. Chester, June 17, 1924). But, when first performed in London, June 14, 1926, at His Majesty's Theater, *Les Noces* was bitterly attacked. The composer's defense against an obtuse press was unexpectedly taken up by H. G. Wells, in a letter that Diaghilev circulated in the audience at the second performance:

... Writing as an old-fashioned popular writer, not at all of the high-brow set, I feel bound to bear my witness on the other side. I do not know of any other ballet so interesting, so amusing, so fresh or nearly so exciting as *Les Noces*. I want to see it again and again, and because I want to do so, I protest against this conspiracy of willful stupidity that may succeed in driving it out of the programme. ...

One of our guardians of culture treats the amusing plainness of the backcloth, with its single window to indicate one house and its two windows for the other, as imaginative poverty—even he could have thought of a stove and a table—and they all cling to the suggestion that Stravinsky had tried to make marriage attractive and failed in the attempt. Of course they make jokes about mothers-in-law; that was unavoidable. It will be an extraordinary loss to the London public if this deliberate dullness of its advisors robs it of *Les Noces*.

The ballet is a rendering in sound and vision of the peasant soul in its gravity, in its deliberate and simple-minded intricacy, in its subtly varied rhythms, in its deep undercurrents of excitement that will astonish and delight every intelligent man or woman who goes to see it. The silly pretty-pretty tradition of Watteau and Fragonard is flung aside. Instead of fancy-dress peasants we have peasants in plain black and white, and the smirking flirtatiousness of Daphnis and Chloé gives place to a richly humorous solemnity. It was an amazing experience to come out from this delightful display with the warp and woof of music and vision still running and interweaving in one's mind, and to find a little group of critics flushed with resentment and ransacking the stores of their minds for cheap, trite deprecations of the freshest and strongest thing that they had had a chance to praise for a long time.

One result of this hostility was that Stravinsky began to believe that English music critics were more prejudiced against him than those of other countries:

The largest proportion of criticism against me comes from England. I ask why. ... After all, English musicians play my music in the most understanding way. Also, it seems to me that my music is not completely foreign to the British temperament. [*Journal de Genève*, November 14, 1928]

Whatever the truth of this, as late as December 11, 1956, a reviewer for *The New Statesman and Nation* could still describe the *Symphonies of Wind Instruments* as "hardly making the effect of a considered composition until the final pages." When the same reviewer wrote of a 1960 performance of *Oedipus Rex* that the singers sound "glorious in music usually reckoned hopelessly unvocal" (*Sunday Times*, January 17, 1960), Stravinsky, in a marginal note, demanded to know the names of the judges of this unvocalness. On the other hand, when *The Times* for November 5, 1958, described *Agon* as an "imitation of Boulez and Arbeau," Stravinsky was so curious to learn about Arbeau that the malice of the review was scarcely noticed.

Yet the London press was aware of itself. Under the title "Catching Up with Stravinsky," *The Times* observed that

... The English never really take great men to their hearts until they are Grand Old Men. Is it a lingering reputation of a self-rejuvenating *enfant terrible* that makes us keep Stravinsky at arms' length still? [October 27, 1961]

Ironically, the composer whom Ernest Newman, Constant Lambert, and others were belaboring was the only major foreign one ever to have become deeply attracted to English music. As Stravinsky told a reporter for the *London Evening Standard,* June 18, 1927: "Of modern English music I know very little, but I know and appreciate old English music." Two years earlier, in New York, he had told an interviewer for *Etude* magazine that "the works of the early English writers for keyboard instruments, such as Byrd, Bull, Gibbons, Purcell, make an immense appeal to me." And, in his American years, Stravinsky owned virtually the complete works of the English lutenists and madrigalists, whose music he knew and loved.

C. F. Ramuz has left a vivid description of Stravinsky at work on *Les Noces:*

Stravinsky had moved from the slate-roofed and turreted villa in the suburbs of Morges [261] to the second floor of a fine, early nineteenth-, perhaps late eighteenth-century house [262] near the outskirts of town. ... A half-concealed wooden stair, shut off by three doors, led to a room he had fitted up as a study in the immense attic.... Each day the music became more aggressive and noisy, each day less acceptable to ... his neighbors.... This was the time when the cart of the bride in *Noces* rolled daily onto the scene, rumbling noisily over the pine floor. ... Each day, seated in her cart in this attic in Morges, she loudly bewailed the fate of her hair, symbol of the loss of her virginity. Her vigorous lament came first in Russian; then she would try to express it in French.

It was the time of *Noces* and its orchestration.... Intended first for mechanical reproduction, it had to be turned over to four pianos because of technical difficulties. The pianos did their best to sound like an Orchestrion, a device that one may call artificial, but which I believe was justified and authentic. *Noces* was at that time titled *Les Noces Villageoises,* and the original plan was to place in the wings those giant boxes which have been seen in our villages since the time of Beethoven, and which we owe to him (a fact too often forgotten). Wedding guests generally slipped in two *sous* to start things going....

The *Noces* music is swept from end to end by a single current.... The bride has hardly finished lamenting when the wedding guests intervene, then the father and the mother, then all of the characters at once.... The invocation is carried to the end of the first part. In the second part we attend the wedding feast.... When the backdrop rises we see an enormous room in a log cabin almost completely filled by a table around which people are seated, eating and drinking. An open door in the background reveals a double bed covered with an enormous comforter. The participants eat, drink, and sing at the same time and all together in what seems like confusion but is not, because, underlying everything, sustaining the entire structure, is the most careful calculation.

The characters lean on the table, or stand apart, grouped or single, quiet one minute, then all talking at once, then again quiet. One hears an invocation to the Virgin, then to the saints; hope is mixed with regret; the experience of the elders is expressed in proverbs; there is chaffing and there are many jokes. . . .

At any given moment there are at least four texts, literary and musical, sometimes interrupted and succeeded by others, sometimes mingled, sometimes resolved in a kind of unison. But the climax of disorder always fits into a most rigorous plan, a mathematical system all the more stringent because the tonal matter appears to be free from it. I know it well. . . . I have tried to work it out for myself, and it was difficult, even though all I had to do was to arrange the syllables. . . . The text could be explicit enough:

> Love your wife,
> Cherish her like your soul,
> Shake her like a plum tree.

Advice of utmost realism shamelessly interrupts the most beautiful passages of peasant eloquence. . . . A man and his wife are selected from among the guests to warm the wedding bed. Everything still specific, as you can see. Even the old drunkard is not missing, never really starting or finishing his song, coming out occasionally with a kind of subterranean rumbling, a hiccough composed of syllables belonging to a word, the words to a line, the line to a sentence, mumbling his story and his opinions to himself as he sits alone in his corner. [C. F. Ramuz, *Souvenirs sur Igor Stravinsky* (Edition Mermod, Lausanne, 1929)]

One project that occupied Stravinsky's mind for a time while he was finishing *Les Noces* was that of composing incidental music for a staging of *Antony and Cleopatra*, using André Gide's translation. On June 26, 1917, Charles Pequin, agent for Ida Rubinstein,[263] wrote to Stravinsky to ask whether he would accept a commission for this. On July 11, Stravinsky wrote to Léon Bakst, in Paris, who was promoting the venture and Stravinsky's participation in it:

Dear Lyovushka! I have just received your telegram of July 7th about André Gide coming here in three weeks for talks with me!!! I find you are wasting a terrible lot of time. Your first telegram says that the music must be finished in 6 *months*. But now an entire month has gone for discussions, and one must still wait for Gide, who, according to your telegram, will arrive only in August. . . . This Saturday (July 14) we are going to the mountains and will remain there until the beginning of September. My address will be: "Les Fougères," Diablerets, Canton de Vaud, Stravinsky. Tell Gide.

On July 30, Stravinsky telegraphed to Bakst:

Notions du réalisme et synthétisme pour la mise-en-scène ne m'explique rien. Attends Gide pour comprendre.

The demand for the concrete is so characteristically expressed that the message could have come from any time in Stravinsky's life, 1971 as well as 1917.

Gide came to Diablerets, Châlet du Revenandray, with Edmond Gilliard, and the composer drew up a scheme for ten pieces of incidental music:

1. Music for the overture to the spectacle.
2. Hymn to the Caesars.
3. Glorification of Cleopatra.
4. Song of the oboes.
5. First entr'acte.
6. Fanfares.
7. Triumphant entry of Caesar.
8. March in the camp of Caesar.
9. Second entr'acte.
10. Music for the death of Cleopatra.

On November 18, 1917, Stravinsky telegraphed to an associate of Ida Rubinstein: "I have started the music; should I continue? Ask Bakst to send the advance to the Banque Cantonale. On November 23, in a military hospital in Montpellier, Lydia Botkin wrote to Stravinsky:

... I saw Goncharova and Larionov, who ask me to tell you that they know our new ambassador very well, and that they will help to let you come to Paris, but say nothing to Diaghilev.... Goncharova made new drawings for *Noces*, and they are marvelous.[264] We like them more than the first ones. Bakst wrote me: Madame Rubinstein telephoned to tell him that she will study your terms for *Antony and Cleopatra* with her business adviser.... I hope you will receive my letter. With the closing of the borders it is very difficult to communicate. What horrible things are happening in our country!

Excuse me that I did not write to you earlier about my conversation with Bakst. I saw him only on the fourth day of his arrival in Paris. The border was still closed, and I sent you a telegram the next day through the office of the commandant in Montpellier.

A letter to Pequin, December 6, 1917, reveals that Stravinsky's interest in the project was still alive at that date, and on the 16th the composer modified his terms. But when Mme Rubinstein failed to meet his financial conditions, she apparently did not inform Gide, since his next letter to Stravinsky did not come until the early spring of 1918, by which time a considerable part of *Histoire du Soldat* had already been composed:

My dear Stravinsky, I have wanted to write you more than once, first of all to tell you, as I would not do on the telephone, how much I share in your grief [265]—again what sadness!—and to tell you also how much I liked your beautiful letter in *Le Temps* (and of the emotion that I had in reading it). Thank you for sending the little musical sketches [266] which I have read with a young pupil.... Did you send any photographs as a souvenir of our meetings?

... Finally, I can tell you that my translation of *Cleopatra* is finished, and that to me it seems good. I can send a marked copy if you wish, indicating the places where music is probably necessary—in particular, the battle of Actium, which takes place offstage but without lowering the curtain. Also, a little later, the second battle should have

a military symphony. . . . I wait for a word from you from Switzerland.
. . . André Gide. [Cuverville, March 8, 1918]

Gide wrote in his *Journal,* January 16, 1923:

Cocteau's play . . . reflects the same feeling that made Stravinsky say
he would gladly collaborate on *Antony and Cleopatra,* but only if Antony were given the uniform of a . . . Bersagliere.

The reader familiar with Stravinsky will doubt that he ever made
such a stipulation, and certainly Stravinsky's letter to Bakst ar-
gues against the likelihood of any such approach.

While waiting for the *Antony and Cleopatra* project to materialize, Stravinsky composed the *Etude* for pianola, a brief
work that was to have a profound influence on his life for the
next decade. The music was conceived not for this instrument
but as an orchestral work, the first sketches containing notations
for strings, piccolo, flute, English horn, clarinet, bassoon, trumpet, tuba, and full percussion. (The 1928 orchestration of the
Etude [267] does not use percussion, except timpani.) Some
slightly later sketches require harp, clavecin, and pianola, in
addition to the wind instruments, thus reflecting the ensembles
of both the 1917 and 1919 scores of *Les Noces.* Still another draft
of the *Etude* is written in the form of a three-piano score, much
like the final version of *Les Noces.*

The first notation for the *Etude,* the figure at measure 10, is
found in a sketchbook, the first pages of which contain entries
for dance pieces (cancan, kazatchok, tarantella), as well as the
tune later used in the bassoon part at $\boxed{5}$ in the music for Scene
I in *Histoire du Soldat.* Then, after experimenting with the figuration eventually introduced in the *Etude* at measures 11 and
12, Stravinsky wrote the first six measures of the opus and completed a draft of it as far as $\boxed{11}$, from which point to the end of
the sketch score a pianola is the featured instrument, the orchestra an accompaniment. The handwriting changes markedly at
$\boxed{11}$, and the music thereafter may date from several weeks
later. At one point in this later section, Stravinsky returned to
the beginning of the piece and orchestrated the first six measures
for wind instruments (flute, clarinets, trumpet, bassoons, horns)
as an introduction to a pianola solo that begins in measures 7
and 8, thus anticipating an idea exploited in the Piano Concerto
of 1924. It should also be mentioned that the first complete
sketch score—dated, at the end, "Morges, 10 September 1917,"
titled *Etudes pour Pianola,* and written on three, four, five, and
six [268] staves—omits the first six measures, though even this
draft contains specifications for winds near the end. The first
audition of the piece—hardly to be described as a performance—
took place in Aeolian Hall, London, October 13, 1921.

Stravinsky had been interested in the pianola [269] long before
composing the *Etude,* and Diaghilev's telegram to him, December 18, 1912,[270] indicates that pianola arrangements were used
by the Ballets Russes at that time. Yet Stravinsky's continuing

infatuation with the instrument is one of the inexplicable eccentricities of his career—not the delight in the novelty of the machine reflected in the *Etude* (which he claimed was the first piece written especially for the instrument), nor even his profligate expenditures of time and labor in transcribing his music for this dodo [271] (since he earned substantial sums of money thereby), but in his musical enthusiasm for it. Another of its strongest attractions for Stravinsky was noted by Béla Bartók:

> ... some famous composers (Stravinsky, for instance) wrote compositions specifically for pianola, and they took advantage of all the possibilities offered by the absence of restraints that are an outcome of the structure of the human hand. The intent, however, was not to achieve superior performance but to restrict to an absolute minimum the intervention of the performer's personality.[272]

Stravinsky was aware of this, of course, as the following statement proves:

> When I played my works at the mechanical piano, the notes did not correspond to my immediate sentiments but were transmitted by electrical means. [*Les Nouvelles Littéraires*, December 8, 1928]

Yet one of the strangest documents in Stravinsky's entire bibliography is an interview in *The New York Times Magazine*, January 18, 1925: "Player Piano, Composer Says, Holds Unplumbed Possibilities in 'Polyphonic Truth.'" But did Stravinsky attempt to "plumb" them? The *Etude* itself, apart from some repeated-note triplets to be executed at superhuman speed—too fast, as well, for standard orchestral instruments in the transcription of the work (at two measures before [8])—does not explore even such possibilities of the instrument as subdividing the beat beyond the techniques of human performers, or writing a glissando for the entire keyboard to be played in the fraction of a second. In fact, Stravinsky's real objectives with the pianola seem to be to assure a rigid rendition of the music and to economize on live pianists. His avowed objectives, however, are truly mystifying:

> I explained to Erik Satie that I was interested in the mechanical piano, wanting to find in it not an instrument to *reproduce* my works but one that could *reconstitute* them. [*Les Nouvelles Littéraires*, December 8, 1928]

But why on earth should Stravinsky wish to "reconstitute" his music? This has never been answered satisfactorily, and the following description of the complications involved in composing for the contraption only deepens the mystery. Ernest Ansermet is writing from London, June 12, 1919:

> I have had two meetings with the expert "*pianoleur.*" He played your piano roll for me several times while I followed with the manuscript score. Unfortunately I heard the piece on a very bad instrument, and, to make matters worse, the expert made *rubati*. In general, I noticed

that the pianola lacks the mechanical strength that I had expected. And your observation concerning the inability of the cimbalom to accent is correct [and applies as well to the pianola]. One feels the intervention of the performer, hence the necessity of an intelligent intermediary. I indicated that a much more rhythmic and vigorous performance was required, and to some extent the expert succeeded in achieving one. I also observed a weakness in all basses not doubled in the octave, but perhaps you intended this.[273] One characteristic of the instrument that must be studied carefully is what I believe they call the "thématie," a device to bring out one element or line more strongly than any other. In the earliest pianolas the use of this thématie was optional; but for mechanical reasons and, no doubt, economic ones as well, the thématie is now integral. You must indicate by a sign in your manuscript exactly which element should predominate. Here are some additional points:

1. The piano roll cannot exceed a hundred feet in length. Your roll, at 30 feet, is among the smaller ones. The quality is less good in the longer rolls because of a quavering in the band.

2. The length of the roll does not depend only on the duration of the piece but also on the number of notes which it comprises. Because of musical factors, the manufacturer cannot determine the length of the roll from the number of measures and their metronomic quotient. Thus a time value in tremolo takes more space than the same value in tenuto. The manufacturer is able to tell the approximate length of the roll if he also knows the number of measures, and the metronome value, and if he has some indication of the content of the measures (long notes or subdivided ones). To give you an idea, the 1812 Overture makes one roll, but one of the longest.

3. The time that it takes to rewind the roll depends on the length of the roll [sic] but this cannot be done in less than thirty seconds. The possibility of a faster, mechanical change is not foreseen at present, but two pianolas can be used, the second beginning when the first ends.

4. Your roll is far from exaggerating the number of notes that can be performed simultaneously. The perforations are very small and quite separate from one another, the roll rather large and strong so that the most formidable chords can be incised without risk. Glissandos crossing each other are possible, but at the point of intersection the notes common to the two lines are not reinforced. Thus one hears only a single note, not two, as the case would be in an orchestral transcription.

5. The tremolo on one note is not as perfect as it is when played by a pianist; but your piece contains only one example of this.

The reader's heart sinks at Stravinsky's statement to the press on arriving in New York in 1925:

I will not compose while in America; that requires too much concentration. Instead, I am making entirely new versions of my works for your mechanical reproducing instruments, forty-four pieces in all.[274] Not a "photograph of my playing," as Paderewski has made of his, through recordings . . . but rather a "lithograph," a full and permanent record of tone combinations that are beyond my ten poor fingers to perform; in effect a new orchestration for the whole piano keyboard.

As late as June 1927, by which date the future of the phonograph vis-à-vis that of the mechanical piano had been assured, Stravinsky made a personal appearance in the Théâtre des Champs-Elysées at a "Gala de la Musique Mécanique" to advertise his

Pleyela version of the *Firebird* Suite—and was warned by Aeolian that this was in violation of his contract with that company. Needless to say, whatever the technical interest in these arrangements, all of them together are not worth the briefest original composition.

Histoire du Soldat

The *Histoire du Soldat* libretto exists in three different versions, the first almost twice as long as the third. The second version, not much shorter than the first, would seem to have been the one that was performed, once only, in September 1918. The score and definitive text were not published until 1924, and Stravinsky changed the music after the first performance. The original play requires a purely musical introduction, then a discourse from the narrator on the kind of theater that the audience is to behold. Also, the narrator speaks throughout the "Royal March," the orchestra participates in the action (by applauding), and the King has a first-person part (spoken by the narrator). His daughter—"Princess Emmeline" in this version and the second one—is addressed by name. Finally, the royal family is presumably fond of Horace, and jokes are made about Latin hexameters and dactylic trimeters. The first *Soldat* was verbose and the music disproportionately short.

The original production was to have been presented in Geneva (October 16, Comédie Théâtre), Winterthur, and Zürich, this last as a part of a series devoted to music and literature, whose next event, also canceled, would have been Rainer Maria Rilke reading his poems. But when the Spanish influenza took its toll of the *Histoire* cast and musicians [275] and frightened people into staying away from theaters, C. F. Ramuz went alone to Zürich, where he read the play without music. Stravinsky also succumbed to the flu but recovered within a week. "Today I am much better . . ." he wrote to Ramuz on October 7, though the next day Ramuz sent a note to the director of the Zürich organization: "Stravinsky still has a violent fever, after eight days."

Stravinsky and Ramuz sometimes worked on the French translations of Stravinsky's vocal music at Ernest Ansermet's home, which was midway between Stravinsky's in Morges and Ramuz's in Treytorrens. According to Ansermet, the idea that led to *Histoire du Soldat* was born during one of these translating sessions:

The poet and composer wanted to form a small traveling theater through which, simply and directly, they could tell a story with music. Their theater would be free of standard theatrical trappings and therefore could visit small towns and villages. . . . Stravinsky knew many popular Russian tales of the kind that were acted or narrated at country fairs, and one of the most striking of his stories [276] was about a soldier with a violin that represented his soul. The Devil, appearing to him in various disguises, finally persuaded him to part with the violin, which he did at the price of his soul. . . . Ramuz and Stravinsky invited René Auberjonois to design the theater, as well as the sets and costumes for the piece that they had begun to create. This began to grow in scope, complexity, and cost, for Auberjonois wanted a change of decors with each scene, as well as several masks for the Devil. Also, since Ramuz did not want to be the narrator, an actor had to be engaged.[277] Furthermore, an unaccompanied violin was too thin, and Ramuz proposed to add a harmonica or a guitar. . . . At this point Stravinsky decided that the violin must be coupled with a string bass, and that two wind instruments, a clarinet and a bassoon, were necessary to fill out the ensemble. "Why two?" Ramuz asked, and Stravinsky explained that two voices from each instrumental family would provide a full range. Then Stravinsky said that he needed a trumpet and trombone—always two—and at this Ramuz's eyes conveyed his fright, except that no one knew whether or not he was acting. Finally, Stravinsky declared that he required a percussionist—only one, but he did not say that this soloist would have to have a shop full of instruments. [From "La Naissance de 'L'Histoire du Soldat,' " in C. F. Ramuz's Lettres, 1900–1918 (Lausanne, Clairefontaine, 1956)]

Another memoir of the beginnings of Histoire du Soldat, by Liudmilla Pitoëff,[278] who danced the part of the Princess, emphasizes the Russian origins of the work:

One day in Geneva [in 1918], Stravinsky called, asked if we had a piano, then said that he would visit us and play something very beautiful. In the afternoon our housekeeper announced that a man whose like she had never seen was at the door. And he did look strange, since, attached to his belt, were cases and boxes of several sizes, containing various percussion instruments. Soon after he had arranged these around the piano, Stravinsky arrived, saying, "It is the Soldier's Tale, the popular story known to all Russian children. You, Georges [Mme Pitoëff's husband], will be the stage director and take the part of the Devil. Liudmilla will be the Princess. Now I will play it for you," Stravinsky said, and with this he pounced on the piano and percussion, while imitating other instruments with his voice. Fireworks seemed to be exploding in our little salon, and Stravinsky reminded me of a devil in a Byzantine icon, so red, so black, so resonant. A doleful melody . . . and the percussion growled, purred, crackled. The fracas at the end [which Stravinsky played on the drums] tore the atmosphere to shreds . . . We were ecstatic, happy, shocked. This story in music, with its tangle of Russian melodies, truly represents the Russian folk tale . . .

We went to Lausanne and lived there during the rehearsals, taking our daughter Svetlana . . . We were dancing mutes. Georges, as the Devil, fluttered and threw himself about, and I was the melancholy, unsmiling Princess, charmed out of her apathy by the soldier's violin. How fascinating were the interminable discussions with Stravinsky, Ramuz, Auberjonois, though the three men were so different that they could never understand each other . . . Stravinsky is captivating . . . His curiosity is so great that he awakens this quality in all those around him and leads them into unknown kingdoms. [Paraphrased from "Souvenirs Intimes," Le Quartier Latin, Montreal, March 23, 1945]

A letter from Ramuz to Stravinsky, February 28, 1918, reveals that, following the form of *Renard*, they intended to conclude and begin the new work, *Le Soldat, le Violin, et le Diable*, with a march. Ten days later, Ramuz wrote to say that Werner Reinhart had promised his support and had already placed 3,000 francs at their disposal. Stravinsky had not yet made the acquaintance of Reinhart, as a letter from him to the composer, April 4, reveals. Later that month, Reinhart came to Lausanne, and Ramuz and Stravinsky described their project in detail. A letter from Reinhart to Stravinsky, May 15, thanks the composer for receiving him in his home and for playing his works—which probably refers to *Les Noces* and some of the songs, since Reinhart proposes a concert of Stravinsky's songs with instruments in Zürich: "Even though Mr. Isler who is in charge there comes from the camp of Reger, I hope that he will understand your music." Meanwhile, more money was needed, and on April 18 Stravinsky signed a letter, written by Ramuz, to Mme Auguste Roussy, a music lover, at La Tour-de-Peilz, asking for 15,000 francs. When this was not forthcoming, Stravinsky approached the Infanta Beatrice of Spain, who had already shown an interest in the work (see Reinhart's letter to Stravinsky, June 10). The *Histoire* project was stalled in May, but Reinhart provided the 15,000 francs (letter to Stravinsky, June 27).

On March 16, Stravinsky composed the coda to the *Tango*, which uses a theme that occurred to him in a dream:

Another letter, dated April 23, discusses the form of this most hybrid of all of Stravinsky's creations before *The Flood* (1962), but the correspondence of the authors does not trace the development of the piece, no doubt because they were meeting almost daily, but also because of increasing reliance on the telephone.[279] (In a letter of July 19, Ramuz says that he was unable to call Stravinsky because ten people had reserved the telephone before him.) On July 7, Ramuz describes a rehearsal with the actor Gabriel Rosset in the part of the Soldier, and, on the 15th, writes to Stravinsky about the possibility of employing a "café-concert actress" for the part of the Princess. But the most intriguing remark of all is found in a letter of September 5 from Ramuz to Auberjonois. After referring to "lively altercations" with Stravinsky that, however, "always end amicably," Ramuz adds:

Stravinsky informed me last evening of his intention to dance the last scene himself. This would be perfect; encourage him.

Ramuz wrote again the next day, explaining that Stravinsky was going to Geneva every two days both to see the publisher, Henn, and to try to settle the question of a hall for the performance. The letter concludes with the observation that the *Gazette de Lausanne*'s music critic "*n'aime pas Stravinsky*."

Since no study has yet been published of Stravinsky's sources for the music,[280] or even of his contributions to the text,[281] it must suffice to say that the pieces were composed in general accordance with Ansermet's account of the gradual enlargement of the ensemble.[282] Thus the violin-and-bass "Valse" was apparently begun first (though not completed until July) and rescued from monotony by the addition, one by one, of the bassoon, clarinet, and cornet. In the earliest sketches, the transition from the *Valse* to the *Rag*[283] is abrupt but worth remarking because the bass continues in the triple meter while the remainder of the ensemble switches to *alla breve*. "The Dance of the Devil" was the next piece composed (but as yet without percussion), followed by the "Chorale," which was written directly in instrumental score, but with changes in harmony and voice-leading from one draft to another.

In the first notations for "The King and the Princess"—eventually the "Royal March"—the unaccompanied trombone announces a fandango:

This is answered by the trumpet fanfare that was later transformed to the *Soldier's March* at [4]. Stravinsky did not use percussion instruments until the beginning of May,[284] hence the *Tango, Ragtime, Soldier's March,* and *Triumphal March* were among the later parts of the score to be composed; the music from [9] to [10] in the *Tango* is dated July 16, 1918, the *Little Concert* (originally called the "Concertino") August 10—though Stravinsky was still revising this on September 19—and the *Triumphal March of the Devil* August 26. On August 30, Stravinsky gave to Ansermet copies of the full scores of the *March*, the *Soldier by the Brook*, the *Music for the Second Scene*, the *Tango*, the *Royal March*, the *Chorale*, the *Valse* and *Ragtime*, the *Dance of the Devil*, the *Devil's Triumphal March*, and the *Introduction to the Second Part*. Only the *Devil's Song* was written after that, and the music between [7] and [13] in the *Little Concert*, these sections being late inserts. In the original manuscript, Stravinsky wrote "Soldier and Princess (finale)" over the music beginning at the third measure of [5] in the *Devil's Dance*. One of the most interesting sketches, that for the *Ragtime* at [34], shows the influence of the percussion on the style of the violin music— although the percussion at this place does not duplicate the rhythm of the violin part, as in the final score, but is the first notation for the percussion solo at the very end of the work.

From the beginning of August 1918 until the premiere of *Histoire*, Stravinsky kept an account book marked "Expenses for *Histoire du Soldat,*" a revealing document in that it indicates the amount of work, apart from composing, that Stravinsky contributed to the preparation of the performance, and the financial restrictions under which he was obliged to live. Characteristically, he does not mention the performance itself, and, no less typically, the entry for the day after the performance is for pharmaceuticals:

EXPENSES FOR "HISTOIRE DU SOLDAT"

August [1918]

2 Telephone to Piotton.[285]
   Telephone to Closset.[286]
   Advance payment to Piotton.
3 Trip for Closset, Geneva-Morges.
4 Telephone to Closset.
9 Telegram to Madame Pitoëff.
10 Boat: return to Ouchy.
   Strings.
   Music paper.
   Telegram to Ansermet.
12 Telegram to Ansermet.[287]
14 Telegram to Ramuz.
   Express letter to Ansermet.
   Telephone Bartholoni.[288]
15 Ticket: Morges-Lausanne-Morges.
16 Boat.
   Supplement for train.
19 Three telephones to Geneva.
20 Boat: Morges-Geneva-Morges.
21 CFF and train Geneva-Morges.
   Boat: Morges-Ouchy.
   Wine.
   Surtax for direct train.
22 Telephone to Winterthur.
24 Boat and DFF: Morges-Lausanne-Morges.
   Restaurant.
26 Telephone to Brandenbourg.[289]
27 Morges-Geneva-Morges.
   Restaurant.
28 Morges-Lausanne-Morges.
29 Telephone to Reinhart.
   Telephone to Ramuz.
   Telephone to Piotton.
   Telephone to Closset.
   Telephone to Rosset.
30 Morges-Geneva-Morges.
   Restaurant.
31 Boat from Morges to Lausanne, restaurant, return by train.
   Telegram, wine, and coffee.

September

1 Lausanne and Morges.

2   Morges-Lausanne-Morges. Restaurant. Train. Telegram. Rosset and home. Supplement. Telephone to Auberjonois.
3   Lausanne-Geneva-Lausanne. Restaurant.
4   Morges to Lausanne by boat. Food. Telegram.. Coffee. Lausanne-Morges. Food.
5   Trip to Geneva. Telephone.
6   Telephone. Reservations Morges-Lausanne CFF. Morges-Geneva-return. To Piotton. Letters. Train. Dinner. Belongings. Hotel and coffee.
7   Surtax. Telephone and tea. Restaurant at the station. Tramway. Telephone.
8   Telephone.
9   Telephone. Morges-Geneva. Stamps.
10 Tea and telephone.
11 Supplement II class.
12 Telephone. Telegram. Telephone to Allegra.[290]
13 Morges-Geneva.
14 Geneva. Lausanne. Dinner and supper.
15 Telephones. Telegrams.
17 Supplement II class. Ticket Morges to Geneva. Tram. Bottle.
18 Telephone. Supplement II class. Music paper.
20 Telephone. Telegram Jacquelet. Telegram Ansermet. Telegram Closset. Telegram Ramuz. Supplement and tip.
22 Telephone. Dinner at the station. Telegram to Ansermet. Supplement.
23 Paid for yesterday's dinner and today's dinner.
24 Telegrams. Supplement. Telephone to Zürich [Ansermet].
25 Telephones.
26 Supplement. Express letter to Ansermet. Emmeline.
27 Automobile. Tram.
28 Restaurant and razor.
29 Pharmacy.

Relations between Stravinsky and Ramuz were not always smooth, and at times the composer was dismayed by his collaborator's inexperience. Thus, as the performance approached, Ramuz wrote to Stravinsky:

I have reached the conclusion that the more abstract the mask, the stronger the effect. A perfectly glabrous mask, such as the one that we had yesterday . . . would be truly diabolical.

Stravinsky penciled in the margin of the letter, partly in French, partly in Russian:

To admit this principle would take us too far from our magic-lantern idea. All of these changes are only proof of the author's uncertainty in the theatrical side of the piece. And I, with my practical sense, know that the fault is usually the author's. He should know that the theater demands precision.

Stravinsky would soon become aware, too, that his collaboration with Ramuz incurred liabilities, as when the French conductor Gabriel Grovlez wrote, November 27, 1918, asking for permission to give the *Soldat* in Paris, but also expressing concern that "Ramuz's text might be too Vaudois for Parisians." When Ramuz revised the text of *Histoire,* in 1923, the composer was by no means pleased to hear about it first from his publisher (letter from Kling, November 20, 1923). Here is an excerpt from an earlier letter from the composer to his collaborator:

My dear Ramuz . . . My role in *Histoire du Soldat* was not limited to composing music for a play that already existed. And yet one would deduce from the "credits" page that the *Soldier* could be played with other music, just as it could be acted (which goes without saying) in front of other decors. Is this how you feel about it now, Ramuz? I don't think it is, for you know only too well the part that I played in the development of the scenario; and that if a genuine collaboration had not existed between us, the "story" of the "Soldier" would be completely different. Do not construe this as a desire on my part to have my name placed next to yours when the text is published separately. As I wrote on my card, I merely propose that this faulty first page be replaced with the page from the program from the premiere. . . . This would be enough to suggest to the reader an intimate collaboration between us for our "Soldier." I stand firm about this, my dear Ramuz, and it pains me a great deal, this unfortunate single page, which you have composed quite consciously and for your own reasons. . . . [Letter of August 23, 1920]

Yet the book of *Histoire du Soldat* was published, by Editions des Cahiers Vaudois, rue de Bourg, 19, Lausanne, with Ramuz's name alone on the outer and inner covers, and, on the third page, the names of Stravinsky and Auberjonois in very much smaller type. Ramuz lists the instrumentation here as including a flute, trumpet, and cornet, but no trombone. As for the cast, he mentions two dancers besides the Princess. A decade after *Histoire,* Ramuz's *Souvenirs sur Igor Stravinsky* surprised the composer, and by no means agreeably. In fact, he considered the book to be a betrayal and exploitation of a private relationship, which explains why he never recommended it to English publishers. His true feelings are evident in the way in which he satisfied with two insignificant details Ramuz's amiable request for criticism. On December 10, 1928, Ramuz sent the third chapter of the book and asked the composer for marginal notes such as "This is false," "This is correct," "I am not of this opinion," briefly giving the reasons. Stravinsky answered, on December 16, 1928:

Dear Ramuz, I thank you with all my heart for your *Souvenirs,* of which volume three is as fine as the preceding ones. These *Souvenirs* have touched me deeply: the *marc* of the past, once deposited, begins its geological life carefully covered over by new layers, and this *marc,* no less potent than those we have drunk together in three quick swallows (your three volumes), has gone to my head—which is spinning, and which turns to you in gratitude for having kept these memories, dear to both of us, in so safe a place. (Your bottle, which still seems to bear the label of three bells, was delivered to me and was uncorked, as you predicted, by my *grand fils.*)
I am astonished by your proposal that I add some "notes" to your text expressing my personal reactions. Of course I have reactions, dear

Concert
IGOR STRAWINSKY
au Conservatoire, le 8 novembre

SUITE DES PIÈCES :

I.*PETITE SUITE DE L'HISTOIRE DU SOLDAT *pour piano, clarinette et violon (1919)*
exécutée par MM. PORTA, ITURBI et ALLEGRA.

II. RAG TIME, *écrit pour 11 instruments, transcrit pour le piano par l'auteur (1918)*.
*PIANO-RAG-MUSIC *(1919)*
exécutés par M. JOSÉ ITURBI.

III.*TROIS PIÈCES POUR CLARINETTE SOLO *(1919)*
exécutées par M. ALLEGRA.

IV.*PRIBAOUTKI (chansons plaisantes) *(1914)*
*BERCEUSES DU CHAT *(1915-1916)*
exécutées par Mlle TATIANOFF. — Au piano : M. JOSÉ ITURBI.

V. HUIT PIÈCES POUR PIANO A 4 MAINS *tirées des deux cahiers de pièces faciles,(1914-1917)*
A. Main gauche facile : Marche, Valse, Polka.
B. Main droite facile : Andante, Espagnola, Balalaika, Napolitana, Galop.
exécutées par MM. IGOR STRAWINSKY et JOSÉ ITURBI.

* Première audition.

Piano de concert BERDUX.

Berceuses du Chat
mises en français par C.-F. RAMUZ.

SUR LE POÊLE.

Dors sur le poêle, bien au chaud, chat.
La pendule bat,
elle bat, mais pas pour toi.

DODO.

Dodo, l'enfant do, l'enfant dormira bientôt...
Aujourd'hui
le chat a mis
son bel habit gris,
pour faire la chasse aux souris...
Dodo, l'enfant do, l'enfant dormira bientôt...
Otera son bel habit,
si l'enfant n'est pas gentil...
Dodo, l'enfant do, l'enfant dormira bientôt.

CE QU'IL A, LE CHAT

Ce qu'il a le chat,
c'est un beau berceau qu'il a ;
mon enfant à moi en a
un bien plus beau que ça.

Ce qu'il a le chat,
c'est un coussin blanc qu'il a ;
mon enfant à moi en a
un bien plus blanc que ça.

Ce qu'il a le chat,
c'est un tout fin drap qu'il a ;
mon enfant à moi en a
un bien plus fin que ça.

Ce qu'il a le chat,
c'est un chaud bonnet qu'il a ;
mon enfant à moi en a
un bien plus chaud que ça.

Pribaoutki (Chansons plaisantes)
mises en français par C.-F. RAMUZ.

L'ONCLE ARMAND

Console-toi, viel oncle Armand :
tu te fais bien trop de mauvais sang,
laisse aller tout droit ta jument
à l'auberge du Cheval Blanc :
là est un joli vin clair,
qui fait soleil dans le verre ;
le joli vin rend le cœur content :
noie ton chagrin dedans.

LE FOUR

Louise viens vite,
viens vite ma fille ; —
la pâte est levée...
cours à la cuisine
chercher la farine.
Les canards commencent à souffler
dans leurs mirlitons crevés.
Voilà le coq qui leur répond,
et les poules tournent en rond.

LE COLONEL

Le colonel part pour la chasse,
tire sur une bécasse,
manque sa bécasse ;
tire sur une perdrix,
la perdrix s'enfuit ;
tombe et cass' son fusil ;
il appelle son chien,
son chien répond rien ;
sa femme l'a reçu,
sa femme l'a battu...
chassera jamais plus.

LE VIEUX ET LE LIÈVRE

Dans une ville en l'air,
un vieux assis par terre.
Et puis voilà qu'le vieux
fait cuire sa soupe sans feu.
Un lièvre, sur la route,
lui demande sa soupe.
Et l'vieux a dit comm' ça,
au bossu d'se tenir droit,
au manchot d'étendre les bras
et au muet de parler plus bas.

L'HISTOIRE DU SOLDAT — PIANO-RAG-MUSIC —
TROIS PIÈCES POUR CLARINETTE SOLO sous presse
CHEZ J. & W. CHESTER
11, Great Marlboroughstreet — London-West !
General Agency for the works of IGOR STRAWINSKY.

November 8, 1919. Lausanne. Program for a Stravinsky concert.

Ramuz; but when someone asks me to write them down, as you have just done, I recoil like a snail into its shell, apprehensive that I will reveal too much. Let me explain: in this instance it is a question, you will agree, of making intelligent statements. Now everyone (myself included) can make intelligent statements; but if I am asked to write them down, to fix them, I am quickly overcome by anxiety. It takes skill to write, as you know very well, and I must admit to you that I have never trained myself to do it. Then, too, I confess that I am slightly lazy. But I will gladly satisfy you with a few remarks which you will find in the Post Script. Here they are:

> 1) It was not by "direct order from God" that Gogol wrote the second part of Dead Souls, but following the advice of his religious mentor, Father Rjevaki, a man of great spiritual qualities.
>
> 2) I have never lived in Candebec-sur-Mer and, consequently, could never have written to you from there—a place not even mentioned in Larousse. Carantec does exist, and I wonder if you could have received my letters from there (in 1920, not 1921).
>
> 3) Some other small errors, hardly worth mentioning.* [291]

Hoping that you will not be too angry because of this somewhat evasive response, I humbly restrain myself from sending you any but the very best of my "souvenirs."

*P.S. See my remarks above.

In November 1918, Liudmilla Beliankina (Stravinsky's wife's sister), her mother,[292] her husband, Grigory, their two children, Ira and Gania, and a nurse, "Baba Ania," crossed part of Russia, Poland, and Germany and on about November 20 reached Lindau on the Bodensee, where they were obliged to stay in the Hotel Bayerische Hof for over a month before obtaining permission to enter Switzerland. This was arranged through the Ukrainian Legation in Berne, by means of intrigue, secret diplomacy, and a deposit of gold francs by Stravinsky in person on December 14. The Beliankins finally joined the Stravinskys in Morges on December 21 and remained with them. On February 25, 1920, Stravinsky wrote to Alfred Pochon:

I have enormous responsibilities at the moment, not only those of my own family but also those of my wife's family, which is without any means of assistance. They are very close to me and to my wife, who receives them from Russia, one after the other, without a penny. All address themselves to me.

The Beliankins went with the Stravinskys to Brittany in the summer of 1920, then to Paris, and in 1921 to Biarritz. Grigory Beliankin became a yogurt manufacturer for a time in Paris, and the proprietor of a restaurant in Biarritz, the Château Basque, which at one time had two "orchestras." Stravinsky subsidized this, and his files contain many messages to his publishers, such as that of May 9, 1929, instructing them to telegraph 15,000 francs to the restaurant. The enterprise, which proved to be about as profitable as Balzac's Sardinian silver mines, had to be closed.

The four-hand pieces, *Pribaoutki,* and the *Berceuses du Chat* were reviewed at the time of their publication (almost two years before performance) by the Rumanian ethnomusicologist Constantin Brailoiu.[293] Though too extensive to be quoted here, Brailoiu's essay, in *La Tribune de Lausanne,* Monday, February 18, 1918, deserves mention as one of the few perceptive articles about Staravinsky's music to appear during the war years.

The *Histoire du Soldat*

re-composed suite became, in effect, a new work. . . . On musical evidence alone, it would be almost impossible to discover which version came first; and the same is true of the other works by Stravinsky which exist in two instrumental forms. . . .[294]

Stravinsky completed the *Dance of the Devil* for the three instruments, violin, clarinet, piano, on November 25, 1918, the *Little Concert* on December 1, the *Soldier's March* on January 18, the *Soldier's Violin* some time before January 17, 1919 (according to a letter to Kling on that date), and the *Three Dances* soon after. In certain places, especially where Stravinsky gives pitches to notes played by percussion in the original septet version, the transcription is arguably more interesting than the original. In the *Tango,* for example,

The percussive sevenths and ninths, which replace unpitched percussion, somehow indicate harmonic shapes without intrusively exceeding the essentially rhythmic function. . . .[295]

The first sketches for the *Ragtime* for eleven instruments were completed on November 27, 1917, though Stravinsky did not finish a full draft of the piece until March 5, 1918. This first version of the score requires a piano, in addition to the cimbalom. A letter from Edwin Evans to Stravinsky, March 14, 1918, reminds the composer that they had "talked about ragtime in Paris," and Jean Hugo recalls:

One day in our apartment in the Palais-Royal, Stravinsky, after having drunk an immeasurable amount, played a ragtime that he had just composed, for an audience of Picasso, Diaghilev, Massine, Auric, and Poulenc.[296]

This music is likely to have been the piano reduction of the *Ragtime* for eleven instruments, for which Picasso had drawn the cover, rather than the more-difficult-to-play *Piano-Rag-Music,* which, in any case, was not completed until June 27, 1919.

The Three Pieces for Clarinet Solo, a gift for Werner Reinhart, an amateur clarinetist,[297] were composed on October 19, 1918 (No. I), October 24 (No. II), and November 15 (No. III). Stravinsky told Edwin Evans that they were inspired by Sidney Bechet's *Characteristic Blues.* A letter dated December 27, 1918, from the Zürich clarinetist Edmond Allegra, who played the opus for the first time, thanks Stravinsky for the copy of the music, received from Reinhart, and asks several questions about accidentals. Allegra says that he intends to play the pieces for Reinhart soon and would like to play them for Stravinsky.

The *Three Easy Pieces*—"Music Hall" pieces, Stravinsky calls them in a letter to Ansermet, March 1916—and the *Five Easy Pieces* were composed in the order: *Polka* (November 15, 1914, Clarens, La Pervenche), *Marche* (December 19, 1914, Clarens), *Valse* (March 6, 1915, Château-d'Oex), *Andante* (January 4, 1917), *Balalaika* (February 6, 1917), *Galop* (February 21, 1917, though the melody at four and three measures before ⑤, titled "Cancan" in a sketchbook, was written at least a year before that date), *Napolitana* (February 28, 1917), *Española* (April 3, 1917). All eight pieces were first performed by Nino Rossi and Ernest Ansermet at a concert in the Conservatoire de Lausanne, April 22, 1918. The source of the *Marche* was a tune (No. 486) from a collection of *Old Irish Folk Music and Songs* that Stravinsky had purchased in London at the end of January 1913:

Stravinsky started to orchestrate the pieces, beginning with a twelve-instrument version of the *Marche*, on March 23, 1915. On March 14, 1916, he wrote to Ansermet: "I have done the instrumentation of the Three Pieces [*Marche, Valse, Polka*] for a small ensemble." On September 22, 1920, Stravinsky wrote to Ansermet from Garches, in response to his request, "The *Marche* is orchestrated, not the *Galop*." The orchestration of the *Galop* and the reorchestrations of the *Marche* and *Polka* were completed by August 1921, according to a letter from Stravinsky to Kling on the 28th of that month. Writing to Hermann Scherchen, September 29, 1925, Stravinsky promised the conductor the first performance of a "Little Suite," consisting of instrumentations of the *Marche, Valse, Polka,* and *Galop;* this premiere took place, under Scherchen, at Frankfurt, November 25, 1925. On October 21, 1925, Stravinsky orchestrated the *Andante,* on December 27 the *Española,* on December 21 the *Balalaika,* and on December 31 the *Napolitana,* then regrouped the pieces in their published order as the two "Little Suites." On April 1, 1926, he wrote to H. Kling:

This new Suite No. I, which I conducted in Amsterdam together with the older Suite, should always be performed before the older Suite when the two are played together—so it seems to me after the experience in Amsterdam. . . . Logically the new Suite should be called "First Suite for Small Orchestra"; when the suites are played separately, the piece must have some kind of name but certainly not "Second Suite."

On August 27, 1930, Stravinsky wrote to Paul Sacher:

. . . in spite of my sincere sympathy for that good virtuoso Mr. Aladár Rácz, I never composed a valse, polka or any other piece for him. These two dances to which you refer . . . are undoubtedly the same that figure in the "Easy Pieces," and Rácz has simply arranged them for his instrument.

But in fact Stravinsky *had* made the cimbalom arrangements, and Rácz had the manuscripts. Finally, in Sacher's concert, Stravinsky permitted Rácz to play the two dances as an encore following the *Ragtime.* Writing to Sacher on the subject, Stravinsky also says:

I must tell you that I never conduct before playing the piano, thus *Apollo* must be placed at the end of the program, with the *Capriccio* just before. [Letter of September 9, 1930]

In the late spring and summer of 1919, Stravinsky and Diaghilev quarreled about unpaid performance fees for *The Firebird* and *Petrushka.* The hostilities were conveyed not directly but through Ernest Ansermet, who was conducting the London season of the Ballets Russes:

May 2. Ansermet to Stravinsky: "Diaghilev promises to send your author's rights and the advance on *Les Noces.*

May 4. Ansermet to Stravinsky: ". . . Wednesday evening . . . I immediately spoke to Diaghilev on your behalf. But in spite of my efforts (and his promises), I have not yet been able to obtain any tangible results. . . . In principle he agrees to pay for each performance of the two ballets since the end of the Argentina tour, but he seems to understand this only in the sense of a payment of author's rights, and he pretends that this sum amounts to very little. . . . He prefers to give an advance on *Noces.* . . . The season here seems to be going well . . . and in the autumn and winter he has engagements in Paris at the Apollo, followed by the Opéra. It seems that the latter will include the premiere of *Noces.* . . . He has given commissions to Picasso, Derain, Delaunay; Ravel; Auric and Poulenc (disciples of Satie)."

May 7. Ansermet writes: "Sunday night, after posting the letter to you, I wanted to talk to Diaghilev about you again, and I found him in a very different mood. He is looking for a position that will insure a certain feeling of solidarity with you but at the same time give him an advantage. He began by lamenting the difficult times, saying that his situation was less brilliant than I had thought, that the present season cost a great deal, that he could not tell me before the end of the week if his financial circumstances would permit him to send money to you under one set of terms or another. Then he complained . . . of the affair of *Noces* and *Liturgie.* He pretends to have promised 15,000 fr. for the one, 10,000 for the other; that you pretended the sums were 20,000 for the one, 5,000 for the other; and that finally you are asking 25,000 for the *Noces* alone. He said that he never contracted to give *Noces* at the Opéra, but simply a new work by you, and that if *Noces* was not suitable, he could mount *The Nightingale.* . . . He added that he was hesitating on the subject of *Noces* in view of the expense that it would entail and the rare opportunities to perform it because of the chorus.

... When I returned to the question of the performance rights of *The Firebird* and *Petrushka,* he said, typically: 'Tell Igor that if I hear any more about his attitude in the *Noces* affair, I will stand on my legal rights. But in spite of everything, we are friends and I will pay him. The question is, how much? ... Legally I owe him nothing. *Petrushka* was published in Germany, and I do not have to pay the rights. *The Firebird* is Russian and not protected. ...' "

May 16. Stravinsky to Ansermet: "Unnecessary to tell you that Diaghilev's assertions are without a word of truth. They are a daydream, but conscious and calculated, and your suppositions concerning the brusque change in his attitude toward me are correct. I know too well this *gaillard-là* to be taken in. ... I ask you to mark on a piece of paper all of the performances of *Petrushka* and *The Firebird,* and their dates."

May 16. Ansermet to Stravinsky: "I seize each opportunity to remind Diaghilev of the necessity of sending money to you. I was at his hotel this morning ... but he answered: 'I have just paid Derain a large advance, and yesterday I had to pay the company. I have no money at the moment but will have some next week, and I promise to send an advance to Igor for *Noces.*' ... How much do you want as an advance for *Noces* and how much for author's rights to *Petrushka* and *The Firebird*? With a single exception, one or the other ballet has been on every program since the beginning of the season, which comes to 18 performances."

May 17. Ansermet to Stravinsky: "After the performance last evening, Diaghilev wanted me to take tea with him. I returned to the charge. ... He said that he had never dreamed of *not* paying for *Petrushka* and *The Firebird* and that he'd also decided to pay 25,000 fr. for the *Noces;* I believe that this is due to the influence of Massine. Diaghilev also said that this decision was not determined by 'rights,' but by a feeling of moral solidarity. ... I would be very happy to receive a telegram from you telling me whether or not to accept this proposition, in principle."

May 23. Ansermet to Stravinsky: "Yesterday, when Diaghilev asked, 'Have you news from Igor?', I answered: 'He is hurt by the manner in which you have treated the question of his performance rights, and he does not want to accept your gift.' Diaghilev said: 'Are we strangers to each other that he does not want to take a gift from me?' I replied: 'In this case he is concerned with a particular thing to which he possesses a right.' Diaghilev said: 'I recognize a moral right ... but not a legal one since no law can constrain me; that I grant this is pure good will on my part.' When you see Diaghilev you will discuss these subtleties ... but he will blame me, saying that I have expressed your thoughts badly. (He already said so, in fact, in the continuation of our discussion.) 'Tell Igor that legally, and at bottom, I owe him nothing' ... Diaghilev is giving sensational interviews here against German music ('Fight the Hun in Music')."

May 25. Ansermet to Stravinsky: "It has been a great joy knowing Derain. He is a brother, French of the people, like Picasso before Olga, ... but does not adjust to the ballet. ... He is the first painter I have ever met who is *très musicien,* and it is astonishing the way he feels the music—just as you feel painting! Picasso and Olga arrive today."

May 26. Stravinsky to Ansermet: "Here are the conditions on which your discussions with Diaghilev must be based, but, before stating them, two words: You will understand how repugnant it would be for me to write to him personally, and the 'moral solidarity,' about which he goes on and on, counts for little compared to the monstrosity of his statement that 'since *Petrushka* was published in Germany and *The Firebird* in Russia' he has the right *not* to pay for them, though, since he is good and generous, he will pay a small sum. . . . To digest this made me truly ill. That he could have recourse to legality in such matters, and could make allusion to it at the very moment when a friend finds himself in such a difficult situation, is a most peculiar way to interpret friendship. . . . As I telegraphed to you, I will wait for the moment when he needs me. . . . For the same reason I will refuse the sums of money that he decides to send to me without recognizing my rights, sums that I see as gifts and will not accept."

May 30. Stravinsky to Ansermet: "Diaghilev, it is true (I suppose), experiences feelings of *amitié* and sympathy, for a moment at least, and after having reflected that I might gain an advantage by creating precedents. For that reason he repeats the same thing: that morally he owes me money for the performance of my works, but not legally. He finds it just and normal that a composer (who is his friend), whose works he plays (and which bring him a certain income), is obliged to beg to right and left, while he, Diaghilev, profits from the success of these works. If Diaghilev finds this situation abnormal and unjust, is it not more logical for him to protest against the injustice of some laws, and declare openly that he, Diaghilev, will never obey them? Is it not more logical to behave in this fashion rather than to do what he is doing? . . . Yet he does not protest. . . . On the contrary, he finds these laws perfectly suitable since they provide the wherewithal to surpass them with his generosity. . . . Diaghilev always dealt directly with me, never with my publishers, though he finds it opportune now to make you believe that I was published in Berlin and Moscow. This is foul play, which can turn against him because he also never fulfilled his obligations vis-à-vis the publishers. . . . *The Firebird* is performed from copied, not printed, material, and the orchestra score is my personal property; I ask you, as you promised, to bring it to me on your return. One means of defense would be to publish a letter in the Paris and London newspapers in which I would ask the public to judge between us."

June 1. Ansermet to Stravinsky: ". . . Diaghilev claimed that 'No pieces of paper exist between [myself and Igor]; all that we can cling to is good faith.' He asked Massine to intervene and to say that he had witnessed your agreement on *Noces* and *Liturgie*. But Massine was not present at Diablerets. When I placed the copy of your contract under Diaghilev's nose, I believe that he was about to thumb his nose at me. . . . Last evening he came to the theater as a spectator, with Karsavina and her husband. I said that I had important things to tell him, but he said that since Tuesday he has had too many other worries. Karsavina must make her debut tomorrow, and the seats have been sold at an elevated price, but she . . . has a sore foot. Also, conflicts have arisen with Lopokova and Tchernicheva in dividing Karsavina's roles."

June 10. Ansermet to Stravinsky: "Diaghilev said: 'I have never seriously contested Igor's author's rights, but the law is the law. . . . If I give 20,000 Swiss fr. to Igor for *Noces*, and if I pay for Goncharova, Massine, and the costumes, this alone will cost 100,000 fr. . . . You tell me that Igor has an extraordinary new idea for the orchestra, God knows what—three or four men, so I understand. But perhaps the instruments cannot be found anywhere. Also, he cannot eliminate the chorus, and no director except Rouché wants to give me one. . . ."

June 26. Ansermet to Stravinsky: "[Your publisher] consulted a 'King's Counsel' and, in effect, [the publisher] has pursued Diaghilev and Sir Oswald Stoll before a tribunal. . . . The reply of the King's Counsel is very clear. It turns out that neither *The Firebird* nor your unpublished works can be copyrighted, nor are the performance rights protected by the Convention. On the other hand, *Petrushka* (because it was first published in Berlin) . . . and the works published in Geneva *are* protected. . . ."

June 27. Stravinsky telegraphs to Ansermet: "Please see Mme Edwards Savoy Hotel and candidly explain my differences with Diaghilev."

June 30. Ansermet to Stravinsky: "I have just had a long meeting with Mme Edwards. She is very concerned about you and will try to arrange a settlement with Diaghilev for your author's rights and a decision on the subject of *Noces.*"

July 11. Stravinsky to Ansermet: "I wanted to come to London to see Mme Edwards myself and to insist that she do everything possible with Diaghilev, since, in spite of his affirmation, nothing has happened and the second contract that you sent is no better than the first: I demand protection for my published works. . . . But at the English Consulate in Geneva I could do nothing. . . ."

July 15. Stravinsky to Ansermet: "Still waiting results of Misia's meeting with Diaghilev."

July 18. Ansermet to Stravinsky: "Diaghilev returned from Paris Saturday evening, and I will see him. . . . He told me that he wants to introduce the *Soldat* in his programs, and I replied that you were not ready to consider this before he had settled the question of your author's rights. 'Oh, that's understood,' he answered. 'Misia spoke to me and I will take care of it very soon.' . . . Diaghilev is greatly preoccupied with *Noces:* 'What is this orchestra, and how do you want me to procure these choruses? Can't Igor make a version without chorus? The Opéra chorus rehearses only three hours a week. . . . Rouché came to see me in person and, with a Parisian smile, said: "I offer 100 musicians and am told that we need only four for *Noces,* and that these four are not part of the orchestra. . . ." ' "

July 20. Ansermet to Stravinsky: "I saw Diaghilev at the Savoy this morning. He began by protesting that he could not be the target of any legal action, and he said that he had talked to his lawyer on the subject. This lawyer's argument is that *Petrushka* is protected by the International Convention of Berlin, but because you are a Russian subject, your rights are not protected in England. In other words, the work, German in origin, is protected, but not the author. . . ."

July 23. Stravinsky to Ansermet: "To compound the irony, a subscription in the New York press is coming to my aid. When I wrote to Otto Kahn protesting his right to pirate my work, he replied very amiably that he never had any such intention—using the pretext that he did not know my address. Now he sends 250 fr. each for five performances (the sum I demanded from Diaghilev), at the same time astutely putting himself at the head of the committee which has been formed to send help to me. Notice how different is this attitude from Diaghilev's, who robs me, or wants to rob me, in a far more disgusting manner, Diaghilev having been my friend until now. . . . Perhaps I should reply through the intermediary of Capell in the *Daily Mail,* under the title 'Why must America open a subscription for Stravinsky when his ballets are so successful at the Alhambra Theater?' If Diaghilev knew that I intended to do this, he would change his mind."

July 25. Ansermet to Stravinsky: "I gave your telegram to Diaghilev. He screamed. Still, he is waiting. And I am impatient for your letter. He will go to Stresa and Venice on vacation."

July 28. Ansermet to Stravinsky: "On the condition that you accept Diaghilev's proposition, I will ask him to make a check to you for 10,000 fr., which I will give to you on my arrival. He leaves Friday for Stresa."

August 7. Geneva. Ansermet telegraphs to Stravinsky: "Received money meet me in the station at Morges, Friday. Train 14:14 hours."

Pulcinella

Jean Hugo writes: [298]

Picasso had shown a large album to me of forty or fifty sketches that he had made for the decors of this ballet. . . . His first idea had been to use contemporary, or nearly contemporary, costumes, with ill-fitting and démodé dresses, and with one side of the skirts hanging lower than the other. When Diaghilev rejected this project, Picasso chose the exquisite colors of male dancers' boleros and of female dancers' tutus, and he made but a single maquette showing the costume that was worn by Massine, the white blouse, the red stockings, and the beautiful black mask with the grotesque nose. The result was a certain, perhaps delectable, disagreement between the style of the costumes and that of the decors in this marvelous spectacle.

"Picasso, the tender mandolinist and fierce picador: How much you would like him!" Cocteau wrote to Stravinsky, August 11, 1916. The friendship between the composer and the painter was initiated by Eugenia Errazuriz, who had championed and helped to support both artists. She had planned to accompany Picasso to Rome in 1917 for his meeting there with Stravinsky, but when illness obliged her to remain in Paris, she wrote to the composer: "I have a strong desire for you to make Picasso's acquaintance because one day . . . you must collaborate with him. What a genius! As great as you are, *cher maître.*"

In Berne, April 2, 1917, Stravinsky obtained permission from the Russian Legation to go to Italy *"pour diriger les spectacles des bienfaisances."* On April 11, at the Costanzi Theater, Rome, the Ballets Russes opened with *Fireworks* and *Petrushka* on the program. The following night Stravinsky conducted *The Firebird, Fireworks,* and excerpts from *Petrushka. The Firebird* was repeated on April 15, and, on the 16th, in the Hôtel de la

1920. Poster for the first performance of *Pulcinella*.

Russie, Picasso drew the first of his three portraits of the composer. On the 17th, the company was in Naples, beginning its performances there on the 18th with *The Firebird* on the program. On the 20th, Stravinsky obtained an exit permit to return to Switzerland. On the 24th, leaving Italy via Como, he was delayed by Italian officials and obliged to leave Picasso's portrait behind, on suspicion that it was a map of fortifications—which, in a sense, was true. On May 4, in Morges, Stravinsky sent a music manuscript to Picasso, but the package was returned on May 30, marked "object seized by the military authorities."

In February 1924, Picasso wished to construct a *"représentation plastique"* on Stravinsky's Octet, for a "kind of Music Hall spectacle" (letter of the 11th from Etienne de Beaumont); the Princesse de Polignac and Walter Berry were among the prospective sponsors. But Stravinsky withheld permission to use his music, reasoning that "already as a symphonic piece the work is presented to the auditor in a plastic form" (letter of February 1924, from Stravinsky, in Biarritz, to E. de Beaumont). In the same month, Mme Picabia wrote to Stravinsky that Picasso would probably do the decors for the Paris premiere of *Histoire du Soldat*. But, on February 23, Stravinsky wrote to Ansermet:

I spoke to Diaghilev ... who is probably afraid that if he does not engage you for the Paris season, you will work with me on the *Soldat* for [Etienne de Beaumont], whose organization includes, 1. Satie, who is furious with my non-concurrence as to the success of his recitatives [*non réussite de ses récits*] in the *Médecin Malgré Lui*; [299] 2. Picasso (?); 3. Cocteau; 4. Picabia; 5. Tristan Tzara. . . .

Stravinsky's first and last recorded comments on Picasso are found, respectively, in a 1915 sketchbook for the *Podblyudnya* choruses ("Picasso must be either weary or nihilistic, since he now says that he does not like Cézanne"), and in a copy of Françoise Gilot's *Life with Picasso*, dated by Stravinsky December 1964 ("Picasso is a monster, who at times, nevertheless, is right").

The original playbill for *Pulcinella* reads: "Music by Pergolesi, arranged and orchestrated by Stravinsky." But Pergolesi's name gradually disappeared—justly, as it happens, scholars having subsequently shown that the instrumental music attributed to him in the ballet is actually not his. Writing to the President of the Société des Auteurs, March 19, 1936, Stravinsky objected that the word "arrangement" was not a proper description of his work on *Pulcinella*.

In an interview in *Comoedia*, January 31, 1920, Stravinsky founded the legend that the score is based

on unpublished themes by Pergolesi. . . . Being in Italy, I ransacked the libraries with M. Diaghilev. We discovered many interesting and unknown themes.

But Stravinsky borrowed whole pieces, not simply themes, and he was not with Diaghilev in Italy during the period before the composition of *Pulcinella*, being too busy feuding with him instead. In fact, traveling from Paris to Venice in August 1919, Diaghilev deliberately avoided seeing Stravinsky on the way. The project of a "Pergolesi-Picasso" ballet to be called *Pulcinella* is mentioned in a letter from Ansermet to Stravinsky, June 10, 1919, but exactly when Stravinsky agreed to collaborate and to undertake the "recomposition" of the music is not clear. The contract was signed in December 1919, three months after he had begun work.

Most of the manuscripts were purchased from the "Casa Musicale" of Professore A. Ricci in Naples, who was engaged in selling copies of music from the Naples Conservatory. He pro-

June and July 1920. Two postcards from Picasso. In the first, June 26, from Marseille, the artist asks for "the manuscript of *Pulcinella*" and says that he will leave tomorrow to look for a house in which he can work without interruptions. The second, from Juan-les-Pins, thanks Stravinsky for the manuscript (probably some sketches); the handwriting in Russian is that of Picasso's wife, Olga Khokhlova, shown with him in photo on reverse of card.

vided the excerpts from *Il Flaminio*, *Il Fratello Innamorato*, Cantata IV, the "Gavotta and Two Variations"—marked "Variations I and IV" in Ricci's manuscript—and the Sinfonia for cello and bass, of which the "Presto" movement became Stravinsky's trombone-and-string-bass duet. The other source was the British Museum, where, in September 1918, the cellist and musicologist E. van der Straeten transcribed into score form the following movements from "Pergolesi's" twelve sonatas for two violins and bass:

Sonata 1:	First Movement
Sonata 2:	First and Third Movements
Sonata 3:	Third Movement
Sonata 4:	First Movement
Sonata 8:	First Movement
Sonata 10:	Third Movement
Sonata 11:	Second Movement
Sonata 12:	Complete

Stravinsky did not use any music from Sonatas 4, 10, and 11, and he took only the Presto from No. 12. His copy of the Allegro from "*Sonata 7 pour clavecin*"—the "Toccata" in *Pulcinella*—also came from the British Museum, but is in another hand. The origin of one other manuscript, a collection of string symphonies, or *concerti grossi* (four violin parts, viola, cello, and continuo), is not known, but the last movement in this set became Stravinsky's "Tarantella." It should be said that he rewrote many of the pieces directly on these manuscript copies—among them that of the "Tarantella," which he dated September 7–10, 1919. He was in Paris then, having obtained permission to go there from the Russian Consul in Geneva on September 1 (and permission to return to Morges from the Swiss Consul in Paris on September 16). On September 8, Picasso drew two figures for the ballet and inscribed them for the composer, but the final form of the libretto—in Massine's hand—was not drafted until a month later.

Stravinsky's progress on *Pulcinella* can be followed in his correspondence with Kling. Thus on October 12 the composer wrote that he was working on *Pulcinella*, though, a week earlier, he had cabled to Diaghilev, in London, to the effect that time was being lost on "the Pergolesi" because of the postponement of the *Noces* premiere. On October 13, Stravinsky cabled to Diaghilev: "*Accepte aucune condition ni termes payement. ...*" But, on October 28, a dozen pages of the new opus were mailed to Kling, with a note asking him not to mention this to Diaghilev because the manuscript was supposed to be given to him. Stravinsky's next letter, November 14, explains that he had delayed answering because his wife had been in a hospital in Lausanne. The engraving had been started, and Kling was disturbed because Diaghilev had expressed his intention of altering the scenario. But Stravinsky's letter assured the publisher that any changes would be impossible because "the work on Pergolesi's music is organic," and because each piece is being "recomposed in both timbre and tonality, thereby obtaining a block for the whole." On December 5, Stravinsky revealed that he was composing directly in orchestra score, and, on the 11th, sent the corrected proofs of the first twenty pages. Pages 29–32 followed on January 3, pages 33–8 on the 10th. On the 10th, too, he instructed Kling to send a copy of the gravure to Diaghilev at the Hôtel Continental, Paris, since the impresario "must be shown at least something." On February 5, Stravinsky and Massine signed an agreement with the Société des Auteurs et Compositeurs Dramatiques.

Meanwhile, in October 1919, Stravinsky's interest was aroused by a project to compose music for the Teatro dei Piccoli in Rome. He had been engrossed in the marionette theater since he first witnessed it, and would have agreed with Adrian Stokes that:

Anyone who enjoys a show of Italian marionettes should be capable . . . of understanding all art. For he appreciates the beauty in the trick of imitation realized by mechanical gestures that are generalizations of action, a treatment which in a more "classical" art can be recognized as the use of conventions. Such generalization, the saying of much in the terms of a very limited medium, is the condition of all art. [From "Pisanello," *Hound and Horn,* 1930]

On October 13, 1919, Stravinsky wrote to Vittorio Podrecca, director of the theater:

Monsieur, I have your card of October 6 and am hastening to reply. I know your Teatro dei Piccoli very well, and I love it. During the war I had the occasion many times to see your "plays" and always had the greatest pleasure. In principle, therefore, I am in accord with you to compose the music. But, before all, you must let me see the libretto (in French, if possible, and with indications for the length of each scene, number, or part of the piece, in seconds or minutes). You must also tell me when you have to have the music, and what instrument, or ensemble of instruments, can be used. When I have your answer to these questions, I will tell you if I can accept (my time already being very taken this year) and give you my conditions. Waiting your amiable reply . . .

But Podrecca did not send the libretto—his company was on a tour in Milan—until February 2, by which date Stravinsky was in Paris for the premiere of the ballet version of *The Song of the Nightingale.* It is regrettable that this venture came to nothing, and that Podrecca did not write sooner, for Stravinsky might have left a masterpiece in a genre unlike any other.

The libretto had been adapted from the Homeric *Batracomiomachio,* "The Battle of the Frogs and Mice," arranged in five scenes with a prologue, and involving many droll characters. Podrecca wanted twenty minutes of music for an ensemble of piano, flute, clarinet, trumpet, percussion, four violins, a viola, a cello, and a bass—conditions that would surely have attracted the composer of *Histoire du Soldat.*

After the Paris *Nightingale*, Stravinsky returned to *Pulcinella*. The remainder of the music was sent in batches, on March 11, 12, 26, 27, and April 10. The overture, written last, was completed on April 24 and mailed on the 26th. The vocal scores for the three singers were posted directly from the publisher to Misia Sert (at the Hôtel Meurice), who gave them to the performers. On May 7, Stravinsky arrived in Paris to supervise the rehearsals, which Ansermet conducted.

It was already the season of outdoor parties and after the first performance of *Pulcinella*, Prince Firouz of Persia gave one . . . in a strange little château, a large hall with balcony all the way around and doors opening from it to rooms—exactly as described in Radiguet's *Le Bal du Comte d'Orgel*. We went . . . in a caravan of automobiles, directed at crossroads by porters with flashlights . . . Stravinsky, Picasso and his wife, Diaghilev and Massine, Misia and Sert, the Princess Eugène Murat, Lucien Daudet, Jean Cocteau . . . others whom I forget, and Radiguet, who immortalized the evening. Prince Firouz—Mirza in the novel—was a magnificent host, and we drank champagne copiously. Stravinsky became drunk, went up to the balcony and the rooms, took the pillows, the slats and the mattresses from the beds and threw them everywhere from the balcony into the hall, where we fought each other with the bed linen until the party finished at 3 in the morning.[300]

Returning to Morges not long after this, Stravinsky began to pack and, on June 2, 1920, obtained permission for himself and his family to leave Switzerland for Paris. On June 8, the Stravinskys left by train for the French capital.

Genealogical Table

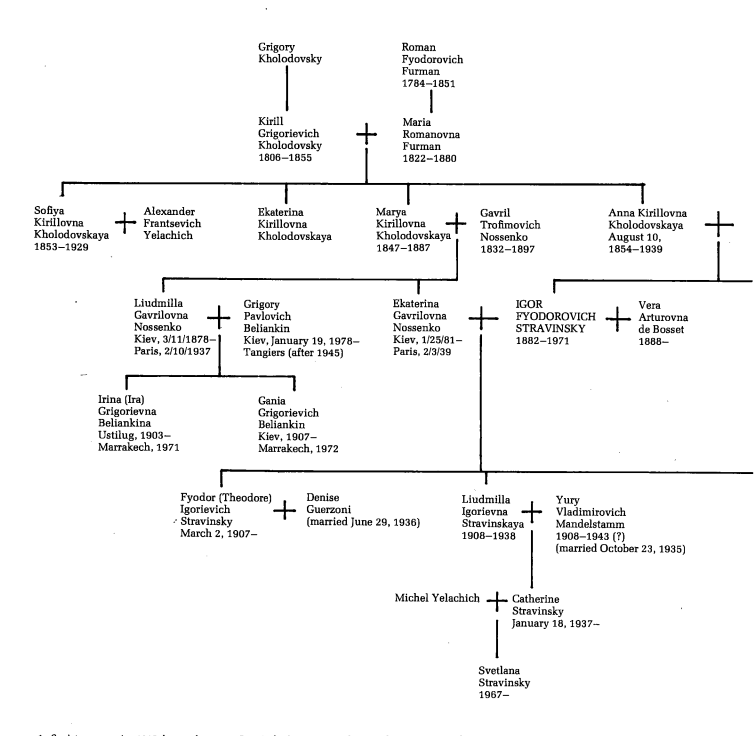

Grigory
Kholodovsky
|
Kirill
Grigorievich
Kholodovsky
1806–1855

Roman
Fyodorovich
Furman
1784–1851
|
Maria
Romanovna
Furman
1822–1880

Sofiya
Kirillovna
Kholodovskaya
1853–1929

Alexander
Frantsevich
Yelachich

Ekaterina
Kirillovna
Kholodovskaya

Marya
Kirillovna
Kholodovskaya
1847–1887

Gavril
Trofimovich
Nossenko
1832–1897

Anna Kirillovna
Kholodovskaya
August 10,
1854–1939

Liudmilla
Gavrilovna
Nossenko
Kiev, 3/11/1878–
Paris, 2/10/1937

Grigory
Pavlovich
Beliankin
Kiev, January 19, 1978–
Tangiers (after 1945)

Ekaterina
Gavrilovna
Nossenko
Kiev, 1/25/81–
Paris, 2/3/39

IGOR
FYODOROVICH
STRAVINSKY
1882–1971

Vera
Arturovna
de Bosset
1888–

Irina (Ira)
Grigorievna
Beliankina
Ustilug, 1903–
Marrakech, 1971

Gania
Grigorievich
Beliankin
Kiev, 1907–
Marrakech, 1972

Fyodor (Theodore)
Igorievich
Stravinsky
March 2, 1907–

Denise
Guerzoni
(married June 29, 1936)

Liudmilla
Igorievna
Stravinskaya
1908–1938

Yury
Vladimirovich
Mandelstamm
1908–1943 (?)
(married October 23, 1935)

Michel Yelachich

Catherine
Stravinsky
January 18, 1937–

Svetlana
Stravinsky
1967–

1. Soviet sources give 1915, but a telegram to Stravinsky from Petrograd, November 20, 1916, reads:
"Uncle Alexander died today."
2. Some sources give 1876. Inna Stravinsky was an actress.

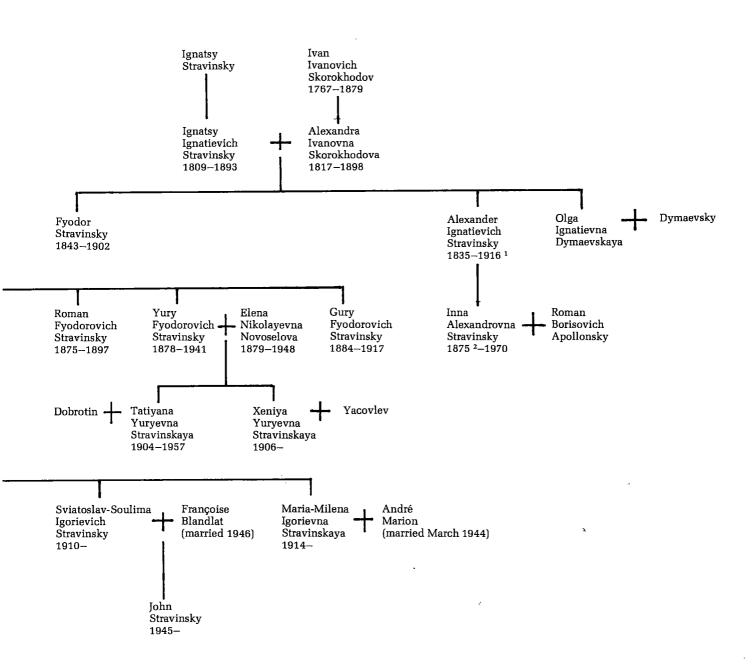

Interlude:

Obiter Dicta*

* From the beginning of his life as a peripatetic concert artist, in the 1920s, and until his death, Stravinsky gave a vast number of interviews. In any selection of extracts from these, his voice and his philosophy and style emerge with greater force than they do in descriptive commentaries. Moreover, these statements, taken largely from newspapers of the 1920s and 1930s, do not depend on contexts. The sources and the languages of the publications are listed at the end, but not the language that Stravinsky used, since in most cases this cannot be ascertained. Interviewers in New York often spoke Russian or German with the composer, but their reports do not mention language. Nor do the Scandinavian newspapers note the original language of Stravinsky's Danish, Norwegian, Swedish, and Finnish interviews. A conversation published in Czech seems to have taken place predominantly in Russian, but Stravinsky approved a French transcript of the article, prepared by his friend, the Prague conductor Tallich. Also, the interviewer for the Berlin Börsencourrier, Heinrich Strobel, always spoke French with Stravinsky. The problem is typified by a 1937 Chicago newspaper headline: "Stravinsky, in German, says he's French."

Un musicien, doit-il parler de lui et de ses oeuvres? Non, n'est-ce pas? [1]

A true creator should not lose his time discoursing about the tendencies and consequences of his art. . . .[2] *[And] I do not want to be a critic. I am in the world to create my own way. . . .*[3] *[Still,] I could make a very exacting criticism of my music. For example, it is not free from dryness. But that is the price of precision. La Bruyère is dry.*[4]

I happen to be a believer; but I do not think that this has anything to do with music. I have been endowed with musical gifts and I know that I must make the best possible use of them. But that is the limit, so far as I see it, of the relationship between metaphysics and art. . . . Music is not an instrument of divine knowledge, but is born solely because of the innate need to create. . . .[5]

I do what was done before, but in a different manner. . . . The problem may be the same, and the problem of creation is to find the relationships that suit the creator. I am enlarging the periphery of a departure point that I consider my own, and the movement produced around it, the curve of its line, is perfectly logical, as exact as that of a wheel around its axis.[6]

My theory? Do I have one? I attempt to erect certain kinds of architectural constructions. My objective is form. My improvisations inevitably evolve into formal constructions.[7] Nevertheless, I do not believe in the triumph of forms on this earth; ideas triumph, not forms.[8]

Divine Order, and not a speculative, artificial one, is the only domain in which order itself can be exercised in plenitude. The struggle against anarchy and the absence of order (more that than disorder) must be manifested in the interior life as well as in its exteriorization through music and painting. In the arts I believe in architecture above all, because it establishes order. Suicide is the most terrible sin because it despairs of order and returns to nothingness from which God has lifted us for and by form. To create is to protest against anarchy and nothingness, and suicide and the absence of order are protests against God. . . .[9]

We do not know about the future. The future does not exist; it is something that will exist. One supposes that it will exist. What will exist? The music that has always existed will always exist. If you ask me about the music of the future, I cannot say because this is music that does not yet exist. . . .[10] As for the past, I prefer to refrain from pronouncing on that, since it no longer exists. And I try to abstain from speaking of the present, not being certain of the justice of my judgments, since I am in them myself.[11] Nonetheless, art is an anticipation of the future. Art is a question of intuition, for the most part, and the artist's intuition expresses things at the moment of their appearance that ordinary people do not understand.[12]

Every revolution presupposes a doctrine. I had none when I was composing Le Sacre du Printemps. I simply wanted to speak my own language, which might seem new, and, at first, incomprehensible, since it was contrary to certain rules, customs, and especially certain clichés. For me this new language was perfectly natural, but to others it seemed revolutionary. . . .[13]

You cannot tell where music is going any more than you can tell where people are going. Each time creates its own needs.[14]

One day upon entering my hotel in New York [in 1925] I encountered a large group of newspaper reporters come to solicit interviews from me. In order to accommodate all of them, I invited them into my hotel room, where they sat on the floor taking notes. They asked a collective question, "What do you think of modern music?" I remained still, motionless. "Gentlemen, you are undoubtedly on the wrong floor. . . ." [15]

What is "modern"? Who is "modern"? No doubt everyone now living and working considers himself modern. Of course, there are some who live with yesterday's wigs on their heads. Yet they are exceptions. Most of us try to give, or to contribute, something fresh and new, man always being under the influence of growth. . . .[16]

It is said that I write music for the day after tomorrow. But my music is in the music of today. Could it be that the public is that of the day after tomorrow? [17]

In France one speaks of a "Compositeur de musique," which seems quite enough. In my passport, I have purposely put "inventor and composer of music" as my occupation. Thus a composer is not only an architect but also an inventor, and he should not build houses in which he cannot live. I fear that many such houses are being built today. After all, anybody can compose, and if one is even slightly talented, the absence of the "inventor" may be overlooked.[18]

The workmanship was much better in Bach's time than it is now.

One had first to be a craftsman. Now we have only "talent." We do not have the absorption in detail, the burying of oneself [in craftsmanship] to be resurrected a great musician.[19]

Romanticism, inspired by the spirit of the Middle Ages and the mystic spirit of improvisation, is not concerned with making objects. . . . At the moment, therefore, art is hostile to Romanticism, feeling closer to classicism because of its clarity of form. But we must be careful with these demarcations. Weber is a classicist in the Romantic period, and so is Mendelssohn. Both of them dress in the clothes of their time, but the skeleton underneath is that of classicism, in the sense of construction and clarity of form. We must also distinguish construction as an esthetic—that of the worst architects, for example—and construction which, in the case of good architects, results from necessity, or utility, which simply means being sensitive to the needs of life. Utility in music is manifest in the proportions of episodes, and in that which is salient in the outline of a construction.[20]

Concerning surrealism, I must confess that I have not fully penetrated its essence and its directives. In any case, I do not identify with it, for I do not work with subjective elements. My artistic goal is to make an object, clearly, and with a natural apportioning in it of my own self. I create the object because God makes me create it, just as he has created me. . . . I cannot accept surrealism or communism, despite my belief that on many points both are right, and that the bourgeois is the one who is not right. . . . I am unable to accept materialism, as proclaimed by the surrealists and the communists, because my religion makes me a dualist, and, in the search for the beautiful, the fusion of material and spiritual is everything.[21]

Expressionism involves individuality, cubism personality. Individuality is suspect, but never personality, which is almost a divine concept, the quality of being as a gift of God. Individuality is recognized in the world of the spirit as a form of refined pride, or egoism. Personality: person: the receiving and the returning. Play a scale in C major metronomically and ask someone else to do the same. The difference in the playing is the proof of the presence of personality. . . .[22]

There are different ways of loving and of "appreciating" music. One of them . . . I would call selfish love, that which asks music for general emotions such as joy, sorrow, the subjects of dreams. . . . But why not love music for itself? Why not love it as one loves a painting—for the good qualities of the painting, the design, the composition? Why not give music a value in itself, independent of sentiments and images? . . . Music does not need an adjuvant. . . . Nothing is more difficult to talk about than music, and the moment one leaves the ground of its technique, one plunges into a wave where one flounders ["on plonge dans *la vague et on divague*"]. Robert Schumann, than whom few can have thought more deeply on the subject, concluded by declaring that in music nothing can be "proven." [23]

The audience? What I ask of it is simply to listen to the music that I have written without trying to discover in it what is not there. A composer is happy, perhaps, if the person who listens to him tries to be in communion with his thought and with his inspiration.[24]

That which is unnatural in form can be mystifying, which is the reason why one stands with some respect before those skyscrapers whose entrances are on the roof and whose tops are on the street. But such structures cannot have lasting value. The machine-man is possible, of course, but only where there is no soul. Besides, he would be interesting only for a very short time.[25] *

Style is not a framework into which the . . . work is inserted, but the work itself. Form is not a means to an end . . . but creation itself. . . . Human work is conceivable only in form. . . . The Russian word *stroi*, loosely translated as "agreement" [expresses what I mean]; we need a working "agreement" between ourselves and the surrounding chaos. . . . When I compose, a great number of musical combinations occur to me. I have to choose and to select. But what standards should I use? Simply that only one form pleases me and the others do not. . . . The result resembles a predetermined physical or chemical experiment. All that we are able to do is to surrender ourselves to the course of the experiment that is being conducted in and by us. . . .[26]

It is harder to be a composer than anything else in the world today, first because of the many noises that one must hear and guard against. The streets, the neighbors, the radios—even when the radio is turned off, the vibrations that I know are going on everywhere, waiting to be released in . . . malevolent sounds from that little box, have the power to disturb. But it has always been difficult to be a composer. A doctor confirmed for me that inside one's ears are the instruments for balancing the whole body. One tiny muscle there is drawn tightly all the time with the effort to receive and transmit the sensations made by the music I am hearing in my mind, together with the impressions or interruptions from the outside, and this affects the whole nervous system. Sometimes I have staggered when I got up to walk about after a long period of concentration and composition.[27]

When the music is not so noisy we feel better, our nerves are better, our nostrils feel better. At home I compose on an . . . upright piano, muted, covered with felt; then I hear everything. I can enjoy. . . .[28]

. . . even when I do not feel like work, I sit down to it just the

* Stravinsky may have been thinking of La Mettrie.

same. I cannot wait for inspiration, and inspiration at best is a force brought into action by effort. . . . Understanding is given only to those who make the active effort, and listening is not enough.[29]

Inspiration is secret, occult. One can be inspired within four walls . . . or in the outdoors, far from the root [the concrete sound of the piano], though outdoors one commits the biggest errors; it is better to be close to the root. The impulse that can come from a machine, from a drug, from any stimulus is not inspiration but something external. . . .[30]

When I start a work, an idea from inside has taken me, and, when starting, I may see the end or the middle but *not* the beginning. That has always to be found, has to be developed in the spirit of the composition, that discovery of the correct entrance to a piece.[31]

I wish people would let me have the privilege of being a little bit unconscious. It is so nice sometimes to go blind, just with the feeling for the right thing.[32]

The idea of the [Piano] Concerto was not spontaneous . . . which is to say that at the beginning of the composition I did not see that it would take the form of a concerto for piano and orchestra. Only gradually, while already composing, did I understand that the musical material could be used to most advantage in the piano, whose neat, clear sonority and polyphonic resources suited the dryness and neatness which I was seeking in the structure of the music I had composed. . . . I never said that my Concerto was written in the style of the seventeenth century. I did say that, while composing it, I encountered some of the same problems as the musicians of the seventeenth century, and also Bach. What are these problems? They are purely technical and refer to the form: how to build with the musical material that comes from my brain—themes, melodies, rhythms—everything that has a power in a spirit dedicated to musical creation. . . . Beethoven had other problems, and you can readily see that those of my Concerto have nothing in common with his, just as Philippe de Champaigne had nothing in common with Delacroix.[33]

I am a musician of my country, but Bach, a German of the great epoch, has all of my veneration.[34] . . . J. S. Bach's music—so formal, *fait à froid,* music of pure architecture, making one think of stone rather than of nuances—is played in symphony concerts by Wagnerian orchestras. As a result, the public, if it were to hear Bach's music in the original sonorities, would find it very ugly and cry "sacrilege." This is what I call a deformation, an attack on music, a great ignorance, a misunderstanding, a stupidity.[35]

I was born under *Das Wohltemperierte Clavier,* and I write in the well-tempered scale. I have heard some of these experiments, Alois Haba and the rest. It seems to be like ordinary music just a little false—Es klingt falsch—all they succeed in writing is quarter-tone Brahms.[36] I hear only in half-tones. Quarter-tones sound to me like portamentos, or glissandos between [half-tones]. . . .[37] Once when I was calling on Hindemith in Berlin, he invited me to inspect a quarter-tone piano. It was an instrument that had been specially constructed in Berlin. It looked like any other piano, but with two keyboards—two floors. . . . Each half-tone had its division into halves, the first division on the upper floor, the other on the lower. After a few minutes I had no difficulty in thinking in quarter-tones: turn everything into quarter-tones and you have the identical thing. As soon as you had got accustomed to the quarter-tones and comprehended what they are capable of, you found it was a construction that had always existed in your head. . . . Through quarter-tones we are richer in the number of notes. But being richer in notes, we are not richer in any other respect. We are enriched only unilaterally. . . . It is true that the Orientals have the small intervals . . . but we are not Orientals. Our music stems from the Greeks, and it is not easy to make over an educational system that has lasted for thousands of years. We would have to be made over ourselves. . . . The Oriental is attached to the symbol, the religious idea; he is concerned with the symbol of thought rather than with the notes. To the Oriental, each melody must have a significance before he can accept it. Theirs is not music for music's sake.[38]

Atonality, polytonality,* those do not concern me, and in fact I think that polytonality is nonsense; I have not been able to find anyone who could perpetuate this principle. . . . But *nothing* should be done according to theory.[39]

The sixth, mi-sol-do, is not at all the inversion of the fifth, do-mi-sol, but an entirely new chord with its own character and expressive construction: a third becomes a fourth. . . . Beethoven and the other old masters understood the character of the sixth perfectly clearly, of course, but the great art of a Palestrina in changing chords by suppressing and doubling notes has fallen into decline. . . . Composition was governed by merciless laws then; nevertheless they cultivated a taste that enabled people to distinguish good from bad.[40]

Color is an inspiration to me when writing music. But when it is written, the music . . . is its own color, [hence,] color, which is its own realm, must be suppressed.[41]

Instrumentation? One instrumentates first and orchestrates afterward, arriving at mixtures of colors. . . . But what interests me is

* "Much of Stravinsky's music, and also of my music, looks as if it were bitonal or polytonal. Therefore the pioneers of polytonality used to regard Stravinsky as one of their fellow polytonalists. Stravinsky, however, deliberately denies this circumstance even in such exterior features as orthography." (Béla Bartók, *op. cit.*)

this: to place the music in the instruments. Each instrument must receive the music for which it has the best voice. . . .[42] But I don't care if you count out tone color altogether and simply give me a piano. Cannot everything be said on the piano that needs to be? [43] Orchestration is good when it corresponds exactly to the character of the composition. It has been said a thousand times that the Brahms symphonies are poorly orchestrated, heavily, that is, and with little variety of color. But this critique is unjust: the instrumentation of these symphonies is precisely what it should be, given the genre of the music.[44]

. . . I had to go through an extensive overhauling of whole sections of [the] piano reduction [of *The Rake's Progress*]. My idea in doing this has been not only to give the piano reduction a better pianistic [style] but also and mainly to bring it acoustically closer to my original orchestra score. . . . Don't waste your time in putting in instrumental indications as they only make the score harder to read. Besides, with my music one cannot have the right idea by reading a vocal score in which the instrumentation is given only piecemeal. . . .[45]

. . . in my stage works . . . I have always endeavored to find an architectural basis of connection. I produce music itself. Whenever music itself is not the aim, music suffers. . . . I have never made applied music of any kind. Even in the early days in *The Firebird* I was concerned with a purely musical construction.[46]

Jeu de Cartes: . . . although related to the dance, the form of the music is strictly symphonic, [nor is] there any descriptive element illustrating scenic action that might hinder the sense of the symphonic development. . . .[47]

Since I am definitely not in a position to take a direct part in your production of *Antony and Cleopatra* [in Gide's translation], my role will naturally amount to composing a certain quantity of musical numbers. Therefore, I must talk seriously with you or with Gide, for I really want to find out how you intend to present Shakespeare. If, as I suspect, you are going to stage him in the spirit of the sumptuous settings of *Saint Sébastien* or *Helen Spartanskaya,* then I definitely cannot imagine a link between the music I would be interested in composing and such a treatment of Shakespeare. I do not feel capable of composing "mood" music, like Debussy's *Saint Sébastien,* no matter how good in itself. Therein lies the most important question.[48]

Practical restrictions I have always welcomed, psychological restrictions, no! People say to me, "Create atmosphere." Comment? Create atmosphere. How can one? I am ashamed. I blush. I am absolutely incompetent to create atmosphere, I say to them. You must create atmosphere for what I write. I cannot artificate.[49]

[You say that] "*Petrushka* inaugurated a new era for us and made us forget the suavities of Impressionism." Well, that is not for me but for music history to decide. And why should we forget what was good in Impressionism? It is enough to forget the bad. If I did not continue in that direction, this was because it was contrary to my nature, and because it seemed to me that what Impressionism had to say had already been said. . . .[50] I have a great veneration for Debussy, to whom a deep friendship binds me. . . . The Impressionists prepared the way for the avant-garde.[51]

So far as the story is concerned, Petrushka—whether pianist, musician, or poet—becomes involved in the most banal plot. But the focus of the action is the Charlatan, the realistic spirit who reveals that Petrushka is full of sawdust. The Charlatan does not hear the melodies in Petrushka's heart, or see the pictures in his soul, but instead makes commerce out of him. This is sometimes called symbolism. But let us call it truth, since the poet never dies.[52]

I feel myself to be far from the aesthetic of Fokine. . . . One evolves, and I have the luck to have very little memory, which is what enables me to begin each new step of my life forgetting the past. We were saturated with Classicism at the time [of Fokine's new ballets], and today it has returned with a new and doubly powerful fervor. . . . I consider Petipa to be the greatest artist of all, the founder of a choreographic canon without rival. . . . When Diaghilev asked me about the "argument" of my *Apollo*, I answered that none exists, and that this is the key to the mystery of Terpsichore. . . . What are the connections that unite and separate music and dance? In my opinion, the one does not serve the other. There must be a harmonious accord, a synthesis of ideas. Let us speak, on the contrary, of the *struggle* between music and choreography. . . .[53]

As to the question of the title of my new ballet, I stick firmly to "*Apollon Musagète*," and I deduce that the conversation which you have had about this was with Diaghilev . . . : but it is absurd to say that the words "*Apollon*" and "*Musagète*" constitute a pleonasm, "*Apollon*" being a name and "*Musagète*" a function. "*Musagète*" means *conducteur* of the Muses, not *constructeur;* Muses, after all, are not houses. . . . What really displeases Diaghilev is that America will give the premiere, and he wants to find something wrong with the title, which he would like to change for his premiere in Paris. I am certain that this is true, knowing Diaghilev very well.[54]

[Francis Poulenc: "One day I came to see Stravinsky while he was composing *Apollo* (1927). He had discovered the poet Boileau, which seems somewhat odd. But Stravinsky thought that Boileau was a marvelous poet. 'Do you like Boileau?' he asked. I said: 'Yes . . . not madly, not like Racine.' He said:] 'What is wonderful is that I have found in the *Art poétique* exactly the couplet that I needed to fill an exergue under the title for a variation of one of my muses.' " [55]

The music [of *Pulcinella*] will be by Monsieur Stravinsky-Pergolesi.[56] The ballet is an original composition that completely transforms the elements borrowed from Pergolesi. *Pulcinella* is not a harmonization or orchestration—which terms constitute the usual meaning of "arrangement"—but a true composition in its own right, the borrowed material having been developed in an original way.[57]

I discovered a new Tchaikovsky, one whom I defend against the success of his Fifth Symphony. . . . Just as a good portrait contains as much of the artist—if he is not a mere copyist—as of his model, so my Tchaikovsky portrait contains Stravinsky. . . .[58] [Tchaikovsky] is reproached for "vulgarity." But it seems to me that to be "vulgar" is not to be in one's proper place, and surely Tchaikovsky's art, devoid as it is of all pretentiousness, cannot be accused of this fault. . . . The "pathos" in his music is a part of his nature, not the pretension of an artistic ideal. . . .[59] This evening or tomorrow you should receive the copy of the two-hand piano score of the first tableau of Tchaikovsky's posthumous *La Vierge des Glaciers*.* [60] The program of the Monte Carlo winter season is posted everywhere around here, and on it is emblazoned "*Le Baiser de la Fée* by Yegor Stravinsky, music to a tale by Andersen." First of all, my name is well enough known not to call me "Yegor." Furthermore, I alone am the author of the libretto, not Andersen, of whom not even a hint has remained. . . .[61]

[Scriabin] is an example of the nefarious influence in Russia of German music at its most sentimental and pedantic. Each time that the influence of French and Italian music has been felt in Russia, the result has been an opening up, a flowering. . . . Tchaikovsky, of course, adored Mozart, but he was an Austrian, which is very different from being a German. . . .[62]

I see from your letter that you do not agree with my criticisms of the works and activity of Glazunov and the other academics. But I am not . . . given to mindless denials. I concede Glazunov's reality and his contribution to the world of academic music. But academicism is a negative phenomenon, nothing but shouting at the top of one's voice, an uncontained evil. The academic is addicted to the shapeless, the unformed, and I cannot respect the person who does not hold himself back.[63]

Russia is a very conservative and old country for music. It was new just *before* the Soviets.[64] The style of Shostakovich's *Lady Macbeth of Mzensk* is extremely disturbing, and the score is a

---

* I.e., of Stravinsky's *Le Baiser de la Fée*.

work of lamentable provincialism in which the music simply serves as illustration. But it was first acclaimed [in New York] by a bewitched public. . . . In Paris two years ago, his First Symphony made a far better impression on me than this opera has done. . . . the music plays a miserable role of illustration, and in an embarrassingly realist style. Formless, monotonous music—a system of recitatives with entr'actes during which the conductor works up the applause of a public delighted at being brutalized at the arrogance of the very numerous communist brass instruments. [As for] this première (and, I hope, dernière) . . . I regret to have to be so hard on Shostakovich, but he profoundly deceived me both in his mentality and in musical value. . . . This is not the work of a musician but the product of a total indifference to music in the country of the Soviets.[65]

The influence of Prokofiev [on Markevich's Rebus] is discernible and should already have been shed. . . . Since the technique is strong enough, the explanation for the failure of the piece should not be looked for in that direction. . . . The young composer is not a Wunderkind but an Altklug.[66]

I went to a concert here [Los Angeles] of Soviet music . . . with utterly hopeless pieces by Tikhon Khrennikov and Kara Karaev. . . . Never have I heard such rubbish . . . and of course I could not leave. . . . I am obliged to smile but would like to vomit. . . .[67] The U.S.S.R. is a nightmare, a madhouse. Stockhausen goes there with pianists, and Nadia Boulanger—why the hell does she have to go there?—and even a festival of my music takes place. . . .[68]

I have read Dr. Zhivago in Russian and am saddened and disappointed by the book. It is awfully old and reminds me of Peredvishniky.* How strange to have written such a book after the event of James Joyce.[69]

Some composers have found their most potent inspiration in folk music, but in my opinion popular music has nothing to gain by being taken out of its frame. It is not suitable as a pretext for demonstrations of orchestral effects and complications, and it loses its charm by being déracinée. One risks adulterating it and rendering it monotonous. . . .[70]

. . . historical and ethnographic exactitude are not of great importance. What does matter is precisely the naïve and dangerous wish (velléité) to imitate what was created instinctively by the genius of a people. Many artists . . . have suffered from the effect of this ultimately sterile tendency.[71] The Greek myths have always attracted me . . . they feed the creative imagination. . . . But I visualized the character of this music [Orpheus] as a long, sustained, slow chant, composed independently of any folklor-

* A group of naïve painters in the 1870s.

istic elements. . . . Even if I knew ancient Greek music, this would be of no use to me. The . . . painters of the Renaissance rendered the stories of ancient Greece or of the Bible in the European landscapes and costumes of their own time. . . .[72]

Movements of all sorts may be introduced into the dance, but on the condition that the canons of the dance and its immutable laws are respected. . . . Well, choreographers who respect these principles have become rare.[73] I proposed to George Balanchine . . . that he give me carte blanche to do a new ballet [Agon] for them. I told him that he had done so well in adjusting dances to symphonies that I would like to write a special symphony with the dance in mind. It is to be a dancing symphony. . . .[74]

I like jazz when it is the simple expression of *la musique nègre.* I like it a great deal less in its Anglo-Saxon transcriptions. Should one borrow from jazz, and should it influence composers today? These are delicate questions, since each musician conceives his own expression according to his own temperament and personality. Jazz remains an art form so long as it does not lose its origins.[75] But jazz does not bring anything new. It emphasizes the rhythmic side of music, which has been neglected for more than a century; yet this is a secondary element, now pushed into prominence. Having been neglected for so long, it is only natural that rhythm in music and dance should now be in the forefront. What needs to be adjusted is not this, however, but the musical verb. . . .[76]

Jazz is not music, if, as aesthetes do, one uses the word to signify a form of spiritual elevation; in fact, one of the great merits of jazz is that it opposes such habits and conceptions. . . . That young people understand jazz as dance music does not concern me; in any case, these people are not going to waltz to the first movement of the *Eroica.* . . . Jazz is not an art created for eternity, but a mode, and, as such, destined to disappear. . . . It also corresponds to the taste for the *ersatz.* . . . After all, style, or mode, created the *ersatz,* which the public prefers to the original. . . . But at present all of the arts are marked by a nervous search for values. Each art is in a problematic situation, since so much contemporary art seems spurious and false. But it is a mistake to see its future entirely pessimistically. Without doubt, it is in the synthetic forms of the present that music will find its future.[77]

Aléatorisme is not a substance but a character of music. . . . *Sérialisme,* which has to do with the very body of the music, is a substance because it has an order. Silence in music is a substance because it has a duration, a beginning, and an end.[78]

[Though difficult to record], the voice is perfect on the telephone. Now I will tell you a funny story. In St. Petersburg, when I was twenty-two, I was a private pupil of Rimsky-Korsakov. The telephone was new then, and he had the telephone at the same time that we had the telephone. I called him every day and he called me. One day I called and said, "Nikolai Andreyevich, can I come to see you tomorrow at three?" "Of course," he said, "that's all right. But you smell of wine." So we laughed together. A great invention, this telephone, so new, so perfect, that when you listen you can smell wine.[79]

I know of nothing more difficult than recording. One has to rehearse over and over again. . . . Then, when the spirit is wilting under the monotony of the work, at that very moment everything must be perfect, since only then does the actual recording begin. I have never had to make a comparable effort. Furthermore, the obligation to listen coldly to myself before an apparatus without taking part in the action, and to be unable to correct an error in the performance, or a mechanical fault—that is worse than the most cruel criticisms. . . . The whole process is governed by a stop-watch and it is not unlike trying for a record in sports.[80]

I received a letter from Stokowski in which he says that . . . he wishes to study the Sacre and to record it if I am willing. Unless this recording has already been made, I am very eager to stop him, not being at all confident of his tempi. You understand that, unlike a concert performance, a recording is definitive. . . .[81]

[When] I am asked "Who is the best conductor?" . . . I answer "myself," without blushing. I don't like performances made without my personal touch.[82] It is fifteen years that I have tried to perform my music as often as possible myself. . . . A composer can be "interpreted" by another conductor, but his music can be "realized" faithfully only by himself.[83]

Please do not think that I do not admire [Chopin]. . . . [But] I have higher honor and admiration for the great Liszt whose immense talent in composition is often underrated.[84] Chopin writes piano music, which comes from the soul of his piano-conceived work, while Liszt usually takes music for other instruments and arranges it for piano.[85] Liszt is a more interesting composer than Wagner. . . . [I have] great feeling for Brahms. . . . You always sense the overpowering wisdom of this great artist even in his least inspired works. . . .[86] What the public likes in Brahms is the sentiment. What I like has another, architectonic basis.[87]

What shall I do? One part of the press says that I should continue to shock. Another part says that I am now making the right music since I have started to compose like Verdi. They are actually unable to hear that I am doing something different altogether![88] Verdi! Verdi! The great mighty Verdi. How many beautiful things there are in his early works as well as in the final ones. I admire him unconditionally, a truly great composer! I prefer Verdi to all other music of the nineteenth century.[89]

I had time before leaving New York to fix with Auden the main lines of an opera [*Delia*] in one act. . . . Auden is "blue-printing" the libretto, and he will complete it with Kallman when the latter (whose collaboration is very valuable) will be back. The theme is . . . a celebration of Wisdom in a manner comparable to Ben Jonson's Masques. Nevertheless, we will not stick to any set style musically or otherwise. The opera will require about six characters; a small chorus, a chamber ensemble of about 18; several tableaux.[90]

Much to the contrary of the traditional concept, which submits music to the psychological expressiveness or to the dramatic significance of the word, in my *Oedipus Rex* the word is pure material, functioning musically like a block of marble or stone in a work of sculpture or architecture. *Les Noces*, in contrast, consists of songs, written in verse according to the Russian words. These do not make much logical sense, but, instead, follow an order suggested by their possibilities in rhythm and sound. *Oedipus* represents a great advance on this, for while the musical work that uses a living, contemporary language has many elements that evoke emotions and sentiments in us, the language destroys the value of the words as pure musical material. For this reason, the use of a dead language is justified, and I prefer Latin to Greek and Slavic because Latin is definitely fixed—as well as universal, thanks to its diffusion by the Church.[91]

I wanted the Hebrew [of *Abraham and Isaac*] to be sung in a different manner than in the religious tradition, which is fixed. I did the same thing in Russian. My *Noces* is not sung like Tchaikovsky or Rachmaninoff, after all. . . . The baritone has a double role, that of a narrator who tells the story, and that of a singer, who comments. . . . The language led me to employ appoggiaturas, as in Arab chant, for example in the repetition of the vowel a-a-a-a. . . . As for the serialism, that is perfectly natural; it is the *other* way which is exhausted. I cannot do otherwise. . . . Schoenberg understood this.[92]

[The public sees continuity in my later music] like people recognize my face even though it is older.[93]

Part Two

FRANCE,

JUNE 1920–

SEPTEMBER 1939

Concert Tours in
Europe,
the United States,
Canada,
Argentina,
Uruguay,
Brazil

Romantic music was a product of sentiment and imagination; my music is a
product of motion and rhythm.—From an
interview in RVL, a Russian newspaper in
Paris, June 1928

Modern music does not exist. We speak in
a different language from that of our
ancestors but say the same things—or express them differently.—From an interview in Mannheim, December 1930

"Modernism" as a movement is not a
scientific idea but a sentimental one. . . .
—From an interview in Bologna, May 21,
1935

A fter Stravinsky moved from Switzerland to France, in June 1920, his music was influenced to an unprecedented extent by the circumstances of his life. On February 19, 1921,[1] he met Vera de Bosset, Mme Serge Sudeikin, the woman who was to be his companion for fifty years. Then, in 1924, he embarked on a career as a conductor and pianist,[2] with a radical effect on his work. For the first time, too, his new music met with avant-garde as well as general-audience resistance,[3] partly because of the increasing popularity of the old;[4] one result of this was that he began to formulate a philosophy of art, something that he had not needed before. Finally, the creative eruption that began with The Firebird, and that had seemed to come almost entirely from within the composer—the exploration of the rhythmic, harmonic, and other possibilities discovered in his first ballets—had run its course. Pulcinella, which followed this extraordinary efflux, was the first of Stravinsky's creations that did not originate in his own imagination. His acceptance of the commission may imply an awareness that he could no longer rely exclusively on his inner resources.

As early as 1911, Stravinsky had decided that someday he would live in Rome. In May of that year, he completed Petrushka in the Italian capital,

which I loved so much that I signed and dated the score in Latin letters, the first time I was to do so with any of my music. [Interview with Renzo Giacomelli, Bologna, May 21, 1935]

At the end of the 1914–18 war, Stravinsky made up his mind to abandon his comparatively secluded existence in Switzerland and to make his home in Rome. But when his friends there were unable to find an apartment for him,[5] he stored his possessions [6] in Paris and spent the summer in Carantec, Brittany, where he composed the Concertino and Symphonies of Wind Instruments.

That Rome rather than Paris had been his first choice of residence must be recognized as essential to an understanding of Stravinsky's entire future. It helps not only to explain his frequent sojourns in Italy, and the disproportionately large number of concerts that he gave there, even with orchestras of the second rank, but also to excuse his political blindness to the country in the 1930s.[7]

In September 1920, Stravinsky and his family, still in Brittany, were rescued by Gabrielle Chanel, who placed at his disposal her home in the Paris suburb of Garches. But, since Chanel soon became his mistress,[8] the presence of a wife and children was awkward, and, in May 1921, he moved them to Biarritz. "On a quitté Garches définitivement," he wrote to Kling on May 26, and Stravinsky himself had already moved to a studio at the Maison Pleyel, 22, rue Rochechouart, by the beginning of April.

The Chanel affair was first publicized by the late Paul Morand, who seems not to have perceived the bragging in her late-in-life memory of it:

... Stravinsky was young and timid, and I pleased him. ... Misia began to suspect that something was happening without her knowledge. ... One day Stravinsky said that he wanted to have a concert of his music [9] in the Salle Gaveau, but that he needed a financial guarantee. I said that I would arrange everything. ... When Misia heard about it she pretended to be "suffoquée par le chagrin" to think that Stravinsky had accepted money from me. ... When the Ballets left for Spain, Stravinsky asked me to come with him. ... .[10]

But no one who knew Stravinsky will believe that he ever considered divorcing in order to marry Chanel, or that he would invite her to accompany him—publically, in effect—to Spain, especially since, by this time, he was having an affair with the Chauve-Souris singer Katinka.[11] Morand concludes with the puerile comment that Chanel

transformed Stravinsky from a self-effacing and timid man to un homme dur et monoclé. ... .[12]

After returning from Spain, Stravinsky installed his family in Biarritz, an arrangement that entailed long periods of separation from his wife and children. The reason for this should now be stated, Stravinsky having at first pretended that Biarritz had been chosen because of its healthy climate and superior educational facilities.[13] But the true explanation was his desire to be with Vera de Bosset Sudeikina, from the time of the Sleeping Beauty revival (November 1921) his constant companion, whom he was to marry (1940) after the death of his first wife (1939). From 1921 to 1939, a triangle was the geometry underlying Stravinsky's existence. Here is an excerpt from a letter to Ramuz, June 16, 1924:

... returning to Paris, I will join my family in Biarritz and leave again in ten days with Catherine for Nice to look for our future home. ...
Here [Paris] I go with Vera in the evenings to the Ballets Russes or to

the Cigale. . . . One sees only *snobisme* . . . and princesses who have nothing else to do but invite you to luncheons. . . .

This resulted in considerable humiliation for both women, since the secret, though open, was unacknowledged. For Stravinsky, it resulted in much loss of time, the logistics of his marital dualism requiring countless letters, which he had to write himself, to agents, hotel managers, and intermediaries; thus he wrote to his Berlin agent, Dr. Peter Sirota, asking him to procure visas "for me and my secretary, Mme Vera Sudeikina, 82, rue des Petits-Champs" (letter of October 3, 1924). On August 31, 1925, he was obliged to write to Alfredo Casella asking him to arrange for a visa for Vera Sudeikina to come to Venice (more difficult to obtain in her case than in Stravinsky's). And, in 1929, he wrote from his home in Nice to his publisher, Gavril Gavrilovich Païchadze,[14] in Paris:

. . . Give the suite [No. 2] . . . to Vera, who comes to join me at Toulon to go with me to Barcelona. She leaves Paris this Saturday.

Stravinsky's double life developed a certain deviousness in him as, for example, when planning to go to Argentina in the spring of 1932 and, in order to have a cabin next to Mme Sudeikina, he arranged for the steamship tickets (the S.S. *Cap Arcona*) to be purchased through influential friends in Germany. (Letter to Willy Strecker, February 20, 1932) He seems to have lived in mortal fear that his mother would discover the truth about his double life, but she never did.

Guilt feelings were one of the many consequences of Stravinsky's personal situation during the 1920s and 1930s,[15] and so was the new religiosity which appeared in his music as well as in his life.[16] As frequently happens in such cases, his wife became extremely devout, and her letters to him contain passages from the Saints, most notably the words of St. Cassian in a note of February 26, 1936, in which she also remarks that "You wrote the truth the other day, that your life is difficult and that you devote it all to us." Visitors to his homes in Nice and Paris describe "an icon of the Virgin with a small flame flickering in front" (*Le Jour*, May 16, 1936)—*La Vierge de Perpétuel Secours* with votary candle. And references to saints begin to appear with increasing frequency in his correspondence. Writing to René Auberjonois, for example, July 6, 1928, the composer looks forward to the painter's summer visit with him "in the country of St. François de Sales, this great saint. . . ." As late as October 24, 1950, Stravinsky wrote to the wife of his elder son asking her to look for

the diptych of Saint Suaire that was always on my piano and that must still be in storage in the Rue Antoine Chantin.

Numerous entries in Stravinsky's sketchbooks and even on his printed music are followed by drawings of the Russian cross—sometimes unexpectedly, as after the "Variation de Polymnie" in *Apollo*—and by references to confessions and communions. Thus the first sketch for the theme at [20] in the Piano Concerto is dated "Tuesday, 17th July, St. Alexis's Day," the cover of Stravinsky's performing copy of the Sérénade en la is inscribed "Nice, April 9, 1926, after Confession and Communion," and his first draft for the music from [198] to [200] in Oedipus Rex, "March 13, after my Confession and Communion, Father Nicolas [Padasseroff] [17] at home."

Like an act of prayer, Stravinsky wrote a Pater Noster [18] during the composition of Oedipus Rex, his largest-scale work of the two decades from 1914 to 1934, imbued in spirit, language (Church Latin), and musical substance, with religious feeling. Its emotional depth far exceeds that of anything he had written before, and the music is expressive in ways entirely new for him. The melos in the part of Oedipus might have been inspired by ecclesiastical chant and by such devices as the pneuma, whose power of feeling had been remarked in the fourth century by Jerome and Augustine. The style of the chorus part frequently evokes the Church, as well, and, with other words, might have been used in a sacred composition. Stravinsky's religious feelings attained their fullest expression three years after Oedipus, in the Symphony of Psalms, though obviously neither the Psalms nor the later religious pieces can be explained simply as products of his divided life. The dichotomy was no more than a catalyst, and no doubt the religious side of the composer's nature would have emerged without it.

The practical side of Stravinsky's new modus vivendi is easier to measure. It required him to spend so much time in transit from Paris to Biarritz [19]—and, later, from Paris to Nice and Grenoble, when the family moved twice again—that the world is poorer by at least one symphony; in fact, and as a letter to Werner Reinhart reveals, Stravinsky was planning to compose a symphony and to finish it by the spring of 1926:

Scherchen is half right about the symphony; I am planning to compose one this year. [August 1, 1925]

In addition to his concert tours, this commuting kept him in almost perpetual perambulation until 1935, by which time his wife's [20] and elder daughter's tuberculosis had worsened, and the family had to be installed in Paris. His daughter Liudmilla ("Mika") died in November 1938, and her mother three months later, after which Stravinsky, who had the disease himself in 1937 and feared a recurrence, entered a sanatorium, where he remained for six months. Until emigrating to California in 1940, the composer was taking ten centigrams of quinine daily against lung infections, one of which was eventually the cause of his death—but thirty-four years later, proof of an astonishingly strong constitution, given the state of his health in 1937.

Stravinsky was present at the revival of Le Sacre du Printemps, London, June 27, 1921,[21] and the next day's Times reported that

M. Stravinsky got a laurel wreath . . . and the whole house roared itself hoarse while the protagonists held their trophies and each other's hands and bowed themselves to the ground.[22]

Jacob Epstein made two drawings of the dancers.

A year later, Cocteau and Mayakovsky, among others, kept notes on their visits to Stravinsky in his studio. This was in a pianola factory, next to Chopin's former rue Rochechouart residence—of all things blasphemous to the memory of the least mechanical of the poets of the keyboard. Stravinsky served as translator for the two writers on an occasion described by Cocteau:

During an interview which I had recently with the Russian poet Mayakovsky, Stravinsky acted as interpreter. The conversation took an unfortunate turn. It was not only a question of running from one language to another, but from one epoch to another. . . . Stravinsky went on translating. I could learn nothing from the expression on Mayakovsky's face, which resembled that of a prodigious baby. The real sight was our interpreter, who was engaged upon a strange sort of smuggling adventure, traveling all alone from one tongue to the other, and only letting through what he chose to let through. . . . [La Revue Musicale, December 1923]

Mayakovsky's impressions of Stravinsky in his extraordinary habitat are dated November 18, 1922:

The soul-searching wail of pianolas being tested floated up even through closed doors. . . . the composer's tiny upstairs room was crowded with grand pianos and pianolas. Here Stravinsky creates his symphonies; he can hand his work directly in to the factory, trying the musical proof on the pianola.[23] He speaks rapturously of the pianola, of composing for eight, for sixteen, even for twenty-two hands! [24]

Here are two further descriptions of Stravinsky in his pianola-factory pad:

To see Stravinsky in Paris, in his rooms over Pleyel's, where he lodges, is to see an animal in its carapace. Pianos, drums, metronomes, cymbals, American pencil-sharpeners, desks, rings, spats, scarves, eyeglasses, pince-nez, [gold] chains. He inherits from N. A. Rimsky-Korsakov orderly habits. . . . On Rimsky's table the ink bottles,[25] pen holders, and rulers revealed the bureaucrat. Stravinsky's order is terrifying. It recalls the surgeon's instrument case. [Cocteau, op. cit.]

The composer lives in an instrument factory whose repair shop is a constant source of interest and pleasure for him. He has only one room, and an alcove containing a single piece of Henri II furniture. . . . Piles of plates are spread on the small table where he eats, and pajamas of all colors are hanging on the wall. The room contains a sofa-bed covered with rough cloth and a small piano at which Stravinsky, with his pelisse on his back, dreams and works, smoking long cigarettes one after the other to the very end. On the walls are the percussion instruments of the orchestra: bass drums, side drum, triangle, xylophone, Chinese bells, chimes. . . . Stravinsky appeared suddenly, under an extraordinary armature of clothing, a small wiry man with a strong nose, thick lips, and the features of an ancient Chinese bronze.[26]

Between the world wars one change in Stravinsky's life with an immediate effect on his music was his new career as a performing artist. This was the result of financial necessity [27] but became an artistic one also.[28] The royalties from his music were insufficient to support a family (increased by his Beliankin relatives). Since even the largest commissions for new works could not compare to the fees that concert artists receive in return for very small investments of time, Stravinsky realized that the podium offered him the most practical means of enlarging his income. Thus, with precious little experience, and at the comparatively advanced age of forty-one, he began to accept engagements as a conductor or pianist, soon having more of these than many performers on the circuit who were not composers.

Stravinsky's conducting technique was by no means highly developed. In fact, he had tried his hand at it only a few times before his official debut, in which he led the premiere of the Octet (1923). But audiences came to see the composer as much as they did to hear the performer, and within two years he was guest-conducting, or playing the piano, from Copenhagen to Venice, Warsaw to Chicago. The most important consequence of this on his composing was in terms of the time subtracted from it, while the chief artistic compensation was that he could provide model performances—a major consideration, since Stravinsky blamed the lack of appreciation of his new music on the way it was played. On this subject, here is a French critic quoting some remarks by Stravinsky to an orchestra during a rehearsal in Paris in December 1930:

The French people possess in the highest degree the gift of precision and the rhythmic sense. This should not be neglected and for this reason *I want you to inherit the right tempo from me.* [Hector Fraggi, in an unidentified Marseille newspaper, December 23, 1930.]

It has also been alleged that Stravinsky acquired a firsthand knowledge of the orchestra and of the technique of orchestral performance from his conducting experience. But did he need this? Has anyone ever known more about both than the composer of *Le Sacre du Printemps,* who had never conducted anything? Chiefly, however, and apart from the effect on his composition, conducting accounted for the largest share of Stravinsky's income for the rest of his life.

Unlike conducting, Stravinsky's piano-playing [29] both determined the medium and shaped the content of about a third of the music that he composed between 1923 and 1935. But first, here is a sensitive description by Elliott Carter of Stravinsky's "electricity-filled piano playing":

I have a very vivid memory of him playing over the score of *Perséphone* (the humanistic rite of spring) with René Maison singing the part of

Eumolpe, at the apartment of Nadia Boulanger in Paris, a few days before the premiere. What impressed me most, aside from the music itself, was the very telling quality of attack he gave to piano notes, embodying often in just one sound the very quality so characteristic of his music—incisive but not brutal, rhythmically highly controlled yet filled with intensity so that each note was made to seem weighty and important. Every time I heard him play, in the Salle Pleyel, in Town Hall, or wherever, the strong impression of highly individualized, usually detached notes filled with extraordinary dynamism caught my attention immediately—and this was true in soft passages as well as loud.[30]

Addressing an audience in Buenos Aires in 1936, Stravinsky said that his *"vif appétit"* for the piano at the time that he wrote the Sonata and the Serenade could be attributed to "the instrumentation of *Les Noces*, which comprises four separate piano parts." In any case, the Piano Concerto, Sonata, *Capriccio*, and Concerto for Two Solo Pianos were designed as vehicles for his own use, and at first were even reserved exclusively for himself.[31] So were the *Duo Concertant*, written for his concert tours with the violinist Samuel Dushkin, and the arrangements for violin and piano of excerpts from the ballets. Like the pianola transcriptions, these are technically interesting, though all of them together are scarcely worth the shortest original composition.

What matters is the extent to which Stravinsky tailored his piano music to his specifications as a performer. He once protested that

to play both the *Concerto en la* [32] and the *Capriccio* in the same concert would require too many rehearsals, each work demanding no fewer than three, while the difficulty of the change of technique involved in such different pieces is enormous. [Letter to the Westdeutsche Konzert-Direktion, Cologne, April 4, 1930]

His keyboard style in any music was marked by a *staccato-sforzando* touch, a *secco* tone,[33] an avoidance of the pedal—all in the interest of that clarity of articulation which is reflected in his own compositions for the instrument. It follows that his abilities and limitations as a pianist are also imprinted on his piano music, for while he was not obliged to solve every conducting problem in his orchestral scores—conductors can and do leave orchestras to their own devices—he *had* to play his Sonata, his Serenade, and his Concerto.[34]

Does this personal requirement restrict the music's technical range? [35] In most types of keyboard virtuosity, Stravinsky cannot be compared with, for example, Rachmaninoff, though their respective performing skills correspond to the different kinds of music that each composed. Yet Stravinsky, if not his compatriot, might have written even more innovatively for the piano if he had had someone other than himself in mind to play the music, as in the case of his arrangement of the *Three Movements from Petrushka* (1921) [36] for Artur Rubinstein.[37] (Perhaps the most richly exploratory piano part in the music of this century is that in *Pierrot Lunaire*, whose composer was unable to play even its simplest passages.)

This obviously overstates the case. The author of *Capriccio* exploits to perfection his own characteristics as a performer. Nor could he have been guided exclusively by his own performing technique in composing the Concerto for Two Solo Pianos, a demanding piece to play by any standards.[38] But the influence of the pianist on the composer is evident in the Concerto, and so, too, is that wretched pianola's, at least in the first movement, which is as mechanical as any music Stravinsky or anyone else ever produced.

Perhaps some of the patchwork impression of the second movement may be attributed to an attempt to counteract the metronomic rigidity of the first. But tempo itself is a problem in the second movement. Stravinsky had not written music of this character and speed before, and he seems less than certain of the way to do it, as one of his rare instrumental miscalculations, the lumbering, foursquare *tutti*, demonstrates. Furthermore, neither the "Russian" tune at the beginning of the movement nor the "popular," all too advertently "contrasting," second tune is in the composer's natural voice; and these melodies, together with the stereotyped accompaniment figurations and the perfect cadences, are ill-assorted stylistic components. Stravinsky was in trouble here, failing for the first time in his twenty years as a composer to concinnate his materials and to make alien ones his own.

Obviously no one could have predicted the form of Stravinsky's emergence from this comparatively bleak terrain. Whatever else, therefore, *Oedipus Rex* must have come as a huge surprise, its sheer size and emotional force being utterly unlike anything that the forty-five-year-old composer had done before. Nor could Stravinsky himself have foreseen the evolutionary path from *Pulcinella* to Sophocles' drama, and on from there to the new esthetic of *Apollo*. The composer's instinct for seeing the new in the old was apparent already in *Pulcinella*, as was his uniquely inverted relationship with the past, for he embodies Borges's paradox about the artist creating his precursors, actually making us believe that "Pergolesi" borrowed from *him*. With the Sonata and the Octet, his future pointed to an increasing dependence on The Uses of the Past.[39]

The variety of Stravinsky's music of this period is bewildering. Only ballet, heretofore *his* form, is missing. Looking back, he drew some conclusions about the origins of musical constructions in the sonorous materials themselves:

The only forms which are worth anything are those which flow from the musical material. . . . We have wind instruments, stringed instruments, percussion instruments, and the human voice: there is our material. The form should derive from the actual use of these materials. . . . [*The Observer*, London, July 3, 1921]

The composer also seemed to be trying to convince himself that he was no longer Russian, at any rate not in a line of descent from Balakirev and Rimsky-Korsakov. But neither was Stravinsky French, of course, being in fact deeply isolated from the French music for which he was to provide so many models. Deprived of his cultural base, he tried to piece together a new one from whatever came to hand: ragtime, early-nineteenth-century *opéra-bouffe*, sonata (the *Three Movements from Petrushka* were first performed—by Jean Wiéner,[40] Paris, December 26, 1922—under the subtitle "Sonata"), theme and variations, jazz fugue, Verdi aria. In 1924, he sketched a vocal work, *Dialogue Between Joy and Reason*, on a text in Old French; some of the music was used in *Perséphone*, but it is worth noting that, after renouncing Russian, Stravinsky turned to an archaic language even before he chose the peculiar Latin of *Oedipus Rex*.[41]

In January and February 1921, Stravinsky wrote eight piano pieces of such extreme simplicity that it seems as if he were trying to rediscover in them both his own roots and the elements of composition.[42] At one point, he began to question former principles of instrumentation, declaring that "sounds struck and sounds bowed do not go together."[43] And, between 1920 and 1926, he eschewed strings altogether except for a solo trio of them to support the voices in *Mavra*. One of his theories at the time was that

the natural difference of the volumes of wind instruments renders the musical architecture more evident.[44]

He was also opposed to the use of nuances, and suspicious of *sfumato* and similar effects.

As the first original opus to appear after *Pulcinella*, the Concertino for string quartet would have been of interest for that reason alone. Where, in what direction, would Stravinsky go? The musical substance of the piece develops logically from *Histoire du Soldat*—and on successive pages of the same sketchbook. But the new work is predictive as well as retrospective. It contains formal elements that anticipate the collage of motives in the *Symphonies of Wind Instruments*,[45] a score that looks back but *not* forward, apart from its concluding Chorale, which is the prototype of the "apotheosis" in the later secular pieces (and of the "*consecratio*" in the sacred ones).

Yet the novel motivic architectural principle was not developed in the Octet, that other perfect creation of the *Pulcinella*-to-*Oedipus* interregnum. Thus the Octet and the *Symphonies* are the *termini, post* and *ante quem*, of Stravinsky's Great Divide, the Octet marking the beginning not only of his neoclassicism— "A much abused expression meaning absolutely nothing," Stravinsky told a Brussels interviewer (*Le Vingtième Siècle*, May 27, 1930)—but of his preoccupation with esthetics, more later.[46] The *Symphonies* score is dated November 30, 1920, the fugato in the Octet, February 1, 1921,[47] hence the index point of this epochal change in musical philosophy can be narrowed to December 1920.[48]

Perhaps no one understood Stravinsky's neoclassicism more clearly than Béla Bartók:

...the *Pulcinella* music is only a preparatory study. [Stravinsky's neoclassical period] really starts with his Octet for wind instruments, followed by his Concerto for Piano (wind instruments and percussion), piano solo pieces, and many other works too numerous to mention here. Just at the beginning of this period, when I once met Stravinsky in Paris, he told me that he thinks he has the right to incorporate into his music any material he believes to be fit or appropriate for his purposes. This belief reminds us of Molière's saying: *"Je prends mon bien où je le trouve."* With this conviction, Stravinsky turned to the music of bygone times, to the so-called classical music of the seventeenth and eighteenth centuries, for a new starting point. This start again shows pure evolutionary principles and is by no means revolutionary in concept.

The opinion of some people that Stravinsky's neoclassical style is based on Bach, Handel, and other composers of their time is a rather superficial one. As a matter of fact, he turns only to the material of that period, to the patterns used by Bach, Handel, and others. Stravinsky uses this material in his own way, arranging and transforming it according to his own individual spirit, thus creating works of a new, individual style. Had he tried also to transpose Bach's or Handel's spirit into his work, imitation and not creation would have been the result.[49]

With *Mavra* and the Octet, each new creation was introduced by a private preview, newspaper article, interview, radio talk, or public lecture—even though Stravinsky protested that "to speak of my own music is more difficult for me than to write it," [50] and though, not long before, he had refused Jacques Rivière's invitation to write for the *Nouvelle Revue Française*. In the case of the Concerto, Stravinsky, with Jean Wiéner at the second piano, played the piece in the Salle Gaveau, May 15, 1924 (a week before the premiere with the orchestra), giving a talk about it beforehand and repeating both the two-piano performance and the lecture that same evening at the Princesse de Polignac's. By the 1930s, Stravinsky had become less reticent about writing articles, and a letter to him from Blaise Cendrars in September 1932 reveals that the composer had agreed in principle to write a book of a polemic nature for an American publisher. This may have developed from a request, received from New York in 1928, to participate in the promotion of his music by new means. On November 27, Stravinsky's New York agent for his pianola recordings wrote to his agent in Paris:

We are extremely eager to have an introduction and commentary by Stravinsky on his Piano Concerto for a demonstration at an audiographic exhibition in January. . . . It has been suggested that M. Dubois go to Stravinsky with a stenographer who could take Stravinsky's conversation by dictation. . . . We will make the translation here and organize the annotations necessary to present this material in a film. . . . As you know, the New York public's impression of Stravinsky is very special and not very favorable. We wish to change this by audiographic means and to make his principles clear as expressed by himself. . . . To this end we have prepared a questionnaire. . . . M. Stravinsky will be able to polish his answers before the document is placed in the Bibliothèque Audiographique.

The questions, titled *"D'un Profane à New York à Stravinsky,"* are unanswerable:

As an artist it is your task to express the beauty that you have discovered. . . . You have succeeded, for your part, since you have seen a new beauty and found the new forms to reveal it. But we have failed, since we do not entirely understand it. . . . For example, when you played your Piano Concerto in New York in February, 1925, we were stirred by the strength of the music but did not grasp its meaning. . . . The critics failed us, moreover, saying that a new beauty cannot exist if *they* have not perceived it. Thus we turn to the last source, the composer himself.

Nineteen largely vapid questions follow, but Stravinsky penciled replies in French in the margins of a few of them, then wrote a section-by-section analysis of the Concerto, translating his text into dictionary English. Here are a few extracts:

Prelude, processional movement.

No. 35: Leaving the theme No. 2, I build up a new period based on the rhythmical development which followed same theme after its exposition.

No. 39: Rhythmical piano-solo cadenza (in its first phase) which determines in its second phase the value of the metrical unity and which allows me to place in its previous movement . . . the processional music of the *Prelude.*

Second Movement: I straight start with solemn and large song.

Third Movement: . . . I straight begin this allegro by a theme which will be developed in fugato form.

No documentation survives to indicate whether or not the *"Profane à New York"* was helped to grasp the meaning of the Concerto.
 In the late 1920s, not all of Stravinsky's apologias were written by him, though he seems to have initiated all of them and certainly kept them on short leash. This is the case, for example, with Arthur Lourié's[51] *"Apropos de 'l'Apollon' d'Igor Stravinsky"* (*Musique,* December 12, 1927). While the score was far from complete when Lourié saw it, his essay interpreted Stravinsky's new musical philosophy in the light of Thomist ideas on the correlation of esthetics and ethics that Lourié, a disciple of Jacques Maritain, had been inculcating in Stravinsky since the beginning of their acquaintance.[52]
 The influence of Arthur Lourié on Stravinsky's thinking in the mid-1920s requires a book in itself. Here it must suffice to say that Lourié was partly responsible for the formulation of Stravinsky's *"homo faber"* philosophy, expressed by the composer in numerous writings. But Lourié would have been remarkable even if he had never known Stravinsky. In Petrograd, two years before the Revolution, Lourié became a friend of Olga Glebova Sudeikina,[53] the first wife of Vera de Bosset's second husband, as well as a friend of Vera Sudeikina herself. In 1917,

when the Sudeikins moved to Yalta, Lourié remained in Petrograd, where, in October of that year, Lunacharsky [54] appointed him commissar of music. In 1920, in faraway Brittany, Stravinsky wrote to the new commissar, whom he did not know—and to an intermediary P. Katzenthal,[55] who had aided the composer's mother during, and in the period following, the Revolution—asking for help in obtaining a visa for her to leave Russia for France. Lourié did intervene, but permission to emigrate was withheld for two more years, by which time he, too, had gone to Paris, where he was introduced to Stravinsky by Vera Sudeikina. Stravinsky respected Lourié's musical opinions, was interested in his philosophical ideas, and enjoyed his company. Lourié soon became Stravinsky's musical coadjutant and was entrusted with proofreading [56] and with such tasks as making the piano reduction of the *Symphonies of Wind Instruments*. Stravinsky gave the original full score of *Histoire du Soldat* to Lourié in gratitude for his work correcting the proofs of *Les Noces*, which he was uniquely qualified to do because of his knowledge not only of music, but also of Russian and French.[57]

Lourié's letters to Stravinsky reveal that the ex-commissar was planning to write a monograph on the composer. The letters range from technical questions about music to such observations as:

I have just read the *Spiritual Exercises* of Loyola, thinking the while that if you were a theologian, you would write in the same way; you have the same dry passion. [November 1, 1924]

Something of Lourié's own qualities, as well as of his role in Stravinsky's intellectual life, is revealed in a letter which he sent from Paris to Stravinsky in Nice, December 17, 1927, after Schoenberg had conducted the world premiere of his Septet-Suite in the French capital:

Igor Fyodorovich, I mourn the death of Sologub,[58] purest and wisest of men. . . . Two events have occurred in the musical life here, Schoenberg and Theremin.[59] Everyone plays Schoenberg—orchestras, chamber groups, even in the salons—and we have also had *causeries, connaissances, convictions.*[60] I went to his concert yesterday [actually December 15] at the Salle Pleyel. The atmosphere was exciting, but I had an extremely poor impression of the music. He seems to want to shock and overwhelm. A big reception was given for him and his wife. . . .[61]

The second event, Theremin, really *was* a sensation. He is an engineer, a gifted technician whom I knew in Russia long ago, now en route from Berlin to London and America. He has invented something fantastic, music without an orchestra, or instrumentation: *electric music!* He improvises on an electric instrument—gesticulating like a conductor, which looks like witchcraft, but after a few minutes you begin to understand and become interested. If the "theremin" is developed, it can be used in the cinema and radio. I was bored, *à la longue,* but I will tell you more when you come to Paris.

Now I must add a disagreeable note. Sabaneyev [62] wrote an attack on *Oedipus Rex* and somehow got Chester [63] to print it. Sabaneyev and

Chester are both scoundrels; the one good thing is that nobody reads the *Chesterian*. It would be helpful if you could write to Edwin Evans, who, perhaps, can print *my* article about *Oedipus*. Or, if not, I might be able to find another review in London. Sorry to bother you with this.

Perhaps Lourié did more than any other critic before Theodor W. Adorno [64] to establish the notion of Schoenberg and Stravinsky as thesis and antithesis, and Lourié's "Neogothic and Neoclassic" (*Modern Music*, March–April, 1928) was profoundly influential in this regard. Countless interviews with, and articles about, Stravinsky at the time begin with statements similar to the following from a "*gespräch*" with him in the *Dresdner Neueste Nachrichten*, Friday, February 1, 1929:

The work of this man embodies one of the elements of the New Music. Arnold Schoenberg's work embodies the other.

No doubt a composer or painter is always mistaken in trying to explain in words what the public does not feel or cannot follow in his work, a fact of which Stravinsky was well aware. His main objective in his writings was to make distinctions, and in this he shows his legal training and philosopher's mind. But he also felt that it was important to inform his audiences of the existence of laws of art and of the imagination with which artists alone are conversant, and to serve notice that to criticize a functioning artist (e.g., himself) is useless. Criticism, it goes without saying, was neither enlightened nor disarmed.[65]

Of the two categories of Stravinsky's writings, dialogues and discourses,[66] he preferred the former—together with *pensées*, which he collected, especially those of Rozanov—since the dialogue allowed for instant changes of subject, and, above all, could take directions chosen by himself. The following exchange, for instance, was obviously dictated by Stravinsky. The so-called interrogator for Radio-Paris (March 23, 1936) was Charles-Albert Cingria, and Stravinsky had just returned from a concert in Spain:

C.: Did you bring back anything [from Spain]?
I.S.: Some impressions and some Sherry—the most remarkable that I could find. Also some Manzanilla.[67]
C.: Were you pleased by Paris on your return?
I.S.: I live here.
C.: Well, what monument pleased you most?
I.S.: The Madeleine.
C.: The exterior or interior?
I.S.: The interior.
C.: How I understand you. If one says the exterior, everyone agrees.

Stravinsky's autobiography,[68] published in April 1935, attempts to summarize his artistic stance in the mid-1930s. But the one statement from this book that still clings to his name—"Music is powerless to express anything at all"—is simply another form of the Kantian hypothesis that, to be truly beautiful, a thing should signify nothing but itself. Stravinsky was merely declaring his belief in the absolute autonomy of music. Lourié's friend Maritain failed to understand this. Writing to Stravinsky on July 28, 1935, the philosopher proposed another line of pursuit than the one that, in any case, the composer had denied:

From my point of view it would be necessary to confirm the existence of something entirely different from the expression of feelings. I refer to "creative emotion" or "creative intuition"; by means of this, the artist, without being aware of it, speaks to himself in his work as God does in the act of creation. I have written several pages on this subject in my *Funèbres de la Poésie* (pages 192–99), and I would be happy to know what you think. . . .

What Stravinsky thought seems not to have been committed to paper, but he was undoubtedly shocked by Maritain's analogy.[69] Few contemporaries have known with the firsthand certainty of Igor Stravinsky that a "creative emotion" exists. As for God, while listening to the *Symphony of Psalms*, one can feel that Stravinsky may also have had some knowledge of Him.

It was on the recommendation of the Godebski family (Misia Sert), who had lived in Carantec before World War I, that Stravinsky moved there in June 1920. Since no piano was available either at the Hôtel Charles, where he stayed,[70] or in the neighborhood, the composer wrote to the Pleyel Company, Paris, on June 9, and an instrument was sent on the 11th. At the beginning of August, Stravinsky, his wife, and her sister Liudmilla Beliankin went to Paris (Hôtel Termines et de la Marine) to see Ansermet (on the 3rd), who was to have brought money from Diaghilev in London. Another purpose of the trip was to find a residence for the autumn and winter. This was to be Gabrielle Chanel's Villa Bel-Respiro, the *art nouveau* Hector Guimard house, Avenue Alphonse de Neuville, Garches, where the Stravinskys were installed by September 15.

The first performance of the *Symphonies of Wind Instruments*, by Kussevitzky and the London Symphony Orchestra, Queen's Hall, June 10, 1921, was a fiasco that Stravinsky, in an interview, blamed on the conductor. Kussevitzky replied in a letter to *The Times*, first bowing obsequiously to Ernest Newman, who had written a vicious review,[71] then describing the music as

devoid of new elements . . . except some false and not convincing harmonies; the *Symphony* [sic] contains also reminiscences of *Petrushka* and *Le Sacre du Printemps*, and to these pages is quite artificially attached a chorale of no artistic value. [*Times*, July 24, 1921]

After reading this, Stravinsky wrote to Ansermet:

Consider, *mon cher*, what it is possible to do in the English press against the letter by Kussevitzky. Artur [Rubinstein] says that K. has

August 1920. Carantec.

discredited himself with this letter even in the eyes of my enemies, but why have my friends not replied to it? Are they all poltroons? [Undated]

Kussevitzky's letter enraged Diaghilev, whose note to Stravinsky on June 29 exposes some of the impresario's snobberies and prejudices:

I enclose an article written by one of your Jewish friends. Being your real friend, I advise you to beware of these Jewish musicians, the price of whose friendship you will begin to learn. I was shaken and furious reading the article by this bastard. . . . But do not answer this criminal letter yourself. In my new letter, addressed to the English public, I will defend you as I already did in my previous one, and I will do it briefly and clearly. Embraces. Serge. P.S. Ask someone to translate every word for you.

That Stravinsky ever forgave Kussevitzky is a wonder, but the conductor arranged a *démenti* through his secretary, Zederbaum, a doctor of medicine, sending him to see the composer about a new chamber-music organization of which Kussevitzky was president. Stravinsky wrote to Ansermet from Biarritz, September 9, 1923:

Kussevitzky is here. . . . Having seen my Octet, [he] wishes to invite me to conduct it. I will see Kussevitzky these days and find out what there is to this affair.

The result of the meeting was that Kussevitzky invited Stravinsky to give the first performance in a concert at the Paris Opéra, October 18, 1923, on the second half of which Kussevitzky conducted the *Eroica*(!).

In his *Chroniques de Ma Vie* (1935), Stravinsky does not blame Kussevitzky for the débâcle of the *Symphonies*, but this account of the event is unreliable. Stravinsky recalls having arrived in London at the last minute [72] and taken a seat in the last row of the balcony, when in fact he attended two rehearsals and, at the performance, was close enough to the stage to take a bow— which must be said in view of Ernest Newman's implication that the applause would not have been sufficient to cover even a fast walker's passage from the rear of the balcony to the stage. Eugene Goossens conducted the piece in London, December 12, 1921; Ansermet, who had performed it in Geneva on November 26,[73] describes the London event in a letter to Stravinsky on December 20:

I had the impression that Goossens had not looked at your score. There were simply no tempi at all . . . it was even worse than Kussevitzky. "Twice as fast," I said at one point. . . . Diaghilev and Nouvel went to the concert and said that they understood nothing, [yet] Newman wrote that "one can consider Goossens's performance as faithful, and our opinion of the work is unchanged." [74]

Stravinsky's creative processes are no less mysterious than those of any other great artist, but some of their patterns contradict the composer's own statements about them. Thus he said that as a rule his works were composed straight through, though his sketchbooks show that this was seldom the case, and that he rarely began at what was ultimately to be the actual beginning. He claimed, too, that his musical ideas always came to him in specific *timbres*, which he seldom changed in later stages. But his sketchbooks belie him. The String Concerto included winds in the original drafts, while part of the first movement of the four-hand Sonata was conceived and scored as an orchestral piece. At one time, too, the *Symphonies of Wind Instruments* featured violin and viola in what later became the duos for flute in G and alto clarinet. This string duet was a continuing idea from the Concertino for string quartet, with its violin and cello obbligati, an idea—two solo string instruments in relief to a wind ensemble—to which Stravinsky returned when he arranged the Concertino for twelve instruments in 1952.

At his first press conference in America, in 1925, Stravinsky stated that

Les Symphonies d'Instruments à Vent was designed as a grand chant, an objective cry of wind instruments, in place of the warm human tone of the violins. [New York Times, January 6, 1925]

But the music was not designed as such at first, and the earliest notations, probably dating from July 1919, are scored for harmonium; [75] thus the anomaly of Stravinsky's wind-instrument masterpiece is that it was not originally intended for winds. In the spring and summer of 1919, his main work was the reinstrumentation of Les Noces for an ensemble consisting of a harmonium, two cimbaloms, a pianola, and percussion instruments. [76]

To judge from the numerous sketches for the harmonium part in Les Noces, it is evident that Stravinsky was much involved with the instrument, and the use of it in a new piece follows naturally. In June 1919, he put Les Noces aside to compose the Piano-Rag-Music, and, according to every indication in the blue and brown sketchbooks which contain the first drafts for that opus and the Symphonies, the latter appears to have been written immediately after the former. As in the Rag-Music and the Three Pieces for Clarinet, Stravinsky dispensed with meters in the Symphonies, as if to say that, except as an aid to performance by larger groups of musicians, bar lines were meaningless in the kind of music he was then composing; but neither does he use meters for the music between 6 and 9 in the first full draft of the score, and, whatever the instrumentation that he had in mind here, at least four players would be required. But work on the Symphonies was suspended for Pulcinella, which, unlike the "harmonium piece," had been commissioned.

The first sketches for the Symphonies are found in the blue book, and the earliest of these is for the music eventually used in the waltz variation in the Octet. The sketches in the brown book are more extensive and include far more material, thematic, harmonic, and rhythmic. The earliest entries are written on two staves and contain registrations for harmonium. When Stravinsky finally abandoned this instrument, it was for an ensemble of violin and viola, cello and string bass. A string quartet of two violins, viola, and cello was indicated in one of the stages in Stravinsky's progress from harmonium to wind orchestra, with the hocket in the opening motif sounded by viola and cello pizzicato, and the duo at two measures before 16 by violin and viola arco. In this duet—the only passage in all of the sketches with a tempo marking (a faster one than Stravinsky was later to adopt)—the opening motif is reintroduced exactly as it is in the final score. At a still more advanced stage, the composer retained the violin and viola in a concertante role, choosing a wind orchestra for the ripieni. Wind instruments seemed to have occurred to Stravinsky's imagination when he first questioned whether at a certain place the music of the violin part might sound better played by a flute an octave higher. Then, while composing the music at three measures before 49, he apparently realized that clarity of articulation and pitch could be provided only by bassoons. After this, at any rate, the scoring is exclusively for winds. But obviously the conception of sonorities underwent considerable evolution.

Resuming the *Symphonies* in June 1920, after moving from Switzerland to France, Stravinsky wrote the final Chorale first, intending it for an album of piano pieces by several composers as a "tomb" for Debussy. The Chorale was apparently completed in a single day, June 20, 1920. On that same date, Henri Prunières wrote to Stravinsky from Paris:

Do not feel that it is necessary to make a piano reduction . . . if the music was conceived for instruments. . . . I will publish it in whatever form you wish, and you are not obligated to do as the others.

A later letter from Prunières refers to the music as a "piano reduction." The Chorale was developed from the following, written while Stravinsky was composing the Piano-Rag-Music, and found among the sketches for that work:

Stravinsky's brown sketchbook contains several variations and elaborations on this motif, showing the relationship between it and such phrases as that at one measure before 2 , and again at 3 , 6 , and in the three measures at 11 .

By July 2, almost the entire piece had been drafted in a two-, three-, and four-stave score, with some instrumental indications. Then work was interrupted, first, by the expansion of the "Marche Triomphale du Diable" [77] for a concert performance of *Histoire du Soldat* that Ansermet was to give in London on July 20; second, by the necessity of correcting the proofs of the new *Firebird* Suite, sent from London on July 28. As for the changes in *Histoire du Soldat*, Stravinsky wrote to Ansermet on July 1 wondering if the revisions could be completed on time. Ansermet replied on the 3rd, questioning the indispensability of the added music, largely repeated material, in a concert performance. But Stravinsky refused to allow the dance to be played without the revisions. On July 2 and 4, he added forty-one measures, beginning at three before 3 , and mailed them on the 5th.

The completion of the Concertino, which Stravinsky had started months before, required a still larger interruption. He wrote to Pochon of the Flonzaley Quartet, February 25, 1920: "I think about the composition for your ensemble all the time, and not only think but from time to time put on paper the things that come to my head through my ears and under my fingers." The full score of the *Symphonies* was finished on November 30, after that of the Concertino. But Stravinsky was dissatisfied with his instrumentation, and, accordingly, the orchestral score was engraved by the Russischer Musik Verlag (RMV 459) but never published. Moreover, the differences in the three versions of the proof score are so numerous that to determine which changes represent the composer's last revisions is difficult. Thus the rhythmic figures at 15, in what seems to be the third set of proofs (identified by the use of horns in the first three measures, versus bassoons in the first two sets), resemble those in the published, 1947 version. Nor can these three unpublished scores be collated, taking the intricate and attractive phrasing of the four flutes at 6 from one score, for example, and the superior, on-the-beat distribution of the trumpet music at 54 from another. The 1947 instrumentation is clearer, harder, and better balanced, but two passages are preferable in all three 1920 versions: the dialogue between bassoon and English horn at 58, and the crossing parts, in legato, of flutes and clarinets at 68.

Apart from changes in instrumental combinations, the sketches reveal that the motif at the beginning was first written a fourth lower than in the final score, indicating that Stravinsky did not always hear a theme or harmonic construction in the pitch at which he eventually employed it. Also, this motif is written as two-part music; the hocket between trumpets and trombones of the ultimate version is a later idea. Finally, the motif leads directly to the bassoon theme, with flute harmony, at 8, which is in the tonality of the final score. The sketches do not indicate the point at which Stravinsky detached the bassoon motif, but this example shows that composition was a matter of knowing where each segment fitted, and of separating as well as of joining together.

Two motifs are conspicuously absent from the first sketches, the threnodic figure at 1, a sustained tutti chord followed by the same chord staccato, and the flute motif at 15. The latter, together with the music at one measure after 13, first appears in a draft for the Concertino, which Stravinsky was composing at the same time and with which, briefly, the Symphonies was entangled. (The motif of the trumpets at two measures before 13 in the Symphonies was originally part of the Concertino.) The first sketches do not contain more of the final Chorale than the musical example quoted above.

There are two additional sketch scores; one curiosity in the first of them should be mentioned, the music that Stravinsky used to fill the gap at 56 before introducing an anticipatory fragment of the final Chorale which would also help to connect it with the body of the piece. He had at first simply felt the need of a section of contrasting music and had written five measures in slow tempo repeating the following figure:

Thus the two "false" beginnings of the Chorale were afterthoughts.

After the first American performances of the *Symphonies*, conducted by Stokowski, in Philadelphia, November 23 and 24, 1923, and in New York on February 5, 1924, Stravinsky wrote to Oeberg, "Russian Easter, 1924," instructing the Editions Russes de Musique to forbid performances by anyone except himself and Ansermet, and specifically withholding permission for a performance by the International Society of Contemporary Music in Prague (at which *Erwartung* was heard for the first time) as well as "anywhere in America." Thus Ansermet became an authority on the work, and his letters to the composer contain numerous questions concerning possible wrong notes, notes beyond the range of the English horn and basset horn, erroneous metronome markings, and the use of substitute instruments for the flute in G and the clarinet in F.[78] On one occasion, Ansermet requested permission to replace the former by an alto saxophone, saying that he had once used this instrument to replace the flute in G in the *Sacre*(!), and the latter by a bass clarinet—peculiar alternatives, since an ordinary flute and clarinet would obviously do less violence to the plan of sonority, the balances, and the character of the music.

In June 1933, Ansermet sent two lists of queries. Should the first bassoon's last note in measure 7 be an A rather than the written B-flat? Stravinsky confirmed that the B-flat was correct.[79] A doubt was raised in Ansermet's mind, too, by the A in the second clarinet, second beat of the fifth measure before 4, and here Stravinsky verified A-flat as the correct pitch. Ansermet also proposed to simplify the interrelations of the tempi, reducing them to *primo, secondo,* and *terzo,* the latter two respectively replacing the written "*più mosso*" and "*ancora più mosso.*" Stravinsky agreed, and the three speeds were established metronomically: I. = 72 (= 144); II. = 108 (II. = 72); III. = 144 (= 72). But, as these numbers show, the entire piece, which involves twenty-one changes of tempo, is based on a single pulsation of 72. A further batch of questions from Ansermet, dated June 30, seems to have irritated the composer, possibly because he was unable to explain why, in the next-to-last measure, second beat, the third horn moves from B to C while the English horn and trombone remain on B. He offered to send the original manuscript.

That Stravinsky did not revise the *Symphonies* until 1947 may be explained both by the lack of demand for the piece and by the circumstances of World War II, during which the publisher of the music, the Editions Russes de Musique, was inactive and inaccessible. In a letter to the present writer, August 29, 1947, Stravinsky says that he has only "a very dirty proof of the orchestra score in the last version made before the war." He goes on to say that he reorchestrated the Chorale in 1945 for a broadcast performance (CBS's "Invitation to Music") on a program with the *Symphony of Psalms,* because of length (to fill the half-hour) and suitability as a companion piece. This rescoring of the excerpt eliminates the clarinets but employs some of the extra flutes, oboes, bassoons, and trumpets required for the *Psalms*. The most striking changes in this unpublished version occur at ☐3☐, where a quartet of oboes is used, versus the mixed colors of the 1920 scores (three flutes, flute in G, two clarinets, alto clarinet, bassoon) and of the 1947 (two oboes, English horn, bassoon); and at ☐6☐, where the B of the chord is sounded in three octaves.

The 1945 arrangement of the Chorale inspired Stravinsky to rewrite the whole *Symphonies*, an intention announced in a letter to his publisher, October 7, 1947:

I have decided to rewrite it in a more practical manner, eliminating the flute-alto and clarinet-alto.

He also promised to complete the score by December and, in a letter of November 4, says that he is working hard to finish. The new version is dated November 25; on December 20, Stravinsky remarks that, although this has taken him two months, and although "the barring is completely different, I have not made many changes in the music itself." The same letter instructs the publisher to destroy the old score.

"Not to be performed," Stravinsky wrote on the covers of the three 1920–1921 proofs, and, in January 1948, he refused Ansermet's request to be allowed to perform "the original version" with the NBC Symphony. The conductor then besieged the composer with telegrams asking for verifications of notes in the new version. Ansermet's broadcast, January 31, was the public premiere, but Stravinsky had given a private one in Hollywood the day before, with a group of film-studio players. Meanwhile, *Time* had published an article about Ansermet, quoting him to the effect that "Stravinsky is a good businessman." The composer telegraphed, January 31: "Do you really think I am a good businessman composing such music?" Ansermet answered on February 1:

Cher Igor, assuredly the *Symphonies*, and, in general, all of your music, has nothing to do with business . . . you have caught me in the trap of my imprudent word. . . . Still, it is true that I have always admired your business acumen, coupled with your sense of the real. . . . Your last-hour telegram was providential. The first trombone part had perplexed me, and I was about to ask, with horror, if you had suddenly been converted to the twelve-tone technique. . . . Thanks to your corrections, the dissonances, which had so terrorized Toscanini [80] at the rehearsal, disappeared in the performance.

To return to the 1920s, in a letter to A. Brooks of Columbia Records in London, Stravinsky says that he loves Tchaikovsky's music in general and *La Belle au Bois Dormant* in particular. In the autumn of 1928, Brooks had invited Stravinsky to record the *Symphonie Pathétique*, and the response was affirmative and even enthusiastic. When nothing came of the idea, Stravinsky proposed (letter of March 19, 1929) that a recording be made instead of *La Belle au Bois Dormant*, which he planned to con-

November 2, 1921. London. The Alhambra Theater. Vera Sudeikina as the Queen, Walter Treer as the King, in *La Belle au Bois Dormant.* "The main color scheme for the courtiers was red, but the King and Queen were in white and gold with long blue trains. Vera Sudeikina, who played the Queen, was a very attractive woman, and she made a breathtaking entrance wearing a huge headdress of ostrich feathers. Her regal carriage and superb gestures were unforgettable." [Lydia Sokolova: *Dancing for Diaghilev* (London: John Murray, 1960)]

duct for the Ballets Russes at a gala performance in Versailles in June.

Stravinsky's espousal of Tchaikovsky dates from the orchestrations, completed in October 1921, of the "Variation d'Aurore" (No. 15) and the "Entr'acte" (No. 18) from *La Belle au Bois Dormant,* incidental tasks that, nevertheless, were to have a lasting influence on the composer of *Le Baiser de la Fée.* (Copies of Stravinsky's manuscript scores of both numbers are in the collection of Mrs. Parmenia Ekstrom, New York.) Diaghilev wished to include these two pieces in his revival of the ballet and, no score of Tchaikovsky's orchestrations being available, the impresario asked Stravinsky to make them from the piano score. As an exercise in Tchaikovskyan style, Stravinsky copied the full scores of parts of the "Variation of Candide," the "Pas de Six," and the "Apparition de l'Aurore." Orchestrating the "Entr'acte," he used trumpets, trombones, tuba, and timpani, none of which appears in the original, and, unlike Tchaikovsky, Stravinsky does not begin with a chord and the violin solo, but gives the violin melody to horn and clarinet, then to the oboe, forming the chord by sustaining their melodic notes. Yet the resemblances between the two orchestrations are more striking than the differences. (It is possible, of course, that Stravinsky still remembered something of the original from his youth.) Clearly the idea for *Le Baiser de la Fée* is rooted in these instrumentations of six years before.

At Diaghilev's request, Stravinsky wrote a letter to him, for publication in *The Times*, on the subject of Tchaikovsky's ballet, and, a fortnight later, Stravinsky amplified his written remarks in an interview in the same newspaper:

La Belle au Bois Dormant is the most convincing example of Tchaikovsky's immense talent. It was not necessary for this cultured man, with his knowledge of folk and of old French music, to enter into archaeological investigations in order to reproduce the epoch of Louis XIV in an appropriate way. He expressed its character in his own musical language, preferring historical inaccuracies to conscious but tortured stylization. Daring such as this belongs only to very great artists.[81]

Quite recently I had the opportunity once again to study the score of the ballet. I orchestrated a few numbers which had remained unorchestrated or incomplete and spent several very pleasant days savoring again the freshness and resourcefulness, the power and mastery of the music. I sincerely desire that audiences in all countries of the world perceive this ballet as I, a Russian musician, have perceived it. . . . [*The Times*, October 18, 1921]

. . . Monsieur Stravinsky was careful to explain that he had not in any way tampered with the score of *The Sleeping Beauty*. He has not added but restored passages that have been omitted from previous productions . . . doing his best to replace them according to the spirit of the original. He pointed out that he was no more adding to the score than the correction of Shakespeare's text from the Folios was rewriting Shakespeare.

"*La Belle au Bois Dormant*," he said, "combines a vivid imagination of the incidents on the stage with an enormous orchestral imagination. An example of this is the entrance of the Princess to trumpets and drums. This could very well have been done with harps and muted strings if a sentimental effect had been wanted, but Tchaikovsky's conception of the nature of the entrance was something different. . . .

"Since the Revolution, there has been a decided reaction against Tchaikovsky. Popular opinion has veered away from him toward Scriabin. Perhaps it is my admiration for Tchaikovsky that makes me regret this so keenly." [*The Times*, November 4, 1921]

The letter provoked less comment in London than in Paris, where Stravinsky's sincerity was doubted and his motive assumed to be no more than that of advertising the Ballets Russes production. He replied to these criticisms in a letter published in *Le Figaro* in May 1922, just before the first performance of *Mavra:*

I wish to emphasize that I have always felt a close communion with the spirit that animates Tchaikovsky's music, as well as with the "sense" of his art. The love that I have for *Boris Godunov*, or for a symphony by Borodin, and my esteem for "The Five," does not imply that I adhere to their tendencies, of which my own music has been mistakenly regarded as a continuation. On the contrary, I feel far closer to a tradition founded by Glinka, Dargomizhsky, and Tchaikovsky. The Russianism of "The Five" is manifested above all in an opposition to the conventional Italianism that reigned in Russia. Also, "The Five" found its voice in a picturesqueness that easily caught the imagination of foreign audiences. But this is over, and the old opposition to Italianism no longer has any *raison d'être*. We now savor anew those works in which the need for the picturesque—which now seems to me to be conventional—has been superseded.

Tchaikovsky may wear a top hat with his Russian blouse and belt, but the boyars' costumes fancied by "The Five" were out of date in the period in which they lived. Tchaikovsky is also reproached for being "German." What nonsense, or is this simply to confound him with the pianist Anton Rubinstein? First of all, Tchaikovsky is a melodist, which is not the case with the Germans, who confuse "melody" and "theme." And is Tchaikovsky's melody not more Russian in essence than are the waltzes of *Sadko* or of *Schéhérazade*?

Stravinsky's disavowal of the Russian Nationalist School in *Mavra* dismayed many of his followers. The one-act *opéra-bouffe* was first heard privately,[82] with Stravinsky at the piano, at a concert given by Diaghilev in the Hôtel Continental, Paris, May 29, 1922, together with pieces by Glinka, Dargomizhsky, and Tchaikovsky, on a program entitled *"La Musique Russe en Dehors 'des Cinq.'"* Later attempts to explain the opus were made by Ansermet—in an article, *"Mavra"* (*Le Radio*, Lausanne, October 18, 1935), written as a preface to his concert performance of the work, October 23, 1935—and by Stravinsky himself. Ansermet remarked that, since *Pulcinella*, Stravinsky had moved further and further away from regionalism and nationalism:

The Russia he renounces is that of blouses and boots; he wants Russians to dress like everyone else, espousing the same objectives and participating in the same diversions as everyone else, but in a Russian manner. In short, Stravinsky has turned his back on the school of Balakirev . . . addressing himself to those who are, as he would like to be, not *"musiciens russes"* but Russian musicians. . . . The choice of Pushkin was perhaps not a very happy one so far as the theatrical action is concerned. . . .

Stravinsky's article was written in Paris, December 4, 1934:

The triple dedication [to the memory of Pushkin, Glinka, and Tchaikovsky] will be easily understood by those who are conscious of the difference between the ideology of the Group of Five (Balakirev, Mussorgsky, Borodin, Rimsky-Korsakov, Cui) and the ideology represented by Tchaikovsky, whose inspiration—like that of the Five—was Pushkin and Glinka. But whereas the esthetic of the Five was directed to the cultivation of the national ethnographic element that they found [in Glinka]—which is not very different from that of films about the Old Russia of the Tsars and the Boyars—Tchaikovsky, like Dargomizhsky and others less well known, continued the tradition established by

Glinka, the tradition of which, even though it employs popular Russian melos, does not fear to present it in a Europeanized aspect.

But Glinka, not Tchaikovsky, was the inspiration for Mavra.[83] The B-minor aria of Parasha, Stravinsky's heroine, may well have been suggested by Liudmilla's aria (in Ruslan and Liudmilla) in the same key, and Stravinsky's ensembles, the duets, trios, and quartet, show signs of having been modeled on those in Ruslan. Stravinsky's most obvious borrowings are found in the Chorus and Romance, numbers fourteen and fifteen, in Ivan Susanin, and in the Prelude to Act Five of Ruslan:

It is also possible that the idea of scoring Mavra for an orchestra of winds may have derived from Ruslan, in which one of the female choruses is accompanied by winds alone. Mavra, in any case, is close in spirit and style to the music of Glinka's stage windband, which plays both by itself and as a supplement to the orchestra in the march and oriental dances in one of Ruslan's most stunning scenes.

Vera Sudeikina was not a professional dancer. She entered the Nelidova Ballet School in Moscow "not to become a ballerina," she says (performing a mock arabesque penchée), since

I was too tall and late-starting. But I wanted to acquire poise, to be able to move less brusquely, and to learn something about bodily expression. The ballet, it seemed to me, was the ideal basic training for an actress, and that is what I had determined to become. One day while I was at the Nelidova School, Diaghilev and Fokine came to look for new dancers.[84] The Nelidova sisters asked me to escort Diaghilev for them, and to answer his questions—which I did. But he was ungracious, plumping himself in an armchair and clapping his hands like an Oriental potentate to signal the girls to start or stop. He offered no comment but chose one dancer for his company, Vera Nemchinova.[85] . . . When I met him in Paris, years later, I did not tell him that I had seen and talked to him before.

During the Nelidova period, Vera de Bosset saw Isadora Duncan perform, and, inspired by her, the student, coming home afterward, removed her shoes, induced her mother to do the same, and cavorted with her parent à la Duncan. In Paris in the 1920s, Vera Sudeikina and Isadora Duncan were neighbors, sometimes dining together.

Vera de Bosset was born on Christmas Day 1888 in her parents' St. Petersburg home, Aptekarsky Ostrov, Pesochnaya Ulitsa, 5. (She counts herself a Capricorn, using the Old Style Russian calendar, and devoutly believes in her horoscope.) Her mother, Henriette Malmgren (also born on Christmas, 1870), was

1893. St. Petersburg. A pouty Vera de Bosset with her mother.

Swedish, her father, Artur de Bosset (born 1867), French. One of her father's ancestors was the Monsieur de Beausset, Prefect of Paris, who brought the portrait of L'Aiglon from the Empress to Napoleon before the Battle of Borodino.

    Vera de Bosset did not grow up in St. Petersburg and, in fact, went to the city only once in her childhood, on a visit to one of her grandmothers. She lived at Gorky (which means "little hills" or "bluffs"), the De Bosset country estate in Novgorodskaya Province, midway between St. Petersburg and Moscow. The De Bosset home was surrounded by forests, fields, and lakes, a landscape that entered profoundly into the child's feelings, for it is still evident in Vera Stravinsky's paintings. Her education at Gorky was entrusted to governesses—Fräulein Erna in the winter, a Parisienne in the summer. Vera was fond of Fräulein Erna,

except when she threatened me: she would say that unless my manners improved I would end up marrying Aneesim, the old peasant who carried logs to the hearths and lighted the fires.

When Fräulein Erna married a doctor and returned to live in her native Mittau, the De Bossets prepared a large trousseau for her. She was a competent pianist, and under her instruction Vera became one too. The pupil had an excellent ear and is still able to repeat the intervals of Kaiser Wilhelm II's automobile horn, which she heard frequently while living as a student in Berlin. Also thanks to Fräulein Erna, Vera de Bosset's second language, like Igor Stravinsky's, was German. (It is Franglais now.) Another teacher, though hardly thought of as such, was her father's gardener, Alexander Kalistratovich. Vera's love of flowers antedates his service with her family, but she says that most of her practical knowledge of plants and flowers comes from—not to say stems from—him.

Vera's companion in the country was her mother. The two rode horseback together, gathered mushrooms together (for stomach, not soul, food in those days), joined in pampering Vera's numerous pets: Mashka the cat, Kashtanka the dog, Mishka and Sashka, the baby bears, Schwetka the horse, Cheezhik the young bull, Petash the pig, La Générale the cow, and Murzilka the goose who honked after Mme de Bosset wherever she went. Other animals, too, appear in Vera Stravinsky's childhood memories, "a small donkey that was owned by our neighbor, the Marquis de Paoluchi. My mother promised that she would try to buy this or another donkey for me if I would speak only French for a whole month. She put a calendar over my bed and crossed off the days, but I always failed and had to start over again and never had a donkey." During "Butter Week" (Maslenitza), the Shrovetide carnival of Petrushka, the De Bosset sleighs were drawn by tame elks instead of by horses. Vera Stravinsky also remembers that the festivities of the same season included contests of blini-eating.

Artur de Bosset owned an electrical-equipment factory in Kudinovo, a village about forty-five minutes from Moscow on the Nizhni-Novgorod line. Mrs. Stravinsky recalls that when the Tsar's train passed Kudinovo, soldiers stood on either side of the tracks pointing rifles toward the houses, the windows of which had to be curtained. Artur de Bosset was a liberal who refused to accept the Order of St. Stanislas, and who named his daughter for the leftist Vera in Goncharov's The Precipice. But Artur's cousin, the Marquis Theodore de Bosset, was an admiral and a personal friend of the Tsar.[86] After the Revolution, Theodore lived in Nice, where he met two Peruvian women, with whom he eventually went to live in Lima (where he is buried). Artur followed him, but to Santiago, where he died and was buried (in

1902. At Kudinovo. Vera de Bosset and Mashka.

August 1937). Before leaving Europe, Artur resided for a time in Berlin, where he obtained a divorce from Vera's mother. Also, he visited his daughter in Paris. His second wife, Irena Mella, a Russian woman, moved to Buenos Aires from Santiago after his death, and, in August 1960, met her stepdaughter there. Vera de Bosset saw her own mother for the last time in 1925, in Paris, after which Mme de Bosset returned to Moscow, where she died during World War II.

Vera de Bosset spent four years in boarding school in Moscow, with the exception of weekends at home and vacations there and in Switzerland. Apart from a *nanya* who called her "Bossic," school was a trial, and Vera was soon leading a hunger strike to protest the rations. "Shall I send to Tiestov's [a four-star restaurant] for lobsters?" the headmistress asked her rebellious pupil, whose answer was that this seemed a capital idea. In Moscow, Vera continued her musical studies under David Shor, of the Shor, Krein, and Erlich Trio, and made an impression at school by including a Scriabin étude in her graduation recital.

Vera's greatest delight in Moscow was the theater, and she would pawn her most prized possessions to buy tickets. It was the heyday of the ballet, of Russian opera—Tchaikovsky's *The Little Slippers* was the first opera that she saw—of Stanislavsky, and she had the astronomical luck, in the first two plays she attended, to see Eleonora Duse and Sarah Bernhardt. Duly imitating these actresses in drama classes at school, Vera de Bosset made a hit by fainting in the Bernhardt manner: "I went down like *that*" (gestures) "and there I was, *par terre.*"

Graduated *cum laude*, gold-medaled, and certified to teach mathematics and French, Mlle de Bosset hoped to continue her studies in Paris. But since the young ladies of her father's acquaintance who had been finished at Parisian schools were less distinguished by their intellectual accomplishments than by their affectations and wanton ways, Artur de Bosset, regarding the German capital as safer and more serious, enrolled his daughter at the University of Berlin. While living at a *pension* there, "kept by a pair of despotic old maids," Vera de Bosset studied philosophy and science (anatomy, physics, chemistry) in her first year, then switched to an art curriculum in her second, attending the lectures of Heinrich Wölfflin—who, she says, "opened my eyes." It was in Berlin, in November 1912, that she first saw Diaghilev's Ballets Russes (in a performance of *Carnaval*), but she did not see, or does not remember seeing, Stravinsky or his *Firebird* and *Petrushka*. After her second year at the university, her formal education was cut short by World War I, and she returned to Russia—both intellectually improved and without affectations, from which, in any case, she has remained free all of her life, being immune to the fault.

When Vera de Bosset appeared as an actress in the Kamerny Theater, she was discovered by movie scouts—or whatever Russians call them. A screen test was arranged and, as a result, in the next two years she played in a dozen film comedies, some of them opposite Marius Mariusovich Petipa, the actor and son of the choreographer of *Swan Lake*. Three of her best-known films,

1915. Moscow. Vera de Bosset, or, as she is listed in the film, "Vera Shilling," as Helen in Protozanov's *War and Peace*. This ten-reel movie was made between February 13 and April 14, 1915, and released by the "Russian Golden Series."

all made in 1914, were *The Arena of Vengeance, Drama at the Telephone,* and *If a Woman Wants, She Will Fool the Devil.* These films, like *War and Peace,* the high point of her cinema career, were directed by Jacob Protozanov, who wrote glowingly of her in his memoirs (Moscow, 1957).

While still at the Nelidova Ballet School, Vera de Bosset married Robert Shilling—"*nyet kopeki* and now a Shilling," her friends remarked, but Shilling was a compulsive gambler, and the newlyweds were constantly at the pawnbroker's. On March 15, 1916, Mme Shilling eloped with the painter Serge Sudeikin [87] to Petrograd, where the couple resided in an apartment on the Ekaterinsky Canal. But this story is told more fully by John Malmstad in his biography of Mikhail Kuzmin: [88]

. . . the Donna Anna of the [poem] is still alive and remembers well the events which the poem describes and also her association with her old friend Kuzmin, whom she vividly discussed in a memorable conversation with me in her New York apartment [Essex House, May 7, 1970]. She is Vera Stravinsky, widow of the composer. Before her marriage to Stravinsky she was the second wife of Sudejkin (after his separation from Glebova), and the poem itself describes their romance in the autumn of 1915. Thus the initials of the dedication are clear, standing for Vera Arturovna Shilling, née de Bosset, and Serge Jurievic Sudejkin. Then in her early twenties . . . Vera Arturovna was infatuated with the theater and was especially interested in Tairov's Kamernyj Theater, which had only recently opened in Moscow. Tairov learned of this interest and of her desire to join his company and paid her a visit. He came, as she frankly admits, because he had heard the rumors that her father was very wealthy. . . . When he asked her why she wanted to become an actress, she replied simply that she loved the theater. To his question about her previous experience, she replied honestly that she had none and thought that she had little talent. Tairov invited her anyway, probably charmed by her beauty and determination. As her husband, Shilling, had no objection, she immediately accepted the offer. She began to attend the rehearsals of the company and remembers how Tairov jokingly liked to remark, punning on the title of an Ostrovskij play, "u nas ne bylo ni grosa, da vdrug Shilling!" The company was then rehearsing Beaumarchais's Le Mariage de Figaro. Sudejkin, in Moscow to design the sets and costumes, fell in love with the beautiful young woman. He was determined that she should have a part in the production. As she had had no experience but had studied ballet, Sudejkin and Tairov created a separate number for her, a Spanish dance for which the artist designed a special costume decorated with tiny stars. Thus the references in the poem to "Ispanija i Mocart— 'Figaro' " are clear (Mozart was used for the incidental music), as are the references to the "heroine's" "ognennye i bystrye tancy." The references to Donna Anna, who, of course, does not appear in Mozart's Le Nozze di Figaro but in Don Giovanni, are also explainable. Sudejkin, who had immediately begun courting her, referred to himself throughout the courtship as Figaro but felt the name Susanna did not suit Vera Arturovna's special beauty. So he began to call her Donna Anna but refused to allow her to address him as Don Juan, as he felt the Don unsympathetic. The romance began in September and continued throughout the autumn and winter. Their favorite place for rendezvous was the Kremlin, especially its great cathedrals, and this too is reflected clearly in the poem (the Uspenskij and Blagovescenskij cathedrals are mentioned by name), as is even the black "subka" she wore at the time. . . .

Sudejkin had by then separated from Glebova, and [on March 15] 1916 he and Vera Arturovna moved to St. Petersburg. At first they took an apartment immediately above the "Prival komediantov." Kuzmin was a frequent guest at the apartment, and the three of them would sometimes stop into the cabaret to see friends. Kuzmin was much taken by the charm and intelligence of the young woman and was delighted by the story of the circumstances of their romance. He was especially intrigued by the fact that the romance had been played out against the background of the old Russia—the Kremlin, the oldest parts of Moscow. Vera Arturovna herself, considered by some, like Thomas Mann, to be a "specifically Russian beauty," had no Russian blood. Her father was of French descent, her mother Swedish. This Kuzmin referred to in the poem's conclusion. . . . As a surprise Easter gift to her, he wrote the poem ("cuzaja" because it is the story of someone else's love affair and is told from Sudejkin's point of view) and presented her with a copy, dated "1916. April. Easter," which is still in her possession. Kuzmin continued to see them often and inscribed several other poems to her, but he lost touch with them after the October Revolution when she and Sudejkin fled to the Crimea and from there to Europe. They never again heard from Kuzmin, and Vera Arturovna did not learn until our interview in 1970 that the "poema" inspired by her had eventually been published. [From *M. A. Kuzmin Sobranie stikhotvorenij* (Munich: Fink Verlag, 1977]

It was during this period in Petrograd that Alexander Blok, encountering Sudeikin in the Summer Gardens, wrote that he was "zhutko," which, in the context, might be translated as "awesome." [89] In Petrograd, too, Vera de Bosset heard Maxim Gorky speak, and she was in the city when Rasputin was murdered, as well as during the Revolution of March 1917, when, as a result of being forced to lie in the snow in a bullet-raked street, she became seriously ill. She returned to Moscow after that and, reunited with Sudeikin, joined the Crimea-bound exodus—of practically everyone who could afford it. There she began to paint. Her first works, silhouettes on glass,[90] were exhibited in Yalta in 1918, and there, on February 11, she married Sudeikin,[91] though in the chaos of the Revolution neither had been able to obtain a divorce.

At Alushta, near Yalta, Vera Sudeikina became a friend of Osip Mandelstam, one of whose most famous poems, "Tristia No. 3," was written for her:

> The thread of gold cordial flowed from the bottle
> With such languor that the hostess found time to say
> Here in mournful Tauris where our fates have cast us
> We are never bored—with a glance over her shoulder . . .
>
> . . .
> Do you remember in the Greek house the wife they all
>   loved?
> Not Helen, the other, and how long she embroidered? [92]

Mme Sudeikina is the "hostess" and "the other" (i.e., Penelope). Mandelstam gave the manuscript of the poem to her, dated August 11, 1917. Three days earlier, he had made a gift to her of the manuscript of Poem No. 84 (in the Struve-Fillipov numbering), signing and dating it "August 8, 1917, Professors' Corner [Mandelstam's residence], Alushta."

Clarence Brown's *Mandelstam* [93] commends the Soviet scholar D. M. Segal for "exposing clearly the enormous role played by classical imagery" in "Tristia No. 3," adding that Segal's analysis is "one of the truly excellent detailed studies of any poem by Mandelstam." But Mrs. Stravinsky reveals, in addition, that the "cordial" was honey, and that the subjects of the embroidery, which she still possesses, were Columbine and Pierrot. The slow movement of the poem, the long lines (alternating fifteen and sixteen syllables), and the anapestic pentameter are strikingly beautiful even to those of us who are unable to appreciate the linguistic structure.

With the invasion of the Crimea by the Red Army in the spring of 1919, the Sudeikins sailed for Constantinople. Mrs. Stravinsky recalls that the father of the late Vladimir Nabokov was on the same Yalta pier, as was the Dowager Empress, who was later rescued by an English cruiser. The Sudeikins' ark was

Vera de Bosset, c. 1904.

Serge Sudeikin, c. 1910. He helped to paint the set for the *Sacre* (receipt from Diaghilev, March 2, 1913).

more modest, a mere thirty-footer loaded with oil drums. A heavy storm came up, and, many queasy hours later, the boat docked not in Constantinople but in Batum, at the wrong end of the Black Sea. From there, the Sudeikins journeyed to Tiflis and Baku, where women still wore veils. For the next year, Tiflis was the Sudeikins' home—a happy one despite the Revolution, to judge from Vera Sudeikina's diaries. In May 1920, she sold her diamond-with-pearl earrings for 3,000 Kerensky rubles to buy passage for herself and her husband on a French steamer bound for Marseille. The couple reached Paris on May 20, during the city's celebrations of the canonization of Jeanne d'Arc.

Mme Sudeikina met Stravinsky through Diaghilev, who invited her to a dinner, February 19, 1921, at which the composer was to be present. "He is moody today, so please be nice to him," Diaghilev said. And of course she was.

This first meeting took place in an Italian restaurant in Montmartre, and Mrs. Stravinsky recalls that the composer was

the wittiest, most amusing [94] man I had ever met. . . . He was always witty, moreover, but though he could be moody, too, and very caustic, he was never that way with me. Most of his tempers were due to impatience with business affairs, but our first *"crac"* occurred in 1926 when I moved to an apartment in the rue de Ranelagh. He had asked me to have a priest consecrate the new home, and, when I neglected to do so, became very angry. I promised to do it the next day, but with Stravinsky everything always had to be done immediately.

Vera Sudeikina had a pack of cards with her at that first meeting, and she told the composer's future, presumably saying something about the Queen of Hearts.

Each of Vera Stravinsky's artistic careers flourished in a different country. She was an actress in Russia (apart from the stint in London in 1921 as the Queen in *La Belle au Bois Dormant*), a costume designer in France, a painter in America. The scene of the middle career was a Paris atelier, which she directed and which employed more than a score of midinettes to provide costumes for the theater and the Diaghilev ballets. On November 1, 1926, Stravinsky, in Nice, wrote to Ansermet:

Vera is very busy at the moment working for Diaghilev, who has asked her to take charge of the costumes for the Goncharova *Firebird* that he is reviving in London in a few weeks. [95]

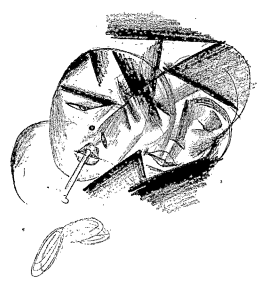

1920. Drawing of Serge and Vera Sudeikin by Ilya Mikhailovich Zdanevich (1894–1975).

PLATE 9

A poster for a 1924 Geneva concert.

1920. *Symphonies of Wind Instruments.* Sketch for the music from before 21 to after 24 . The parts in black ink were intended for solo violin and viola, those in red ink for woodwinds.

March 6, 1920. Baku. A watercolor
cartoon by Serge Gorodyetsky (legs on
table), from Mme Sudeikina's autograph album. The picture represents
"The Round Table," a group of poets
and writers who were friends of the
Sudeikins. L. to R.: Valery Bryusov
(his *Angel of Fire* is the source of Prokofiev's opera), Fyodor Sologub (the
demon in his glass signifies his most

PLATE 10

famous book, *The Little Demon*), Alexey Remisov, Viacheslav Ivanov (the large head indicates that he was considered to be the greatest of the symbolists), Alexander Blok (shown with wings because of his angelic character), Mikhail Kuzmin (*Wings* was the title of his homosexual novel), Andrey Biely, Konstantin Balmont. The verses at the bottom of the picture, by Gorodyetsky, contain jokes about each writer portrayed. Stravinsky composed music to poems by Gorodyetsky and Balmont.

1917. "The Stupid Viasma Drowning in Priyaniki," says the title of this watercolor by Vera de Bosset, painted in Yalta. "Priyaniki" means "cookies," and Viasma, a city in north Russia, was a famous maker of them.

March 1921. Paris. Rasorial "Firebird" by Sudeikin, with first theme of *The Firebird*, in pencil, added by Stravinsky, with his dedication "To Madame Vera de Bosset Sudeikina, Igor Stravinsky, Paris, March 1921." Two weeks later, Stravinsky copied in Vera Sudeikina's autograph album the eight measures from *Les Noces* beginning at 127 , with the text: "This one is fantastically good. If you don't touch her she costs one ruble, but if you fuck her she will be worth two rubles." (The French, German, and English translations expurgate the Russian text.) Over this music, to the same rhythm, Stravinsky changed the words as follows: "To the lady, this one, charming one, this one, beautiful one, this one, nice one, Vera Sudeikina."

PLATE 11

Mme Sudeikina redesigned Marie Laurencin's sketches for *Les Biches,* after Diaghilev found them incomprehensible, and, when drastic adjustments were required in Rouault's *Le Fils Prodigue* (first performed May 1, 1929), Diaghilev again entrusted this task to her. She also designed and supervised the making of some three hundred costumes—at the Maison Verame, Paris—for a production of *Carmen* in Amsterdam conducted by Monteux, November 17, 1928. In a letter to Dr. Enrique Telemachus Susimi, February 18, 1932, Stravinsky recommended Vera Sudeikina to make the costumes for a production of the *Sacre* in Buenos Aires, saying that since Mme Sudeikina would be coming with him, this would be especially convenient.

During this period, Mme Sudeikina's closest friend was Stravinsky's niece, Ira Belline, who moved to Morocco at the end of World War II:

I talked . . . in Marrakech with Ira Belin [sic], a Russian who was more or less a dealer in antiques, knew everyone, and collected stray dogs. She was a niece of Stravinsky's and, though she could dance hardly or not at all, she had been allowed to appear in Diaghilev's ballets [Nabokov's *Ode*] because of her supreme beauty. She told me that hers had been the face in the famous photograph by the Baron [de Meyer] that Elizabeth Arden used for several decades to advertise her cosmetic products.[96]

On March 13, 1925, at the Metropolitan Opera House in New York, Stravinsky experienced a public but incomplete meeting with Serge Sudeikin. After a performance of *Petrushka* (on a double bill with *Pagliacci*!) for which Sudeikin had designed the sets,[97] the composer started onstage to acknowledge the applause, saw Sudeikin approaching from the other side, froze, bowed alone, departed rapidly. The *Philadelphia Inquirer* pursued the story, and the newspaper's Sunday magazine section, March 29, 1925, devoted a full page to the "feud" between Stravinsky and Sudeikin—"TRAGEDY OF THE FAMOUS ARTIST'S LOST WIFE"—illustrating it with a cover photograph of Vera Sudeikina. By the time the Sudeikins saw each other again, in New York, December 29, 1940, both had remarried.

In Biarritz, in 1922, Stravinsky told his wife about Mme Sudeikina, and in February 1925, while Stravinsky was in America, Vera Sudeikina met Catherine Stravinsky in Nice, at her request and Stravinsky's. Later, the two women became friends, and in the 1930s most of Stravinsky's letters from his wife contain messages for Vera: "How good that you've made it possible for Vera to move to another apartment . . . This is good for her in many ways . . . it will lift her spirits as she'll be doing this while you're gone and will make your absence seem shorter" (February 22, 1936); "And how is Vera? Won't her cold interfere with her going to London?" (October 15, 1937); "What of Vera? She must be arriving soon, or has she already come?" (November 6, 1937). Since Stravinsky's letters from America to Mme Sudeikina reached her in Paris before those to his wife, who was in the country, Mme Sudeikina always telephoned his news to Mme

August 1923. Paris. At work with the Pleyela. Stravinsky's assistant in recording his works for the Pleyela was the composer Jacques Larmanjat (1878–1952). Photograph by Vera Sudeikina.

Stravinsky. After the Stravinsky family moved to Paris, the two women saw each other on many occasions. Thus Mme Sudeikina wrote to Stravinsky in Buenos Aires, April 14, 1936: "I found Katia looking extremely well and on Friday I walked with her on the avenue Gabrielle. She sent beautiful pink roses for Easter."

Stravinsky's interest in mechanical instruments continued until the late 1920s, though he later became a confirmed enemy of electronic music.[98] One of the first to observe this aspect of the composer's work was C. F. Ramuz:

Stravinsky's piano coincided with the carpenter's handsaw and the engines of the garage man. For kinship or sympathy with it one would go, not to the lawyer's office, the neighboring bourgeois apartments, the women in the square, the passers-by with handsome new straw hats, but to the workshop. There, suddenly the machines begin to revolve, the transmission belts to glide over the shaft wheels, and the gears to engage. Each part of each machine in Les Noces had its own special noise and pace, while from the superimposed sounds, and the superimposition itself, comes a new rhythm, the simple persistent consequences of all of these many opposed forces.[99]

In the autumn of 1922, Stravinsky was in Berlin for several weeks waiting to meet a Soviet ship bringing his mother from Petrograd to Stettin. On August 27, he had written to Ansermet from Paris:

I will wait here for news of my mother (who will soon be leaving Petrograd), then meet her in Germany and take her to Biarritz.

The composer wrote again on September 2: "I am still here waiting for news of my mother." The scheduled sailing was postponed several times, in fact, and Stravinsky was obliged to remain in Berlin, since, if he were not actually on the Stettin dock, Anna Stravinsky would not have been allowed to disembark. He lived in the Russischer Hof and almost daily saw his friend Ernest Oeberg, the representative of the Russischer Musik Verlag, and became a friend of Pavel Tchelichev,[100] yet the only published memoir of Stravinsky at the time is the embroidered one by George Antheil.[101] This greatly annoyed Stravinsky when he first read it, but he did not deny the truth of some of Antheil's stories, including the following:

One night Igor Stravinsky and I decided to walk home instead of taking a cab. . . . It was well past midnight. Berlin was full of . . . streetwalkers. We went through the famous Brandenburger Tür. When we got out on the Tiergartenalleestrasse we saw about fifty girls running toward us. . . . I would not have known how to get out of such a jam. But Stravinsky spoke to [them, saying] that we had just come from entertaining six girls, three apiece, and that we were really very, very tired. They would, he felt sure, understand. . . . They broke up and left us. Professional etiquette . . .

Stravinsky avoided all Berlin teas; but at last there occurred a very important one, attendance at which he could not possibly get out of.

During this tea a third-rate German composer caught him in a corner . . . : "Dear Herr Stravinsky . . . I have been wanting to meet you for such a long time. Would you do me the very great honor of looking at my new Symphony in B-flat?" Stravinsky, who could not escape, . . . said: "Come to my hotel tomorrow at four o'clock." The next day at four the third-rate composer came gleefully, his briefcase bulging with a 300-page symphonic score. . . . Stravinsky . . . gave him short shrift. "I cannot look at your symphony today. I'm sorry. Good-by!" . . . "But Herr Stravinsky, you distinctly said, yesterday, that you would look at my symphony today at four o'clock. . . . Would you, therefore, please be so kind as to make an appointment for me for tomorrow, the day after, or any time which suits your best convenience?" Stravinsky looked at him coldly. "Ah, yes . . . I will arrange it, but first I must get my appointment book. Let's see [thumbing it], tomorrow is impossible. . . . The day after is no good. . . . The week after? No, I'll have a lot of things to do around Berlin getting ready to leave for Paris. The week after? No, I'll be leaving for Paris. Next year? No, I won't be coming back to Berlin again. The year after? No, not then, either." He came to the end of the appointment book, took out a pencil and looked up brightly. "Fine!" he said triumphantly. He scribbled down on the last page, "Never!" and looked up brightly. . . . "Eh bien— 'jamais'—voulez-vous?" 102

On November 4, Stravinsky wrote a concert ending for the Nightingale's aria in his opera of that name. On November 10, his mother landed in Stettin, and, three days later, obtained a permit for transit through Belgium. Anna Stravinsky and her son arrived in Paris on the 14th, and, shortly after the concert of the 25th, they went together to Biarritz—as a letter from the composer to C. F. Ramuz, December 7, reveals.

From 1914 to the mid-1930s, Ernest Ansermet was one of Stravinsky's closest musician friends, the one with the keenest appreciation of his music. As early as 1914, Ansermet wrote in the *Cahiers Vaudois*:

Igor Stravinsky directs the course of musical evolution today, and his arrival in our musical life is the most important event since Debussy, an event on the order of a Wagner or a Beethoven. [April 20, 1914]

Ansermet wrote the first important essay on Stravinsky's music, in *La Revue Musicale*, Paris, July 1921, and Stravinsky's letter to Henri Prunières, editor of this periodical, recommending that he commission the article from Ansermet, is the most important statement of Stravinsky's high opinion of the conductor's critical and musical intelligence.

The correspondence between the two men, which did not begin on Stravinsky's side until 1919 but then continues, with large lacunae, to his eighty-fifth birthday, covers a longer span than any other in his life. The exchanges are also the most useful, the contents being largely concerned with questions of performance, and the most voluminous—some 450 letters, postcards, telegrams—though Ansermet's communications greatly outnumber, and are much lengthier than, Stravinsky's. Outside of

November 25, 1922. 3:00 P.M. This was the first time that Stravinsky conducted *Fireworks, The Nightingale* excerpts, and the 1919 *Firebird* Suite in Paris.

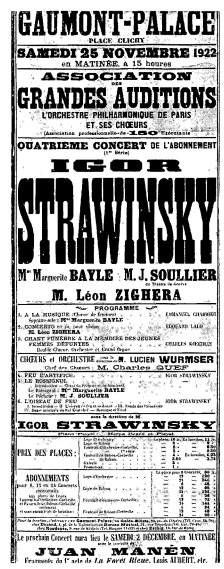

Winter 1923. Paris. In the Café Gaillec. Photograph by Vera Sudeikina.

music, however, the two men are diametrically different, Stravinsky being a believer, Ansermet a skeptic, Stravinsky a concrete thinker, Ansermet a theorizer, Stravinsky a scourge to academics, Ansermet a born schoolteacher. From the late 1920s, moreover, the central fact of the association is the rivalry that arose between the two as conductors of Stravinsky's music, Ansermet defending "the way it was played originally," Stravinsky changing with every performance. Stravinsky began to show his irritation when Ansermet was credited with preparing a work for Stravinsky to conduct and, in at least one case, with actually conducting it. Thus when Abbé Juan Ma Thomás of Mallorca sent an issue of the music magazine *Philarmonia* asking Stravinsky to inscribe some measures on it from the *Symphony of Psalms,* he answered

I see that your correspondent was not present at the [Paris] concert, since it was not Ansermet who had the brilliant success [with the *Psalms*] that your critic attributed to him. I conducted the work in Paris. . . . [May 2, 1931]

Stravinsky seems never to have withheld a criticism where Ansermet was concerned. For instance, Stravinsky wrote to him, November 17, 1932:

1923. Paris. With Prince Argutinsky.

Winter 1923. Paris. In a bar. Drawing by Michel Larionov.

May 1923. Monte Carlo. With Ernest Ansermet at the time of the first rehearsals for *Les Noces*. Stravinsky wrote on the reverse of the photograph: *"Nos repas chez la veuve Delorme à Monaco."*

Yesterday I heard the broadcast . . . of your concert in London . . . from the last *Nocturne* of Debussy to the end. I was satisfied with the tempi of the *Sacre*, but the tempo was the only aspect of the performance that I was able to judge. . . . I have only one reproach, the nervousness in the first measures of the "*Danse Sacrale*"; and, later, the reprise was too hurried at the beginning for the timpani to achieve their natural allure.

Nevertheless, the two men were dependent on each other for many years. Ansermet was a valuable champion and disciple, and, as for the other side of the relationship, he describes it himself in a letter to Stravinsky, December 22, 1925: "In this human marsh in which one sinks, my thoughts cling to you as to a stone."

The breach between the longtime friends was the result of Ansermet's highhandedness with *Jeu de Cartes*, which he proposed to cut by about one-third for concert performances, defying Stravinsky's refusal to give his permission to do this:

Jeu de Cartes, played in concert, no more warrants cuts than does *Apollo*.[103] . . . What particularly surprises me is that you are attempting to convince *me* to make these cuts. . . . [Letter of December 14, 1937]

The conductor was not deterred by this, however, and, five days later, Stravinsky fired off a second missive:

The absurd cut which you suggest completely spoils my little March. . . . you are not *chez vous, mon cher* . . . [*and*] I never said to you, "Well, you have my score and you may do whatever parts of it that please you." . . . Either you play *Jeu de Cartes* as it is, or you do not play it at all. [December 19, 1937]

Finally, on January 3, 1938, Stravinsky wrote to his publisher, Willy Strecker:

Since Ansermet is apparently suffering from a strange megalomania and has continued to play the piece with cuts, the orchestra parts must be recalled.

At the beginning of the quarrel, Ansermet defended his position in a letter (October 22, 1937) that Stravinsky did not answer, except in marginal comments:

It is not the form that people appreciate, it is the substance. If you find this to be an absurd distinction . . . and if, like the new physicists for whom "mass" is "movement," you believe that the musical substance is only form, then you must recognize the qualities of forms and precisely those concerning which one could say that they are more or less substan-

Stravinsky has underscored and questioned the first sentence.

My God, what philosophical jabbering.

tial. . . . Can you tell me why [your] *Chant du Rossignol* is never played? God knows that I have often [conducted it] and always with the same unsuccess.[104] This is not because the work is not constructed—and certainly the listener may find individual passages delectable—but because the form is of a kind that disorients him. . . . I do not know how you can invoke the *Symphonies of Wind Instruments* as a parallel example. . . . The formal structure of *Jeu de Cartes* is infinitely more complicated and more delicate than the symphonic dialectic with which the concert public is familiar. . . . I do not say that the success of the shortened version would be more authentic because based on *une impression plus consciente*. . . . The arrangement would be similar to what you yourself did with *Le Baiser de la Fée* and with *Petrushka*. Most people stopped going to Wagner operas after learning to appreciate such concert excerpts as the Forest Murmurs, the Good Friday music, etc. . . . I have to take responsibility vis-à-vis my audience. . . . And I have some reason to be confident in my judgment since it has helped me to make an effect with new music in a country where the new is . . . tolerated, at best. . . . I have heard many echoes from Venice [106] and people say things to me that they do not say to you. . . .

A great many other good pieces are not played.

Thanks for informing me.

Because this piece has the same unsuccess.

Here Stravinsky has inscribed a question mark in the margin.

This is the reasoning of a Protestant minister.

Myself, yes, but not others.

Is it really possible that he makes this comparison?

But not vis-à-vis me?

Gretchnevaia Kasha.[105]

This remark is the equivalent of an anonymous letter. I could also tell you that people say very different things about you than to you, except that I would never make an allusion such as this, which I find to be very inelegant.

One must heed the manifestations of the public.

If I cannot discuss questions such as this with you . . . without being received by your brutality it would be better to bring the matter to an end.

This is dangerous. One could become Stokowski this way—but probably that is what you would like to become.

But who is the author of this eight-page, ill-humored dissertation?

Ansermet was banished from Stravinsky's counsels after the *Jeu de Cartes* affair, and a long silence [107] began between the two former friends, during which they talked *about* each other instead, and in surprisingly vituperative terms. In America, after World War II, Ansermet tried to effect a reconciliation, but his and Stravinsky's musical creeds were further apart than ever. The two men did not meet again until October 26, 1951, and then accidentally, on a tram in Geneva. Later in the day, Ansermet, trembling with emotion, called on him in his rooms at the Hôtel des Bergues and invited the composer to dinner, which the composer accepted, at the Ansermet home. The two musicians met again in Geneva, May 1, 1954, and in New York occasionally in the later 1950s. Ansermet attended two of Stravinsky's rehearsals with the New York Philharmonic in January 1957, and a year before, on January 11, 1956, Ansermet visited the composer in his suite at the Gladstone Hotel, East 52nd Street, where the following scene, described by the conductor, took place:

> ... Stravinsky tried to persuade me to interest myself in serial music, notably in the works of Webern: "They are pearls," he told me. "But my dear Igor, I am writing a book which shows that this music is contrary to the laws of hearing. ... Sounds are organized in their simultaneity as well as successively. Suppose that the author of a play ... assigned each syllable of a phrase to a different actor and directed all of the actors to speak them at the same time, would you understand the phrase?" "Certainly not," he said, "but ... it would be an effect."..."Agreed," I said, "but in music the effects must have a clear significance." Stravinsky ... answered me, in a bass voice: "You know that I pay attention to harmony; in the horizontal, one arranges the 'file' as one wants, but the vertical assemblages are something else. They must justify themselves before God!" [Ernest Ansermet and J.-Claude Piguet, *Entretiens sur la Musique* (Neuchâtel, 1963)]

This anecdote reveals not only the gulf between the two men—Ansermet shows that he was not prepared for Stravinsky's interest in the "effect" of everyone speaking at once, though this response is characteristic of the composer—but also Ansermet's misunderstanding of Stravinsky's philosophy of art, for what he meant is not that he "hoped to God" that the vertical combinations would be "right," but that he had to make them right in his art, since rules did not exist.

In 1958, writing to Harold Box of the Voice of America, for whom Stravinsky had taped many interviews, the composer deplored "Ansermet's reputation as an authority on my music," adding that the conductor is "getting old and is hostile to the entire progressive world" (letter of December 13). Meanwhile, Ansermet had openly criticized Stravinsky's revisions of his early works, had conducted the premiere of Stravinsky's Mass on the stage of La Scala, and had published *Les Fondements de la Musique dans la Conscience Humaine*,[108] which Stravinsky regarded primarily as an attack, if ineffective, on himself. There were no meetings after this, and when Ansermet attended a performance of *The Rake's Progress* in Carnegie Hall in November

1962, the two men avoided each other. But in New York, four years later, Ansermet sent a note to Stravinsky:

Our old friendship has more weight than all circumstances and we are, both of us, too near the end of our lives to forget it. [July 13, 1966]

Stravinsky answered, July 15:

Your letter touched me. We are both old enough *not* to think of the end of our days, and I would not like to finish mine under the weight of a painful enmity.

In Brussels on January 14, 1924, Stravinsky conducted the Octet, *Pribaoutki, Mavra,* and the 1919 *Firebird* Suite, in a program that also included the Three Pieces for String Quartet and the Concertino. Ansermet was to have led the concert, but when he became ill, it was offered to Stravinsky. A week later (January 21), an article appeared in *Comoedia,* by J. van Cotton:

On the express from Antwerp, between an apoplectic lady and the celebrated composer Igor Stravinsky . . . I was able to ask the young Russian maestro several questions without giving him the feeling of being submitted to an interview. He answered with the marvelous indifference of a banker explaining his minor business affairs to an agent of the Sûreté.

January 1924. Brussels. With the Pro Arte Ensemble, musicians and doublebasses. Photograph by Vera Sudeikina.

About forty years old, a monocle covering a deep-set brown eye ... and in his voice the native charm of all Slavs ... M. Stravinsky spoke to me first about the young French school, and of the fact that they give the feeling of being mildly obsolete.

"Ravel? But Ravel is ten years older than I am." Having made the statement, it is as if he saw himself ten years hence in a state of advanced decrepitude. "As for Ravel's talent, it is Rimsky-Korsakov's fifty years younger. . . ." M. Stravinsky goes on to discuss the music of "The Six" [109] whose principles and methods are most closely related to the current methods of the Russian master. . . . Don't forget that Stravinsky is constantly evolving. . . . Even if his admirers know where he comes from and where he is at the moment, they have no idea where he is going. . . . "I, who am conveniently described as a revolutionary, am guilty of having borrowed from Pergolesi for my *Pulcinella*. What is more, Liszt provided the example."

In the same light mood I threw in the name Wagner, and suddenly the smile gave way to a grimace. "Wagner ... is certainly not a real musician. He has had recourse to the theater at every moment in his career, and this remains an obstacle to his musical ideas, whose progress is hindered by his philosophy. Every time Wagner was tempted by pure music, he was hit on the nose. . . ."

Stravinsky is not only a composer of great talent ... and a pianist of the first rank, but he is also a fine scholar, a true artist, and an amiable speaker who uses the French language faultlessly.

We arrive at the subject of Belgian musicians.
—Do you know any of our composers, maestro?
—Who? César Franck!?
—The moderns . . .
—No . . .

Stravinsky did not hold Hindemith's music in high regard—the Russian composer used to describe the German's *Ludus Tonalis* as having "all the juice and flavor of cardboard"—and Stravinsky wrote to Ansermet, September 9, 1923:

I do not regret having made the trip to Weimar: [110] 1) Scherchen's performance of the music of the *Soldat* was very good; [111] 2) the German public gave the piece a good reception and me an ovation—which could be useful in the future when normal life is resumed in Germany; 3) I saw with my own eyes the gigantic abyss that separates me from this country, and, in fact, from the inhabitants of all of *Mitteleuropa*. *Kubismus* is stronger than ever here, and, what is most ridiculous, it goes arm in arm with the *Impressionismus* of Schoenberg. In the concerts, I heard interminable . . . lieder [Das Marienleben] by Hindemith, a kind of H. Wolf. Too bad. I was expecting something different. Scherchen says that Hindemith composes too much. Perhaps. I also heard a complete *Abteilung* of piano pieces by Busoni played by a very good pianist, Petri, from Berlin. Some of Busoni's more recent small compositions for piano [*Fünf kurze Stücke zur Pflege des polyphonen Spiels*, 1923] were not bad at all. I also made the acquaintance of this "master" who was seated next to me and who was so moved by the *Soldat* that he wept hot tears during it.

Stravinsky and Hindemith were good friends, nevertheless, and their paths crossed frequently in the 1940s and 1950s. The two composers regularly exchanged musical presents, from birthday

November 1924. Amsterdam. With the Amar Quartet: Licco Amar, Walter Casper, Paul Hindemith, and Maurits Frank. A few months after this photograph was taken, Hindemith read the part of the Devil in a broadcast of *Histoire du Soldat* from Frankfurt-am-Main — conducted by Scherchen and with Karl Ebert as the narrator.

July 1924. Copenhagen. On July 18, Stravinsky played his Piano Concerto in a concert in the Danish capital. On July 15, he was photographed in Brussels on the way to Copenhagen, and, on the 27th, back in Paris, he wrote to Ramuz: "It is absolutely intolerable to lose entire days in consulates (which was the case with my trip to Copenhagen) filling out pages of answers to stupid questions, such as the color of the hair of my father's mother. The Germans have given me a visa for six months, and though the pigs charged me dearly, at least I do not have the nuisance and the loss of time." Photograph by Vera Sudeikina.

canons to books. Thus Hindemith sent his 1950 Hamburg Bach lecture with the inscription: "To the great Westerners with best wishes from the modest East-coasters."

The *Tribune de Lausanne*, September 30, 1956, contains a description of a meeting between Stravinsky and Hindemith. Stravinsky is rehearsing the Orchestre National de Paris at the Festival de Montreux:

"...*Monsieur le triangle*, I ask you, please do not forget to enter.... *Madame la harpe*, please put an accent on the G-sharp eight measures before the end of the movement...." Paul Hindemith is there, watching with concentrated interest the manner in which his illustrious colleague directs the rehearsal. After it, Stravinsky, descending from the podium, encounters Hindemith—an effusion, a spontaneous accolade, and an expression of joy.... [By Henri Jaton]

In January 1929, Stravinsky expressed interest in Hindemith's *Cardillac*,[112] yet when Willy Strecker, Hindemith's publisher, sent an orchestra score of *Neues vom Tage*, Stravinsky thanked Strecker for the gift (letter of December 27) but avoided commenting on the work. Thirty-two years later, Stravinsky heard part of a rehearsal of this opera in Santa Fe, New Mexico, conducted by Hindemith himself; and, a few weeks after that, the two composers saw each other for the last time:

August 30, 1961. New York. The Pierre Hotel. Varèse and Elliott Carter for lunch. Stravinsky not being ready on time, I precede him, and, in the elevator, run into the Hindemiths. When Varèse recovers from the surprise of seeing me emerge with the wrong composer, he asks me to introduce him, but by this time Hindemith is several yards away. Then when I catch up and convey the request, in the very moment that he starts to say "yes," Frau H. does say "no." As Varèse watches them hurrying away, I can think of no other excuse than that Hindemith isn't feeling well, which can scarcely accord with Varèse's impression of him a short time later in the hotel restaurant satisfying a huge appetite and positively leaping from his seat to greet Stravinsky when *he* arrives. Afterward, Stravinsky, Varèse, Goddard Lieberson, and I listen to my recording of *Deserts*, in a tape-editing cubicle at 52nd Street and Seventh Avenue. [From R.C.'s diary]

Between 1924 and 1929, Stravinsky played his Piano Concerto in more than forty concerts. Naturally he was asked many questions about it, and, finally, on December 28, 1928, he prepared a written answer, of which the following is a brief excerpt:

The short, crisp dance character of the Toccata, engendered by the percussion of the piano, led to the idea that a wind ensemble would suit the piano better than any other combination. In contrast to the percussiveness of the piano, the winds prolong the piano's sounds as well as provide the human element of respiration.

On December 27, 1924, Stravinsky sailed on the S.S. *Paris* for a three-month concert tour in America, playing his Piano

November 1924. Amsterdam. By the stage door. "The Artist as Duke of Omnium." On the day that this photograph was taken, Stravinsky played his Piano Concerto in a concert directed by Willem Mengelberg. Photograph by Vera Sudeikina.

Concerto and conducting. After four days of rough weather, the docking was twelve hours late. *The New York Times*, January 6, describes him on his first day in New York:

Igor Stravinsky put in his first full day in America yesterday by holding a morning rehearsal of his music with the Philharmonic Orchestra in Carnegie Hall, glimpsing the newer skyscrapers of Fifth Avenue from snow-bound taxicabs . . . telling a dozen interviewers his plans . . . and going out at evening to dine and to hear on its native hearth the dance music that the Old World has called American jazz. . . . On his crossing on the liner *Paris*: "We had a great storm without as much sun as a twenty-franc piece." Mr. Stravinsky, monocled . . . heavy gold bands on both wrists for a watch and other matters, stood, as he talked, by an open piano. . . . A box of flowers being brought to his door, he exclaimed: "I hope not my immortal crown." [January 6, 1925]

Three months later, in Barcelona, asked if he liked being called "modern," Stravinsky said that he had been asked the same question in New York:

All that modern, avant-garde stuff, all that which wants to limit art to a mode, a fashion, is repugnant to me; the epoch of "isms," programs, manifestos is over. . . . [*La Veu de Catalunya*, March 1925]

Stravinsky conducted the New York Philharmonic on January 8, 9, 10; participated as pianist in a concert of his chamber music at Mrs. Astor's, 840 Fifth Avenue, on the 15th; played his Concerto in Boston on the 23rd and 24th; conducted the Philharmonic Orchestra in Philadelphia on the 30th and 31st; played his Concerto with the New York Philharmonic under Mengelberg on February 5 and 6; conducted the Cleveland Orchestra on the 12th and 14th; played his Concerto under Reiner in Philadelphia on the 15th; conducted the Chicago Symphony on the 20th and 21st, the Detroit Symphony on March 3, and the Cincinnati Symphony on March 6 and 7. The programs included the *Scherzo Fantastique, Fireworks, Firebird* Suite, *Song of the Volga Boatmen, Song of the Nightingale,* and *Pulcinella* Suite. *Le Sacre* had been on the New York Philharmonic program, but Stravinsky canceled the piece. (See Appendix B, note 57.)

But the most celebrated concert of the tour was "An Evening of Chamber Music with Igor Stravinsky," in Aeolian Hall, New York, on January 25. The program consisted of the Octet, *Ragtime,* and *Renard,* which the composer conducted, and nine of his songs, sung by Greta Torpadie [113] with Stravinsky at the piano. The program had been rehearsed by Carlos Salzedo (who played the cimbalom part in *Renard* on the piano [114]) before Stravinsky's arrival. On December 30, 1924, the *Musical Digest* published a thumbnail portrait of the composer by Salzedo:

His rhythmic innovations, his increase in the use of percussion, were revolutionary fifteen years ago. Now . . . next to Varèse's *Hyperprism,* Stravinsky's use of percussion seems mild. In the minds of the modernists,[115] Stravinsky is already a classic. . . . When I was preparing *Re-*

nard, he sent a kind letter, in answer to queries of mine, in which he outlined with the greatest consideration and thoughtfulness the various problems which he knew would arise in its performance. That letter was a perfect key to the character of the man. It was coolly calculating and logical. . . . He can stop or begin work at will. . . . He keeps a tradition among composers by being far from what one would call rich, yet he is Russian in his generosity.

Salzedo asked Stravinsky to compose a work for harp and instrumental ensemble, but whereas Salzedo's letters to the composer in 1925 and 1926 refer to the hoped-for piece, none of Stravinsky's to Salzedo (Paris, July 9, 1925; Nice, December 26, 1925; Nice, February 10, 1926) mentions anything except the fee for the American premiere of *Les Noces.* Salzedo and Varèse were organizing a performance of this, to be conducted by Stokowski in Carnegie Hall, February 14, 1926, with Casella, Enesco, Tailleferre, and Salzedo as the pianists. Varèse had written to Stravinsky's London publisher in the spring of 1924, requesting the parts for *Les Noces.* The letter was forwarded to Stravinsky, who determined the amount of the rental himself but asked his representative in Paris, Robert Lyon, to write to Varèse. Lyon's letter is dated March 26, Varèse's answer April 8, but on May 7 Varèse cabled that the performance would have to be postponed for lack of a chorus. Varèse, in Paris, wrote to Stravinsky on June 22, asking for a few minutes in which to discuss the matter. But Stravinsky seems not to have answered, which would explain Varèse's conspicuous absence during Stravinsky's New York visit in January 1925. In fact, the two composers did not meet until August 1961, when they were introduced by this writer.

Between the dress rehearsal and the concert, the critic Paul Rosenfeld managed to extract what has become probably the most famous of all Stravinsky interviews:

Stravinsky was a good thirty minutes late [116] for rehearsal the afternoon I interviewed him. . . . [He] came rapidly onto the stage from the wings, a metallic insect all swathed in hat, spectacles, muffler, overcoat, spats, and walking stick; and accompanied by three or four secretarial, managerial personages.

The man was an electric shock. In a minute, business was upon the entire assemblage.[117] There was a sound of peremptory orders . . . a little personage [118] who looked like someone in a Moscow Art Theater performance rushed forward to the composer and started stripping him of his coats and helping him . . . and Stravinsky, simultaneously resembling a bug, Gustav Mahler, and a member of the Russian Ballet, began rehearsing. If he had been late, there was no laggardliness in his mind at all. Never a doubt as to exactly what it was he wanted and the means to arrive at his end! He himself might not be able to play all the instruments assembled before him; still he could tell the musicians how [to] get the effects wanted. The bassoonist had some difficulty with the high notes. Stravinsky told him how he could reach them. At the moment when the bass drum enters, Stravinsky stopped the orchestra. "Deeper," he said in German. The drummer struck again. "No," said Stravinsky, "it must sound the way it does in the circus. You will need a heavier drumstick." In passages of complicated rhythm, he stopped the orchestra, sang the measure very quietly, and then left the musicians to play it after him. Once there was a dispute. He stuck his nose into the score, read a few bars carefully, then said to the instrumentalist, "You must make it this way," and sang the notes.

Most of his talking was done in German, but he spoke French with Salzedo, Russian with one of the men, and indicated the passages by numbers given in very correct English. . . . The man was abrupt, impatient, energetic, but never ironic either of himself or of his interlocutors; most exemplary in his relations with the players. It was apparent they were working out a little problem together, and Stravinsky had some suggestions which might enable them all to solve it. A kind of interest radiated from him to the musicians, who began entering into the spirit of the animal comedy, and kindling him in return. He commenced singing the words in Russian, even danced a little in his pink sweater up on the conductor's stand. . . . His arms at all times mimed the rhythmic starts and jerks, till one could actually perceive where his music came from. . . .

When the rehearsal was over . . . the little Stanislavsky type was helping on with coats and hat; and I found myself before an oval, olive, excessively sensitive face from out some fine old Chinese print, and a man . . . at once nervous, intelligent, and master of himself. I heard myself saying in French that I had some questions which I wanted to ask him, and that I regretted I spoke French and German equally badly; and was relieved to hear Stravinsky answering quietly that he would converse in the language we both spoke.[119] . . .

He measured me for a moment, then said suddenly, "We are going to exchange roles. It is I who am going to interview you. I want you to begin by telling me exactly what it is you mean by 'personal emotion.'"

I laughed. "But, Mr. Stravinsky, I am not a genius."

"Neither am I," he retorted. Then after a moment, "Suppose you went out and narrowly escaped being run over by a trolley car. Would you have an emotion?"

"I should hope so, Mr. Stravinsky."

"So should I. But if I went out and narrowly escaped being run over by a trolley car, I would not immediately rush for some music paper and try to make something out of the emotion I had just felt."

"... In their very effort to escape from romanticism, people are committing the most grotesque errors. Take Schoenberg. . . . [He] is really a romantic at heart who would like to get away from romanticism. . . . But even the romantic composers aren't as 'romantic' as people have tried to make them. Schumann, for instance. I know I could play Schumann for people so that he wouldn't have that particular sort of sentimentalism which we don't admire today. But then people would say it wasn't Schumann."

"... What interests me most of all is construction. What gives me pleasure is to see how much of my material I can get into line. I want to see what is coming. I am interested first in the melody, and the volumes, and the instrumental sounds, and the rhythm. . . ."

. . . As we went through the door . . . and while Salzedo was talking to Stravinsky about the music of Varèse, a young fellow who had been listening to the conversation from a little distance rushed up to the composer, declared he admired his work, and begged to be allowed to shake his hand. There was a half-embarrassed moment, Stravinsky bowing like an oriental potentate, and doubtlessly enjoying, for the thousandth time, the sweetest of all homages, that of young people.[120]

In Brussels in 1930, Stravinsky returned to and developed some of these ideas in a conversation in which his interviewer was trying to draw parallels between the musician's art and that of Le Corbusier:

For me, constructive form is predominant, and all of my music, even of the early years, is constructive. It seems to me that the tendency of all art today is constructivist. . . . [Le Vingtième Siècle, May 27, 1930]

On his return to Paris from America, Stravinsky was interviewed by Eugene Jolas:

M. Igor Stravinsky, famous Russian composer and iconoclast of rhythm [sic], arrived in Paris from the S.S. Aquitania last night,[121] after being lionized in New York, Chicago and other cities of the North American continent during a triumphant stay of more than three months. "I expect your country to bring us the new things in music," Stravinsky told The Tribune at the Gare Saint-Lazare. "Your skyscrapers impressed me as leading to new visions in art. What work! What energy there is in your immense country!" . . . American jazz gave him a real thrill, he admitted, although he said he had heard much of it before going to America. "The music of the future will have to take it into account, no matter what the tendency of the composer."

Stravinsky then went directly to Barcelona, where, on March 28, at the Gran Teatro del Liceu, he conducted the Orquestra Pau Casals in a concert consisting of Fireworks, The Song of the Nightingale, the Pulcinella Suite, Ragtime, Petrushka. On April 2, he conducted a second concert: Scherzo Fantastique, excerpts from The Nightingale, the Three Japanese Lyrics, Pribaoutki, Pastorale, Tilimbom, Octet, Suite from Histoire du Soldat, The Faun and the Shepherdess, and the Firebird Suite.
    While Stravinsky was in America, his niece Tanya, daughter of his brother Yury, came to France to learn secretarial work. She stayed with the Stravinsky family in Nice until October, then went to Paris, and eventually returned to Leningrad because of nostalgia—or so Yury wrote to his brother. In a long letter dated "Leningrad, May 8, 1925," the elder brother explains to the younger one that the State Philharmonic wants to have him conduct his more recent works and implores him to come. In another letter, June 21, Yury asks Igor not to be offended but says that

you look rather old in your photographs; probably we do too, in the photographs that Tanya brought to you. We are grateful for your kindness to her.

But Yury's next letter, July 16, criticizes Igor for refusing to come to Leningrad, and predicts, accurately, that they will never see each other again. In September 1925, Mme Taropiano, a busybody whom Stravinsky used to describe in the most unflattering terms—but who must have known him well since she addresses him with the familiar "tu"—wrote that your brother Yury looks shabby and lacks proper shoes and clothing. Benois is going to Russia. Couldn't you give a package to him for Yury?

In the beginning of 1947, Stravinsky received a letter from Yury's widow giving the details of his brother's death. It seems that, one day in May 1941, Yury had telephoned from his office and said he felt very ill, and that a few moments later he had lost consciousness. The cause of death was apparently a stroke. The letter says that Yury had written not only about his science of engineering, but also about the architecture of Leningrad. Elena adds that:

I live with Xenia and her thirteen-year-old daughter. We have two rooms in the apartment of Napravnik . . . better than . . . the apartment at No. 66. Tanya lives separately, with her husband and eighteen-year-old son. . . . Xenia married a second time, three months ago.

Stravinsky answered this on February 17, 1947, but his greatest sorrow seems to have been for the loss of his father's library.

To return to 1925: on August 18, Stravinsky wrote to Mme Brussova, at the Commissariat of Education in Moscow:

Owing to numerous prior engagements abroad, extending into the fore-seeable future, I am unhappily obliged to decline your kind invitation to undertake a concert tour of Moscow, Leningrad, Kiev and Odessa.

I thank you very much for your kind words, in any event, and I hope that in the future it will be possible personally to acquaint my countrymen with my art.

Pray, Madame, accept assurances of my utmost respect.

Igor Stravinsky
Paris

P.S. Forgive me, Madame, for not answering you in Russian, but I do not have a typewriter with Russian letters.

On October 1, 1925, Stravinsky wrote to the Secretary of the Composers' Union in Leningrad, declining still another invitation.

But the performance of his music in the U.S.S.R. was a matter of great interest to Stravinsky. Writing to Kling, July 2, 1924, the composer says that he has received a letter from A. W. Hawk, conductor of the Théâtre Académique in Leningrad, inquiring about fees for the performances of Renard, *Les Noces*, and *Histoire du Soldat*, and, on the 23rd of October, Stravinsky wrote to Kling asking if he had heard from Leningrad.

On April 24, 1926, Weber, the representative of the Russischer Musik Verlag in Berlin, wrote to Stravinsky that Dr. Fritz Stiedry had had a triumph in Leningrad with *Le Sacre*:

. . . it was so successful that the orchestra representative made a speech calling the event the greatest in the history of the orchestra. It was impossible to obtain tickets for the performances, and hundreds of people were turned away. Stiedry performed the *Sacre* four times in all, and he has been invited to return next year, also giving the *Sacre*.

On May 3, 1926, Stravinsky answered a request of the Première Ensemble Symphonique in Moscow concerning a Russian translation of *Histoire du Soldat*. And, in December 1926, *Les Noces* was at last performed in its composer's native city. As he told a reporter in 1927:

The *Noces* was given in concert in the middle of last December, in the Pevtcheskaïa Kapella (which translates better in German than in French: "*Singkapelle*"), which, in the past, was part of the Imperial Court.

Stravinsky appears not to have answered an invitation of March 30, 1929, from his concert agent in Vienna, Kugel (then in Leningrad, but relayed through his Austrian office), to conduct in Leningrad that same year.

Stravinsky's 1925 American tour was the most lucrative of his life, and on his return from Paris to Nice, in late July 1925, he employed a chauffeur,[122] whom he describes in a letter to Ramuz, July 29, 1925, as

... very nice, very expensive. At every moment he introduces me to one of his ex-chauffeur friends—one of them the proprietor of a bistro, another of a bicycle shop—saying "here is my new *patron*.". . . Apart from the automobile rides, I bathe each morning in the sea, then compose regularly, then, in the afternoon, do my correspondence and practice the piano (in order not to lose the technique that I acquired last year). This letter appears to be very correct but seems to me very boring to read, for which reason I must now put a period.

The fine flower of international snob society was gathered in the salon of the Princesse de Polignac . . . women and their male companions crowded around the Russian musician . . . the rolling of "r's" in "mon

September 7, 1925. Venice. With the Princesse de Polignac on the balcony of her home, the Palazzo Contarini dal Zaffo. The Princesse's letters to Stravinsky at this time address him as "Cher grand ami" and are signed "Singer Polignac." Photograph by Vera Sudeikina.

cherr" sounded like a swarm of bees. Someone offered [Stravinsky] another cup of tea, and everyone stopped talking to hear his answer: "For a Russian, tea is the center of all our nostalgias. In the West there are no samovars and the taste of tea is altogether different. *C'est un autre goût.*" [G. F. Malipiero in an unidentified Venetian newspaper]

Artur Rubinstein was in Venice at the time, and the two friends were often photographed together. Also on this trip Stravinsky met the violinist Alma Moodie, with whom he was later to give the first performance of his Suite from *Pulcinella*, arranged for violin and piano. Stravinsky was in Venice to play his Sonata.

On October 13, 1924, writing to Guido Boni in Rome, Stravinsky says that if Venice wants him as a conductor of his works, it must at least learn to distinguish him from Borodin, the composer of *Prince Igor*, who had died forty years before. Venice did not want Stravinsky to conduct, however, but to play his Sonata on a program with works by Ruggles, Louis Gruenberg, and others, and for this the composer of *Le Sacre* demanded a high price. The Venice committee asked Werner Reinhart for assistance, and his letter to Stravinsky, July 29, 1925, seems to indicate that Schoenberg's participation in the festival might have been considered a factor in Stravinsky's reluctance to take part:

I need not tell you of the pleasure that we will have to see you there [in Venice] and to hear the work performed by yourself, but I also understand that it is difficult for you to make the trip for only one work. I ask you frankly, therefore, to tell me the conditions that would make this possible. Perhaps you know that Schoenberg is coming, to conduct his Serenade.

Stravinsky may have heard the Serenade (his bill at the Hotel Danieli shows that he was in Venice on the night of September 7, the day of the Serenade performance, as well as on the 8th and 9th); also, he had not yet given a title to a piano composition-in-progress of his own that, soon after, he was to call "Serenade." The popes of modern music did not meet, in any case, and by this date they were clearly not on friendly terms.[123] Schoenberg composed his *Three Satires* after the Venice festival.[124]

On September 8, in the Teatro La Fenice, Stravinsky played his Sonata, written the year before, partly in Biarritz (the first movement, completed August 21, 1924) and partly in Nice (the second movement, completed October 6, and the third movement, completed October 24).[125] On August 4, 1925, Prokofiev wrote to Miaskovsky:

Stravinsky has written a dreadful sonata, which he plays himself with a certain chic. The music is Bach but with pockmarks.

At the end of July 1924, Stravinsky and his wife had gone from Biarritz to Nice in search of a new home—". . . last week I was in Nice with my wife looking for a new habitation, which we

September 8, 1925. Venice. Stravinsky is wearing gloves, this being the day of the miraculous cure of his thumb.

found but at such a price" (letter to Ramuz, August 6, 1924)—and on September 25, 1924, the Stravinsky family moved from Biarritz to Nice, Villa des Roses, Montboron. Soon after, all four Stravinsky children had diphtheria (letter of October 14, 1924, to Oeberg).

I dined at [Stravinsky's] house in Nice [126] and listened to him talk. . . . The after-dinner conversation centered mainly around my host and his recent appearance as pianist at the Venice festival of the International Society for Contemporary Music. It seems that Stravinsky had been contracted to play his piano sonata at the festival for a five-hundred-dollar fee. A short while before leaving for Venice, he got an infected finger and was seized by fear of being unable to appear at the concert; on the eve of the event he visited a church and prayed fervently for his finger's recovery. Stravinsky appeared on the concert platform, his finger bandaged, and made a short speech of apology, pointing to the bandage and begging the audience's indulgence. Just before attacking the sonata, he removed the bandage and, Eureka!—the infection had subsided and the finger functioned normally.[127]

But another infection was always present in Stravinsky's homes in Nice and elsewhere: tuberculosis. A 1925 letter from Pierre de Lacretelle, in Villefranche-sur-Mer, tactfully explains to Stravinsky that Cocteau, who has come to work on Oedipus Rex, has been warned by his doctor not to enter the Stravinsky household, that the disease is highly contagious and Cocteau extremely susceptible. Lacretelle asks Stravinsky if it would be possible to meet with Cocteau in the garden. In a letter to Elie Gagnebin, January 27, 1926, from the Hôtel Welcome, Villefranche-sur-Mer, Cocteau says that he has just had "a visit from Igor," which would seem to indicate that Lacretelle's words had had an effect.

On October 9, 1925, Stravinsky finished the "Romanza" of his Serenade (the Cadenza-Finale had been completed as long ago as May 9) and gave the first performance of the opus (possibly incomplete) at the home of Werner Reinhart, for a group of his friends. The first public performance took place, the composer at the piano, on November 25, at Frankfurt-am-Main. Before the Frankfurt premiere, he had played his Piano Concerto in Basel (November 14) and Berlin (November 21). On November 26, Stravinsky and Vera Sudeikina went to Copenhagen, and on December 7, returned to Paris, where Mme Sudeikina's mother came from Moscow, and where one of Stravinsky's close friends, Ernest Oeberg, died:

I have just spent ten days in Paris, very unhappy ones due to the death of Oeberg, of whom, as you know, I was very fond. My poor friend suffered so, first from a liver disorder, then a burst appendix, peritonitis, surgery, and death. [Letter to Ansermet, written on the Paris-to-Nice train, December 20, 1925]

Igor Stravinsky and Vera Sudeikina not only traveled together but sometimes wrote letters together. Here is one to Diaghilev:

VERA: Dear Sergei Pavlovich: I was very touched by your telegram and very pleased that the costumes were successful. Igor is in Paris now and would like to see you.

IGOR: You pig. At least you could have sent a telegram as you did to Vera, to say that the music pleased you. Come. Since I am here I expect to stay for about two weeks longer. I embrace you. Igor. [Paris, December 31, 1925]

December 2, 1925. Copenhagen. The Restaurant Nimb, after a concert in which Stravinsky played his Sonata as well as conducted the *Pulcinella* Suite, *Ragtime*, *Histoire du Soldat*, Suite for Small Orchestra. On December 6, Stravinsky conducted *Petrushka* for the Royal Danish Ballet. Stravinsky is in the center of the photograph, Vera Sudeikina to the right. Carl Nielsen (white hair) stands directly behind Stravinsky.

May 14, 1926. Milan. Teatro alla Scala. Poster.

In 1926, in Nice, Stravinsky received a visit from Vladimir Eduardovich Napravnik, son of the Czech conductor and composer Eduard Napravnik. Vladimir arranged a concert for Stravinsky in Belgium, May 20, 1930. In Nice, April 13, 1926, Vladimir Napravnik witnessed the contract between Stravinsky and J. & W. Chester for the First Suite for small orchestra, and for the orchestral version of *Tilimbom*.

On May 12, Stravinsky had conducted *Petrushka* at La Scala (on a double bill with *Hansel and Gretel*), and, on May 16, he was to conduct *The Nightingale* and *Petrushka* on a triple bill with the Humperdinck opera between. The chorus master for *The Nightingale*, Vittore Veneziani, was in the same post twenty-five years later when Stravinsky came to La Scala to rehearse *The Rake's Progress* for its premiere in Venice. The stage director for *The Nightingale*, Giovacchino Forzano, celebrated as the librettist of *Gianni Schicchi*, was also to encounter Stravinsky again. In the Vatican, on June 12, 1965, after a performance of the *Symphony of Psalms* in his honor, Stravinsky stepped forward to receive a decoration from the Pope, slipped, and Forzano, standing a few rows away, rushed to the composer's aid.

In Paris, December 12, 1925, Stravinsky received a license to drive, and he was a member of the Automobile Club of Nice and the Côte d'Azur until December 1932. In the summer of 1926, he purchased a Hotchkiss, and, in January 1927, a Citroën. But, the first time he drove the Citroën, he was given a ticket for parking at the wrong hour in front of Hermès (where he had gone to buy a cravat), and, shortly after that, he drove to St.-Germain-en-Laye in low gear—unwittingly, of course—and burned out the motor. The Citroën was sold in June 1933, but he had meanwhile bought a Mathis, in which, on October 29, 1927, he and Vera Sudeikina left Paris for Nice, reaching Valence at 2:00 P.M. and Nice at 1:00 A.M. (according to a note by the composer). The Mathis was still in his possession in September 1935,

June 1926. By the Seine. In Vera Sudeikina's Renault, a gift from Stravinsky, January 22, 1926. Mme Sudeikina was living in the Hôtel de l'Acacia at the time, while repairs were being made in the apartment in the rue de Ranelagh to which she later moved.

August 1926. On the road, Paris to Nice, with Vera Sudeikina and Jean Cocteau.

in which month he rode in it from Voreppe to Venice. His next automobile was a Peugeot *bleu-nuit*, given to Vera Sudeikina.

Much of the correspondence between Stravinsky and Cocteau concerning *Oedipus Rex*, beginning with the composer's invitation to the writer, dated October 11, 1925, has been published, but not the timetable of the composition. The first notations date from January 2, 1926, when Stravinsky entered in his sketchbook the music at one measure after 2 and the words *"peste serva nos qua Theba moritur."* On January 6, he composed the music for *"Oedipus, serva nos,"* and, on the 13th and 14th, the chorus *"e peste libera urbem."* By the end of the month, he had completed the opening chorus, and, in the beginning of February, he went with Cocteau and Vera Sudeikina for a short holiday to Marseille. The composition was resumed on March 26, "After returning from a concert tour in Holland, Budapest, Vienna, Zagreb," as the manuscript says. The other dated entries are as follows:

March 28. Paris. Composes the music at 22 .

April 1–15. Composes Creon's aria.

April 19. Composes the music from 45 through the fourth measure of 55 , then interrupts work until August. He conducts

Petrushka and *The Nightingale* at La Scala, May 9, 12, 14, 16; returns to Paris; is again in Milan for concerts on June 17 and 18, playing his Piano Concerto under Scherchen, who also conducts Part One (only!) of *Le Sacre*; after the Milan concert, goes with his wife for a two-week vacation in Italy (Florence, Rome, Naples, Capri, Pompeii), and, on July 8, flies from Paris to London for the English premiere of *Les Noces*. Back in Paris, Stravinsky dined with Cocteau on July 30, and with Diaghilev on the 31st, then, the same evening, left for Nice by car with Vera Sudeikina, Cocteau, and Guy de Matharel. At 4:00 A.M. on August 1, the party stopped at Moulin. They had *déjeuner* at La Palisse and slept in the Hotel Majestic at Grenoble. On August 2, they dined at La Mure and at Dignes, reaching Nice at 2:30 A.M., August 3.

August 6. Resumes the composition at 56 . (See illustrations below.)

August 9. Composes the music at 60 .

August 10–17. Composes the *"Delie"* chorus.

August 18–26. Completes Tiresias' aria.

August 27. Begins *"Invidia fortunam odit."*

September 1. Composes *"Stipendarius es, Tiresias!"* Writes to

August 6 and 7, 1926. Two sketch pages for *Oedipus Rex*.

Païchadze: "Very soon I will send the first act, having decided, in view of the considerable length of the opera, to divide it into two parts."

September 2–7. Completes Act One.

N.D.: Begins Jocasta's aria with the notation for the triplets at [100], then writes her part at [96].

October 15. Develops the music at [100].

October 20. Completes the aria through the first measure of the reprise of the *tempo primo.*

November 1. Completes the music to Oedipus' "Pavesco" (after [117]).

November 16. Completes the duet as far as "*Sciam!*" For the passage from the entrance of the Messenger to the end of the chorus "*monstrum resciscam,*" the sketchbook contains the French text as well as the Latin.[128]

January 6, 1927. Begins the music at [168].

January 12. Begins "*Divum Jocastae caput Mortuum!*"

January 18. Composes the chorus at [179]. (Stravinsky's wife undergoes an appendectomy.)

February 2. Telegraphs Diaghilev at Monte Carlo asking him to come "today."

February 9. Completes the music through [196]; goes to Paris on February 18, returning to Nice on March 10.

March 9. Paris. Receives $250 partial payment from Editions Russes de Musique.

March 12. Nice. Composes the music at [197].

March 13. Composes the music from [198] to [201].

March 14. Completes the sketch score.

March 28. Orchestrates the "Gloria" chorus.

March 31. To Païchadze: "I wrote a letter to you yesterday in great haste and nervousness. Today I will tell you in detail what I had no time to say yesterday. . . . First, I finished the orchestra score of Act One. . . . As for staging *Oedipus* in Diaghilev's season, unfortunately Cocteau has not yet succeeded in enlisting the financial support on which he has been counting. I am very disturbed about this in view of the short time left in which to engage singers."

April 8. Asks Diaghilev to see him "today."

April 11. To Païchadze: "I ask you to write to Diaghilev (Hôtel de Paris, Monte Carlo) concerning the rental of the material, since I do not want to be involved in these questions. Yesterday I gave Diaghilev the means of mounting *Oedipus*—seeing no possibility of involving myself with Cocteau in this question. I will not conduct, and I therefore renounce my honorarium. I will help Diaghilev with money that I hope to obtain from Mme de Polignac for the realization of my opera. I told Diaghilev that he must deal directly with you for the orchestral and choral parts. I also renounce the honorarium for the 'world premiere,' since the work was always promised to Diaghilev. . . . " [129]

April 17. To Païchadze: "Tuesday I will send the piano score of the first act. . . . do not be upset since the rehearsals will not begin before the 20th of May. The performance will probably take place on May 30."

April 25. To Païchadze: "Together with these lines, I send the copy of the piano score. . . . You can give it to Nouvel, who will pick it up from you and give it to the chorus director, who must study it before . . . rehearsing it. . . . If the . . . printers are ready before my arrival in Paris (2nd, 3rd, or 4th of May), then make the proofs. I will correct the remaining faults in Paris immediately."

April 27. To Païchadze: "Herewith the manuscript of the first act together with the first proofs of the piano score. Do not be frightened by the number of corrections in this second proof, for they are not complicated. . . . I will apply myself immediately to the job of revising the first proof of the second act. . . . And do not worry about the copyright, which is protected by the collaboration of Cocteau. My music will not be stolen without the text."

May 3. Goes to Paris.

May 29. Evening. The *"avant-première"* (Stravinsky's note on his program) of *Oedipus Rex,* at the home of the Princesse de Polignac, Avenue Henri-Martin, the composer accompanying the soloists, chorus, and speaker, at the piano.

May 30. Théâtre Sarah-Bernhardt. Conducts first performance (on a program with *The Firebird,* in which Balanchine is Kastchei, Danilova the Firebird). Oedipus: Belina-Skupevsky: Jocasta: Hélène Sadoven; Creon: G. Lanskoy; Tiresias: K. Zaporojetz; Narrator: Pierre Brasseur.

August 15. To Païchadze: "Cocteau . . . has sent his French text to rue d'Anjou. . . . I feel from his letter that he needs money at the moment and think that it would be wise to pay this last installment. . . ."

The August 6 draft for the instrumental phrase before *"Sphynga solvi"* resembles the final version in harmonic outline (including the bass), but the melodic lines differ. On August 7, Stravinsky added a chord but did not alter the melody, hence it was between this sketch and the final score that he conceived the melodic progression in the inner voices—G-flat, F, F (an octave lower)—and, to give due prominence to the line, assigned it to the horn. Two further improvements effected between the sketches and the final score are the substitution of eighth-notes for the dotted rhythm (which seems brusque here), and the shortening of the meretricious five-note turn (at the end of the third measure) to the simple resolution of the trill in the final score.

A comparison of the sketches for the music at "*Sphynga solvi*" shows the composer lightening the string accompaniment at the entrance of the voice and emphasizing the G-flat and the second beats and off-beats—a rhythmic pattern that, together with the cello trill, provides exactly the right degree of agitation. The rhythmic figuration in the earlier sketch is less effective though more aggressive, filling each measure with syncopation and unnecessarily reinforcing the metrical accents, thereby tending to cover the beautiful first interval in Oedipus' part.[130]

Despite the lyric style, new for Stravinsky, the rhythmic profile of the music is no less sharp, and the accompaniment figurations are no less important, than in his ballets. But the rhythmic substance, Stravinsky's principal instrument of dramatic tension, is simpler than ever before. The vocal parts are always uppermost, and the role of the orchestra is secondary, the only purely orchestral passages being brief introductions and connecting links. Yet much of the effect of the music depends on the instrumentation.

The seventh chords and sustained bass in the harmony at "*Sphynga solvi*" might be described as chastely Wagnerian, whereas the vocal line could have been inspired by Byzantine chant. The repeated D-flat in the tenor part gives the D-natural in the third phrase a power of change that few single notes have exercised in any music of the last fifty years. Finally, the extension of the last phrase (see the left side of the August 7 sketch) and the resolution of the harmony—G-natural—are in Oedipus' own part, which may or may not be an example of musical symbolism.

The third measure of the August 6 sketch provides a lesson in Stravinsky's approach to word-setting. The "*Carmen*" in the canceled version can be articulated only by aspirating every note and is clumsy even then, but in the rewritten version (above the staff) the melismas trip along gracefully, two notes to a syllable, and the repetition of the word puts the hard "*c*" on the beat both times. By eliminating the first quarter-beat, too, Stravinsky interrupts the regularity of the meter and lightens the entire phrase. The reader will note that the metrical accent falls on the second syllable of "*clarissimus*," that a chord in the orchestra sets off the tenor's entrance on this word, and that "*iterum divinabo*" has been omitted, perhaps by oversight.

Even before the first performance of *Oedipus Rex*, Prokofiev wrote to Miaskovsky:

The libretto is French, the text is Latin, the subject is Greek, the music is Anglo-German (Handel), and the money is American—true cosmopolitanism. . . . [Letter of May 26, 1927]

After the premiere, Francis Poulenc wrote to Stravinsky:

Votre art est arrivé à une hauteur qu'il faudrait le langage de Sophocle pour en parler.

Two months later, Ravel remarked that

Stravinsky is, happily, never content with his past achievements. He is seeking. His neoclassicism may be something of an experiment, but don't think that Stravinsky has stopped. His last work, *Oedipus*, showed that while he plays with old forms, he is actually finding something new. [From an interview in *The New York Times*, August 7, 1927]

But when Schoenberg attended Klemperer's enormously successful staged performance in the Kroll Opera, Berlin, the Viennese master could find nothing good to say about the work:

I do not know what I am supposed to like in *Oedipus*. . . . It is all negative: unusual theatre, unusual setting, unusual resolution of the action, unusual vocal writing, unusual acting, unusual melody, unusual harmony, unusual counterpoint, unusual instrumentation—all this is un, without *being* anything in particular. . . . All Stravinsky has composed is the dislike his work is meant to inspire.[131] [February 24, 1928]

Far more perceptive are the comments of the young Benjamin Britten:

Stravinsky's *Oedipus Rex*—opera-oratorio after Sophocles, text by Cocteau (put into Latin by Daniélou)—was performed under Ansermet at Queen's Hall on February 12th. The enthusiasm of the conductor did not seem to have spread to the performers. The chorus sang accurately enough, but with dull tone and not much vitality. The attitude of the orchestra seemed the same: while the soloists, with the exception of Oda Slobodskaya who sang beautifully, though the part of Jocasta lies too low for her, seemed quite at sea. Oedipus was entirely miscast; the bel canto of a Latin tenor is needed rather than the teutonic "Tristan" style.

One of the peaks of Stravinsky's output, this work shows his wonderful sense of style and power of drawing inspiration from every age of music, and leaving the whole a perfect shape, satisfying every aesthetic demand. And, of course, the established idea of originality dies so hard, it is easy to see why the later works of Stravinsky are regarded with such disfavour. Another hard nut to crack is the typical later-Stravinsky method of the drama. The combination of set, stylized sections in the music, the Latin words, the masks worn by most of the actors, gives the impression of an impersonal comment on Sophocles rather than a re-enaction of the drama. . . . One London gentleman expressed amusement at Jocasta's great and beautiful aria in Act II. But perhaps it is a compliment in itself to have stirred him to any emotion at all. [*Diary*, February 12, 1936]

Another acute appreciation of *Oedipus Rex* is found in Leonard Bernstein's 1973 Charles Eliot Norton lecture:

I remembered where those four opening notes of *Oedipus*

came from. . . . And the whole metaphor of pity and power came clear: the pitiful Thebaïs supplicating before their powerful king, imploring deliverance from the plague . . . an Ethiopian slave girl at the feet of her mistress, Princess of Egypt. . . . Amneris has just wormed out of Aida her dread secret. . . . Why Verdi of all people, who was so unfashionable at the time *Oedipus* was written, someone for musical intellectuals of the mid-twenties to sneer at; and *Aida*, of all things, that cheap, low, sentimental melodrama, the splashiest and flashiest of all the Verdi operas—*why?*

At the climax of Oedipus' *"invidia fortunam odit,"* where the orchestra plays a

diminished seventh chord . . . that favorite ambiguous tool [132] of suspense and despair in every romantic opera. What is it? Of course; *Aida!* . . . Was Stravinsky having a secret romance with Verdi's music in those supersophisticated mid-twenties? It seems he was. . . .[133]

Mr. Bernstein was right, and the reader of the present book may already have wondered about the photograph of Verdi incongruously adorning the wall over the pianola in Stravinsky's studio in 1923 (see page 242). Stravinsky knew and loved Verdi's operas, and, in order to hear them on his concert tours, would maneuver the dates of his own performances, if possible, as he did for a *Macbeth* in December 1931 in Hanover—when, too, it might be mentioned, he met Kurt Schwitters. "I like Donizetti very much," Stravinsky told Domenico di Paoli, when this critic was beginning his biography of the composer (1933):

As for Bellini, he is too genial to be understood. But if I had been in Nietzsche's place, I would have said Verdi instead of Bizet and held up *The Masked Ball* against the music of Wagner.[134]

And, in Buenos Aires, three years later (May 1936), the newspaper *El Pueblo* described an encounter between Stravinsky and "a self-styled avant-garde writer in search of some peppery comments":

"Maestro, what is your opinion of *La Traviata*?" Stravinsky looked severely at the interviewer and threw back at him: "Recently I had the pleasure of listening to its delicious waltz and never in my life would I be capable of composing anything to equal that." The journalist fled.

On July 17, 1927, the London *Observer* published an interview with Stravinsky in which, asked about the text of *Oedipus Rex*, he remarked that he had chosen Latin because it was "the most exact and unalterable language." The statement gave a boost to Latinists, and Sylvia Pankhurst, the daughter of the famous suffragette, promptly sent a telegram to Giovanni Peano, the mathematician and philosopher who, since 1913, had been

publishing his international review of mathematics in unin-
flected Latin:

*Secretario de comitatu pro Lingua Internationale de British Associa-
tion interroga si Latino sine inflexione pote exprime subtitlitates de
philosophia et "Belles Lettres." Sed Stravinsky dic Latino es lingua
maximo exacto et inalterabile.*

While composing *Oedipus*, however, Stravinsky sometimes forgot that Latin is not always accommodative to the claims of a
musical prerogative in contradictions between musical and verbal stress. Bernardino Molinari—who earned some of the highest marks that Stravinsky ever gave to a conductor—appears to
have been the first to point out to the composer that

the word *cecidi* is evidently a voice of the verb *caedere* (to kill) and not
of the verb *cadere* (to fall). According to Latin grammar, the accent is
on the second syllable and not on the first: *cecídi* and not *cécidi*. Since
the correct accentuation is not in accord with the musical rhythm, I
propose the following modification. . . . [Letter of April 1937]

Yet Stravinsky did not change this passage when he prepared a
new edition of *Oedipus* ("entirely revised by me, with corrections, supplements, and alterations . . . October 10, 1947").

Stravinsky's fifty-year friendship with Cocteau probably had
more low points than high ones, and because of some remarks

Summer 1925. Juan-les-Pins. Cocteau,
Picasso, Stravinsky, Olga Picasso.
("Cigarettes are good for you.")

in *Le Coq et l'Arlequin* (1918), Cocteau was not in Stravinsky's good graces for four years. Ansermet wrote to Stravinsky from London, July 7, 1919:

On the subject of Cocteau, Mme Edwards told me that you should not mind his chatter, since, she said, no one is duped by it.

Then, on August 11, 1922, Stravinsky wrote to Ansermet from Biarritz: "Cocteau writes to me frequently; now we are friends."
A glimpse of the relationship between the two men at a later period is found in a letter to Stravinsky from one of his early biographers, André Schaeffner: [135]

Maître, when it comes to Cocteau, there is always something disagreeable to be said. I am sorry to tell you that the soirée at the Vicomte de Noailles's has been postponed indefinitely, thanks to one of Cocteau's unpleasant whims. He does not want you to see his film before he has had time to make some cuts in the scabrous passages, which might offend your religion. It is regrettable that he did not think to delete these scandalous sections before. Now he is condemning himself, the more so since he is the author of the *Letter to Maritain*. This delayed repentance is at the same time comic and harmful. [July 1931]

Throughout the 1920s, Stravinsky continued to transcribe and record for the mechanical piano, and though the question of a gramophone recording of *Petrushka* had been broached as early as 1919, he did not become convinced until 1928 that

the phonograph is now the best instrument with which to transmit the music of modern composers. [*Les Nouvelles Littéraires*, December 8, 1928]

He complained about the limitations of early recording techniques, the physical effort that making records entailed, and the often discouraging results:

A month ago in Paris I recorded the *Firebird*. It was my second such experience, for I had already recorded *Petrushka* in England. . . . One has to rehearse over and over to try to obtain the best performance. Then, precisely when everyone is most exhausted, when nerves are strained to the breaking point, when the violinists' arms are ready to drop . . . at that very moment everything must be perfect, since only then does the actual recording begin. . . . Even after the final satisfactory test performance, the piece must still be played three times more. It is from these three that the master disc will be chosen.

The pitch of the phonograph recording is determined by the speed with which the work is performed. Thus a movement must be rendered in 3 minutes and 50 seconds, and the conductor must begin again 3 times in succession at exactly the same speed. The whole process is governed by a stop-watch and is not unlike trying for a record in sports.
To judge from my experience, the phonograph is not yet the new instrument it claims to be—but could become if composers were to write expressly for it and for its particular sound, as I did for the mechanical piano. [*Les Nouvelles Littéraires*, December 8, 1928]

Autumn 1927. Paris. Photographed by Vera Sudeikina in her rue Ranelagh apartment. C. F. Ramuz wrote to Stravinsky in 1928 asking him to send a copy of this "photograph in which you resemble Ramses the XXXXVIth, with cane."

December 6 and 15, 1927. Poster for
two "Concerts Jean Wiéner."

In later years, Stravinsky was again critical of recording:

"I am disappointed about recording in the last decade. You have a
good record, and in a few years they throw it away and start a new
system." He objects to the way recordings are "improved" by the technicians after the performance has been given. He believes a recording
should be an exact reproduction of the performance, "like a snapshot."
[Sydney *Telegraph*, November 22, 1961]

On January 4, 1928, Stravinsky wrote to Païchadze:

I am finishing the composition of the *Musagète*, and I am this very
moment working on the "Apotheosis." If all goes well, I will be able to
send the piano transcription of the ballet by the end of next week. You
will copy it and send the copy to Washington together with the scenario which I will add to it. I do not think it will be possible to send
the scenario before, since I have a great number of things to do and the
scenario, as I envisage it, requires mature reflection.

Stravinsky himself wrote a publicity release which says in part
that

January 1928. Draft of the final page of *Apollo*. The chords in the first five measures and the recapitulation of the beginning of the ballet (dotted rhythms) were composed a week earlier than the music on the remainder of the page. Stravinsky's problems had been to find the link between [97] (in the published score) and the middle of the measure before [98]. The Russian script says: "Finished the third day of [Russian] Christmas, 1927"—i.e., January 9, 1928—and the writing seems to express Stravinsky's exuberance on completing the composition.

Stravinsky is preparing an important new work, a classical ballet which is called "*Musagète*."... Its theme is that of Apollo and the muses. The Library of Congress in Washington has acquired the premiere of the work, and afterward the manuscript will be part of its collection.

By March 1928, the new ballet was called "*Apollon-Musagète*."

The first performance, in Washington, D.C., in April 1928, conducted by Hans Kindler, was announced as "*Apollon-Musagètes*," as were the first performances, conducted by Stravinsky, in Paris (June 12, 1928), at the Théâtre Sarah-Bernhardt, and in London (June 25, 1928), in His Majesty's Theater. *Apollon*, of all Stravinsky's works, was the one that he most often conducted in staged performances in the United States during World War II, and at that time the ballet was invariably entitled *Apollo,* the name that Stravinsky continued to prefer until the end of his life.

On April 6, 1927, Pleyel forwarded a cable to Stravinsky from Washington, by way of Carl Engel in Berlin, conveying an invitation from the Library of Congress to write a pantomime for three or four dancers and small orchestra on a subject of his choice,[136] the performance to take place the following April, the commission to be $1,000. On July 11, 1927, Engel wrote to Stravinsky informing him that

. . . Adolph Bolm will be in charge of the production of your little ballet and will be one of the dancers in it. Our hall is not equipped with a regular theater fitted with wings. The present setting is permanent. (I am enclosing a view of it.) Therefore any scenery required will have to be specially adapted and should be technically as simple as possible. . . . The orchestra pit is sunken . . . and it holds easily twenty people. . . .

In an interview eight months later (*L'Intransigeant,* December 2, 1927), Stravinsky reveals that he expected *Apollo* to be heard by "a small circle from the White House"; in fact, the subtitle of the same article—the main title being "Stravinsky speaks to us of the 'Duce' of the Muses"—is *"Une Première à la Maison Blanche."* As for the "small orchestra," Stravinsky wrote to Balanchine, in New York, November 22, 1935:

The news of your forthcoming staging of *Apollo* at the Metropolitan Opera House has provided a welcome opportunity to express my joy and complete confidence in you. My memories of our collaboration during the staging of *Apollo* for Diaghilev in 1928 are among the most satisfying in my artistic life. . . . Knowing what a good musician you are, I count on you to observe the metronomic tempi. . . . The string sextet should consist of thirty-seven players in all, and the number of violins should not be increased because of the extra cellos. The balance was carefully calculated so that the two violin sections correspond to the two sections of cellos and to the one section of violas and one of contrabasses. The sections must consist of 8, 8, 6, 5, 5, 5.

Since much has been written about the influence on *Apollo* of Delibes and Tchaikovsky, it should be mentioned that, before starting the composition, Stravinsky wrote to his publisher in Berlin asking for four-hand scores of the quartets of Mozart and Beethoven, piano scores of the St. Matthew and St. John Passions of Bach, four-hand scores of the first three symphonies and two suites by Tchaikovsky, and a piano score of the same composer's *Snegourotchka.* (He also asked for a new edition of Tchaikovsky's letters that had recently appeared in the U.S.S.R.)

Stravinsky began the composition on July 16, 1927, with, among others, notations for the measure at ⬚3⬚ and the accompaniment figure at [4].. Two days later, more ideas were entered in his sketchbook (now in the collection of Paul Sacher, in Basel), including a version of the music at the third measure of [64], and with them this description of the "Prologue: The Birth of Apollo":

Ilithye [137] *arrive à Délos. L'enfantement saisit Léto et elle se sentit près d'accoucher. Elle jeta ses deux bras autour d'un palmier et elle appura ses genoux sur un tendre gazon, et la terre au-dessous d'elle sourit, et l'enfant bondit à la lumière. Les déesses lavent l'enfant d'eau limpide, purement et chastement. Elles lui donnent pour linges un voile blanc léger, frais tissu, et l'assujettirent avec une ceinture d'or. Thémis lui présente le nectar et l'ambroise.*

The notation for the "Pas de Deux" (after [64]) was not used until a late stage of work on the ballet; in fact, that movement and the "Apotheosis" were the final ones to be completed. The remainder of the timetable for the composition is as follows:

July 19. Writes the melody at [4].

July 20. Writes the beginning of the score; at this point, the ensemble includes harp and piano.

July 21. Tries variant forms of the "Pas de Deux" theme (after [64]) in the key of D-flat, and composes a version of the upper melodic line at [41].

July 22. Resumes the development of the Lento (sic) "Introduction."

July 23–27. Sketches the Allegro of the first movement.

July 29–31. Completes the Introduction and the beginning of the Allegro.

August 5. Writes scansion marks (without pitches) for a phrase of music, underneath which Boris Kochno has written (in Stravinsky's manuscript!): "My dear Igor Fyodorovich."

August 10. Begins the violin solo in the "Variation d'Apollon."

August 15–20. Composes the "Variation d'Apollon."

August 29. Echarvines. Composes the violin melody at [25].

August 30–September 15. Composes the "Pas d'Action."

September 30. Monte Carlo. Diaghilev writes to Lifar: "I have visited Stravinsky, heard *Apollo*, and seen the composer off on the train to Paris."

November 2. Composes the melody at [40].

November 3. Writes the "Variation of Calliope" in the form of scansion marks (without pitches.).

November 5. Composes the cello solo at [41] and enters in his sketchbook the couplet from Boileau that became the epigraph for the "Variation of Calliope."

November 8. Finishes the "Variation of Calliope."

November 9–13. Composes the "Variation of Polyhymnia," starting at ⌈48⌉.

November 16–19. Composes "Terpsichore."

November 22. Makes notations for the "Pas de Deux," then interrupts work.

December 12. Completes the "Variation d'Apollon."

December 14. Resumes work on the "Pas de Deux."

December 16–27. Completes the "Coda," then writes the word "*zakluchainiye*" ("the solution"), referring to the discovery of the final form of the "Pas de Deux."

January 21, 1928. Telegraphs to Diaghilev at Monte Carlo, asking him to come with Balanchine "Tomorrow at four."

Before conducting the European premiere of the ballet, Stravinsky explained the title of the piece in a dedication, written in his score, but which could not be published at the time: "*Voici cet 'Apollon' dit 'Musagète,' c. à d., qui amène la Musa Ver'igor.*"

On July 9, 1928, Prokofiev wrote to Miaskovsky:

I am disappointed in *Apollo*. The material is poor, taken from all the miserable pockets of Gounod, Delibes, Wagner, and even Minkus. All of this is presented adroitly and skillfully.... Stravinsky missed the most important thing, and the work's a terrible bore. Yet on the last page he shines and makes his disgusting theme sound convincing. In the piano score you will not understand this [ending], for you must have the orchestra.

Apollo was widely publicized before it was performed:

I lunched yesterday with Serge Diaghilev, who talked about *Apollo*: "[It] contains a dance adagio in which the first musical part plays at a speed twice as fast as the second, three times as fast as the third, and four times as fast as the fourth. Thus the same melody has four different aspects...." [Michel George-Michel, *Excelsior*, Paris, October 27, 1927]

July 22, 1930. Marseilles. Bouillabaisse. Mme Sudeikina has just noticed the S.S. *Souirah* (on which she arrived in Marseilles from Russia in May 1920) entering the harbor.

In addition to conducting the stage premieres of *Petrushka*, *Le Sacre du Printemps*, and *The Nightingale*, Monteux gave the first concert performances outside of Russia of *Petrushka* and the *Sacre*, that of the latter reversing the scandal of the ballet production of the year before. On April 6, 1914, *Comoedia* published an encomium from Stravinsky:

Mon cher Monteux, I am very happy to be able to express my appreciation of your performances last season with the Ballets Russes. Everyone can appreciate, as I do, your enthusiasm and integrity with regard to contemporary music in all of its diverse tendencies, which you have defended at every opportunity.

1928. Vera Sudeikina at home. Photograph by Stravinsky.

Today I am moved to see you spontaneously offer your expertise to works that, although received with hostility by the public, represent a real artistic effort to you. You do this willingly, moreover, with no fear of being criticized by opposing factions.

In the light of your truly artistic performances of my works, I must express not only my personal gratitude but also the thanks of my French colleagues who are encountering difficulties similar to my own.

I attach the greatest importance to the dedicated and meticulous collaboration of the remarkable musicians who support you so intelligently in the interpretation of compositions which I know to be extremely difficult.

March 15, 1928. Barcelona. The Hotel
Ritz. With Pierre Monteux.

Stravinsky's opinion of Monteux was to change drastically in
the 1920s, and, when the conductor balked at being asked to
turn over his orchestra for a recording of *Capriccio* to be conducted by Ansermet, Stravinsky described the hero of the *Sacre*
premiere as a *"mesquin et vaniteux individu"* (letter to Ansermet). When Stravinsky, to help promote his own Columbia recording of the *Sacre*, provided that company with an open letter
elaborating on his distinction between an "interpretation" and
an "execution," Monteux naturally identified himself as the un-
named "interpreter" and complained to Stravinsky:

Since you are no longer content with my interpretations, I have refused the offer from the Société Philharmonique de Bruxelles, thus leaving you to indicate directly the conductor of your choice. [Letter of February 3, 1930]

Stravinsky answered saying that, whatever the reasons for Monteux's attitude, surely they were not "of a musical order":

Your recording of the *Sacre* is an execution, not an interpretation ... but you are the victim of bad recording (engineering) technique. As for myself, I believe that I possess sufficient authority and technique to make the public understand what I want. . . .[138]

Stravinsky was irritated, no doubt, because his recording had sold less well than Monteux's.
    Writing to Jean Bérard, January 15, 1930, Stravinsky referred to Monteux as

a man of very limited vision, very large vanity, and very small spirit, which is so often the case with orchestra players. . . . Since 1910 Monteux's career has always been one of turning everything to his advantage.

Yet the composer was no less outspokenly critical when writing to the conductor directly:

. . . I never had any intention of putting the name of the orchestra on the recording. . . . When I recorded the *Sacre* with the Straram, the question never arose. . . . Excuse me if I have again wounded your self-esteem, but I am convinced that not only Ansermet but also any other artist who has my confidence would be equally badly viewed by you. . . . [Letter of April 19, 1930]

It should be said, however, that many of Stravinsky's letters of this time were harsh, and that his concert agents, Wolff and Sachs, actually asked him not to write so roughly any more. Stravinsky answered:

. . . I must tell you that the often disagreeable tone of my letters to you is a consequence of your inexact replies and of the negligence in reading my letters by your agency, this putting me in a state of nerves. I ask you not to judge this too severely, in view of the enormous and differ-

April 10, 1928. Poster announcing a long evening at the Rome Opera. On April 8, Stravinsky wrote to Païchadze: "I have worked hard all day rehearsing *The Nightingale*. . . . I am in agreement about Diaghilev and I wrote to him a half-hour before leaving Nice. I know Diaghilev's ways, but I have never understood how he calculates his percentages. It is impossible to climb out of his complications. First, he must pay what he has promised (for *Apollo*)."

ent kinds of work that I have to accomplish each season, and not to conclude that if you find certain sharp expressions in my letters, I am working with your firm against my will. You must know that each time I find something inexact, or some omissions by you, I express it directly, and that this is what gives you the feeling of *"unfreundlichkeit"* in my letters. . . . [Letter of May 17, 1930]

To return to Stravinsky and Monteux, the two men were on good terms in their California years, and in the 1940s Monteux regularly invited the composer to conduct the San Francisco Orchestra. In 1955, Stravinsky wrote a *Greeting Prelude* for Monteux's eightieth birthday, and, after the conductor's death, composed a brief orchestral canon to his memory, on a melody from *The Firebird*.

Serge Kussevitzky played three roles in Stravinsky's life: first, as one of his publishers (Editions Russes de Musique, 1911–14, 1921–30, 1932–4); second, as his patron, having commissioned the *Symphony of Psalms* and the *Ode*; third, as a conductor, for Kussevitzky led the first performances of the *Symphonies of Wind Instruments*, the Piano Concerto, and the *Ode*, as well as the first concert performances of *Le Sacre du Printemps* (in Moscow and St. Petersburg, February 1914). Yet Stravinsky was sharply critical, even contemptuous, of Kussevitzky's conducting. Reading in the *Chesterian*, July 1937, that

May 1928. En route from Calais to Dover, Vera Sudeikina and Andrés Segovia. Photograph by Stravinsky.

August 1928. The Villa Warens, Combloux. With Serge Kussevitzky and Serge Prokofiev.

In *Le Sacre du Printemps* it depends on the interpretation of the opening bars [and] Kussevitzky turns them into an awe-inspiring portal. . . .

Stravinsky wrote in the margin, "One naturally wonders what Kussevitzky had promised the author."

Stravinsky's letters, interviews, and marginalia bristle with abuse of conductors.[139] He once told Guido Gatti (*L'Ambrosiana*, Milan, August 26, 1931):

The conductor I envy is the director of the military band, who keeps a revolver strapped in a holster by his side, and a notebook in which he marks a player's mistakes and, for each one, sends him to jail for a day.

Stravinsky's chief criticism of conductors is that they try to "substitute their own ideas for the composer's." But another factor in his conductor phobia ("careerists and intriguers," he calls them in a letter to Ansermet, June 1932) is surely the lack of recognition of his own skill in performing his works. Here is a typical statement from a review:

[Stravinsky] is a workaday conductor. With any of his scores Mr. Kussevitzky far outdoes him. [*Boston Transcript*, October 13, 1928]

Stravinsky reveals his true feelings about Kussevitzky in a letter to Ansermet, September 3, 1930:

This contrabassist, who has never learned to play a piano, became the American Star with no more than his conductor's baton. But a genius

does not need to study at the piano, since, for this inferior job, he can always hire someone to play the music for him, and over and over until he is filled up to his ass with it.

Stravinsky wrote to Ansermet from the Ansonia Hotel, West 73rd Street, New York, February 2, 1935:

I will see Kussevitzky and speak to him; if only something would come of that, but you know yourself that he is as false as a counterfeit coin, promises everything and does nothing.

Stravinsky wrote again on April 4, 1935, from the Powell Hotel, 28 East 63rd Street, New York:

I spoke to Kussevitzky about you, but in spite of his remark—"[Ansermet's] name is at the head of my list of my conductors conducting my orchestra during my vacations"—it is important not to believe a single word that he says. This same Kussevitzky once said to Lourié, in an access of frankness, "I am somebody who has the weakness to promise and the strength not to fulfill."

Nevertheless, Stravinsky wished to rent Kussevitzky's Paris house while the conductor was in America (letter of May 3, 1933, to Païchadze), and when the composer was preparing his lectures for Harvard and planning to live in Boston or Cambridge, he appealed to Kussevitzky for assistance. On July 18, 1939, Stravinsky, then in a sanitorium at Sancellemoz, wrote to Alexis Kall in Los Angeles, saying that Kussevitzky had come to Sancellemoz and enlightened him on the difficulty of finding a suitable servant, and on the greatly increased cost of domestic help in the United States. Stravinsky had been planning to keep house with Kall in Cambridge, but after Kussevitzky's visit the composer realized that a "$300-a-month budget" was insufficient. While in Sancellemoz, Kussevitzky invited Stravinsky to conduct the Boston Symphony in the fall and spring.

And, during the 1940s, Kussevitzky continued to be a gift-horse provider of lucrative concert engagements.[140] In that decade, Stravinsky led the Boston Symphony more frequently than he did any other American orchestra, but after Kussevitzky's retirement was never invited to conduct the Boston Symphony again. The tone of Stravinsky's letter to Nicolas Nabokov on Kussevitzky's death is not particularly warm, saying little more than that newspapers and magazines had made a great fuss, and that, although Time's request for a statement had been complied with, Stravinsky's remarks had not been published. (Letter of June 13, 1951) On page 132 of Robert Siohan's monograph on Stravinsky, which discusses the composer's relationship with Kussevitzky, Stravinsky not only questions Siohan's assumption that the two musicians were "friends" but writes "quel idiot!" over the text. And when a reviewer in the May 1931 issue of Latinité mistakenly says that the Symphony of Psalms is dedicated "to the Boston Symphony and to its conductor Kussevitzky," Stravinsky, in a large marginal "non," protests the inclusion of Kussevitzky.

Stravinsky respected Klemperer more than almost any other conductor, and the two men were friends until the composer's death. In the earlier California years, Klemperer's concerts were among the few that Stravinsky attended; this writer recalls the composer's particular pleasure in a series of Klemperer-conducted Brandenburg Concertos at the University of Southern California. At one time, Klemperer was Stravinsky's choice to conduct the first performance of *The Rake's Progress,* as a letter from him to Boosey & Hawkes reveals. The last Klemperer performance that Stravinsky heard was of *Fidelio,* in Zürich in October 1961, and on that occasion the conductor published a homage to the composer:

Stravinsky's switch, some years ago, from tonal music to the twelve-tone row changes only the style of his music. His face remains the same, and, since the death of Arnold Schoenberg, he is without doubt the greatest living composer. Though he will be eighty years old next year, he is as vigorous and strong as a man of forty. . . . In these times, which celebrate the triumphs of mediocrities, we are happy that Stravinsky is still among us. Where he enters is life. [*Die Tat,* Zürich, October 10, 1961]

Stravinsky's next opus, *Le Baiser de la Fée,* was composed between July and October 1928. Mme Ida Rubinstein had written, December 5, 1927, saying that she and Benois were very eager to talk about a project, and, when Stravinsky answered that he could not come to Paris before February, she wrote to the composer, December 12, to say that Benois was sending a letter describing the plan. Mme Rubinstein's next letter (December 23) reveals that the "Tchaikovskyana" was not Stravinsky's idea, but hers and Benois's. On January 7, 1928, Stravinsky stated his terms—$6,000, depending on length and exclusivity—which Mme Rubinstein accepted on the 15th, asking for the new work by the end of the summer.

The ballet is based on Hans Christian Andersen's "The Ice Maiden," [141] which was Stravinsky's original title, though he changed it after finishing the first tableau; a letter to Païchadze, August 20, 1928, gives the new title, as well as a description of the stage action at each of the score's rehearsal numbers. Before beginning the composition, Stravinsky went for a holiday (July 9 and 10) to Thonon-les-Bains, [142] his conducting schedule between May and June having been exceptionally strenuous. He led the first performance of *Oedipus Rex* in England (May 11), several Ballets Russes performances of *Apollo* in Paris, a Salle Pleyel concert with the *Sacre,* the recording (his first) of *Petrushka* in London, and the English premiere of *Apollo* (June 25). For one other concert, May 19 in the Salle Pleyel—in which he played his Piano Concerto under Bruno Walter on a program that included Mahler's Fourth Symphony—Stravinsky did not receive his fee ($500) and was obliged to bring a lawsuit against M. Firmin Gémier of the sponsoring organization, the Société Universelle du Théâtre. Stravinsky won the case, [143] but after weeks of testifying and of time-consuming correspondence.

Returning to his summer home, Châlet des Echarvines, Talloires, on July 11, Stravinsky worked for a few days on the instrumentation of his *Etude* for pianola, then began the composition of the new ballet. On July 16, he wrote to Païchadze, asking him to send Tchaikovsky's "songs for children" (presumably the collection of sixteen), and, on August 2, wrote again to "*Dorogoi Gavril Grigorievich* [Païchadze]" saying that the first tableau had been sent in piano score.

The original scenario is more detailed and specific in Stravinsky's sketchbook than in the score, using the names Ruby and Babette, for example, and identifying the lake as Interlaken. Also, the first scenario includes a preliminary outline of the musical pieces, among them a barcarolle in the sixth section of the third tableau, each with estimated timings. A note at the head of the first page reads: "*Romances*, Opus 51, for the scene at the Mill, *Nata Waltz* (for wind instruments)," but this is the only reference in Stravinsky's manuscript to his Tchaikovsky sources.

The sketchbook reveals that the sequence of the melodic materials in the first tableau did not occur to Stravinsky's imagination in final form. The first tableau was completed in two-hand piano score on July 25, and the second was begun on the 29th. By August 7, he had sketched the music at 96 , 98 , 101 , and 102 , and, on the 16th, completed the movement. On August 12, Stravinsky wrote to Alexander Benois, who was to design the sets and costumes:

... First of all, I have changed the title of the ballet. It will not be called "*La Vierge des Glaciers*" but *Le Baiser de la Fée*. The complete title on the cover of the score will be:

THE FAIRY'S KISS

Allegorical Ballet

in 4 Tableaux
by
Igor Stravinsky
inspired by
the Muse of Tchaikovsky

Gradually, as the composition progresses, I find myself retaining only the skeleton of the story, the plot that develops among the three characters in the tale: a fairy marks a young boy in his infancy with a mysterious kiss. She claims him from the arms of his mother, and, on the day of his greatest happiness, claims him from life, in order to possess him and thus to preserve an unchanging happiness. Again, she marks him with her kiss.

I will write a brief preface to the score and the program saying that I relate the fairy to Tchaikovsky's Muse—hence the allegorical meaning of the ballet, for the Muse similarly marked him with her fatal kiss, the mysterious imprint of which one senses on all the works of this great artist. . . . I do not want to give precise specifications as to time, place, and action for the décor and the production, but you will find exact indications in my score for the appearances and actions of the characters, as well as some more or less vague titles regarding place. Here are the titles:

> 1st Scene (Prologue)
> > Lullaby in the storm. Fairy's Kiss.
> 2nd Scene
> > A village festival.
> 3rd Scene.
> > At the mill.
> 4th Scene (Epilogue)
> > Lullaby of the eternal dwelling place.
> The Fairy's Kiss.

I believe that everything will work out well this way, and that all is accounted for. I will be in Paris for several hours on the first of September on my way to Holland. . . .

Stravinsky finished the 5/8 movement of the "Pas de Deux" on August 26, and the Variation in C on the 31st, inscribing it "Echarvines, Lac d'Annecy." After returning from Scheveningen to Nice, he resumed the composition (September 15) with the Coda and completed the movement on the 23rd. The sketch score of the *Fée* is dated October 15, and the two-hand piano score, October 16. The next day he wrote to Païchadze:

I hasten to share with you the joy of finishing the music for the *Fée*. . . . I am sending the whole end of the piano score to you in a few days for engraving, not for familiarizing Ida with it, or Nijinskaya or Benois. . . . It is necessary for people such as they are—not particularly initiated—that I play the music for them myself. Therefore I ask you not to let anyone look at it before my arrival. Nijinskaya will howl, but do not pay any attention to that.

Ten days later, on October 27, Stravinsky wrote again to Païchadze:

Pass on immediately to Ida and Nijinskaya that after the final scene of the third act with the young man, we will not let his bride come out, as we had initially proposed. Thus her role ends at the Coda. I am informing Nijinskaya about this particularly (although everything was indicated quite precisely in the piano score) for fear that she would not pay attention to the text and take the absence of the bride's last appearance as an omission, or as forgetfulness on my part. I hope that she hasn't reached this part in her staging, and that my letter to you hasn't arrived too late.

The piano score contains numerous stage directions by the composer, despite his letter to Benois. The orchestra score was completed at midnight, October 30, in Nice, and, on November 5, Stravinsky left for Zürich, where he played his Piano Concerto the following day. On the 7th, he was in Paris, where he recorded the *Firebird* Suite on the 8th, 9th, and 10th. On the 16th and 17th, he conducted concerts in the Théâtre des Champs-Elysées, giving the first performance of the newly orchestrated pianola *Etude*. On the 27th, at the Paris Opéra, he conducted *Le Baiser de la Fée*. No one seems to have appreciated the music, and when Stravinsky himself first saw the ballet in an audience, in Brussels, December 7, 1928, he attributed the failure of the spectacle to the "five-to-eight-minute pause between the tableaux which sabotages the work." (Letter to Ansermet, December 11) In the first week of January 1929, Stravinsky again wrote to Païchadze:

In a half-hour, I will go to Monte Carlo for the rehearsal of the *Fée,* which will be performed in a matinée this Sunday. It is a mystery to me why Ida Rubinstein offers it only once, since that is hardly worth the expense to which she has gone. . . . But no one in the artistic world today is as mysteriously stupid as this lady.

Le Baiser de la Fée destroyed Stravinsky's friendship with Diaghilev, and, in the final year of the impresario's life, the two men exchanged letters only once more and spoke to each other in person only once (in Monte Carlo, the time of the last photograph of the two together, in the street, Stravinsky in knickers). On August 8, 1928, Diaghilev wrote to Stravinsky from the Hotel Europa in Venice:

. . . The [London] season went well, thanks to friends who made our performance a place of rendezvous for English society. . . . *Apollo* was done five times with great success. But what is this I hear about *Apollo* with Ida Rubinstein? *Apollo* is a big success in England, and it has large groups of avid admirers. We will play *The Firebird* on the tour. Beecham wants to conduct *Le Sacre* in London, and I think that this will be good because he is becoming a first-class conductor—something that we do not have in Paris, and this includes the great Ansermet. I would like to see you here in Venice, where I will stay for another month before going to Athos.[144] I found a Russian typewriter for you,[145] although with great difficulty.

Stravinsky answered on August 15:

Dear Serge, I thank you and Boris [Kochno] very much for the Russian typewriter, but since I have not yet picked it up at Païchadze's, I am typing these lines in French—in answer to your handwritten letter.
    I am happy for you and for the Ballets that you have found someone (Beecham) to replace the late Rothermere. But to put Beecham above the "great Ansermet" makes me think of Gogol's "Although Alexander of Macedonia was a great man. . ." So much so that I find considerable difference between the King of Macedonia, who never improvised his battles, and Beecham, who only improvises the movements of the works of others. But if you recognize genius in Beecham, why not in Kussevitzky?
    I go to Holland toward the end of August for my concert at Scheveningen, then, after ten days, return to Nice, where I will finish my work for Ida Rubinstein. This will take from mid-September through all of October; hence it will be possible for me to see you only in Nice.
    You ask about "this business with my offer of *Apollo* to Ida Rubinstein." It is a question neither of "business" nor of "an offer," unless you are referring to inquiries addressed to my publisher concerning my ballets. But since you seem to be particularly interested in this case, I can tell you that Rubinstein, like many other theatrical entrepreneurs, has inquired from Païchadze about *Apollo.* I myself never offer my works to anyone, either directly or indirectly.

When do you leave for Mount Athos? I must tell you that your trip to this holy place interests me more than anything else. I would like you to bring several icons (en oléographies) for me, and a wooden cross, and to have them blessed at the same place. Since I know that your main reason for going to Athos is to search for books, I would also be grateful if you would bring me a catalog of every book for sale there in Russian and Slavonic. . . .

Embrace Lifar [146] for his kind letter, which gave me great pleasure, and tell him that I am sending the "Saintes Ecritures" that I promised. He will receive it in a few days.

On December 20, 1928, Stravinsky wrote to Païchadze:

Did you read Diaghilev's interview in the December 18 "Vozrozdenie" [a Russian-language journal published in Paris]? I don't approve of it. His appraisal of that "poor Russian woman," as he calls her, is completely accurate, but it was foolish and tactless for Diaghilev to lower himself to criticizing her, especially since he was appearing immediately after her in the Paris Opéra. I felt embarrassed for Diaghilev's sake.

Here is a timetable of the last months of Diaghilev's life in relation to Stravinsky:

April 8, 1929. Nice. Stravinsky writes to the Princesse de Polignac: "I have just spoken to Diaghilev about the project, and he says it would not be possible to perform *Renard* in your home."

May 15–18. London. Stravinsky records at Aeolian.

May 21. Paris. Théâtre Sarah-Bernhardt. Stravinsky and Prokofiev conduct *Renard* and the *Prodigal Son*, respectively, on a Ballets Russes program.

June 11. Stravinsky and Vera Sudeikina go to London on the night train, via Dunkirk-Tilbury. Before leaving, he writes to Ansermet at the Fürstenhof in Berlin: "I must advise you that the affair is not going very well between me and Diaghilev. After your departure and our conversation on the subject of the cut in *Apollo*,[147] Païchadze sent a registered letter to Diaghilev, who did not sign it but said that he had not changed his promise to restore the Variation. . . . Diaghilev said that he was astonished by my severity with him and indulgence toward the Staatsoper, which plays *Pulcinella* under horrible conditions and frequently changes the order of the numbers in the ballet. . . . I will arrive at the Friedrichstrasse station on June 14 at 5:17 in the afternoon and go directly to the Fürstenhof."

June 12. London. Rehearses his Piano Concerto with Goossens.

June 13. 3:00 P.M. Queen's Hall. Performance of the Piano Concerto.

June 17. Berlin. Staatsoper. Plays the Piano Concerto on a program that includes *Apollo* and *Les Noces*, the three works conducted by Klemperer.

June 19. Paris. Writes to Ansermet in Cologne asking him to tell

Diaghilev that "I will be in London at the same time that he is there, and living at Albemarle Court, where he usually stays."

June 23–24. Diaghilev and Markevich, Stravinsky and Mme Sudeikina are on the same train, see each other, but do not exchange greetings or speak.

June 25. Geneva. Ansermet writes: "Diaghilev left Berlin for Paris without saying *au revoir,* but also without having addressed a single word to me since the first rehearsal. . . . The high point was the first spectacle at Charlottenburg, where *Apollo* had a great success and the *Sacre* long ovations. . . . Nouvel is not going [to London] and [no one knows] whether Diaghilev is going to Albemarle or to the Savoy."

June 25. London. Stravinsky rehearses, morning, afternoon, and evening.

June 26. Stravinsky rehearses, then, with W. Strecker, visits Hampton Court.

June 27. London. Kingsway Hall. Stravinsky rehearses in the morning and conducts a BBC concert, *Apollo* and *Le Baiser de la Fée,* in the evening.

June 28. Returns to Paris with Vera Sudeikina.

July 9. In Talloires.

July 22. (Monday). London. The Ballets Russes perform the *Sacre.*

August 8. Diaghilev arrives in Venice.

August 11. The seventy-fifth birthday of Stravinsky's mother; the family goes to Lyon.

August 19.[148] Venice. Diaghilev dies, "alone in a hotel, like a vagabond" (Ansermet to Stravinsky).

The lives of the people in the picture opposite and of the photographer were closely involved, Olga Sudeikina and Vera Sudeikina having been successively married to the same man, while Olga and Tamara were successively married to Lourié (though Olga's marriage was of the "common law" variety). Furthermore, Lourié and Olga, Serge and Vera Sudeikina once shared the same Petrograd apartment (Champs de Mars). Then, too, Serge Sudeikin left Olga for Vera, who left him for Stravinsky, who was responsible—through his friend at the Quai d'Orsay, Alexis St. Léger (St.-John Perse)—for facilitating Olga Sudeikina's emigration from the U.S.S.R. to France. Finally, these same people were intimately associated with some of the era's greatest poets, Blok,[149] Akhmatova, Mandelstam. Olga Sudeikina seems to have been Blok's mistress for a time, thereby precipitating the suicide of Vsevolod Knyazev, whom she had rejected. (Mrs. Stravinsky testifies that Sudeikin did not believe this to be the real cause, or that Olga had had an affair with

Blok.) After separating from Sudeikin, and before the liaison with Lourié, Olga shared an apartment with Anna Akhmatova, who was attracted to both of these men.[150] Visiting Oxford shortly before her death, she brought a silhouette that she had made of Vera Sudeikina c. 1916 and entrusted it to Isaiah Berlin, who gave it to Mrs. Stravinsky in New York. "Naughty girl," the poet had written on it (in c. 1916)—i.e., for taking Sudeikin.

Olga, on the other hand, did not mind losing Sudeikin, and she and Vera de Bosset remained on good terms for the year and a half before Vera left Petrograd in the spring of 1917, as well as later, in Paris. From 1913 to 1915, Olga performed—acted and danced, semi-professionally—in the St. Petersburg cabaret "Brodiachaia Sabaka" ("Stray Dog"),[151] which had panneaux by Sudeikin, who had also designed her costumes.[152] Mrs. Stravinsky describes Olga as

a fluffy blond, rosy, slender, naturally flirtatious. She was unable to remember enough poetry to be able to recite any, and she could dance nothing but polkas, but she had charm.

Finally, the grouping in the photograph aptly symbolizes Lourié's 1920s and, to a lesser extent, 1930s relationship to Stravinsky, which was that of musical assistant and philosopher-éminence grise, Lourié having adopted the name "Arthur" out of admiration for Schopenhauer. Lourié emigrated to France at about the same time as Stravinsky's mother, and, in January

1924, accompanied Stravinsky to Brussels, where he had gone to conduct. On January 14, Vera Sudeikina wrote in her diary:

Lourié is so pleased to be present and to be talking to Stravinsky that he blushes.

Lourié's letters to Stravinsky are crammed with religion—prayers copied out for the composer, requests for the composer's prayers for him (letter of November 24, 1926), glosses on the Evangelists (letter of December 21, 1926), progress reports on the conversion, from Judaism, of Lourié's wife, Tamara. In a letter to Stravinsky written on returning to Paris after a visit with him in Nice, Lourié says that he has seen Mme Sudeikina, whose "paganism" he contrasts to his religion.

Stravinsky's confidence in Lourié increased to the extent that on December 12, 1929, the composer wrote to a representative of Columbia Records in London proposing that Lourié be invited to give a series of "conférences" on Stravinsky's recordings in conjunction with his forthcoming concert tour in Germany (Berlin, Leipzig, and Düsseldorf). And, on numerous occasions, Stravinsky recommended Lourié as an authority on his music. In the following letter, for example, Stravinsky tells Universal Edition in Vienna that the preface to the pocket score of *Renard* is unacceptable:

... although written in an incredible French, I could make out the sense well enough to understand that the author has scarcely even an acquaintance with the musical language of my time. . . . I ask you to suppress this article and to replace it by another one . . . written by Ansermet or Arthur Lourié. [Letter of August 30, 1929]

As for Lourié's music, on August 17, 1929, Ansermet wrote to Stravinsky:

... I have studied the *Sonata Liturgica* by Lourié. I am not without hope of being able to grasp the logic and perhaps the wisdom of it, but, for the moment, I do not perceive the pleasure. . . . If this music did not make allusions to Catholicism, one could believe that it came from a Protestant austerity or from a strange stylization of the Jewish Jeremiads.

Stravinsky quarreled with Lourié shortly before coming to America in 1939, and, despite the efforts of mutual friends, the breach was never healed. Here is a note from Vera Stravinsky's diary, New York, February 9, 1945:

The Dushkins come this afternoon to try to effect a reconciliation between us and Arthur Lourié, but Igor will not listen.

When Lourié died, Stravinsky was in Honolulu. Back in Hollywood, he read an obituary by Henri Masson in *Le Monde*, titled "Compositeur déraciné et méconnu" and containing the statement, "Bach, Mozart, Stravinsky knew each other well and mutually influenced each other." On January 14, 1967, writing to

1929. In his Salle Pleyel studio. During World War II, Stravinsky entrusted these percussion instruments to his niece Ira Belline, but they have been missing since 1945. Photograph by Lipnitsky.

Suvchinsky with reference to the *Monde* article, Stravinsky said he was unaware that Bach and Mozart had been influenced by each other, let alone by himself, and he added that he had never seen a single page of Lourié's music, nor ever heard a note of it. But this cannot be true. Correspondence from Willy Strecker to Stravinsky suggests that he must have seen the scores of at least the *Concerto Spirituale* (1929) and the *Sinfonia Dialectica* (1930), and a letter from Ansermet to Stravinsky, December 31, 1929, confirms his acquaintance with other Lourié scores as well:

I received a letter from Lourié radiating joy because of the interest that you have shown in his work.

July 25, 1929. Sketch of the cadenza in the *Capriccio*. The arrow indicates that the ending is on the preceding page. Stravinsky composed the third movement first, beginning it on the day before Christmas 1928, with, among other notations, the music between [70] and the third measure of [71]. The second movement was completed next and the first movement last. On October 23, 1929, Stravinsky wrote to Païchadze, "In a few days, I will finish the instrumentation of the first part of the *Capriccio*."

Here are two impressions of Stravinsky's *Capriccio* in performance, the first by Ezra Pound:

I have heard a great mass or mess of so-called piano concertos, but I have never heard but one *composition* for piano and orchestra, namely Stravinsky's *Capriccio*—there the piano and orchestra are as two shells of a walnut. I sat in the top gallery in Venice [September 11, 1934], while Igor led and his son played the solo part . . . of the *Capriccio*.

Stravinsky played his new work, a *Capriccio* for piano and orchestra; he had in every way a distinguished and critical audience. Not a seat in the huge hall [the Salle Pleyel] was vacant, and when the last chords had sounded, the genial Igor was the recipient of a marked and vociferous ovation. I think it was a tribute to him, not only for the immediate work he had given, a work as ingenious and vigorous as anything he has done, but for all that he meant to that audience—Stravinsky, the innovator, the scholarly and erudite musician, Stravinsky, the man of powerful insight and individuality, probably the most fecund and original musician today. He must have completed the *Capriccio* a few weeks ago; he had been working on it since last January. . . . [Leon Edel, *Montreal Star*, December 7, 1929]

The *Capriccio* was first performed in a program with a Brandenburg Concerto, a Haydn Symphony, Debussy's *Rondes des Printemps*, and the Mussorgsky-Ravel *Pictures*. Shortly after the concert, Stravinsky received a letter from Jacques Maritain:

Mon cher maître et ami, since you admire Leon Bloy,[153] I would like to send a copy of his *Letters to My Godsons*, published by Stock, wherein you will really discover our "godfather" in his familiarity, his kindness, and his admirable simplicity. May this book serve as a token of our enormous admiration, and of the incomparable joy you have given us with your *Capriccio*.

There is something about which I must speak to you. I know that some unpleasant lines have appeared about you in an article by Nicolas Nabokov. Be assured that he is very unhappy about them. He is un *grand enfant sauvage*, but without a shade of malice. He deeply loves and admires you, and the thought that you are angry with him disturbs him greatly. Call it a great blunder on his part, but forgive him in the name of Christian charity and believe what I know to be true: that he never meant to offend you.

In fact, Stravinsky was surprised and infuriated by Nabokov's article, published in *Musique* (November 15, 1929), the more so because, on October 4, Stravinsky had written to Ansermet expressing pleasure in Nabokov's symphony, "which he has just played for me on the piano," and because Stravinsky had liked Nabokov on their first meeting, in Paris in October 1927—here recalled by Nabokov:

Diaghilev and I heard steps on the winding staircase and two diminutive figures surfaced from below; first . . . Nouvel, and behind him, . . . familiar from portraits and photos, but wrapped in shawls and mufflers, Stravinsky's head, hidden by a wilted black felt hat. What caught my immediate attention were the neat light-gray spats and, when he took off his raincoat, the gold chains that crisscrossed his waistcoat.

I had known that Stravinsky was small, but I was startled by his size, perhaps because he was so wiry. . . . There was something ancient, Assyrian, in Stravinsky's face . . . and at the same time, something of a fairy-tale magician from out of the dark Russian woods, a *lešovichok*, a forest imp of Russian lore. . . .

How gloriously kind and charming Stravinsky was that afternoon after the gloomy lunch *chez* Prunier, and, God, was I scared to play my music for him! . . . Stravinsky sat very close to me on my left, his spectacles raised onto his forehead. "Must you write so sloppily?" he said, looking at my untidy, penciled manuscript. "One can barely read it!". . . Stravinsky stopped me and said, "Sing just the soprano, I'll figure out the bass myself." . . . When we came to the end of the piece, . . . Stravinsky turned to Diaghilev and said, . . . "You know what it's like? It's as if it were written by a predecessor of Glinka, someone like Gurilyov or Alyabiev." And then smilingly at me, "From where do you know all this Russian salon music of the 1830s? It is unmistakably and naïvely Russian. . . ."

Once in the taxi, Stravinsky . . . laughed when I told him stories about my teacher Rebikov. "I knew him," Stravinsky said. "He may have been un *original*, but his music was not." [154]

Stravinsky's riposte to Nabokov's article in *Musique*, printed in the next issue, is utterly characteristic of its author. He begins by quoting Nabokov but deliberately avoids any mention of his name:

"Diaghilev's part in Stravinsky's work, in my opinion, is enormous. Two facts seem to prove this: Diaghilev appears to have given Stravinsky the idea for *Petrushka*, and certainly he gave Stravinsky the original idea for the 'Liturgie,' which eventually evolved into *Les Noces*. Here the mark of Diaghilev's inspiration actually touches on the creation itself. He supplied the original idea and influenced the music in very definite ways."

Without criticizing these lines, I must state—and I think I may do so without discrediting Diaghilev in any way:
1) That the idea of *Petrushka* was not his;
2) That I never had any intention of composing the so-called Liturgie which Diaghilev was urging me to do, an idea that I had always rejected; moreover, he broached the subject when I was already fully involved in the composition of *Les Noces*. On the contrary, I remained quite deliberately removed from all outside influences while composing *Les Noces* and even refrained from letting Diaghilev know about individual tableaux as each was completed.

In future when claims are made about me, may I ask that you verify them with me before publishing them, in order to make certain of their authenticity? A wrong opinion is often less harmful than a statement of fact made without verification. Igor Stravinsky

In an interview in *L'Etoile Belge*, May 22, 1930, Stravinsky said:

I have finished the first part of a choral symphony . . . a composition of a great simplicity inspired by a biblical text of Saint Jerome.

On September 14, 1929, Stravinsky had written to Païchadze:

Symphony for Boston: I have decided to accept this proposition and ask you to establish a contract with Boston so that I can sign it as soon as possible. The payment should be half on the signing of the contract, the other half on the delivery of the material, in all six thousand dollars.

On October 23, the composer again wrote:

I read in *Poslednie Novosti* [a Russian-language journal in Paris] that Prokofiev and I have been given an order by Kussevitzky for the composing of (I don't remember what sort of) things for the Boston Philharmonic. . . .

But not until three months later, December 12, 1929, was the contract with "the Boston Symphony Orchestra, Inc." a reality. The agreement provided that the manuscript would become the property of the orchestra, which also held the right to give the first performance and to make the first recording. No mention is made of a chorus. Stravinsky also wrote on the 12th asking to modify the condition about the first performance, so that if the Boston orchestra failed to give it by November 15, 1930, he would be free to play the piece in Europe.

In the flyleaf of his sketchbook for the *Symphony of Psalms*, Stravinsky pasted a drawing of the Crucifixion, inscribed "*Adveniat Regnum Tuum.*" Then, after completing a part of the com-

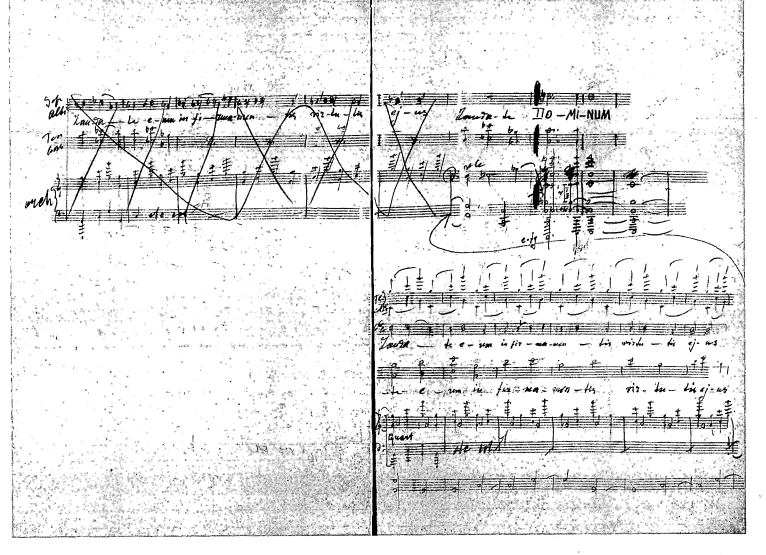

position, he made a revealing statement about his religious convictions, in an interview in *Le Vingtième Siècle*, Brussels, May 22, 1930:

1930. A page from the sketchbook of the *Symphony of Psalms.*

The more that one separates oneself from the canons of the Christian Church, the further one distances oneself from the truth. These canons are as true for musical composition as they are for the life of an individual. . . . Inspiration is secret, occult. . . . The impulse that can come from a machine, from a drug, from any stimulus [is not inspiration but] something external. . . . The machine is a very beautiful form, but superficial; it could not directly inspire an art of any interest. Art is made of itself, and one cannot create upon a creation, even though we are ourselves graftings of Jesus Christ. . . . The overflowing of the framework in art testifies to a lack of internal discipline, which weakens the work. . . .

Stravinsky has stated that he began the *Psalms* with the Russian text, later switching to Latin. And, indeed, the Russian is found above the Latin in his sketches for the first movement. Yet, in a copy of the program booklet for the first performance, Brussels, December 13, 1930, he deleted an annotator's remark that the rhythmic motive in the horns says, simply, *"Laudate Dominum"*; by coincidence, this is the same rhythm as that which undoubtedly says in Stravinsky's heart: *"Gospodi pomilui."*

The most surprising discovery in the sketch shown on page 295 is that originally full strings were intended. The reader may also note the change in the tenor and bass parts in the rewritten six measures (lower right); the addition of the A-flat, G, A-flat ostinato, which, transposed, was to become the thematic basis of the choral chant in the first movement; and the doubling of the flutes by the horns, which, in the final score, play the A-flat, G, A-flat motif.

As in the case of the *Capriccio*, the third movement of the *Psalms* was composed first—it is dated "April 27, 1930, Nice, Sunday, a week after Ascension"—then the second, dated July 17, and, finally, the beginning, signed "August 15, Assumption Day in the Roman Church, Echarvines-les-Bains." On January 6, 1930, Stravinsky copied the Vulgate text of Psalm 39 in his sketchbook and entered eleven notations, marking one of them, the core of the piece, to be repeated six times:

Concert engagements obliged Stravinsky to postpone the composition until March 4. In mid-January, he went to Berlin, and, on the 19th, attended a performance of *The Magic Flute* at the Kroll Opera. On the 23rd, he played the *Capriccio* at the Staatsoper under Klemperer, who also conducted *Le Baiser de la Fée* and Mozart's Symphony No. 40. On the 26th, Stravinsky directed a matinée concert of *Apollo* and *Le Baiser de la Fée* on the Berlin Radio and afterward heard *The Threepenny Opera*. He then went from Berlin to Leipzig, the Hotel der Kaiserhof, and, on the 29th, in Leipzig, he and Vera Sudeikina sat through *Rienzi*(!). The next day he played his *Capriccio* under Otto Klemperer in the Gewandhaus,[155] after the Chaconne from Gluck's *Orpheus* and before Brahms's Symphony No. 1. Stravinsky conducted in Düsseldorf on February 6, and in Bucharest on the 16th. In Prague, on February 26th, he played the *Capriccio*. Back in Nice, he resumed work on the *Psalms* but without finding his way. Then, on March 10, he entered the text of Psalm 150 in his manuscript book, wrote the music for the word "Alleluia," and, in the following weeks, composed the movement virtually in its final form.

Part of the first movement was sketched on June 11 and 12; on the 13th, he turned to the second movement, completing the instrumental fugue between June 14 and 17. Four days later, he introduced the second subject, at first doubling the sopranos with tenors at the octave. On July 10, the music was completed to [12], and, on the 17th, the entire movement, as well as the orchestration of its final measures and the instrumental interlude after [12]. He and Vera Sudeikina then went for a holiday (Avignon on July 19, Fontaine Vaucluse on the 20th, Marseille on the 21st and 22nd). On July 29, he wrote the beginning of the first movement and, two weeks later, completed the full score.

The provisional title for the opus was "*Symphonie pour Chant et Orchestre*," and, at the head of the first page in Stravinsky's sketchbook for Psalm 150, the words "*Symphonies Psalmodiques*" have been incompletely erased. On August 12, 1930, he wrote to André Schaeffner:

It is not a symphony in which I have included *Psalms* to be sung. On the contrary, it is the singing of the *Psalms* that I am symphonizing.

The title was fixed sometime in the next two weeks, as a letter to Ansermet reveals:

I finished my *Symphony of Psalms* (as I have named it), and I already possess the photo-copy of the orchestra score—which I wrote in calligraphy that would arouse the envy of the finest copyists. Païchadze has made several scores for our performances in Europe. The chorus parts are engraved, the orchestra parts are in manuscript. This Symphony is composed in three continuing parts: I, Prelude, II, Double Fugue, and III, the symphonic allegro, which you know. I am impatient for you to become acquainted with the other two parts. [September 3, Echarvines]

The following note appeared in *Le Journal*, August 1930, at the time that Stravinsky was completing the *Psalms:*

Sometimes toward sunset one can see a slender man of medium height walking with measured steps from Mount Boron, where he lives, to Nice. Bareheaded, wearing a bright red vest open at the neck, a navy-blue, white-striped jacket with a belt at the waist, and white pants reaching to his sandals, he has tortoise-shell glasses and his hair is smoothed back. The people in the neighborhood glance discreetly toward him, for he is one of the greatest musical geniuses of the epoch: Igor Stravinsky.

Stravinsky first played the *Psalms* for Kussevitzky in the Casino(!) at Plombières-les-Bains, "on an old casserole in B-flat," the composer writes. (The conductor did not have a piano.)

This was ten days ago. Lourié was there with his odious book about Kussevitzky, commissioned by its subject in the belief that his genius would be immortalized through Lourié's pen. [To Ansermet, September 3, 1930]

After the first performance of the *Symphony of Psalms*, Francis Poulenc wrote:

... Stravinsky has never deceived us, but rarely, also, has he offered such a beautiful surprise. ... What is particularly to my taste in this new masterpiece is the absence of grandiloquence. ... It is a work of peace. ... One can only marvel at Stravinsky's powers of renewal. I salute you, Jean-Sébastien Stravinsky. [*Le Mois*, February-March 1931]

Stravinsky recorded the *Symphony of Psalms* in the Théâtre des Champs-Elysées, February 17 and 18, 1931.

Ernest Ansermet has described Stravinsky at his morning exercises but placed a somewhat paranoid interpretation on one incident:

During our journeys together, or when I stayed with him at Morges, or Nice or elsewhere, often living in the same room, we used to do our matutinal exercises together. Once, after we had finished, and he had left the room apparently to make his toilet, I noticed that, instead, he was continuing his gymnastics in another room—to be certain of gaining an advantage over me. Sometimes these exercises ended with a wrestling match in which, since he was more muscular and more agile than I was, I could not count on my greater weight. The struggle was a little like that of a colt and a young ox. [*Entretiens sur la Musique* (Neuchâtel, 1963)]

Stravinsky was still exercising thirty years later:

... Stravinsky's appearance hasn't changed much in the ten years since I first met him. He's still slight, slim and neat. His rather large hands still gesture youthfully. Perhaps there are fewer strands of beige-colored hair plastered across his cranium and there may be another line or two in his narrow, oriental face. But the wide-mouthed smile is still the same, and the hazel eyes, behind pale, horn-rimmed spectacles, are as bright as ever. On the podium, he's apt to give the impression of austerity. When he's among friends, he's as lively and amiable as a terrier. With a little urging, he'll stand on his head to demonstrate one of the ways he keeps physically fit. "A brief head-stand," he says, "rests the head and clears the brain." It's something he picked up from a Yogi. And no day passes without a quarter-hour of calisthenics. ... [William King, *Cue*, April 24, 1948]

Autumn 1924. Berlin. Hotel Fürstenhof. Exercising during a concert tour in Germany. On July 23, 1923, Stravinsky, in Biarritz, wrote to Ernest Ansermet: "I do my gymnastics every morning and I sunbathe from twelve to one o'clock." Photograph by Vera Sudeikina.

Throughout his life, Stravinsky experimented with *à la mode* diets and health regimes and followed one or another of the leading gurus of physical culture. Nicolas Nabokov describes Stravinsky's diet in 1930:

Usually he went out for lunch, with Lourié or Vera Arturovna de Bosset, whom I had met two years earlier at a Diaghilev rehearsal, or with other friends. ... But sometimes we would walk over to the Russian restaurant across from the Russian church on the rue Daru. We would drink vodka and eat a *pirozhok*, and then Stravinsky would say: "Now you order whatever you want. I am ... on a diet and can eat only raw things."

Then Stravinsky would explain to the waiter:

"Bring me a plateful of sliced raw potatoes and tomatoes with no salt or pepper, but with half a lemon and some olive oil on the side." I would order ... Côtelettes Pojarsky. Stravinsky would say to the waiter: "Bring him three. He is big, hungry, and needs meat." And then, when I was full after two *côtelettes*, Stravinsky would pick up the third, cover it with sour cream, and ... say, "I want to astonish the raw potato in my stomach." [156]

Two years later, as Stravinsky noted to C. F. Ramuz, the diet had changed:

... I am on the third day of a *régime* prescribed by my Russian doctor ... in the morning a little porridge and half an apple, at noon some mashed potatoes, one egg, and another half of an apple; at six o'clock half a glass of water and at eight some mashed potatoes. This is all for twenty-four hours. I think I would be better off to eat nothing at all than to suffer with a menu like this, but it seems to be the only way to end the colitis that I have had since last June. [Letter of January 1, 1932]

Ramuz answered, recommending "tablets of effervescent calcium: colitis is a sickness of the soul." Six months later, at the beginning of July 1932, Stravinsky captioned a photograph of himself: *"Hérissy (séjours de quelque jours, soin de la colite) près Fontainebleau."*

Whatever Stravinsky's diet may have been in the following year, on April 1, 1933, Ida Rubinstein, in Paris, telegraphed a dinner invitation to him in the Carlton Hotel, Budapest:

Cher maître et ami please give me the great pleasure of coming to my house next Friday April 17 with Mme Debussy and Nadia Boulanger Stop We will all dine according to your diet. ...

In July 1936, he wrote to Victoria Ocampo:

The twelve days of the voyage *ont rendu un mauvais service à mes intestines que je suis en train de soigner en ce moment-ci.*

And on the second of July 1937, Stravinsky, in Paris, wrote to Ramuz:

We are going to the country (near Annemasse, château de Monthoux, a pension), the whole family. ... The move will take place about July 13. As for myself, I will have to follow the severest diet until September, since two ulcers have been found, one in the stomach and the other in the intestine. ...

This *"régime"* must have been effective. René Kendyk wrote in *Gringoire*, October 22:

He has a good digestion and proves it. He rushes to the Villette or to rue Saint-Denis for his meals. Snails and grills give him the vitamin Z which his inspiration requires. ... At three o'clock in the morning he enters, foulard wrapped around his throat, carrying some bottles of champagne.

In Santa Barbara, in September 1941, Stravinsky became a disciple of Siposh, the Hungarian masseur, hydropathologist, and gymnast, and survived him to fall under the influence, a decade later, of Dr. Sigfrid Knauer, with his homeopathic prescriptions, his system of diagnoses by pendulum, and his belief in rejuvenation by the ingestion of minced fetuses. In Zürich, October 8, 1961, Stravinsky was examined by the celebrated Dr.

Niehans, with a view to following a course of his treatments, but the composer decided against this because of the cost in time.[157]

An interview in the summer of 1931, in Voreppe [Isère], reveals some of this preoccupation with health:

"Let's have a promenade in the park," Stravinsky said, "I like this slightly wild landscape. Each morning I drink a glass of water and walk in the park. It is very healthy. Do you know Kneipp? I would like to read a book about him. Please find it for me. Kneipp was an extraordinary man. He was also a priest." [158] . . .

"How are things in Berlin? Will we always be hearing the same old music? And how is it with the newspapers? Always they must pigeonhole, while I am doing something different. It is this, of course, that maddens them. . . . Always, too, they must associate me with someone—Diaghilev, Picasso, and now Cocteau. I recently received a clipping from a . . . German magazine in which I am said to be *dependent* on Cocteau."

Going inside, tea and *pâtisserie* are served. "Our cook is from Trieste," Stravinsky said, "and her specialty is sweets." Starting to talk about his forthcoming concerts, Stravinsky was not very gentle on the subject of conductors, but he spoke well of Zemlinsky and Hans Rosbaud. We listened to rehearsal records of the *Symphony of Psalms.* [Heinrich Strobel, the *Börsencourrier*, August 1931; Stravinsky had written to Strobel on August 17 explaining that he would be obliged to stay in Grenoble and come to Voreppe on the 2:43 train on Sunday next.]

A large portion of Stravinsky's letters are addressed to doctors and pharmacists:

Je vous prie de . . . m'envoyer . . . trois tubes de la pomade (pour le nez) numéro 104440 . . . d'après une recette du Dr. F. Gaudichon. . . . [Letter of May 2, 1932]

And many of the composer's letters begin with complaints about his health. On September 15, 1921, for example, Stravinsky writes to Ansermet that he had barely returned from Paris when he caught the grippe, and in another note to the same correspondent, in December 1926, the composer says that he has been rather ill with grippe. *"Je me sens au point de vue des nerfs très mal,"* he writes to Païchadze, July 15, 1927; and to Don Gelasio Caetani, from Nice, March 12, 1928, Stravinsky says that he is tired because of a slight grippe, which, he explains in a letter the next day to Païchadze, is "a head cold: *Je me prépare pour le voyage par des cachets d'Eurythmine."* To Païchadze, August 31, 1933, Stravinsky writes that he has been in bed these last three days because his bile has poisoned his intestines, but that finally a diet and forced rest have purged him, although leaving him feeble.

Many interviewers comment on his precautions against drafts:

Igor Stravinsky unwinds his muffler. . . . Sharp-witted, cunning as a fox . . . [After the interview] he wraps himself up again in his scarf, leaving only his sharp nose sticking out, and departs, muttering: "Not heated here, not heated." [Gustave Rey, in *L'Intransigeant*, December 2, 1927]

Stravinsky is wearing his cap, and his neck is wrapped in a yellow scarf; he lives in Nice and is afraid of catching cold [in our climate]. [*L'Etoile Belge*, May 22, 1930]

In fact, Stravinsky *was* extraordinarily susceptible both to colds and to the enteritis bacillus. His illnesses also crowd his wife's diaries: "New York, December 23, 1940: Igor starts a cold." . . . "California. Igor has the beginning of a cold." . . . "New York. Igor has the flu." Yet *Life*, March 23, 1953, accurately described him as "moving, at the age of 70, with the springy grace of a high-school basketball player." The same article quotes W. H. Auden saying that Stravinsky had told him:

Every morning for fifteen minutes I pray, for fifteen minutes I exercise, and for fifteen minutes I shave.

The *Life* article goes on, from other sources, to describe Stravinsky's morning:

He gets up at eight, drinks a cup of Italian coffee, smokes exactly one cigarette, and does special Hungarian gymnastics, including eyeball rolling, for fifteen minutes. He then has breakfast alone with his newspaper and starts to work at 9:30. At 11:00 the mail arrives and Stravinsky knocks off to answer all important letters immediately.

Janet Flanner wrote about Stravinsky in the 1930s:

He's a hypochondriac who worries about his health, his family's health, everybody's health. "How are you feeling, I'm not feeling very well," he began a letter to a friend. He hurries back and forth between homeopathy, allopathy, and symptoms. For years he has taken daily gymnastic exercises before an open window and has the pride of the small male in his magnificent muscles. . . . When fully dressed, he has a great deal on even in mild weather—scarf to his ears, spats, sweater, tweeds, stick, cigarette-lighter, *étui*, wristwatch, complicated double lenses for his myopic eyes, sacred medals and fetishes pinned to his underwear—for he is superstitious—and over all, for fear of draughts, often two coats, one of fur. His friend Chanel once made and gave him a tremendous astrakhan-collared traveling coat and cap he became partial to. . . . In rehearsals, he wears scarves and a sheepskin coat.[159]

Here is still another account of Stravinsky's health during his first American tour. The interviewer is the Cincinnati critic Charles Ludwig, the time, the winter of 1925.

[Stravinsky said that] "The American composer [John Alden] Carpenter took me through the famous stockyards in Chicago, and then, to put the finishing touches on my American education, Henry Ford invited me, while in Detroit, to inspect the Ford automobile factory, but I caught cold in Detroit and was unable to go. . . ."

Stravinsky was still suffering from the cold. He came into Emery Auditorium heavily bundled in sweater and overcoat, and even carried a huge shawl to protect himself against drafts. He was so indisposed Wednesday that he had to remain in his room at the Hotel Gibson while Fritz Reiner took his place on the conductor's stand at the rehearsal.

Stravinsky said before he took the baton Thursday that he still felt ill—and he asked Reiner to hold his bottle of medicine for him. But as soon as the music started, Stravinsky forgot all about his cold. His overcoat was thrown across the railing of the conductor's stand. Soon he became so warmed up that he peeled off his coat too. The last time he did this there was disclosed a pink sweater. This time it was a white woolen sweater cut short like a vest. In ten more minutes, Stravinsky, bathed in perspiration, wrapped a towel around his neck and repeatedly wiped his forehead with it. . . .

Stravinsky's appearances in Vienna were rare. The first, since the "sabotaging" of *Petrushka* in January 1913, took place in March 1926. Conscious then that he was in Schoenberg's native city, he told a reporter for *Die Stunde*:

It is difficult for me to speak about the character of my music. I only want to emphasize for the sake of those who do not know my work that anyone who thinks that I am atonal does not understand me. Maybe they understand Schoenberg; his work can be atonal. [March 17, 1926]

But another writer (unidentified), quoting Stravinsky on the same occasion—a press conference in his room at the Imperial Hotel—interpreted his meaning differently:

Atonal? Everything is valid depending on the results, the reality of the sounds. For me harmonic problems are secondary. . . . I like Weber,[160] Schubert, Chopin, Gounod, Bizet, Debussy.

(Oddly, Weber's name provoked some letters.) According to this same newspaper (also unidentified), Stravinsky said, too, that he knew all of the great Russian literature in his youth and that he had been especially impressed by Turgenev. A few days later, at a press conference in Mannheim, Stravinsky announced that "My music is not atonal, and in fact atonality does not exist."

In Vienna (in 1926), other newspapers described Stravinsky as an eccentric:

Conductor Dirk Fock rehearses *Petrushka* and the *Firebird* Suite, and when Stravinsky arrives he knows exactly what to expect. He enters in the middle of the rehearsal, a small, swift-stepping, elegant gentleman, and immediately creates a sensation by reaching for his glass cigarette holder and lighting a cigarette. Herr Botstieber, the general manager, turns pale, since it is the first time that anyone has ever smoked in the hall. But Stravinsky smokes and, as a Russian, insists on drinking tea.

Stravinsky talks to Herr Kugel [an impresario] in Russian, then begins to rehearse the Piano Concerto, his fingers flying over the keyboard like a group of dancers on a stage.[161] He leaps from the keyboard to the conductor's podium and back to the piano with the agility of a dancer, and, at the end, stepping down in youthful waltz-like movement, lights another cigarette. [Unidentified newspaper clipping]

On March 17, 1926, the *Neues Wiener Journal* published an in-

February 1930. Prague. Between Ansermet and Alexander von Zemlinsky (Schoenberg's brother-in-law). Drawing by Benedikt F. Dolbin.

terview conducted by Julius Bistron, who refers to the combination of East and West in Stravinsky's culture, then asks him:

"What limits do you feel or find in modern music?"

Stravinsky: "That is a philosophical question, and of a kind that one expects in Vienna. I would like to answer it but must declare myself incompetent. My conceptions are much too mirrored in my own creative beliefs and knowledge; I cannot verbalize them. . . . My own artistic perspectives come from within myself and from the surroundings in which I live. I live in Paris because the meaning of French spiritual life attracts me and keeps me there. But you would be wrong to assume that French guidelines are also mine. Perhaps I am old-fashioned in finding so much good in the past, but I love Gounod and Bizet, and I claim them as spiritual brothers, just as I do Debussy. Debussy was able to put impressionism into music, and, if his tones were to be transposed into colors, his works would surely hang in the Louvre. . . . The problems of harmony today do not affect me; the *dernier cri* must be the living music. . . . All that matters for the productive artist is to be able to form and to inspire.

Stravinsky had begun to travel by air in 1926, to avoid the Paris-London boat train. (In a letter to his elder son, September

November 29, 1930. Vienna. The photograph was taken after a performance of the *Capriccio* conducted by Martin Spanjaard.

OPPOSITE TOP:
October 1930. From the 25th to the 31st, Stravinsky traveled in the Rhineland. He conducted in Mainz on the 25th and was photographed there that day in front of the house where part of *Meistersinger* had been composed. On the 26th, he went to Wiesbaden, where, on the afternoon of the 31st, he played the *Capriccio* in a concert led by Ansermet, conducting a program of his own music that night. On the 28th, he and Vera Sudeikina dined at the Mumms' and Stravinsky was photographed in front of the Metternich Palace. Vera Sudeikina had been a friend of Olga Mumm in Russia and knew her daughter, Elena, later Mrs. Edmund Wilson, in Davos and in New York. On October 29, Stravinsky and Vera Sudeikina saw a performance of the *"Urfaust."*

OPPOSITE BOTTOM:
April 25, 1931. Venice. Arriving by aquaplane from Trieste, after a concert there.

April 26, 1931. Venice. In the Piazza San Marco. Photograph by Vera Sudeikina.

12, 1954, the composer recalls that he was very frightened on his first flight.) Vera Sudeikina's first airplane trip was this one from Trieste to Venice, whose final stage is pictured here, and her reason was the same as Stravinsky's had been five years earlier: she was violently seasick during a Channel crossing, January 25–6, 1931. On that occasion, Stravinsky wrote a poem for her, "Sleep, Vera Arturovna, sleep," that mentions such details of the experience as pressing a hot teapot to the solar plexus, and which, in a footnote, expresses satisfaction at "having found a rhyme for Calais"—*"tibiéh"* ("to you").

April 27, 1931. On the Ponte dei Mendicanti, looking toward San Michele. Photograph by Vera Sudeikina.

Forty years later, on April 15, 1971, Stravinsky's mortal remains would be borne under the Ponte dei Mendicanti for burial on the island toward which he is gazing. On the day that this picture was taken, he visited Diaghilev's grave, still without tombstone, and photographed it. The Rio Mendicanti was the main waterway in one of Stravinsky's favorite Venetian neighborhoods. In the late 1950s, the autumn of 1960, and September 1962, he was obliged to come each week to the Scuola di San Marco, Venice's hospital, for examinations of his blood. He was also fond of the San Zanipolo (where his funeral service was to take place). And, finally, across the Rio from the church was the palazzo of his friend Countess Giovanni ("Mussia") Antonini, a Russian refugee, married at one time to the pianist Borovsky. She had known Stravinsky and Vera Sudeikina in Paris in the 1920s, and in 1940 was to live with them for a time in their Hollywood home.

During the 1930s few people were closer to Stravinsky than his publisher, Willy Strecker, director of B. Schott's Söhne, Mainz:

I spent much time together with Stravinsky when he was composing the Violin Concerto: "I want to write a true virtuoso concerto," [Stra-

vinsky said] "and the whole spirit of the violin must be in every measure of the composition. . . . For me the first idea is always the strongest, because it comes from a higher force—is God-given and hence cannot be improved by the art of man. . . ." [Strecker, *op. cit.*]

The first notation for the Violin Concerto, dated October 27, 1930, was for the music at $\boxed{7}$, but conceived in triplet figures. The next four months were almost entirely occupied with concerts, and it was not until March 11, back in Grenoble, that he was able to resume work. The first movement was completed there on March 27, and the other three, in their sequence in the published score, between, respectively, April 7 and May 20, May 24 and June 6, and June 12 and September 4. Only one of the sketches is dated, that for the passage between $\boxed{103}$ and $\boxed{107}$, composed on August 10–11, 1931.

The Violin Concerto was slow to enter the repertory, and as late as 1967 Stravinsky wrote in the index of Szigeti's autobiography,[162] "Why is my Violin Concerto not mentioned by Szigeti? It is not a bad work." In Paris, on October 28 and 29, 1935, Stravinsky and Samuel Dushkin recorded the Concerto for Polydor. After the last session, Stravinsky read a statement on a radio broadcast giving his views on recording. This, in effect, says that

March 18, 1932. Venice. Taking flowers to Diaghilev's grave on San Michele. Stravinsky conducted in Venice on March 19.

his recordings should be considered not only as documents of his wishes but also as guides for others, and should serve as protection against arbitrary interpretations; the text was published in *L'Intransigeant,* October 29, 1935. Nearly twenty years later, he said virtually the same thing to the *Seattle Post-Intelligencer:*

When I conduct, the music is presented pretty nearly the way I want it. That is why I've been conducting recording sessions of most of my music. In the future there will be no doubt as to how it should be played. [March 5, 1954]

For these, as well as financial reasons, Stravinsky began to record his music at every opportunity in the 1930s, and the following schedule, covering only eleven months, is typical:

May 6 and 7, 1932:	*Histoire du Soldat.*
May 9, 1932:	Octet.
April 6, 1933:	The *Pastorale* (violin and winds); the violin-and-piano arrangements of the "Danse Russe" (*Petrushka*), "Berceuse" (*Firebird*), "Chinese March" (*Nightingale*); the "Cantilène" (*Duo Concertant*).
April 7, 1933:	The remainder of the *Duo Concertant,* and the "Serenata" and "Scherzino" (*Pulcinella*) for violin and piano.

The following year, he recorded the *Sérénade en la* on July 5 and 6 and, on the 13th, the *Ragtime* for eleven instruments.

Toward the end of his life, Stravinsky was increasingly disaffected with the recording process and with the industry. Also, he began to realize that, although his recordings enabled him to establish models for other conductors to follow, he could not compel them to do so. And he was rarely content with recordings of his music by other conductors. In a letter to the present writer, October 7, 1947, Stravinsky complains that the new RCA discs of his Octet and *Histoire du Soldat* do not follow his own European records, that a pedal drum is used in *Histoire du Soldat* "to facilitate the job of the percussion," and that "the drum coda entangles the pitches of the different drums." The letter concludes with the fervent hope that these records will never be published.

Comparison between this draft of the "Dithyramb" (*Duo Concertant*) and the final score reveals few alterations of a conceptual nature but many refinements. How vastly superior, for instance, is the group of five notes in the second score-system to the four-note phrase in the upper score. The "X" above the third score-system directs the composer to the rewritten version of the same music at the beginning of the second page. The inscription in the lower left margin of the first page, "*Pour la fin, à trois temps, cette mesure,*" was carried out, but it is remarkable that the ending of the piece had occurred to Stravinsky so soon after

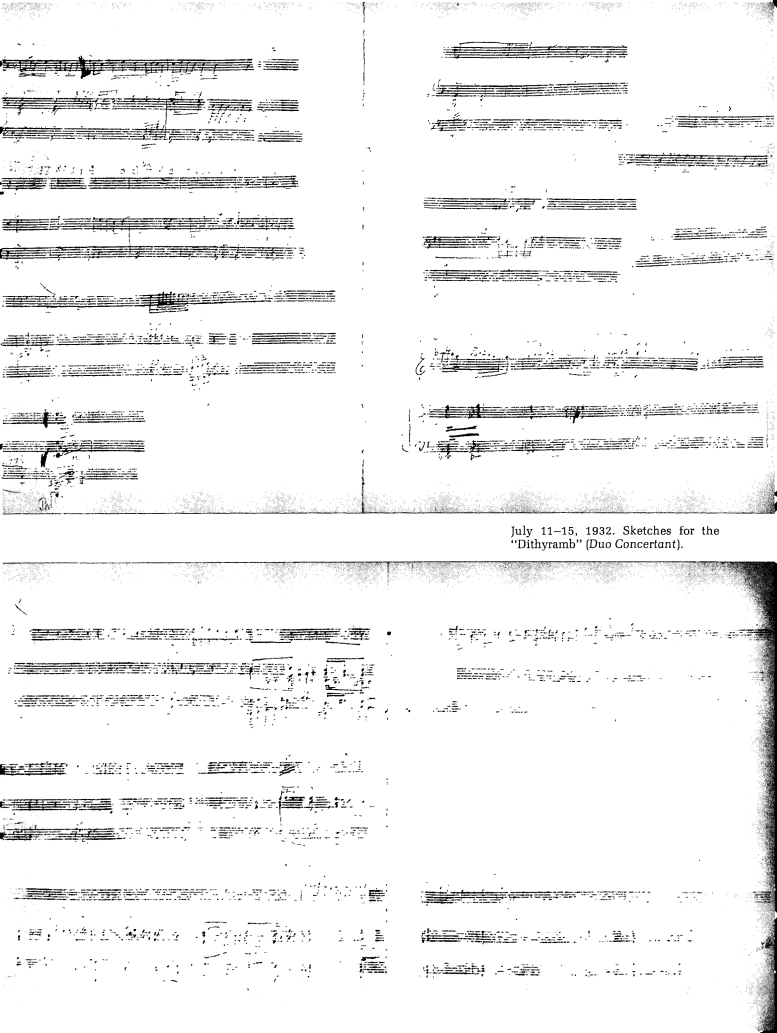

July 11–15, 1932. Sketches for the "Dithyramb" (*Duo Concertant*).

the beginning. Some of the piano fingerings here are not included in the published score, proof that he was concerned with the performance of the music in the very heat of composing it—or the "cool," for the melody is elegant and restrained.

The *Duo Concertant* was begun on December 27, 1931, but interrupted on January 17, "the day of departure, Paris-London," as the manuscript says. Returning to Paris and Voreppe, Stravinsky composed until February 9, completing the first movement up to the final ten measures, then departed again for concerts. Work was also interrupted by visitors and promenades. The pictures in the composer's photograph albums of the time contain such captions as: "Promenade in auto, Mâcon to Paris, May 4," "Lunch with the Louriés near St. Cyr, May," "Visit from Mme Belaiev and N. Vinogradov, Voreppe, 8–9 June," "Visit from H. Rosbaud, June 12," "Promenade with Ardèches to Mme Fougeral's home," "Lunch with Strecker, Wiesbaden, June 24," "Lunch at Heidelberg, June 26." The "Gigue" is dated "June 16, Voreppe," and the entire score was completed a month later.

While preparing the *Duo Concertant* for recording and for concert performance, Stravinsky . . . described . . . the Eclogue No. 1 with its irresistible motoric drive [as] a *Kazatchok*. . . . But the most unexpected—and . . . extremely apt—illustrative guidepost came when Stravinsky "interpreted" the first Trio of the Gigue. He jumped up from the piano and . . . danced and hummed and mimed [the following] refrain from Johann Strauss's *Fledermaus*, in impeccable German:

> "Glücklich ist
> Wer vergisst
> Was nicht mehr
> Zu ändern ist." [163]

In Berlin, October 31, 1932, Stravinsky and Vera Sudeikina attended a concert, conducted by Furtwängler, that included Beethoven's Fourth Symphony, Prokofiev's Fifth Piano Concerto (with the composer as soloist), and *Harold in Italy* (with Hindemith playing the viola obbligato). Stravinsky and Prokofiev became friends after a concert in St. Petersburg, December 31, 1908, which Stravinsky attended, and in which Prokofiev played some of his own piano pieces. But the friendship lacked a natural basis in music, in religion—where they were prototypes of the believer and non-believer—and in politics, where these roles were reversed. Among the many instances of strained relations between the two men, the following is especially curious. After a concert in Warsaw, Stravinsky had traced his hand in a woman's autograph album, in his case a not infrequent form of responding to a request for a "souvenir." (The composer Ellis Kohs, one of Stravinsky's Harvard pupils in 1939–40, possesses a copy of Stravinsky's *The Five Fingers*, on the cover of which the composer has traced his left hand.) Later, when Prokofiev was asked to sign the same book, he inscribed a mocking remark under the drawing. Stravinsky read about this in a Paris newspaper and wrote to Prokofiev:

June 20, 1932. Châlons-sur-Marne. With Vera Sudeikina. On June 19, Stravinsky left Voreppe for Frankfurt. In August, he took another holiday with Vera Sudeikina, driving from Valence to Arles on August 17, photographing gypsies on the road to Montpellier on the 19th, stopping at Carcassonne on the 20th, and at the Hôtel du Palais, Biarritz, on the 22nd. The 27th and the 28th were spent at Gavarny with the Marquis Lur-Saluces (Château Yquem). On September 1, Stravinsky, Vera Sudeikina, and M. and Mme Blaise Cendrars were in Bordeaux at the start of a *tour gastronomique* to Paris.

Dear Seriozha: I send this clipping, which appeared recently in the Paris newspapers. I suppose that your interpretation of your joke in the album of the Warsaw woman had another character than the one given to it by these unknown-to-me slanderers in the newspapers. Surely it cannot have been your intention to laugh at me as a pianist—for, after all, I play only my own compositions—or even as a conductor. My hand, drawn in the album, both plays and conducts, and not so shamefully, I think, that people might make stupid and nasty fun of me. No doubt many people object to my activity as a performer, but it is the only way to avoid the grimaces of other interpreters of my music. Devotedly and with love, Igor Stravinsky. [December 20, 1933]

Prokofiev answered on December 21:

I much appreciate your indulgence for this affair in the newspapers. It has afflicted me terribly. Now it is time to forget that whole period— when you spoke badly about my music [164] as well as about what I wrote in the woman's album.

After Prokofiev's return to Russia, Stravinsky heard from him directly only once again, a telegram of condolence, from Moscow, December 11, 1938, on the death of Stravinsky's elder daughter.
Stravinsky's diary for November 27, 1959, contains an entry:

Luncheon here in Gladstone [Hotel, New York] with Bill Brown. Went with him to see, in Museum of Modern Art, the most stupid and provincial Russian film *Ivan the Terrible*, first part, with very embarrassing music of the poor Prokofiev.

Mr. Brown recalls that Stravinsky complained that "the Russian is so bad I can understand it only by reading the English subtitles and translating back."

October 23, 1932. Berlin. With Serge Prokofiev. Photograph by Vera Sudeikina.

Perséphone

The following excerpts from letters reveal something of the origins of Stravinsky's largest creation of the 1930s, the melodrama *Perséphone*. One of the principal figures in the correspondence is Gavril Païchadze, the most skillful diplomat among those who attempted to manage Stravinsky's business affairs and at the same time maintain a cordial personal relationship with him. Next to Walter Nouvel, Païchadze was Stravinsky's closest Russian-émigré friend in the 1930s, and it is typical of Païchadze that, after completing some difficult negotiations with Diaghilev for seven performances of *The Firebird* in London in November and December 1926—Diaghilev's position was that the Ballets Russes were entitled to perform the piece without paying royalties—Païchadze wrote to Stravinsky asking him to confirm the understanding with Diaghilev, and adding that "a 'thank you' is never too much."

OPPOSITE:
January 21, 1933. Hamburg. A rehearsal of the *Capriccio* under the direction of Eugen Pabst. This is one of the rare photographs of Stravinsky actually playing the piano. Nine days later, on January 30, Hitler came to power in Germany.

February 1, 1933. Wiesbaden. With André Gide. The following day Stravinsky and Dushkin gave a recital, after which Thomas Mann visited with the composer.

One of Païchadze's first letters to Stravinsky concerning *Persèphone* shows that the composer believed that Valéry was to be the librettist:

Your suppositions about Paul Valéry were wrong. The day of your departure I had a long conversation with Ida Rubinstein, who told me that she had André Gide in view, and that he had written a remarkable piece for her, the subject of which will please you. I understood that it is a classical text, with chorus. She would like Gide to be in communication with you as soon as possible, but I explained that you are on a concert tour now and are unavailable until the end of February, at which time you will be able to see Gide and to talk to him. I telephoned to you many times but could not get through.

I have the impression from my conversation with Ida Lvovna that we can obtain better conditions than we had expected. I hope that the fees will be the same as for *Le Baiser de la Fée,* but you must be more diplomatic and less impulsive.

Gide called me the next day, wanting to see you as soon as possible and even to go to Berlin. I told him that you have many rapid changes of address and would not be in Berlin at all. I promised to find out where you will be and to inform him. Perhaps he can come to Italy? Or even to Voreppe?

He asked me to send this letter to you, and if you want me to answer it by telephone, I can do that. But I feel that it would be better for you to do it, since only you can arouse his enthusiasm, which he will then transmit to Ida and thus make our talk about terms much simpler. I would like to know which fee is the more important to you, the one for the commission or the one for conducting? I think that we should discuss the commission first, and the conducting much later— as we did with *Le Baiser de la Fée.* . . . [Letter from Paris, January 24, 1933]

Stravinsky answered by telegram from Wiesbaden four days later, saying he was delighted by the choice of Gide and inviting him to come to Wiesbaden immediately. On the next day (January 29, 1933), Païchadze telegraphed that Gide would come on Monday morning, then two weeks later (February 14) wrote that he had received

a call from Ida Lvovna, who knows that you are coming to Paris on the 15th of March and who asks you to meet with Gide and with her at the same time. Would it be possible for you to come with Gide to her house for lunch on the 16th? Please let me know. I must give her an answer.

Meanwhile, on February 24, Gide wrote to Stravinsky:

Dear Igor, your express letter has just come. I sent the first tableau to you in care of Ida Rubinstein in Milan.[165] Fortunately I have a copy in hand (a unique one) which I am sending with this letter. I would propose to come to you in Voreppe but am afraid of the fatigue and the cold since I have not been well recently. What bothers me most is not working. I hope to be able to send the remainder of the text to you in a week or so (the provisional parts of it, that is, for they must be redone— so much the worse). Very affectionately, André Gide.

On the same day, Païchadze wrote to Stravinsky:

I had two short conversations with Ida Rubinstein. She thinks that we should wait until you are in Paris to formulate all of the conditions with all the details. She says—and I concur with her—that she can sign the contract only after your final agreement with Gide. . . . All that I wanted was her assurance that the new contract will have the same terms as that for *Le Baiser de la Fée.* . . . Gide has gone away for a short time. . . . I told Ida Lvovna that you will come for her luncheon on the 16th of March and of course she was delighted.

Three days later (February 27), Païchadze wrote again:

Gide wants me to send this package to you; it is a rough sketch of the first part of the new piece.

On March 5, Stravinsky, in Voreppe, wrote to Gide at Le Lavandou (Var), thanking him for the end of the Second Tableau and above all for "the beautiful verses with which the play is filled." Stravinsky asks for "a little tranquillity" in which to look at the libretto from the point of view of the theater, both in general and in this play, in order to be understood with absolute clarity. He also declares that his love for Gide's work is serious and profound, and claims to have been "seduced by the beauty of his magnificent words celebrating the ancient mystery of *Perséphone.*" Finally, Stravinsky says that he aspires with all of his powers to erect a monument in sound that will stand by the side of Gide's in words, yet this monument must be an independent musical organism serving neither to embellish the text ("beautiful in itself") nor to color it, nor to guide the public in the various evolutions of the drama as in the *leitmotif* of Wagner. Then, perhaps remembering Cocteau's visit to Leysin in March 1914, and the nuisance of having a house guest, Stravinsky says that, although in his last letter he had invited Gide to come to Voreppe, the bad weather does not recommend this plan, for Gide would be uncomfortable in the small and unheated room.

On March 13, Stravinsky and Dushkin gave a recital for the BBC in London. The next day, Stravinsky returned to Paris, where, on Sunday, March 19, 1933, Count Harry Kessler wrote in his *Diary*:

A visit from André Gide. . . . He told me that he and Stravinsky are writing a ballet, *Perséphone*, for Ida Rubinstein. . . . Later we drove to a Stravinsky concert at the Salle Pleyel [5 o'clock].

The program that Stravinsky conducted consisted of the *Symphony of Psalms*, a group of songs with instruments (Parasha's aria, the *Pastorale*, *Tilimbom*, excerpts from *The Nightingale*), sung by Romanitza, and *Le Sacre du Printemps*. The musicians were those of Monteux's Orchestre Symphonique de Paris. Stravinsky then went to Winterthur for a recital with Dushkin (on the 25th), and to Budapest, where, on April 3, he conducted a program of *Fireworks*, the *Petrushka* Suite, the Piano Concerto, and the *Firebird* Suite. The soloist in the Piano Concerto was a nineteen-year-old American girl, Rosalind Kaplan, who had played the piece in Chicago at the age of fourteen(!).

A little more than a month later, Païchadze wrote to Stravinsky:

Yesterday I telegraphed the news that I had signed the contract with Ida Rubinstein for *Perséphone*. Now I have sent the first payment of 25,000 francs to you. It was not easy to find the right form for the contract since I, the publisher, am guaranteeing that *you* will compose the music. Your dates for the delivery of the material are the same as those that we worked out together at our last meeting with Ida Lvovna. I had to yield on point 6 concerning symphony and concert performances, especially those in Paris. She insisted on this because later in the spring, or autumn, she wants to repeat her season and naturally wishes to avoid a coincidental concert performance. Since she will spend a tremendous amount of money for the staging, it would be unfair to stop her from repeating her performance. . . . It will always be possible to give *Perséphone* later in concerts.

About the payments. Ida Lvovna wishes to make the last one on the first of December, this being more convenient for her than the first of November. I consented, remembering that you had said she could arrange the payments as she wished. . . .

It was difficult to reach an agreement about your conducting. Ida Lvovna thinks that this need not be stipulated in the contract. Of course she is delighted that you will conduct the first performance—and the others—but as the dates are not yet fixed, she prefers to wait. What seems important to me is to fix a date for the *first* performance. Understand that she is afraid of being tied down if her date is not convenient for you, and to avoid this I added a clause (10), which is somewhat complicated and vague. I want to explain to you that Ida Lvovna is obliged by contract to offer the conducting of the performance to you but that you are not obliged to accept if you have a conflicting concert engagement.

I am certain that she will invite you to conduct all of the performances—also next year's—if the piece is a success. She has agreed, but it was not easy to include this point. . . . Also, she was slightly uneasy in that I alone signed the contract, but I promised her that you will sign it too. Please do so now. . . .

On May 3, Stravinsky informed Païchadze that the work was under way and that Eumolpus [166] had started to sing. On July 7, the composer wrote to ask why Mme Rubinstein had inquired about his progress in the piece from Païchadze,

since she telephoned to me from Paris several times and only yesterday called to say that she has found a convenient apartment for me there (which, if true, will solve one of my greatest worries).

Païchadze answered on July 8:

Why are you so astonished that Ida Rubinstein talks to *me* about your work? What else can she talk to me about? She wants to know not only from you but from other people, too, which only shows the trepidation and respect she feels for you. I hope *you* are not jealous of *me!*

On September 7, Stravinsky informed Païchadze that the second tableau was almost finished. On November 13, Mme Rubinstein telegraphed to Stravinsky in Milan:

André Gide asked me to tell you that he thinks incessantly of the project, in which he is sustained by you. . . .

Stravinsky wrote to Païchadze the same day, saying that the letter had come from Gide, and that the business agreement which they had reached in Wiesbaden specified an equal division of the royalties:

since *Perséphone* is not a ballet libretto but a book by Gide that already existed, his share of the royalties belongs in a higher category.

These letters omit all mention of the stage director, Jacques Copeau, with whom Stravinsky became embroiled in a misunderstanding. The composer wanted his son Theodore to design the sets and costumes, but by the time Copeau was informed of this desire—in January 1934, by which month the full score was completed (on the 24th)—he had already chosen André Barsacq.

Stravinsky's differences with Gide were to become more serious, and they worsened steadily until the time of the performance and after. Next to the text of Eumolpus' "*Perséphone confuse,*" Gide had written the direction, "*Le rhythme accéléré de la musique, ironique et stridente,*" and, at another place, "*Eclat de rire dans l'orchestre. . . .*" Stravinsky underlined these instructions and wrote, in Russian, on the margin of Gide's manuscript: "What a mentality."

But Gide's original libretto contained numerous remarks of the sort, and his stage directions are almost as long as the text itself. He wrote the libretto in three parallel columns, the first one for the sung parts, the second for the spoken parts, and the third for the action. Yet Gide seems at first to have been eager to exchange ideas and to "collaborate" with Stravinsky, as the following excerpt from one of the novelist's letters indicates:

I think that it would be better if Perséphone were to pronounce her short tirade *after* Eumolpus, in order to put some distance between *this* song and the "*C'est ainsi*" that he sings between the tableaux. Or do you think that the March of Descent to the Underworld will provide sufficient separation?

Stravinsky followed the suggestion and switched the order.

It should be mentioned that Stravinsky composed the chorus "*Les Ombres ne sont pas malheureuses*" directly on Gide's libretto, which is one reason why a facsimile edition of this manuscript with the corrections, comments, and notations of both authors would be of great interest.

Stravinsky's setting did not please Gide, who did not attend any of the performances (April 30, May 4 and 9, 1934), but when the libretto was published, Gide sent a copy to Stravinsky, inscribing it: "*En amicale communion.*" Stravinsky answered as follows:

"*Amicale communion!*" Why, my poor Gide, did you believe it incumbent to add the dedicatory formula, "André Gide to Igor Stravinsky," which remedies nothing and cannot hide the absence of rapport which was so manifestly your attitude? [May 26, 1934]

Yet Gide sent a moving letter to Stravinsky on learning of the death of his daughter Liudmilla, in 1938. And a card from David Diamond, in Nice, October 7, 1948, tells Stravinsky that "Gide came for a visit this morning and . . . spoke of you so warmly."

After *Perséphone*, Stravinsky's friend Charles-Albert Cingria wrote to the composer advising him to be content in future to "compose for God and for the Philadelphia Orchestra" (the *Symphony of Psalms* having been dedicated "to the Glory of God and to the Boston Symphony"). Cingria's letter gives a picture of French literary cliques at the time—for example, in a reference to Claudel as "the Buddha of the Noailles." Cingria also suggests that Stravinsky advise the Protestant C. F. Ramuz to "read Claudel's *Sur la Présence de Dieu*, which is terrifyingly beautiful." Cingria wanted to write about *Perséphone* for the *Nouvelle Revue Française*, and he persuaded Claudel to broach the matter with Jean Paulhan, who replied favorably but warned that Gide would oppose it.

Four years after *Perséphone*, Ida Rubinstein again approached Stravinsky, this time proposing Claudel as librettist. Stravinsky disliked Claudel personally, and had recently been irritated by his essay "The Wagnerian Poison" (*Le Figaro Littéraire*, March 26, 1938), writing in the margin: "Really, is it worthwhile to renounce Wagner in order to exalt the beauties of Berlioz? This is too stupid." Nevertheless, in a letter to Strecker, June 1, 1938, Stravinsky says that discussions had begun the day before, and that the piece would be "of large proportions, with chorus and declamation (an oratorio with staging)." Strecker then met with Mme Rubinstein on Stravinsky's behalf, and, on June 21, wrote to him in detail about the business agreement. But Stravinsky and Claudel could not agree on a subject, Stravinsky insisting on *Prometheus*, Claudel on the *Book of Tobit*. On June 21, Claudel wrote to Stravinsky from 11, rue Jean Goujon, Paris, rejecting *Prométhée*, and, a week later, wrote again, from the Château de Branques (Isère), poetically describing some music by Stravinsky but saying that "the inspiration has come for *Tobit*. . . ."

To return to 1934: on September 11, Stravinsky conducted his *Capriccio* in the Teatro alla Fenice, Venice, on a program that included Alban Berg's *Der Wein*. Berg and Stravinsky met, and the two composers seem to have been curious about each other; Berg gave an autographed photo of himself to Stravinsky as a souvenir of the occasion. Fortunately, Berg did not know that Adriano Lualdi, chairman of the Festival Committee and the head of Mussolini's Sindaco dei Musicisti,

. . . an intransigent Fascist and an ardent admirer of Nazi theology, wholly antagonistic to Schoenberg and his circle [167]

was on excellent terms with Stravinsky; the correspondence between them was to continue for three more years. Then, in 1938, Stravinsky programmed a Piano Concerto by Vittorio Rieti for a concert in Turin and was ordered to replace it "with a work by an Italian composer" (Rieti being partly Jewish). Stravinsky stood his ground, at least for a time, and answered: "I cannot agree to replace the Rieti with *another* Italian work."

The publisher Victor Gollancz wrote of *Perséphone:*

André Gide's poem touches the profoundest issues of human destiny and of existence itself; and Stravinsky has made of it an intensely moving expression of the *lacrimae rerum,* and, above that, of a hope that does not merely strive with despair but lies at the heart of it. . . . *Perséphone* . . . in its variety of expression betokens not only a great musician but a man of the widest human sympathies . . . a man of deep religious faith. I do not understand how anyone who knows *Perséphone* can . . . deny Stravinsky a place among the great composers of any age. [*Journey Towards Music* (New York: Dutton, 1965)]

Two nights before the concert, Gollancz and his wife had dined with Stravinsky:

It was at Covent Garden during . . . the Wedding March at the end of *The Firebird* that we practically became engaged. Fourteen years or so later Stravinsky was dining with me at the Langham Hotel before a concert he was giving across the road and I told him about this; whereupon he asked for a piece of notepaper, wrote out a bar or two of the music, and added *"Pour Mme Ruth and Victor Gollancz, souvenir de Igor Strawinsky, qui était en quelque sort témoin de leur union matrimoniale. Londres le 26 Nov 34."* . . . I recollect that Stravinsky ate nothing on that occasion but smoked salmon, of which he had two large helpings. [*Ibid.,* pp. 27–8]

A year after the *Perséphone* premiere, Stravinsky told an interviewer in Rome that he preferred the work in concert rather than in staged form because the latter "involves too many elements—scenographic, choreographic—that dissipate the center of attention." (*Il Piccolo,* May 27, 1935) The composer may have been reacting to the revival then taking place in Paris with choreography by Kurt Jooss.

Two years after the premiere, Stravinsky's Argentine friend Victoria Ocampo (to whom he gave the manuscript of the sketch score, now in the Morgan Library, New York) asked him to approach Gide for permission to make a Spanish translation. The composer replied that he had not been on good terms with the *"poète"* since the performance, adding, however, that Jean Paulhan had given his assurance that Gide, then in Senegal, would not object to the translation being made if he were to receive a fee. The Spanish version (1936) was done by Jorge Luis Borges. In one of Ansermet's last letters to Stravinsky, July 25, 1966, the conductor discusses *Perséphone:*

What seemed somewhat strange to me was the syllabic declamation. This shocked my sense of the language, which is not made up of syl-

November 28, 1934. Poster announcing the first performance of *Perséphone* in England.

lables but of words provided with certain tonic accents. In the performance,[168] however, I noticed that the music made one forget its syllabic nature, the vocal and orchestral parts bringing into focus a certain bucolic character.

1934. Page from a pocket English dictionary, compiled, as well as designed—by pasting the letters of the alphabet in alternating blue and red in the margin of a lined notebook—by the composer. (From the archives of Vera Stravinsky)

The dictionary above exemplifies not only Stravinsky's preoccupation with linguistics but also his painstakingness in all things. Entries are included under every letter except K, and the translations are given in German, French, and Russian, these three languages also being drawn upon for illustrations of pronunciation. The spelling is British ("harbour"), and, to a large extent, so are the vocabulary and usage ("he minds very much"). Among the oddities, Stravinsky devises no fewer than thirteen instances of "stick" as a verb; and, as an example of "have you not?" in an ironic sense, he quotes a sentence from Charles Morgan's *The Fountain*, the first English novel that the composer read in that language.

Side by side with this dictionary, Stravinsky kept a copy—bound in beige buckram with leather spine and gold lettering—of *The English Class* by P. Dessagnes (Paris, 1925). This is no less interesting than the dictionary, thanks to the composer's annotations, cross-references, translations in Russian, German, and French, and, especially, corrections—for he takes issue with the author several times, changing, for example, "The line begins in A and ends in B" to "*at* A" and "*at* B."

By the time of his second American tour, in 1935, Stravinsky did not like having his English corrected:

. . . Stravinsky sat perched on a sofa in his room at the Hotel Mayflower until his foot went to sleep. Then, jumping up and down in a lithe dance and grimacing behind his thick glasses, he called a halt to a lengthy interview and sought quietude at the motion pictures. The one he chose was *Roberta*. Once he paused, puzzled at a question, and then with meticulous pronunciation gave the question in French as it should have been done. "I correct your French," he said, "because people are always correcting my English." [*Washington Post*, March 24, 1935]

While Stravinsky was applying himself to English, Vera Sudeikina began to study the language with Serge Nabokov, brother of Vladimir. She has preserved two volumes of English lessons with her teacher, dated May 23, 1931, and November 2, 1934. They contain, as well as several extraordinary aids for the shopper—"Please let me see some stockings in mole color," and "Where can I buy a mauve cravat?"—at least one actual incident of autobiography:

I was a young girl with a pink dress and a big hat with flowers on the top, and I was very happy to be in a Berlin music hall. In order to be more comfortable I removed my shoes, and at the same time a trained monkey on the stage rode a bicycle and jumped and did many funny things. Suddenly the monkey threw away his bicycle and jumped into our box. I cried with all my might and ran along the corridor without any shoes. The moral of this story is never to take off your shoes in a public place.

Coincidentally, the very first entry in these exercise books, and the first English that Mme Sudeikina learned, was the Edward Lear poem that, thirty-five years later, Stravinsky set to music for her and that was to be his last completed composition:

> *They sailed away for a year and a day,*
> *To the land where the Bong-tree grows. . . .*

Mrs. Stravinsky has kept two of her later English notebooks, begun, respectively, on October 2, 1939, and March 2, 1944. The first, in preparation for her emigration to America, also contains verses, but of a different kind—"All Alone," by Irving Berlin.

June 18, 1932. At Voreppe with his mother. This is La Vironnière, the country mansion near Grenoble where Stravinsky spent the summers of 1932, 1933, 1934, and 1935. The house was in a walled park with a woods where, weather permitting, the family used to dine under a large tree.

Stravinsky rarely mentioned his mother—in the last twenty-three years of his life, at any rate—and never with affection. But he did not deny the truth of the following story from George Antheil's description of her and her son in Berlin in 1922:

... When, finally, Stravinsky's mother did turn up in Berlin, she brought with her a great pile of Stravinsky's earliest attempts at composition; but she also brought with her a faint but typical Soviet Russian contempt for his present "mercurial" (as she considered it) reputation in Paris. . . .

One evening, while I was sitting with both of them, I heard Mrs. Stravinsky and her son break into a heated prolonged argument. She would not give in, and finally Stravinsky almost broke into tears, so wrathful did he become. At last he turned to me and translated: he, Stravinsky, no longer able to stand his mother's inordinate admiration for Scriabin (when, after all, she had a son destined to become more famous than Scriabin would ever become!), admonished her, criticizing her taste, and finally admitting to hating Scriabin. Whereupon she had answered: "Now, now, Igor! You have not changed one bit all these years. You were always like that—always contemptuous of *your* betters!"

Stravinsky shrugged his shoulders and again looked absolutely forlorn, hopeless.[169]

In 1934, Stravinsky was interviewed by Janet Flanner:

Igor Stravinsky . . . was born on and named for St. Igor's Day, June 5th (Russian-style calendar), in 1882, in Oranienbaum, a St. Petersburg suburb across from Kronstadt. His father, Fyodor, descended from the Polish Counts of Soulima,[170] was a celebrated basso at the Imperial Theater and created the role of the drunken Monk in *Boris*.[171] . . . At nineteen, [Stravinsky] played his first composition to Rimsky-Korsakov, with the warning that should it fail to please, he would continue composing just the same. At this time, Stravinsky's parents were having him educated not as a musician but as a lawyer at the University of St. Petersburg. . . .

The Stravinskys have just taken a flat in Paris in the rue du Faubourg St.-Honoré by the President's palace. . . . Stravinsky likes practical old furniture, modern paintings, and—out of doors—landscapes that look like modern paintings.

Stravinsky . . . has a strange, prehistoric face—lean, bony. . . . He's an agitated little man with the will of a giant, fine formal gestures, and a cyclonic temperament. His is an inventive, contradictory, complicated mentality bent on comprehending everything immediately and from the ground up. . . .[172]

He loves to talk,[173] has the drawing-room charm of the verbal virtuoso, and when he listens gives the perfect attention of a clock-maker hearkening to a new movement. In an argument he always takes sides and, since he ignores concession in any form, always thinks his side is right. He hates to be alone, is always at the boiling point of gaiety or despair, has a tremendous capacity for *joie de vivre*, smokes forty bad French cigarettes a day, is a connoisseur of claret, which he buys in the barrel at Bordeaux and has bottled for his special use, sensually enjoys fine brandy, champagne, and foods when he isn't concerned with conscience or diet, occasionally overeats, invariably keeps all Church festivals.

[Stravinsky] composes three hours every morning. . . . His working desk is bureaucratically neat; his manuscripts, which used to be in colors, like liturgies, are now in mere black and white, but museum pieces for meticulousness. After all, he was trained to be a lawyer. . . .[174]

Others amplify this picture. Thus a correspondent from Rome remarked that

Stravinsky is both cordial and reserved, with something of the diplomatist and of the prelate about him. [*Il Piccolo*, May 27, 1935]

And few observers fail to mention his articulateness:

Like all intellectual Russians, Stravinsky has a gift of immediate communication . . . his language is colorful but precise. [*Il Resto del Carlino*, Bologna, May 21, 1935]

Sol Babitz was in the Berlin audience at the first performance of Stravinsky's Violin Concerto (see page 307), but this eminent musicologist and violinist did not make the composer's acquaintance until February 1935, when Stravinsky conducted the Los Angeles orchestra, of which Mr. Babitz was a member. After Stravinsky moved to Los Angeles in 1940, he and Babitz became close friends—the composer was the godfather of Babitz's daughters, Eve, who has become a well-known writer, and Miriam—and Stravinsky consulted with Babitz on every question concerning violin technique. "Did you see [Babitz's] excellent *Principles of Extensions on Violin Fingering?*" Stravinsky wrote to Alexander Schneider, September 26, 1947 (a letter that the composer signed "So long").

On December 27, 1934, Stravinsky and Samuel Dushkin sailed (from Villefranche) on the S.S. *Rex* for New York and a three-month coast-to-coast American tour. The composer visited California for the first time and enjoyed that part of the trip more than any other. "*Que la Californie est appétissante,*" he exclaimed at a Paris press conference in June 1935 to promote the first volume of his *Chroniques de Ma Vie,* and he offered some observations on the American character:

... there are more students than gangsters, after all. . . . Life is more crude there, and human relations tend to be excessive in character, impulsively inclining toward the good as well as toward the bad. Also, the Yankee generosity covers a thin, rather vague hypocrisy that comes straight from England, though at the same time, the traditional British puritanism is often stopped at its roots. ["Igor Stravinsky, Globe-Trotter and Man of Letters," *Candide,* June 6, 1935]

Stravinsky returned to Europe on the S.S. *Ile de France,* leaving New York on April 13 and arriving in Paris on the 19th. He then gave concerts in Copenhagen, Bologna, and Rome, including *The Sorcerer's Apprentice* on his program in this last city, in memory of Paul Dukas, who had just died. During the Roman visit, Stravinsky was received by Mussolini and Ciano, and the composer gave press conferences in which he had many good things to say about the dictator. The reporters, however, seem to have been more interested in the musician's impressions of Hollywood than in his appraisal of their political bosses, and, ironically, Stravinsky's first recorded remarks about his future home city, Los Angeles, appeared in Italian and in a Fascist newspaper:

This past season I was in Hollywood, a very interesting place. I visited several film studios, each of which is a kind of principality, with its own borders, trenches, police, cannons, machine guns, as well as its ministers for the various technical and artistic operations. At Metro-Goldwyn-Mayer [in Culver City, February 25], I saw forty salaried composers, all working from morning to night to produce music. This way the directors avoid re-runs of music that already exists and do not have to pay royalties to the composers. . . . I wanted to meet the head of the company, Signor Mayer, and an interview was arranged. I was led through a grey corridor to a grey room crowded with others, waiting like myself. I remained there a long time, during which everyone talked about Mr. Mayer, though no one had seen him and he might have been a myth. But at long last a door opened and a little man with a large

February 1935. Los Angeles. Rehearsing the Los Angeles Philharmonic. Photograph by Edward Weston, with a dedication by Stravinsky to Sol Babitz. Of the countless descriptions of Stravinsky rehearsing, the following dates from the start of his conducting career: "He underlines the design of the music with the movement of his body.... According to the character of the passage, he dances lightly, or rebounds, and groans like a wounded man after a detonation from the brass. ... He pounces like a feline, and, full of Slavic ardor and spirit, mimes his music, now violently, now caressingly...." [Le Soir, Brussels, January 15, 1924]

beak appeared, followed by two lieutenants. He approached me, nodded, said, "I am a man like others, with a lot to do," and, with this, shook my hand and left. At least I can testify that Mr. Mayer is not a myth. [La Gazetta del Popolo, June 1(?), 1935]

Stravinsky later came to know Louis B. Mayer, and, on May 31, 1942, dined with him at his home to help in planning a benefit for Russian War Relief.

Neither was Mr. Goldwyn a myth. As Time reported, July 26, 1948:

One day Producer Sam Goldwyn, who buys only the best labels, summoned Stravinsky, and asked him to write the music for a picture on Russia. The conversation went something like this:

GOLDWYN: How can you write music for this picture; you're not a Communist?

STRAVINSKY: How can you produce it; you're not a Communist?

GOLDWYN: I understand it's twenty-five thousand you want?
STRAVINSKY: Whatever my agent says.
GOLDWYN: Well, you have to have an arranger.
STRAVINSKY: What's an arranger?
GOLDWYN: An arranger! Why, that's a man who has to arrange your music, who has to fit it to the instruments.
STRAVINSKY: Oh.
GOLDWYN: Sure, that'll cost you $6,000. And it'll have to come off your $20,000.
STRAVINSKY: I thought it was $25,000. . . .

Another time a Hollywood studio offered Stravinsky $100,000 for three musical scores a year. Stravinsky replied: "To turn out one worthwhile piece of music in a year is enough. To guarantee three is to make a deceit of art." Stravinsky likes to see movies, particularly Westerns ("Just the shooting of the guns and the simple plot") and the "picture comique." But he refuses to write music for them. . . . "I cannot submit myself to their rules and laws."

Stravinsky's most powerful creation of the 1930s, the Concerto for Two Solo Pianos, baffled its first audiences. Raïssa Maritain's diary contains a typical reaction: [175]

Saturday, 23rd of November 1935: Yesterday evening [176] heard Igor Stravinsky's double piano concerto at the Salle Gaveau. Admirable technically, but without the slightest inwardness; it gave me no pleasure in hearing it except such as one gets from any good professional job. There is no *song* in this music. It does not proceed from any lyrical germ but only from a musical *idea*.[177]

The concerto also puzzled a better musician than Mme Maritain. Serge Prokofiev wrote to Miaskovsky, December 24, 1936:

In Paris I heard Stravinsky's Concerto for Two Pianos played by himself. It is difficult to follow, with lots of notes jumping on each other, but the piece is interesting and one has to listen to it again and again. Now Stravinsky has fallen from the heights of *Apollo* and *Perséphone* to a gambling den to compose a ballet in four deals—his own libretto—for America. I saw only a few pages, very well done. He has gone to America to conduct Mozart and Tchaikovsky's Third.

"Why [was] the new concerto for two pianos written without an orchestra?" an interviewer for the New York *Musical Courier* asked Stravinsky, who answered:

I did that for the reason that I wished to give the instruments and players every possible chance. In composing for piano and orchestra, I never could think of the keyboard as something apart from the rest of the ensemble, but felt that it should be fused in the symphonic whole. [January 16, 1937]

The following excerpt from Stravinsky's pre-curtain briefing on his Concerto for Two Solo Pianos is typical of his etymological obsessions, especially in asking his audiences to think of familiar musical terms in obsolete senses, and of his propensity for enumerating what *not* to expect, including extra-musical "programs." Although his remarks concerning classifications are edifying, they must have seemed somewhat remote to listeners struggling for a foothold in the music:

Etymologically the word "concerto" refers to a musical work of a certain size, in several parts, affecting the architectural structure of the sonata form of the symphony. In the *concerto grosso*, for example, one or more instruments play a role "in concert" (*concertant*), an expression deriving from the Italian *"concertare"* which means *concourir*, to complete or participate in a contest. Hence a "concerto" presupposes a contest among a number of instruments in concert, or between a single instrument and an ensemble in opposition.

But "concerto" has now come to mean a work for a solo instrument without opposition and in which the role of the orchestra is usually reduced to that of an accompaniment. . . . My four concertos adhere to the older formula: I have opposed several instruments to the primary one, or to groups of instruments also playing *concertant*.

Just as the harmonic order is the natural form of the accompaniment of a concerto for solo instruments without opposition, so a contrapuntal order is required in the concerto of the *"concours concertant"* type. I have applied the latter principle in my new work, in which two pianos of equal importance assume a *concertant* role in relation to one another. . . . It is this formula that enables me to call the work a concerto.

The word *Notturno*, the title of my second movement, is not used in the sense in which Field and Chopin characterized those dreamy, formless fragments that they call Nocturnes. My meaning is closer to that of the *Nachtmusik* or Cassation so popular with eighteenth-century composers. But in my piece the separate sections with which compositions of this sort are generally comprised have been condensed into a single movement. . . .[178]

The main event in Stravinsky's public life in 1936 was his tour in South America (April, May, June). In Barcelona for concerts on March 12 and 15, he gave an interview to the newspaper *La Noche* (March 12, 1936), that was published under the title "Igor Stravinsky and Surrealism," partly for the reason that Stravinsky rode in the train from Madrid with Salvador Dali. But the composer talks about Picasso:

I am a great friend of Picasso, and I admire him in all of his tendencies; he is always and consistently a great artist. But I have not seen him for some time. Both of us are solitaries, essentially, and we run into each other only from time to time. Of myself, I have to say that in Paris, where I live, I go almost nowhere, not to artistic balls, not to the theater, not to concerts. But I go to the movies.

My art is the product of Christian dialectics, and this is a reason why I cannot accept surrealism or communism. . . . I am Christian-Orthodox, but I sympathize with Catholicism and recognize that in religious matters, the neuters, who abound in the bourgeoisie, above all in France, are more prejudiced than those who openly combat the church, as in Soviet Russia. It is clear that I am in opposition to both. Esthetically I am unable to accept materialism, as proclaimed by the surrealists and by the communists.

Schoenberg, in my judgment, is more of a chemist of music than an artistic creator. His investigations are important, since they tend to expand the possibilities of auditory enjoyment, but—as with Haba, the discoverer of quarter-tones—they are more concerned with the quantitative than with the qualitative aspects of music. The value of this is evident, but limited, since others will come later and look for and find "eighth-tones," but will they be able to make genuine works of art with this? I admire Schoenberg and his followers but I recognize that the chromatic gamut on which they are based only exists scientifically and that, consequently, the dialectic which is derived from this is artificial. . . .

Stravinsky sailed from Boulogne-sur-Mer on April 9, on the S.S. *Cap Arcona* (cabin 247), whose ports of call were Vigo (April 11), Lisbon, Madeira, the Fernando Islands, and Rio de Janeiro, where he spent the day of April 21 on shore. The steamer docked again at Santos on the 22nd, and, on the 24th, at Montevideo. On April 30, *El Debate*, a leading newspaper of the Uruguayan capital, published a statement by Stravinsky:

It has been twenty years since *Le Sacre du Printemps* was modern; today it belongs to an already past period. The musicians who continue in the musical direction of the *Sacre*, together with those who lean upon jazz and black music, seem to be incurably devoted to the past. . . . The present hour demands a totally different music, in which the decorative element surrenders to the spiritual and intellectual. The composer must renounce coloristic orgies in order to develop healthy and strong concepts. Perhaps it seems strange to hear this from me. I do not deny my past, however, but only hope to make it understood how my music of today differs from that of my youth. Today my music is more intimate and more compact, even if less brilliant.

The Buenos Aires *Herald*, April 25, described the composer as his boat reached Argentina:

Immediately after Stravinsky's arrival on the S.S. *Cap Arcona* he was invaded by newspaper photographers, reporters, and admiring members of the public who surrounded the great little musician. . . . M. Stravinsky posed while photographers snapped him from every angle, somewhat nervously handling a cigarette all the while, and chatting with a great many people at once until he was whisked away by friends to the private residence where he is staying during the time he will spend in Buenos Aires. Today he begins rehearsals at the Colón.

On April 25, *La Nación* (Buenos Aires) published an interview with Stravinsky:

My timing is [different and] the movement of my work is rapid . . . which explains the lack of comprehension and of the necessary preparation to penetrate the sense of my new concepts.

For the moment I am not considering the publication of a new volume [of my autobiography]. Perhaps this will come later. There has been an amount of incomprehension in relation to this. I did not intend to present an anecdotal life. The picturesque aspect of my behavior and my confidences are no one's concern. I simply proposed to myself to express what I think, employing clear, simple language, exactly as I do in music, not a doctrine but the practice of the life of a creator. . . .

I can say that there are a few composers today that I like very much and many who do not interest me in the slightest. . . . Dimitri Shostakovich is a talented young composer. I am familiar with some good works by him, but his *Lady Macbeth* has a detestable libretto and is backward in its musical spirit, its musical tendency being out of Mussorgsky's era. This confirms what I was saying, namely, that the general public in Russia is fifty years behind the truly original creator. As for the past, I am for Italianism, Cimarosa, Rossini, Bellini, and Verdi, whom I adore. I also have a great veneration for Debussy, to whom a deep friendship binds me. . . . The impressionists prepared the way for the avant-garde.

The following agenda contains some of the main events of the tour:

April 27–8. Rehearses.

April 28. The newspaper *Los Recortes* quotes Stravinsky in an interview:

I am not a revolutionary of the symphonic art, but simply an investigator, searching—which is so difficult in the realm of art—for the best ways to achieve emotion and innovation, without stripping the old molds of their fundamental structures.

9:45 P.M. Teatro Colón. Concert: *Pulcinella,* Piano Concerto, *Symphony of Psalms.*

April 29–30, May 1–2. Rehearses.

May 2. Teatro Colón. Concert: *Fireworks, Capriccio,* Two Little Suites, *Symphony of Psalms.*

May 5–7. Rehearses.

May 6. Los Recortes criticizes Stravinsky for a

deplorable decision. The Teatro Colón customarily broadcasts its performances, and Stravinsky apparently rejected this proposal. Thus he stands accused of being elitist, and of depriving the people of the opportunity for cultural enlightenment.

May 7. Teatro Colón. Conducts ballet performances of *The Firebird* and *Petrushka.*

May 8–9. Rehearses.

May 9. Teatro Colón. Concert: *Fireworks, Capriccio,* Piano Concerto, and the *Sacre.*

May 10. Teatro Colón. Conducts ballet performances of *The Firebird* and *Petrushka.*

May 11. The Teatro de la Comedia. Attends the Buenos Aires Wagner Association's broadcast concert, conducted by Juan José Castro, of the *Song of the Nightingale,* Little Suite No. II, *Capriccio, The Firebird.*

May 12. Rosario. Teatro de la Opera. As the guest of El Círculo, Stravinsky gives a *"Conferencia sobre las obras"* and, with his son, plays the Concerto for Two Solo Pianos.

May 14. (Goes to the cinema in the morning.) 9:45 P.M. Teatro Colón. Conducts ballet performances of *The Firebird, Le Baiser de la Fée, Petrushka.* Bronislava Nijinska is the choreographer for *Le Baiser de la Fée.*

May 15–16. Rehearses *Perséphone* and *Apollo.*

May 17. Teatro Colón. Conducts *Perséphone*—with Victoria Ocampo as narrator—and *Apollo.*

May 18. Victoria Ocampo sends a note to Stravinsky (her house guest):

Angélica [Victoria's sister] tells me that at ⟨31⟩ the orchestra covers the voice. As for the phrase, *"La brise vagabonde a caressé les fleurs,"* this verse can hardly be shouted. Also, for the last speech . . . I force myself to follow the orchestra and hurry all the time, which is not good for the recitation. Can you give me a little more time?

6:00 P.M. Teatro Colón. Repeats the *"Conferencia,"* and, with his son, plays the Concerto for Two Solo Pianos.

May 19. Montevideo. The Hotel Lamata.

May 21. Mundo Uruguaya publishes a Stravinsky issue, with several photographs of the composer.

May 22. The Club Uruguay presents a concert of music by Uruguayan musicians, members of El Centro Stravinsky, and, in the second half, Stravinsky's Concerto for Two Solo Pianos, which he plays with his son.

May 23. 8:30 P.M. Estudio Auditorio. Conducts a concert with the Orquesta Sinfónica del Sodre, consisting of the *Pulcinella* Suite, *Capriccio, Scherzo Fantastique, Divertimento.*

May 27. Sails on the S.S. *Almanzora.*

May 30. Santos.

May 31. Rio de Janeiro, the Copacabana Palace.

June 5. Teatro Municipal. Conducts the *Firebird* Suite and *Perséphone* (Victoria Ocampo).

June 6. Photographs the *Hindenburg* zeppelin.

June 10. Dines with Dagmar Godowsky and Mr. and Mrs. Josef Hofmann at the Gloria Hotel.

June 11. Victoria Ocampo leaves Rio for Buenos Aires.

June 12. Ocampo cables from Santos: "We miss you greatly. Embraces." Stravinsky conducts second concert in Rio de Janeiro.

June 13. Sails on the S.S. *Cap Arcona.*

June 22. Lisbon.

June 23. Victoria Ocampo writes:

In spite of the disagreements, the heat, the inedible food . . . I had an unforgettable memory of our sojourn in Rio.

June 24. Plymouth, Boulogne-sur-Mer, Paris.

June 29. Paris. Attends the wedding of his elder son.

. . . ne vous étonnez pas de me ranger le mariage de Theodore parmi les autres soucis qui ne cessent de me tracasser. . . . [To Victoria Ocampo, Paris, July 10, 1936]

In New York at the end of the same year, Dagmar Godowsky, daughter of the pianist Leopold, and silent-screen partner of Rudolph Valentino, began to manage Stravinsky's life. On December 24, arriving on the S.S. *Normandie,* somewhat ill, he stayed in his bed at the Sulgrave. Miss Godowsky noted that

Stravinsky is certainly the most devout man I have ever known. A Greek [sic] Catholic, he would cross himself before and after—a concert, a dinner, everything, but everything—

this last "everything" referring, of course, to the sexual act. Then, when Stravinsky

. . . got out of bed, I took him to the New York premiere of *Amelia Goes to the Ball* at the New Amsterdam Theater. A new composer [179] was born that night [but] I.S. [was] patronizing about him.

Later, Miss Godowsky became a nuisance, stowed away on a transatlantic liner, and appeared in Paris, where she—or, rather, Stravinsky—made a "scene," as this note, sent to him in Brussels, where he was conducting, makes clear:

My beloved one . . . to have you send me away, when all I care about is you. . . . It is so sad to love someone to whom one is merely an incident. And it is really you I blame, who made me feel as I do. . . . You send me away coldly, unfeelingly, with only one thought, not to complicate your life.

A letter from Stravinsky to Balanchine, dated November 16, 1935, reveals that the choreographer had asked for a "classical ballet." Nor would Balanchine be more specific, and on June 30, 1936, only a few days after Stravinsky's return to Paris from South America, he wrote complaining of being unable to work without a clear plan of the succession of episodes. In the same letter, he asks Balanchine why he has proposed Hans Christian Andersen as a source, "the new ballet not being a divertimento." Its plot is simple to follow, Stravinsky continues, the performance time of the score will be from twenty to twenty-five minutes, and only a few solo dancers, a normal orchestra, and a

December 2, 1935. The first sketches for *Jeu de Cartes*. The theme around which Stravinsky has drawn a frame was used at the very beginning of the work. Just above this notation is the theme from the Coda to the *Deuxième Donne*. It should be remarked that Stravinsky's first notations occur in keys, such as A major and D-flat major, that are prominent in the final score, and that his first notation was for the rhythmic figure eventually used at 92 . The music to the right, middle of the page, was used in the third variation.

single set are required. Stravinsky does not describe the plot, and in a letter to Dushkin, August 12, 1936, seems to indicate that the ballet did not have a title, yet the sketch score (finished December 3) contains numerous indications for dancers ("cards") and choreography throughout. When the music was completed, Stravinsky asked N. Malaïeff to help him write a brief synopsis of the ballet in French, but this was simply taken from the score. (Letters to Strecker, November 24 and December 10, 1936)

Almost a year after the premiere of *Jeu de Cartes*,[180] Stravinsky talked about it to a French reporter:

I composed a ballet to be *danced,* and I wanted it to contain the minimum story, one with an easily perceptible subject. . . . For this reason I chose the card game. What could be easier to understand than the different combinations, the cards by themselves, as well as their respective values when they enter into the game? For maximum comprehension I chose poker, a simple game to follow and one in which the movement of the Joker is interesting. . . . I ignored the nonsense of amorous intrigues among the cards. [*Le Jour,* Paris, March 4, 1938]

Ansermet remarked about the piece when he performed it (with cuts) in Geneva, October 27, 1937:

Jeu de Cartes is a new example, a new appearance in a new tone, of this world of Stravinsky's, a world of action and of characters, in which the evil spirit seeks to dominate and must be conquered: the Joker against the group of hearts, as, before, Kastchei against the Firebird and Ivan Tsarevich, the Moor against Petrushka and the Ballerina, the Devil against the Soldier. . . . [Program of the Orchestre de la Suisse Romande, October 27, 1937]

On December 18, 1936, Stravinsky sailed on the S.S. *Normandie* for America and a four-month tour ending at the Metropolitan Opera House in New York with the first performance of *Jeu de Cartes.* His first concert was in Toronto's Massey Hall, where, thirty years later, he was to make his last appearance as a conductor. On this first visit, he arrived on the morning of January 4, 1937, via the (slightly late) night train from New York:

Igor Fyodorovich Stravinsky, probably the world's greatest living composer, leaned back in his fur-lined overcoat and pondered. The scene was the foyer of the Royal York where the great composer rested for a moment before dashing off to rehearsal for his symphony appearance. . . . He waved his cigarette holder reflectively and kept on pondering. . . . M. Stravinsky was trying to think of the English name for his favorite movie: *"Je le sais! . . . Il s'appelle 'Bullets or Ballets.' "* [181] M. Stravinsky said he liked all sorts of movies. . . . But he wished to point out that better than the movies he liked the theater of his Russia . . . : "That it was infinitely superior is incontestable," he said. . . . "Hemingway's [182] last book I have been able to read for myself in English," said M. Stravinsky proudly. "I study English in Paris and I can read it quite well, but for the speaking . . . I have not the *pratique . . .* the practice." Of jazz, the composer said: "It has been tremendously vital in its time, but that is past." [*Evening Telegram,* Toronto, January 4, 1937]

Returning to New York for two weeks of concerts with the Philharmonic, Stravinsky granted a number of interviews, the most important of which appeared in the *New York World-Telegram,* January 23. The reporter asked Stravinsky if he believed that "the way of future progress might lie through a smaller division of the scale." He replied in the negative and was questioned "about the resolutions and so on." Stravinsky replied:

But it's the same thing. . . . The result is meager. . . . What, I asked myself, does it add? Only quantity, not quality. The whole thing is like the nouveau riche whom we make fun of. He doesn't know what to do with what he has. He makes a great deal of money without acquiring other qualities in proportion to the new wealth. After quarter-tones we might have eighth-tones, but they would only be a fictitious quantity. . . . I am acquainted with Haba, by the way. He has made experiments. But if you were to do the same things in our conventional music, they would be very commonplace. Haba's experiments have not resulted in anything unusual.

To another interviewer, Leonard Liebling (*Musical Courier,* January 16), Stravinsky spoke almost entirely in German, but Liebling scrupulously respected the composer's request that "nothing was for publication," and nothing was published. Apparently no such restrictions were placed on the reporter for *Musical America* (January 10, 1937) to whom Stravinsky complained of the difficulties of being a composer. On February 6, Stravinsky finished the *Preludium* for jazz ensemble, then left New York for Cleveland, whose orchestra he conducted both at home and on tour. He was no less generous with reporters here:

Interviewed at Princeton, N.J., where the composer-conductor took over the baton of the Cleveland Orchestra,[183] Stravinsky revealed that he is writing a new symphony, to be produced sometime next year with an American orchestra.[184] [*Cleveland Press,* February 20]

Actually, Stravinsky's first notation for this symphony

is dated March 3 and is written on stationery of the Orrington Hotel, Evanston, Illinois, where he stayed while giving two recitals with Samuel Dushkin in Winnetka.

Back in Cleveland, in his suite at Wade Park Manor, Stravinsky was described as "All gesture. His face lights up, the thin, slender hands grasp the air for meaning, the low voice turns from French, to German, to English, for the precise word":

Abstract music! What does it mean? The effect of music depends, does it not, upon the culture of the listener's ear? See, now in the room we shall suppose an audience of four—a savage from darkest Africa, a laborer on the street, a doctor, a musician—and we play music for them, a good, sweet melody.

Is it music to the savage? No. "This is terrible," he cries [since] for him music is boom! boom! boom! His ear is not cultured. To him it is abstract. So each listener calls that which is familiar to him, music. . . . [*Cleveland News,* February 22]

Another Cleveland interviewer wrote that

The first time one sees Stravinsky a distinct shock is in store. He is only five feet two and weighs only around 115 pounds. He doesn't help his small stature any by stooped shoulders, and a forward-craning neck. But he is wiry and strong, walks with long strides, and is absolutely oblivious of his size—in fact he revels in it. This is best illustrated by a story he tells on himself. He played in Rome several years ago—an all-Stravinsky program—and the next day was invited by Mussolini for an interview. When he arrived, Il Duce was sitting behind his huge desk with both hands on the table and his notorious black eyes piercing through the distance at the composer.

"Maestro," the Italian leader slurred through his white, gleaming teeth, "I know you." The air was charged, the composer said. A moment's silence, then Stravinsky answered in perfect Italian: "Il Duce, I know you, too." . . .

American broadcasting methods came in for their share of criticism by the composer. He chuckled over the lack of strings in a broadcasting symphony orchestra, while wind instruments and brasses are all doubled in number. "That might be fine for radio reception, but the broadcasters do not take the studio audience—like that of Carnegie Hall—into consideration. To them the small number of string instruments must be laughable. And, also, they place the soloist at one end of the stage with a microphone and the accompanist at the other end— a mile away at another 'mike'—and we are supposed to play together. That's ridiculous—no?"

During the 1935 visit to Hollywood, Stravinsky and Chaplin discussed a project on which they intended to collaborate. The concept of the work, as outlined in a letter from Willy Strecker to Stravinsky, November 8, 1935, seems extremely naïve, and at first Stravinsky was not attracted ("*Je ne trouve pas ça . . . une idée utopique . . .*"—letter to Strecker, November 17, 1935), but evidently Chaplin was interested, at least at the time of the meeting. Stravinsky wrote to the actor from Paris on June 8, 1937, but he did not receive an answer. Nevertheless, Stravinsky's letters

March 1937. With Charles Chaplin at his home.

until January 1938 contain references to the project and a belief that it might be realized.

While in Hollywood, too, Stravinsky saw a Warner Brothers film *The Firebird*, starring Ricardo Cortez, Lionel Atwill, and Anita Louise. The sound track included fragments of Stravinsky's score, which he had sold to Warner Brothers, knowing that in the United States, in any case, the music was in the public domain. But promptly on returning to France, alleging that the film was damaging to his ballet of the same title, Stravinsky filed a 300,000-franc suit against Warner Brothers for the theft of the title and for using his music in a scene in which the heroine is excited to "*mouvements du revolté et enthousiasme.*" The case was heard on May 3 in the Third Chamber of the Civil Tribunal, but judgment was not reached until the following February. On the 4th of February, *Paris-Soir* reported:

Stravinsky said, "Would you believe that there is a parrot on the billboard? I would not have complained if at least it had been a nightingale. . . ."

After seeing the film, the judge paid homage to M. Stravinsky's talents but stated that the film . . . had been based on a Hungarian play.

Actually, the story of the play, Lajos Zilahy's *The Firebird*, on which the film is based, is of a young girl who dreams of dancing in Stravinsky's *Firebird*. (Letter from Gilbert Miller to Stravinsky, August 10, 1932; Miller had been introduced to Stravinsky by Diaghilev in the Savoy Hotel, London.)

Dr. Alexis ("Woof") Kall was a St. Petersburg schoolmate of Stravinsky's and one of the very few people whom Stravinsky tutoyer-ed. Kall was an accomplished pianist who had emigrated to Los Angeles, living there by giving lessons. Stravinsky stayed in Kall's house on this first visit to that city, in 1935, after which Kall became the composer's principal American factotum. In 1939, when planning his living arrangements at Harvard, Stravinsky wrote to Edward Forbes requesting that an exception be made to college rules so that Kall could live in Eliot House, which had been chosen as a residence for Stravinsky; the letter describes Kall as a musician and philologist. When the request was denied, Stravinsky wrote once again saying that Kall's presence was important to him for "psychological and moral reasons," since "after the last two terrible years my nerves are not yet completely *d'aplomb,*" and since

Kall has already given up his own work in Los Angeles to share my solitude and to look after me throughout my stay in America.

But the request was not granted, and Stravinsky did not live in Eliot House but with the Forbes family. Kall came to Cambridge, where he prepared synopses in English for Stravinsky's public lectures and assisted him at his meetings with students. Stravinsky's affection for Kall is very evident in letters, which usually

AUSPICES OF THE
Art Commission of San Francisco
RUSSIAN MUSIC SOCIETY PRESENTS

Dr. Alexis Kall of Hollywood
in a lecture with musical illustrations

"IGOR STRAVINSKY
as I know him"

. • .

CENTURY CLUB
1355 FRANKLIN STREET

Monday, March 22, 1937 •» 3 o'clock

Tickets on sale at Sherman, Clay & Co.
or at the Century Club

March 22, 1937. San Francisco. Handbill for a lecture by Stravinsky's St. Petersburg school friend, and, in 1939–1940, secretary, Alexis Kall.

begin with "Dear Woof" or "Dear Fat Man." But Kall's bouts of inebriation made him an unreliable secretary, and, later, in California, Stravinsky was obliged to dismiss his old friend (who died in 1948). In February 1966, while in San Francisco to conduct three concerts (on the 23rd, 24th, 25th), Stravinsky received a note from Mrs. Bruce, a former piano pupil of Kall's, who, as the second sentence reveals, will be a source when a full biography of Stravinsky is written:

I remember going twice with Kall to hear you conduct *Petrushka* at the Shrine Auditorium. . . . He wrote such interesting letters during your stay together in Boston. . . . We celebrated his last birthday with him in his studio on South Mariposa where my husband made a sound movie of him.

Stravinsky conducted the *Symphony of Psalms,* and, on March 24, left for New York, where he supervised rehearsals of *Jeu de Cartes,* conducted the ballet's first two performances (April 27 and 28), and arranged Parasha's Aria (*Mavra*) for violin and piano. Later, after his return to Paris, the composer said that he liked neither the decors nor the costumes, but that "the dances composed by G. Balanshin [sic] I admired very much." (Letter to Willy Strecker, May 20) Arriving in Paris on May 11 (he had left New York on the S.S. *Paris,* May 5), he was soon planning new tours:

We interviewed Stravinsky on the evening of his return from New York. He was seated in an armchair beneath a large eighteenth-century

March 11, 1937. Los Angeles. The Shrine Auditorium. Conducting the dress rehearsal for a stage performance of *Petrushka.* The bath towel and hat are defenses against the infamous drafts of this barn-like hall.

March 22, 1937. San Francisco. With Pierre Monteux, twenty-four years after Le Sacre du Printemps.

oil portrait of a beautiful woman [the Empress Elizabeth Petrovna], in a room with Louis Quinze paneling. . . . In a twelve-month he will cross the Pacific to give concerts in Australia. "I want to know the country of the lyrebird," [185] he said. [L'Intransigeant, May 16, 1937]

The blossoming twigs of the chestnut trees of the Champs-Elysées almost touched the sitting room of his apartment [rue du Faubourg St.-Honoré]. The order in the room was impeccable: no book or bibelot could be imagined in any other place. . . . An armful of Darwin peonies opened in a large vase. . . . [Le Jour, May 16, 1937]

Stravinsky spent the summer of 1937 at Château de Monthoux, Annemasse, where he wrote the first movement of the Concerto in E-flat:

As for myself, I compose, and if the uncertainty and anxiety about my wife's health were not always uppermost, the summer would be a very good one for me. [Letter to Dushkin, August 8]

Catherine Stravinsky's letters to her husband in the autumn of 1937 are a depressing chronicle of her losing struggle against tuberculosis:

. . . Yesterday I had my first injection of camphor but [the doctor] prescribed a dose five times too strong . . . The result was that I coughed up fifty times and felt such a ravaging in the trachea that I had to take codeine. . . . My temperature this morning was 37.7, which, I think, might be a new manifestation of my illness, though perhaps it is simply a reaction to the chills I had yesterday. . . . [October 11]

My dear Gimochka . . . I am glad that you are not going to stay very long in London. . . . Please take your fur coat with you so that you don't catch cold after the concert . . . I hope that Vera's cold is not serious. . . . Our dear small hot water bottle broke, the one that served us so long and so well . . . To judge by the way I feel, my temperature is not a fever, but was brought on by my cough—forty more times yesterday. . . . As for Salmanov's injections, ask him, if you don't forget, whether the number should be gradually decreased instead of abruptly discontinued . . . May God and the Holy Mother be with you. Katia. [October 12]

My Gimochka, So now you too have caught a cold . . . Since early this evening I felt as if I might be catching a chill . . . Yesterday I coughed up thirty-seven times. My temperature this evening is 37.4. [October 13]

. . . I have come down with a cold and [Dr.] Tobée . . . said that I must lie in bed for three days and take plasters . . . Evening temperature 37.8. Yesterday I coughed up thirty-five times. [October 15]

I cannot cheer you but, on the contrary, must disappoint you with the news of another fever . . . At the moment my cough is rupturing and frequent . . . and I have a temperature of 39.3. I'm sorry to tell you this because I know it will cause you much grief. [October 28]

Last night all I did was think of you . . . and about how my letter must have upset you . . . The coughing has been stronger since morning, but, my dearest, I am not at all worried. What news from Vera? [October 30]

My cough has become strained and the hoarseness in my chest interferes with my sleep . . . Mama writes that on Saturday you went with Ira to the cemetery. . . . Fedya must see the doctor without fail as . . . he's always got a head cold and a runny nose . . . I hope that I get a letter from you tomorrow and I'd also like to know what Vera writes from Germany. . . . My temperature this evening is 37.4. [November 1]

I've been coughing more in the last two days and yesterday I coughed up thirty-five times. [Dr.] Degeorges says that I have fluid in the lungs again. I've been taking camphor, but, for the results, all I can really say is that I do not have that tearing sensation when I cough a great deal . . . [November 6]

The *pourparlers* for the commissioning of the Concerto from Mrs. Robert Woods Bliss [186] had taken place while Stravinsky was in America, but when no money was forthcoming, Stravinsky asked Nadia Boulanger to send a cable, which he dictated:

Stravinsky desires to know should begin composition for you suggest 2500 dollars accepts compose music Brandenburg Concerto dimensions.

A letter to Dushkin dated October 24 reveals that

the first part of the Concerto is composed and orchestrated, and probably there will be two more parts. Finally the first payment has come from Bliss. The delay was due to a distraction on Nadia's part since she did not send the letter of agreement until after she returned from her holidays.

A letter to Strecker, January 20, 1938, informs the publisher that the instrumentation of the Concerto's second movement ("which I call Intermezzo"—letter of January 3 to Strecker) is almost finished and that the transcription for two pianos is entirely finished—which offers a view into Stravinsky's working methods. The Concerto was completed in March 1938. (Letter to Strecker on the 29th)

Another project of the period, to compose music on the subject of Orozco's frescoes at Dartmouth, was transmitted by Severin Kavenoki, Stravinsky's New York agent, to whom the composer wrote of his dread of "*sinusite, cette désagréable et absurde maladie Newyorkaise.*"

Stravinsky's final years in France were unhappy ones, first because of the deaths of his elder daughter, his wife, and his mother. His daughter Mika's death shocked him,[187] and, though she was gravely ill, the end must have been unexpected, since her mother wrote to him in Turin on November 29, 1938, only one day before. Second, Stravinsky was sensitive to an increasing opposition to his music in Paris and to the neglect by impresarios there.[188] *Perséphone* had had a lukewarm reception—attributed by the composer to the work's idiosyncratic French diction—and *Jeu de Cartes*, the last of his ballets to have been conceived [189] and completed in Europe, was staged in Germany

May 1938. A dinner by Misia Sert. L. to R.: Jacques Février, Serge Lifar, the Vicomtesse de Noailles, Stravinsky, Vera Sudeikina, Chanel.

(Dresden) but not in France.[190] The final work of the period, the Concerto in E-flat, was apparently more successful at its Washington premiere, conducted by Nadia Boulanger, than in Paris, a month later, conducted by the composer—though, in a letter to Mrs. Bliss, July 26, 1938, he describes the Salle Gaveau audience as abundantly appreciative. Stravinsky reacted to his changed position in an interview in *Le Journal de Paris*, October 13, 1938:

STRAVINSKY: From January to May [1937] I conducted the New York Philharmonic, the Cleveland Orchestra—splendid groups. Then I went to Toronto and Montreal, and from there to San Francisco and Hollywood. Before sailing back, I conducted the premiere of my new ballet, *Jeu de Cartes*, at the Metropolitan Opera in New York.

RENÉ SIMON: And are you saving nothing for Paris?

I.S.: Paris, a city I adore, does not give me the opportunity to exercise either my art [composing] or my profession [conducting]. Here no one seems to realize that I am not only an occasional conductor. . . .

R.S.: And . . . the composer?

I.S.: Frankly, he is not much happier. . . . I do not have a single work in the French repertory.

R.S.: The symphony orchestras play your music.

I.S.: Yes, the *Firebird*, *Fireworks*. But the theaters ignore me.

R.S.: Wasn't your marvelous *Symphony of Psalms* presented at the Exposition?

I.S.: Yes. But it was only by accident that *I* conducted it,[191] my admirable friend Pierre Monteux being indisposed. . . . It is rather curious, you will agree, that having at present fourteen scores, operas and ballets, performed throughout the world, not a single one is now in France.

Two months later, after *Jeu de Cartes* had been heard in the capital, the composer gave an interview to *L'Intransigeant*:

STRAVINSKY: *Jeu de Cartes* has finally been played, on December 5, by the Orchestre National, arousing a great deal of unsatisfactory curiosity. A long time before the premiere, M. [Jacques] Rouché very kindly asked me to let him know which of my works I would like to see presented in his theater [Paris Opéra].

Q.: Was he thinking of *Jeu de Cartes*, of *Petrushka*?

I.S.: I mentioned other ballets to him, those which I felt would most suit the stage of the Opéra: *Le Baiser de la Fée*, created by Ida Rubinstein, and *Pulcinella* and *The Firebird*, from the former Diaghilev repertory—well-known pieces with which the risks would be considerably smaller than with new works. I did not hide from M. Rouché that I wished to see them together. A "Stravinsky festival" would cause less astonishment than one of my works alone.

Q.: But . . . *Jeu de Cartes*?

I.S.: The music is too recent, and I would have had to conduct the rehearsals and the performance. It was created by the great choreographer Balanchine, and he was too involved in New York, with his American Ballet, to come here.

Q.: Are there no notations referring to the original choreography?

I.S.: No . . .. Apart from certain rudimentary notations used for certain North African dances [we have no choreographic scores].[192] . . .

That is why I would like to call on the authors of those three ballets
. . . Massine to do *Pulcinella,* Fokine *The Firebird,* Bronislava Nijinska
Le Baiser de la Fée.

Q.: That would take a great deal of money?

I.S.: Probably. Also, for the moment I have had no response to my
suggestions. [December 19, 1938]

Another factor in Stravinsky's disaffection with France was
his humiliating defeat—in 1935, the year after he became a
French citizen—as a candidate for the French Academy. The
story of this débâcle is well known, but not Stravinsky's comment about it in *Le Figaro:*

MY CANDIDACY FOR THE INSTITUTE

Much has been said in the newspapers, and the commentaries have
been varied. I would like to reply to some of the better of them, as
summarized in the article by Guermantes in *Le Figaro,* "*Le Sacre de
l'Automne.*"

"Monsieur Stravinsky's candidacy for the Institute is indeed astonishing," Guermantes writes. "I realize, of course, that this same question is posed each time that a highly original artist, independent in
expression and attitude but approaching his fiftieth year, suddenly
discovers the road to the Bridge of Arts. . . ."

It would have been indiscreet of me to have answered before the
vote of the Institute, but I can do so now. I stood as a candidate for one
reason only, because a few of my friends insisted upon it,[193] and because I could not refuse them the gesture of respect for this venerable
French institution of which they are members, and as a member of
which they believed that I might be useful.[194] I was not soliciting an
honor but performing a favor.

Guermantes remarks that until now I have taken pains *not* to display any "visible ornament of this sort." But how could I display any
ornament when I do not have one?

As for Guermantes's strange question, "What kind of metamorphosis has occurred that Stravinsky's talent and spirit could suddenly accommodate themselves to this kind of glory?" the answer is in my
music, and in my autobiography, the second part of which, containing
my ideas and opinions clearly set forth, has just been published. These
are the same ideas that I would have brought to the Institute, where I
could have defended and supported them.

Guermantes continues: "I do not say that one ought to despise
honors, but only that Stravinsky's works seem to say 'No' to them." It
is not for me to decide whether or not my works say "No," but for the
Institute to say "Yes"—or "No." I received only 5 votes out of 32.[195]

Guermantes concludes: "A moment occurs in the life of an artist
when he no longer consults his youth." This is true, of course, as well
as natural, and to deny it would be to deceive. But I have never forgotten my youth, and I do not regret it. I have not reached the age where,
all too often, people live only in the past; I still look ahead with joy.
Let us suppose, Guermantes, that a miracle occurred and made me
twenty years younger—something that I am very far from desiring.
Would I then be a living anachronism, looking older than I am in
reality? Do you see how ridiculous are those wrinkled revolutionaries
who did not progress but continued to repeat themselves over and over

and to fight blindly for ideas long since dead? I detest artificial youth and plastic aesthetic surgery, internal as well as external.

I am not ashamed of my age and am not afraid of it. At my age Bach composed his finest cantatas, Beethoven his last symphonies, and Wagner—which I say for the sake of the Wagnerians—his *Meister-singer*. It is revolting to see older people flattering the young, when this flattery is dictated only by the fear of being regarded as backward. Do the old ever consider what a cruel disappointment they are preparing for the young when, egotistically, they fail to guide them, but, instead, flatter them today and drop them tomorrow? Goethe said: "The greatest art in life is to endure." Finally, why does Guermantes give a pejorative sense to "*Le Sacre* of Autumn"? The season of the harvest is beautiful, the season of Pomona is full of riches, a blessed season, certainly worthy of a *Sacre*.

July 14, 1935. Gisor. Vera Sudeikina. Photograph by Stravinsky.

Part Three

THE UNITED STATES, 1939-1971

Concert Tours in
Mexico,
Cuba,
Venezuela,
Canada,
Europe,
Japan,
Colombia,
Peru,
Chile,
Argentina,
Brazil,
Australia,
New Zealand,
South Africa,
Israel,
the U.S.S.R.

Nous vivons avec, et de votre musique.
Parce que vous êtes là il nous semble que
le chemin n'est pas si sombre.
    —*Letter from Nadia Boulanger,*
         March 6, 1942

*It is wonderful to know that you exist, an
island of genius and integrity in this disas-
trous world. . . .*
    —*Letter from Lincoln Kirstein,*
         December 26, 1947

*We hope that the stupidity in this country
will not kill you.*
    —*Jane Heap, of* The Little Review,
    *writing to Stravinsky on his arrival
    in America, January 6, 1925*

HELMUT DANTINE: *"Who was that man
with whom you came to the airport? His
face looks so familiar."*
NICOLAS NABOKOV: *"Stravinsky."*
HELMUT DANTINE: *"That's what I thought.
But what is he doing in Hollywood?"*
    —*Nabokov:* Old Friends and New Music
      (Boston: Little, Brown, 1951)

*The only way to escape Hollywood is to
live in it.*
    —*Stravinsky, from a 1940s interview.*

*[When I met Stravinsky he said,] "You are
. . . the new director [of] [Columbia] Mas-
terworks. I am a Masterwork!"*
    —*Schuyler Chapin:* Musical Chairs
      (New York: Putnam, 1977)

T he events of almost every day of Stravinsky's thirty-two years in America can be reconstructed from diaries, letters, and other documents. Yet the sum of the parts is less than the whole, a casual remark by the man himself often casting more light than pages of biographers' details. Thus his observation that "It is impossible for the brain to follow the ear and the eye at the same time" [1] reveals the totality with which music absorbed his brain; and the exactness of the analogy, "Film music should have the same relationship to the film drama that somebody's piano-playing in my living room has to the book I am reading," suggests an extraordinary power to visualize. Dicta such as these [2] are obviously worth more than any amount of commentary on the composer's "listening habits" and "visual imagination."

Throughout the 1920s and 1930s, France played a diminishing role in Stravinsky's life, the United States an increasingly important one. His widespread fame there had begun with the tour of the Ballets Russes in 1916, but his music had been played in concert before then. In 1919, a New York newspaper reported that the composer was living in a Swiss garret on the verge of starvation. Two rescue operations were organized,[3] and, on the 2nd of June, Stravinsky received 1,913 francs, 40 centimes, "from his admirers in Boston [via] the American Consular Service in Geneva and Ignace Jan Paderewski"—who must have wondered what his neighbor had done to provoke such philanthropy.

On June 10, an additional 10,450 francs arrived from still more "American admirers and friends," an amazingly generous and altruistic gift from a public that had never seen Stravinsky and had been shocked and irritated by what little music of his it had heard. But the dire-need rumor lived on, and, as late as December 20, the New York *Evening Post*, reviewing the American premiere of *Pribaoutki* in Aeolian Hall, added that the composer was even then "lying ill and hungry in Switzerland." At this point, a large new envelope marked *"Affaires Américaines"* appeared in Stravinsky's files.

The 1925 tour was a great success, both artistically and financially. One consequence was that, throughout the remaining years of Stravinsky's residence in France, the majority of commissions for new works—the Serenade, *Apollo, Symphony of Psalms*, Violin Concerto, *Jeu de Cartes*, Concerto in E-flat, Symphony in C—came from the United States. Naturally his thoughts turned increasingly toward America, though a still more compelling reason for his eventual settlement in Los Angeles was the discovery, during a concert tour in 1937, that his lung disease had been arrested in the then-beneficial California climate and air.

A different Stravinsky must be distinguished at every stage in the American years, but especially between the first and last decades. The composer-conductor of the 1940s, still struggling to earn a living from his "art" as well as his "profession," is remote from the world figure of the 1960s, just as the Stravinsky who used to visit the National Parks in a second-hand Dodge,[4] eating in drugstores and sleeping in fleabag motels, is far removed from the elderly VIP who was whisked from airport to hotel in police-escorted limousines. So, too, the Stravinsky who was the personification of *joie de vivre* is understandably different from the man who, after the age of sixty-nine, lived under the constant threat of paralysis from a blood disease. And, finally, the Stravinsky surrounded by a retinue of nurses contrasts sadly with the man who once did everything for himself and permitted absolutely no intrusion on his privacy.

With age, too, Stravinsky's ambivalences became more pronounced. He was the proudest Russian in Hollywood during World War II, rejoicing in the victories of the Red Army, actively participating in Russian War Relief, and even going so far as to listen to Shostakovich's Symphony No. 7 [5] when it was broadcast on July 19, 1942. Then, immediately after the peace, the mere mention of the U.S.S.R. was enough to offend Stravinsky. He protested against the Waldorf Conference and refused to add his name to a composers' telegram welcoming Shostakovich to the United States. Still strongly anti-Soviet at the time of Sputnik, Stravinsky fiercely berated the hapless headwaiter in a Baden-Baden hotel who first broke to him the news of this Russian achievement. As late as 1960, Stravinsky told a reporter:

Under Lenin, the Soviets invited me. I couldn't go. Stalin never invited me. . . . I saw their paintings in Venice. Seventy-five years ago, people painted that way. . . . *The Nightingale* was played just before the Soviets came to power in 1917. I was in Switzerland and had a big correspondence about it. My younger brother wrote to me about the performance, so I know it was very good. . . .[6] [*Washington Post*, December 24, 1960]

Yet, only six months after this statement, Stravinsky accepted an invitation from the U.S.S.R. to conduct concerts in Moscow and Leningrad. Moreover, these proved to be the most gratifying public occasions of his life, as well as revealing how deeply defensive had been his former bitterness against his homeland.

The American years also heightened certain contradictions in the composer's personality. Dickens himself [7] could not have created a more parsimonious character than Igor Stravinsky, who, during his second American tour, complained that he had "paid in tips to Pullman porters what amounted to one concert," [8] who once entered in an expense-account diary a ten-cent donation to a panhandler, and who noted on the sketch of a piece sent to Hindemith in Switzerland thanking him for a birth-day canon, "Sent on June 25/57 by ordinary mail." [9] Yet the composer was a generous man and the very opposite of miserly, helping to support friends, relatives, former domestics, impov-erished artists and writers.[10] Still another inconsistency was his attraction to the formalism of religions (as exemplified by his belief in the efficacy of ritual prayer and the rejection of the spontaneous, personal kind) versus his extremely rare atten-dance at religious services.

The post–World War II years reverse the paradox of the pre-war period in France, the most conspicuous events during Stravinsky's second and third decades in America taking place in Europe. In the 1950s and early 1960s, his music as a whole attained a far greater measure of success in Europe than in Amer-ica, while the quality of a performance such as that of Ingmar Bergman's *Rake's Progress* has never been duplicated in the United States. Also reversing the situation of the 1920s and 1930s, more commissions for new works came from Europe (and Israel) than from America, beginning with the Concerto in D (1946), and including the *Canticum Sacrum, Threni, Move-ments, Monumentum, A Sermon, a Narrative and a Prayer, Abraham and Isaac,* as well as the English-language opera which had been planned for an American stage but was finally paid for by the Italian government and first performed in Venice.

When Stravinsky arrived in New York on the S.S. *Manhat-tan,* September 30, 1939, it was not with the intention of making his home in America but to fulfill concert engagements and to give the Charles Eliot Norton Lectures at Harvard. The texts of these six talks were written between March and June 1939, not by Stravinsky alone but jointly with Roland-Manuel, who had collaborated with Stravinsky in writing his *Chroniques de Ma Vie* five years earlier. In a letter to Stravinsky, June 18, 1939, Roland-Manuel says that

You have greatly honored me and given me the greatest joy by inviting me to collaborate in this work, in which I am so passionately interested.

Another of Roland-Manuel's letters indicates how the work was accomplished, Stravinsky talking and Roland-Manuel taking notes which he then wrote in essay form ("*J'ai rassemblé mes notes et commencé a composer . . .*"; letter of March 24). Roland-Manuel came to Sancellemoz—where Stravinsky was composing the Symphony in C—in March and again at the beginning of June but, in other letters, Roland-Manuel says that further conversations with Stravinsky are necessary in order to develop certain ideas. Roland-Manuel also worked with Pierre Suvchinsky, who understood the Russian expressions behind the French ones. "I saw Suvchinsky this morning," Roland-Manuel wrote to Stravinsky on June 22, returning to Paris after two weeks in Sancellemoz, and "we have put the final details of the fifth lecture in order. Suvchinsky has added an appendix."

Why did Stravinsky never officially acknowledge his collaborators, since he also did not deny their share in his work? Thus when Daniel Lesur, reviewing the first publication of the lectures in France, remarked that the language and paradoxes sounded like Roland-Manuel (*La Gazette des Lettres,* April 13, 1946), Stravinsky did not protest the remark, as he would certainly have done had the statement been untrue. When a full biography of Stravinsky is written, his association with Roland-Manuel must be examined in detail. Roland-Manuel introduced the composer to Freud (through Dalbiez's book), and wrote letters for the composer that he copied without changing a word and to which he affixed his name.[11]

Stravinsky was in Sancellemoz when he and Vera Sudeikina heard the news of mobilization, whereupon she took a taxi to the nearest railroad station, purchased two tickets on the next train to Paris, returned to Sancellemoz to help Stravinsky to finish packing, and, an hour later, boarded a train with him that, to their surprise, was only half full. Shortly after arriving in Paris, at Mme Sudeikina's apartment in the rue de l'Assomption, an air-raid alarm sent them to the basement. The all-clear signal was sounded an hour later but, as Mme Sudeikina's diary continues,

Igor is in a terrible state of nerves, and we decide that he will stay at Nadia's country house until he leaves for America. He takes a dozen suitcases—for only two weeks!—and Olga [Sallard]'s husband [a taxi driver] drives him there, after which Igor gives the automobile to him. [Five nights later:] We have had an alarm every night, and already the stores are advertising "pajama styles for the basement," which is very French.

Stravinsky returned to Paris from Mlle Boulanger's, at Gargenville, to learn that the S.S. *Manhattan* would sail not from Cherbourg but from Bordeaux, on the 25th. Nadia Boulanger's friend Katherine Wolff accompanied him there on the boat train.

Stravinsky's inaugural Norton Lecture offers the first public glimpse of him at the start of what was to become his American period:

Around 7:30 on Wednesday evening, October 18 ... ushers in black ties lined the walls of the Harvard music department.... Then ... sleek limousines began to drive up with Beacon Hill dowagers radiating white hair, evening dresses, diamonds and dignity.... No sooner had we settled down to Beacon Hill than the New Lecture Hall rustled again. This time it was for Kussevitzky.

Eager, tense, the audience waited for Stravinsky.... He made a sweeping entrance in tails, and then, after a low, courtly, athletic bow ... began his *Prise de Contacte*. Reading a manuscript of beautifully written French,[12] he spoke slowly, distinctly, with a soft Russian accent. He looked up from his paper infrequently, and then jerkily.... Wild applause greeted [him] as he concluded.... He bowed ... almost to the ground, shook Dr. Forbes warmly by the hand and breezed out, his tails flying behind. [Frederick Jacobi, *Modern Music*]

The next day, at Stravinsky's request, the *Boston Herald* reviewer wrote to the composer informing him that

the microphone unfortunately picks up other sounds, and thus it was possible to hear your breathing at times a trifle too loudly.... Once or twice I lost a word at the end of a sentence.

Here it should be mentioned that Boston was a stronghold of Stravinsky's music in 1940 and continued to be one throughout Kussevitzky's reign as conductor of the Symphony. The orchestra not only played more Stravinsky than did any other in America but regularly invited him to conduct it. Apart from that, in Boston his reputation as foremost composer of the age was unchallenged, this being due in considerable measure to Nadia Boulanger,[13] whose advocacy took even stronger hold in French-provincial Massachusetts than in Paris.

The terms of the lectureship required periodic meetings with the students, and, accordingly, on Tuesday and Friday afternoons, Stravinsky worked at Eliot House with about a dozen pupils. One of the two weekly meetings was devoted to a lecture, the other to a student composition, played by its author, and followed by comments from Stravinsky. A reviewer for the *Christian Science Monitor* attended the session of November 21, 1939, and published his report of it the next day:

Seated at the piano, Mr. Stravinsky; grouped about him, would-be Stravinskys of the future. Professor Merritt announces the purpose of the session, and Mr. Stravinsky invites a volunteer to play for him.... After some urging, a Mr. Jan La Rue of Ann Arbor ... produces a clarinet and a manuscript. As he begins to play Mr. Stravinsky comes and stands beside him.... Throughout the playing ... [Stravinsky's] face is devoid of expression. [Afterward,] sitting beside his pupil, Stravinsky proceeds to analyze the work in detail. "The musical thought is a little difficult to follow in places," he says. "This motif should be developed, restated; that idea should be repeated, not verbatim but with interesting variations. See, in this composition of mine," he says, and plays an illustration on the piano. "Like that." ... With Mr. La Rue once again, he hums over another passage, objecting to this F-sharp as out of place.... Students leaned forward in their chairs. Others in the room [include] William Denny, American composer ... Vladimir Ussachevsky, [and] William Austin, who plays two piano preludes. Sitting beside [Austin] and turning the pages, Mr. Stravinsky occasionally inserts a note in the bass. . . . He reserves comment until the end. Then, rather harshly, he points out a mixture of styles, a lack of form. . . . "Square-cut" is his word for some of the phrases. . . . Then, always punctual, methodical, practical, Mr. Stravinsky notes the time and suggests that the meeting should close for the day.

Another of the students was Robert Stevenson, later a professor of music at UCLA. He wrote to Stravinsky twenty years later:

In November of 1939 you allowed me to begin taking a series of weekly "advices" with you of an hour each. At first Dr. Kall was present, but from the second "advice" onwards we were conversing in French without his attendance. I am writing to you now in English only because I have been assured by Dr. John Vincent that your English has become as fabulous as your French. During that year I came to see you once a week, first at the house of the Forbes's, where you were residing on the top floor, then, after you married, at your house near the Christian Science Headquarters at Symphony Hall.

Still another student was Ellis B. Kohs, who wrote to Stravinsky on January 29, 1966:

I still cherish the lively recollection of my work with you at Harvard University, and your overwhelming kindness in actually sitting down to the keyboard with me to help me perform the first movement of my string quartet. . . .

In an interview at the end of his stay in Cambridge, Stravinsky confessed that

The lectures were like concerts: the performance was given and then "au revoir." . . . But the meetings with students . . . those were the good things that filled me with the best impressions and interest. . . . With this terrible war disrupting all art in Europe, it seems as though the Good Lord sent me specially to Harvard. Here I have hours for work. . . .
    I like to take short walks when the weather is good.[14] The weather has not been good . . . so I stayed indoors and your climate has made me give all the more time to my new symphony. . . .
    No effort is required to listen to the radio. One turns a knob. One can listen without hearing, as we can look without seeing. . . . It is indispensable to learn to read music. The secrets of creation are perhaps in the artist—the secrets of nature. But it is no difficult matter to see how the music is made. That . . . can and should be learned.

The content of Stravinsky's Harvard lectures [15] is too well known to warrant discussion here, but one aspect that may be worth remarking is the composer's wariness not only of the music of the future [16] but also of that of his contemporaries. Only Hindemith was even implicitly endorsed, and, though the lecturer conceded that Schoenberg "knows what he is doing," from all indications Stravinsky did not know, at least at the time.[17] The lecturer suggested that a young composer on whom some hopes might be pinned was Henri Sauguet,[18] though the audience must have felt that one or two Americans were as worthy of notice.

It should be said, too, that opinions such as these were more widely circulated than the themes of the lectures, for Stravinsky's disciples had made him the *arbiter elegantiarum*. Nor did it matter if the opinions seemed perverse. Thus, if Haydn's masses, symphonies, quartets, and piano trios had any special significance for Stravinsky,[19] he said nothing about it in the lectures, which is remarkable if only because he spoke with such enthusiasm about the music of Charles Gounod.[20]

On November 27, 1939, Stravinsky wrote from Cambridge to the American Ambassador in France, Robert D. Murphy, asking for his aid in securing a visa for "my best friend, a friend for a very long time, Mme Vera Sudeikina." Stravinsky says that they have decided to get married and that, being unable to leave America himself, he has asked Mme Sudeikina to join him. He guarantees to post the $500 bond required before Mme Sudeikina will be permitted to enter the United States and says that she will come as a member of the Union Féminine Française, at the invitation of the American branch of this organization. Mme Sudeikina has a Nansen passport, he adds, and he gives her Paris telephone number, JAsmine 64–40. In conclusion, he asks the Ambassador to keep the matter between themselves so that it will not become an object of publicity.

On November 28, Stravinsky began rehearsing the Boston Symphony Orchestra for a series of concerts (*Jeu de Cartes, Capriccio*, excerpts from *Petrushka*, the *Symphony of Psalms*). On December 6, he went to New York, and from there to San Francisco, for more concerts (Tchaikovsky's Second Symphony, *Jeu de Cartes, Petrushka* Suite). On December 12, the *San Francisco Examiner* published an interview:

Seven minutes were all that the busy and efficient Igor Stravinsky . . . could grant. . . . For seven minutes, tidy, intelligent opinions poured from his lips in overflowing measure. . . . "I will not speak until you have finished taking my picture. I must be photographed plainly, seriously. I detest being snapped in so-called action, with the mouth open. . . . War can never be good for the arts. The cannons speak, not the violins—not even the cymbals. . . ."

On December 17, Stravinsky went to Los Angeles, where, with George Balanchine, he visited the Disney Studios to see what they had done with *Le Sacre du Printemps*. The composer's anger at the alteration of the sequence of movements in this score blinded him to other aspects of the film, yet this experience may have spared him worse ones, for it bred a distrust of producers, whose lucrative offers he continued to reject for the same reason, the unwillingness to relinquish control over the manner in which the music would be used.[21] He returned to Cambridge, perhaps having learned more from his fury at the treatment received in Hollywood than from the enlightenment of his semester's teaching at Harvard—if it is true that "The tigers of wrath are wiser than the horses of instruction."

On December 23, from the Beverly Wilshire Hotel, Beverly Hills, Stravinsky cabled travel money to Vera Sudeikina in Paris. Then, after spending Christmas with Kall, Stravinsky left for Washington, D.C., where he stayed at Dumbarton Oaks with Mr. and Mrs. Robert Woods Bliss until the beginning of January, when he went to New York to rehearse the Philharmonic. Mrs. Bliss had commissioned the Symphony in C in the summer of 1939—Stravinsky acknowledges a $1,500 payment from her in a letter dated September 23, 1939, "on board the S.S. Manhattan"—but the piece was not yet designated for the Chicago Symphony. (On September 7, 1940, the Library of Congress purchased the manuscript full score for $1,000.)

Vera Sudeikina arrived in New York on January 12, 1940, and, on the 15th, went with Stravinsky and Kall to Pittsburgh for concerts (Apollo, Petrushka Suite, Jeu de Cartes, Firebird Suite). At the beginning of February, after a day or two in New York, Stravinsky left for Cambridge, Vera Sudeikina for Charleston, South Carolina, to spend a month with a Parisian friend.[22] On the 1st of March she went to Boston just as Stravinsky was returning there from concerts in Chicago (Jeu de Cartes, Petrushka Suite, Tchaikovsky's Second and Third Symphonies, Firebird Suite). On March 9, the couple was married in Bedford, Massachusetts.

In Los Angeles, in July 1940, the newlyweds applied for Mexican visas, went to Mexico City to establish quota qualifications, and, immediately on re-entering the United States, filed declarations of intent to become American citizens.[23] A concert tour in the autumn and winter took them to Chicago for the premiere of the Symphony in C, and to New York for Balustrade, Balanchine's ballet based on Stravinsky's Violin Concerto. Returning to Hollywood, they purchased a home at 1260 North Wetherly Drive [24] and moved there on April 6, 1941, thirty years to the day before the composer's death.

Stravinsky was fifty-eight when he began a new life in California, yet he was to change continually and more profoundly there than ever before, both as a composer—from the very first months in Los Angeles, he was more accessible to new ideas and influences than he had been in his final years in Europe—and as a man. The metamorphosis of the man was largely due to his remarriage, but the informality and the radically different "life style" of southern California were contributing factors. Those who knew him both in Europe before World War II and in Los Angeles during and after it are unanimous in this opinion, and the following comment is typical:

[Prince Argutinsky] introduced me to . . . Stravinsky [in the 1920s], and I did not at first like him as much as I did . . . when he came out to Hollywood, and I grew to love him. At this first meeting I thought him conceited and ungracious.[25]

That he was more approachable as a person is attested to not only by his friends, moreover, but also by the photographs in sandals and shorts, or Navy pea jacket—compared to his 1920s portraits, bemonocled and looking remarkably imperious.

When the present writer first entered Stravinsky's California household (1948), the language, friends, and habits of the home were almost exclusively Russian. But the Stravinskys' courtesy and hospitality were such that they spoke English with each other when not alone and tried to adapt themselves to American ways. The Stravinskys' closest Los Angeles friends [26] in the early 1940s were Russians—Balanchine, Eugene Berman, the Adolph Bolms, the Vladimir Sokoloffs [27]—and so were the doctors, cooks, gardeners, dressmakers. The remainder of the composer's circle was comprised largely of refugees—the Werfels, Szigetis, Montemezzis, Castelnuovo-Tedescos, Artur Rubinsteins, and others less well known—with whom the Stravinskys spoke either French or German. Therefore, except for the peculiar case of Mr. Ernest Anderson, to be discussed below, the present writer was Stravinsky's only monolingual, native-born American associate.

At the beginning of the American period, jazz was the new music to which Stravinsky was most susceptible, though probably his most successful use of it is in *Agon* (1957). In an interview on the subject in New York in 1925, he had said that

In jazz you have something that is not the result of ostentatious theorizing, that almost sneaked in on us from an out-on-the-corner cabaret. ... We don't like to admit it, but *real* music *has* such simple origins. ... I have written something in the jazz rhythm. It is not really rag. It is a portrait of rag. [*Musical America*, January 10, 1925]

He expressed interest in jazz again in an interview in *Die Stunde,* March 17, 1926, but, soon after that, became more critical.

Jazz is evident in the majority of Stravinsky's compositions between 1940 [28] and 1947, the Symphony in Three Movements—bits of which might have been introduced practically unnoticed at the Copacabana, between stretches of bossa nova— no less than the Concerto that was custom-made for Woody Herman. Stravinsky's early-1940s music is remarkable, too, for its grasp of the features of prevalent styles and moods. But, as Eliot said of Baudelaire,

The man who has the sense of his age is exposed to its follies as well as sensitive to its inventions

and Stravinsky did not always escape the banalities of the genres in which he trafficked, as in those parts of Scènes de Ballet that openly emulate Broadway.

It might also be said of some of Stravinsky's music of this period that the rhythmic element is lacking in subtlety, the standard of judgment being his own use of the same devices to perfect effect in earlier scores. Yet each of his little masterpieces-for-money is at least genial, and the inventiveness outweighs the weaknesses. In sonority, for example, he continues to be, as he always was, new in every piece—in the use of saxophones and guitar [29] in the *Scherzo à la Russe*,[30] in the canon for bassoons in the Symphony in Three Movements, in the guitar-like accompaniment to Orpheus' "Air." Nevertheless, he was openly aiming at the commercial market, and not many works of the time can be said to have been born purely of inner necessity.

The "Kyrie" and "Gloria" for a Roman Catholic Mass that Stravinsky composed at the end of 1944 are the exceptions. Why did he write these pieces, which were not in fulfillment of a commission, or intended for a specific occasion? His avowed reasons were that he was inspired to compose a more liturgical kind of music than he found in Mozart's Masses, and that he required instruments, which are forbidden in the Russian Orthodox Church to which he belonged. Yet his Mass is no mere exercise in musical style but a work born of religious faith. He believed in the Devil Incarnate, and in a literal Hell, Purgatory, Paradise. At the same time, he was deeply superstitious, forever crossing himself and those around him, wearing sacred medals, and performing compulsive acts without which the auguries for the day were certain to be unfavorable. He believed in miracles, both large and of the Houdini sort, and never questioned the provenance of any sacred relic.[31] He venerated the Turin shroud, kept a photograph of it next to his studio desk, and, from the 1930s, collected writings about it, but not those accepting the statement in the Bishop of Troyes's 1389 statement to the Pope that the forgers of the shroud had confessed. It goes without saying that dogmatism was another part of his religion, as it was of Stravinsky himself; that so many of the opinions of this least Socratic of men, in maieutic method, have appeared in the form of dialogues is ironic, even though the form was artificial and, in Stravinsky's mind, closer to Hebrew versicle and response than to Platonic question and answer. But a more powerful force than dogma ruled Stravinsky, that of an abiding intellectual curiosity, of openness to ideas and irresistible attraction to new ones, in a limitlessly receptive mind. And, finally, the genius of his artistic instinct overrode all else.

That Stravinsky had reached a spiritual crisis in 1944 is evident in his reading, which consisted of Bossuet's *Lettres sur l'Evangile* (but the composer read Bossuet almost daily for many years), Bloy, Bernanos, and parts of the *Summa*. In that year, too, Stravinsky visited Santa Clara, the convent of the Dominican sisters in Sinsinawa, Wisconsin, and he was often with Jacques Maritain. At about the same time, Stravinsky filled the margins of Ramuz's *Questions* with criticism of its "Protestantism," while endorsing the Roman Catholic views of C.-A. Cingria in the margins of *his* books. Yet none of this accounts for the creation of a Mass for a church which Stravinsky never joined, and which disappointed him by failing to use the work in its services.

The character of Stravinsky's music as a whole is radically different in the early California period from that of the last years in Europe. Compared to the Concerto in E-flat (1937–8) and the first two movements of the Symphony in C,[32] which are marked by the domination of classical models as well as by the insistence on diatonicism and the basic tonality, the new "American" music is "freer" and more "experimental." The first two movements of the Symphony in C are among the peaks of refinement in Stravinsky's art, but they are also a cul-de-sac. Contrast them with the two "American" movements of the same work, and with the first and last movements of the 1945 Symphony, in which, whatever else, the sheer physical energy of the music seems so much more abundant, and the ideas—such as the fugue for trombone, piano, and harp—so much bolder.

From the first, America provided Stravinsky with the most diverse opportunities to display his versatility in fulfilling commissions. Thus the *Circus Polka* (1942), with its march rhythms, pop tunes, tuba-and-piccolo instrumentation, and acrobatic leap into the *Marche Militaire*, fairly smells of sawdust and the Big Top.[33] But some of the trapeze artistry—musical or otherwise—in connection with the scores that followed this elephant ballet is no less breathtaking. The middle movement [34] of the *Ode*, for instance, had originally been intended as music for the hunting scene in the Orson Welles film *Jane Eyre*.[35] Then Kussevitzky commissioned a work in memory of his wife, and Stravinsky placed the hunting music between an "Epitaph" (composed between May 19 [36] and June 1) and a "Eulogy" (composed between June 9 and 25), adroitly re-characterizing this liveliest of his "three songs for the deceased" as

a *concert champêtre* suggesting an outdoor "musical," an idea cherished by Natalie Kussevitzky and brilliantly realized in Tanglewood by her husband.[37]

Stravinsky's other compositions of the time include a piece for the Paul Whiteman band that had originally been conceived as an *a cappella* sacred chorus; a Symphony, sections of which, from all three movements, had been intended for episodes in films; a two-piano Sonata, of which part of the first movement was adapted from an orchestral piece [38] conceived for a film; a ballet for a Broadway variety show; a biblical cantata commissioned by a Hollywood composer who was buying his way into better musical company and whose contract required that Stravinsky's score (as well as one by Schoenberg [39]) be played and recorded together with one of *his*; an *Elegy* for unaccompanied viola, a piece which demonstrates that Stravinsky could produce music of deep feeling "to order," for he scarcely knew the deceased,[40] was not particularly "moved" by his death, and in fact wrote the work only at the insistence of Nadia Boulanger [41] and of the player who was to perform it.

Despite his protestations to the contrary, the idea of composing for film undoubtedly attracted Stravinsky beyond the financial motive. An incurable movie addict, he had been flirting with film projects from as early as 1919, in which year he wrote to Blaise Cendrars [42] saying that *Don Quixote* did not conform to his conception of the cinematographic spectacle,[43] and reminding his correspondent of their conversations on the matter (letter of October 13). Three months before, Stravinsky had written to Ansermet about a certain critic's comments on the subject of film music, saying that the critic, whom he calls an "asshole," compromised everything that he touched. Stravinsky imagines with horror what would become of music if it were to "express" the film as the critic advocated, and wonders that people are always so preoccupied with "expression," even in the cinema, and that they have never understood the charm of music played parallel to a film. In 1932, in the era of the sound film, he prepared a statement for the review *Candide* on the same subject:

N'étant pas partisan de l'expressionisme en musique je pense que le rôle de cette dernière n'est pas d'exprimer le sens d'une pièce ou le sens de son texte, ni de créer une "atmosphère" du spectacle. On demandera, alors, selon quel principe s'opère une collaboration entre le jeu de la musique et l'action du spectacle. Selon le principe de l'indépendance d'une de l'autre, voici ma réponse. Chaque vrai art est nécessairement canonique, possédant ses loix à lui qui le régissent et le gouvernent. Ce principe s'appliquant à tout spectacle de scène (théâtre) je ne trouve aucune raison logique de ne pas l'appliquer également à tout spectacle d'écran (cinéma).

A quarter of a century later, the subject of film music provoked Stravinsky to one of the clearest formulations of his artistic philosophy:

I realize that music is an indispensable adjunct to the sound film. It has to bridge holes, to fill the emptiness of the screen, and to supply the loudspeakers with sounds. The film could not get along without it, just as I myself could not get along without having the empty spaces of my living room walls covered with wallpaper. . . . But music is too high an art to be absorbed by the subconscious mind. . . .

Music expresses nothing of a realistic character. . . . If a movement in a ballet should happen to be a visualization of the words "I Love You," then this reference to the actual world would play the same role in the dance (and in my music) that a guitar would play in a Picasso still-life: something of the real world is caught as pretext or clothing for the inherent abstraction. Dancers have nothing to narrate and neither has my music. Even in older ballets like *Giselle*, descriptiveness has been removed—by virtue of its naïveté, its unpretentious traditionalism, and its simplicity—to a level of objectivity and pure art-play. . . .

It is the individual that matters, never the mass. . . . When Disney used *Le Sacre du Printemps* for *Fantasia*, he told me: "Think of the numbers of people who will now be able to hear your music." Well, the numbers of people who consume music is of interest to somebody like Mr. Hurok, but it is of no interest to me. The mass adds nothing to art. It cannot raise the level, and the artist who aims consciously at mass-appeal can do so only by lowering his own level. The soul of each individual who listens to my music is important to me, not the mass feeling of a group. Music cannot be helped by means of an increase of the quantity of listeners, be this increase effected by the film or any other medium. It can be helped only through an increase in the quality of listening, the quality of the individual soul. . . .[44]

Whether or not Stravinsky's preoccupation with film music was motivated by the desire for money, that apparently was the sole object of his acceptance, in March 1941, of a private pupil, the only one in his lifetime, a certain Ernest Anderson, to whom he gave approximately 215 lessons. Stravinsky did not enjoy teaching, but, as he told an interviewer (*Opera*, San Francisco, October 1946), "a composer brought me a Symphony of two hundred pages and wanted me to give him lessons; I know nothing about teaching, so I spent two years rewriting his Symphony, and I learned a great deal while doing it." In a letter to Samuel Dushkin, December 29, 1941, Stravinsky described this pupil as "a composer who is far from young, but who is trying to improve the style of his composition by watching me rewrite his symphony from top to bottom."

It is regrettable that the result has disappeared, both because Stravinsky apparently did recompose almost every note of the piece, explaining, wherever possible, his reasons for the changes, and because his work on it was contemporary with the first movement of his own symphony, from which Anderson's might have received some residue, or contain vestigial hints. Regrettable, too, is the failure of the pupil to leave an account of his experience, any portion of these putative "Anderson tapes" being worth a dozen of those "personal memoirs" in which Stravinsky the composer never appears.

The Anderson story becomes less mysterious with the discovery of its relevance to the Stravinsky budget. On January 2, 1942, the name appears in Mrs. Stravinsky's diary next to the comment: "Igor very worried about our financial situation." And, in Stravinsky's own diary, the lessons are scheduled five and six together after the arrival of large household bills, thus arousing a suspicion that the pupil's accelerated ascent of Parnassus may not have been the teacher's main objective. But Stravinsky's financial worries were justified. Concert engagements were scarce, his music not being in the highest demand in the first place, and, in the second, requiring extra, and expensive, rehearsal time. Conducting the New York Philharmonic in January 1940, he was obliged to prepare two programs, one, of his own music, for the Carnegie Hall audience, another, of Tchaikovsky's, for the Sunday broadcast.

Apart from work, the data of Stravinsky's life in the 1940s can be compiled from Mrs. Stravinsky's diaries,[45] from letters,[46] and from the descriptions of visitors. From the diaries, for example, we learn that, one night in July 1942, Stravinsky had already gone to bed when footsteps sounded on the stairs leading to his front door. He opened it to a tall, shy man who apologized in Russian for the lateness of the hour, saying he had been told that Stravinsky worked until midnight. The composer of *The Firebird* then recognized his visitor as the composer of the Prelude and asked him in. Rachmaninoff had come to invite Stravinsky to dinner—promising that music would not be discussed—and to present him with the gift of a jar of natural honey. Rachmaninoff had heard, correctly, that Stravinsky liked honey—in edible, not thickly mellifluous aural, forms. On July

22, Stravinsky went to the dinner and, on August 8, returned the hospitality at his own home, the last time the compatriot-colleagues were to meet. The following March, while changing trains in Chicago, Stravinsky caught sight of a newspaper headline announcing Rachmaninoff's death.

Also from the diaries we learn that on April 25, 1942, Stravinsky was notified of a requirement to register for defense work. But his contribution to the war effort, apart from benefit concerts, was to be limited to keeping a flock of chickens ("I like their rhythmic clucking," [47] he told a reporter) and cultivating a Victory Garden; on May 16, 1943, the Stravinskys dined on borscht made from beets that the composer had planted and tended himself.

One tantalizing entry in Mrs. Stravinsky's diary is that of August 1, 1943. After receiving an invitation to dinner at the Werfels', she wrote: "Igor asks if Schoenberg has also been invited"—but failed to indicate whether this meant her husband did or did not want to see him. (She came away from the dinner with a recipe for "petits pois à la Mahler.") On the 26th of the same month, the diary records that the composer had attended a lunch at Warner Brothers, this time not to discuss a proposition to compose film music but to be interviewed by the casting department to play the role of himself in a film about Gershwin.[48]

The diaries record that, on March 6, 1944, Stravinsky first heard an Evenings-on-the-Roof concert. This Los Angeles chamber-music society, together with its offspring, the Monday Evening Concerts, introduced him to music from Josquin to Ives that he would not otherwise have known; the organization also gave the first performances of nearly twenty of Stravinsky's own smaller-scale pieces, originals as well as arrangements.

Finally, the diaries are a scrapbook of press cuttings compiled from concert tours, some directly quoting the composer, others merely describing him and the vicissitudes of his travels. Thus a business-minded Dallas newspaper informed its readers:

While transferring from one station to another the Stravinskys lost a bag containing music and clothes. This will be an opportunity for Dallas merchants, since most of Mrs. Stravinsky's clothes, as well as the conductor's dress suit, will have to be replaced immediately. [March 13, 1946]

In New York to conduct the premiere of the Symphony in Three Movements, January 24, 1946, the composer was pictured by the Times's Howard Taubman

... sitting in his room at the Sherry Netherlands ... and speaking of his work with careful and exact choice of phrase. His English was thoroughly reliable but occasionally he reverted to French for the mot juste. ... He felt that music in Russia had gone backward. ... What about Prokofiev? He replied that he found Prokofiev less interesting than he used to be. ... As a man who has always been interested in jazz and its contributions to music [sic], Stravinsky says that what he has heard lately is of little interest. ... [January 29, 1946]

Even after a quarter of a century, *The Rake's Progress,* Stravinsky's final work of the 1940s, is still misunderstood. This may be attributed to two obstacles, the opera's undeniable dramatic flaws [49] and its musical idiom, the audience never being quite certain of the composer's intentions, or even whether or not he is pulling its leg. Stravinsky is a "modern" composer, after all, yet what is modern about these diatonic melodies, consonant harmonies, harpsichord recitatives? This difficulty for audiences may be expected to disappear, however, and future opera-lovers will be able to hear the music untroubled by the composer's indifference to the "modern" opera he did not write because he believed that the form had completed its evolution at some point in the past. As for the dramatic weaknesses, *they* can be decisively diminished by a talented director. Ingmar Bergman made most of them practically invisible.

The length of the opera, three times that of any other work by Stravinsky, was a burden on his mind throughout its composition. In fact, the thought that he might not be able to complete *The Rake* may have been responsible for a duodenal ulcer, the discovery of which caused him to consider temporarily shelving the opera in order to compose a short piece for which he had been offered a handsome fee. That almost all of his more than one hundred compositions *are* short, and that his life work includes practically no incomplete ones and even few unused sketches, says much about the character of the man. It follows that two of the attractions of *The Rake,* and these the ones that kept him to the task of completing it, were the structure, which had been established before he began to compose, and the completeness of each "number" in itself.

Stravinsky began these numbers in accordance with a strict procedure, first adding scansion marks (as well as, occasionally, the musical meter), then memorizing the lines while pacing up and down repeating them aloud. Finally he timed each number according to a tempo that he had decided would be most suitable for the words. The last is puzzling, for how could he know the duration of a passage of unwritten music? Yet the musical speed does appear to have been predetermined from these verbal recitations. Stravinsky worked in the same way in February 1946, while studying Robinson Jeffers's *Medea* for the possible inclusion of a prelude and an entr'acte, clocking to the second— "6:52," "3:45," "1:05"—not only the two instrumental sections but also each of the play's speeches in which music might be involved.

Stravinsky's practice of writing rhythmic values above the syllables and only later notating intervallic or melodic ideas is not true of his vocal music generally, nor always true of *The Rake.* The same method is used in some of the Russian-language pieces but, beginning with *In Memoriam: Dylan Thomas* (1954), rhythm was the secondary consideration, pitch the primary one. Sometimes, in *The Rake,* Stravinsky confused French and English quantities, allotting, for example, only one quarter-note for "earnest," and later (March 27, 1951) changing it to two eighths.

But the discovery of this kind of error embarrassed him, and only through Mrs. Stravinsky's diplomacy could he be induced to add a stem for the second syllable. When the opera was first performed, and singers asked whether the noteless syllables should be sung or spoken, he stubbornly refused to reply—though the missing note was obviously meant to repeat the preceding one.

Stravinsky also misunderstood certain lines, reasonably in the case of "Indeed, let all who will, make their joy here of your glad tidings." The comma after "will" was missing in Stravinsky's copy of the text, and, trying to make sense of the words, he changed "here" to "hear." His setting implies a comma after "joy," and, in order to preserve the rhythm of his music—after the mistake was discovered—and to erase the ambiguity, Erwin Stein sensibly suggested changing the words to "Let all who will share your joy, hear of your glad tidings." (Letter of June 1, 1951) But this solution was not adopted. It should also be mentioned that, at one time, Stravinsky thought of writing a different version of the vocal parts for each translation. In a letter of October 13, 1950, he argued that, since most of the musical links between words or syllables and notes are lost in translations, the music should be written according to each translated text.

Stravinsky's feelings for The Rake were intensely personal. Apart from the berceuse that he composed for Vera Sudeikina in Perséphone, he had never written love music before, and now, at nearly seventy, he was inspired for the first time to do so by a text. He identified the love of Tom and Anne in their last scene with that of himself and his wife, and the Duet "In a foolish dream, in a gloomy labyrinth," as well as the Arioso "My heart breaks"—music instinct with the anticipation of death—were written for her first of all, and only then for "the world." Having played the score at the piano with him, page by page as it was written, the present writer recalls the occasion when Stravinsky first unveiled the music of this last scene for her. As was customary at these readings, he took the bass parts himself, sometimes also singing them, though occasionally he would strain, in a painful half-falsetto, to indicate some of the tenor music as well. The performance was as loud as his muted piano permitted, for he was also testing the harmonic relationships and trying to hear them with distinctness. But since he would repeat a chord without warning, yet explode with irritation when all four hands were not precisely together, the results bore little relation to the way that the music was intended to sound.

The Rake's Progress was an end, in the sense that Stravinsky's music in the fifteen years after the opera does not extend from it. But the following statements, recorded ten years after the opera and on the other side of the world, in Australia and New Zealand, are wholly characteristic of him at any time in the last three decades of his life:

Stravinsky, who spoke with the mental agility and energy of a much younger man, said that he did not compose music for any particular group of people: "I feel that I need to speak, and surely I speak to someone who needs it. . . ." On his own early works, Stravinsky stated that "my attitude to them is just to leave them alone; I am moving, they are probably not moving.". . . Stravinsky moves in a world that takes no account of geography. His compositions are unaffected by the accident of where he may be living at the time. "I compose under the influence of ideas, and climate cannot change my ideas or my techniques." [*Wellington Evening Post*, November 16, 1961]

Someone mentioned that as recently as 1953 people at a Melbourne concert had walked out on *The Rite of Spring*. "Only *nine* years ago? . . . But fifty years ago was the time to walk out on it, not nine years ago. . . .
　"When I die, I leave you my music. . . . It is music that followed rules that were not written, but I hope I have added something new to what was existing." [*Melbourne Sun*, November 25, 1961]

I have a feeling, although it is not of complaint, that M. Deesney rests too much on his formula. [Stravinsky, quoted in the *Toronto Evening Telegram*, January 4, 1937]

　In spite of this misgiving, when Harry Fox, an agent for Walt Disney, wrote to Stravinsky's publishers seeking permission to use *The Firebird* in an animated cartoon (letter of April 12, 1938), Stravinsky replied that Disney's proposition "gave me an idea to compose some original music for his *dessins animés.*" (Letter to Strecker, May 15, 1938) When nothing came of this, and Disney turned to the *Sacre*, Stravinsky instructed his New York attorney, Maurice J. Speiser, to sign a contract with Walt Disney Enterprises for

December 1939. Hollywood. With Walt Disney.

the irrevocable right, license, privilege, and authority to record in any manner, medium, or form Rites [sic] of Spring for use in the film Fantasia. [January 4, 1939]

The sum paid was $6,000. Another provision of the agreement was that Disney could use the music in other films, which he did in Monsters of the Deep (February 1956), a movie otherwise fitted with a score of "what appears to be original music written by George Bruno" (letter to Stravinsky from Harry Fox). When Stravinsky saw Fantasia in Los Angeles in December 1939, he was not impressed by the synchronizing of his music with swooping pterodactyls and orogenic explosions, but, despite his later accounts of the visit,[50] he seems not to have protested at the time.

After a second screening at the Disney Studios, on October 12, 1940, Mrs. Stravinsky noted in her diary that her husband was

appalled by the bad taste, by Deems Taylor . . . making a boring speech, and by Stokowski climbing a staircase in a flood of red light.

The Sacre was undoubtedly Stokowski's, not Disney's, choice. As early as 1927, Stravinsky had written to Païchadze:

I received a letter from Stokowski in which he says that he will not conduct this season because of an injury to his arm (the result of an automobile accident), but that he intends to make recordings and wishes to study the Sacre, and, if I am willing, to record it. . . .[51]

Despite Stravinsky's criticisms of Fantasia, on October 23, 1940, two Disney directors called on the composer to discuss the possibility of making an animated film of Renard, and, on October 28, he sold an option to Disney for Renard, Fireworks, and The Firebird, probably realizing that the music would never be used. A few months later, in Boston, Disney's New England representative wrote to Stravinsky requesting an interview

on your impression of Mr. Disney's handling of The Rite of Spring, or, if you do not care to go so far, just talk for a short while about your visit to Mr. Disney's studio.

Stravinsky later became an enthusiast of Disney's nature films, except for the way in which they use music. An entry in Mrs. Stravinsky's diary, July 10, 1953, notes that, after seeing a Disney water-bird film:

Igor says he is getting tired of the synchronization of animal movements to Liszt's Second Hungarian Rhapsody.

But, to return to 1939, on New Year's Eve, Vera Sudeikina left Paris for Genoa, from whence she was to sail for America on the ship of a neutral country. The following excerpts from her diary for the next fortnight give a picture of their writer:

December 31, 1939: It was good that we drank martinis in the station bar, as Ira [52] suggested, so that we would be brave and not cry when the train started.

January 1, 1940. I had a couchette to Chambéry. At midnight I wanted to say "Happy New Year" to three officers but was tired and slept until 5:25, when the train stopped. I thought we were in Chambéry, but the conductor said that we were late; he promised to wake me at 6 and to transfer my baggage to the other car, which he did. At last we were in Genoa, Hotel Colombia, where I drank tea and ate sandwiches, wrote postcards, went to bed.

January 2. At 11 A.M. I went aboard the S.S. *Rex,* cabin 565, tourist class. On the advice of someone who had made the trip before, I gave twenty dollars to a steward to get a better cabin. At lunch, the pretty woman I met in the train, Eve Charpentier, proposed to share the same table with me, but a fat woman came also, saying she wanted French conversation. This woman, Signora Honda, proved to be very gay and nice.

January 3. Naples. A beautiful view. I throw in the water all of the flowers that I received in Paris.

January 4. Gibraltar. An endless stop. On the deck, one Jewish refugee to another: *"Was ist es für eine Station?"* I tell them that we are not in the subway yet. At 2 P.M. we finally start for Lisbon.

January 6. I send a cable to Igor, *"Bon Noël,"* and the telegraph operator says, "You are late." I explain that tomorrow is *Russian* Christmas.

January 8. We see the Azores in the morning. It is foggy, but the boat is rocking more and more. The best thing is to go to bed. Mme Honda comes to see me and says that the dining room is empty.

January 9. I go up to receive a cable from Igor. What a joy! I order Asti Spumanti at lunch, but the rocking is stronger, and I lack courage to see the movies.

January 10. I stay in bed until 4, then get up and play cards, read, and look at the waves. How slowly the time passes; trips like this are for old people. This evening a gala dinner and dancing. Red ropes are everywhere, as if for a Hollywood film preview, except that these are for safety. People are dancing in the bar, falling over each other and over tables, and with drinks in their hands. Some Russian Bolsheviks are at one table; what ugly, vulgar faces. They do not eat much but try to look like intellectuals.

January 11. The sea is calm, but because of the Gulf Stream the air is stifling. And—horreur—I have lost my voice, but absolutely! How will I tell them tomorrow about Paris? I try several remedies but nothing helps. I am disgusted.

January 12. My voice has still not returned. I am impatient and look at my watch every five minutes. (We have to change the hour again, putting our watches back forty-five minutes.) I pass the time repeating English phrases. At 5 P.M. I see New York, in a fog, but like thousands of stars in a blue mist. How beautiful! We enter the harbor very slowly, docking only at 7 P.M. Some of the passengers are shut in a salon with a sign on the door, "Ellis Island." How humiliating! Somehow I find a porter to take my baggage. I can see Igor on the pier, with Kall, Dushkin, Bolm, and Kyra.[53] I feel: now they will take care of me. My voice comes back a little, and I ask a woman next to me to shout down to my friends: "She is all right but has lost her voice."

May 18, 1940. Miami. Aboard the S.S. *Seminole.*

How wonderful to end this voyage! Bolm suggests that we go to the hotel first and have drinks in the bar, "Then we will show her things that she has never seen before; yes, yes, a cafeteria." We go to the hotel, the Great Northern, and I am half drunk from all the excitement.

January 13. Everything is so strange! Igor cannot come and chat with me in my room. It is forbidden because I am not his wife. I can still feel the pitching of the ship. We go to the cafeteria—I like it—and at 3 P.M. to Kussevitzky's concert in Carnegie Hall. I am in a loge with Alexandra Tolstoy and during intermission I meet Elena Mumm.

On March 2, Vera Stravinsky wrote in her diary: "I arrive in Boston [from Charleston, South Carolina] at midnight, and Igor brings me back to the Forbes home." Four days later she wrote:

I am divorced. A lawyer, John Divine, comes, and later a judge. . . . I am very tired and Igor thinks I am not well. No; I am preparing myself to be soon Mrs. Stravinsky.

As aforesaid, the marriage took place at 12:30 P.M., March 9, in Bedford, Massachusetts. On the 28th of April, Stravinsky completed the third movement of the Symphony in C, dating it according to the Russian calendar, "Easter, April 15, Boston: This part of the orchestra score is finished. 154 pages." The Stravinskys then made arrangements to move to California.

The composer had spent his last day in Boston at the home of a dentist (who made a movie of him), and his last evening there (May 6) with George Balanchine, listening to a black jazz band. The next day, the Stravinskys went to New York by boat, and, on May 15, they left for Galveston on the S.S. *Seminole.* Vera Stravinsky's diary describes shipboard life as

nice, intimate, with bingo, poker, movies, and the radio broadcasting horrible news. On the 19th we attended a Mass in the salon. The ocean is blue and calm, so calm that I caught a little bird. On the 20th we endured a big dinner party and entertainment at which Dr. Kall recited Turgenev's "How beautiful were the roses," the only poem by Turgenev that I hate. In Galveston [May 21] we buy all of the newspapers and are sick with the bad news from Europe. We take the train to Houston and later to Los Angeles.

Nine years later *The Houston Post* elicited from the composer further information on the Galveston episode, publishing it under the title "Heretofore Unknown Visit to Houston":

The Russian-born master and his wife set out from New York on a honeymoon trip to the Grand Canyon. The first stage of the journey was made by boat, which landed the couple in Galveston. They didn't like it. They hurried directly to Houston, took a look at the city—and gave up.
"It was a terrible trip in every way," Stravinsky said. "The boat was bad—very bad—and so was the ocean that year—and at the end there was Galveston. We wanted to rest—but not there. We took the first train to Houston. We got off and looked around—then got back on and went home. That honeymoon—it was a French *débâcle.*"

Shortly after reaching California, in May 1940, Stravinsky wrote to Carlos Chávez, in Mexico, saying that life had become a constant anxiety "because of the tragic news of our poor old Europe."

On July 20, 1940, Vera Stravinsky wrote in her diary:

After a long wait at El Paso, the train creaks across the Rio Grande Bridge and stops at a miserable station, where Mexicans with guitars, babies, and bundles crowd on board. Next to the station is a café, the "Caballero," and in front of it in the middle of the street a dead cow. A gendarme tells Igor that he does not have all of the necessary papers and asks him to come to the Immigration Office. I go along, since I will not stay in the train alone—it could suddenly leave. Finally everything is in order and we depart, stopping at even the smallest village, where Indians come to the windows of the train to sell things and to beg. An endless desert. Once, three horsemen, with braided hair and solferino-pink shirts, ride up alongside us trailing clouds of dust. Every hour or so all night long the train stops, then, after a long while, jerks and rattles ahead.

Guadalajara is a very fragrant city, full of flowers; perfumes are made here. We take taxi drives. In the Mexico City station, a crowd with journalists and photographers. [From V.A.S.'s diary, July 22]

Two days later, at a press conference, the first subject on Stravinsky's mind was the war.[54]

July 22, 1940. Arriving in Mexico City.

In his apartment in the Reforma Hotel, the Maestro was chatting with . . . Adolfo Salazar, Alfonso Reyes, Maestro Chávez, and Arqueles Vela: "I left France September 16th, a few days after war was declared. . . . There was sadness, alarm, uncertainty, perhaps because the people had a presentiment of catastrophe.". . . The conversation turned to music. "Some people—races, rather—are naturally musical, while others make themselves musicians by dint of study. . . . The [Mexican people] have a musical heritage. I had proof of it this afternoon, rehearsing the Orquesta Sinfónica. . . . Paul Valéry explained everything biologically, a strange mania of his. He said that the writers, musicians, or painters who made his glands work were the people who really produced the sensations of those arts. And so these Mexican musïcians . . . put my glands to work.". . . Turning to Alfonso Reyes, [Stravinsky] told him that . . . his book Vision of Anahuac taught him more about Mexico than all the histories he could have read, because the ideas were expressed with such harmony: "That is the great difficulty in all art," Stravinsky concluded, "to put ideas in their necessary order." [Excelsior, Mexico City, July 24, 1940]

Stravinsky conducted two different programs with the Orquesta Sinfónica: on July 26, the Divertimento, excerpts from Petrushka, Cherubini's Anacreon Overture, Tchaikovsky's Symphony No. 2, and, on August 2, Apollo, the Divertimento, Jeu de Cartes, the Firebird Suite. On August 3, he recorded the Divertimento for RCA Victor Mexicana, but, because of noise from a nearby factory, the recording had to be remade the following year. On August 5, the Stravinskys left by train for Los Angeles, and, on the 8th, at 12:50 P.M., in Nogales, Arizona, entered the United States as Russian Non-Preference Quota Immigrants:

Igor receives Number 1053425 and I have Number 1053429. We are in Nogales for 3 hours, to sign the papers and undergo medical examinations. I am nervous and no doubt my blood pressure is high, but the doctor is understanding: "My wife has it very often," he says. Finally we are back in the train, the Consul himself driving us to our Pullman car. [From V.A.S.'s diary]

A week after reaching his rented house in Beverly Hills, Stravinsky completed the Symphony in C (August 17). On October 14, he finished a Tango for voice (without words) and piano. With Stravinsky's approval, an orchestral arrangement of this piece was made by Felix Günther, and the first performance took place July 10, 1941, in Robin Hood Dell, Philadelphia. On July 16, the publisher of the Tango, Leonard Feist, wrote to Stravinsky at the Hotel Reforma, Mexico City:

The Philadelphia performance was a great disappointment [in] the manner in which it was conducted. . . . I [thought] that a dance band conductor like Benny Goodman would have a feeling for the Tango . . . but Mr. Goodman did not take the trouble to study the score to know sufficiently what he was doing. . . . The audience . . . was no great help. There were ten thousand jitterbugs there who came only to hear Benny Goodman.

On August 14, back in Hollywood, Stravinsky sent his arrangement for the "Star Spangled Banner" to Feist with the explanation:

. . . Upon studying the theme I found it . . . lent itself naturally to the form of a sacred chorale. . . . It is my hope and wish that one day Congress will pass an act standardizing my harmonization. My version will be premiered here September 9th. . . . My original manuscript is being bound and embossed in gold and will be presented to President Roosevelt at this concert which will be nationally broadcast. . . .

Actually, Stravinsky had thought of harmonizing the piece many months before, and the idea of exploiting a new arrangement in this way was not his, but was suggested to him by his lawyer, Aaron Sapiro.

After finishing the Tango (in October 1940), Stravinsky began *Danses Concertantes*, the first notation for which, the theme of the "Pas d'Action," had been written the year before, on October 19, 1939, while he was working on the Symphony in C, this theme being an outgrowth of the beginning of the "Allegro" in the finale of the Symphony. Returning to *Danses Concertantes* in October 1940, the melody that he composed—on a Western Union telegram form—was used at 107, and the variation in which it occurs (No. III) is the first part of the piece that he was to complete; [55] "one of eight variations," he wrote next to the notation, though he was to compose only four. The "Thème" was written next, then the first two variations, the opening march (called "Marche de Présentation" in the sketchbook), and, finally, the "Pas d'Action" (begun June 4, 1941). Two themes for this last, used at ⎡34⎤ and ⎡38⎤, may have occurred to Stravinsky while he was in Robert's Cleaning and Laundering shop at 8874 Sunset Boulevard, since they are jotted on a calling card from that establishment. The fourth variation was completed on October 20, and, by December 1, except for the final "Marche," Stravinsky had finished the entire score. The expression "O.K." occurs for the first time in Stravinsky's manuscripts in the sketches for *Danses Concertantes.*

According to Vera Stravinsky's diary, her husband played *Danses Concertantes* for her on November 12, and, on the same day, Balanchine telephoned from New York with the proposition to compose the *Circus Polka.* The next day, Stravinsky received the news of the death of his brother Yury in Leningrad six months before, and, on the 16th, attended a Panikheda service in his memory. In San Francisco for concerts at the beginning of January, Stravinsky made notes for a telephone conversation with Balanchine: "The elephant's name is Medoc [like the wine]?"; "How many minutes? The less the best." But in fact Stravinsky had already begun work on the piece by the end of December 1941—after conducting concerts in St. Louis, where he was humiliated by objections to his arrangement of the national anthem. On January 20, he telegraphed to Dr. Milton Bender, a New York dentist who was also Balanchine's manager: "Discussion of contract takes time. I start working only afterward," yet Mrs. Stravinsky's diary notes that her husband played the finished piece for her on February 6. On the 15th, Stravinsky telegraphed to Balanchine: "Miss Modoc's Dance composed expect second payment." On March 11, Balanchine telegraphed from Sarasota, "Rehearsals begin Monday please send score," and Stravinsky replied:

Kindly ask Ringling to Air Mail last payment and I shall be glad to send him also by air just finished score.

The *Circus Polka* was first performed in Madison Square Garden, April 9, 1942, in an arrangement for band by David Raksin, conducted by Merle Evans. (Stravinsky wrote the orchestra score later, completing it on October 5, 1942.) The program described the piece as:

A ballet for fifty elephants and fifty girls, featuring Old Modoc and Vera Zorina, directed by George Balanchine, with costumes by Norman Bel Geddes.

The *Daily News,* April 10, wrote

. . . Newest and biggest of the spectacles is the "Ballet of the Elephants" staged by Balanchine and danced last night by his screen star wife. In this, what seemed like several thousand girls in brief red costumes spun and hung from the maze of ropes above the arena while the mastodons cavorted below to the music of Merle Evans's swell circus band which was doing a Town Hall job with the Igor Stravinsky music.

The New York Times, same date, said that

... The "Ballet of the Elephants" ... was breathtaking. Igor Stravinsky wrote the music for it and George Balanchine directed it. The cast included fifty ballet girls, all in fluffy pink, and fifty dancing elephants. They came into the ring in artificial, blue-lighted dusk, first the little pink dancers, then the great beasts. The little dancers pirouetted into the three rings and the elephant herds gravely swayed and nodded rhythmically. The arc of sway widened and the stomping picked up with the music. In the central ring Modoc the Elephant danced with amazing grace, and in time to the tune, closing in perfect cadence with the crashing finale. In the last dance fifty elephants moved in endless chain around the great ring, trunk to tail, with the little pink ballet girls in the blue twilight behind them. The ground shook with the elephants' measured steps. . . .

After the Circus Polka, Stravinsky wrote the first movement of what was to become the Symphony in Three Movements, though he did not give it that title until the entire work was completed; the earliest sketches are dated April 4 and 9, 1942. When the movement was finished in its first version, on June 15, Stravinsky wrote the Four Norwegian Moods, the homage that he had had in mind since the Nazi invasion of Norway, completing the full score on August 18 (V.A.S.'s diary). Shortly before the premiere of the Moods, Stravinsky informed an Associated Press reporter that the new work had been written

after studying Norwegian folklore. . . . I used a style similar to that employed by Joseph Haydn in his treatment of folk material.

The "Song" (No. II), originally called "Fisherman's Song," came from the Norwegian Her Hjemme (Home), and one of the melodies of "Cortège" (No. IV), originally to have been the third piece in the suite, was one of a collection of Danses Norvégiennes. When the Norwegian Moods was performed in Lewisohn Stadium, New York, by Efrem Kurtz and the New York Philharmonic, July 1944, General de Gaulle attended the concert.

Stravinsky remarked on more than one occasion that the first movement of the Symphony in Three Movements was conceived as a piano concerto, yet none of the early sketches contains any piano part at all; the piano solo at $\boxed{39}$, for instance, was originally scored for bassoons, the piano part at $\boxed{76}$ for strings. The movement was composed sectionally, and in complete units, the first of which extended from $\boxed{71}$ through the second measure of $\boxed{80}$. Another section, with a B-flat-minor key signature, began at the upbeat to the measure before $\boxed{59}$ and continued to $\boxed{70}$. This was followed by a draft of the first part of the third movement (!) through the canon for bassoons. The next sections to be composed contained the music from $\boxed{34}$

to [56] and from [61] to [93], where, at [81], the piano makes its appearance for the first time. The beginning of the movement was written next and the end last, which explains the non-development of the opening figure, so puzzling to commentators.

One of the more fully scored sketches for measures 143–172 is marked "new, with piano," and since these same measures were completed in a five-stave score without piano in the June 15 draft of the movement, it can be established that Stravinsky did not decide on the piano obbligato role until he embarked on the full score (completed October 15). In fact, the first draft of the complete movement (from measure 1) still does not use the piano in the ostinato figure at [8].

The opening theme of the second movement did not occur to Stravinsky at the start, his first notation, dated February 15, 1943, being for the two-flute music at [119]. The sketches for this movement differ in many ways from the composition in final form. To mention only one of the changes, the flute solo between [125] and [127] was originally assigned to a horn. This movement was completed March 17, 1943, the third movement not until August 7, 1945.

In December 1940, when Stravinsky was in Minneapolis conducting Dimitri Mitropoulos's resident orchestra, and Mitropoulos was in New York conducting the Philharmonic, Mitropoulos sent a telegram welcoming Stravinsky in well-meant, if unusual, English:

It is too great an honor for me and my colleagues that the greatest living composer is going to collaborate with us. Please accept my limited admiration for your genius. [December 16]

Stravinsky's compositions of 1944 are varied in the extreme: he finished the *Scherzo à la Russe* and the Sonata for Two Pianos, wrote the short cantata *Babel*, the *Giselle*-inspired *Scènes de Ballets*, and the first two parts (Kyrie and Gloria) of the Mass. *Babel* was completed in sketch score on March 29, and in full score on April 12; the first performance took place in the

July 20, 1944. Hollywood Bowl. With Dimitri Mitropoulos, who had just rehearsed — played and conducted— Prokofiev's third piano concerto.

Wilshire Ebell Theater, Los Angeles, November 18, 1945, conducted by Werner Janssen. The "Gloria" of the Mass was completed December 20, the "Kyrie" either just before or just after that date. 1944 is also the accepted date of the *Elegy* for unaccompanied viola; in a letter of November 5, 1944, to Germain Prévost, who was to play the first performance—in the Coolidge Auditorium of the Library of Congress, January 26, 1945—Stravinsky refers to the music as having just been composed (*"le pièce p. alto que je viens de composer pour vous"*). But a graphological comparison with the sketches of *Danses Concertantes* would seem to indicate that the *Elegy* was written immediately after that work. Perhaps Stravinsky returned to the already completed opus when asked for a new one, as he returned to, and used, the "Dialogue Between Reason and Joy" in *Perséphone*.

After the *Elegy* premiere, Prévost wrote to Stravinsky, then in New York, thanking him for his "words from Thomas Aquinas," and saying that on February 7, at the home of some friends in New York, the Pro Arte would play Bartók's Fifth Quartet as "a surprise for its composer." Prévost also wished to play the *Elegy* for Bartók but wanted coaching from Stravinsky. This was duly given on the morning of the 7th,[56] but Stravinsky declined Prévost's invitation to attend the Bartók soirée.[57]

While in New York, Stravinsky gave an interview to a newspaper, *Pour la Victoire:*

... I have no "*manière*" in composition, and I do not try to obey any preconceived system. My esthetic resembles that of certain Latin classicists, and of . . . Pascal . . . I have a general idea before I compose, but ideas come to me only while I am composing, following each other, each one the logical consequence of its predecessor—though more than ideas, obviously, are needed to compose music. When I start to work, I am not certain *what* I am going to do but I know exactly what I *want* to do . . . The creative process is very complex. One must limit the portals of what is called "inspiration," which is popularly thought to be an onset of emotion that sets the creative imagination in motion. I disagree with this conception. Composition begins with an appetite, or taste, for discovery, and the emotion is born after the discovery, following rather than preceding the creative process . . .

Though I do not impose any system upon myself, I nevertheless submit to the strictest discipline, and it is this "submission" that brings me close to the spirit of classicism. Gide had defined the attitude: "*L'oeuvre classique n'est pas belle qu'en raison de son romantisme dompté.*" The elements which the imagination receives must be passed through a sieve . . . and, like the sounds of nature, become music only after they have been organized, or controlled. The more controlled the art, the more free. . . . And the composer must find unity in multiplicity, choose the reality of a limitation over the infinity of a division. [February 24, 1945]

Stravinsky's experiences in New York extended beyond theorizing about his art, as a story in the *Cincinnati Enquirer*, February 25, shows:

A recent remark by a New York bus driver is causing considerable mirth among musicians. Igor Stravinsky . . . had come . . . to appear as guest conductor of the Philharmonic Symphony. . . . One afternoon he had just tried to step off a bus and the door closed ahead of him. Calls back and forth got the door open again and at last Mr. Stravinsky stepped off onto the sidewalk. He was about to cross the street directly in front of the same bus when the light changed and the bus started off. Stravinsky stepped back, the bus stopped. Stravinsky started off again, and so did the bus. Brakes screeched and both stopped once more . . . The bus driver shook his head pityingly. Pointing to Stravinsky, he mumbled: "There's one born every minute."

The third movement of the Sonata for Two Pianos was composed in September 1943 (begun on the 9th), the first movement in October 1943, and the second movement in January and February 1944; the fugato variation is dated January 30, the end of the movement February 11. Copies were soon circulating, and, on March 19, Marcelle de Manziarly wrote to Stravinsky from New York saying that she and Harold Shapero will "play the piece for Balanchine next Tuesday." The first public performance, by Nadia Boulanger and Richard Johnston, took place at Edgewood College of the Dominican Sisters, Madison, Wisconsin, August 2, 1944. On July 28, Mlle Boulanger wrote to Stravinsky that she was preparing a Palestrina mass for the program with the new piece. One of the most distinguished early performances of the Sonata took place at Hamline University, April 1, 1946, when the pianists where Dimitri Mitropoulos and Ernst Křenek.

Like the Sonata, the *Scherzo à la Russe* was begun in 1943. The Second Trio, originally a wordless choral duet in A major, was titled and dated by Stravinsky "little chorus for children, discanti and alti, January 18, 1943." He later rewrote this as a four-voice instrumental piece in the same key. The First Trio, in B major, was composed next, also in four harmonic parts. Then Stravinsky rewrote the Second Trio, this time in C and with sixteenth-note figuration. Since the opening portion of the *Scherzo*, in its first form, was a piece for two pianos, the opus was actually made up of three separate numbers. Shortly before the premiere, which took place at 11:30 P.M., September 5, 1944,[58] on a Blue Network broadcast by Paul Whiteman, Stravinsky was asked for program material. He replied that his ideas had had no extra-musical association, but in fact the music was intended for a score to the film *North Star*. The commission from Whiteman came later, and the orchestration for Whiteman's band was made in 1944: 4 violins, 2 violas, 1 cello, 1 bass; piccolo, flute, oboe; 2 alto saxophones, 2 tenor saxophones, 1 baritone saxophone; 3 trumpets, 1 horn, 3 trombones, tuba; guitar, piano, harp, xylophone, timpani, bass drum, snare drum, tambourine. Stravinsky's contract with the Blue Network is dated July 13, 1944, and the score was given to Whiteman soon after that. It should be mentioned that Whiteman had offered a commission to Stravinsky almost twenty years earlier, in 1925, and that the composer had seriously considered accepting this because the band had an excellent cimbalomist.

Whiteman's broadcast did not reach the West Coast, but Stravinsky eventually heard the music in a recording made for him by Associated Music Publishers. In the meantime, David Diamond wrote from New York that he was enchanted with the piece, whereupon Stravinsky sent a note to Hugo Winter at AMP:

I conclude [from this] that [the *Scherzo*] was not too disfigured by the performance. [Letter of September 16]

The scoring for symphony orchestra was completed in May 1945, according to a letter from Stravinsky to Winter on the 31st of that month.

The *Scènes de Ballet* began with a telegram from Billy Rose to Stravinsky, June 8, 1944, inviting him to compose a ballet for a Broadway show to be called *The Lively Arts*. He asked for $15,000, which Rose refused, but, by June 16, Stravinsky had accepted $5,000, and, on that same day, devised the scenario in collaboration with Anton Dolin, who was to choreograph the ballet. This was called *L'Etoile*, at first, after Markova, its star, and the outline drawn up that morning—in the afternoon Stravinsky plotted another one, with Balanchine, for *Danses Concertantes*—is essentially the same as that of the final score:

L'ETOILE

Giselle p. 67	1. Ouverture	1 minute 40 sec.
see also p. 55–6	2. Corps de ballet lento, accel., lento	2½ to 3 min.
Giselle p. 65	3. Entrance of *l'Etoile* and her Variation (Like the entrance of Giselle)	40 sec.
Pas d'Action		
Coppélia p. 119 (Aurora)	4. Pantomime: he looks, she disappears, rejoining for the "Pas de Deux"	1 to 1½ min.
Swan Lake p. 131	5. Pas de Deux, adagio	3 to 3½ min.
Giselle	6. Variation (him)	40 sec.
	7. Variation (her)	40 sec.
Giselle p. 87	8. Corps de ballet	1½ to 2 min.
Giselle p. 90–91–92	9. Final	2 minutes

On June 27, Stravinsky wrote to Hugo Winter:

... Anton Dolin is coming to see you to discuss the scenario and the title. ... These are evidently his, as the author of the idea and its choreographic realization. ... There is no libretto in the literal sense of the word, but only some choreographic numbers bound together by a general literary and psychological idea. This ensemble of numbers will form a ballet of a romantic character with a title that will be Dolin's property. The point here is that we will want this title for my music without having to make any ridiculous pecuniary sacrifice. ...

L'Etoile, or *Scènes de Ballets,* inspired by *Giselle,* was written very rapidly, in spite of the composer's active social life throughout the summer of 1944, and of which the following entry from Mrs. Stravinsky's diary is typical:

June 27. We go to dinner at the Werfels'. The food is bad and Werfel has to go to bed, but Igor has become good friends with Alfred Hitchcock, and we stay until midnight.

On June 22, Stravinsky sketched the "Variation" at ⟦89⟧ and, on July 3, wrote the "Pantomime" at ⟦58⟧. By July 23, he had composed the music from ⟦40⟧ to ⟦42⟧, as well as the first dance for the corps de ballet (at ⟦5⟧); that same night he talked with Mitropoulos until 2:00 A.M. On August 6, Stravinsky wrote the second "Pantomime" (at ⟦103⟧), and, on the 11th, he played the score for Dolin and Markova. On the 23rd, the "Apotheosis" was completed in full score, and, on the 29th, the "Introduction." On September 12, under Stravinsky's supervision, Ingolf Dahl recorded his piano reduction of the score for the dancers to use during rehearsals, and, on September 16, Stravinsky sent the full and piano scores to New York.

Seven Lively Arts opened in the Forrest Theater, Philadelphia, November 24, 1944, and in the Ziegfeld Theater, New York, on December 7; since the show did not close until Saturday, May 12, 1945, *Scènes de Ballet,* or a part of it, was performed during twenty-five weeks. On November 30, Stravinsky received a telegram from Dolin:

Ballet great success stop . . . can the Pas de Deux be orchestrated with the strings carrying the melody this is most important to insure greater success. . . .

Stravinsky telegraphed "Satisfied great success."

In New York on December 5, Vittorio Rieti was invited to an orchestra rehearsal by Rose's musical director, Maurice Abravanel—who had conducted *Mahagonny* in Paris, and had met Stravinsky after one of the performances there. Rieti reported to Stravinsky that the players were capable, that the conductor knew the music, and that, in spite of all the cuts—the ⅝ music was too difficult—the piece did not sound mutilated. Abravanel had telephoned to Stravinsky on December 3 for permission to make cuts, though, from the full text of Dolin's telegram, it is clear that the ⅝ music had already been dropped before the first Philadelphia performance. Stravinsky's response was to demand that the piece be billed as "excerpts" from *Scènes de Ballet*. Then Rose called to say that the orchestra would have to be reduced to twenty-eight players—40 had been guaranteed by the contract—and Stravinsky refused, proposing a two-piano reduction as an alternative. Nevertheless, on January 6, 1945, the tuba, one trombone, and seven strings were eliminated. But a possibly even greater obstacle to appreciating the music than the cuts and the incomplete orchestra was—as Mercedes de Acosta telephoned to Stravinsky after the New York opening—that the piece was used as an overture to the second half of the show, and that people were walking down the aisles throughout.

When *Scènes de Ballet* was first performed in Paris, Arthur Honegger hailed it as

a ravishing catalogue of orchestral effects. . . . Even the comic is not absent, in a pompous cornet theme repeated by the full orchestra against a triplet accompaniment of the purest Meyerbeer. . . . Stravinsky is still in full possession of his powers. . . . [*La France*, December 27, 1945]

On June 24, 1946, Stravinsky, Balanchine, and Eugene Berman met to plan a new ballet with the music, but this project was not to be realized.

After completing the Symphony in Three Movements (in

1946. Adam in Eden (1260 North Wetherly Drive, Hollywood).

August 1945), Stravinsky composed the *Ebony Concerto*. This was the brain-child of Aaron Goldmark of Leeds Music Corporation, who suggested the piece both to Stravinsky and to Woody Herman, and who negotiated the commission. After a vulgar publicity story had appeared about the "collaboration," however, Stravinsky withdrew (September 24, 1945) until persuaded by his lawyer, Aaron Sapiro, that no offense had been intended. Finally, on October 24 he wrote to Woody Herman asking for "records and scores of your repertory, swing and jazz . . . ," but signed the letter "Beatrice Bolm." Music and recordings of "Caldonia," "Out of This World," "Laura," and four other pieces duly arrived, together with a letter from Herman's manager, Herman Goldfarb, informing the composer that Woody Herman

performs as soloist, usually reserving the saxophone for sweet melodious parts and the clarinet for jazz passages.

In a letter of November 4 to Nadia Boulanger, Stravinsky complained of being unfamiliar with the genre and of having difficulty with the unusual combinations of instruments (which at that time included an oboe), yet he sent the complete score of the first two movements to Herman on November 22, that of the third movement on December 10. (The second movement was composed between November 5 and 13, and, by the 19th, Stravinsky had composed as far as the glissandos in the third movement.) Walter Hendl, an assistant conductor of the New York Philharmonic, was chosen by Stravinsky to conduct the premiere (letter of February 11, 1946, from Goldfarb to Stravinsky in the Waldorf-Astoria Hotel), but it was the composer who first rehearsed the players, backstage at the Paramount Theater, New York, where they were appearing. Members of the advertising department of Columbia Records in Bridgeport, Connecticut, attended this three-hour session and, after it, concocted an "Appreciation of Woody Herman by Igor Stravinsky," which, on February 25, was read over the telephone to Stravinsky, then in Miami en route to Havana for concerts. Incredibly, Stravinsky approved this fatuous article, in which he is made to speak fulsomely about "Mr. Woody"—the players call Stravinsky "the professor," of course—and even to say that the Concerto was composed as a gift for the clarinetist.

The premiere took place in Carnegie Hall, March 25, led by Hendl. On the 29th, the music was broadcast on ABC, this time conducted by Alexei Haieff, who then toured with the Herman band, directing the piece in Baltimore, Boston, and other cities. On April 2, Marcelle de Manziarly wrote to Stravinsky from New York, describing the performances there (and giving her impressions of two visitors from Paris, Vercors and Camus). Stravinsky first conducted the Concerto in Hollywood on a "Columbia Workshop" national broadcast, August 18, and he recorded the opus the next day.[59]

The revised versions of the *Firebird* Suite and of the complete *Petrushka* also date from 1945–6. The stimulus for the former was a guarantee from the Ballet Theatre to give the new version thirty times; accordingly, in April 1945, Stravinsky prepared the so-called "third" *Firebird* Suite, working from the pirated Kalmus edition of the 1919 score for most of the music, and, for the reorchestrated added sections, using his copy of the complete ballet. The first performance, conducted by Jascha Horenstein, took place at the Metropolitan Opera House, October 24, 1945. But whereas the publisher Leeds had commissioned the new *Firebird*, Stravinsky undertook the new *Petrushka* to satisfy himself; he had been making notations for a revised edition since 1915, when Gabriel Pierné wrote to ask about the meters and subdivisions in the "Dance of the Wetnurses." The conductor Antal Dorati has described Stravinsky revising a passage in *Petrushka* in the 1930s:

... the emendations and new draftings made by Stravinsky are innumberable. Even after they were finished, [Stravinsky] made corrections in [his compositions] again and again, for decades. ... In 1933 or 1934 he visited me in my [Paris] hotel room to give me hints for a [performance of *Petrushka*]. When we came to [a certain] passage [Stravinsky said]: "Well, to be quite frank, the way it is written makes it rather difficult to get what I had in mind." Having said this, he sat down and ... proceeded to jot down some twenty versions until he seemed satisfied by the one in our illustration. [*Hungarian Book Review*, May-August 1972, which reproduces the manuscript of the revision that Stravinsky had given to Dorati]

With Alexei Haieff, Ingolf Dahl was Stravinsky's closest professional associate from the early 1940s to 1948. The older musician invited the younger one to lunch, October 23, 1942, and, in 1944, commissioned him to make the piano reduction of *Scènes de Ballet*. As a multi-lingual European, Dahl collaborated with Stravinsky in a number of interviews, including those in the *Musical Digest*, Hollywood, 1946, and in Mina Lederman's *Modern Music*, summer of 1946. The following excerpt is from the latter:

People always expect the wrong thing of me. They think they have pinned me down. Then all of a sudden—*au revoir*. ... It is not up to me to explain or to judge my music. That is not my role. I have to write it—that is all. ... I do not have any ultimate viewpoint of composition, and when I write my next symphony it will be an expression of my will at that moment. What this is going to be at that moment I do not know.

Stravinsky worked with Dahl in writing program notes (as is revealed in a letter from Stravinsky, December 8, 1945, to Bruno Zirato, manager of the New York Philharmonic) and entrusted the English translation of the *Poétique Musicale* to him (and to Arthur Knodel, a French scholar, who, like Dahl, taught at the University of Southern California). Dahl's knowledge of Stravinsky's music was complete and his love of it consuming. On more than one festive occasion, Stravinsky exchanged canonic greetings with him. At USC, Dahl gave a course in the music of Stravinsky that was one of the most popular and successful in the curriculum of the School of Music. Finally, Stravinsky chose him as the pianist for the first performance of *The Owl and the Pussy-Cat* (1966). Dahl died in Switzerland in the summer of 1970, not far from where Stravinsky was living at the time (on Lake Geneva).

Here Stravinsky is about to leave to rehearse for a concert in Town Hall, April 11, 1948, in which he conducted the *Symphonies of Wind Instruments* and *Danses Concertantes.* A few days after this event, Stark Young, novelist, drama critic, and friend of Stravinsky's for many years, wrote to him:

I am wondering—as happens to me very rarely in art—how these incredible patterns of form and tone appear to any soul, how can the wonder and beauty of what you say come to anyone like that . . . all the miracles of the ancient, barbaric, passionate world are there, and all the human heart is there. . . .

April 9, 1948. New York. In the Ambassador Hotel.

On April 28, 1948, at the New York City Center, Stravinsky conducted the first performance of his ballet *Orpheus*, commissioned by Lincoln Kirstein on May 7, 1946, but postponed until the completion of the "Basler" Concerto. The *Orpheus* sketches, the last in which Stravinsky uses the Russian language to any extent, contain few dates, but reveal that his first notation, October 20, 1946, was for the wind chords at 2 ; that by April 5, 1947, he had started the "Dance of the Angel of Death" (28); that by May 10, he had sketched the "Pas d'Action" (through 98) as well as the music at 112 . On May 25, Kirstein was still looking for a theater, and Stravinsky telegraphed to him that forty-three players were required. The second "Interlude" was completed July 8. On the 18th, Stravinsky wrote to Kirstein:

I am absorbed by *Orpheus* and hope to finish it by the beginning of September. . . . Badly need to get in touch with Pavlik [Tchelichev]. What is his Arizona address?

Kirstein replied on July 22 expressing the fear that Tchelichev's work might be wholly unrelated to the spirit of the music, and enclosing a typescript of Yvor Winter's *Orpheus* "in memory of Hart Crane." On October 16, acknowledging the receipt of the completed score, Kirstein confirmed that Tchelichev would not do the decors. Esteban Frances [60] was then considered, Stravinsky having been delighted with his costumes for Balanchine's 1946 *Renard*. Isamu Noguchi was the next, and final, choice.

The *Orpheus* production being costly, Stravinsky reduced his conducting fee,[61] and even Balanchine became a sponsor:

When *Orpheus* was in rehearsal in 1948, it was discovered at the last moment that a billowing white silk curtain had to be paid for in cash— $1,000 worth—which nobody could procure that quickly. Between rehearsals, Balanchine disappeared. When he showed up again in two hours, he had the money in bills, and the only explanation he ever offered was "I did not steal it." [Emily Coleman, *New York Times,* December 1, 1957]

Orpheus was a great success. Stravinsky acknowledged the applause from the stage—not, however, as reported in *Time* (May 10), which provoked a letter from Kirstein that is worth quoting since it accurately portrays a part of Stravinsky's stage manners at almost every concert in his life:

In describing Igor Stravinsky at the triumphant premiere of his new ballet *Orpheus* . . . you say that the greatest living composer of ballet scores "took his bows on stage with the dancers, his feet crossed in his best Position III." Mr. Stravinsky, who has been writing ballets since 1909 . . . knows very well the logical anatomical basis of the Five Absolute Positions. In the Third Position (the heel of one foot locked against the instep of the other, weight equally distributed, with completed turnout), Mr. Stravinsky would have found it awkward to execute the traditional stage bow derived from the Imperial Russian Theater. He took it in Fourth Position—with weight equally divided, the forefoot twelve inches in advance of the back.[62] [*Time*, May 31, 1948]

In October 1949, in response to a request from Allan Kayes of RCA Victor to promote Stravinsky's newly released *Orpheus*, the composer recorded a talk about the piece. Kayes had sent six questions, which Stravinsky answered in English—a measure of the change in his life in one year, for the original libretto, in his hand, is in Russian (except for one episode, written in French, on the Chicago–Los Angeles train "The Chief"). The talk was broadcast on WQXR, New York, November 1, 1949, at 10:05 P.M.:

Three years ago, in 1946, Lincoln Kirstein . . . president of Ballet Society, asked me to compose a ballet for his company. The artistic director of this company, George Balanchine . . . suggested the . . . legend of Orpheus. I had worked with Balanchine many times before and was very glad to have him again as choreographer for a new ballet. [Also] the Greek myths always attracted me . . . they feed the creative imagination. . . .

The original staging of *Apollo* by George Balanchine was very beautiful and his subsequent stagings in New York and Buenos Aires were even more impressive. . . . The elements of melancholy, of love, and of mystery in the Orpheus tragedy [have] always fascinated me. Orpheus, the demi-god, a son of Apollo and the Muse, Calliope, introduced the arts and civilized life among the savage peoples. [Orpheus] was a poet and a prophet, also learned in medicine and in the history of the heavens. Orpheus, by the power of song, tamed savage beasts, made the trees follow him, and awakened inanimate nature into life and rapture. He played so divinely on the lyre that all nature stopped to listen to his music. When his wife Eurydice died, he [sought] her in Hades, [where] the strains of his lyre softened even the stern gods of the dead. Eurydice was released and followed him to the upper world.
    I did not use the whole story of Orpheus. . . . When Balanchine spent the summer of 1946 in Hollywood, we settled the main lines of the legend, and decided . . . the exact duration of each movement. . . .
    I begin [at] the moment when Orpheus weeps for Eurydice, his beloved wife, who has died of a serpent bite. His friends bring him gifts and offer him expressions of sympathy, but he is overwhelmed with grief, he is inconsolable. He . . . plays upon his lyre, and his sorrowful

song attracts the Angel of Death, who pities him . . . comforts him, and promises to take him . . . to Hades, the abode of the dead, in search of Eurydice, in the hope that he may find her and bring her back to Earth-Life. And the dark Angel of Death leads Orpheus through the obscuring mist of the between-worlds to Hades. There the Furies [try] to frighten him. Threatening and agitated, they dance crazily about him. But the Lost Souls, chained and bent under their heavy burdens, implore Orpheus to play to them. He [plays] his lyre [and his] magic music calms the Furies, charms into sleep the Lost Souls, and penetrates even the walls of the hidden sanctum of Hades' ruler, Pluto, [who] also is moved by Orpheus' song and [who] restores Eurydice to Orpheus.

Eurydice appears, the Furies join the lovers' hands and bind Orpheus' eyes, for . . . he may neither look back nor upon her during their return to Earth. Eurydice follows the blindfolded Orpheus through the shades of the between-worlds. Although he must not look upon her, she pleads with him, caressing and cajoling him. No longer able to withstand his longing for her, Orpheus tears the bandage from his eyes [whereupon] Eurydice . . . slips from his arms and falls dead at his feet. Orpheus looks everywhere for his vanished Eurydice. He is alone; everything has been taken from him; he has not even the solace of his lyre and is restored to Earth without it. . . . Lost in his immeasurable grief, he scorns the Bacchantes, the jealous Thracian women, and in a frenzy they tear him to pieces. Orpheus is no more, but his song lives. Apollo appears radiant in sunlight, the god raises the lyre of Orpheus, lifting his deathless song to the eternal sky.

One of the few accurate descriptions of the composer in the home in which he lived longer than in any other is Nicolas Nabokov's account of four days there in December 1947:

It was a little past noon on December 22 when Balanchine's wife Maria [Tallchief] [63] stopped the car on an incline of winding North Wetherly Drive. On our right a low white picket fence was overtopped by a wall of tall evergreen shrubbery.[64] Some two hundred and fifty feet behind . . . stood a small and flat one-story house, rimmed by a narrow porch in front and a large terrace. . . .

From behind the shrubbery we heard hasty footsteps and Russian voices. A minute later both Stravinskys appeared at a small gate near the garage. They were dressed in breakfast clothes—she in an impeccably white negligee,[65] which made her look large and stately, he in a polka-dotted burgundy bathrobe, with the striking addition of a narrow-brimmed, wilted, black felt hat. . . .

"Give this to me," said Stravinsky, picking up my bag. "Heavens, what is in it . . . ?"

"It's only music," I replied, "and a couple of bottles."

"You brought my scores," said Stravinsky. "Good for you. Only . . . I don't need them any more. I mean the Handel operas. I found most of them here.. . . ."

"Go to your right, through the living room," said Vera Arturovna as we reached the small entrance hall of the house. I crossed a spacious, sunny room filled with spring flowers, modern pictures, light-colored furniture, and several bird cages, and entered a smaller room, lined on two sides with bookcases. Across the room, turning its back to the terrace window, stood the sofa.

Vera Arturovna ordered me to take off my shoes. "The first thing we do is to measure the prospective sleepers."

"Here they are, all of them," said Stravinsky, and he pointed to ... marks and signatures written in pencil on different levels of the door frame. "See, this is tiny Mrs. Bolm. She was the smallest of them all. And this is Olson,[66] the tallest.". . .

"Come here [said Stravinsky]. Stretch out on the sofa. You see," he turned to George Balanchine, "he fits perfectly: from socks to hair. Like a violin in its case.". . .

After lunch . . . Vera Arturovna introduced me to the lesser . . . members of the household. "Here is Popka," she said, taking a small gray parrot out of a cage and seating him on her husband's shoulder. "He is two years old. . . . He usually eats with us at the table when we are alone." [67] . . . Besides the parrot, the feathered household consists of a . . . canary, whose name is Lyssaya Dushka (Bald Darling), . . . and a flock of about eight lovebirds.[68] . . .

Dushka's and Popka's cages stand in the living room, each near a window. Opposite a large white mantelpiece, as if to tease them, hang several engravings of falcons, eagles, and other birds of prey with large protruding beaks. . . .

She turned away from the [cages] and pointed at a big black cat stretched out in the sun. "And this is our only quadruped—Vasska.[69] His full name is Vassily Vassilievich Lechkin. . . . When I used to run a picture gallery, I always sent him a printed invitation and wrote on it: 'Please do come—fishbones, cocktails.'. . ."

A soft, narrow couch . . . stood behind the piano in [Stravinsky's] study. On one end of its dark silk surface lay a neatly folded plaid rug, and on the other a dainty little pillow. . . . Stravinsky's love for clear terms, for laconic definitions and adequate translation, manifests itself in his enthusiasm for dictionaries, with which his study is filled. Of all of them he prefers the Grand Larousse. . . . His own remarks generally have a Laroussian precision as well as wit and imagination. . . . But particularly sharp and picturesque are his remarks about people. An over-emotional conductor . . . reminds him of a . . ."belly dance seen from behind.". . . His workroom is another example of the precision which orders his music and his language. . . . In a space which is not larger than some twenty-five by forty feet [70] stand two pianos (one grand, one upright) and two desks (a small, elegant writing desk and a draftsman's table). In two cupboards . . . are books, scores, and sheet music, arranged in alphabetical order. Between the two pianos, the cupboards and desks, are scattered a few small tables (one of which is a kind of "smoker's delight": it exhibits all sorts of cigarette boxes, lighters, holders, fluids, flints, and pipe cleaners), . . . chairs, and the couch Stravinsky uses for his afternoon naps. (I saw him on it the next day, lying on his back, with an expression of contained anger on his face, snoring gently and methodically.)

Besides the pianos and the furniture there are hundreds of gadgets, photographs, trinkets, and implements of every kind in and on the desks and tables and tacked on the back of the cupboards. [Stravinsky's] study [has] all the instruments needed for writing, copying, drawing, pasting, cutting, clipping, filing, sharpening, and gluing that the combined efforts of a stationery and hardware store can furnish (and yet he is always after new ones). A touch of nature in the midst of all this . . . is provided by a bunch of fresh roses in a white china vase which stands on his desk. His wife cuts them for him every morning from his special rosebushes. . . .

Vera Arturovna appeared in the entrance [71] to the study and announced that the Balanchines had arrived. "George and Maria are here," she said, "and Genia Berman is waiting for us with vodka and *zakousska*. It is time to go, Igor. Come, Nika."

"*Seytchas, seytchas,*" answered Stravinsky. . . .

Half an hour later we were driving down to Eugene Berman's apartment. On the front seat of the car, squeezed in between Vera Arturovna and myself, was Stravinsky's tiny figure, dressed in a pea jacket and a yachtsman's hat. (He bought the pea jacket at a navy surplus sale and is proud and fond of it.) . . .

We entered the hall of Berman's apartment house and went to the desk. Vera Arturovna announced our arrival. The telephone operator, an elderly lady with glasses, looked at Stravinsky and, recognizing him in his nautical apparel, said, "Aren't you the author of . . . *Firebird?*". . . He smiled charmingly and answered, "Yes, madam, *Firebird* is a bird of mine."

The dinner at the Napoli was gay and happy. . . . Stravinsky was in wonderful form—voluble, witty, and at the same time extremely attentive to all of us. As usual, he ordered the best food and, especially, the best wines. . . .

[Back at his house] I looked around for books and found a few rare Russian editions on a shelf that contained a pell-mell assortment of French novels, Russian classics, murder stories, and biographies. There were no books on music except Mozart's *Letters*. Among the books were the epigrammatic works of . . . Rozanov (whom I knew Stravinsky liked very much and whose works he rereads and quotes constantly, comparing Rozanov's ideas and style to Gogol's and Dostoevsky's). . . . [Nicolas Nabokov, *Old Friends and New Music* (Boston: Little, Brown, 1951)]

Here are some further views of Stravinsky in his Hollywood home, from the diary of the present writer:

July 1, 1949. Stravinsky does not have "perfect pitch," which is to say that he cannot, out of the clear, distinguish G from F-sharp (for example). If his record player happened to render the *Jupiter* Symphony in B instead of C, he would complain about a slower tempo but probably not about the key.

Stravinsky cannot whistle, and, except while composing, he rarely sings, though when he does, it is in a one-syllable ("ta-ta-ta") *solfeggio*, far from the actual notes. Apart from his work-in-progress on *The Rake,*

March 22, 1949. Drawing by Stravinsky after a visit to Palm Springs in March 1949, in a letter to Robert Craft.

the only tune I have heard him carry this summer is *"und der Haifisch"* from the *Dreigroschenoper,* which he "sang" not for the music but for the words.

When Stravinsky composes, he must be alone, even closing the windows of his studio as if to seal himself in, and, when emerging, is either silent or grumpy. But when orchestrating he likes companionship, often asking me to read to him, though interrupting from time to time to say "just a moment" (i.e., "be quiet"), then, a moment later, "and?" When V.A.S. did not feel well and remained in bed one afternoon last week, he brought a table from his studio to her bedside and orchestrated there—ostensibly to keep her company, but he was the one who did not want to be alone.

Stravinsky talks constantly about rules in art and the necessity of obeying them. Every element of musical composition has its rules, he will say, and he means textbook rules, those that have been deduced and formulated from the works of the masters. Yet his own rules are those of thumb.

Stravinsky has a passion for copying music and has actually duplicated entire scores of his own music as well as of other people's, especially when he wishes to learn the music thoroughly.[72] This is a hobby and a relaxation, he says, but it is also the exercise of his talents as a calligrapher.

July 2, 1949. Stravinsky seems to have almost total recall of his intensely active, creative, and usually technicolor dreams, which form the subject of most breakfast conversations. As Sir Thomas Browne wrote, "And the slumber of the body seems to be but the working of the soul." In Stravinsky's case, the origins of many of his compositions have been in dreams, as well as the solutions of musical problems.

Beneath Stravinsky's intellect lurks an athlete, all muscle and bone, and the man is a constant reminder of one's own indolence and sloth. Ordinarily my first view of him each morning, on the porch adjoining his studio, is face-to-feet, and he will hold this inverted position, head on a straw mat, bandy legs skyward, for as long as ten minutes, then execute a manual of toe-touching, torso-twisting, knee-bending exercises, concluding with a dozen "chins" on a crossbar in his bedroom closet.[73] Not until he wraps himself in his white terry-cloth robe and sets off for the shower am I reminded of how completely this particular athlete is lacking in brawn.

No one is allowed to disturb the sacred rites of Stravinsky's afternoon tea. This is never served in a cup but only in a glass with a metal holder, *podstakanniky* (under the glass). Also, the tea must be very hot and very weak ("In St. Petersburg, we could see Kronstadt through our tea"), and pumpernickel or black bread, cakes, and jams should be served with it. Stravinsky then plays a game of solitaire (two, if he loses the first), eats some of the bread but does not drink the tea until just before rising to leave, by which time, as he says, it is "lukey warm."

July 4, 1949. Though professing to loathe parties, when actually attending one Stravinsky becomes its voluble epicenter. (V.A.S. recalls that in their first years in Hollywood they would return from movie stars' parties and read Dostoevsky together, "to remind ourselves about human beings.") We go to a poolside party for Stravinsky, but the guest of honor keeps well away from water, and not only externally.

Stravinsky uses English translations of the Russian gender pronouns instead of the English articles. After swatting a fly, for example, he will refer to the corpse as "she." But the idiosyncrasies of his English are not always traceable to Russian constructions. "I finded it," he will say, "later one" (for later "on"), "close the towel" (for "fold"), "rape" ("rapez") the cheese, and "please pass the language" (for "tongue"). Also, conductors and critics are uncompetent, though sometimes a review is "eulogious."

When speaking Russian, Stravinsky is by no means shy of the earthy and indelicate.[74] His customary skeptical response to all ribald gossip, a result, perhaps, of his early legal training, is *"Kto dirzhal ich za nogee?"* ("Who was holding their legs?") Among his workaday critical expressions are *"oo meenya nee sty-eet"* ("It doesn't give me an erection"), *"hooey golandsky"* ("Dutch penis," this in reference to someone of exceptional *mental* density), and *"mandeet"* [75] which is not found in any Russian dictionary. He also uses a portmanteau word, *"podmivatsa,"* which means to wash one's private parts. A few days ago he told an uncomprehending wine steward who had served a corky Chablis to "pour it into a bidet and *podmivatsa."* Among the favorite words classified by his Russian friends as Stravinskyisms is *"krivo- sachka,"* this being used to refer to "a woman who cannot piss straight, but in a curve." Always graphic, he illustrates her difficulty with pencil and paper, drawing a *"primaya liniya"* (————) and a *"krivaya li- niya"* (⌒⌒).

He is especially devoted to the word "drag," which he learned in Purcell, both in rehearsing an orchestra and in his business correspondence: "Don't drag, please." According to V.A.S., he has a substantial Ukrainian vocabulary, though all that I have learned of it (apart from words like "hospodar," which are in the English dictionary) is *"ne vihiliates,"* the laconic direction in railway cars that Stravinsky likes to contrast to the German version: *"Das Hinauslehnen des Oberkörpers aus dem Fenster ist wegen der damit verbundenen Lebensgefahr strengstens verboten."* German usages are frequent targets of his ridicule, though at the same time many of his favorite words and sayings are in that language—*"plopper"* (for someone who talks too much and to no purpose), *"Eingeschachtelt"* (and he always shows the exact shape and size with his hands), *"feine Gesellschaft," "mit langen Zäh- nen,"* and Wilhelm Busch's *"Erstens ist es anders, zweitens als man denkt."* [76] Not surprisingly, Stravinsky's English is as polyglot as *Fin- negans Wake,* from the morning's first *"so-so la-la"* (one of his standard responses to "How do you feel?") to the last comment of the evening on the performance of a piece of music: *"grosso modo."*

Stravinsky is addicted to inter-language puns, especially to those involving words that are proper in one tongue but improper (*"unan- ständig,"* he says) in another; yet V.A.S. says he is an inveterate punster in Russian as well. (The tendency to play with words as things in themselves—and thus to diminish their primary value as sign functions—is said to be a withdrawal-from-reality symptom, but in Stravin- sky's case no other behavior corroborates the diagnosis.) At the moment he is interested in homophones, such as "puny" and "puisne," but especially those with diametrically opposite meanings, like "raise" and "raze." A sizable part of his conversation is concerned with language, at any rate, and his pursuit of English equivalents for Russian, German, and French idioms can interrupt a meal or conversation for a quarter of an hour while he disappears among the dictionaries in his den, obliging us to await his findings. He is also very fond of declensions and can be started on them by accidents such as my use at lunch yesterday of "enthusiasm," which is the same word in Russian. *"En- thusiasmum* is the accusative, *enthusiasma* is the dative, *enthusiasmu* is . . . ," *et cetera.*

July 9, 1949. The household routine is shattered by the discovery that Popka is female. This morning, finding an egg in the parakeet's nest (a wine cradle in the kitchen closet), Yvgenia Petrovna [77] keeled over and had to be given a whiff of smelling salts. Popka is the most pampered of Stravinsky's feathered pets, and though sometimes caged or held in jesses, the bird more often has the run of the house, including the dinner table, trampling on the food, eating and excreting, tracking butter on the linen, until Stravinsky extends a forefinger, orders the bird to perch there, and lifts it to his shoulder.

Stravinsky abhors clumsiness in any form, one of the reasons, no doubt, why he loves cats and goes into conniptions when people drop, spill, stumble. He is prejudiced against anyone with a loud voice, too—among them the Reverend James McLane, of whom he is otherwise very fond—and V.A.S. attributes some of the perfect harmony of their marriage to her very quiet one.

All noise is painful to Stravinsky. He will jump out of his chair if Yvgenia Petrovna drops a spoon, and even the most distant bombination of a hammer or drill drives him "mad." Moreover, he notices noises heard by no one else, having an especially keen ear for discrepancies, from one block to the next, in the engine of his wife's automobile. Reynaldo Hahn was the first to write about, if not to observe, this hypersensitivity: "Théophile Gautier said, 'I am a man for whom the exterior world exists.' Stravinsky could say, 'I am a man for whom the sonorous world exists.' No resonance, no perceptible vibration, escapes his attention, a plate striking against the table, a cane rubbing against a chair, the rustling of cloth, the grating of a door, the sound of a step—his infallible ear perceives them all, analyzes them with a marvelous certainty, and draws from each sound a new instrumental idea." [*Journal de l'Université des Annales*, Paris, January 14, 1914]

August 8, 1949. Stravinsky is obsessed with mirrors, not, I think, out of any metaphysical wish to go through the looking glass (although, like Alice, it could be a question of "I'm never quite sure what I'm going to be, from one minute to another"), but simply to assure himself, constantly and from all angles, that everything is in place. (Curiously, he does not recognize his voice on a record, as he mentioned in a recent interview: [78] "Why is this? I have asked many engineers. No one can explain it.") He is interested in mirror-writing, too—that sign of neurological impairment at certain tender ages, and of unusual intelligence at others. Still another of his obsessions is with scissors, apparently because, like many nearly bald men, he is forever trimming his remnants of "haars"—a form of the plural that he insists should be admitted in cases such as his. Many other utensils fascinate him also. Dentists' tools, for example. And hardware stores are magnetic lures whose spell can be broken only by the purchase of a bag of nails, a shiny new monkey wrench, or an implement for his gardening or carpentering. One of his hobbies is making picture frames, for which he has had a diamond glass-cutter built to his specifications.

Stravinsky collects small ivory, metal, leather, wood, papier-mâché boxes,[79] of which he has no fewer than forty, and the contents of which he alone remembers. Inordinately, even fetishistically, fond of the smell of leather, he will hold a wallet, pouch, or tefillin to his nose as others would sniff a carnation. Otherwise, his favorite smells are of coffee—especially the aroma when a tin of it has been newly opened—and tobacco. He rolls his own cigarettes, partly because the handwork appeals to him (he also likes to wrap packages), but mainly for the olfactory gratification.

Stravinsky perfectly fits Freud's description of the anal personality: the cataloguing; the thrift; the accumulating, hoarding (he picks up every piece of string and saves it), retaining; the exactness, tidiness, and neatness, for he cannot resist wiping the ring left on a table by the glass of a guest or dinner companion; the possessiveness, which extends to people (he demands absolute fealty from his friends and total subservience from servants); the exaggerated fears—of funerals, of illnesses (he will leave a room in which someone has coughed or sneezed), of being without money, of intestinal irregularities (especially oppilations). As for the last, the sheer volume of his talk about *govno* is impressive. This Russian word, which also means "black," is more literally suitable than the French, German, and English ones because of the charcoal that he munches before drinking champagne, as an anti-flatulent—and it should be added that he talks about "breaking wind," or "crepitation," as frequently as Mozart does in his letters. No breakfast or lunch passes without reference to his *"poire"* (syringe), while three times this summer he has described an auto-coprophagous experiment in his childhood. (It was *"sans goût."*) It might also be concluded by anyone who happened to see Stravinsky's surprisingly large collection of photographs of himself in the nude that he is exhibitionistic. Certainly he likes sunbathing and is proud of his muscles, but, at the same time, he does not bother to cover himself, or to wear a bathing suit—which he does not have, in any case, since he cannot swim.

Stravinsky's sexual utopia is mammary, his sexual type the opulent Rubens goddess (the uberous bosoms, that is; the mesial features of the back do not excite him). The psychogenesis of the attraction might well have been an insufficiency on the part of his wetnurse, but it is not an undifferentiated desire (any port in a storm) nor even a "desire" at all, perhaps, but a fixation. Inspired by a robusty woman at a neighboring table in a restaurant, he will wean himself from the view just long enough to sketch the "heaving embonpoint" on the tablecloth. And whereas his portraits of Picasso and others are characterized by radical abbreviation, these forms are fully filled (*formosa*) and complete with areolas. Nor is it any use to tell him that if you've seen one you've seen them both.

Stravinsky is vain to the point that he will not go out to dinner because of a pimple on his nose. And he is a dandy, a collector of silk scarves, handkerchiefs, pajamas, cravats. He will spend as much as ten minutes in selecting the proper neckwear; V.A.S. recalls that at the Princesse de Polignac's, after the premiere of Falla's *Retablo*, Stravinsky and the Spanish composer were observed conversing animatedly in a corner, not about Falla's new opus, as she later learned, but about his necktie. ("Nothing is unimportant about a great man," Schoenberg wrote, adding that he would like to have watched Mahler tying a necktie.) Before going out to dinner tonight, Stravinsky says, "I'll wear a sincere tie."

September 1, 1949. Stravinsky would be happy going to the cinema every day, and the worse the film—bad Westerns preferred—the more he seems to enjoy it. "Good" cinema, on the other hand—socially significant drama, Method Acting—generally annoys him. In these three months with him I have seen more films than in the previous three years.

V.A.S. tells a story that reveals an aspect of Stravinsky's character. It seems that Cocteau's *Les Enfants Terribles* provoked a wave of shop-lifting in Paris. In fact she tried it herself, pocketing a magnet while accompanying Stravinsky in a hardware store, but when she told him, he stalked out in anger without making his own purchase. At home she discovered that the stolen article was not magnetized, and he maintained that this retributive justice was divinely inspired.

September 2, 1949. Before we drive to San Diego today, Stravinsky obliges us to sit for a minute in silence, as Arabs do before traveling, then to stand while he makes the sign of the cross. This *"prisyest"* is to ensure our safe return, a Russian superstition, like throwing spilt salt over one's left shoulder, or dabbing one's fingers in spilt wine (or mopping it with bread, like intinction), and then touching behind the ear with them, which the Stravs never fail to do.

September 4, 1949. Tijuana. We join Eugene Berman and Ona Munson for the *corrida.* The squalor, dust, and stench are revolting, yet Stravinsky, usually super-squeamish about the cleanliness of cutlery, plates, drinking glasses, does not scruple to eat a tortilla that has been bare-handled by the vendor. Our seats being on the sunny side of the ring, Stravinsky makes a sombrero from a newspaper, a work of art, no matter how unfashionable as a hat.

Stravinsky seems to regard himself as an aficionado, though what he actually likes about bullfighting is the pageantry—the parade of the matadors and their *cuadrillas*—and, for a wonder, the noise: the shouts, boos, catcalls, fanfares, blaring brass band. He watches transfixed as the bull charges into the ring, and shouts "bravo" when the animal vaults a barrera and scatters the hecklers in the front row. But during a crisis, when the crowd leaps to its feet, Stravinsky cringes and cannot bring himself to look. And he is plainly horrified when a picador's nag is gored, spilling steaming entrails; when a muleta misses its mark and blood expulses from the wound like water from a hand pump; and when a team of mangy plough horses drags each carcass out of the arena while workers in overalls sprinkle sand over the sticky ground as matter-of-factly as if the ring were a stockyard and the sacred *taurobolai* a purely commercial transaction. Then, for a moment anyway, he would make over his estate to the SPCA.

On our return to the United States, an Immigration Officer asks Stravinsky where he was born. "St. Petersburg," he says, hoping to pass as a Floridian, but his accent leads to further questions and eventually to "Russia." Ordered to "pull over," he is subjected to a barrage of inane questions ("What was your grandmother's middle name?" as he retells it), which infuriates me because he suffers from the refugee's abiding fear of border police and customs inspectors. During World War II he felt humiliated because he was required to carry "Alien Registration Receipt Card No. 5893409," and back in Hollywood he complains bitterly of being a "second-class citizen."

The house sits well back from the winding road by which it is reached, and it was on the flagstones that we encountered Mrs. Stravinsky . . . She retraced her steps, for fear that her husband, busy in his soundproof studio, might not hear the doorbell. She led the way : . . to the drawing room, and, opening the studio door, said, *"Igor, il y a quelqu'un pour vous voir."* The room was long with windows looking on the gardens in front of and behind the house . . . There were satin-wood tables and a writing desk, pictures and mirrors, a comfortable divan, and objets d'art . . . Mr. Stravinsky shook hands cordially . . . pointed to the divan, pulled up a chair and sat facing us. He offered us cigarettes from a box on the table and lighted one for himself. "Do you agree that writing music is a spiritual process?," we asked. "No, it is a vocation." [*Opera*, San Francisco, October 1946]

Vera Stravinsky is the most naturally aristocratic person on earth. From the time I was able to see, during the time children see adults and find them all phony and creepy, Vera always remained outside that circle of judgment, because Vera's innocence is so charming and so purely about life that you have to have been there, you have to have heard her laugh, you have to have seen her roomful of flowers and her purple satin capes made in Rome lined with iridescent taffeta to know that it is possible. . . . Stravinsky was tiny and happy and brilliant and drank. He used to slip glasses of Scotch to me underneath the coffee table, when my mother wasn't looking, when I was 13. At my sixteenth birthday party, I wore white (very low-necked, of course) and he slipped rose petals down my top when my mother wasn't looking.
. . . For Christmas one year my sister and I gave him an ant farm but, alas, he told us, all the ants died. He collected insects in glass cases, beautiful ones. . . . (From *Eve's Hollywood*, by Eve Babitz [New York: Delacorte, 1972])

Stravinsky first met Aldous Huxley through Victoria Ocampo [80] in 1925. A decade later, she wrote to the composer, from Buenos Aires:

Aldous Huxley has written some pages on "The Case for Constructive Peace" that are truly admirable. I am so enthusiastic that I cabled to

July 17, 1949. On the terrace at 1260 North Wetherly Drive. Photograph by John Kuypers.

him. I would like you to read this. In addition to everything that I expect from him, there is something that is new and somewhat surprising. It is that he has humanized himself and that the quality of this humanity is precious, magnificent and rare. All that had been missing from him (in my view) I have rediscovered. This so pleased me that I wrote "*Joie, joie, pleurs de joie*" (Pascal). When I love something, I want to love it completely . . . Most affectionate thoughts to Vera. [June 24, 1936]

In the late 1940s and 1950s, the Stravinskys and the Huxleys lunched together two or three times a week at Jolanda's, in Hollywood's Town and Country Market. At this time, the Stravinskys considered the Huxleys to be their closest friends in California. On December 3, 1946, Maria Huxley wrote to her son Matthew:

Today we had a most delightful dinner with the Stravinskys. . . . I must say it was delightful to listen to Stravinsky. He pours out—what pours out is very intelligent—it is often very new—sometimes quite difficult to explain but always immensely worth listening to, and the French, not perfect, is intelligent and colorful. There were also books, and reproductions, and everything. A vegetarian dinner for Aldous, just right, simple, good. She is so easy and very nice. . . . The house is nice, easy, straggling, full of things. . . . Stravinsky is so extremely polite, I suppose the old school of politeness but quite all right and unnoticeable at the same time. Then suddenly, at ten, they asked us if we wanted some champagne. It startled me so much. Of course I said no. So did Aldous, but when they opened it all the same, we had it, and it was such a symbolic thing somehow. We quite easily and unostentatiously drank each other's health, but I felt it was a gracious act of hospitality and also a gesture of particular friendship. I believe they have a real friendship for us. We like them very much. . . .

Two weeks later Mrs. Huxley again wrote to her son:

Stravinsky has been curiously kind and considerate to me, gone out of his way to be kind about nothing in particular as if he had a second sight about my despair.

Mrs. Huxley's niece, Claire Nicolas, visited the Stravinskys in 1947 and published a description of the experience:

The Stravinskys are epicureans and collectors. One is immediately shown Madame Stravinsky's collection of shells, Mr. Stravinsky's collection of driftwood. "This is a Rodin," Stravinsky will say, twinkling maliciously and pointing to the most shapeless piece of wood in the collection. . . . At any moment Stravinsky is likely suddenly to perform his gymnastic exercises, "a special mixture of Swedish and German techniques," he explains seriously. Sometimes he invites people to walk on his stomach to test the effectiveness of the technique. In the evening he plays a . . . very complicated version of Chinese checkers. . . .
    When Stravinsky speaks, one is struck by the precision of his words and ideas. His conversation often takes the form of parables. He quibbles over exact meanings and frequently refers to the dictionary. There is great conviction, almost stubbornness in the way he argues. . . .
    Music critics, he says, are as bad in America as anywhere else,

August 1949. With Aldous and Maria Huxley at the Town and Country Market.

although he concedes Virgil Thomson a superior place to his colleagues because "Thomson is the only critic clever enough always to avoid discussing music. . . ." [*Junior Bazaar,* May 1947]

Miss Nicolas's article provoked a fuss, which is only worth mentioning because Huxley, writing about it to his son, June 17, 1947, mentions an aspect of Stravinsky's character that no one else had noticed, at least in print:

We have just seen Stravinsky, who tells us that he has received a letter from Claire telling him that you had told her that he didn't like her article. You shouldn't have made remarks about Stravinsky in a quarter from which they might easily be returned to him. We did our best to soothe Stravinsky's obviously ruffled feelings, but the net result was that he probably won't be too cordial when he sees you again, as he seems to have something of the elephant's memory for real or fancied slights.

A letter from Maria Huxley to her son, May 13, 1951, offers still another glimpse of the Stravinskys:

Vera Stravinsky rang up . . . they could not bear going to another cinema, could they visit us? So I said yes, the programme would be good but not the refreshments, and they came at 9. We are very fond of them. Stravinsky still looks like Father and is very sweet really. Always the same programme. Stravinsky, Bob Craft—almost an adopted son of theirs, 26 and very clever, knows everything, terribly nervous and not a pansy—and Aldous stay in the music room and Vera and I stay somewhere else. . . . They play music and we chat. . . . Stravinsky arrived in an enchanting costume . . . narrow effect in little blue jeans, and a blue jean zipper jacket open on a deep red wine jersey and silk scarf with pin. He looked enchanting and was really pleased with himself. I must not forget the always white socks and sandals. I do not know what he makes me think of, a voltigeur in the circus, a leprechaun with the little elegant legs, or what? A cyclist? And Aldous will turn the heat off when I am gone and poor little Stravinsky shivers and dares not ask and Aldous notices nothing. So finally he came to sit on my bed, and Vera inside the open window in a décolleté dress under a lace shawl and velvet bows in her hair looked immense next to the little shivering elfish man. I am very fond of him and I like her and we are very good friends. Bob too is very nice. . . . They are all going to Venice where the world premiere of the opera on *The Rake's Progress* is taking place in September. . . . I wish we could be there.

On July 18, 1951, Huxley wrote to thank Stravinsky for a gift:

Que vous êtes gentil! Je vous remercie mille fois et de tout mon coeur. You do me too much honor in calling me the Rake's godfather. At most I am only the go-between who happily continued the meeting of those eminent Lesbians, Music and Poetry, who, for these past thirty centuries, have stuck together so notoriously. . . .

Four days earlier, the Stravinskys had been to dinner at the Huxleys' in the open lean-to behind the Huxley house. Julian Huxley is there, and Gerald Heard, Isherwood, Haddow (the British Consul), the Hubbles, the Kiskaddens. Conversation is highly competitive in the display of up-to-date scientific information, but Aldous and Gerald are so quick at the game that no one else even has a chance to play. In gatherings such as this one Aldous speaks trippingly (as always), Gerald with a just noticeable strut. At one point, when Aldous advances a somewhat shaky hypothesis, his brother gently teases him about his credulity. But Aldous is skepticism itself compared to Gerald, whose talk consists in large part of the rashest speculations. Yet the essential difference between the two Angeleno sages is one of temperament. Aldous would shine most appealingly in a girls' college, Gerald in a lamasery—if such inextinguishable but entertaining verbosity is imaginable in a holy place. What bravura performers both! [From R.C.'s diary]

In March 1952, Aldous Huxley wrote an article about Stravinsky, and, as was the case with many visitors, the author of *The Perennial Philosophy* remarked on the extraordinary amount of light the windows admitted to the Stravinsky house. On the composer himself, Huxley wrote:

What precisely goes on in the mind of someone who responds to experience with the *Symphony of Psalms?* . . . I find it hard indeed to imagine. Hence the pleasure I always find in reading the books, or listening to the talk of a musician at once as eminent in his own field as Stravinsky and so articulate, at the same time, in the field of verbal expression. . . . Stravinsky is one of those happy amphibians who are at home on the dry land of words as well as in the ocean of music, and whose prowess ashore has never spoiled them as swimmers. . . . Good in English, better in French, and presumably, best of all in Russian, Stravinsky's talk has a curious and fascinating quality all its own. One begins, for example, with a discussion of aesthetics and the problems of expression. . . . From abstraction one passes in due course to the particular case and concrete example . . . to the agreeably acid tone of the *flûte à bec*. . . . Then the talk takes a literary turn, and we pass from Tolstoy (whom Stravinsky does not greatly admire [81]) and Dostoevsky (whom he does) to Rozanov and Shestov, and from Gide on Chopin to the musical bad taste of Marcel Proust. . . . Stravinsky's energy . . . is enormous. . . . He is a prodigious worker, never satisfied with any achievement however high . . . [and] the will to perfection never fails. [*Vogue*, February 15, 1953]

Stravinsky used to consult Huxley as if he were a mobile encyclopedia. If the information that the composer sought could be provided very briefly, Huxley would telephone it, but, if more complex, send a note, such as the following:

Septiformis—adjective, in ecclesiastical Latin. "Sevenfold." Used by St. Augustine of the Grace of the Holy Spirit. "*Septiformis gratia Spiritus Sancti.*" I think in your sheet-music there is a misprint. It should be "*Septiformis Paracleti gratia*"—the sevenfold grace of the Paraclete. Without the seven graces? I don't know, but St. Augustine did. Aldous. [May 3, 1955]

Maria Huxley was to write a month before her death:

Aldous . . . was refreshed by our dinner at the Stravinskys. We are such a happy family with them. Vera and myself always the only women—red wine of good quality, only just enough of the main course, but a large dessert . . . then music and books. . . . They have wonderful art books. He works *very hard* and all those concerts are for the sake of money. They spend every penny and sometimes more, but live easily. Vera has a one-man show in Rome and Aldous is to write the notice. We love what she does. [January 10, 1955]

The Stravinskys' friendship with Christopher Isherwood was even longer-lasting than that with the Huxleys. Isherwood has said that:

I always think of Stravinsky in a very physical way. He was physically adorable; he was cuddly—he was so little, and you wanted to protect him. He was very demonstrative, a person who—I suppose it was his Russianness—was full of kisses and embraces. He had great warmth. He could be fearfully hostile and snub people and attack his critics and so forth, but, personally, he was a person of immense joy and warmth. The first time I came to his house, he said to me: "Would you like to hear my Mass before we get drunk?" He was always saying things like that. He seemed to me to have a wonderful appreciation for all the arts. He spoke English fluently, but it astonished me what an appreciation he had of writing in the English language, although he was really more at home in German or French—after Russian. . . . When I was seeing a great deal of him, I was usually drinking a great deal, too, because he had these wonderful drinks. I recall a fatal, beautiful liquid called Marc—Marc de Bourgogne—made out of grape pits, colorless but powerful beyond belief. I used to think to myself, Godammit, I'm drunk again, and here is Igor saying these marvelous things, and I won't remember one of them in the morning. And along came Craft's books years later, and I recognized that this was the very essence of what he'd been saying. . . . When I think of those days, I really seem to have behaved very oddly. I remember once I'd actually passed out on the floor, and, looking up, I saw at an immense altitude above me, Aldous Huxley, who was very tall, standing up and talking French to Stravinsky, who never seemed to get overcome, however much he drank. And Aldous, who I think was very fond of me, was looking at me rather curiously, as much as to say, "Aren't you going a little far?" It's not like me to behave like that, or so I imagine. Perhaps it is. But I suddenly realized how relaxed I felt, how completely at home. It didn't matter if I blotted my copy book. . . . You can get drunk in many ways, but the Stravinskys projected the most astounding coziness. Because Vera Stravinsky was a part of it, she had enormous charm and style, and she's very amusing. Going out with them was always an experience.[82]

And here is an excerpt from Isherwood's diary:

On July 8, 1950, Bill Caskey and I were invited to drive to Sequoia Park with Igor and Vera Stravinsky and Bob Craft. We began, needless to say, by talking about Korea. Igor said he does not expect World War Three to break out, but there may be an indefinitely prolonged border struggle between the two world powers. Then, as we were crossing the San Fernando Valley, he asked us to excuse him: "I have to think about my opera for ten minutes." So we all kept quiet. I found the situation thrilling. Here was Stravinsky meditating on *The Rake's Progress*, ob-

1961. Hollywood. Photograph by Michael Barrie.

viously creating a powerful "field," as Gerald Heard would say. I decided I would profit by it and try to meditate on my novel. And I actually did have several quite valuable technical insights. This is the first time in my life that I have deliberately practiced "artistic meditation"!

Shortly before we entered Sequoia Park, I told Igor, who had never been there before, that he would find the landscape strangely out of perspective—because, as you enter, you are surrounded by very small trees, birches, while, at the same time, you look up and see the giant trees on the skyline, hundreds of feet above you. Igor seemed to understand what I meant. He answered promptly: "Just like Shostakovich at the Hollywood Bowl."

Later we visited the General Sherman Tree, which is supposed to be the largest living thing on earth. Igor stood looking up at it for some time; it was an awe-inspiring confrontation. At length he said, "That's very serious."

Then we climbed out on the Moro Rock. Igor said that Derain had told him that a mountain is the most difficult of all objects to paint. He showed tremendous energy, scrambling up the trail. He has a huge appetite. On the drive home, he really suffered because we couldn't find a restaurant the very moment he decided that it was time for supper.

Isherwood's biographer, Jonathan Fryer, tells the story of the opening night of *I Am a Camera*, at the Empire Theater, New York, at the end of November 1951:

Christopher and John van Druten walked back and forth across the back of the auditorium to catch the feel of the audience. During the interval Christopher went into the lobby, where Stravinsky rushed up to him, embraced him, and murmured, "Inferior to the novel!" Marlene Dietrich then approached Stravinsky with a wild *"Cher Maître."* [83]

Gerald Heard, the last of the triumvirate (with Huxley and Isherwood) to become friends with the Stravinskys, was a once-a-week dinner guest between 1950 and 1965, and, in the 1950s, Stravinsky was one of Heard's faithful flock, seldom missing his Sunday-morning lectures:

June 28, 1953. Lunch with the Huxleys and Gerald Heard, after hearing Gerald's sermon in the Ivar Street Temple; the talk is marred only by a reference—quite regular when Stravinsky is in the congregation—to "atonal music," which Heard seems to believe is something Stravinsky invented. At table, Heard does not have, as Maugham claimed for him, that "affluence of conversation which Dr. Johnson loved in Burke," but probably for the reason that I have none at all; Gerald simply goes on and on about the Adamites and chiliasm, and about hyperthyroids through the ages: "Ambrose of Milan, Teresa of Avila, and Joseph of Copertino had pop-eyes, gaping-mouths and swollen throats." At one point, when Stravinsky bemoans the necessity of disposing of his canary, because it is old and Yvgenia Petrovna devotes too much time to it, Aldous says: "But old canaries can be taught new tunes; surely you remember the serinette, the organ, mentioned by Diderot, used for teaching the bird."

In the afternoon, Stravinsky plays his newly completed Septet

with me, four-hands, but at night he is nervous about his forthcoming
prostatectomy, and I fetch Aldous, who hypnotizes and massages him
to sleep. [From R.C.'s diary]

The Rake's Progress
A Chronology

1947

May 2. Chicago. The Art Institute. Stravinsky sees a Hogarth
exhibition.

September 26. Hollywood. Writes to Ralph Hawkes (of Boosey
& Hawkes), saying that after completing the Mass, the next project will be to compose "the opera discussed at our last meeting."
> As librettist . . . advised by my good friend Aldous Hux-
> ley whom I see frequently here, I suggest that you con-
> tact W. H. Auden.

September 30. New York. Auden meets with Hawkes, who
writes that the poet "is intensely interested and is free to go to
work immediately."

October 16. New York. Lincoln Kirstein writes to Stravinsky:
> . . . Wystan Auden spent the evening with me talking
> about *The Rake's Progress.* He has wonderful ideas. I
> am so glad you are working with him; for me, he is the
> greatest English poet of our time. He is not only a su-
> perb technician, an amazing mind on a purely intellec-
> tual level, but a very passionate and touching lyric poet
> as well. He adores opera; he spends half of his time
> playing records of Mozart and Verdi. For him opera is a
> ritual. You can tell him just what you want, and you
> will get it—but to a degree of intensity and perfection
> that is quite stupendous. I very much wish Hawkes had
> made it possible for him to see you in Hollywood. He
> has not enough money to go by himself, but perhaps
> you can do it all by letter; you would enjoy him so
> much; he is so kind, so generous and a most remarkable
> mind. He is going to Italy in April.

November 4. Hollywood. Writes to Hawkes:
> . . . I have invited Mr. W. H. Auden to be my guest in
> my home and am paying for his flight here. . . . I wish
> you could bring me from London that remarkable pub-
> lication of Byrd's work that I saw there in 1937, and

maybe there is a similar [edition] of Purcell.

November 9. Writes to Hawkes asking for orchestra scores of four Mozart operas, the "source of inspiration for my future opera."

November 11–18. Auden is at Stravinsky's home, where he and the composer complete the scenario.

> As soon as Wystan Auden accepted Igor Stravinsky's invitation to stay at his home in Hollywood, the composer and his wife began to search for a clue to the most important fact that they needed to know about the poet: his height. Would he be too tall to sleep on the couch in the den? Finding no hint in his writings, the future hosts turned to photographs for possible prosopographical leads, and concluded that in all probability he would not fit. This apprehension was confirmed the minute the poet crossed the doorstep. Then Stravinsky was obliged to improvise—something he would never do in music—by extending the "bed" with a chair and pillows to accommodate his guest's legs and feet.
>
> During the following week the two men shaped the content, plot, form and characters of *The Rake's Progress*. On two evenings the Stravinskys entertained friends and, on two others, the hosts and their guest attended performances of *The House of Bernarda Alba* and *Così fan tutte*, the latter in the parish hall of a Hollywood church. As for Southern California's natural and architectural wonders, the poet shrank at the very mention of them and refused even to glance in the direction of the ocean. In fact he ventured from the house only one other time, to visit a doctor to whom he complained of sudden deafness, and who miraculously restored the hearing faculty by extricating some formidable accumulations of earwax. Like the World, the opera scenario was created in Six Days. On the Seventh the makers separated, only then realizing how extremely fond of each other they had become. [From "The Poet and *The Rake*," by R.C.]

> [At first] I [was] scared stiff. . . . Rumor had it that Stravinsky was a difficult person with whom to work. Rumor had lied. What [I] feared to find was a Prima Donna: what in fact [I] found was a professional artist, concerned not for his personal glory, but solely for the thing-to-be-made. Of Stravinsky the man, I can only repeat what I have said elsewhere about somebody else, namely that he embodies the truth of Logan Pearsall Smith's aphorism: "Hearts that are gentle and kind and tongues that are neither—these make the finest company in the world." [W. H. Auden, 1967, Columbia Records Album Note]

November 20. New York. Auden writes:

> First, an account of my stewardship, I have (a) posted the letter to the Guggenheim Foundation. (b) Called Miss Bean. (c) Called Mr. Heinsheimer. The journey was a nightmare. The flight was cancelled; I was transferred to an American Airlines local which left at 7 A.M., stopped *everywhere* and reached New York at 4 A.M. this morning. The meals, as usual, would have tried the patience of a stage curate, so you can imagine what I felt, after a week of your luxurious cuisine. And finally, of course, I got back here to a pile of silly letters to answer—a job I loathe.
>
> The only consolation is the pleasure of writing you this bread-and-butter letter (how do you say that in Russian?). I loved every minute of my stay, thanks to you both, and shall look forward with impatience to the next time we meet.
>
> Greetings to Vassily,[84] Das Krankheitliebendes Fräulein,[85] Popka, Mme Sokoloff,[86] La Baronesse des Chats.[87]

November 25. Writes to Hawkes:

> Wystan Auden spent seven days with me. . . . The complete opera scenario is: three acts and 8 scenes; 4 leading and 2 minor parts; chorus; an orchestra of about 35. . . .

December 11. Composes the Prelude to the graveyard scene. Inspired by his vision of the drama, Stravinsky immediately composed the string quartet which begins the second scene of Act III. Back in New York, Auden also set to work, in collaboration with his friend Chester Kallman, the subject of whose participation had not been broached in Hollywood; Auden did not reveal this partnership until it was a *fait accompli* and the first act of the libretto had been sent to Stravinsky. Both because he had not been consulted, and because it was Auden alone whom he wanted, the composer was upset by this, though he said nothing. Twelve days later he received and accepted the manuscript of Act Two, on which Auden's and Kallman's names again appeared as co-authors. The final act was delivered to Stravinsky—in Washington, D.C., where he was conducting—by Auden in person, no doubt to smooth over the question of dual authorship. The poet then sought to reassure the composer that "Mr. Kallman is a better librettist than I am," that "the scenes which Mr. Kallman wrote are at least as good as mine," and that "Mr. Kallman's talents have not been more widely recognized only because of his friendship with me." Stravinsky magnanimously answered that he looked forward to meeting Mr. Kallman in New York. [R.C., *op. cit.*]

1948

March 3. New York. Hawkes writes:
> Auden has demanded a great deal more [money] than I had anticipated.

March 22. Hawkes telegraphs:
> I am worried about your attitude over Auden's libretto.[88] Auden would come to Washington if necessary but is pressing me for completion of contract which I do not desire to do unless you are satisfied. Alterations can be made to your liking.

Telegraphs to Hawkes:
> Will be in Washington morning March 31 Hotel Raleigh. . . . If Auden coming there already 31st am almost sure alterations could be made in a few days.

March 26. Writes to Hawkes:
> I am sure we will now have time enough to discuss with Auden and to make alterations in his otherwise brilliant libretto . . . which seems to me from time to time a little complicated for musical purposes.

March 31. Washington. The Hotel Raleigh. Works with Auden.
> The dinner in the restaurant of the Raleigh Hotel was memorable mainly as a study in contrasts, not only in culture, temperament, and mind, but also in appearance, for the shabby, dandruff-speckled, and slightly peculiar-smelling poet (attributes easily offset by his purity of spirit and intellectual punctiliousness) could not have been more unlike the neat, sartorially perfect, and faintly eau-de-cologned composer. At table, too, while the poet demolished his lamb chops, potatoes, and sprouts, as if eating were a chore to be accomplished as quickly as possible, and while he gulped Stravinsky's carefully chosen Château Margaux oblivious to its qualities, the composer fussed over his Châteaubriand, and sniffed, savored, and sipped the wine.
>
> These habits illustrate an essential difference between the two men. While with Auden the senses seemed to be of negligible importance, with Stravinsky the affective faculties were virtual instruments of thought. Though a powerful observer, Auden displayed little interest in the optic sense, being purblind to painting and architecture and even to "poetic" nature: he was more concerned with the virtues of gardening than with the beauty of flowers. And whatever the acuteness of his aural sense, the idea of music appealed to him more than music itself, music with words—opera and Anglican hymns—more than Haydn quartets and Beethoven symphonies. That the music of Auden's poetry is not its strongest feature, therefore, should hardly surprise us. A conceptualizer in quest of intellectual order,

he was above all a social, moral, and spiritual diagnostician.

There were other contrasts between poet and composer. Thus, both were religious men, equally keen on dogmas, ritual, faith in the redemptive death; but the poet had evidently arrived at his beliefs through theology, the composer through "mystical experience" (however diligently he may have applied himself to the *Grammar of Assent*). Theology, at any rate, was a frequent topic in Auden's conversation with Stravinsky, and an exasperatingly difficult one to follow, except when the poet digressed on biblical symbolisms (e.g., the moon as the Old Testament, the sun as the New), or on the argument of "*sui generis*" (that "man's image is God-like because the image of every man is unique"). But Auden preferred to theorize as to whether or not "angels are pure intellect," and to postulate that "If two rectangles, with common points between them, can be described on a face, that face is an angel's"—which sounds like a put-on but could have been scholastic exercitation.

The conversation in the Washington restaurant began with a reference to an announcement of a forthcoming New York performance of Stravinsky's *Oedipus Rex* in a new translation by e. e. cummings (the entire text, not just the Narrator's part). Auden was prepared to vouch for cummings's awareness of the composer's intentions and was certain that only the speeches would be in English—an especially welcome comment since it indicated that Auden was acquainted with the piece. Thereafter the talk about music turned to the Wagner and Strauss operas that the poet most admired but that were far from Stravinsky's present interest, and, in the case of Strauss, familiarity. (Auden did not subscribe to Strauss's estimation of himself as an epigone of Wagner, maintaining that "Wagner is a giant without issue.")

Begging indulgence for her English, Mrs. Stravinsky asked Auden how to improve it. He advised her to "Take a new word and use it in ten different sentences." She chose "fastidious," and, with no implicit criticism of her mentor, started with "My husband is very fastidious." Auden's English, mumbled and heavily accented, was an obstacle for the Stravinskys. Aware of this, he offered supplementary bits in German ("*unbequemt*") and French, thereby adding to the Stravinskys' confusion, since his pronunciation of these languages constituted a further impediment; he was obliged to write "*au fond*" on the tablecloth, for example, before the Stravinskys could understand what he was saying.[89] His vocabulary seemed odd, too, not in obscure or classical-root words but in such British expressions as "fribble," and "grouting" (referring to the work of certain

PLATE 12

December 18, 1954. With Ingolf Dahl, at the home of Oscar Moss, sponsor of the Monday Evening Concerts.

June 1942. A page from the sketch score of the first movement of the Symphony in Three Movements.

1950. *The Rake's Progress.* Sketch for the introduction to the first aria of Act III, Scene 2. On December 9, 1959, Stravinsky sold the manuscripts of both the full and piano scores of the opera to the University of Southern California.

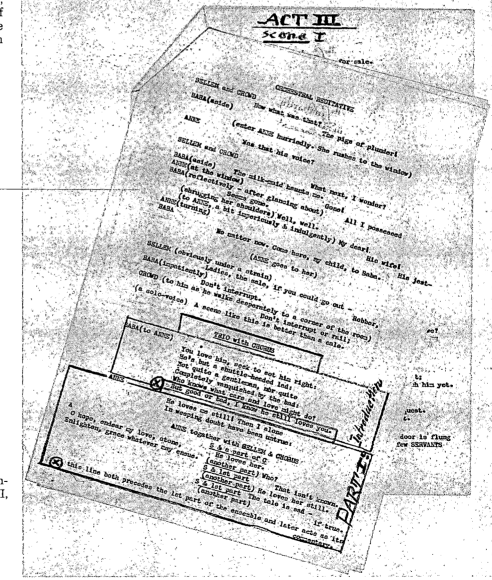

1950. *The Rake's Progress.* Stravinsky's typescript of the libretto, Act III, Scene 1.

PLATE 13

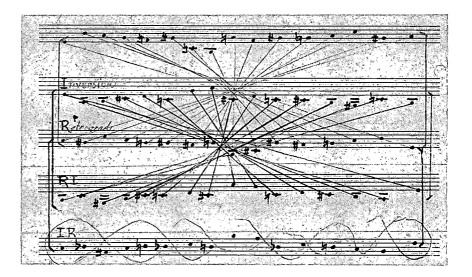

The Rake's Progress. Draft of a passage from the Chorus, Act I, end of Scene 2.

1952. Serial chart for the *Septet.*

PLATE 14

PLATE 16 ▷

PLATE 15

August 1965. Sketch for *Requiem Canticles*.

OPPOSITE:
August 21, 1957. Salisbury Cathedral. From Salisbury, the Stravinskys went to London, Paris, and Venice. Photograph by Gjon Mili.

September 16, 1957. Venice. Composing *Threni* in the basement nightclub of the Hotel Bauer Grünwald. Photograph by Gjon Mili.

PLATE 17

March 28, 1959. Leaving Honolulu for Wake Island. Photograph by Robert Craft.

April 5, 1959. Kamakura, Japan. With the Buddha. Photograph by Vera Stravinsky.

April 5, 1959. Kamakura. A toy booth. Photograph by Vera Stravinsky.

PLATE 18

April 1959. Kyoto. On the steps of a temple. Photograph by Vera Stravinsky.

April 17, 1959. Kyoto. Entering Nijo Castle. Photograph by Robert Craft.

February 2, 1962. New York. I.S. smooching Mrs. I.S. at a party at Arnold Weissberger's.

ET-HADAVAR HAZEH V'LO
the deed   this one   and didst not
KHASHAKHTA ET-BINKHA ET-YEKHIDEKHA
withhold   thy son   him only one.

17 KI VAREKH AVAREKH' KHA
That bless   I will bless thee,
V'HARBA ARBEH ET-ZAR'AKHA
and multiply I will multiply, thy seed
K'KOKH(A)VEI HASHAMA'YIM V'KHAKHOL
as the stars of the heavens, and as the sand
ASHER AL-SFAT HAYAM V'YIRASH
which (is) on the shore of the sea; and (it) will inherit
ZAR'AKHA ET-SHA'AR OIVAV:
thy seed   the gate of his enemies.

18 V'HITBARKHU   VZAR'AKHA KOL GOYEI
And (they) will be blessed in the seed all the nations
HA'ARETZ EKEV ASHER SHAMA'(A)TA
on the earth because that thou hast hearkened
B'KOLI ||VAYASHAV AVRAHAM EL-NA'ARAV
to my voice. And (he) returned Abraham to his boys,
VAYAKUMU VAYELKHU YAKHDAV
and they rose and went together
EL-B'ER SHEVA VA'YESHEV AVRAHAM
to Beer-Sheba and dwelt Abraham
BIV'ER SHEVA.
in Beer-Sheba.

PLATE 20 ▷

PLATE 19

1962. A page from Stravinsky's working text for *Abraham and Isaac*.

OPPOSITE ABOVE:
1964. Variations. A Sketchbook page.

OPPOSITE BELOW:
October 15, 1964. Variations. Draft score of the variation for twelve wind instruments. On October 27, Stravinsky composed measures 130–4, and, the following day, finished the opus.

May 23, 1959. Copenhagen. Looking at the giraffe, Stravinsky remarked: "What must it be like to have a sore throat?" (Perhaps a similar thought inspired Dali's *Giraffe on Fire*.)

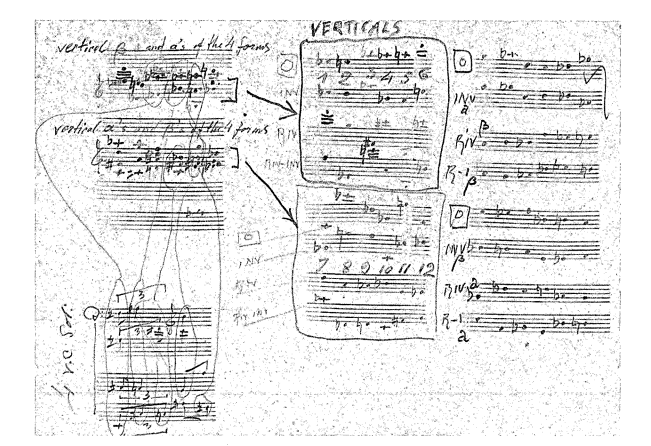

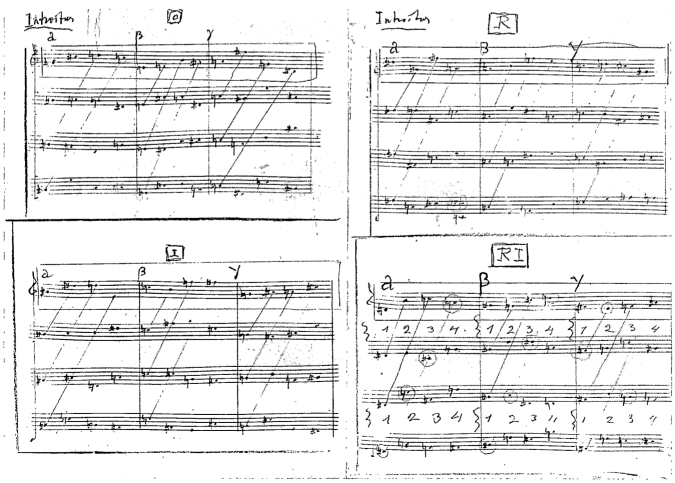

PLATE 22

OPPOSITE ABOVE:
July 18, 1960. With Paul Horgan and
Robert Craft in Canyon Frijoles, New
Mexico. Photograph by Vera Stravin-
sky.

OPPOSITE BELOW
AND BELOW:
February 1965. Serial chart and first
page of the sketch score for the *Introitus*. The first words of the *Introitus*
(and the *Graduale*), "Requiem eternam dona eis, Domine," and "Lux
perpetua luceat eis" derive from the
apocryphal Hebrew book of *Esdras*.

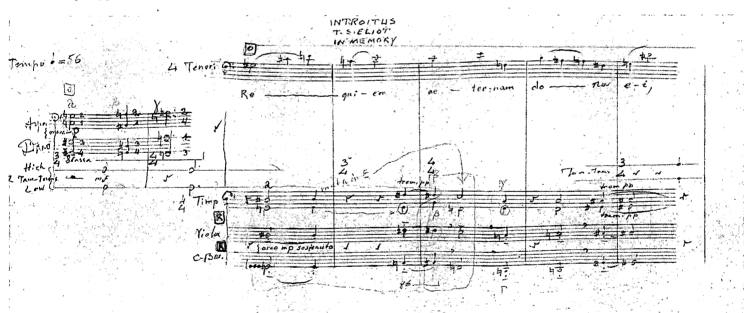

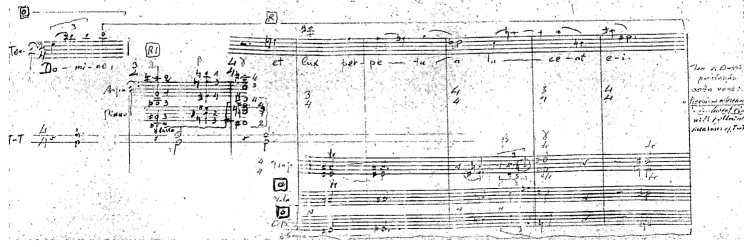

OPPOSITE:
September 18, 1966. New York. Hotel
Pierre. Studying the score of the *Requiem Canticles*. Photograph by Arnold Newman.

October 1, 1966. New York. Hotel
Pierre. Turning a page in the *Requiem
Canticles*. This is the finest photograph ever made of the back of Stravinsky's head and of one of his ears;
regrettably, his death mask, unlike
those of Pascal, Blake, Wagner, Berg,
Diaghilev, and others, is an impression only of the front of the face and
does not include the ears. Stravinsky
was interested in death masks, and
Willy Strecker has recorded that
when he showed Beethoven's to Stravinsky, he said that he found it "more
human" than the life mask. Photograph by Arnold Newman.

April 27, 1966. Final page of the *Lac-
rimosa* (*Requiem Canticles*).

PLATE 24

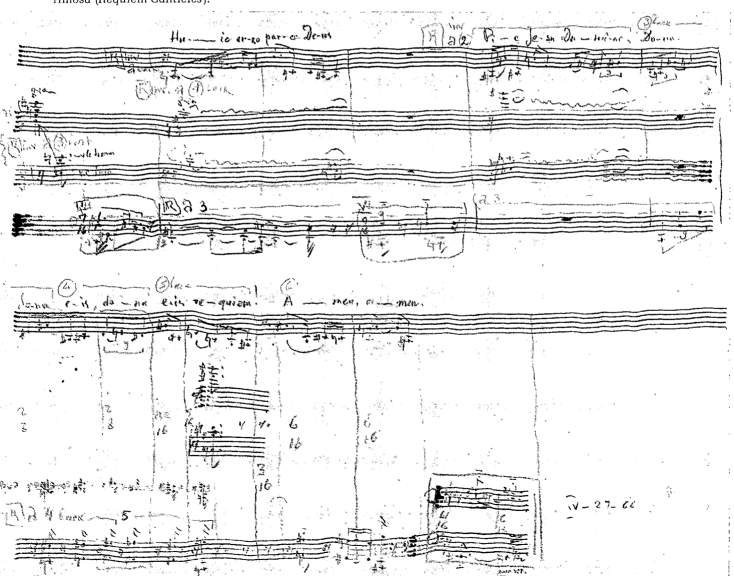

March 20, 1968. Phoenix. At the Casa
Blanca Motel. Photograph by Vera
Stravinsky.

March 20, 1968. Phoenix. Photograph
by Vera Stravinsky.

PLATE 25

A page from Stravinsky's instrumentation of Hugo Wolf's "*Wunden trägst du*" (*Spanisches Liederbuch*). Completed on June 28, 1968, this is the second song by Hugo Wolf that Stravinsky orchestrated in May and June of that year.

January 1970. In the Essex House before going for a drive.

PLATE 26

June 14, 1970. 6:00 P.M. The Stravinskys in the dining room of their suite
in the Hôtel Royale, Evian-les-Bains.
Photograph by Arnold Weissberger.

March 16, 1971. New York. In the living room of the Stravinsky suite in the
Essex House. Fittingly, in this last
photograph of the composer, he is
with the person who meant most to
him in his life. Stravinsky liked to listen to his wife's stories this way, forefinger extended like a perch, which
she would touch. (The story of the
four billiard-like balls is told under
January 16, 1971, in the present
writer's *Chronicle of a Friendship*.)

PLATE 27

writers). The problem of comprehending his speech was still further aggravated in later years by the installation of loose-fitting dentures.

Answering a question about his travel plans, Auden said, "I like to fly and am not afraid of crashing. It is simply a matter of whether one's time is up. My time will be up when I am eighty-eight." (The present writer heard him reiterate the last statement so frequently as to wonder whether the seer was finally betrayed not by his destiny but by his too intelligent understanding of the future.)

Suddenly Stravinsky switched from "Ow-den" to the poet's first name and was enthusiastically met on the same basis with "Ee-gawr," a cultural gaffe since the use of the given name without the patronymic is inadmissible to Russians. The composer overlooked it. At departure still another cultural difference was exposed when Auden, his body wobbling from his pumping handshake, charged for the door, only to be detained there by the Stravinskys' Russian-style hugs and kisses. [R.C., *op. cit.*]

April 5. New York. Stravinsky meets Chester Kallman.
The composer was quickly won by Chester Kallman's intelligence and sense of humor. Furthermore, Kallman was easier to understand than Auden, and could bring out the poet's sometimes dormant affability, as well as subdue his tempers, of whose advent the poet himself often gave warning: "I am very cross today." Bluntly stated, the Stravinskys were happier with Auden when Chester Kallman was present. On the trip from Washington to New York, Stravinsky had read the opera's final act and hence could give his blessings to the partnership, telling the librettists how delighted he was with *their* work.[90] Then Auden went to Ischia for the summer and Stravinsky to his Hollywood studio to compose the first scene. [R.C., *op. cit.*]

May 8. Hollywood. Begins work on the first act.

June 16. Writes to Hawkes: "I am exceedingly busy with *Rake's Progress.* . . ."

June 13. Completes the recitative which ends: "You are a rich man."

August 2. Writes to Hawkes:
Many pages have already been achieved, but I am not quite through the first scene. This work affords me great joy and freshness, and no one need worry about my losing a moment. The music will be very easy to listen to, but making this easiness is very expensive with my time.

September 13. Completes the Duettino (Scene 1).

October 5. Begins the chorus music in the Bedlam scene.

October 8. Writes to Craft:
> My *Rake* progresses (starting the 2nd scene), but not as fast as Ralph Hawkes wants it. . . . I am in complete agreement with you not to speak at all about *Rake*.

1949

January 9. Plays Act I for Eugene Berman, whom Stravinsky has chosen to design the sets.

January 16. Completes Act I.

February 3. New York. Plays Act I for Auden.
> Coming east again in the winter for concerts, Stravinsky expected to play the completed scenes for Auden on the very morning of arrival in New York (February 3). At 6:55 A.M., Auden met the train in Pennsylvania Station—this time inclining toward the Stravinskys, the better to receive their Russian embracing—explained that he had jury duty, and asked that the audition be postponed until evening. In their hotel suite at dinner time he was elated at "having hung the jury and obstructed injustice in the trial of a taxi-driver who would have been a victim of the prejudice of car owners." Then, questioning Auden about legal processes, the Stravinskys appalled him by revealing that they had never voted, thereby receiving a stern lecture from him on their civic responsibilities.
>
> The poet was less voluble after hearing the first act of the opera, but he asked the composer to "change the soprano's final note to a high C," as well as to take fewer pains in making every word audible, for, in the interests of verbal distinctness, Stravinsky had tended to alternate the voices in duets and trios, rather than to blend them. As for the "C," the composer complained that the word was unsuitable for the upper octave, whereupon Auden, after some "uh-uh"-ing and "now let's see"-ing, wrote a new last line on the spot. Auden stood behind Stravinsky as he played, trying to follow the music over his shoulder, unaware of how irritated the composer was by this and other violations of his strict rule of silence. [R.C., *op. cit.*]

February 21. Works with Auden.
> On February 27, Stravinsky conducted part of a concert in Town Hall, and had invited Auden to read a group of his poems on the program.[91] In contrast to his normally untidy, unwashed, uncombed, unpressed appearance,

at concert time the poet was uncomfortably well-groomed. His restlessness and impatience were intensified by stage fright, and since the event was a pre-martini-hour matinée, his chain-smoking accelerated. Leading with his chin, and moving awkwardly, he read "In Praise of Limestone," "The Duet," and "Music Is International." His voice spluttered and barked, thus adding to the "gentle hound" impression that he sometimes gave. Yet by sheer force of intellect he was always in total command of the audience. He acknowledged the warm applause with a surprised grin, a spastic bow, and a rapid exit such as he normally made at dinner parties upon discovering that it was past his bedtime.

Auden went to Ischia [92] again in the summer, and Stravinsky again returned to his Hollywood studio. [R.C., *op. cit.*]

April 21. Hollywood. Writes to Hawkes enclosing a new page 165, with words and alterations in the music.

June 6. Writes to Erwin Stein (chief editor at Boosey & Hawkes): "Touched by what you say about the *Rake*." [93] The letter includes corrections for Act I.

June 19. Telegraphs to Betty Bean (of Boosey & Hawkes): "I hope to finish my opera in about 18 months [and] cannot give performance information now."

July 8. Craft writes to Stein: "... Mr. Stravinsky is ill.... [He] will send the first installment of the *Rake* score in a few days."

August 2. Sends the full score thus far completed to Betty Bean.

September 16. Writes to Sylvia Goldstein (of Boosey & Hawkes): "I can only tell you that I hope to finish [Act II] in January or February...."

October 3. Begins the Terzetto, "Could it then ... ?"

November 12. New York. Craft writes Stravinsky to say that Auden's teaching schedule will not permit him to come to California.

November 20. Hollywood. Writes to Hawkes expressing the desire to conduct the premieres in each city and to have Paul Breisach conduct the subsequent performances: "I don't put Reiner's name forward despite my sincere appreciation of his gifts and techniques, because I feel that my Mozart-like *Rake* is more in the line of a Breisach-type conductor."

December 29. Completes Baba's music through "Oh no!, no, n(ever)."

January 3. Writes to Hawkes:

> I realize now that our preceding conversations and correspondence on the subject of the *Rake* premiere under my direction have never meant to you anything but mere and vague talk.

January 10. Begins the Arioso, "Oh Nick."

January 17. Hawkes writes to say that the thousand dollars which Elizabeth Mayer wants for the German translation is too much.

February 6. Cables to Ernst Roth (of Boosey & Hawkes) saying that the third scene of Act II in sketch score and the second and third scenes in full score are being sent.

March 1. The Lombardy Hotel. Works with Auden.

> The two men conferred together several times in the composer's hotel rooms, Stravinsky by this time visualizing every detail of the dramatic action. How long, for example, would it take to wheel the bread machine onstage? Auden, responding swiftly, and as if he had had a great deal of experience with baby carriages, jumped to his feet, extended his arms, and crossed the room pushing an imaginary vehicle of that sort while Stravinsky held his stop-watch like a starter at a track meet. This somnambulistic exercise had little validity, however, since no one knew the dimensions of the stage on which the opera was to be performed. The music at the beginning of this scene is generally found to be too short.
>
> Stravinsky wanted an American premiere, preferably in a small New York theater, where he believed the opera might survive a brief "run," a notion that seized him after attending *The Consul.* Lincoln Kirstein helped to approach potential backers, the most promising of whom was Huntington Hartford, until he insisted that Stravinsky play the score for him, which the composer refused to do for any non-musician. Eventually, Billy Rose's opinion was sought (if not his money); but, like the others, he wanted to hear the piece, and therefore had to be smuggled, like Odysseus among Polyphemus' sheep, in a group of Stravinsky's musician friends for whom the composer had agreed to play the opera. After a very few minutes Mr. Rose's countenance implied that Tom Rakewell could expect a crueler fate in the commercial theater than in Bedlam. [R.C., *op. cit.*]

March 15. Sends corrections for Act I (full score) to Stein, writing on the carbon copy of his letter: "Sent to Stein with answers and a short letter by Bob."

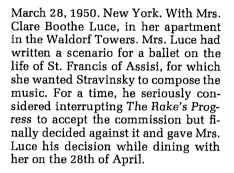

March 28, 1950. New York. With Mrs. Clare Boothe Luce, in her apartment in the Waldorf Towers. Mrs. Luce had written a scenario for a ballet on the life of St. Francis of Assisi, for which she wanted Stravinsky to compose the music. For a time, he seriously considered interrupting *The Rake's Progress* to accept the commission but finally decided against it and gave Mrs. Luce his decision while dining with her on the 28th of April.

March 17. Works with Auden.

October 6. Hollywood. Writes to Betty Bean saying that he has asked Arnold Weissberger to discuss with a Mr. Ricketson the possibility of performing *The Rake* at Central City.

October 13. Writes to Betty Bean:

> The third and last act is made of three scenes . . . plus a short epilogue. It is not only the longest but also the most dense of the three acts. . . . It is impossible to make a translation . . . without losing most of the musical links between words or syllables and notes. . . . I suggest that you ask Auden, who is now back in New York . . . to give his author's okay. As to the musical correctness of the German translation, why not ask Nicolas Nabokov, who is also back in the U.S., and who knows both German and my music very well. . . . That's enough writing for today. I'd better go back to my *Rake.*

[W. H. Auden wrote, after Stravinsky's death,] that when Chester Kallman and I were offered the opportu-

nity to write the libretto of *The Rake's Progress*, we felt, of course, immensely honored, but at the same time rather alarmed. . . . Though, as lovers of opera, we both knew that musical and spoken rhythmical values cannot be identical, we were afraid, particularly since Stravinsky had never set English before,[94] that he might distort our words to the point of unintelligibility. But, from the moment we started working with him, we discovered that our fears were groundless. Going through our text, he asked for, and marked into his copy, the spoken rhythmical value of every word. In one instance, only one, did he make a mistake. He thought that in the word "sedan-chair," the accent fell on the first syllable of "sedan." When we pointed this out to him, he immediately altered his score. In one number in the opera, the Auctioneer's aria in Act III, Scene 1, it is dramatically essential that the sung rhythms conform pretty closely to the spoken. They do. In the rest of the work, whatever occasional liberties he took, none of them struck our English and literary ears as impermissible.
. . . [W. H. Auden, "Craftsman, Artist, Genius," *The Observer*, April 11, 1971]

October 16. Writes to Stein complaining about the vocal score of Act II, adding that
> . . . You will very likely have the visits of Nadia Boulanger and Markevich. They will ask you to let them have a look at the *Rake*.

October 17. Sends "the completely corrected and extensively rewritten" vocal score of Act II.

November 1. Begins the tenor aria "How dear . . ."

November 6. Writes to Betty Bean referring to the "cagey attitude proving [that Ricketson] was only willing to give his sponsorship in order to reduce his taxes." Stravinsky says that he has been approached by Carl Ebert and Dr. Raymond Kendall, who wish to give the premiere of *The Rake* at the University of Southern California Opera Department.

December 1. Stein writes:
> . . . It was a great pleasure to see the solutions that you have found for the piano. They are so ingenious that we can hardly blame [Stein's assistant] if he did not find something similar. . . . I admire the way in which you have taken up the conventions of opera for a new purpose. . . .

December 6. Writes to Stein:
> I sincerely appreciate your words about the music of *Rake's* . . . a sharp eye and ear . . . fortunately you have it. . . .

December 31. Composes end of scene, "Methinks it is no shame."

1951

January 19. Writes to Betty Bean saying that he has sent the vocal score of the first two scenes of Act III and expects to send the orchestra score by the end of the month.

January 24. Cables to E. Roth, director of Boosey & Hawkes: "Have accepted conducting world premiere Venice September 12."

January 26. Receives a letter from Roth, who is indignant that Stravinsky has negotiated the Venetian premiere independently:

> ... in Venice you will find yourself in a turmoil of disorganization which requires improvisation in the smallest matters ... the situation for us is extremely awkward.

Stravinsky cables:

> Venice is no improvisation [Mario] Labroca gave every guarantee outstanding performance original English version....

January 28. Completes "In a foolish dream."

January 31. Sends corrections to Stein for Act III, Scenes 2 and 3 (orchestra score).

February 6. Signs a contract with the Biennale di Venezia agreeing to conduct the first performance and to supervise the second and third, also giving broadcasting rights to the Biennale. The RAI Orchestra, Rome, is specified for the performance.

> The Venetian premiere was arranged by Nicolas Nabokov after a year-long struggle against the pococurantism of Italian culture officials. As soon as Auden discovered the terms, he asked for help: "7 Cornelia Street, N.Y.C., 16/2/51. Dear Bob, It's wonderful news about Venice. But there are one or two matters which—strictly *entre nous*—Chester and I would like to know about. It seems to us that, if there is, as I understand, a *large* sum of money being paid for the premiere rights, we are entitled to ten per cent thereof. What do you think? As the contract is not being negotiated through Boosey Bean,[95] we are completely in the dark as to the facts. Could you use your discretion and, if circumstances are propitious, mention the matter to *Il Maestro*?
>   "Hope Cuba is fun. Love, Wystan." [R.C., *op. cit.*]

February 7. Writes to Bean saying that he is ready to send "a big portion already completed in summary sketches of Act III, Scene 3."

February 9. Writes to Roth explaining that the delay in answering was in order to finish the third scene. Stravinsky defends his contract with Venice on the grounds that he has had no remuneration for his work, and he compares the failure of the various American offers with the $20,000 from the Italians simply to *conduct* the premiere:

David Webster called on me here last week just two days after I received your last telegram. When he asked how my work was progressing, I told him that Venice had just secured the premiere for next September. He nearly fainted. [But] he did not mention that he would have been willing to pay me money. . . . I mailed Act III, Scenes 1 and 2, to Betty Bean on January 26.

February 16: Writes to Auden:
It is not my responsibility to provide for your active role [as advisor to the stage director] with Kallman. I have not sold La Biennale anything but my conducting and musical supervision. . . . Contact Ferdinando Ballo at La Biennale as I am sure he will be most willing to do his utmost to be able to use your services. . . .

February 17. Composes "Where have you hidden her?"

February 18. Carl Ebert comes to discuss the staging.

March 17. Writes to Betty Bean concerning a recording project, saying that he has heard from Dario Soria.

March 19. Writes to Stein:
On my return from Cuba . . . I am carrying on with my orchestrating of Scene 3. . . . This new transcription of yours for piano is much easier to use than the others, and I believe that I will have less to do myself in the way of alterations. . . .

March 26. Writes to Stein saying that the orchestra score of the last scene has been mailed.

March 29. Roth writes:
Auden called at the New York office and inquired about the premiere in Venice, complaining that he was not consulted and that no financial arrangements were made for him and Kallman. . . . I explained . . . that any fee paid to you was the fee for your services and not for the right of the first performance. . . . What exactly is Chester Kallman's work? . . . Mr. Kallman wants to see the proofs of the score which may mean a considerable delay.

April 2. Writes to Roth:
. . . Auden and Kallman have to give up any idea of altering the prosody. . . . I have checked the first two acts with Auden a year ago, and for the third act I have consulted with Robert Craft, who is an excellent musician and can do the job as well as Auden and Kallman.

April 7. Completes the Epilogue.

April 9. Roth writes explaining Auden's request that he and Kallman be invited to Venice "first-class round trip and three weeks stay there paid."

April 14. Writes to Roth:
> . . . There will not be a civil war in Italy just for the sake of *The Rake.* . . . I think they will come to terms through some traditionally Machiavellian *combinazione.* . . . I have just finished the Epilogue.

April 19. Writes to Roth:
> Please tell your people in Würzburg to keep sending the proofs as soon as they can do it, even in small bunches. . . .

Stein writes, informing Stravinsky that he has neglected to compose music for the line "All men are mad."

April 21. Writes to Stein:
> Today I have completed my corrections of the *Klavierauszug* Act III, Scene 3. . . . I have just been informed by Wystan Auden that he has arrived in Italy from India.

April 23. Sends music for "All men are mad."

April 27. Writes to Roth describing a visit from Chandler Cowles concerning a proposed production of *The Rake* in the Mark Hellinger Theater, New York.

May 1. Writes to Stein:
> A phrase has obviously been withdrawn from the English vocal score. Strangely enough the German translation appears to conform with the English phrase which has mysteriously disappeared.

May 2. Betty Bean writes:
> . . . Auden and Kallman seem to feel it very important that they check proofs as far as the libretto is concerned, as there were certain changes . . . that may not have been picked up.

May 3. Sends the Epilogue, and the orchestra score of the Prelude.

May 10. Roth writes:
> Pulls from the second proofs will be sent to Chester Kallman directly from Germany. . . . Auden was here last Tuesday from Rome. . . .

June 5. Writes to Stein:
> . . . I must tell you that the version you read in my score was actually composed by Auden himself a year ago, but from what I see now, it is likely that the authors have thought of doing some improving.

June 25. Roth writes:
> La Scala has assumed all artistic responsibility for the performance in Venice.

June 27. Writes to Stein: "Originally I had had the sound of a harpsichord in mind, but I fear that in Act III, Scene 2, the harpsichord might be inaudible." Stravinsky also says that he did not set his mind on the harpsichord from the start because he was afraid to encounter difficulties with it and wanted to be able to decide only after completing the work. Now that the time has come to make up his mind, his decision is to give the whole cembalo part to a piano. He adds that "I would like very much to have the full German translation. . . . I enjoy it immensely . . . it is a perfectly beautiful job."

June 30. Writes to Roth:
> I had recommended Eugene Berman to Ballo, but, since Berman is no longer available, I suggest John Piper. As to the stage director, Dr. Carl Ebert . . . he was here many times and we have already discussed at length all the problems of the staging. . . . As to the conductor . . . I would be very glad if they would ask Igor Markevich.

July 6. Roth writes that Schwarzkopf and Tourel have been engaged.

July 10. Writes to Stein enclosing corrected proofs and adding two measures:
> Kindly excuse me for giving you this trouble. Such things may happen when working under pressure.

July 16. Writes to Stein:
> It is all right with me if the authors prefer "My heart is cold" instead of "I cannot laugh."

July 16. Roth writes asking Stravinsky to conduct all three performances:
> The Italians do not want to use Markevich because they do not want him for the performances in Milan.

July 18. Sends corrections to Stein, adding:
> I am most worried about the third act, not yet received. . . . I am here for eleven more days only.

July 21. Writes to Stein:
> Please do as the librettists want. I have reached an agreement with Auden on this. But do not fight to have the German translation match exactly whatever alterations are made in the English text.

In the period between finishing *The Rake's Progress* and leaving for Europe to conduct its first performance, Stravinsky was disturbed by two deaths, one of them that of a close friend, the other of his greatest colleague:

April 16, 1951. The death of the dancer Adolph Bolm, a friend of Stravinsky's since 1910, shocks and saddens the composer and his wife. They had known that Bolm had been in a La Jolla hospital recently, yet did not suspect that he could be seriously ill.[96] Death, from myocardial infarction, occurred shortly before 8 A.M. The milkman, looking through the open window of Bolm's room, saw that he was not breathing, went to the front door, rang for Mrs. Bolm and gently warned her: "Be sure to say a prayer before you go to wake your husband."

During an afternoon drive with us, the widow tearfully recalls the first time that V.A.S. met the beloved "Adya"—in Paris, on V.A.S.'s name day, September 30, 1920. My own memories of Adya are of an exceptionally kind and considerate man, the most helpful to me of Stravinsky's friends when I first came to California. True, his account of the first *Apollon Musagète*, in which he wore a Louis Quatorze costume ("exactly what Igorfyodorovich wanted"), soon became familiar, and his fund of anecdotes about Nijinsky was by no means inexhaustible. It must also be admitted that Bolm's garrulous culture-talk barked at the composer's shins, although he played Patience during it, drumming his fingers on the table and nodding noncommittally. But when Stravinsky had the floor, Adya would prostrate himself at the composer's feet: *"Da, da, da* Igorfyodorovich," he would say (making a synaloepha of the first two syllables of the patronymic, and reducing the rest of it to *"itch"*).

Most condolences seek to convince the bereaved that the deceased is "better off where he is now" (wherever that may be), on grounds that if he or she had lived, then he or she would only have had to endure more suffering. Thus the object of grief is switched from the dead to the living, and the mourner, released from the obligation to mourn, can continue with plans for his own deathless future.

July 14, 1951. While we are at breakfast, Miss Brown, secretary of Evenings-on-the-Roof, telephones the news of Schoenberg's death last night. Stravinsky is far more upset by this than he was a few weeks ago by the death of Kussevitzky, whom he knew well. Within the hour, a telegram is dispatched to Mrs. Schoenberg: "Deeply shocked by saddening news of terrible blow inflicted to all musical world by loss of Arnold Schoenberg. Please accept my heartfelt sympathy. Igor Stravinsky." Stravinsky is silent all day.

Schoenberg's death ends a uniquely tangential relationship, a *coincidentia oppositorum,* the only bond between the two composers being the forty-year antinomical coupling of their names.[97] Apart from this, they knew practically nothing about, yet were deeply interested in, each other. "Soirée at the Werfels' with Stravinsky," Thomas Mann writes in his diary, in 1943: "Talked about Schoenberg."

July 19, 1951. Dinner at the home of Frau Mahler-Werfel,[98] who has the bosom of a pouter pigeon and the voice of a barracks bugle in one of her first husband's symphonies. Being entirely in German, the conversation is strenuous for me. Moreover, this survivor of distinguished husbands and consorts is deaf, and her wines, champagne, and cordials are both befuddling and unrefusable, since they are needed for her incessant toast-making. To Stravinsky, she quotes Mahler's "only those who can create can interpret," letting us know that the remark is aimed at her neighbor, Bruno Walter. When the subject turns to Schoenberg, she tells the story of the composer's objection to the illogical American system of addressing mail with the number before the street. To prove the illogicality, Schoenberg once instructed a taxi driver: "Take me to number forty-five. I will give you the name of the street when we get there." Recalling the night of Schoenberg's death, she says that, because the downstairs clock was several minutes fast, Mrs. Schoenberg thought that midnight had passed and, with it, her husband's superstitious fear of dying on the thirteenth; she then went to his bedroom, found him dead, and noticed that the clock in his room had not reached twelve. After dinner, Anna Mahler, Frau Alma's sculptress daughter, unwraps the death mask that she made of Schoenberg. This visibly moves Stravinsky, the more so after she tells him he is the first to see it. *Absit omen!* [From R.C.'s diary]

August 10, 1951. Aboard the S.S. *Constitution*. In the center, standing, are General and Mrs. Patrick Hurley and daughter.

For Stravinsky, the crossing to Naples on the S.S. *Constitution* was perilous. Always sensitive to air-conditioning,[99] he was confined to bed from the fourth day at sea, suffering from a cold that he attributed to the unadjustable air-cooling system in his stateroom (No. 118). On debarking in Naples, he had pneumonia. Mr. and Mrs. Theodore Stravinsky and the composer's granddaughter, Catherine,[100] came to meet the boat, the first time father and son had seen each other in twelve years. Auden and Kallman were also on the pier, and Ferdinand Leitner, who was

August 1951. On the train, Naples to Milan.

to prepare the singers and orchestra at La Scala before Stravinsky's arrival. In Naples, on August 24, Stravinsky signed a contract with Columbia Records to record the opera.

On August 27, at 9:00 P.M., the first rehearsal with orchestra, chorus, and some of the principals took place at La Scala. Afterward, at midnight, at Biffi Scala, the painter Ratto showed his maquettes: a Piranesi Bedlam; also the pinks and blues in the other scenes are Southern Italian, not English.

August 28. Rehearsal at 10:00 A.M.: Schwarzkopf, Tourel, Cuenod.

August 29–September 4. Rehearsals.

> The preliminary rehearsals took place in Milan, where Stravinsky and Auden were constantly together and closer than at any other time in their lives. Stravinsky lived in the Duomo Hotel, but since the librettists had neglected to make reservations, they were obliged to reside in a bordello, where, they said, "the girls were very understanding, but the rooms could be rented only by the hour and so were terribly expensive." Auden came to rehearsals in a white linen suit, polka-dotted with Chianti stains. He was assigned two jobs, coaching the chorus in English, no word of which could be understood, and advising the *"maestro della scena."* He ignored the second, since he disapproved of everything in the staging: "It could hardly be worse if the director were Erwin Piscator and the singers were climbing and descending ladders." Nor was Auden fond of the sets, particularly a Neapolitan-ice-cream-colored "London," but he openly objected only to the one of Truelove's home in the country. "With a house as grand as that," he told Signor Ratto, who had probably not read the libretto, "the 'Rake' would be better off marrying the daughter right away and foregoing his 'Progress.'"
>
> The outstanding event during the sojourn in Milan was a dinner that Auden gave for the Stravinskys. After it, everyone attended a performance of Giordano's *Fedora,* which was deeply disappointing in comparison to Chester Kallman's hilarious preview of it. At such times, Auden relinquished the limelight, except to contribute scraps of background information or to alert the Stravinskys to imminent high points. He was proud and happy. But, then, Wystan Auden's devotion to Chester Kallman was the most important fact of the poet's personal life, as well as the real subject of the libretto (the fidelity of true love), even transcending the confession of Auden's most popular lyric. More touching still, when Chester Kallman was unable to attend the second performance of the opera in Venice, Wystan Auden quietly left the theater before the end, not wishing to risk

having to bow alone and receive credit that ought to be shared with his friend.

It seems to this writer that Kallman was indispensable to Auden in at least one considerable area of his work: the older poet could never have written libretti without his younger colleague. What is more, in everything that Auden wrote, he relied on Kallman's critical judgment. No less important, Chester Kallman, though hardly the personification of bourgeois behavior himself, succeeded in imposing some of his Brooklyn common sense on his partner. Kallman was also the domesticator—if only to a degree, for the tamer was so mild that the animal was never entirely housebroken. Finally, and appearances to the contrary, the two poets understood each other. Kallman always knew, despite Auden's protective friends, that, no matter how "lost" his librettist colleague might seem to be, he was actually capable of finding his way home, of handling his business affairs, and of attending to his physical needs.

[W. H. Auden wrote that] Stravinsky, in his attitude towards Past and Present, Tradition and Innovation, has set an example which we should all do well to follow. . . . Those who were scandalized by Le Sacre du Printemps seem to us now to have been old fogies, but their reaction was genuine. They did not say to themselves: "Times have changed so we must change in order to 'be with it.' " . . . To do this is to reduce art to an endless series of momentary and arbitrary "happenings," and to produce in artist and public alike a conformism to the tyranny of the passing moment which is far more enslaving, far more destructive of integrity and originality, than any thoughtless copying of the past. Once more, Stravinsky: "What, may I ask, has become of the idea of universality—of a character of expression not necessarily popular but compelling to the highest imaginations of a decade or so beyond its time?" This, as we all know, his own compositions have achieved. If any young artist hopes to do the same, let him begin by forgetting all about "historical processes," an awareness of which, as the master has said, "is probably best left to future and other kinds of wage-earners." [W. H. Auden, The Observer, April 11, 1971.]

[Auden also commented, on a 1967 Columbia Record Album Note:] Too often in my life, I have met persons whom I revered but found myself unable to love; less often, I have met persons whom I loved but found myself unable to revere. I have met Igor Stravinsky and find myself able to do both: what a joy that is!

September 5. Train to Venice.

August 30, 1951. Milan. The Teatro alla Scala. With W. H. Auden during a rehearsal of *The Rake's Progress.*

September 11. Venice. At the Taverna La Fenice, after conducting the first performance of *The Rake's Progress,* with Nicolas Nabokov, Vera Stravinsky, Wystan Auden.

September 6. Teatro La Fenice. Afternoon rehearsal of Act III, evening rehearsal of Act III.

September 9. 9:00 P.M. Stravinsky conducts the dress rehearsal.

September 10. Ferdinand Leitner conducts the final rehearsal.

Auden returned to New York shortly after the premiere, but Kallman went back to Ischia. He wrote to Stravinsky from there, outlining a proposed revised version of *The Rake* with an additional scene for the third act. This subject was discussed with Stravinsky in Naples, when he conducted there in November, and it was during this stay that the Stravinskys and Kallman became close friends. (In later years, the Stravinskys endured the mayhem of Kallman's birthday parties, which fell on the same day as Mrs. Stravinsky's Russian-calendar celebration.) Regrettably, plans for two further collaborations came to nothing. A second libretto, whose protagonists were to be "Rossini (the man of heart), Berlioz (the man of intellect), and Mendelssohn (the man of sensibility)," did not develop beyond the talking stage. But the text of *Delia,* the masque written especially for Stravinsky, is complete, awaiting a composer with some of the same gifts of a Stravinsky—or a Mozart.

Stravinsky and Auden remained good friends after *The Rake's Progress* and until death parted them. Here is a glimpse of the poet three years later in Hollywood:

March 16, 1954. Auden and Isherwood for dinner. Auden suddenly seems to have aged, as if he had just returned from Shangri-la, and his face now has the craquelure of an Old Master—which, of course, he *is*, but not *that* old. He is becoming more moral by the hour, too ("It is profoundly wicked not to pay one's bills by return mail"), and at this rate will soon be sounding like Moses. Also, he seems to be growing more and more fond of ugly words, especially those associated with mining (tump, adit, buddle, gangue). After borrowing Stravinsky's copy of Von Hügel's *St. Catherine of Genoa,* the lecture-circuit bard departs, listing from the effects of five martinis and two decanters of wine. God rest his liver! . . . Later, Stravinsky says that when Auden was living with him while working on the scenario of the *Rake,* Yvgenia Petrovna reported that the soap, towels, and washcloths that she put out each day were never used, and that she never found even a trace of moisture in the shower or the sink. Stravinsky also says that when Lisa Sokoloff sat next to the poet at dinner and could not resist observing aloud that his fingernails were remarkably dirty, Auden did not reply but asked Stravinsky later: "Who was that extraordinary woman?" [From R.C.'s diary]

From New York, December 18, 1951, Stravinsky wrote to his daughter and her husband, Mr. and Mrs. André Marion, in California:

I was at Balanchine's all day yesterday, playing *The Rake* for him and discussing all the staging problems. The next days we will meet with Auden and Balanchine to fix the points that I made with Balanchine. . . . On the 28th the Met gives *Così fan tutte*—important for me to hear certain singers for *The Rake.*

Mrs. Stravinsky had written to the Marions on December 6:

Every day there are lunches, dinners, concerts, theaters. It is difficult to resist a Scotch or a cigarette. . . . *Papa n'a pas résisté.* . . . *La vie à New York est très palpitante,* but I want to begin to work at my painting.

None of the accounts of Stravinsky rehearsing for the first performance of *The Rake's Progress* in Venice reveals as much about him as does Martin Mayer's report of the recording sessions of the Metropolitan Opera's production of the piece in New York a year and a half later:

The biggest event of the 1952–3 Broadway season was not a play . . . but an opera, *The Rake's Progress,* at the big, brown, inefficient Metropolitan Opera House. . . . By the beginning of February, with first night only two weeks away, the public-relations bubbles were shimmering all over town. Stravinsky himself came across the continent to quarrel with conductor Fritz Reiner about the proper way to perform the music. . . . Bonwit Teller . . . decked out its windows with papier-mâché figures of the opera's prominent characters. . . . The premiere was scheduled for a Saturday matinée, to let the Met's large and financially important radio audience share the excitement, and . . . on February 15, 1953, at two o'clock, in a great hush of expectancy, the splendid gold curtain went up. . . .

Igor Stravinsky, who was seventy-one last June, is a very small, wiry man with a quick manner, a large nose and extraordinarily large ears. He always seems to be listening to something. He has associated throughout his life . . . with the most prominent figures in art, literature, and ballet . . . and he is himself a cosmopolitan intellectual, with a precise and surprisingly deep knowledge of half-a-dozen fields. . . .

Before *The Rake* he had never written "a real opera. By real," Stravinsky says, "I mean conventional." . . . The opera had its world premiere, September 11, 1951, as part of the Fourteenth Biennial Festival of Contemporary Music at the Fenice Theater in Venice. . . . The Met got to it in seventeen months, which is something of a speed record for the Monster, Sloth of 39th Street. And the first recording session was held fifteen days after the first performance at the Met. . . .

The clans assembled at seven o'clock Sunday night, March 1, at Columbia's studio, formerly the Adams Memorial Presbyterian Church, on Thirtieth Street just off Third Avenue in Manhattan. . . . Stravinsky stood on a podium almost in the center of the hall, facing the booth. In front of him was a 44-piece orchestra, less than half the full Met ensemble. Stravinsky likes his music soft. . . . "At home I compose on a Baldwin upright piano, muted, covered with felt, then I hear everything. I can enjoy. . . ."

Stravinsky . . . wore a white shirt open at the neck with a white muffler tucked inside—he is susceptible to chills. . . . Robert Craft, a young conductor . . . , [was there]. Stravinsky had asked him to come. "When I conduct I do not hear," he says. "Robert is my ears." Craft has remarkable ears; throughout the sessions Stravinsky deferred to his judgment in matters of pitch. . . .[101]

Stravinsky is a professional conductor, but his beat is sometimes hard to follow and his tempos for the recording were usually different from those to which Reiner had trained the orchestra and the cast.[102] There was, to put it mildly, trouble; but the troubles were fewer as the sessions wore on. Aside from his occasional involuntary gesture of annoyance when [the recording director] stopped the music, Stravinsky through more than fifteen hours of conducting never once lost his temper. . . . [He] established between himself and the orchestra an affection more important than any amount of technical wizardry, and the orchestra played better for [him] than it has in years for any of its regular conductors. . . .

At the start of each break Stravinsky would go to a closet of a dressing room off the hall, put on a sweater and dingy herringbone jacket, and take a nip of Scotch. Then he would dart up the half-flight of stairs and into the booth, light a cigarette (a cautious man, he smokes filtered cigarettes in a filter holder), hunch over the score and listen. The soloists, too, would sit in the booth and listen, keeping an eye on Stravinsky's reactions. . . .

Vera Stravinsky, the composer's tall, cheerful, blonde wife, sat through it all—music and break—in a corner of the room, reading a pocket mystery which to her delight was generally mistaken for a miniature score. . . .

Stravinsky was pleased; when the bells sounded through the loud-speaker in the graveyard scene he even interrupted his listening to turn to Craft and say, "I dreamed once in Switzerland that sound." . . . After four hours of recording, Stravinsky came up to the booth for a brief consultation. [The director] suggested that he take a rest before going back to work. "I have no time to rest," Stravinsky said. . . . [He] darted to his dressing room for a last shot of Scotch before putting [Hilde] Gueden through her big aria once again. . . . Then the seventy-one-year-old Stravinsky, who had been doing the actual physical exertion of conducting, came scurrying out of the dressing room and across the floor, and took the three steps to the podium at a jump. "I always," Stravinsky says, "have much more strength than I know."

Stravinsky liked the records, probably more than he liked the Met's performance, which was disfigured by unimaginative direction, the usual hideous sets and the Met's peculiar acoustics. Stravinsky had written a harpsichord accompaniment to the recitatives, but conductor Fritz Reiner told him that a harpsichord couldn't be heard in the Met and he'd have to take a piano. He took a piano. He had written for a small, Mozart-like orchestra, with woodwinds by twos, and "they made me take five, as though it was *Elektra*, by Strauss." And then his fine, transparent orchestration, through which the voices cut so cleanly, became muddied by numbers, and Reiner had to hold down the volume so that the singers could be heard. "The Met is a wonderful hall," Stravinsky says earnestly, ". . . but it is not even. Some places you don't hear."

May 19, 1952. Paris. Leaving the stage of the Théâtre des Champs-Elysées after conducting *Oedipus Rex*. Jean Cocteau, the Narrator at this performance, is in the foreground. (Writing to an official of the Gulbenkian Foundation, in Lisbon, April 13, 1966, Stravinsky said that "The *Oedipus* narration . . . always was an embarrassment.") Later in 1952, Cocteau sent a copy of his *Le Chiffre Sept* to Stravinsky, inscribing the volume "*à mon cher et admirable Igor, roi des nombres.*"

. . . Stravinsky likes records . . . , though he understands why most other composers don't. "The piano is not faithful," he says, ". . . and they have not learned to capture just the sound of the violin, either. But the woodwinds are perfect. The brasses are almost perfect. The percussion is almost perfect." Stravinsky listens to records on a prewar Stromberg Carlson with an LP turntable plugged in. Mrs. Stravinsky thinks they should get a new machine. [Martin Mayer, *Esquire*, December 1953]

For Stravinsky's *Oedipus Rex*, Cocteau had designed masks in which the parricide's eyes were popped out, like *truite au bleu*. Two performances of this semi-staged version were given, and at the second, on a double bill with Schoenberg's *Erwartung*,

both pieces conducted by Hans Rosbaud, the audience erupted in a demonstration against Cocteau:

During Cocteau's last speech, whistles, hisses, and boos from the upper part of the theater. When the noise subsides, Cocteau shrewdly asks the public to show respect for *Stravinsky's* work. This statement provokes applause which is followed by more boos, then by counter-applause. The war between the claques continues at the end of the performance, too, but Igor has disappeared at the beginning of the fracas and is waiting for us in the hotel. [From V.A.S.'s diary]

A letter from C.-A. Cingria to Stravinsky a day or so later advises him that

The public incident with Cocteau should not be exaggerated. . . . But there was an element in the hall which would have preferred the Hellenism of the repertory. . . . I understood why you left the hall, and finally I had a glimpse of you.

Stravinsky made the acquaintance of Albert Camus earlier in the month, and a letter to Stravinsky, July 29, 1952, from his son Theodore, who had recently seen Camus, reveals that the writer was as taken by the composer as the composer was by him.

Stravinsky was invited to celebrate his birthday in Holland, at the beginning of 1952.

Queen Juliana, her ministers, ambassadors, generals: I have never seen so much pomp and gold galloon, so many epaulettes, medals, and swords. Stravinsky and I are the only non-uniformed guests not in white tie. At intermission, following Mozart's Serenade, K. 361—or, rather, about half of it, and that in absurd tempi—the Queen sends for Stravinsky, bids him sit next to her, declares her admiration for his "works," and is not only taken aback but made speechless by his re-

June 4, 1952. The Hague. With Queen Juliana, at the opening of the Holland Festival. .

sponse: "And which of my works do you admire, Your Majesty?" The program ends with his String Concerto, in which nearly everything, including the relationships of tempi in the first movement, is wrong. Yet the conductor, Van Otterloo, when presented to the composer afterward, asks how he liked the performance. Stravinsky: "Do you want a conventional answer or the truth?" Van O. manfully opts for the latter, which is "Horrible!" [From R.C.'s diary]

Stravinsky's music was always warmly received in Holland, which was also the first country to name a street after him, the "STRAWINSKILAAN" in Voorschoten. The 1952 Holland Festival featured his music and so did the 1969 one, which he was planning to attend until prevented by illness.

Shortly after this photograph was taken, the Stravinskys, Alexei Haieff, and the present writer drove from Flint, Michigan, where the Stravinskys had purchased a Buick at the factory, to Los Angeles, by way of Glacier National Park, Lake Louise, Spokane, San Francisco. Here is a vignette from the trip, the day of Stravinsky's seventieth birthday:

June 18, 1952. We drive 150 miles along the Baltic-like shore of Lake Superior to Duluth, where an attempt is made to celebrate Stravinsky's birthday in a restaurant called "The Flame." But the proper liquid

June 5, 1952. The Hague. Cutting a birthday cake.

ingredients are lacking, and the only available bottle of wine, a Beaujolais *rouge*, is served in an ice-filled bucket. Not having adjusted to the improbability of finding well-stocked wine cellars in hinterland America, he is furious, but Alexei defuses him with a fit of giggling. Reverting to his restaurant routine, Stravinsky asks the waiter to remove the ice-water; demands "*un couteau qui coupe*" (this even before trying the one that he has); orders "a tall empty glass" (as an *étui* for his spectacles); tests the legs of the table for unevenness (and, when a wobble is discovered, inserts wedges under all four legs); insists on the instant removal of used plates, and, in exasperation, pushes them himself to a vacant table.

In the afternoon, V.A.S. drives, her husband next to her, giving directions from a road map spread on his knees. Not having been properly slaked from the noon meal, he resorts to a thermos, thereby flooding the car with a redolence of whiskey and a phosphorescence of discourse. But at night, in a motel in Bemidji, Minnesota, she tells Alexei and me that Stravinsky is offended because we neglected to include him in our backseat conversation about Bach—which we considered too trivial to interest him. [From R.C.'s diary]

Life obtained a report from Haieff of an event that took place a day or two later:

Stravinsky was making an automobile trip with his friend, the composer Alexei Haieff, in Glacier National Park. They were climbing a high peak and as they negotiated the curves of the steep road, Stravinsky began to give increasing signs of temper. When they reached the top, Stravinsky got out to look at the view. "I despise mountains. They don't tell me anything." [*Life*, March 23, 1953]

A few years later, Stravinsky read books about geomorphology and, after making flights over Greenland and Alaska, about periglacial movement, but he always disliked travel-brochure views:

At Niagara Falls, looking at the roaring water, he broke out in German, French, and Russian: "It's something like a revolution—it's terrible." [*Newsweek*, January 23, 1937]

What attracts Stravinsky in a landscape is composition, frame, dimension perpectivized by architecture—the castle on the Italian hilltop, the arch of the broken aqueduct in the pasture. The unique landscape on the walls of his studio is a Zen-like Rembrandt drawing of a black fence bisecting a field of snow. Stravinsky's indifference to mountains is surprising for someone who lived so long in Switzerland, but he dismisses the Alps as "Wagnerian." [From R.C.'s diary, July 30, 1948]

In July 1951, after finishing *The Rake's Progress*, Stravinsky composed "The Maidens Came," for mezzo-soprano, two flutes, and cello. On February 2, 1952, he resumed work on this Cantata of anonymous Elizabethan lyrics, with the piece that was to become the mezzo-soprano and tenor duet, "Westron Wind"; in its first form, however, the movement was to have been purely instrumental, and the ensemble included horns, trombone, bass, and "woods." On February 8, he began to compose "To-Morrow

Shall Be My Dancing Day" and, only after finishing it, returned to "Westron Wind," adding the two vocal parts and completing the score on March 21.

"To-Morrow Shall Be My Dancing Day" marks the first effect on Stravinsky of Schoenberg's serial principle, for, although cancrizans of the kind found in this Ricercar were employed centuries before, Stravinsky came to them here by way of his contemporary, having heard some of the Viennese master's music, as well as much discussion about it, in Europe in the autumn of 1951. Stravinsky's typescript of the poem "To-Morrow Shall Be My Dancing Day" contains musical notations in the margins opposite the lines "To call my true love to the dance," "The Jews on me they made . . . ," and "Before Pilate the Jews . . ."; and the pitches and some of the rhythms are the same as in the final score. The notation for "Before Pilate the Jews . . ." consists of nine notes derived from "The Maidens Came" (at "We will therefore sing no more"), and to these nine Stravinsky has added two more at the end, then drawn a chart of the four orders—original, retrograde, inverted, retrograde inverted—of his eleven-note "series."

While composing "To-Morrow Shall Be My Dancing Day," Stravinsky attended rehearsals, conducted by this writer, of Schoenberg's Septet-Suite. After the first of these, on February 12, Stravinsky asked numerous questions about the construction of the piece, as he did after rehearsals on the 17th, 20th, 21st, and 24th. (On February 17, he composed the music for "And rose again on the third day," and, on the 22nd, for "The Holy Ghost on me did glance": the piece was not written in the order in which it appears in the final score.) On March 12 and 21, April 12 and 14, he also heard this writer's rehearsals of Schoenberg's Serenade. At the end of April, after arranging the 1920 Concertino for an ensemble of twelve instruments (completed on Easter Day), Stravinsky flew to Europe, where, in Paris, he attended performances of *Wozzeck* and *Erwartung*, both wholly new to him. Returning to Hollywood, June 29, he composed the "Lykewake Dirge," thus completing the Cantata (on July 21, according to one of his letters to E. Roth).

The first movement of Stravinsky's own Septet, begun on July 22, was completed August 8, on which day he started to make a fair copy of the sketch score. The first notation for the second movement, the Passacaglia, is found on a sheet of eight-stave music paper, on one side of which is the series of Schoenberg's wind Quintet, in the hand of the present writer, together with a demonstration of the way in which Schoenberg deployed the twelve pitches harmonically; on the other side, Stravinsky has drawn the series of his Passacaglia, clearly using the Schoenberg as a model. The Passacaglia was composed between mid-August and November 6, 1952, during which period Stravinsky heard the present writer conduct four Schoenberg memorial concerts and their numerous rehearsals. Stravinsky began the Gigue finale immediately after finishing the Passacaglia, but he did not complete it until January 21, 1953, after conducting concerts and recordings in Cleveland and New York. The first performance took place an entire year later, at Dumbarton Oaks, Washington, D.C., January 24, 1954. After it, Stravinsky wrote to his wife:

Dearest Vera . . . Septet received indifferently well by a young audience. Today the audience will be different, probably indifferently bad. . . . Tuesday is the premiere of the *Rake* at the Met [of the opera's second season there], but I record the Septet that night. . . . [Original in English]

Stravinsky continued to explore the possibilities of composing with series in the *Three Songs from William Shakespeare*. These date from the late summer and autumn of 1953, the first of the group, "Musick to heare," having been completed on September 7, the last, "When Daisies pied," on October 6. But 1953 was not a productive year for composition. Stravinsky was in New York until March 11, recording and conducting concerts there and in Baltimore, and, from March 31 to June 4, was again

December 1953. Philadelphia. The Museum of Art. With Vincent Van Gogh. Photograph by Adrian Siegel.

on a concert tour that took him to Havana, Caracas, and Boston. In July, he began to compose music for a poem by a friend, Edward James, but, on the 23rd, entered the Cedars of Lebanon Hospital (Los Angeles) for a prostatectomy. This was performed the next day by Dr. Elmer Belt, the Leonardo collector; after returning home (August 3), Stravinsky suffered from spells of dizziness, which his physicians attributed to the spinal anesthetic. Later in August, Lincoln Kirstein commissioned the ballet that was to become *Agon*, and, on September 25, Stravinsky wrote to his publishers to say that he had accepted the offer and would compose "a kind of symphony to be danced." In November, Stravinsky conducted concerts with the Los Angeles Philharmonic and, on December 20, flew to New York for concerts with the Philadelphia Orchestra.

Stravinsky wrote *In Memoriam: Dylan Thomas* in February and March 1954, finishing the "Song" on March 14, the instrumental Prelude on March 21, and the Postlude in June, after a concert tour in Europe. During July, he arranged his *Balmont Songs* (1911), "The Flower" and "The Dove," for the same combination of instruments that he had used in 1913 in the *Three Japanese Lyrics*.

"Where's Vera? Is she painting?" This used to be Igor Stravinsky's first question as he emerged from his workroom, and the answer, that she was indeed painting, assured him that, in the center of his world, all was well, for the marriage between this tall, gentle, calm, soft-voiced, quintessentially feminine woman and the tiny, bony, anxious, basso-profundo, masculine man was as nearly perfect a match as can be imagined. When the two did not complement each other in their likes and dislikes, it was only because these were the same: their love of birds and flowers, for example, and of animals and paintings. Every day, Vera Stravinsky would make a list of errands and business chores to be accomplished, and, every day, Stravinsky would write at the top of it: "First you have to kiss me." When the Stravinskys moved to Hollywood, Mrs. Stravinsky opened an art gallery, La Boutique, and resumed the painting that she had not practiced since the Russian Revolution. When visiting Los Angeles in 1954, Gasparo del Corso, director of the Galleria Obelisco in Rome, invited her to exhibit there, and, in the following year, she held her first one-woman show at his gallery. For nearly twenty years, the composer and the painter unveiled their work to each other before anyone else heard or saw it. And, for twenty years, the composer was the painter's most helpful critic:

Mr. Stravinsky has always encouraged me. Of course he criticizes and says what I should have done here and there, but if he likes something, he says, "That's marvelous, I'll take it and hang it up." [*Mexico DF News*, April 8, 1961]

Stravinsky had an unerring eye for composition in painting, as well as the eye of a cartoonist for the characteristic feature, the essential detail. He so cherished his wife's pictures that to

OPPOSITE:
1954. At home, 1260 North Wetherly Drive. This photograph, by Michael Barrie, is Vera Stravinsky's favorite photograph of her husband.

August 1957. Dartington Hall, Totnes.

exhibit them before him was to risk having one or more impounded in the already overcrowded gallery, museum, flea market of his studio. As for the painter's criticisms of the composer, no one has ever heard of any, but the Stravinskys' closest friends can testify that he wrote all of his music for her first, that the first sharing of his discoveries with her was sacred to him, that her response was more important than "the world's."

Nature—leaves, flowers, seashells, clouds—is the material of Vera Stravinsky's painting. But she prefers nature in a certain mood, rainy rather than sunny. "I like the mélancolie in a landscape," she says, "and I like early-morning mists, woods, and fields blurred by rain, night scenes with mysterious explosions of light." Her first American pictures were inspired by automobile trips through the swamps of Louisiana and the redwood forests of the Northwest. (The Stravinskys traveled extensively by automobile in their early years in the United States and between 1950 and 1954 crossed the continent six times.) Oil rigs near Ventura, California, were another source of inspiration, "but at night, when they look like Christmas trees." Mrs. Stravinsky continued to paint on each return to Europe in the 1950s and 1960s, most rewardingly on the Bosporus, in the great city that her boat did not reach in 1919.

Yet her pictures are not really "of" any of these places nor "of" any "thing." She does not copy and does not sketch, nor even take notes, except for verbal reminders of colors in a composition of nature. To her, color is composition, and her greatest gifts are her color sense and skill in color manipulation. She says that her imagination

is ignited from the outside, though I paint entirely from the inside, depending on imagination alone. I try to forget the relationship with the object when I begin to paint. Birds, fish, fragments of objects, natures mortes: they must retain no more than a soupçon of reality in the painting.

Vera Stravinsky's techniques are her own. She has been a gouache painter first and foremost, partly because she likes the velvety texture, partly because of circumstances. While on concert tours with her husband, she never had sufficient time for oils to dry, and acrylics and siccatives had not yet been developed. Needlework was another occupation on these travels; she designed and stitched more than a score of very attractive rugs while attending backstage.

Vera Stravinsky applies paint with spatula, sponge, palette knife, sable brush, the flat of her hand, then rubs the paint with paper, scratches it with a table fork, or even washes it in her bathtub. In the case of work that displeases her—and her touchstones tell her immediately—this washing is an act of purification, the need to begin with "a clean slate." She will briefly immerse a gouache in the bath, and, once the baptismal waters have dried, paint a new surface over the palimpsest of the old.

After her husband's death, Vera Stravinsky did not paint.

Then one day, many months later, she copied a poem by Kuz-min, forming large Russian letters in bright colors, and surrounding and intertwining them with flowers, weeds or seaweeds, starfish or stars. It was the most "Russian" picture she had ever painted, a vision of Stravinsky's grave in the Russian corner of the cemetery island in the Venetian lagoon. Though a painful revelation of her feelings, the picture was a good one, and it broke the barrier. She began to work regularly thereafter, and with new inventiveness, for she possesses some of her husband's phenomenal powers of self-renewal. In the dreaded lonely moment of finishing a picture and wanting to show it, she would start toward his room, which she had never entered since his death. Eventually she did go there, and begin to paint there, and now she works exclusively in his room and seems happier in it than anywhere else in the house. Stravinsky, of course, would be—or, as the present writer prefers to think, is—happy too. The answer to his "Where is Vera? Is she painting?" is "Yes."

The favorite twentieth-century painter of both Stravinskys was Paul Klee. In 1966, Mrs. Stravinsky found a statement by Klee which she translated as follows:

Let art sound like a fairy tale and be at home everywhere. Let it work with good and evil as do the eternal powers. And to men let it be a holiday . . . a transfer to another world. . . .

One day shortly after Stravinsky's death, she discovered that he had pasted this motto on the flyleaf of Claude Roy's *Paul Klee aux Sources de la Peinture*.

Here are two impressions of the painter:

ABSTRACT OIL PAINTER: MRS. STRAVINSKY, A GIFTED WIFE

"Hullo . . . hullo . . . hullo." With charming informality, Mrs. Stravinsky complies with her husband's request "to be presented to these people" at his press conference yesterday. She sat beside him (as she has so often done at similar conferences). One sensed the feeling of complete accord between the couple, who have been married since 1940. Mrs. Stravinsky listened intently to all the questions fired at her husband, and, at times, with an expressive shrug of the shoulders or a wave of the hands, she seemed to anticipate the reply.

A glamorous figure in a black frock, the painter wife of the famous composer quickly established friendly relations with the women who had come to interview her. Mrs. Stravinsky, who travels for six months of the year with her husband, paints abstracts in oils. Though she is intensely interested in music, it is not the inspiration of her paintings. These have been exhibited in many capitals of the world, and she is planning an exhibition in New York next January.

Her home is in Hollywood, where, she said, "we are very spoiled." The Stravinskys have had the same Russian cook for fifteen years. "We like simple food, but very well prepared. We suffer when we travel.

Coffee must be Italian espresso. Bread must be dark—rye or pumpernickel—and roast beef must be pink, not red or brown. These things are not always easy to find in hotels. In two weeks, however, we will be back home," she added with a wave of her hands. [*Wellington Evening Post,* New Zealand, November 1961]

Mrs. Stravinsky told us she would rather be at home preparing for her New York exhibition in January. "New York is my favorite city," she says. . . . "I shall always put my husband's music before my painting. . . . Of course I read *Dr. Zhivago*. Not because Boris Pasternak is Russian, but because everyone insisted. It had some moving passages, some not so good. You know, the mention of snow, trees, and the countryside appeals very much to Russians, who wept over the book. . . . In Hollywood we have only three weeks of green. The rest of the time it is yellow, or yellow and brown, as far as can be seen. . . ."

Often there will be a concert of recorded music at home from Stravinsky's collection. Other composers send tapes of their works for his critical appraisal.[103] Perhaps one evening, though, it will be an all-Beethoven concert, or Schoenberg. . . .

To be badgered and bullied by hard-boiled philistine reporters and photographers; to guard her husband's frail health by playing the role of buffer against public molestation generally (rather in the manner of Tolstoy's wife); in short, to be the wife of the greatest living composer demands a great degree of patience, tact, and self-sacrifice. Madame Stravinsky, who is a true cosmopolitan, reveals all three qualities, tempered with a relaxed charm and straightforwardness which quickly takes the sting out of over-inquisitive journalists.

Madame Stravinsky attends all of her husband's concerts, and she thinks that perhaps he has taken notice of her criticism of certain passages in his music. "I can generally tell if the program he has chosen to conduct is right for a particular audience." [*New Zealand Listener,* December 1, 1961]

Stravinsky had agreed to compose a third ballet, to form a trilogy with *Apollo* and *Orpheus,* shortly after the first performance of the latter. As early as December 2, 1949, he wrote to Lincoln Kirstein, saying that "the ballet is always in mind, but *The Rake's Progress* will take another year to complete." At the beginning of December 1953, Stravinsky composed a version of the opening fanfare of the new ballet scored for three trumpets, a complete piece in ten measures that can be performed separately. The following month, in New Orleans, where he had gone to conduct a concert, he referred to the "third ballet" publicly, but said that

I can't write anything when I'm running around this way. All that I can do is to sleep, rehearse, conduct, and take care of a cold brought on by rapid changes of climate. [*Times-Picayune,* January 30, 1954]

The name *Agon* was not chosen until August 1954, when Stravinsky wrote the final form of the first movement. By September 26, he had composed the work through the "Triple Pas de Quatre" (then called simply "Coda"); by October, the "Prelude"; and, by November, the "Saraband-Step" and the "Gailliard," this last completed on the 29th. The "Pas de Trois," which follows,

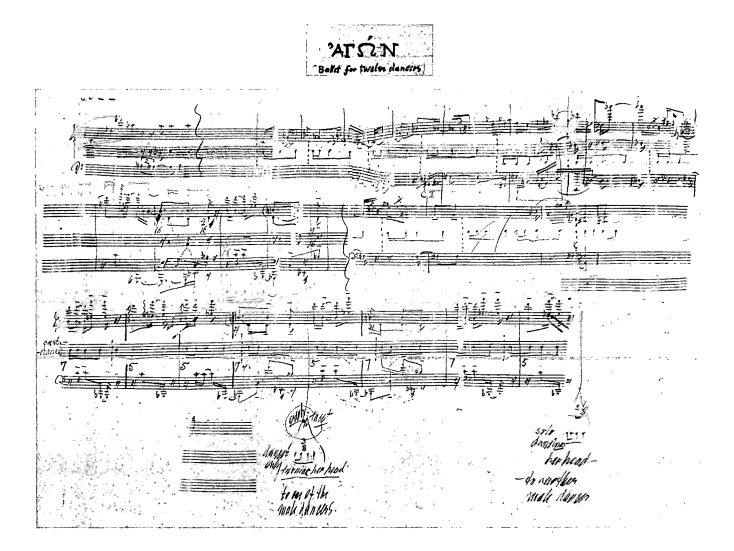

was completed on December 23, but, three weeks before, on December 4, Stravinsky had written to Alessandro Piovesan, director of music at the Biennale in Venice, agreeing, in principle, "to compose a Passion according to St. Mark on the Evangelical Latin text." *Agon* was put aside at almost the halfway point for the *Canticum Sacrum* and the *Vom Himmel hoch* variations. On September 11, 1955, Stravinsky wrote to Nicolas Nabokov saying that *Agon* was half completed and, on March 15, 1957, wrote to him saying that the ballet would soon be finished, [104] but that "such music cannot be composed in a hurry." Balanchine himself contributed a program note for the first performance of the ballet: [105]

June 8, 1956. This draft of the "Bransle Gai" (*Agon*) shows that the castanet solos, dividing the music into stanzas, were an afterthought. More important, the page reveals that Stravinsky visualized choreographic movement as he composed; the *Agon* sketches include diagrams of the positions of the dancers at the beginning of each movement.

Agon . . . [was] planned by Stravinsky and myself for twelve of our ablest technicians; it has no story except the dancing itself; it is less a struggle or contest than a measured construction in space, demonstrated by moving bodies set to certain patterns or sequence[s] in rhythm and melody. . . . In order to compose dances for *Agon*, I have abandoned my attitude as a cook and tried to put myself in the state of mind of a carpenter. The cooking has all been done by a master before I was needed to provide any accompaniment. I must try to find some visual equivalent which is a complement, not an illustration. Such music as Stravinsky's cannot be illustrated. *Agon* was invented for dancing, but it is hard to invent dances of a comparable density, quality, metrical consistency, variety, formal mastery, symmetrical asymmetry. Just as a cabinet-maker must select his wood for the job—palisandre, angelique, rosewood, briar or pine—so a ballet-carpenter must find a dominant quality of gesture, a strain or palette of consistent movement, an active scale of flowing patterns which reveals to the eye what Stravinsky tells the sensitized ear. There is the skeleton frame; there is the division into panels or drawers; then there is the inlay work which is so invested into the structure that it is never merely decorative or rhetorical. . . . [New York City Center program booklet, December 1, 1957]

On December 9, Kirstein wrote to Stravinsky:

Agon has become a popular success; we have changed our programs to accommodate six additional performances.

In an interview in Rome, April 7, 1955, Stravinsky talked about his trips to Etruscan archeological sites and to Ostia—where the perfect acoustics of the Roman amphitheater astonished him—and about the Sibelius medal, which, Stravinsky said, he would not go to Finland to receive because "Helsinki is . . . too near to a certain city that I have no desire to see again." The interviewer described Stravinsky "climbing the Spanish steps, now full of azaleas before Easter," and added that

to be near Stravinsky one immediately has the impression that this man is *al corrente* concerning the whole literary and artistic activity of the world. Of his Roman friends he spoke especially about the books of Carlo Levi, the paintings of Guttuso. His knowledge of old music is profound. Concerning new music he says that "Webern has opened many doors."

But the most surprising of Stravinsky's remarks was the statement that he was already at work on a *"passione secondo San Marco."* On April 18, he was in Venice, testing the acoustics of Santa Maria della Salute and of the "Frari," with the aid of a group of musicians from the orchestra of La Fenice, this in the event that the Basilica of St. Mark might not be available for the performance of the new Passion—eventually the *Canticum Sacrum.* From Venice, he went to Switzerland and Germany for concerts, and, in Stuttgart, gave a broadcast interview (with Eric Winkler), one of the composer's rare public talks in German. On May 4–5, he flew from Copenhagen to Los Angeles on the newly inaugurated polar route, which, at the time, included a stop on the west coast of Greenland, as well as at Winnipeg. At the beginning of June, he started to compose the *Canticum Sacrum,* completing the *"Dedicatio"* on the 8th, and *"Surge Aquilo"* on July 20. On July 27, he wrote to his publisher about my new work for which I have finally got the right title, *Canticum Sacrum ad Honorem Sancti Marci Nominis*. [It will be in] five movements [and] I composed it after the Vulgata. The phrases of the first and last movements are those of the St. Mark Gospel's last verses, the parting words of Christ to the Apostles. The texts for the other movements are taken from . . . [the] *Canticum Canticorum*, from *Deuteronomy* and from the *Psalms*. . . . Today, by surface mail, I am sending the first 17 pages of the full score. . . . Do not let anybody see this music before it is completed. . . .

The *Caritas* section was completed on August 7, and, on the 29th, Stravinsky wrote to his publisher again:

. . . Please tell Mr. Roberto Barry that Buenos Aires and Montevideo are out. . . . As to my *Canticum Sacrum* . . . though I always [refuse] any interview on this subject, I found it suitable to give my friend Robert Craft some details concerning the text, music and construction to enable him to write about it. . . . Nobody will know better than he, who is a first class professional musician and writer.

Stravinsky completed the "Virtues" movement on September 30, his wife's name day, for the words Viera Nadiezhda Lyubov stand for Faith, Hope, Love, in the Russian Orthodox Calendar. On November 2, he finished the *"Brevis Motus Cantilenae."* His editor in London, Erwin Stein, wrote on November 3:

I saw the beginning of your *Canticum Sacrum* and am enormously impressed . . . one recognizes your mind and hand in every bar. . . . I am fascinated by your contrapuntal style. . . . Your 12-tone rows will cause an upheaval in the musical world and will keep analysts busy. I do not know whether you should help them by the arrows you have indicated in the score. It is a question of principle about which I should be happy to know your opinion. Is it necessary that the listener knows the rows or is it sufficient that he feels the unity of form which the rows provide? . . ." [Here Stravinsky wrote in the margin: "as always, I forgot to delete the arrows."]

Stravinsky answered on November 14, enclosing the repeat of the last section of *"Caritas"*:

. . . I decided to enlarge this section by repeating it because of the new text (First Epistle of St. John). . . .

On November 21, nearly a year ahead of schedule, he completed the *"Illi autem profecti."*

The *Canticum Sacrum* being comparatively short, Stravinsky decided to orchestrate and "re-compose" Bach's *Vom Himmel hoch* variations for performance as a companion piece with the *Canticum*, employing approximately the same instrumental ensemble, and also containing five movements—like the number of St. Mark's domes, of the prongs of a gondola, and of the *sestiere* of the great sinking city itself. (Stravinsky did not, however, base the *Canticum* on an architectural analogy—as, for example,

August 1956. Venice. Trying on a shoe.

Pointing to it, smiling.

Leaving the shop.

In the street.

On the way to the Piazza, glancing toward the Frezzeria.

Returning to the hotel, after an espresso at Florian's.

Busoni did in a fugue inspired by the proportions of the Palace of the Popes at Avignon.) Variation I was completed on December 29, 1955, and Variation II about a week later, both in the Gladstone Hotel, New York. On January 11, 1956, Stravinsky left by train for Los Angeles, where he finished the final three variations on January 20 and 26 and February 9, respectively. The chorale was composed last, and the full score completed—and dedicated to this writer—on March 27.

Concerning the program of the first performance, Stravinsky wrote to his publisher:

> I suggested to [the Biennale] that R. Craft conduct old Venetian music before I conduct the *Canticum*. Piovesan probably does not understand my reasons which are: Craft has a great deal of experience conducting and recording this music whereas I have none; the *Canticum* is by far the most difficult work of mine to sing and for the whole ensemble. I anticipate such conducting problems for myself that I do not want to take on the additional worry of conducting Baroque music. . . . Now Piovesan will probably re-propose that I conduct a program all of my own music. But I know the *Canticum* will suffer if first performed together with any of my earlier compositions, and I know better . . . what kind of piece the *Canticum* is. . . . I have never heard trombones and trumpets in any Italian orchestra of the caliber I need. . . . [Letter of May 1, 1956]

The premiere of the *Canticum Sacrum* took place on September 13, 1956:

> In Venice one night last week, 3,000 special guests . . . followed purple-robed Cardinal Roncalli, Patriarch of Venice,[106] into the Byzantine Basilica of St. Mark for one of the strangest events in its 1,000-year history. Outside, thousands more were gathered around loudspeakers to hear Igor Stravinsky's latest work. . . . Later . . . somebody asked [him] why he wrote in the twelve-tone system. "Who says it's twelve-tone?" Stravinsky snapped. [*Time*, September 24, 1956]

> Even for those who have believed implicitly in Stravinsky's ability to master any form, it was a source of wonder that the composer, now in his seventies, should have so regenerated his ideas as to fuse his once revolutionary methods with that other important development, the twelve-tone technique. . . . After the concert Stravinsky was heard saying to a reporter that perhaps he was still too young to appreciate the importance of mathematics. "For," Stravinsky said, "mathematics *is* important." The over-all effect of the *Canticum* is Byzantine rather than Roman Catholic. . . . After hearing it repeated at rehearsal and in performance, it seemed to one listener to blend marvelously with the mathematics and metaphysics of the great basilica. [*New York Times*, September 1956]

> An astounding degree of both integration of the material and balance of form is achieved, notwithstanding the music's diversity. The five movements enclose a circle, whose very center, the middle section of the third movement, consists, again, of five small divisions—by the alternation of soloists and chorus. This center is surrounded by the two other sections of the third movement, which correspond with each

September 26, 1956. Berlin. Tempelhof Airport. With Nicolas Nabokov.

other in that a choral canon is included in both of them, while the whole movement is connected by the ritornello. Pieces for solo voice are placed before and after the third movement, for tenor and baritone respectively. And the whole is encircled by movements that are mirrors of each other. The elaborate organization of its structure makes the form of the *Canticum Sacrum* very consistent. There is a distinct contrast between the texture of the first and last movements, on the one hand, and that of the rest of the work on the other: the one is harmonic, the other contrapuntal. I feel that the less pliable structure of the outer movements—those on the circle's circumference—contributes to the consolidation of the whole. The song *Surge Aquilo* is a piece of great lyric beauty, perhaps the purest lyric Stravinsky has written. . . . [Erwin Stein, in *Tempo*, Summer 1956]

Stravinsky scarcely mentions the event in his own letters, though he described the premiere as a success when writing to Aaron Sapiro, September 15. On the same day, Vera Stravinsky wrote to her friend and Hollywood neighbor Catherine d'Erlanger: [107]

The concert is over. The atmosphere in San Marco with all the lighted candles and the gold of the mosaics, was unforgettable. The Patriarch of Venice wanted the concert to be broadcast for those who could not afford to pay. [September 15]

The day before conducting a concert of his works in Montreux, September 25, 1956, Stravinsky underwent a hematological analysis in the laboratory of Dr. Simon Berenstein, Lausanne. The results showed that certain components were elevated, but not alarmingly. Then, a week later, while conducting the end of the first movement of the Symphony in C in a concert in the Titania-Palast, Berlin, Stravinsky suffered a stroke. He managed to finish the Symphony and to complete the concert, though, during intermission, he complained of feeling ill. The next morning (October 3), he was unable to articulate words clearly, complaining of numbness on the right side of his body, as well as of difficulty in coordinating the movements of his right hand. Yet he refused to see a doctor, and, instead, lunched with his friend Eric Winkler, went for a drive in Zehlendorf and Grünwald, and, at 11:00 P.M., received Hermann Scherchen, with whom he drank *Sekt* and ate goose livers and apple strudel. Feeling slightly better the next day and refusing to admit that anything serious could be wrong with him, Stravinsky flew to Munich.

On arriving in the Hotel Vier Jahreszeiten from the airport,

October 14, 1956. Munich. In the Red Cross Hospital.

Stravinsky complains of a heavy tongue, increasing numbness, loss of balance, and his reflexes are poor. Moreover, the unpressurized airplane from Berlin has given him an excruciating headache. Against his orders, I oblige Karl Amadeus Hartmann to call a doctor. At 5 P.M. Professor Diehl examines Stravinsky and informs V.A.S. and me that a slight stroke has occurred, but that a "massive" one is a possibility within 24 hours. Diehl returns in the evening to take Stravinsky's blood pressure, which is still 200. [From R.C.'s diary]

On October 5, Mrs. Stravinsky canceled all of her husband's forthcoming concerts, and George Balanchine flew to Munich from Paris to see his stricken friend. On the 6th, Stravinsky's blood pressure was almost normal, but his mouth was fish-like at the side, and he was feeble. Dr. Diehl would not say whether the danger was over.

On the 10th, at 5:00 P.M. Stravinsky was taken to the Rote Kreuz Hospital on Nymphenburgstrasse and Dr. Diehl diagnosed "eine multiloculäre Encephalomalacie, bedingt durch atheromatösarteritisch-thrombotisch-spastische Prozesse im Bereich des Cerebrums." In the hospital, the patient rapidly improved, and soon the main danger came from his self-awareness.

"What happened to me?" I.S. asks when we arrive at the hospital this morning. "One side feels as if it were on a different level from the other. I try to force my brain, but it is an effort for me to talk." He is better but still has that fish-out-of-water look and is slow and distant. He becomes agitated, too, if more than one of us talks at the same time. His talk consists largely of self-recriminations, accusing his brain of being unclear. He is obviously unable to manage an orchestra rehearsal, let alone a concert, yet Diehl has given permission for him to conduct in Rome. [From R.C.'s diary, October 11, 1956]

On the 23rd, in an effort to persuade Stravinsky to give up smoking, Dr. Diehl told the patient the whole truth about his thrombosis, but the only effect of this was to reduce the consumption of cigarettes to two a day. Stravinsky was upset by the death of Walter Gieseking, reported by a nurse, and, in the beginning of November, by the Hungarian crisis, which made him anxious to leave not only the hospital but also Europe. On November 11, he was very pleased by a telegram from Paris signed "Soulimas": "Profoundly moved by the beauty of the *Canticum*" (at a performance conducted by the present writer). Discharged on November 17, the composer, with his wife, left Munich by night train on the 22nd for Rome, where, on the 29th, he conducted the *Canticum Sacrum*.

I.S. conducts for the first time since his stroke, in the crowded Teatro Eliseo. At the last minute, he obliges me to do *Vom Himmel hoch* for him. Then, in the *Canticum*, he takes everything differently from his rehearsal, beginning, for example, in a fast 4, after having rehearsed in a slow 8. Nevertheless, the performance has a salutary effect on his morale, and he does not leave the reception for him until 3 A.M. [From R.C.'s diary]

Stravinsky was examined in Rome, in London, and in New York. Here is a letter from his doctors in the last of these three cities:

Report of Drs. Jules Pierre, M.D., 115 East 72nd Street, New York, and Dr. Walter Redisch, M.D.

Maestro Igor Stravinsky has been a patient of one of us (Dr. Pierre) whenever in New York. When he came to New York from Europe this time, he gave a history of having had two "small strokes" within the past ½ year and of having been treated by venesection. He was seen by both of us in consultation, and it was found that there was no focal neurological sign except for facial weakness on the right side, and that he was in mild failure. Hematological work done in England showed that he had polycythemia with a high hematocrit and that the hemogram had improved markedly after bloodletting. Laboratory work here showed the following: between December 24 and January 22 the red blood count rose from 5,150,000 (over 5,270,000 on January 7) to 5,420,000; his hemoglobin rose from 17.5 G to 18.8 G. His hematocrit from 54% to 59%. There were no abnormalities in the white blood cell picture, the count ranging between 8,800 to 9,200. His failure responded promptly to digitalization with digoxin, and he is now on a maintenance of 9.25 a day. He was advised to stay on a low-salt diet since a truly low-sodium one would render him unduly unhappy. He has been on minimal doses of tromexan. Since his prothrombin time showed no deviation from normal, this medication was discontinued; as you know, ineffective doses of anti-coagulants are undesirable. There was one slight complication in early January when he developed a localized thrombophlebitis of one of the minor posterior tibial branches; he responded to conventional treatment.

The Maestro is leaving New York in good shape. However, we are aware of the fact that his polycythemia is again rising. Whether it is a true, primary polycythemia or whether it might be secondary to pulmonary fibrosis and emphysema would not be easy to decide at this stage. . . . We had no occasion to do better pulmonary studies on a sternal marrow. However, we feel that in view of the VVAs and the tendency to the development of thrombophlebitides, his polycythemia should be treated. There is no doubt about venesection being excellent treatment, but it should be considered that he is a 74-year-old man with arteriosclerotic heart disease and that repeated phlebotomies might not be entirely innocuous. We therefore suggest that the patient be treated with P32. There remains the question of the use of anticoagulants which, as you know, is still debatable. There would be no objection, in our opinion, against keeping his prothrombin time at a slightly elevated level (about 20", never higher than 25"); best to consult with someone else in Los Angeles on these therapeutic questions. We would suggest Dr. Julius Bauer of the College of Medical Evangelists.

As every genius, Mr. Stravinsky is, of course, a high strung personality. During the trying days of his performances here, which he discharged marvelously, we have found Miltown in small doses quite helpful.

Helpful for whom? From this date until 1970, the problem of the containment of Stravinsky's "polycythemia" governed his life. His blood was analyzed almost every week, controlled by anticoagulants, and thinned by phlebotomy or radioactive phosphorus approximately every month. The treatment during those fourteen years did not change very radically, except that the medicaments became more sophisticated. Stravinsky kept medical diaries and filed all of his laboratory reports, but he also developed an objectivity about the disease, frequently joking about it, as when, after he swallowed one of the capsules of phosphorus, "Now I will light up like a firefly," and, in a rehearsal of *Apollo,* referring to the "Variation of Polyhymnia" as the "Variation of Polycythemia."

Some months before his seventy-fifth birthday, Stravinsky

FIRST 3 pieces of the
FOUR ETUDES

The ostinato of the end-
lessly repeated (and endlessly
varied (ostinato) (woodwinds chant
almost regularly interrupted at varied distances by
the same row of 4 notes gave
me the impression of a dance
movement, and I called this
first piece DANSE

The second piece called
EXCENTRIQUE was written
in the memory of the nu-
merous manifold and eccentric
appearances of the unforgetable
English clown Little Tich (hope the spelling
correct).

The third one CANTIQUE
a Canticle was called by me
this way because of a choral
religious character of this piece

decided to collect his notes and conversations into books, but he
discovered that publishers were interested only if his name appeared as the sole, unaided author. When one of them offered to
compromise to the extent of allowing a collaborator's name to
appear as "translator," Stravinsky replied, as follows, in a letter
to Deborah Ishlon, who was acting as his agent:

The title of the book is "Conversations with Igor Stravinsky by Robert
Craft." It must appear that way in all editions. . . . This isn't Bob—who
is in fact at fault the other way in not wanting his name on anything—
but he did write the book, it is his language, his presentation, his
imagination, and his memory, and I am only protecting myself in not

wanting it to appear as though I write or talk that way. It's not a question simply of ghost writing but of somebody who is to a large extent creating me. Also, my Autobiography will be reissued in a few weeks. The difference between the two books is so great as to make what I have said even more urgent. If American publishers do not want it that way, I'll have it published by Boosey & Hawkes. . . . [March 15, 1958]

Despite this statement, the "by" was changed to "and" in all of the books. Yet, as the illustration indicates, Stravinsky *did* write the books, and most of the language, with its more foreign than English vocabulary,[108] *was* his. The "presentation" was the work of the present writer.

Much of "conversations with Igor Stravinsky" was written in Venice, where topics would arise during dinner and, in the absence of engagements with friends, or an invitation to the theater or to a concert, could be "composed" during the course of an evening. Stravinsky did not own a tape-recorder until his eighty-fifth birthday and since he never traveled with one, his

September 4, 1957. Venice. Stravinsky's draft of some statements about Mussorgsky.

only taped "conversations" were those made in radio, recording, and television studios—or in his own home, as in the case of the NBC Wisdom Series, in May 1957. Only one of his conversations with the present writer—"Listening to the composer, Igor Stravinsky"—was recorded commercially, by the Silver Burdett Company, for inclusion in a textbook; Stravinsky signed a contract for $2,000 on January 30, 1964, the recording having taken place in Manhattan Center, West 34th Street, New York, the day before, after he had recorded *Apollo*.

Regrettably, all of the autobiographical material in the "Conversations" was bowdlerized by the composer himself, as indicated by this excerpt from a letter to Nigel Gosling of the London *Observer*:

I am sorry that I cannot allow the cuts I made in my manuscript to be restored. I do not care so much about the implications of Diaghilev's homosexuality as about Benois's romance; Benois is still alive. Pierné's daughter is alive too and I know her. "Balalaika" we use commonly in Russian for someone who just talks—"*bavardage*." [May 2, 1958]

Stravinsky became an inveterate interviewee early in his career, and, in the mid-1920s, had discovered that he could write the questions as well as the answers, or at least control the questions by naming his interviewers—Arthur Lourié, Cingria, and, later, Ingolf Dahl and this writer. (The Stravinsky archives contain several interviews for the French Radio in the 1930s, with both the questions and answers in his own hand.) That some listeners and readers placed a high value on these occasional exchanges is evidenced in the statement of the late Oscar Levant:

Stravinsky's books . . . in conjunction with Robert Craft, contain some of the most ironic, savage, and saturnine wit of our time. [*Op. cit.*]

In later years, interviewing became a big business with Stravinsky. In a letter to William Glock of the BBC, September 15, 1961, the composer says that he cannot agree to be interviewed *gratis* and without writing out his material, and that he recently recorded an interview for CBS in New York for $3,500 and has just refused a similar sum from the CBC in Toronto. On January 4, 1966, in response to a request transmitted through his London publishers, Stravinsky cabled instructions to say that he was willing to appear in a televised talk with Karajan, but for a considerable sum. Not wishing to involve himself personally in further negotiations, Stravinsky then answered the next letter concerning the project, signing the name of this writer, who copied Stravinsky's letter and mailed it.

For various strategic reasons, Stravinsky frequently wrote letters or sent telegrams which he signed with someone else's name, and many letters, from every period of his life, inscribed "secretary to Mr. Stravinsky," are actually letters from the composer himself. The main reasons for this name-borrowing were that Stravinsky did not want any direct connection with the

Sonozes Paris
Television française most
make to Stravinsky official
money offer for each of their
three propositions you mention

Sincerely,
Robert Craft

Apr 20/66

April 20, 1966. Letter by Stravinsky to
which he has signed the name "Robert Craft."

December 27, 1949

Mr Ralph Hawkes
30 W. 57 St. NYC

Dear Mr Hawkes,

Mr Stravinsky is confined to bed with a cold and has asked me to
write to you concerning a letter he has just received from Mr Stein.
In preparing to print the SYMPHONIES OF WIND INSTRUMENTS Mr Stein
had sent Mr Stravinsky the "calques" of the old 1921 version. He is
apparently unaware of the new 1947 version which is of course the
one which must be printed as the old version is completely impracticable.
As Mr Stein does not have this score would you kindly send him the
copy in your N.Y. office.

Happy New Year.

Sincerely,

December 27, 1949. The same.

August 24, 1949

Mr Erwin Stein
Boosey and Hawkes
34 Regent St
London, England

Dear Mr Stein,

I enclose an errata sheet for the full score of the new edition
of SACRE DU PRINTEMPS. Mr Stravinsky has checked these, and hopes
it will be added to the score. He also would like to know if there
will be a new set of parts to conform to the new score.

Sincerely,

August 24, 1949. The same.

THE UNITED STATES, 1939–1971   441

addressee, and that he was wary of autograph hunters. On December 27, 1949, for example, he was in good health and it was the present writer who had the cold (double pleurisy), nor did the latter know the word *"calques"* at that time. As the 1966 letter shows, however, the Stravinsky of seventeen years later had become remarkably adept at imitating this writer's stylistic mannerisms (not to say affectations). Still more remarkable was the composer's habit of answering the telephone in his own undisguisable voice, and the door in his own undisguisable person, and saying, "Stravinsky isn't here." Joseph Szigeti wrote that once when he telephoned to Stravinsky—in California, where the two men lived only a few miles apart—"The Russian handyman . . . answered [his] telephone . . . : 'Sorry, Mr. Stravinsky out. Please, again call, he will be back an hour ago.' " [109] But this sounds like Stravinsky himself impersonating his gardener, Dmitri Stepanovich Mirov, who was employed by the composer from May 1941 to May 1955, but who never answered his telephone.

Writing to Mr. Arthur Rhea of Baltimore, May 21, 1964, Stravinsky copied his son-in-law's signature, "André Marion," [110] but forgot in whose name the letter was being sent:

The *Elegy for J.F.K.* . . . is written by Mr. Stravinsky in two versions. . . . The first version was performed here . . . the 6th of Apr. . . . The mezzo-soprano version will take place in a . . . concert which I [!!] organize in New York . . .

In the tradition of the Russian Grand Dukes, Stravinsky was also ready to sell his attendance at concerts and other events. Thus, in a letter of January 3, 1950, he complained to Ralph Hawkes that, many conducting engagements having been lost during the composition of *The Rake,* "I am interested in cashing in on personal appearances." On February 29, 1952, in a letter to E. Roth, Stravinsky gave permission to engage his presence at *The Rake* in Paris, providing that what he saw and heard at the rehearsals met with his approval. It should also be said that, in September 1961, only five days after the aforementioned letter to William Glock, Stravinsky agreed to be interviewed by some Swedish composers if their questions were submitted in advance. After reading them, he wrote on the top of the paper that the questions were collectively composed, and that he did not think collectively, yet he penciled in replies to several of them. In fact, Stravinsky always favored the catechetical, Aquinas form, and it goes without saying that his favorite chapter of *Ulysses* was the penultimate one. During the 1930s, he even preferred an *abrégé* of the Bible—De Bottière's *Demandes et Réponses,* published in 1809—to reading The Book itself. Here are two excerpts from the unintentionally droll De Bottière:

D.: *Pourquoi ne fait-on qu'un chapitre du livre de Jérémie et de celui de Baruch?*
R.: *Parce que le sujet et le style se resemblent.*

D.: *En quelle année et quel endroit est mort Daniel?*
R.: *Il est mort en Perse, vers la fin du règne de Cyrus, 525 ans avant Jésus Christ.*

Arriving in Venice by train from Paris, August 27, 1957, Stravinsky went directly to the outdoor restaurant of his hotel:

Thomas Beecham is there but does not see Stravinsky, nor does the composer make himself known, since Sir Thomas is in mid-tantrum, apparently owing to an unsuccessful attempt to escape crème caramel. "I told you that they have no tinned peaches in Italy," he reminds his wife (and everyone else): "The maître d'hôtel is a nincompoop." Our waiter also complains, but about the sirocco. *"Tempo brutto,"* he says, but, touching his parabolic, *commedia dell'arte* nose, reports that this infallible barometer forecasts rain. Stravinsky orders a trout, which he flenses and bones like an ichthyologist dissecting a rare specimen. [From R.C.'s diary]

On September 14, Stravinsky heard Werner Egk's opera *The Inspector General* at La Fenice. Rolf Liebermann recalls that:

At the end of the performance we went without saying a word in the direction of Stravinsky's hotel, walking slowly for he already used a cane. We were burning to give our opinions but could not do so before the master had given his. This silent promenade lasted about a quarter of an hour, then, arriving at the hotel, we embraced each other and bade each other good night. Stravinsky, who had begun to climb the steps, suddenly turned and said, *"C'est gênant."* Not another word, just this epithet, so perfectly exact, and so unexpected as the definition of an opera. Moreover, we always spoke English together, but he said this in French because, of course, *"gênant"* is untranslatable.[111]

Stravinsky had begun *Threni* at the piano of the nightclub of his Venice hotel, on August 29, 1957, composing the opening measures through the word *"incipit."* Liebermann has described an incident during his negotiations with Stravinsky for the commission of this work:

[Stravinsky] had the generosity of a Russian prince and, at the same time, the sordid avarice of a usurer. . . . I offered ten thousand dollars for *Threni*, that too rarely played masterpiece, and he accepted. But the next day, at seven o'clock in the morning, I was wakened by a telephone call from our mutual friend Nicolas Nabokov: "Listen . . . Igor did not close his eyes all night: he wants a thousand dollars more and is embarrassed to ask you." I would have been stupid to cancel the creation of a work by Stravinsky for a sum that our Hamburg Maecenases could raise in a few minutes. I accepted, and the money was found the same morning. But Igor was so pleased that he invited us all to the best restaurant and ordered mountains of caviar and cases of champagne, which cost at least a thousand dollars.[112]

On September 25, 1957, just before going to dinner with Elliott Carter, Stravinsky completed *Threni* through measure 65. A few days after that he was in Munich rehearsing for a concert, then in Baden-Baden, Paris, Zürich, Donaueschingen, Rome, all for rehearsals or concerts. On October 29, he sailed from Le Havre on the S.S. Liberté for New York, where he stayed only eight days—missing the ballet premiere of *Agon*, so impatient was he to continue with *Threni*. The *"Vide Domine"* was completed on November 25 and the *"Plorans ploravit"* on the 27th. Then, turning to the first part, he wrote measure 11 on December 1, measures 106–72 between December 14 and 15, measures 179–87 on December 20, measures 189–90 on December 22, measure 191 on December 24, and measure 193 on December 28. After a concert trip to Houston, January 2–8, he resumed the composition at measure 204 on January 13, and, on the 16th, reached measure 230. On February 14, he composed measures 344–57, and, by the 23rd, had completed the music through measure 383.

Then two deaths occurred which greatly affected Stravinsky: those of Willy Strecker and Alessandro Piovesan, music director of the Biennale. The present writer, in New York to conduct a concert that included the *Symphony of Psalms*,[113] returned to Los Angeles to find the composer in a state of depression. He wrote to Adriana Panni on March 16: "It is with a double sorrow that this cold disagreeable spring of 1958 begins." On March 21, the *"Oratio"* of *Threni* was completed, though not yet with the separation of the solo and choral parts.

The commissioning of the work by the North German Radio, Hamburg, was engineered by Nicolas Nabokov. According to a letter to Nabokov, June 21, 1957, Stravinsky had a twenty-minute piece in mind, which he had already started to compose. He wrote to Nabokov on February 19, 1958, announcing that the score would soon be completed, and, in a letter of March 27, said that it *was* finished and took thirty-five minutes to perform. At the end of July, Stravinsky left for Europe to conduct several performances of *Threni*. He sailed from New York to Genoa, having been assured that he would see the newly erupted volcanic island in the Azores—which so interested him that he had pasted an aerial photograph of it in his composition sketchbook.

August 2, 1958. Aboard the S.S. *Cristoforo Colombo*, in the Azores. At about 10 A.M. the new volcanic eruption comes into view, a geyser of seething steam, like that of dry ice ablating in water. We distinguish three fumaroles, ebullitions of lava boiling into the sea. Stravinsky is on the bridge, the captain having invited him to use the telescope, but comes down to describe a maelstrom near the newborn island and to say that a neighboring island has had to be evacuated, and that its white village and terraced slopes are already shrouded in ashes. More than an hour later, a plume of white smoke from a water-level crater is still visible beyond the horizon. [R.C.'s diary]

The Stravinskys debarked in Genoa, stayed there for two days, then drove to Venice by way of Piacenza and Cremona.

In Venice, on Sunday, August 17, Stravinsky went to San Lazzaro degli Armeni,

where a French-speaking monk escorts him from the dock as bells peal and bearded brethren emerge from every direction and converge on the church. The service, that of the third day of Assumption, includes a grape-eating ritual, but if the sense of taste is satisfied, the others are not: the incense chokes, the chanting is out of tune, the floor punishes the knees, and the pyrotechnical effect of a crescendo of candlelighting is spoiled at the climax with supplementary electric beams. Afterward, we go to "Byron's Room" for tea and rose marmalade, served by a femininely fussy monk who assures us that the scandalous poet's writings are safely banned from the island. The windows look over gardens toward the casino on the Lido, a short stretch of water but many long centuries away, where Byron used to ride tantivy on the deserted dunes. Opening the door to leave, Stravinsky finds the entire Mechitarist brotherhood lined up waiting to collect his autograph. Although reputedly very learned, they are also prepubertally childlike.

From San Lazzaro we cross the lagoon to San Francesco del Deserto, now more than ever aptly named since only fifteen friars remain. And no wonder. The island is an aviary, and the squawks, trills, twitters, hoots, warbles, boul-bouls (nightingales) are literally deafening. Most of these noisemakers are unseen, but a peacock parades on the main pathway, and pigeons and plovers, swallows and "lecherous sparrows," ouzels and owls (?—I am no birdwatcher!) are visible in the trees and gardens and in the cloisters and eaves of the church. In the church, too, are lizards with orange gullets that inflate like bubblegum.

The human population is also in retreat in the shallows near the island, where birds shrilly protest as men in boots gather mollusks. The buoys here are shrines as well, and some of them are carved like *rimmonim*; the fishermen supply them with candles and adorn them with flowers.

In the Campo San Bartolomeo tonight our thoughts are with Alessandro Piovesan, whose haunt this used to be. Piovesan, ever late on his way to a crisis—underarm briefcase never containing the important papers for which he was always searching in it—is now too early dead. At last year's farewell dinner, when he proposed a toast "To next year," my thoughts went to Stravinsky. But it is Piovesan we are mourning, and whom we now remember, as we always will, by his own word, "*Spirituale.*" [From R.C.'s diary]

Stephen Spender and Stravinsky first became acquainted when they found themselves sitting together at a concert in the Foro Italico, in Rome, in 1954, and when, just before the performance of a concerto by Karl Amadeus Hartmann, Stravinsky wrote, "Fasten your seat belt" on a piece of paper and handed it to the lanky poet. On another occasion, Spender gave a copy of the 1929 Nonesuch Press edition of *The Latin Portrait* to Stravinsky, inscribing it:

Spender's simple spondees/ offer this/ Latin/gift to Stravinsky making a/ dactyl to/ honor his/ eightieth/ birthday

After conducting the Venice premiere of *Threni*, Stravinsky led further performances in Switzerland, Hamburg, and Paris. While he was in Hamburg, Rolf Liebermann took him to Lübeck,

the world capital of marzipan as well as the city of Buxtehude, Bach, Buddenbrooks (the family home now containing a beauty salon), and

September 16, 1958. Venice. The Cavallino Gallery. At Vera Stravinsky's vernissage, with Stephen Spender. In New York, September 26, 1965, Spender wrote in his journal: "Dined with the Stravinskys and Robert Craft. Stravinsky seemed in very good form, talking a great deal—much about the Soviet edition of the works of Chekhov. He said how stupidly this was edited: e.g., in a stage direction, it says that a character wears a *pince nez*. A note explains '*Pince nez*, a French expression.' I.S. pointed out that anyone could tell it was French. If a note were required it should be to explain what a *pince nez* is.... He said that the Soviets had a very selected and edited notion of Chekhov ... I.S. seemed very content, going to and fro among his guests, offering them caviar and sandwiches. At dinner we got drunk..." [Random House, 1978]

Bernstein (amber stone, that is). After herring and green Mosel wine in the Schabbelhaus, we visit a twelfth-century hospice that is still used by old men who live in cottage-like cubicles, each with flowerpot and mailbox. The residents sit before their doors, some puffing meerschaums, nearly all wearing seamen's caps which they doff for Stravinsky. But the object of our excursion is the Marienkirche. Here we climb to the organ loft, where Stravinsky tries the instrument which, though almost entirely rebuilt, was once played by Johann Sebastian Bach. On Palm Sunday 1942, British bombs struck the church, dislodging two huge bells. There are still embedded in the floor, frozen in their molten state just as they had begun to "run," like over-ripe Brie. [From R.C.'s diary, October 9, 1958]

At the beginning of November 1958, Stravinsky went to London to conduct the BBC. While there, he dined at the home of the novelist Henry Green and attended a luncheon with Harold Nicolson, Nigel Gosling, Peter Heyworth, Stephen Spender, Edward Crankshaw, and Sir Isaiah and Lady Berlin. Nicolson, recording the event in his diary, seems not to have been in the least surprised with the discovery that Stravinsky had read *Lord Carnock*, a relatively obscure book—though the composer was interested in studies of diplomacy and, partly for this reason, had read every book that Harold Nicolson had published:

I lunch in a private room at the Connaught at a luncheon given by David Astor for Igor Stravinsky. He greeted me warmly. He tells me how much he enjoyed *Some People*, and what a delight *Journey to Java* had been to him and his wife. I groan inwardly. "But, of course," he adds, putting his hand on my shoulder,[114] "your best book is your life of your father [*Lord Carnock*]." I was overjoyed by that. He said that as a composer he admired technique, and that he felt my technique was superb. I swelled with pride. He said how much he envied us writers, who had finished our work when the book was published. It was so different for a composer. His compositions, when played at Buenos Aires or Melbourne, were often entirely different from anything he had composed or intended. [Sir Harold Nicolson, *Diaries and Letters, 1945–1962* (London: Collins, 1968), entry for December 4, 1958]

From Stravinsky's diary:
January 4, 1959: Concert at the Town Hall under Bob's wonderful conducting. American premiere of *Threni*. Very big success. Was obliged to bow. Endless boring people. Extreme nervousness.[115]

Threni was controversial. Vittorio Rieti, one of the composer's faithful followers, wrote to him after the New York performance saying, in effect, that this was no longer music. On the other hand, Boris de Schloezer,[116] Stravinsky's champion in the 1920s but apostate in the 1930s and 1940s, thanked the composer after the Paris performance for

. . . the profound joy that you have given me. I have attacked you violently in the past, in the same measure that I have admired you, but the grandeur of this score, its formal unity, austerity, beauty, its rejection of all compromise, all "effects," all sensual seduction, all personal sentiment, gives proof once more, after your Mass and cantata to St. Mark, of the continuing youthfulness of your genius. [Letter of November 14, 1958]

Francis Poulenc told an interviewer:

Picasso and Stravinsky are very different cases, though what I shall say does not by any means diminish Stravinsky. It is that he will have a troubled old age—because at seventy-five he asked himself: "Is it my path to compose serial music?" Picasso, on the other hand, will have a serene old age because he does not give a damn about anything.[117]

Poulenc had attended the premiere in the Scuola di San Rocco (Venice), characterized by *Time* as

the fall's most eagerly awaited musical event. In hushed expectation, beneath a Tintoretto ceiling, [the audience] watched 76-year-old Igor Stravinsky, with a clawlike motion of his right hand, launch the orchestra into the premiere of his latest work. What followed was some of the finest—and most complex—music of Stravinsky's career. The 33-minute work . . . was presented by Venice's International Festival of contemporary music. Stravinsky's text and title—Threni, id est Lamentationes Jeremiae Prophetae (Threnody: Lamentations of the Prophet Jeremiah)—come from three of the familiar elegies from the Catholic Vulgate Bible. Written in the tone-row technique that Stravinsky once scorned but has lately adopted, the work has a spare, transparent orchestral accompaniment that for long stretches consists of no more than an occasional chord. To prepare the Hamburg Radio Chorus for the taxing job of staying on pitch while unaccompanied, conductor Robert Craft rehearsed the group more than 20 times. . . . [October 6, 1958]

W. H. Auden has said of Stravinsky's baffling changes:

Stravinsky's career as a composer is as good a demonstration as any that I know of the difference between a major and a minor artist. . . . A major artist is always newly finding himself, so that the history of his works recapitulates or mirrors the history of art. Once he has done something to his satisfaction, he attempts to do something he has never done before. It is only when he is dead that we are able to see that his various creations, taken together, form one consistent oeuvre. [The Observer, April 11, 1971]

The French novelist Michel Butor was one of those who made high claims for Threni:

It is evident that Stravinsky's most moving works are those inspired by religion: the Symphony of Psalms or the Mass. The echoes in these works go back further than Mozart, to a deeply rooted . . . musical tradition.
But while Stravinsky works with earlier musical forms, he has taken account, in his latest compositions, of the music of Schoenberg and his disciples, music he had formerly regarded with a good deal of distrust. The new system brings to his art a real contemporaneity. Inevitably, this new music was bound to become the framework of all of Stravinsky's present compositions.
This striking composition we may consider as the beginning of Stravinsky's third period, far more conventional than the other two, and, to me, far the most desirable. The disparities of style for which he had been very ignorantly condemned have always been integrated at the core of his work by an overriding internal structure. In this third period, however, structure itself becomes the composition's most powerful element, as is indicated, for example, by the title Agon (combat). And the resonances which in the Symphony of Psalms have transversed the entire spectrum of classical forms and reached as far back as Byzantine music, are even stronger in Threni.
You know that few contemporaries of Bach and Beethoven appreciated their late works. That is unfortunate. But you are still Stravinsky's contemporaries. Make the most of it. ["Stravinsky le Méconnu," Artes, September 27, 1960]

OPPOSITE:
January 5, 1959. New York. Leaving CBS's East 30th Street studio after a recording session for Threni. Paul Fromm, the midwest Maecenas of modern music, is in the background, behind Alexander Schneider, a violinist and friend of Stravinsky's for several years. Stravinsky's shuba (fur coat, but not the one made by Chanel) is now in the Paris Conservatoire. Photograph by Gjon Mili.

Whether or not Stravinsky's "most moving works are those inspired by religion," the composer would never discuss the religious attitudes and content of his music, or admit that he worshipped God through it—even though the *Symphony of Psalms* and the Symphony in C were inscribed *"A la gloire de Dieu."* [118] The following remarks in a letter from Ernest Ansermet so deeply offended Stravinsky that he never wished to see or speak to the conductor again:

You place too much emphasis on your technical powers and on your knowledge and not enough on the music itself and on your instincts. No matter what you say about art being simply a "product," in the end it is made by a man, and when you decided to make this Mass, it was not that you merely wanted to create a kind of Flemish motet in your style. You are also a believer who wanted to pay homage to his God. [Letter of February 8, 1949]

On April 8, 1959, Stravinsky wrote in his diary: "Kabuki!!! *formidable*!!!" On the 14th, a Tokyo newspaper reported that

Stravinsky, speaking before a news conference here, said that he has been inspired by Kabuki music. He indicated strongly that several musical ideas are already forming in his head, but he warned the newsmen that "The audience will not recognize it when they hear it." He said he has been impressed by the "rhythmical orderliness of Kabuki."

A year later, June 27, 1960, back in California, Stravinsky noted in his diary:

With Chr. Isherwood to "Kabuki" at the Greek Theater: Export stuff (after what I saw in Tokyo last year!).

The Tokyo *Asahi Evening News* reviewer of Stravinsky's May 1 concert with the NHK Symphony Orchestra in the Osaka Festival Hall was surprised that

the conductor used no baton but only his bare hands, and even these he used sparingly. . . . At times, apparently satisfied that the orchestra caught the beat, he let both arms drop and merely looked on for several bars until a change in rhythm or tempo needed his attention again.

Mainichi (Tokyo) reported that Stravinsky's Tokyo concerts

were unique artistic events in the history of the Japanese capital. . . . Stravinsky was accorded a hero's triumphant welcome [by an audience] well aware of the fact that it was the world's greatest living composer whose personal appearance had graced the musical scene in the city of 9,000,000.

The author of this article, Klaus Pringsheim (Thomas Mann's brother-in-law), added,

I remember the comical bewilderment thirty years ago, caused by the Berlin premiere of *Le Baiser de la Fée* . . . Tchaikovsky . . . in those days being looked upon with disdain in the circles of the New Music.

1959. In the "Dylan Thomas Room" of the Stravinsky home. Photograph by Gjon Mili.

Pringsheim had conducted the *Symphony of Psalms* in Tokyo, June 9, 1932.

Nicolas Nabokov wrote to Stravinsky on March 11, 1958:

> Would you be prepared (after having finished *Threni*) to write a piece for piano and orchestra—or, rather, for piano and a group of instruments of your own choice—for an excellent young Swiss pianist? The length should be approximately 15 to 20 minutes. It would be commissioned by a Swiss industrialist who also owns several hotels in Arosa. His name is *Weber*. If you were interested, this gentleman would be prepared to pay $15,000 for exclusive rights during a season (i.e., roughly 6–8 months). I am confident that this sum would be free of tax.

Stravinsky's answer was prompt and characteristic. Since Nabokov did not mention that the industrialist was the husband of the pianist, Stravinsky assumed that the latter "must be a pederast, otherwise Herr Weber would hardly be so ready to pay." Stravinsky accepted the commission and gave instructions to deposit the money in his account "in the Société des Banques Suisses, Bâle, either in my name or Vera's." [119] Contractual details were then entrusted to Mrs. Weber's New York agent, Thea Dispeker, and Stravinsky rewarded Nabokov with ten percent

($1,500). At a later date, Karl Weber purchased the manuscript from the composer and also gave a considerable sum to him to help pay for the New York concert at which the piece was first performed.

Stravinsky met Frau Weber in Zürich, September 27, 1958, the day before he conducted *Threni* there; by this time, the first and second movements (the latter originally including a vibraphone part) were already completed (on July 9 and September 7, respectively). In February 1959, he sent as much of the music to her as he had composed (the third movement is dated February 14), with a request not to show it to anyone (letter of February 23). Then, on March 23, by which date he had sketched most of the fifth movement, he wrote again to Mrs. Weber, because she had not commented on the piece when acknowledging the receipt of it (March 4), and asked her to tell him frankly whether

the style and technique of the music are alien to you; if so, I will return the advance on the commission.

But the Webers kept to the bargain, and, on April 9, Stravinsky wrote from the Imperial Hotel in Tokyo to tell them that, late in May, he expected

to discuss the premiere of my new concerto—which I call *Movements*—with Rolf Liebermann in Copenhagen

and inviting the Webers to the Danish rendezvous as well. Stravinsky spent the time just before his return from Copenhagen to California (May 26) with the pianist, correcting mistakes that she had found in the score. He wrote to her from Hollywood on May 30:

Chère Madame, I was so happy to see you in Copenhagen, and I hope to see you again in Venice in September. . . . Can you send a list of the errors in the *Movements* that we corrected in the restaurant just before taking the airplane? Please indicate the measure numbers. . . .

The fourth movement was completed on July 30, 1959, the four interludes on August 16. Stravinsky spent August 28–9 in Princeton (at the Princeton Inn), to meet with Robert Graff and discuss the new composition that was to become *The Flood*, to visit with Roger Sessions, and to converse with Sessions's students:

Stravinsky, with poetry and precision, talked about his life and music, providing an informal new chapter, so to speak, in the recently published *Conversations*.[120]

On September 25, Stravinsky, in Venice, wrote to his publisher:

Margrit Weber has been here for a few days . . . and studied with me every day my *Movements*. . . .

Stravinsky's recording of *Movements,* with Charles Rosen as pianist, was warmly reviewed in *The New York Times,* but Stravinsky circled and added three question marks beneath the newspaper's statement that

there is more than a trace of tonal thinking, [which is] mainly a result of the basic and structural use of repetition and doubling.

After the first European performances, in Cologne, in June 1960, one critic wrote that

Stravinsky's. . . . manner of construction remains as personal as the sound of his orchestra, and the result is a work which moves forward and is beautiful to listen to, which is brief yet highly concentrated, which at every point reveals a master who has both a precise and original ear and a fastidious mind to direct his ear. . . . The wisdom of great age and experience speaks through this music, but there is no suggestion of relaxed mellowness: on the contrary, the music is taut and has something of the devotional intensity of *Threni.* The only pity is that Stravinsky's clarity, his sense of proportion, and his ear for new and beautiful sounds no longer seem to be the aim of younger composers.

One younger composer, Charles Wuorinen, writing to thank Stravinsky for his participation in the Lili Boulanger Award, which Wuorinen had won, added that

Your recent magnificent serial compositions . . . are inspirations to all reasonable musicians. [Letter of April 1961]

Stravinsky would have liked to be a zoologist, and after his younger son visited a game preserve in Mozambique, in 1953, the father determined to do the same—a wish that came true when he spent three days in Kruger Park in 1962. As a touring artist, Stravinsky visited the zoo of every city in which he performed, and photographs of him on many of these occasions survive—for example, in the zoo of Antwerp (with Gabrielle Picabia), January 1924; in the Cagnes-sur-Mer zoo in the summer of 1925; at the London zoo in May 1929. Here is a typical entry in Vera Stravinsky's diary:

Zoo, buying books, then Igor gives me a lesson in modulations. [Leipzig, January 31, 1930]

On December 11, 1925, Stravinsky was at the Cirque de Paris with his close friend Count Guy de Matharel, and with Vera Sudeikina and her mother (on a visit from Moscow). Matharel, turning his back on a cage of lions, received a blow from one of them and was hospitalized and confined to bed for some weeks. On November 9, 1926, a Paris tribunal reached a judgment in his favor. Stravinsky was his witness. Then, in January 1927, the case was reopened by the Cirque de Paris on grounds that Matharel had provoked the animal and that a guard had warned people against approaching the cages. Stravinsky testified again, but did so by letter from Nice.

In March 1959, the Danish Embassy in Washington informed Stravinsky that he had been chosen to receive the first Sonning Prize. (He had been awarded the Busoni Prize in 1950.) On May 21, the Stravinskys flew from Los Angeles to Copenhagen to accept the $7,272 award. Rolf Liebermann, Nicolas Nabokov, Karl and Margrit Weber, and Pierre Boulez came to the Danish capital to see the composer, and, at a gathering in his honor at Christiansborg Palace, he met Isak Dinesen, whose *Out of Africa* he greatly admired. On this occasion the Prime Minister addressed him as follows (in part):

... Denmark has the opportunity to honor the outstanding personality in the world of music. ... As Albert Einstein ... was able to change our picture of the world so that it would never be the same, so have you, Mr. Stravinsky, through your life work, been able to transform the music world of your time. Your life ... is an apex which towers over an epoch in the history of music and which has marked an era for all time.

On May 25, Stravinsky conducted his Octet and *Firebird* Suite for an audience that included the Danish King and Queen.

Stravinsky arrived in London September 3, spent a few days in Edinburgh (September 9–13), and went to Stratford on September 7 for a performance of Olivier's *Coriolanus*. The composer wrote in his diary afterward: "Unforgettable." The present writer also confided in his diary:

I have never before been so struck by the soldiers' amatory language— though it is not that but the Neo-Platonic, Renaissance idealization of friendship. Still, in the case of such up-to-date lines as Menenius' "I tell thee, my fellows, thy general is my lover," the contemporary audience can hardly be expected to keep in mind that "lover" in Elizabethan is synonymous with "friend." Coriolanus himself seems to prefer his officers to his wife, and his mother to everyone, though the remark "There's no man in world/ More bound to's mother" is unbelievable, partly because of the exaggeration of some of his rhetoric about her (e.g., "The honored mould/ Wherein this trunk was formed"). But on this point the performance must be faulted; Olivier's Coriolanus overpowers the Volumnia, who in this case is far from a Lupine matriarch. Also, his staging does not distinguish Romans and Volsces at all clearly, and the final scene is richly confusing, Coriolanus dying not in Corioli or Actium but, apparently, on the Tarpeian rock—which hardly accords with his "Cut me to pieces, Volsces; men and lads/ Strain all your edges on me. . . ."

We return to London with Stephen Spender in his Jaguar—with one stop, to pick up a hitchhiker, which makes Stravinsky nervous. At 3 A.M. back at Spender's house and drinking claret, Stravinsky mentions Eliot's remark at dinner yesterday, that Shakespeare was more interested in *Coriolanus* the play than in its poetry. Yet the weaknesses of the play, foremost among them its unlikable hero, nearly sink it. Consider, on the other hand, such lines as

> *Break ope the locks o' the Senate and bring in*
> *The crows to peck the eagles.*
>
> [From R.C.'s diary]

Mention should be made here of Stravinsky's arrangements of music by Carlo Gesualdo di Venosa (1560–1613). In rehearsals, concerts, and recording sessions, in Hollywood in 1953 and 1954, Stravinsky heard many of Gesualdo's madrigals and some of the sacred music, being sufficiently impressed with *"Io pur respiro* (Book VI), among other examples, to make a copy of it— a practice of Stravinsky's with other music and writings that he wished to memorize. In the winter of 1957, he obtained microfilms of the part-books for twenty *Sacrae Cantiones* (Naples, 1603), of which the *sextus* and *bassus* had been lost. When he found that the final piece in the collection, *"Illumina nos,"* [121] required seven (not six) voices, and that only two (not three) parts were missing, he decided to complete the motet, which he did on May 5.

Then, in September 1959, in Venice, he added the missing parts for two other motets in the same volume, *"Assumpta est Maria"* and *"Da pacem Domine,"* having discovered that one of the lost parts in each piece was canonic; the *quintus* in *"Assumpta est"* is marked *"canon in diapason et diapente"* (at the octave and fifth), the tenor in *"Da pacem," "canon et diapente"* (at the fifth). In *"Da pacem,"* too, the rhythmic distance between the canonic parts is indicated by a *signum congruentiae*, yet the final cadence here was problematic. As the Gesualdo scholar and musicologist Dr. Glenn Watkins wrote to Stravinsky, in September 1959,

I received a note from Mr. Craft in which he informed me that you would like some reassurance about the F's in the last three measures of *Da pacem*. I have rechecked the originals, and they are, assuredly, F-naturals. I suspect that at least part of the cause of your suspicion stemmed from the fact that if the last note of the Resolutio were F-sharp, it could be sustained to the end. Considering that the voice is derived a 5th above the tenor (which is B), and that it is the final note of the piece in that voice, one might argue for the validity of the perfect 5th above B as a resolution. This, however, leads to even greater conflict because of unquestionable F-naturals in the Altus, Quintus, and Tenor in these last three measures.

Instead of attempting an academic reconstruction, Stravinsky seemed to avoid what might appear to be the prescribed solutions. What he tried to do in all three motets was to recompose the whole from the perspective of his added part or parts. But whereas Gesualdo could have written the notes that Stravinsky added, Stravinsky's seconds and sevenths being at least philologically justifiable, the frisky rhythms that he joins to measures 22 and 23 of *"Assumpta est,"* and the inverted motion that he introduces at the beginning of *"Illumina nos,"* are not characteristic of the Neapolitan master.

Stravinsky's greatest contribution to the appreciation of Gesualdo is in the *Monumentum pro Gesualdo di Venosa (ad CD*

Annum), of March 1960, a "recomposition" for orchestra of the only three madrigals from the Fifth and Sixth Books that Stravinsky considered to be suitable for instrumental transcription. "To Bob, who forced me to do it—and I did it—with love," Stravinsky inscribed the present writer's copy of the manuscript score, and on June 9, 1960, Stravinsky recorded the opus. George Balanchine's choreographic version of the *Monumentum* has long been in the repertory of the New York City Ballet.

Paul Horgan, the novelist and friend of the composer, wrote:

The Stravinskys and Craft [went] with me for a picnic to the cliff dwelling and pueblo ruins of El Rito de los Frijoles, in the Bandelier National Monument. . . . We set out with hampers of food and wine in my car at mid-morning. . . .

Coming to the canyon we went idling along the trails leading to the excavated ruins of houses and kiva on the valley floor. . . . Craft climbed to the high levels and made his way in and out of several of the chambers. . . . Nobody said much—the place completed our thoughts. . . . Presently we went to a delicious little grove of tall cottonwoods which made a shifting mosaic of shade over some weathered tables and benches set out for picnickers. . . . Madame and I faced Stravinsky and Craft across the table. . . . Stravinsky's face opposite me suddenly assumed a paralyzed astonishment, and lifting his hand as little as possible for fear of inviting a wrong response pointed past me and Madame to something behind our backs. I could not tell whether he was in extremities of fear or of delight. He conveyed the necessity of absolute stillness as he stared fixedly into the near distance behind us. Good God, I thought, what of the several possibilities could he be staring at—a rattlesnake? a deer drawn by the scent of food? a bear? Madame said something to him in a low voice, in Russian. He did not answer. His pointing hand began to tremble, he dramatized a stupendous event. I began making wildly conjectural plans to deal with whatever . . . creature or condition he saw. I turned. In a small pool of dappled sunlight, seated on his haunches, and inquiring of us with its nose what we might have to offer, was a red squirrel. [*Encounters with Stravinsky*, New York: Farrar, Straus and Giroux, 1972]

Two weeks later, on August 1, Stravinsky was in Mexico City beginning a Latin American tour, the inspiration for which had come in November 1959 from his friend Victoria Ocampo, who spoke on behalf of an Argentine film festival which had offered to pay all expenses. At the end of January 1960, he wrote to Señorita Ocampo to say that the trip no longer seemed feasible owing to his basilar stenosis—the pinching of an artery in the brain that had affected the movements of his right arm and right leg. (Letter of January 27) But, on April 23, he wrote to Señorita Ocampo again to say that his health was good, and that she could expect him.

Stravinsky was in Rome in November to conduct a concert. He went from there to Paris for a few days and then to New York, where he learned of the death of his Hollywood neighbor Catherine d'Erlanger, an event that was to affect his life, for he later purchased her house and moved into it.

HOTEL HASSLER
ROMA

November 15, 1960. Rome. An example of Stravinsky's bookkeeping.

December 15, 1960. New York. The St. Regis Hotel. A telegram from John Walsh informs the Stravinskys of the death, in Paris, of Catherine d'Erlanger, my landlady for eight years and part-time employer—as a reader—for four. During this period we devoured a prodigious amount of print together, entire shelves of books and some authors in toto; moreover, I still recall much of the reading matter, probably from having had to recite it aloud. What these sessions meant to her, apart from a pastime, I cannot say, but the book that made the strongest impression on her was Obermann, from which she borrowed a motto: "Let us perish resisting, and if it is nothingness that awaits us, do not let us act as if that is a just fate."

My most vivid memories of the Baroness are of those readings. A chronic toper by then, she would sip Benedictine while lounging in regal déshabille on a sofa that was not only moth-eaten, but worse: My occupational hazards were pruritis, and the bites and stings of centipedalians and of other creatures black and hairy. Her cats, Sita and Terra Cotta, used to join her, plumping themselves on either side like courtiers, jealous of each other and of every caller. (Callers of better times, the Sitwells, Michael Arlen, Cocteau, were caricatured on the walls in the Baroness's own, genre Marie Laurencin, portraits.) On some days a tiara adorned her inconsistently orange hair, on others, metal curlers. But her clothing was less varied. At any rate, I seem to remember her always in the same maroon flannel sack, which was often inside out; and in the same woolen socks, one of them halfway to the knee, the other all the way down, like Hogarth's Bedlamite, except that the Baroness's preferences were French; she used to refer to herself as *"La Folle de Chaillot."*

My recollections of her dinners are no less clear, expecially of drinking wine from silver goblets tasting of tarnish. I see Stravinsky on one occasion precipitating his empty plate in her direction and the Baroness precipitating it back. He used to refer to her as *"notre dame des tapettes,"* and she *was* a patroness of interior decorators, being dependent on them in her commerce in *bric-à-brac,* since she was continually dispossessing herself of her rummage-sale surroundings.

Toward the end she grew corpulent and seldom ventured out. One day while walking in her garden she fainted, and, characteristically, her first thought on reviving was to introduce the people who had come to her aid. It soon became apparent that she could no longer live alone, yet she would tolerate no companion apart from the Russian girl who came in the afternoons to paste newspaper cuttings in scrapbooks, a futile task reminding one of Bouvard and Pécuchet. After another, more serious fall, the police had to be summoned to lift the Baroness to her bed, which prompted her son, the Director of BOAC, to send an airplane to take her to his residence in Paris. The last time I saw her was the day on which she learned of the arrangements for this cruel if unavoidable abduction, for she would have preferred to die in her own home. By this time she had been bedridden for months, but a friend, John Walsh, whose responsibility it was to tell her of the trip, promised: "You will soon be up again and then we'll have fun." At this, during no more than three or four seconds, and conceivably for the first and last time in her life, the stoic old lady started to cry. [From R.C.'s diary]

The Argentine mathematician F. G. Asenjo wrote to Stravinsky, January 11, 1961, from Georgetown University, Washington, D.C.:

Mr. Robert Craft was kind enough to invite me to the recording sessions [of *The Nightingale,* in Washington] . . . but you were so desperately busy that I could not bring myself to impose on your attention. . . . In your *Musical Poetics* you mention the phenomenon of "polarity" in music: that is to say, the *organization* of the various elements of a piece of music around certain main elements that you called "centers" or "poles." As you suggested, there are several ways of obtaining polarity: by harmonic means, by grading the intensity of sound, by orchestral color . . . I am concerned here with the first way.

September 16, 1961. Göteborg, leaving for Stockholm. Stravinsky is here at the start of a two-and-a-half-month trip that took him to Germany, Yugoslavia, Switzerland, England, Egypt, Australia, New Zealand, Tahiti.

... My question is this: do you feel that there is some musical system of relationships in atonalism that is a substitute for tonal polarity? Is there any harmonic polarity in atonalism? If there is not, this is not so much a fault as an absence. Atonal music has proved itself already, as Webern and your magnificent *Threni* show beyond any doubt. But polarity is without question an essential characteristic of every kind of art, the characteristic that is principally responsible for giving a work the feeling of being an organic whole, a living thing, instead of an accumulation of unrelated parts. Hence, is it not important to develop a principle of harmonic attraction in atonalism, if this principle—as I feel—does not yet exist?

Stravinsky answered, in part, as follows:

Since harmony is thinkable only as a product of the tonal system, it seems to me that there cannot exist any "harmonic attraction in atonalism."

Stravinsky had arrived in Australia—Kingsford Smith Airport, Sydney—on November 9, 1961, several hours late, his plane having been delayed in Bangkok because of a mechanical breakdown (*Sydney Mirror*, November 8, 1961). He left for New Zealand on the 11th and returned to Sydney on November 20, conducting there on the 23rd. On November 29, he conducted in Melbourne, and the next day flew to Sydney, where an Air France flight to Noumea and Tahiti was delayed three hours to enable him to make the connection. Of the many interviews that the Stravinskys gave while in Australia, those by the composer's wife are the most candid:

He is very temperamental when working and I always keep out of the way. Sometimes he slips out into the garden to think. . . . He is very nice when he thinks not about music. [*Sydney Sunday Telegraph,* November 12, 1961]

The Melbourne newspaper *Age* wrote, November 25, 1961:

When someone asked Mrs. Stravinsky if living with a genius could be difficult, [she said] "Why should it be?" Mrs. Stravinsky never misses her husband's concerts. "He needs me. You know what men are like— 'Where is my white cravat?' "

Stravinsky was described on his arrival in Melbourne, November 24, as "carrying a string bag full of books" and "wearing dark glasses ('Wouldn't you if you had to face this all the time?' he explained as photographers' flash bulbs shone"). (*Age*, November 25, 1961)

Back in California, in December, Stravinsky wrote to Nicolas Nabokov saying that the story of his illness is "a regular lie of the newspapers," caused in this case by his unwillingness to be interviewed upon landing in Sydney, just after having flown halfway around the globe. He explained that he had promised to speak to reporters at his press conference the next day, and not after a sleepless night and a flight from Cairo, but the result was an AP telegram, "Stravinsky is sick!"

The letter also says that the "White House question" is settled and that he is going there for dinner on January 18. He defends his telegram to Mrs. Kennedy,[122] saying that she had not invited his wife, and asking if a man of eighty years should be expected to fly all alone to Washington on a day that he would like to spend with his wife and friends. He adds that the "Casals business" at the White House nauseated him, being all publicity-seeking and social-climbing on the part of certain American musicians: "No one in Washington has any real regard for my music, but only for my name."

Stravinsky also justifies his forthcoming visit to Israel, remarking that it will not detract from the performance of "the *Isaac* piece" in 1963—if he can finish it by then. He must give concerts abroad each year, the letter continues, and Israel is ideal. He adds that he will never conduct in Paris again, after the reception of *Threni* there by the public and the press.

Ingmar Bergman had written to Stravinsky at the Grand Hotel, Stockholm, September 11, 1961:

Your music has been of great importance to my work, especially in the *Psalms Symphony,* and during many years has been a source of spiritual power in my life. With my respectful thankfulness and warmest personal regards.

Bergman later told an interviewer that his film *Winter Light*

is closely connected with a particular piece of music, Stravinsky's *A Psalm Symphony.* I heard it on the radio one morning during Easter.[123]

September 16, 1961. Stockholm. With Ingmar Bergman.

Recalling one of his meetings with Stravinsky in Stockholm in September 1961, Bergman remembered that

Stravinsky once said something good. I heard Blomdahl and him discussing Alban Berg's *Lulu*.[124] They were discussing a singer. Stravinsky said she was a bad Lulu because she was so vulgar. Then Blomdahl, as I remember it, said, "But Lulu's the vulgarest female alive." And Stravinsky said: "Yes, and that is why she must be played by an actress who hasn't a trace of vulgarity in her—but can play it." [125]

Bergman also said:

Listen to some piece of music by Stravinsky . . . and you'll hear reminiscences from the whole history of music. Though he mixes everything, he has his own ideas, a vision of his own. He has something to say, and he uses whatever he likes to say it.[126]

Bergman's staging of *The Rake's Progress* was seen for the first time at the Royal Opera, Stockholm, April 22, 1961:

The Swedish audience was headed by King Gustave VI, Adolphe and Queen Louise, who stayed on to applaud fourteen curtain calls. . . . Swedish critics regarded Bergman's production as an historical event in Swedish opera. . . . Around the beginning of the year he started to memorize the music of *The Rake's Progress* with the help of his wife, pianist Kevi Laretei. . . . Bergman had the stage built out to cover half of the orchestra pit. This way the stage gained increased depth, particularly useful for the crowd scenes. Most of the changes of scenery took place without bringing down the curtain. The audience saw the cast freeze in their positions until the new sets had been lowered into place. . . . Bergman created striking crowd scenes in which each person had an individualized character. . . . He divided the nine tableaux into two sections; the first one was made up of five tableaux and the second of four.[127] [*Christian Science Monitor*, May 8, 1961]

Bergman has been quoted as saying:

I have always felt close to Stravinsky. His way of thinking is close to mine. His very severe, very cold-hot way of expressing himself fascinates me. [*New York Times*, May 1961]

And the *Times* commented:

Bergman, whose preoccupation with man's relationship to God is reflected in his various productions, denies that Stravinsky is bent merely on cerebral maneuver. *The Rake's Progress* was inspired by the paintings of the same name by Hogarth, "an artistic moralist." Stravinsky, Bergman says, is "a religious moralist, and there is a heaven's distance between the two."
    . . . In mounting the production here—a translation into Swedish from the original English—Bergman extended most of the stage out over a part of the orchestra pit. Gray settings, suggesting the engravings of Hogarth and placed only on that central section of the stage behind the extension, are carried in and out or are lowered after the members of the cast are in place. Some action may take place just outside the set. The conventional use of the curtain to separate scenes is dispensed with.

All this, Bergman says, is his way of breaking the intense realism he often develops in portraying the Rake's downward path to death in an insane asylum. When the audience is especially moved, the mood must be broken, "because Stravinsky wants to tell you something," and that "something" is the moral of the morality play: "The devil finds work for idle hands." [*New York Times*, May 1961]

When Stravinsky conducted part of a concert in Stockholm two years later, Bergman wrote to him from Bastad:

Unfortunately I am shooting my new picture and unfortunately I am on location at the moment. I can hardly explain to you how terribly sorry I am not being able to attend your concert. As you probably know I keep a very close watch on the treasure we have in common, *The Rake's Progress*. We rehearse carefully before each new performance. The performances are acclaimed by a wider and more enthusiastic public each time. Next year I hope to be able to produce at my own theatre *Histoire du Soldat*, a play which I always loved. With my deepest reverence and admiration. Fondly, Ingmar Bergman [June 17, 1963]

Stravinsky's first notations for *The Flood* are dated February 7, 1961. By the 5th of March, he had composed the score through God's first speech and made a notation for the violin part of the choreographic movement "The Flood," marking it "Lento." By May 5, he had completed the music through Noah's speech, "Thy bidding, Lord, I shall fulfill." On the 15th, he began "The Building of the Ark," completing it June 23. On July 6, in Santa Fe, he wrote the first six measures of "The Catalogue of the Animals," completing this movement on the 31st. He began "The Comedy" back in Hollywood on the 21st of August, then interrupted his work for concerts, resuming it, in Hollywood, January 4, 1962, with "The Earth is Overflowed with Flood." On February 7, after a month in Toronto, Washington, and New York, Stravinsky noted in his diary that a revised typescript of the last three pages of the libretto had been sent to the television producer who had commissioned the piece, Robert Graff. On February 10, Stravinsky wrote the word "RAIN" in his diary and began the dance "The Flood," continuing from the sketch made nearly eleven months before. This was completed on March 4, and, on the 6th, God's last speech was composed. On the 14th, the full score was finished, and, on that same afternoon, Balanchine arrived to discuss the visual realization with Stravinsky:

March 19, 1962. Hollywood. Self-portrait.

... am so happy to have finished *The Flood*. This weekend will start the recording. ... I have Balanchine here these days discussing the staging of *The Flood*. [Letter of March 15, 1962]

Georges [sic] Balanchine came from NY to work with me and Robert Craft on *The Flood*. We established the scenario on the full score—the ... different entrances ... of the characters (before and during the music ...). [Letter of March 16, 1962]

Meanwhile, the orchestra parts were extracted, albeit with countless errors, now immortalized in the recording. The latter was completed on March 31, at the Sunset Boulevard studio of

March 28, 1962. Studying the score of *The Flood*, 1260 North Wetherly Drive, Hollywood. This library was an enlargement, built in April 1960, of the guest room, in which Auden, Nicholas Nabokov, and others had slept. The architect, Perry Neuschatz, was an amateur recorder player for whom Stravinsky made the two-recorder arrangement of an excerpt from the final scene of *The Rake's Progress*.

June 28, 1963. Playbill of the first Italian performance of *The Flood* (on a program with *Oedipus Rex*).

Columbia Records. The television crew had arrived from New York on the 27th of March, and the tape-editing was finished April 6. On June 14, 1962, when *The Flood* was shown on American television, Stravinsky was in Hamburg. He never saw the film.

On November 16, 1961, an announcement appeared in the Wellington (New Zealand) *Evening Post*:

The famous composer speaks about the operatic work he is now composing under commission to American television. He said it did not concern him that the work was being done for TV: "I don't know what TV is."

Stravinsky's own celebration of his eightieth birthday is, quite naturally, another new work: a "biblical allegory" for speakers, singers, chorus, orchestra, and dancers entitled *The Flood*. . . . [The] only trace of octogenarian self-indulgence is that it was composed for television and is therefore "popular" in approach. This is a situation in which Stravinsky has always delighted: to undertake a commission under what seem to be impossible conditions for serious composition, and then to turn them about into exactly what he wanted and needed to compose. He seems to take a special pleasure in carefully fulfilling the letter of such a commission so that the commissioner gets precisely what he has asked for, but hardly what he expected.

Evidently *The Flood* appeared equally enigmatic to the people at Breck Shampoo and CBS Television, who jointly commissioned and presented it. . . . Those responsible for the hour-long TV program entitled *Noah and the Flood*, however, managed even more effectively to prevent the least idea of the musical or dramatic nature of *The Flood* from being conveyed without actually having to change or omit a single note. Their technique was to crush the delicate and refined music of *The Flood* between the millstones of a pseudo-profound anthropological prologue having to do with Flood myths, and a long, disorganized, totally inappropriate review of the Stravinsky-Balanchine collaboration. The remaining time was, of course, filled by Breck Shampoo commercials accompanied by their own distinctive, if uncredited, music.

However extensive the damage done to mass culture, the essential fact is that a new and interesting Stravinsky work was called into being, and slipped . . . past the heavy-footed promoters. This, of course, was part of Stravinsky's joke, an external counterpart of the "inside" games that run throughout *The Flood* and are an inseparable part of its specialty. . . .

The richest *double-entendre* in *The Flood* is unquestionably the whistling wind music in the ballet section depicting the flood itself. This consists first of fragments, then the whole of a twelve-tone row is repeated in an insistent and literal *ostinato*. The idea works remarkably well as a "stage" effect, but its hidden appropriateness is still more fascinating. One is reminded of classical "storm" music—Beethoven's *Pastorale* Symphony most notably—that inevitably included sweeping runs over the chromatic scale. . . .

Altogether, this section is one of the most interesting and original in the work: the remarkable burbling flutter-tongue woodwind sounds (obviously intended to portray the aquatic aspect of the calamity) are the freshest instrumental sounds heard since *Movements*. But these also function on more than the simple level of onomatopoeia or striking sound-invention. They are, in fact, merely the central instance of the tremolo ideas around which the entire work is built. One seems to hear every possible variety of repeated sound, of which some are familiar from earlier Stravinsky works, but others are new. Up to now, Stravinsky seems to have avoided much explicit use of tremolo, probably because of its association with the Romantic. . . . [But his] intention of making *The Flood* his work of the tremolo is unmistakable from the very outset: the string tremolandos of the opening section, introducing the story of the *Creation*, a parallel that was probably intentional. Another level of the tremolo idea is the recurrence throughout the work of a characteristic series of chords. In the dialogue between God and Noah, these chords themselves are played as tremolos over the wonderful, slow drum-roll that always presages and accompanies the voice of God—or, rather, voices, since it was Stravinsky's happy idea to have God speak in a two-voice, polyphonic texture resembling the medieval motet. . . .

The "Building of the Ark" ballet section, which reminds me of the opening and last three sections of *Agon* and also parts of *Threni*, begins with parts of repeated sounds, then gradually builds up into a veritable polyphony of tremolos going at various speeds (the five successive trombone blasts are unforgettable), and then subsides into pairs again. After the flood section itself, where nearly every note is attacked with a flutter, a roll, or a tremolando, the opening sections are reintroduced—a structural parallel of the repetition of notes and the recurrences of chords. The final words of Noah's last speech, "And so a world begins to be," occasion the return of the opening *Creation* music, and the cycle seems to begin again, with the reprise of Satan's music (Satan's "pride" is like Oedipus', by way of the Shakespeare Songs), and, finally, a second choral "Sanctus." The linear twelve-tone idea that opens the work also presides over the fading-out textural dissolution with which *The Flood* ends. . . .

From the recording alone, *The Flood* seems . . . to contain some of the most distinguished movie music ever written. [Benjamin Boretz, "Stravinsky's Flood of Genius," *The Nation*, July 28, 1962]

As early as 1960, Rolf Liebermann planned to present *The Flood* on the stage of the Hamburg Opera:

We reached an agreement in New York [that] Günther Rennert would stage the work and Robert Craft conduct it. . . . All that remained was to find someone for the decors, and for this simple biblical story we naturally thought of Chagall. He would have to meet with Stravinsky, whom he had not seen since the [1945] *Firebird*, and who had begun to detest painters because, as he used to say, "They make as much money in twenty minutes as I do in three months." Briefly, I left for Paris to see Chagall . . . who quickly agreed to participate in the project and said he was ready for a meeting with Stravinsky. We chose Nicolas Nabokov's Paris apartment as the meeting place, and Stravinsky came from [Rome], myself from Hamburg, Chagall from [Rouen]. . . . The rendezvous was set at five-thirty in the afternoon [of December 1, 1960], and Chagall, his wife and I arrived precisely at that time. But at six o'clock we were still alone. Some time after six-thirty the telephone rang: it was Mme Stravinsky, mortified at having to say that her husband was on his bed dead drunk after a lunch washed down by an incalculable number of bottles of vodka and of champagne. "It is impossible to wake him," she said, and I told her to let him sleep but to come herself with Robert Craft. "I will try, but it will not be easy because he is also drunk." A quarter of an hour later Vera Stravinsky made her entrance at Nabokov's.[128] . . . Chagall was not impressed by the story, and his wife's reaction was still more severe. . . . At two o'clock in the morning Stravinsky woke up with a terrible thirst and wanted to drink with me at his hotel. There he was, in his pajamas, with two bottles of Dom Perignon, in buckets of ice. I tried for the last time to arrange the affair. "Listen, Igor. Telephone to Chagall or write a word to him." "Impossible," he said, because "I don't *want* any decors by that *con*." [129]

On April 15, 1962, Stravinsky wrote to the producer of the work, Robert Graff of Sextant, Inc., saying that, after listening to the revised record (i.e., with the Prelude repeated before the last words of the Devil), he is now certain that nothing should be changed and that the piece should be heard as it stands. Stravinsky says that the total length will be at least twenty-five minutes, not by the repetition of unrepeatable music but by the lengthening of pauses: at the beginning; before Lucifer's first aria; after the expulsion from Eden; and between the Flood and the Covenant. Stravinsky says that these pauses will also help to pace a piece that moves with great rapidity. He adds that the Prelude is not a curtain-raiser, or accompaniment to credits, but part of the action, hence the conductor should not be seen.

Difficulties with the promotion of Stravinsky's recordings began with *The Flood*. Columbia Records had launched a project to offer the "complete works conducted by the composer," but the composer was unable to conduct *The Flood*, having had no experience with music of this kind. On April 7, 1962, Stravinsky wrote to an official at Columbia Records, remarking that if *The Flood* had required two orchestras, "like Stockhausen," then the use of two conductors (the present writer being the other one) would be justified, but, otherwise, to say that two people conducted the piece, but not to specify which one conducted which, would be to invite speculation.

On November 22, 1935, Stravinsky had written to Balanchine saying that the news of his forthcoming staging of *Apollo* in the Metropolitan Opera House has provided a welcome opportunity "to express my joy and my complete confidence in you." In the same letter, the composer remarks that his

memories of our collaboration during the staging of *Apollo* for Diaghilev in 1928 are among the most satisfying in my artistic life. . . . Knowing what a good musician you are, I count on you to observe the metronomic tempi.

One of my most beautiful memories is of the celebration of [Stravinsky's] eightieth birthday in Hamburg. . . . His preferred cities were Venice and New York [and] except for our friendship, he had no reason to celebrate his eighty years on the shores of the North Sea. He had signed the contract a year before. [Also] I had proposed to mount his three "Greek" ballets a year before [and] George Balanchine and his New York City Ballet were to take part. . . . [Stravinsky] received one of his most extraordinary ovations.[130]

But the climax of the eightieth anniversary came four

June 18, 1962. Hamburg. On his eightieth birthday, walking to the Staatsoper with George Balanchine. On this occasion, Stravinsky conducted *Apollo*. Seventeen years before, on another Stravinsky birthday, Balanchine had telegraphed from Mexico City: "If Apollo's mother was Leto, then certainly his father was Fyodor [signed] Jorge Balanchine."

June 18, 1962. Hamburg. The composer chose to spend his eightieth birthday with the performing organization closest to his heart, the New York City Ballet. Here he is onstage with the dancers after the performances of *Orpheus*, *Agon*, and *Apollo*. Stravinsky framed the three photographs this way himself and kept them on the wall of his studio.

months later, in Russia. At the time, the trip was widely regarded as merely another step in the composer's pattern of reversals. Hosts and guests alike had been vilifying each other for more than thirty years, and, by the date of the trip, neither side had recanted. Officially, Stravinsky was still the U.S.S.R.'s arch symbol of capitalist decadence, and a rapprochement seemed improbable, to say the least; not until after his death, in fact, was Stravinsky's music played to any extent in the U.S.S.R. But the return of the native in 1962 provided the impetus. A historical switch occurred, not comparable to Constantine's conversion of the Empire, perhaps, but, at any rate, to the cessation of persecution before that event.

Stravinsky's feelings about this trip were ambiguous. On

June 12, 1961, he wrote to his Paris friend Pierre Suvchinsky that there had been an international festival in Los Angeles in which he had conducted his Violin Concerto and *Symphony of Psalms,* and that the festival had included a concert of Soviet music. Stravinsky says that he could not leave the hall since these same Soviet musicians had visited him the day before and invited him to come to Moscow to celebrate his eightieth birthday. He says that he has "painful and uneasy" thoughts about this trip. Finally, Stravinsky says that he already hears about his acceptance in the press and on the radio but is not ready for the experience and does not believe that people in the U.S.S.R. have changed their opinions of his music. In a postscript, Stravinsky says that he knew Yastrebzev,[131] and that he was a complete idiot.

A week later, Stravinsky wrote to Suvchinsky again, saying that the official invitation to come to Moscow has been received and accepted. But, on August 18, in another letter to Suvchinsky, Stravinsky announced that he was going to Helsinki. He says that it would be nice to see Yudina [132] there, if she could get permission to leave Russia, but she, "who is really devoted to my music, cannot even cross the border."

A year later, nevertheless, Stravinsky was in Russia. Of this tour, *The New York Times* reported on one occasion:

LENINGRAD HAILS A SON, STRAVINSKY

Leningrad, October 8. Igor Stravinsky evoked for the people of his native city tonight memories of pre-revolutionary Russia and a vision of more freedom in music. It was an evening of sentiment and intellectual excitement as the 80-year-old composer conducted the first of two concerts of his works in Leningrad's Philharmonia Hall. Members of the Soviet elite and devotees of music who had begun applying for tickets a year ago showered Stravinsky with bravos, flowers, and their unrestrained affection.

Stravinsky would have preferred to conduct works more modern than those on the program for the two Leningrad concerts. . . . The management of the Leningrad Philharmonic Orchestra, which Stravinsky conducted tonight, had selected the music. Although Stravinsky found the members of the orchestra fine instrumentalists, the composer's more modern works were termed too far out of their range of experience. . . .

The electric excitement in Philharmonia Hall, especially among the younger intellectuals, was indicative of the importance attached to Stravinsky's appearance here. His presence alone signified a more liberal attitude by Soviet officials toward the modern music of the West, and his concerts may accelerate this trend. There is also a feeling that Leningrad is finally reclaiming Stravinsky after the bitter Stalin years in which his music was denounced as decadent and bourgeois. . . .

Stravinsky was introduced to the audience tonight by Valerian Bogdanovich Gerisovsky, Soviet composer. He said Stravinsky, now a naturalized American, had left Russia when it was still under the oppression of the Czars, "but he always remained a Russian artist spreading the glory of Russian art." Stravinsky was summoned to the podium again and again after he had conducted *The Firebird.* The audience crowded to the foot of the stage to acclaim him. Addressing the audience in Russian, Stravinsky recalled that he was in Philharmonia Hall with his mother sixty-eight years ago for a Tchaikovsky concert, two weeks after the death of the composer. The hall was then known as the "Assembly of the Nobles." [Seymour Topping, *New York Times*, October 8]

Leningrad, October 8. Igor Stravinsky gave a lecture for more than 100 student composers today after a rehearsal with the Philharmonic Orchestra. He reviewed the latest developments of music and particularly emphasized his most modern compositions. Later the young musicians pressed the composer for more details, while Tikhon Khrennikov, President of the Soviet Composers Union, listened carefully. Members of Stravinsky's party said that Stravinsky had implored Mr. Khrennikov, guardian of Soviet policy in music, to take his most modern music seriously. They said Mr. Khrennikov had so far resisted the idea. [Associated Press.]

STRAVINSKY COMPLETES CONCERT TOUR IN SOVIET

Leningrad, October 9. Igor Stravinsky wound up his homecoming concert tour of the Soviet Union tonight with a warmly applauded performance.

A capacity audience of 2,000 in the Grand Hall of the Philharmonic building refused to stop applauding until Stravinsky appeared on stage in his overcoat and bowed out.

A few minutes earlier, members of the audience had surged down the aisles for a closer look at the 80-year-old composer, who was born near here and is now an American citizen.

Stravinsky appeared moved by the attention, but declined to lead the Leningrad Symphony in more than one encore, *The Song of the Volga Boatmen*. Earlier he had conducted the orchestra through spirited renditions of *Fireworks* and *The Firebird*. [*New York Times*, October 10]

Wearing a navy blue coat, a gray felt hat, and with his chin hidden in a white woolen scarf, the famous Russian-American composer Igor Stravinsky arrived last night at Orly from Moscow, where he had given four concerts. "I discovered Moscow with a profound emotion. I had never seen it, having spent only five hours there some sixty years ago, and I am eighty-one. It is a very lively city, full of beautiful things. . . . The Russian public is touching. One must talk to them very gently, as one talks to children, before offering what they expect from us. . . . I have not yet sorted out my impressions. But rediscovering some of my family was the greatest happiness of all. My Leningrad niece is a grandmother now, and her three-year-old grandson has the name 'Igor.' " [Jacqueline Leuilliot, Paris, October 12]

In Hollywood, April 16, 1964, Stravinsky sent a telegram to Nikita Khrushchev: "Wishing you continuing health and a very happy birthday."

In New York at the time of the American premiere of *Abraham and Isaac*, Stravinsky told an interviewer:

In my Christian religion, the Abraham sacrifice is the greatest sacrifice, other than Jesus, of course, but we are talking of the Old Testament. It seems to me to be very close to the philosophy of Kierkegaard, which

I esteem very highly. [Leroy Aarons, from the *New York Journal American*, December 13, 1964]

Stravinsky began the composition of *Abraham and Isaac* in Santa Fe, August 2, 1962, and continued it in September in Venice. By January 31, 1963, he had composed as far as measure 135; by February 16, as far as measure 190; and on March 3, the score was completed—almost a year and a half before it was performed. "It all began three years ago," wrote Nicole Hirsch (*Paris Express*, September 6, 1964):

Stravinsky was at Oxford at the home of his friend, the philosopher Isaiah Berlin, who had read some passages from the Bible for him in Hebrew and with ancient scansion. Deeply impressed by the musical quality of the language, Stravinsky dreamed of using Hebrew in a vocal work. In 1962, invited by the Festival of Israel, Stravinsky made a memorable tour, and at that time the commission was proffered. . . . Stravinsky later refused the money and gave it to the fund for the restoration of Massada. . . . The Israeli listener is very conservative . . . with the tastes of the Viennese bourgeois before the War. "[Stravinsky] is old," the audience seemed to say, and "It is important to have seen him."

Rolf Liebermann was a good and loyal friend to Stravinsky as well as a most articulate and knowledgeable interviewer. They sometimes traveled together. Commenting on Stravinsky's highly developed sense of his audience, and sense of circum-

April 21, 1963. Bremen. With Rolf Liebermann.

November 10, 1957. New York. With Balanchine during a rehearsal of *Agon*. The choreographer once quoted the composer correcting an interviewer who had called him "a turning point in the history of music"—to "I am a turning-*around* point." [Metropolitan Opera program, February 14, 1953]

April 1937. New York. Stravinsky and Balanchine at a rehearsal of *Jeu de Cartes.*

stance and occasion, Liebermann wrote that, in a concert in Zagreb, in May 1963,

all the spectators were in their shirt sleeves, and, though accustomed to more mondaine dress, Igor showed no surprise. On the contrary, when the acclamations greeting him had subsided, he said, "Excuse me, but I too am very warm," and, tranquilly, he removed his tails, then his vest, then his white tie, and then began to unbutton his shirt, the enthusiasm of the hall augmenting, of course, with each stage of this strip-tease.[133]

Liebermann has also told how

In an airplane between Chicago and Los Angeles,[134] I was present at an unforgettable duel: Igor scribbling on sheets of toilet paper from the washroom in search of a twelve-tone series. He was attempting to notate the nucleus of a new composition, and this true struggle between the creator and his material lasted three hours. One can imagine his happiness in finally finding the series a few minutes before landing.[135]

One of the many projects besides *Abraham and Isaac* that occupied Stravinsky in the early months of 1963 was the fitting of movements and passages from his Octet and *Histoire du Soldat* to a film of Jean Genet's *The Balcony*.

Stravinsky flew from London to Dublin, then to Hamburg, Stockholm, Milan, conducting in the last four of these cities. On June 29, he returned to New York and, on July 1, to Los Angeles. At home, he arranged Sibelius's string *Canzonetta*, Op. 62a, for an ensemble of eight instruments (clarinet, bass clarinet, four horns, harp, string bass), completing and sending the score to Helsinki on July 10. The arrangement was intended as a gesture of gratitude for the Sibelius Prize, which Stravinsky had twice received, and he chose the *Canzonetta* because it was the "signature tune" of the Canadian Broadcasting Company's symphony in Toronto, ending each of the orchestra's broadcasts.

The deaths of friends toward the end of 1963 greatly upset Stravinsky, and, one more was soon to follow, that of Michel Larionov. Stravinsky's faithful correspondent Howard Rothschild wrote to the composer from Izmir, Turkey:

I sent to Mrs. Bolm the last news of Larionov. All very upsetting and sad. . . . Suddenly on the way from Pergamum—Lesbos shadowing the azure bay where Agamemnon's fleet anchored on its way to Troy— *L'Oiseau de Feu* on the taxi radio . . .

Stravinsky was deeply shocked by the assassination of the President. He told an interviewer:

The Elegy is in memory of somebody I knew, and whose loss I infinitely regret. We were at a concert in Sicily when it [the assassination] happened. I was conducting my Mass there. I told the Italian audience I would play this Mass in memory of Kennedy. I never saw such sym-

May 7, 1964. Toronto. Massey Hall. Listening to a rehearsal.

pathy of strangers as in Italy. All the walls were covered with his portrait. The day of his burial I repeated my concert in the cathedral [of Santa Maria Sopra Minerva, Rome]. It was the only open [edifice] in the city. Everything was closed. [Aarons, *op. cit.*]

The draft score of the variation for twelve violins was completed August 12, 1963, and measures 63–71 on January 3, 1964, but in a form different from the final version, which was written on January 24. After composing measures 73–5 and measures 61–2 (on February 22), Stravinsky interrupted the composition to write the *Fanfare for a New Theater* and the *Elegy for J.F.K.* (completed, in the version for baritone, April 1, 1964). On May 22, he resumed work on the Variations at measure 86, and, on August 13, completed the fugato.

The *Introitus* sketches offer a simple example of Stravinsky's technical procedures in his final period. What is not shown is that he set the text first, without harmony and without rhythm (quarter-notes only), to a series of twelve different pitches in five different forms: original, retrograde, inverted, retrograde inverted, inversion of the retrograde inverted. Each phrase of the text corresponds to one of these forms of the series, or, rather, has been made to do so by means of repetitions; also, Stravinsky alternates the phrases between tenors and basses, so that the tenors sing the first segment of the text in the original and retrograde forms, then the basses sing the second segment in the inverted form, then the tenors sing the third segment in the retrograde inversion, and, finally, the basses sing the fourth segment also in the retrograde inversion but with repeated intervals

May 28, 1965. Warsaw. Poster for a concert that included the first European performance of the Variations.

July 23, 1966. New York. Philharmonic Hall. Greeted by Marianne Moore, after conducting the Symphony of Psalms.

and octave transpositions. But whereas, in his first sketch, Stravinsky had given the last phrase (the inversion of the retrograde inversion) to the tenors, he later decided to unite the choir at the end, hence the tenors sing the last phrase in retrograde form and the basses sing it in retrograde inversion.

The serial chart shows that Stravinsky constructed three additional series for each of the four orders, O, I, R, RI. Thus the second series of O has been formed by starting with the second interval of the original series and by using its *intervals* (not its pitches!) from this new starting point. So, too, the third series of O begins with the third interval of the first form, the fourth from the fourth interval. All four series of each order are divided into three segments, A, B, and Y. This structure is shown by the slanted lines, and the notes circled in red reveal the derivation of the four-pitch chords played by piano and harp in the first two measures of the composition. The other features of the music are apparent, such as the contrasting sonorities (harp, piano, and tam-tams between the choral phrases, strings and pitched drums accompanying the singers), and the rhythmic imitations from one instrumental group to another and from voices to instruments.

On July 14, 1966, Stravinsky flew to New York for a festival of his music organized by Lukas Foss. On the 15th, Stravinsky attended a concert of his *Ragtime*, choreographed by Balanchine, and of *Histoire du Soldat*, with Elliott Carter as the Soldier, Aaron Copland as the Narrator, and John Cage as the Devil. On the 16th, Stravinsky heard Kyril Kondrashin conduct *Petrushka*. On the 18th, the Stravinskys went to dinner with the Elliott Carters at the Côte Basque, where Stravinsky was approached by Frank Sinatra, who asked for and received an autograph. On the 20th, the Stravinskys attended a staged performance of *Oedipus Rex*.

Mrs. Stravinsky stood up and booed . . . while the composer himself fled to a nearby reception room. What the Stravinskys didn't like was the accompanying "visual representation" by artist Larry Rivers. He had dressed Oedipus as a prizefighter. . . . "It was a mishmash!" Mrs. Stravinsky said. "But later, backstage, Larry Rivers asked me what I thought. I don't like to lie: I do it only to make somebody happy. So I said, 'Oh, I'm an old lady and very old-fashioned. Don't ask me. . . .' "
[*Sunday Oregonian*, February 19, 1967]

Stravinsky's first notation for the *Requiem Canticles*, in March 1965, was for the music between measures 166 and 174. Returning to the work in the summer, he began at approximately the same place, drafting, this time in score, measures 163–75 (July 25–6). Measures 153–8 were composed on July 28, and the music between 176 and 183 was completed on August 29. The "Exaudi" was written next, in November, then the "Prelude," the "Dies irae," and the "Tuba mirum." The last part of the "Tuba mirum"—from measure 115—was written on January 7, 1966, and the "Rex tremendae" was completed through measure 213 on March 29. The "Libera me" was sketched in Lisbon at the

end of May, and the Postlude was completed in Hollywood, August 13.

In April 1968, George Balanchine presented the *Canticles* in a semi-staged version, in memory of Martin Luther King, for which event Stravinsky contributed a program note:

I planned my *Requiem Canticles* as an instrumental work, and I composed the threnody for wind instruments and muffled drums first. Later, I decided to use sentences from six texts of the traditional *Requiem* service, and at that time I conceived the instrumental frame of a string *Prelude*, a wind-instrument *Interlude*, and a percussion *Postlude*. . . . I am honored that my music is to be played in memory of a man of God, a man of the poor, a man of peace.

"Traditional Requiem service," Stravinsky writes, but in fact his text and form were borrowed from Verdi, along with at least three musical ideas: the trumpets in the "Tuba mirum," the unmeasured "Libera me," and the unison triplet for the three syllables of "Libera" at the end of the movement. The present writer's copy of Verdi's score contains several notations in Stravinsky's hand, especially in the "Libera me."

Stravinsky accepted the *Requiem* commission from Stanley Seeger, Jr., Frenchtown, New Jersey, in a letter to him dated February 22, 1965. The first performance took place at the McCarter Theater, Princeton, on October 8, 1966:

The *Requiem Canticles* . . . performance was advanced to enable the composer, now in his 85th year, to hear it at the earliest convenient date. . . . The new work is in nine comparatively short movements: six vocal and three instrumental. A spiky Prelude for strings, with a five against six syncopation, introduces the "Exaudi" movement for chorus. . . .

June 1963. New York. Editing a recording at Columbia Records. Photograph by W. Koenig.

There are occasional correspondences with passages in works by Stravinsky. . . . The phrasing of the repeated chord that frames the separate sections of the Interlude (the first part of the *Requiem Canticles* to be composed) recalls the similar phrasing that is so characteristic of the *Wind Symphonies'* chorale. The return of the trumpets halfway through the "Tuba mirum" echoes the Messenger's flourish in *Oedipus Rex* when he bursts on the stage to announce Jocasta's death, and in the "Exaudi" movement the final phrase of the chorus is interlocked with the orchestra ritornello in a similar way to the close of the "Agnus Dei" movement in the Mass. . . .

Stravinsky's conducting of the *Symphonies of Wind Instruments,* the *Three Sacred Choruses,* and the Mass was splendidly intense and resilient. At the end of the concert he received a standing ovation from the enthusiastic audience, for it was clear to everyone present that the new *Requiem Canticles,* though brief, are of great originality and invention, variety and contrast, and are likely to prove his most impressive and accessible serial work to date. [London *Times,* October 11, 1966]

Shortly before the beginning of the concert, Dr. Robert Oppenheimer sent a note to Stravinsky, backstage:

We shall try to see you briefly at the intermission or the end. If you are in Princeton Sunday, let us bring you home for a few minutes. In respect and devotion, Robert Oppenheimer.

Of the approximately 150 concerts that Stravinsky conducted between 1947 and 1957, he shared the podium with other conductors only very rarely. Between his seventy-fifth and eighty-fifth birthdays, however, 1957–67, he led the halves of approximately 144 programs, the remaining portions being directed by the present writer. In the peak year, 1962, that of the eightieth anniversary, Stravinsky participated in thirty-five concerts, having refused requests for at least that many again. By 1965, this number had fallen to only nine concerts. But how did the two conductors work together? Here is an account of a rehearsal from the Sydney (Australia) *Morning Herald,* November 23, 1961:

Every now and then Stravinsky stood up and conferred with Craft, sometimes speaking in French. . . . Stravinsky had a glass of cold beer brought in at his request from a nearby hotel, pushed his dark glasses onto his forehead and chatted with the players. Robert Craft, a quiet-voiced conductor, whose glasses appeared always to be slipping from his nose, was not to disagree with the man with whom he had been closely associated since 1947, but at one point in the rehearsal Craft gave the orchestra unusual advice, "Don't watch me, just count: Mr. Stravinsky will be conducting this music tomorrow night. We don't agree about how to do it, and I do not want to impose my own interpretation on how it should sound."

Mrs. Stravinsky told an interviewer:

When [Stravinsky] conducts I'm never in the audience. I'll have heard him and Craft talking—"Watch the tenor, he doesn't know his lines," or "Someone in the orchestra isn't doing right"—they speak about it all the time so I'm always waiting for a catastrophe. I think it's better to wait backstage. Nothing ever happens, of course. [*Sunday Oregonian,* February 19, 1967]

Frequently asked to recommend conductors of his music, Stravinsky was always generous in his remarks about this writer:

The three best conductors of my music are Pierre Monteux and Fritz Reiner, who have both become lazy, and Robert Craft, who is a very good and active conductor of my works, the old ones, the new ones, and even those not yet written. [Press conference, Tokyo, April 8, 1959]

On May 20, 1959, Stravinsky wrote to his European concert agent, Ada Finzi:

Mon caché à moi est, comme vous le savez probablement, $1,500 en Europe, et celui de R. Craft $250. Nous partageons quelquefois avec lui le programme ... mais c'est surtout à lui seul qu'il donne des exécutions remarquables de la musique dites d'avant-garde. Rome, Naples, Turin, Vienne, Paris, Bruxelles, Baden-Baden, Hambourg, etc., ont eu ces dernières années l'occasion d'apprécier ce musicien d'une haute culture et ce technicien de grand talent.

On November 13, 1961, the *Auckland Star* printed an interview with Stravinsky:

I shall conduct only half the concert. I would like to take it all but for some years I've had a thrombosis which makes it absolute torture to endeavor to stand and conduct for more than an hour. In Robert Craft, who will take the first half of the concert, I have been fortunate in finding a young man who is a fine conductor of both the music of our time and of earlier periods, and who knows very much what is in my mind when interpreting my works. . . .

On May 1, 1966, Stravinsky wrote to the Gulbenkian Foundation in Lisbon:

For twelve years I have shared programs with Maestro Craft all over the world. . . . If a man conducts, then his name is given [the Gulbenkian wanted Stravinsky's name alone on the program]. If the Shepherd in *Oedipus* is listed, then so must be the conductor of *Le Sacre du Printemps.* Maestro Craft has conducted the premieres of my later music, and everywhere he does about ninety percent of the preparation. . . .

The *Honolulu Adviser* said, on November 18, 1966:

Igor Stravinsky sat in the darkened fourth row of Honolulu Concert Hall last night huddled over the score of his Symphony in Three Movements, while ... Robert Craft rehearsed the Honolulu Symphony. . . . Stravinsky might have been conducting himself, so intent was he, his hands impulsively pointing to the violins, the brass section, the clarinets. Stravinsky said he is happy to be in Honolulu. "I sit in my hotel room and have a wide view of the ocean. . . . And there is lots of oxygen. In Los Angeles the smog is terrible. It bothers the eyes especially."

Mrs. Stravinsky says she keeps trying to persuade her husband to move to New York City. . . . "So many of the people we used to know in Los Angeles have either died or moved away," she said sadly.

In old age, Stravinsky's conducting helped to sustain his morale, and it was a great blow to him when, four years before his death, he was obliged to retire from the podium. He continued to attend performances of his music after that, in concerts and in the theater; *Le Sacre du Printemps* at the Paris Opéra in November 1968 was the last of his theater works that he was to see. The following description of Stravinsky rehearsing, less than two years before his retirement from the concert stage, would apply to any of his later appearances:

He walked to the podium looking frail and bent and old, leaning on a cane. But when the rehearsal began he seemed to become a different man. His whole length straightened until he stood on the tips of his toes with the arms uplifted, seeming to hover above the orchestra. His movements were sure and energetic as he moved the orchestra through . . . the *Firebird*. He encouraged, chided, and praised the musicians. "That's not quite right. Play it faster, more staccato. Once again. That's good. My compliments." For more than an hour he kept the musicians at it, repeating and polishing difficult passages, appearing as fresh when it was over as when the rehearsal began. [*Vancouver Sun*, July 12, 1965]

November 30, 1966. A page from Stravinsky's diary.

After the Princeton concert with the *Requiem Canticles*, Stravinsky conducted in Portland. The *Oregonian*, Tuesday, December 6, 1966, noted:

... Once on the stand Stravinsky seemed to absorb vitality from the project before him. Directive gestures in his *Symphonies of Wind Instruments* were thrifty, sometimes amounting to no more than a twist of the wrist. ... When it came to his *Pulcinella* Suite ... his gestures were more sweeping.

On December 27, 1966, Stravinsky conducted in Chicago and repeated the program on New Year's Day, 1967:

Stravinsky's clean, regular pulse may be given with a finger or a wrist, but it is there, and most of the necessary entrance cues are indicated as well. The wiry indomitability of personality remains, and the broad grin which broke across his face as he was summoned back after the concert would have lighted a house twice the size. [*Chicago Tribune*, December 30, 1966]

On January 11, 1967, the Stravinskys flew from New York to California, and, on the 18th, the composer conducted his last recording, the 1945 *Firebird* Suite. He was to conduct only four more times after that—in Miami, Los Angeles, Seattle, Toronto. He flew to the first of these cities on February 19, grieving at the news of Robert Oppenheimer's death. The next day, Nicolas Nabokov telephoned from Princeton saying that Oppenheimer had left a letter "to be opened after his death" which requested that the *Requiem Canticles* be performed at a memorial service. On February 23, 1967, the *Miami News* reported:

The feared and famous composer arrived in the Dade County Auditorium. ... Suddenly the music failed to please him and the lamb became all lion. He loosened his tie, took off his coat, brushed a music stand aside. ... Then he mounted the stage and took a firm hold on ... the rehearsal of *The Firebird*, proving there's plenty of fire in the old bird yet.

Stravinsky gave interviews in conjunction with all of his last concerts. The *Miami News* reported:

The Maestro appeared, slipping quietly into the room, guiding himself a bit with a cane that he did not appear to need. Asked about his newest composition, he said firmly: "I like to compose. I do not like to talk about it." Then he talked about it. "No, everything I do will not necessarily be 12-tone. It's the serial system which interests me. Maybe tomorrow I will compose in 13 tones. The style always changes with the subject and character of the music. I never know what my style is. Many people write and talk about my style, but no one is right." ... The octogenarian has lost ... little of his fire. "If a lion eats me, you will hear the news from him. He will say that the old man was a tough but tasty meal."

In Seattle, Stravinsky conducted *Histoire du Soldat*:

Stravinsky . . . appeared on stage and the crowd broke into applause which he acknowledged with a wave of his left hand. But the clapping wouldn't stop, and Stravinsky turned, made a half-bow and once again waved. . . . The evening was a personal triumph for Stravinsky. He conducted the ensemble . . . with a vigor that belied his years. [*Seattle Post-Intelligencer*, March 2, 1967]

After the performance, Stravinsky spoke to reporters:

"You can't tell where music is going any more than you can tell where people are going. Each time creates its own needs." [*Seattle Post-Intelligencer*, March 2, 1967]

In the last concert of all, in Massey Hall, Toronto, Stravinsky conducted the *Pulcinella* Suite:

In his shaping of phrase, subtle dynamics, and detailing of rhythms [Stravinsky] demonstrated remarkable control and musicianship. . . . There were brilliant moments and these . . . contributed to a memorable performance. [*Globe and Mail*, May 18, 1967]

On this occasion, Stravinsky received the Canada Council Medal "in the hope that it honors you," as the citation read,

and in the knowledge that it honors us to award it. This is the first time that the medal has been given to an artist from outside our borders . . . but [your] music has crossed all borders.

In New York, on May 23, Stravinsky cabled to his London agent, Robert Paterson: "Diaghilev film possible in Hollywood in late June." Stravinsky had agreed to participate in a documentary about the impresario, but the project was abandoned. While in New York, the composer was subjected to several medical tests, the results of which were sent to Hollywood:

June 2, 1967. As Stendhal says, "Une partie de la biographie des grands hommes devrait être fournie par leurs médecins." Item: The New York doctors' reports of their examinations arrive today, addressed to V.A.S. and not intended for her husband's eyes, but he sees the envelope and confiscates it. Nor is any harm done. On May 24, Dr. Donald Simons found him "Very alert, bright . . . An electrocephalogram was made in my office. It reveals a normal, well-formed 9/sec alpha pattern. There was no trace of any abnormality in the left central-parietal area. There was no evidence of the slowing of the frequencies which is commonly found in elderly people. . . . The patient stated that he has some difficulty in comprehending women's voices, but he was able to hear fingers rubbing at twelve inches, which is much better than most people at his age can do. . . . When asked to multiply 7 by 11, he gave the answer as 77 and said there was 23 left over." (Looking for a point to the question?) "He admits to getting angry at least once a day"—I like that "at least"—and "he has an alert intellect." This leaves the patient feeling conceited. A letter in the same mail from Dr. La Due addressed to Stravinsky remarks on his "voracious consumption of books" and reassures him that "no impairment whatsoever to your mental faculties has occurred." [From R.C.'s diary]

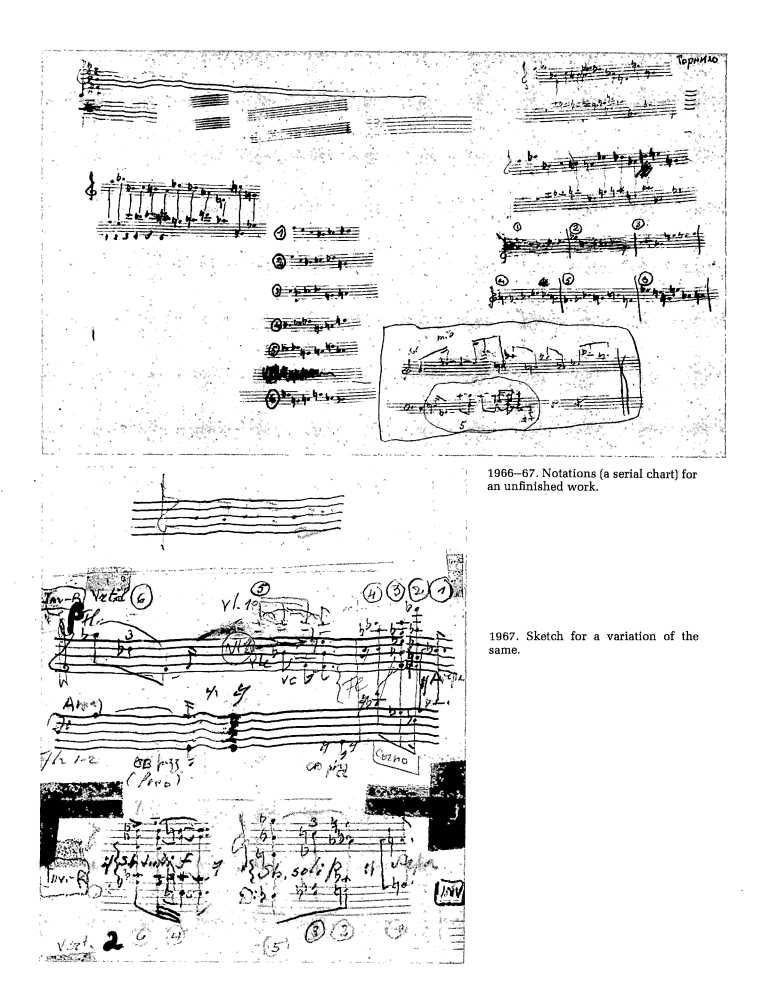

1966–67. Notations (a serial chart) for an unfinished work.

1967. Sketch for a variation of the same.

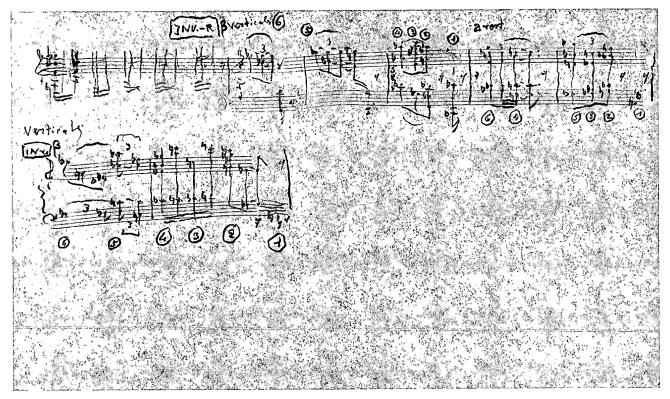

1967. Sketch for a variation of the
same.

1967. Variation of the same, timpani
and three trombones.

The creation of great works of art by anyone of advanced age is rare in any medium. Stravinsky was seventy-four and eighty-four, respectively, when he wrote *Agon* and the *Requiem Canticles*, which is a more remarkable phenomenon, whatever else, than the composition, at twenty-four and thirty-four, of respectively, the Symphony in E-flat and *Renard*. In the case of the final decade and a half of Stravinsky's productivity, the continuing growth and flexibility are the more amazing because of his precarious health. Despite his apparent immunity from normal aging processes, he was afflicted during the whole of this period with a serious disease, polycythemia, whose worst side effect, the unconcealed incertitude of the doctors as to methods of containment, was almost as great a burden as the illness itself. After the two strokes in 1956, body and soul fell further and further asunder. Yet, in the decade between 1956 and 1966, Stravinsky composed more music than he had in the 1930s.

Like other artists in their eighties who continue to create (and not just to produce), Stravinsky's sense of isolation increased, the ferocity of his impatience grew, and his *saeva indignatio* kindled more quickly. Like that of some others, too, his art of these years is marked by a greater concentration—spareness, severity—and by a tendency to sacrifice surface attractions to structural ideas. But, unlike any octogenarian artist except Michelangelo—he, at least, is the only other to come to mind—Stravinsky did not lose his lifelong sense of risk. Nor did he regard his past achievements with a sense of resignation, of "the life-work fulfilled." Though few composers have been able to round out their lives and their work so fully, Stravinsky never doubted his continuing musical fecundity, which explains the struggle of his last four years not to compose but to regain the health that would enable him to compose. At an advanced age, though considerably less advanced than Stravinsky's, Hokusai seems to have felt with similar intensity that he had not done all that he wanted to do:

At seventy-three I learned a little about the real structure of nature, of animals, plants, trees, birds, fishes, and insects. . . . When I am eighty I shall have made still more progress.

He's very neat [Mrs. Stravinsky says]. Everything has a place and everything must be in its place. In the hotel on the dresser he puts a napkin and then lays out everything in a row—scissors, razor. . . . In my room everything is scattered. Yet I'm the one who can always find things; he can't. . . . I know his habits, what he likes. . . . He's very spoiled. He thinks he isn't and I tell him he is spoiled in a special way. He likes breakfast in bed, so the tray is prepared, just the way he likes it. . . . But he is very particular, likes the spoon just so. . . . [Vera Stravinsky in the *Sunday Oregonian*, February 19, 1967]

Stravinsky read Henri Troyat's *Life of Tolstoy* during his trip to Arizona and talked about little else. But he also kept a notebook with such entries as:

I sent a clipping from the *Domaine Musical* to P. Suvchinsky to show how complicated are the writings about Webern and his music, and how little they correspond to the simplicity of his thinking and his style.

In September 1968, the Stravinskys flew to New York and from there to Zürich, where, on arrival, the composer said that he never wanted to return to America. While in Switzerland, he worked on a choral composition, visited his bank in Basel (where he made his wife the sole heir), received such friends as Lina Lalandi, Suvchinsky, Nicolas Nabokov, and the latter's future wife, Dominique, who made many excellent photographs of the composer. Stravinsky also visited the Wagner Museum at Triebschen, which revived childhood memories of Lucerne. One musical experience made a considerable impression on him, the singing of the Benedictine monks in the abbey church of Einsiedeln. After a month in Switzerland, however, he grew restless and wanted to go to Paris.

We fly to Paris from Zürich in mid-afternoon and are met at Orly by Suvchinsky and Lawrence Morton. At the Ritz, Stravinsky complains that the furniture is *"décoratif mais pas très utile,"* whereupon Count Zembrzuski, the managing director, calls for a more effulgent lamp, and promises to install an electric buzzer between Stravinsky's room and that of his wife. Furthermore, a piano, probably unheard in these sedate precincts since the death of Chopin across the street, will be brought in next week. A notice posted in the bathroom advises guests IN CASE OF FIRE BE SURE TO INFORM THE VALET OR MAID. Another notice, USE ONLY FIREWOOD IN THE CHIMNEY GRATES AND CALL IN THE VALET TO LIGHT THE FIRE WHEN REQUIRED, turns one's thoughts to the Louis Quinze chairs, if it should come to that. While a valet helps Stravinsky to unpack, Mrs. Stravinsky worries aloud about a missing garment. *"Un rien vous habille, Madame,"* the valet retorts, making one reflect that whatever the truth of the dictum "Paris is too good for the French," such gallant wit exists nowhere else. As for my room, it is acoustically ideal for listening to the chauffeurs in the Place Vendôme discussing their employers. [From R.C.'s diary, October 23, 1968]

Stravinsky's visit to Paris was very active. He saw Maurice Béjart's *Sacre* at the Opéra, went for excursions almost every day, received such old friends as Nadia Boulanger, and listened to new music. But when cold weather came he decided to return to California. There, toward the end of December, he suffered an attack of herpes zoster, and had no sooner recovered from that than, on January 16, an aneurysm was discovered above his left knee.

This has been the worst week since the siege of November 1967. Two weeks ago a clot was detected above Stravinsky's left knee, blocking the circulation in the lower portion of the leg. The anti-coagulants were too strong, moreover, and at one frightening moment the heart action was disrupted. . . . Yet the response to the last injection was good, and he is decidedly better. . . . His nights—and ours—are almost wholly sleepless, and it is surprising that he still functions according to so-called circadian rhythm. How much suffering he has had to endure since December! . . . We desperately need a doctor for the whole man, someone who can talk to him and earn his confidence. Instead of this

May 1, 1969. Room 1716, Hotel Pierre.
Orchestrating Bach. Photograph by
Dominique Cibiel.

May 27, 1969. Last page of Stravin-
sky's instrumentation of the B-minor
Fugue, Book I of the *Well-Tempered
Clavier.*

we have specialists who will come only for huge fees, and only after we plague them with telephone calls. [R.C. to a friend in Rome, February 1, 1969]

The nurses' log books for February 1969 make depressing reading, except that Stravinsky's fighting spirit shows through on every page. Here, for example, is the beginning of an entry for February 5: "6:00 A.M. Threw his pillow at me but later calmed down." The reasons for the calm may be attributed in part to the following medications:

10 A.M.	1 Pronestyl
11 A.M.	100 Mg. Heparin
12:30 A.M.	1 teaspoonful Butisol
3 P.M.	½ Comp. Tylenol
4 P.M.	1 Comp. Pronestyl
6:30 P.M.	1 teaspoonful Butisol
9 P.M.	Myloran tablet. Darvon tablet.
9:50 P.M.	Pronestyl capsule, Placidyl tablet (500 mg)
12:25 A.M.	Placidyl 200 Mg. p.o.
2 A.M.	Placidyl 200 Mg. p.o.
3:45 A.M.	Placidyl 200 Mg. p.o.
3:50 A.M.	Pronestyl 250 Mg. p.o.
6:15 A.M.	Tylenol tablet p.o.

Yet, even during this difficult time, Stravinsky worked at the piano for forty minutes each day, took a promenade each afternoon, and, in the evenings, listened to music for an hour or two. Toward the end of February, the reports generally conclude: "Had a good day." His health continued to improve throughout March, and, in April, his doctors declared him well enough to go to Paris. Soon after his arrival in New York, however, two embolectomies were performed on his left leg, and he was hospitalized for six weeks. Released on his eighty-seventh birthday, he returned to Hollywood for the summer, flying back to New York again in September.

At the beginning of April 1969, Stravinsky began to instrumentate four preludes and fugues from the *Well-Tempered Clavier*. He chose minor-key fugues in 2 voices (E minor, Book I), 3 (D minor, Book II), 4 (B minor, Book I), and 5 (C-sharp minor, Book I), and decided to use string orchestra for the preludes, clarinets and bassoons for the fugues. This plan was changed when he saw that the D-minor fugue was best suited to three clarinets (without bassoon) and that the B-minor should continue with the strings of the prelude. In the E-minor prelude, Stravinsky adds lower-octave basses on the first and third beat of every measure, omitting them in the détaché Presto section, and reintroducing them in the last four measures of the piece. The score is dated April 11. The fugue is a duet for clarinet in A and bassoon, with the string orchestra entering in the last measure, the basses playing pizzicato. A note at the end reads: "All dynamics after Czerny's piano solo . . . April 14, 1969." The C-sharp-minor prelude, completed on April 18, introduces the basses in measures 13–14 and again for the two final notes (G-sharp and C-sharp). Stravinsky seems to have intended the music to be played softly throughout; in any case, "piano" is the only dynamic indication. The fugue, for three clarinets in A and two bassoons, was the first piece in the set to be completed in New York, in the Hotel Pierre. In the D-minor prelude, Stravinsky does not use the basses at all, and the score contains few performance marks (two indications for "non divisi," and a line to show the continuation of a cello part in the second violins). The fugue is scored for three clarinets in B-flat. The B-minor prelude was completed on April 27, but the fugue, on which Stravinsky's work was interrupted by major surgery, was not finished until May 27. Stravinsky had to overcome a bout of pneumonia (May 20), and to get out of his hospital bed five or six times each day in order to add a few measures, yet his handwriting appears to be steadier than in the manuscripts of the Wolf songs, written a year earlier. In two places, he wrote notes below the range of the violins and violas, unless he intended to resort to scordatura. The basses play only at the end of the fugue.

On July 9, the Stravinskys flew from New York to Los Angeles, where management of the household became intolerably difficult, as the following entry from Mrs. Stravinsky's diary attests:

We receive letters and telegrams: "What a joy you are back here." But why are people happy to have us here? In our home sweet home nothing is commode. The cook has quit. The television does not work. The record player is in the library, and, in order to use it, Igor must come downstairs, which tires him. I must climb the stairs a dozen times a day, and carry the noon meal on a tray for Igor and his nurse. And every day we have five or six people for dinner, for which I do all of the work, buying provisions, cooking, dishwashing. We have a handyman who is anything but handy yet receives huge wages. . . . Also Montapert comes every day with schemes that we distrust. [August 3, 1969]

Here is a page from another diary, the present writer's:

Auden is ornery before dinner and not on his best mettle during it. His uppermost concern nowadays is to adhere to the split-second timing of his daily routine. He replies to Stravinsky's "How are you" with "Well, I'm on time, anyway." Since, for the poet's sake, dinner has to be served at exactly seven o'clock, it must be as carefully planned as a bank robbery. He even gets sozzled on schedule, and to the extent that, so far as he is concerned, the Château Margaux could be acetified Manischewitz. At one point he makes a totally unrelated, outré exclamation: "Everybody knows that Russians are mad," which might be described as emotion recollected in alcohol—except that the recollecting is ahead of time, this emotion being tomorrow's. Toward the end of the evening, while V.A.S. looks on in horror, he opens three closets before finding the urgently needed one. But finally the refractory mood gives way to one of deep affection for Stravinsky, who becomes the object of a tender speech in German.

After Auden leaves, his hosts speculate on the reasons why his

standard of living has failed to keep pace with his income, why he inhabits the same kind of hovel that he did twenty years ago, and why he is still wearing some of the same clothes. Are the dark glasses, the tattered coat, the frayed bedroom slippers that he uses for winter social outings a protective disguise for "the greatest living poet"? Not according to his own interpretation of the psychology of clothes, anyway ("they enable one to see oneself as an object"). Whatever the answer, if he had had a tin cup in his hand, it would have been filled with coins shortly after he reached the street, especially since he sang so merrily on the way out.[136]

December 18, 1969. Essex House. In the Stravinsky living room, with Balanchine, Kirstein, and W. H. Auden. Photograph by Edwin Allen.

The same writer also communicated to a friend in Rome in January 1970:

The suite in the Essex House is larger than the one in the Pierre, but the neighborhood is more dangerous, and, even though the Stravinsky car is in a garage only a block away, transportation for Mr. Stravinsky is more difficult to manage. For him, in fact, the hotel is a prison, from which every escape must be carefully planned. In Paris, he could at least stroll in the Place Vendôme, which was worth the bundling up and the long trek through the hotel corridors. . . . His hands look shriveled, as though they had been too long in water, yet he has gained twenty pounds since leaving the hospital, thin and chlorotic, last June. (Who could have predicted then that he would be alive to celebrate—

or did he deplore?—the beginning of the 1970s?) Mrs. Stravinsky, on the other hand, is showing the strain of constant worry about him—for she reflects every fluctuation in his health—and of worry about the financial and other responsibilities now thrust on her for the first time in her life. Did you know that she is four years older than the date on her passport? Sudeikin made the adjustment in Tiflis when applying for new documents, the old ones having been destroyed in the flight from Sebastopol; she was born in 1888.

The following excerpts from Paul Horgan's *Encounters with Stravinsky* and from the present writer's letters and diary offer glimpses of the composer in 1970 before his trip to France in June:

Mr. Stravinsky has suffered new setbacks, including an attack of cystitis three weeks ago, and a small thrombosis, which is manifested in a severe headache followed by a day or two of drowsiness, then recovery. Even so, the doctors say that nothing is seriously wrong—no disequilibrium in the components of the blood, no weakness of the heart. . . . Much of our time is wasted with lawyers, and I note your warning that in the world of the Bar one goes from Scylla to Charybdis—or, rather, from Jarndyce to Jarndyce—the fees being prodigious, the work accomplished minuscule. [R.C., letter of March 5, 1970]

Paul Horgan describes a dinner with the Stravinskys on March 19:

. . . I saw that the book [Stravinsky] was reading was Henri Troyat's biography, *Pouchkine*. Merely to make sounds, I asked, "Is it a good book?" Stravinsky replied, so softly that Craft leaned down to him and repeated the words to me: "A biography of Pushkin is no ordinary affair," and bowed in the old way of confirmation of his own statement. The dictionary he held was in French. Even in his high literacy in that language, he enjoyed meditating on even familiar words with the aid of a lexicon—a lifelong habit. This meant that he was reading slowly. Time itself was still his to command. His profile was now heroic, craggy, when seen in the scale of the diminishment of all else about him. He volunteered no remarks, but his awareness was so keen that as Craft and I talked commonplaces, he followed our words from one to the other as if watching a tennis match. He was participating in our society in silence, which rather reminded me of how autistic children enter their surroundings . . . while seeming not to do so. . . .

After dinner Stravinsky was established on a sofa, his shoeless feet in neat plain black socks resting on a cushion on the floor, while Madame and I sat together at another side of the room. Craft, after bringing scores, set the phonograph going. He came to sit beside Stravinsky to read the score with him, turning the pages. . . .

They played the first three movements of Beethoven's string quartet op. 127, and the last movement of the piano sonata op. 111. When I say "played," I mean that they participated; that music was never more powerfully conveyed to me than by their active musical intelligences; that Stravinsky's concentration was so complete and consuming that I felt in the presence of an act of creation. [From *Encounters with Stravinsky*, pp. 257–60]

According to a letter written ten days later:

Dr. Lax has just given permission for Mr. Stravinsky to fly to Europe—but not to go by boat (the fragility of old bones!). We plan to be in Paris by the first week of June. Think, only, that a year has passed since the embolectomies! . . . The Stravinskys' financial affairs are in a parlous state, and the California house has been sold for less than two-thirds of the sum that was once considered an acceptable minimum. They have considered auctioning manuscripts but are deterred by the "protective reserves" required from the seller. . . . I cannot pretend to be very confident about the trip, but since a move is inevitable, it may as well be a big one. Stravinsky fears the French political situation, and wildcat strikes in Paris are more and more frequent. Yet surely the unrest there is no worse than it is here. [R.C., letter of April 1]

Three weeks ago Mr. Stravinsky was hospitalized with pulmonary edema. He recovered rapidly from that but developed a kidney infection. Granted that his medical scheduling is a computer-sized project, can you believe that even with private and staff nurses he was not watched closely enough and had to be returned to intensive care with uremic poisoning, or nephritis, or something of the sort? But he is home at last. [R.C., letter of April 29]

Balanchine, soon to leave for Europe, comes to say *au revoir* but digresses about a recipe for making *bitochki*. Stravinsky appears, wearing pajamas and a beret, the crooks of his arms black and blue from injections. He listens with close attention and mounting appetite, but seems bewildered by the point of the talk, and when Mr. B. finishes, Stravinsky demands in a loud voice, *"Kogda?"* ("When can I *eat* some?") [From R.C.'s diary, May 7]

Horgan's picture of Stravinsky eleven months before his death is striking:

[Stravinsky's] face seemed to have receded about his eyes, so that they had a newly prominent look. He was stooped as he sat. His great hands were like exposed roots in winter, all gnarl and frosty fiber. About his throat was a scarf, with its ends tucked into his cardigan. He was placed at the head of the table, still the patriarch at his own board. I was seated to his left, Madame to his right, [Edwin] Allen next to her, Craft next to me. A current of good feeling went from each to the other of us. It was, despite everything, a joyful condition that we were all together with Stravinsky. In one of those small silent marvels of communication of which he had always been capable . . . he made us feel his own pleasure. . . .

Stravinsky looked deliberately around the table at each of us. It was in no sense a bestowal of a lingering farewell, though I for one, and possibly others, could not but think of the notion. On the contrary, his gaze was an expression of the keenest social pleasure and fondness, and when his survey ended with me at his left, he lifted his glass—weakly at an angle so that its contents were almost tipped out—and with beautiful formal manners, he said "Pol, hier haben wir eine sehr gemütliche Gesellschaft." [From *Encounters with Stravinsky*, pp. 262–3]

Shortly after:

. . . We plan to fly to Geneva and to go from there to the Beau Rivage in

Ouchy until the July dog-days are over and Stravinsky has recovered from the trip—assuming, of course, that he can make it at all. If this happens, it will be in early June and at a moment's notice. I cannot report on his condition. He will be eighty-eight in a few weeks, which is miraculous in itself considering the events of the last two months. He lusts for music and still grunts at the great places a split second before they have happened. [R.C., letter of May 18]

Stravinsky's first visitors—at Evian, not Ouchy, as it happened—were Arnold Weissberger, Milton Goldman, and Rufina Ampenoff, the last a representative from his publisher in London. After her visit, she wrote that she was relieved and happy to see Stravinsky "looking and acting so much better than in New York last October." (Letter of June 20.)

Enfin trouvé un Littré, cher Igor, mais $60 . . . Je n'ai pas osé le prendre. Si vous le voulez, vite un mot. . . . Il me semble probable qu'on en trouve d'autres. [Letter from Nadia Boulanger, in Avon, Connecticut, November 7, 1941]

Stravinsky did not buy the dictionary, having found one meanwhile at a better price in Los Angeles.

Was there anyone in the world who was better read? He was such an omnivorous reader that it was nearly impossible to give him a book. . . . Once a book had been published, Stravinsky, within the shortest possible time, had read it and filed it alphabetically in his library, where, with a sweet smile of triumph, he would pluck it out to show it to you just as you were about to present it to him as a gift. [Goddard Lieberson, *Gramophone*, June 1971]

It is from Stravinsky's marginal commentaries in books and articles, in fact, that his own philosophy can best be reconstructed, his personality most sharply drawn. Thus, when *Life* said that "in his relations with people Stravinsky can be warm or frosty, depending on his mood" (March 23, 1953), Stravinsky contradicted this in a superscription, writing that his mood depended on the people that he met. In the case of books such as Igor Glebov's [137] monograph on him, these marginalia constitute a devastating critique. Stravinsky's copy of Glebov's book is profusely underlined, strewn with question marks, decorated with marginal rubrics. "What well-thought-out nonsense," the composer writes at one place, and, when Glebov notes:

We must not forget that *Les Noces* is an incarnation of the ancient cult of birth and multiplication,

Stravinsky underscores the "We must not forget" and adds: "It would be better to forget, for this has nothing to do with it."

Stravinsky's underlinings in his copies of Bernanos's *Nous Autres Français*, for instance, and in Chesterton's *Chaucer* single out statements, phrases, and stories that the composer might have uttered himself. We have, from the latter:

NEW ENGLISH-RUSSIAN
AND
RUSSIAN-ENGLISH
DICTIONARY
(NEW ORTHOGRAPHY)

BY

M. A. O'BRIEN, M.A., PH.D.
THE QUEEN'S UNIVERSITY, BELFAST; MEMBER OF THE ROYAL
IRISH ACADEMY

NEW YORK
DOVER PUBLICATIONS

August 7, 1970. Evian. "Property of Igor Stravinsky," the composer has written (in Russian) on the flyleaf of this addition to his library of dictionaries.

Civilizations go forward in some things, while they go backward in others. . . . The medieval world . . . was intensely concerned with ideas as ideas, and not in the least concerned with them as modern ideas. But the . . . modernists are intensely concerned with the fact that modern ideas are modern. . . . Chaucer was not . . . troubled about ideas being new. It was quite enough for him that they were there. . . . Up to a certain time life was conceived as a dance, and, after that time, life was conceived as a race.

It is regrettable that Stravinsky did not publish a commonplace book, an anthology of such passages as these chosen from the whole breadth of his library.

Few creative artists can ever have been so deeply cultured as Igor Stravinsky,[138] though, in a musician or a painter, this is sometimes thought to be a dubious asset. His appreciation of the other arts, however, was rooted in his own talents—graphic, histrionic, and verbal. Although he was trained in the law, philosophy was the subject that most attracted him in school, and he had a lifelong interest in, and grasp of, philosophical ideas. He encountered such of his friends as W. H. Auden and Alexis St. Léger [139] on their home ground, yet his native culture—and who knows the extent of this?—was Russian.

Claude Debussy's first recorded observation (1911) about Stravinsky is a remark concerning the power of his intellect. George Jean-Aubry quoted the French composer:

"What a mind Stravinsky has!" Several times Debussy repeated to me the following phrase, clenching his teeth as he emphasized the adjective: "He has a *redoubtable* mind."

The first fiction about Stravinsky that needs to be corrected is the one of the purely "instinctive" (versus the "thinking") composer, a view, like its opposite, that was put forth by Stravinsky himself. G. Jean-Aubry also wrote of Stravinsky:

He is not very worried [about reactions to his music]. Later I will try to describe all that inspires me in this musician, from the impressions I have had of him from hearing his conversation and from talking to him myself—this astonishing intelligence that ranges beyond music and this, perhaps unique, union of the most startling ingenuity and the most refined wisdom.[140]

True, Stravinsky described himself as "the vessel through which *Le Sacre* passed"—borrowing the image from Pascal's "the thinking reed"—but he was also the vessel in which *Le Sacre* was conceived and, with peerless creative imagination and intelligence, made perfect. Moreover, Stravinsky's range of emotion, from the savage [141] to the most sophisticated, was as large as that of any artist.

On August 25, 1970, the Stravinskys returned to New York.

We tried to telephone on our final day in Evian but calls to Rome involved long delays. . . . You characterize our return as folly, yet the move was inevitable, the Essex House apartment having been leased for two years. And in Evian the Stravinskys were simply drifting along, hoping that something would develop; they never visited the town, the buvette or the Casino, and when the hotel prepared to close for the season, the Stravinskys had to leave—were, in fact, the last guests to do so. We looked at houses in Switzerland, but they were ugly, expensive and inconvenient. . . . Stravinsky's blood is normal—no traces of his polycythemia, which, after 15 years, appears to have given up on him—and his heart is strong. Thanks to a new therapist, he is also walking better than before, which boosts his sense of coenesthesia. (The chief obstruction to walking is a thirteen-year-old inguinal hernia.) Oddly, in a man of his age, his teeth give him more trouble than anything else, probably because of his constantly changing weight. He will soon have two extractions. [R.C., letter of September 3]

Two weeks after our return, Stravinsky's bronchial condition was aggravated by a heat wave and by a pall of carcinogenic air. He also suffered from a reaction to a transfusion. . . . The search for an apartment has not been successful, the prices being out of sight. [R.C., letter of September 30]

Stravinsky has not had any new crisis. . . . Nabokov comes regularly, and Lucia [142]—also Natasha,[143] who is patient and helpful, playing card games with him and reading to him in Russian, cheering, if also tiring, him. . . . He likes automobile outings, but in New York these are next to impossible. Mrs. Stravinsky shudders at the mention of a winter in the South and, admittedly, the logistic problems of such a move would be formidable. But Mr. Stravinsky always smiles when these projects are discussed and immediately wants to know exactly when we plan to be under way. . . . Francis Steegmuller asked for and received Mrs. Stravinsky's blessing to his request to write a life of her husband . . . [R.C., letter of November 2]

The composer Elliott Carter described, three months before Stravinsky's death:

. . . this remarkable man with his penetrating, brilliant, and original mind and dedicated spirit in action. A highly concentrated inner force, although then considerably reduced in expression, seemed to govern him even during my last visit in December 1970, when we listened to recordings and followed scores together of *The Song of the Nightingale* and the last act of *Magic Flute*, which he particularly enjoyed, shaking his head and pointing out special beauties on the page. [*Perspectives of New Music*, 1972] [144]

At about the same time, the present writer told a friend:

Don't believe the newspapers. The truth is simply that Mrs. Stravinsky purchased an apartment on East 73rd Street, four rooms on the Park, for possession in February. Life there will be quiet and infinitely more *commode* than in the Essex House, and Stravinsky will be able to go out more often; certainly he will *want* to, for he hates the hotel elevators and lobby. But the purchase was also a necessary economy. Gift-tax laws have changed, and he is no longer able to bequeath his manuscripts to the Library of Congress in return for deductions. His medical

PLATE 28

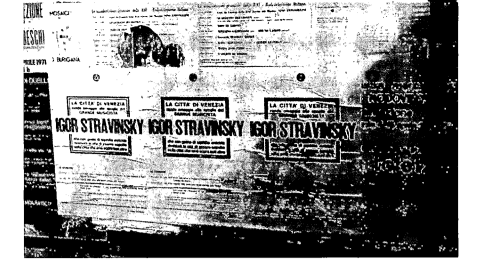

April 13, 1971. A wall in Venice.

IGOR STRAVINSKY,

HONNEUR

DE NOTRE TEMPS *

April 15, 1971. The service in Santi Giovanni e Paolo. The Archimandrite is in the background.

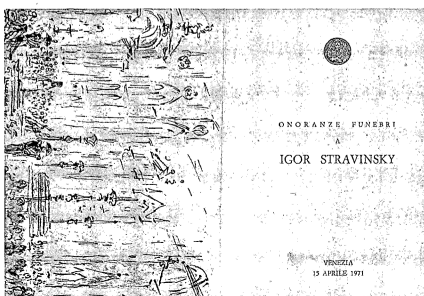

ONORANZE FUNEBRI

A

IGOR STRAVINSKY

VENEZIA
15 APRILE 1971

Sepia drawing on the invitation to the funeral, by Antonio Lucarda.

*St.-John Perse, in an inscription in his *Anabasis*, January 1962.

The recessional, carrying the coffin to
the funeral gondola.

Ezra Pound leaving Santi Giovanni e
Paolo after the service.

Pound once wrote that "Among composers . . . Stravinsky is the only living musician from whom I can learn
my own job" (March 1935), and that
"Stravinsky's music makes me, as
workman in a different art, want to go
back to my own *métier*, overhaul my
technique, and be ready to do a better
job next time" (January 1937).

PLATE 29

PLATE 30

Approaching the Ponte del Cavallo.

The water-hearse in the Rio dei Mendicanti.

The water-hearse in the lagoon.

The water-hearse approaching San Michele.

The funeral procession in the Camaldolensian Cloister.

The inhumation. "She was his necessity, his reason for living . . . and with her he was utterly romantic. It was very beautiful to see, and one could cry to think of it. . . ."* "A special bracelet with the letters 'I love you' linked together encircled her left wrist, a birthday present from her husband." †

* Goddard Lieberson, Gramophone, June 1971.
† From the Wellington Dominion, November 17, 1961.

"My dearest Perséphone," he used to write to his wife before they were married. When he sent the Perséphone lullaby to her,* "Sur ce lit elle repose," he added a note saying that she must learn to sing it by heart, with all of the verses, before his return. And he wrote and enclosed a rhyming poem with the music:

Na pamiat o liete udushlivykh znoi-
   nykh nediel
Kogda dorogaia moia Persefona
Za stavnei prokhlady ishcha i
   pokoia
Skryvaias ot kuchi znakomykh i
   znoia
Ot neizbiezhnykh niei skrytsia
   zvonkov telefona
S utra na vies dien zabiralas v
   postiel†

*From Voreppe,
August 21, 1933.

†In memory of a summer of
   oppressive summer weeks
When my dear Persephone
Behind a shutter seeking
   cool and calm
Hiding from a crowd of
   friends and humidity
From the unavoidable,
   that she cannot hide
   from, rings of the
   phone—
From morning on for the
   whole day snuggled in
   bed.

August 1975.

NIGHTINGALE: . . . and over there beyond the wall is another garden. . . .
DEATH: I like to hear you singing. Why have you fallen silent? Sing on!
[The Nightingale, Act III]

PLATE 31

expenses last year were $100,000, while, at the same time, the income from concerts and commissions has ceased. [R.C., letter of December 16]

August 24, 1970. Evian. Photograph by Lord Snowdon.

Mrs. Stravinsky received a letter from Theodore Stravinsky who has apparently equated a newspaper story to the effect that the manuscripts are worth $3,000,000 with a sale at that price. The letter would not matter except that, even before asking his stepmother for an explanation, he has retained a lawyer, and now, of course, she can only answer him through lawyers—the beginning of an endless fight that no one can win. . . . [R.C., letter of December 25]

Stravinsky was so much better that I decided to go away for a few days at Christmas, the longest separation from him since I conducted *Wozzeck* in Santa Fe four and a half years ago. No catastrophe occurred during my absence, but if there had been one, I could have returned in two hours, as I did last April, which would not be possible from abroad. . . . I found him cast down, on my return, and his outlook has unquestionably brightened as a result of the music we have listened to together since then. Seeing that I can affect his morale this way, I should do all that I can for however long I will have the opportunity. Dr. Lax says that, according to the neurological evidence, no thrombosis has occurred in nine months, and that the heart, circulation, blood pressure, and lungs are in good order. Still, we are only at the beginning of winter. Incidentally, Dr. Lax and the hematologist, Dr. (Miss) Brown, are now convinced that Stravinsky did not have polycythemia *vera* but polycythemia *spuriosa*. Apparently the symptomological imitations were not discernible as such in the 1950s and 1960s, but if Stravinsky had really had p.v., he would have died years ago. [R.C., letter of January 12, 1971]

Carlos Chávez, at 4:30, goes to his knees while talking to Igor, and hardly manages to hold back the tears. This disturbs Igor greatly, of course, and he is upset all evening. [From V.A.S.'s diary, January 31]

Nabokov comes in the afternoon to say goodbye to Igor—before going to Berlin—but makes the mistake of asking him how he is. "You can see how I am, miserable," Igor shouts at him, and so angrily that N. leaves with tears in his eyes. Igor tells him to get out. [From V.A.S.'s diary, February 12 [145]]

We are at this minute sitting on packing cases which are to be moved to the new apartment today and unpacked throughout the weekend. . . . It is something of a miracle that two people of nearly eighty-three and eighty-nine years, respectively, can look forward to setting up a new home. [R.C., letter of March 25]

Stravinsky was to live in the new home for only one week. Here are the last entries in Vera Stravinsky's diary:

April 1: Madeleine Malraux's concert. I did not go. Igor very sick.

April 5: We are not sleeping. Very disturbed. Dr. Lax three times. Dr. Brown, Dr. Moldow last night.

April 6: Igor dies 5:20 A.M.

Mrs. Stravinsky shares the traditional Russian fear of the dead body, believing that the spirit remains in it for forty days. She entered her husband's room only once, heard the doctor say that the body was still feverishly warm, touched the right cheek, then looked to be certain that no mirror was uncovered, for it is another Russian belief that mirrors should not be exposed in a room with the dead.

One day, in Venice in 1960, he left a note for her, in verse form and in that gentleness of tone which he used with her alone:

Why are you going to the cemetery? Do not go; I will not accompany
   you.
I see that you think of my old age and think that it is time to choose a
   tomb.

She wrote beneath these lines:

No. That is not the reason. It is so peaceful at a cemetery.

Appendix A

THE TRIAL BETWEEN
R. FORBERG AND J. & W. CHESTER
CONCERNING *THE FIREBIRD,*
AND STRAVINSKY'S DEPOSITION

On July 29, 1926, after negotiations with Stravinsky in London, J. & W. Chester concluded a new agreement with the composer for the 1919 *Firebird* Suite, annulling the contracts of May 26, 1926, and December 9, 1925, the former signed by Stravinsky in Paris, the latter signed by him in Mainz, in the offices of B. Schott, the representatives of J. & W. Chester in Germany. On December 23, 1926, Stravinsky wrote to Harry Kling, son of Otto, who had died:

> The *Forberg-Jurgenson affair*: I knew nothing about this until a month and a half ago when I received a telegram from Mr. Forberg asking me to stop all exploitation of the new *Firebird* Suite, since he owned the rights of Jurgenson. I replied that I was not the proprietor and referred him to you.

On January 15, 1927, Stravinsky again wrote to Kling, saying that a trial was to take place on February 9 of Kling, himself, and Schott, who was managing the defense, and for which Stravinsky had obtained a procuration. In fact a tribunal in Leipzig had already decided the case in favor of Forberg, and on May 19, 1927, also in Leipzig, an agreement was signed between Forberg and J. & W. Chester Ltd. for the rights to the work. Then, on August 12, 1927, J. & W. Chester asked Stravinsky to reimburse them for the sum of £300, and, in November, when he ignored the request, brought a suit against him for selling publication rights to *The Firebird* that he did not rightfully own. Stravinsky retained an attorney, Louis Gallié, with whom he had a lengthy correspondence on the subject. The argument continued until July 18, 1933, when B. Schott's Söhne purchased both *The Firebird* Ballet and the 1919 *Firebird* Suite from Forberg. Stravinsky severed his relations with Chester in 1928. Here is the composer's deposition, made in March 1927, and titled in his hand:

LITIGATION BETWEEN J. & W. CHESTER IN LONDON AND ROBERT FORBERG IN LEIPZIG CONCERNING *The Firebird*

In 1910, I composed the ballet *The Firebird*, which I sold to the Jurgenson Company of Moscow.
During the War and the period following, I happened to be out-

side of Russia and consequently was unable to establish rapport with the publisher, who remained in Russia, where he is at present and where his company has been nationalized by the Soviet Government.

In 1918 and 1919, I undertook the major work of completely reorchestrating certain numbers from the ballet to form a new *Firebird* Suite. This involved more than six months of labor.

It was impossible to offer this composition to Jurgenson, for the reasons stated above.

In 1920, the publisher O. M. Kling, of the firm of J. & W. Chester in London, entered into discussions with me for the acquisition of the said Suite. Chester had acquired many of my compositions completed during the War.

During the War, Chester was Jurgenson's representative in England and hence was perfectly aware that Jurgenson was the proprietor of the original *Firebird*.

My negotiations with Chester concluded with a contract,[1] according to which the publisher acquired two of my pieces, the new *Firebird* Suite and the *Ragtime* for piano, both together for the sum of 500 pounds.

During these same negotiations, Chester requested a letter of release from me vis-à-vis my connection with Jurgenson, in view of the moral rights of the latter as the original publisher of *The Firebird* music.

Five months after signing the contract with Chester and receiving my honorarium, I sent this letter, bearing the date of the contract.

I did, in fact, write the letter at that time but did not send it, since I considered this a matter of no importance.

I understood that a complete release from Jurgenson was an impossibility, for they were the original publishers, even though nationalized by the Soviets.

Chester acknowledged my letter and continued with the printing of the Suite, which they published some months later.

In 1926, a Leipzig publisher, Forberg, protested the publication of this Suite, claiming himself to be the owner of Jurgenson's rights, and declaring that *The Firebird* was protected by the Berne Convention.

Forberg sued Chester and won, the decision of the Leipzig court being that Chester must stop all exploitation of the Suite and give to Forberg all monies from exploitation in the past.

The two publishers reached an agreement whereby Chester would pay to Forberg 60% of all receipts for the Suite, which Chester would continue to exploit.

Now Chester has turned against me and demanded that I reimburse them for the sum of 300 pounds (the part of the Suite in question of the sum of 500 pounds), as well as pay the costs of the Leipzig trial.

Chester's argument is that I had sold rights to them that did not belong to me, and without warning them, so that the case was prejudiced against them.

My Argument

The new *Firebird* Suite constitutes a new work on my part, and one which cost six months of my time.

Under normal conditions, I would certainly have offered this new work to Jurgenson, as the original publisher of the ballet, but I would have demanded the same financial conditions from Jurgenson that I did from Chester.

In the present circumstances, I can do nothing, since, until 1925, I had never heard of Forberg and had not known that he had acquired Jurgenson's rights.

Forberg himself never informed me of his acquisition.

In the contract with Chester, I indicated that I was ceding the rights to the work in my capacity as owner, not having sold them to anyone before.

It was Chester's obligation to inform themselves about the state of affairs, and whether the publication of the new Suite could lead to complications and risk. But Chester did nothing in this regard. Chester felt certain that the work was free for publication, but the Leipzig trial demonstrated the contrary.

As the representative of Jurgenson in England, Chester could not be unaware that *The Firebird* ballet was the property of P. Jurgenson in Moscow; Chester was also aware of this when they acquired my Suite.

Chester undoubtedly believed that Jurgenson's editions were not protected by the Berne Convention, or that the Jurgenson Company was not in a position to defend itself, hence Chester chose to take the risk.

Chester's position became clear during the Leipzig trial, as well as in two letters to me (1919 and 1922) before and after acquiring the new Suite. The letters were in reply to my stated opinion that Jurgenson's publications were protected because of the company's mark "Leipzig-Moscow"; Chester held that this was not sufficient to protect in other countries works printed and published in Russia. In still another letter, Chester informed me that they would discontinue the publication of all of my works originally published by Jurgenson because of the lack of necessary funds.

Chester demanded a letter affirming my release from Jurgenson, but the letter that I provided certainly could not effect this release, at least according to the first letter from my adversaries to [my attorney] Maître Gallié.

In these circumstances, if Chester had not wanted to accept the risk of publication, they should have ceased publication and asked me for the return of the sum paid to me, or at least insisted on sending the letter of release vis-à-vis Jurgenson.

Instead, Chester continued with the publication of the work, which appeared some months later.

Stravinsky to Païchadze, March 21, 1927:

> I append to these lines the [above] documents prepared by the lawyer of Schott with my remarks and the letter from Strecker. Please be good enough to examine the document and to give your opinion as to whether it is all right this way. It seems to me . . . that the lawyer did not insist strongly enough on the fact that the Jurgenson Suite is literally the same thing as the ballet. This is very important since the ballet, of which I possess the printed orchestra score, was edited and published in Russia, a point that Forberg can never contest. I send to you herewith a cover of the piano score of the ballet that appeared in Russia after the Revolution . . . and on which the house of Jurgenson is indicated as a publisher *in Moscow* and not *in Moscow and Leipzig.* The piano scores, like the orchestra scores of the ballet in my possession, are marked on the last page, "engraved and printed in Moscow," something which is lacking in the copies from Forberg.

Appendix B

LE SACRE DU PRINTEMPS

Stravinsky, Nijinsky, Dalcroze, and Le Sacre
Stravinsky, Diaghilev, and Misia Sert
The Montjoie! *Affair*
The Revisions

Stravinsky, Nijinsky, Dalcroze,
and Le Sacre

At first glance, *Nijinsky Dancing* [1] would seem to belong in a Godiva chocolate shop, but to dismiss the book because of this would be to overlook the gold beneath the glitter of the cover. Though primarily a photograph album, which may explain the confectionary wrapping, the text is substantial and should engage every balletomane. In addition to showing Nijinsky dancing, it reopens the controversial subject of Nijinsky choreographing. As noted in Anna Kisselgoff's *New York Times* review (despite her false parallel):

> It is Mr. Kirstein's brilliant scholarship that allows him to put forth an idea in this book that is by no means universally accepted. That idea (disputed by Nijinsky's associates, Igor Stravinsky and Alexander Benois) is that Nijinsky was as revolutionary a choreographer as he was a great dancer. [December 13, 1975]

In another review, by Gabriele Annan, Stravinsky's name again appears among the skeptics of the thesis that Nijinsky *was* a choreographer, revolutionary or otherwise. Mr. Kirstein's book includes his newly commissioned translation of Jacques Rivière's 1913 essay on *Le Sacre du Printemps*, which Lady Annan finds

> still pretty heavy going—almost as heavy as Nijinsky's choreography. The Diaghilev company performed Nijinsky's version only a few times and then threw themselves with relief and gusto into Massine's, which was also more to the liking of Stravinsky himself. [*Times Literary Supplement,* February 13, 1976]

This statement is misleading in several ways. At the time of Massine's version (1920), only five dancers who had participated in Nijinsky's (1913) were still members of the Diaghilev troupe, and none of them could recall enough of Nijinsky's to be able to reconstruct it; if the company did throw itself with "gusto" into the new choreography, it could hardly have been with "relief" from the old one. Finally, too little has been made known of what actually happened onstage, of what the ballet looked like, to justify the aspersion "heavy."

If Nesta Macdonald had extended her *Diaghilev Observed* [2] ... to include French, Russian, and German critics—in addition to English and American ones—a complete account of the dance movement in Nijinsky's *Le Sacre* might have been pieced together. She does reprint the one important English review; [3] but this should be published along with Jean Marnold's essay [4] and whatever factual information can be gleaned from the mountains of subjective commentary by other European critics. In 1924, Stravinsky was given a book-size collection of reviews from the Paris press of the *Sacre* premiere. Every one of them is characterized by highly emotional opinions and by a corresponding absence of simple reports on the stage action. Even Cocteau seems to have noticed nothing except the scandal, his one remark, that the choreography lacks counterpoint to the music, being the exact opposite of the truth. "Ugly" is the most common epithet for the dancing— though in which ways the writers fail to mention. What is more, none of these reviewers ever questions his own qualifications to judge the new creation, or doubts that the nature of ballet is inalterable.

As for *Diaghilev Observed by Critics in England and the United States*, the one significant criticism to be made of the book is that its main contents are *ipso facto* tangential, the first runs of most of Diaghilev's productions having been in Paris. And, if few of the English critics of the time are worth reading today, *none* is among the Americans, who generally have less to say about the artistic achievement than about the box office ("there was not a single vacant seat"). Even a few lines by an informed observer, especially an inside one, are more valuable than this book's hundred pages of provincial newspaper clippings, as is shown in the following comments from Ernest Ansermet to Stravinsky about Diaghilev's first American tour:

> Diaghilev ... reproaches me for everything: the curtain, the tempo, when the horns crack on a note, even when the dancers make mistakes. ... *Petrushka* has had more success as a stage spectacle than *The Firebird*, though it seems to me that the music—too direct—has not been truly understood.[5] ... The American public is accustomed to consider nothing in any artistic enterprise except "stars," hence all publicity in all of the cities of the tour [is concentrated on] Nijinsky and Karsavina, without whom the Ballets Russes is thought to be nonsense. ... [From the Majestic Hotel, Philadelphia, March 1916]

Anyone concerned with the question of Nijinsky's talents as a choreographer must focus on *Le Sacre du Printemps*, despite the lack of a complete description of the original. First, *Le Sacre* was the one ballet—Nijinsky choreographed only three others—in which he himself did not dance, and to separate the creative and performing aspects of his art, particularly in *L'Après-midi d'un Faune*, must have been, as it still is, a formidable task. Second, with *Le Sacre*, unlike his ballets for music by Debussy and Strauss, Nijinsky was working in close collaboration with the composer, with whom, moreover, he spoke the same language and shared the same cultural background. In the first edition of the four-hand score, the *mise-en-scène* is credited to both men.

Lady Annan's statement that Stravinsky preferred Léonide Massine's choreography to Nijinsky's is unverifiable, though some of the composer's comments when Massine's version was being launched in Paris and London may seem to support such a conclusion:

> What enlightened Massine was to hear [Le Sacre] in concert . . . thus from the first he perceived that, far from being descriptive, the music was an "objective construction." Massine does not follow the music note by note, or even measure by measure. . . . Take, for example, this measure of four followed by one of five: Massine's dancers stress a rhythm of three times three. . . .[6] ["Les Deux 'Sacre du Printemps,'" Comoedia, December 11, 1920]

> The choreographic construction of Nijinsky was one of great plastic beauty but subjected to the tyranny of the bar; that of Massine is based on phrases, each composed of several bars. This last is the sense in which is conceived the free connection of the choreographic construction with the musical construction. . . . [Le Sacre] exists as a piece of music, first and last. [The Observer, July 3, 1921]

The real preference expressed here is not for the work of Nijinsky or Massine, but for concert rather than staged performances. By 1920, Stravinsky was much less interested in Le Sacre as a ballet than he had been in 1913, partly because the ballet had been so violently abused, the music by itself, in 1914, so wildly acclaimed. (Here it should be mentioned that after Monteux's performances of Petrushka in Paris, March 1 and 15, 1914, he wrote to the composer—whom he had asked to play the piano part!—"How this music gains by being played in concert, since all the details are heard," and that Stravinsky underscored the statement in red pencil.) These interviews show that, consciously or unconsciously, Stravinsky had forgotten the original choreography, which also was based on "phrases composed of several bars." Nor is the composer entirely accurate in saying that the work exists as "music, first and last," since the choreographic visions that inspired him partly determined the musical form.

Stravinsky's deprecation of Nijinsky's musicianship and of his choreography of Le Sacre first appeared in the composer's autobiography,[7] which was written two decades after the event and seven years after he had temporarily abandoned ballet for other musical forms. By then, the first Sacre was so far from his thoughts that the Autobiography both misdates the premiere and contradicts every public and private reference to Nijinsky's work that Stravinsky had made at the time of the first performance, May 29, 1913. Only in 1967, with the recovery of the score that he had marked for Nijinsky and used in rehearsals with him, did Stravinsky recall the original conception and reaffirm his former approval of Nijinsky's realization of it. In 1968 or 1969, Stravinsky read Irina Vershinina's monograph on his early ballets (Moscow, 1967), and, after his death, it was discovered that he had made a marginal emendation saying that criticism of Nijinsky's choreography had always been "unjust."

The truth is that in 1913 Nijinsky was the only choreographer whom Stravinsky would consider as a collaborator for new works. As he told an interviewer who remarked that ". . . some said [Nijinsky's choreography of Le Sacre] was alien to the music,"

> They are wrong. Nijinsky is an admirable artist. He is capable of revolutionizing the art of ballet. He is not only a marvelous dancer, but he is able to create something new. His contribution to Le Sacre du Printemps was very important. [Gil Blas, June 4, 1913]

The composer's letters consistently bear out this high regard for Nijinsky as choreographer. Thus, when Nijinsky married (in Buenos Aires, September 10, 1913), Stravinsky, quick to realize that Diaghilev would dismiss his protégé, wrote to Benois:

> For me, the hope of seeing something valuable in choreography has been removed for a long time to come. [Letter of October 3]

Stravinsky did not confide his ideas about *Le Sacre* to Diaghilev until several weeks after the first performances of *The Firebird* (June and July 1910). The reason for this secretiveness was that Diaghilev had quarreled with Fokine, the choreographer of *The Firebird*, and, though Stravinsky would not have chosen Fokine to stage the new "choreodrama," as the composer then referred to *Le Sacre*, he nevertheless wanted Diaghilev to present it, rather than the Imperial Russian Theater, which was the alternative. The break between Diaghilev and his chief choreographer was averted for two more years, hence the continuing assumption that the *Sacre* would be assigned to Fokine. When Diaghilev and Nijinsky visited Stravinsky in Switzerland in 1910, the music that he played for them was not *Le Sacre* but the Second Tableau of *Petrushka*, and the completion of this new ballet, and its performance the following spring, postponed all consideration of the *Sacre*, which was not commissioned until July 1911.

Stravinsky, as always, worked with an exact plan of stage action in mind, which he not only discarded but also denied had ever existed once the ballet had been completed:

> [Massine] and I have suppressed all anecdotal detail, symbolism, etc. [that might] obscure this work of purely musical construction. . . . There is no story at all and no point in looking for one . . . and no subject. The choreography is constructed freely on the music. [*Comoedia, op. cit.*]

The changes in the scenario explain why the titles in the score do not include all the episodes or even correspond to the program at the first performance. Nijinsky, meanwhile, was not apprised of the first scenario and probably was unaware of the others until the summer of 1912. Thus his statement in an interview in Madrid, June 26, 1917, is true of only the last four dances:

> At . . . times I collaborate with the composer, as in *Le Sacre du Printemps* by Stravinsky; in fact, we created it together, and the music and ballet were composed together: they were born at the same time. . . . [I] prefer to dance to modern music, of course. I love and admire the older music, Chopin, Schumann, but I respect it as I do my parents, from whom I always feel distant, as well as ahead of them. I have a different spirit from theirs. Modern music is closer to me, it corresponds to my aspirations. . . . Modern music is "my music.". . . In general it is the music which suggests the ballet to me, and then I put all of my energy into choreographing the dance according to the idea and the spirit of the music, in such a manner that the ballet does not appear to be stuck onto the music but, instead, is propelled by the music. . . . My collaboration with Bakst now is the same as my collaboration with Stravinsky; we are very close, in fact so identified that the idea of one is the idea of the other. [*Hojas Musicales de la Publicidad*]

In the summer of 1912, at home in Ustilug, Stravinsky expressed his growing concern about the choreography in a letter to Schmitt, and in August went to Lugano and Venice to teach the music to Nijinsky. A second meeting took place in the fall, and, at the end of November and beginning of December, after the score had been completed in abbreviated form (November 17), Stravinsky spent two weeks supervising rehearsals with Nijinsky and the dancers in Berlin, where the company was performing with great success.

> Stravinsky ... small and wiry, sat like an intense focus of electric flame darting over the piano. ... [8]

According to Dame Marie Rambert, paraphrased by Lincoln Kirstein in a letter to the present writer,[9]

> The company had worked on *Le Sacre* a month before Stravinsky arrived. [I] was one of the four small girls; there were four big girls, too. The Elders moved exactly twice as slowly as the youths. The company hated all this ... why were they trained as artists of the Imperial Ballet and graduates of the Academy? For this? Stravinsky arrived and flew into a rage because the tempi were so slow. He yelled, banged his fists on the piano cover; he was appalled at the way rehearsals were going. Nijinsky was made very nervous by Stravinsky. There was a dreadful scene at a rehearsal—which was stopped. [Rambert imagines that some sort of conference took place with Diaghilev that night, for the row was made up and the rehearsals proceeded.]

Even before Stravinsky's visit to Berlin, the decision had been made to seek help from Jacques Dalcroze, the inventor of modern "eurythmics," to teach the unprecedentedly complex rhythms to the dancers. Accordingly, Diaghilev engaged Dalcroze's pupil Myriam Ramberg,[10] who assisted Nijinsky from then until the premiere and contributed at least one Dalcrozian idea to the choreography, the divisions into small groups. On January 7, 1913, Dalcroze himself wrote to Stravinsky,[11] then in Vienna:

> You are a man of genius who can create, and you hold in your hands the future of the dance. You are the only one who understands and can compose not mere *divertissements* but pure dance works. ... You have already regenerated the ballet, but you are perhaps not yet aware of all the resources, [since] the musician must know the human body, just as the human body must be impregnated with music. ... M. Nijinsky is also un *homme très rare*, whom I find admirable in certain things but despair of in others, such as *Le Spectre de la Rose*, in which he dances against the music. ...

The letter ends with an appeal for Stravinsky to spend two weeks in the Dalcroze Academy at Hellerau, near Dresden, but the composer appears not to have answered, probably because he was so upset by the hostile reception of *Petrushka* by the Viennese.

Apart from that, the music at the climax (192 to 201) is based not on rhythmic units but on melodic ones, or a "dialectical structure of phrases" (Stravinsky to Ansermet, January 30, 1926). This refers to two alternating motifs (and their variants), each of which is contained in single phrases of either two or three measures. The motifs could hardly be more clearly contrasted: the direction of the first is upward, its intervals are comparatively wide, and it is played by the full orchestra; the direction of the second is downward, its intervals are narrow, and it is played by horns and strings alone. Obviously the choreography must identify these motifs. It follows, too, that a purely rhythmic approach to the music would be featureless. But, to judge from Dalcroze's own compositions, he could hardly have understood this, at least at the time, or have realized that at the turning point (which occurs in the two-measure phrase at ⎡197⎤) the metrical patterns of twos and threes are broken. Here, where the second motif disappears, the meter expands, once only, to four, a stunning pivot.

In London, during the first two weeks of February 1913, Nijinsky and Stravinsky rehearsed the dancers and gave interviews that do not conform in their descriptions of the choreography. Nijinsky stated that

> It will be danced only by the *corps de ballet*, for it is a thing of concrete masses, not of individual effects,

an essentially correct analysis, even though it overlooks the not-yet-choreographed solo dance of the Chosen Virgin. When Stravinsky returned to Switzerland, Pierre Monteux, who was to conduct the piece, wrote to him about discrepancies between the orchestra score and Nijinsky's piano reduction; and, indeed, there are many, for by this time Stravinsky had rephrased much of the music for the choreography.

We are all in debt to the author of *Nijinsky Dancing* for his part in the founding and direction of the world's greatest ballet company. But, curiously, the New York City Ballet has never produced *Le Sacre du Printemps*,[12] and of recent European stagings, the Mary Wigman, Béjart, MacMillan, and others are irrelevant, while only that of the Budapest Opera Ballet even attempts to follow the outlines of the original. Surely the City Ballet, which can hardly avoid *Le Sacre* during the approaching Stravinsky centenary, should recognize an obligation to present the Nijinsky version, as preserved in Stravinsky's and Dame Marie Rambert's promptbook scores. Thus, at last, justice might be done to Nijinsky's, as well as to Stravinsky's, masterpiece. And what could be more fitting homage to Mr. Kirstein than to prove his belief in Nijinsky the choreographer?

Stravinsky, Diaghilev, and Misia Sert

New and forthcoming books about "Misia" née Godebska (1872–1950) could familiarize American readers with her name in the same way that the Bloomsbury revival did for Lady Ottoline Morrell's. Recently, for example, Paul Morand's *L'Allure de Chanel*,[13] a confusing mixture of reminiscence and quotation, featured Misia as a subject of recollections, many of them poisonous, by the fashion dressmaker and intimate friend. And Richard Buckle's *Diaghilev* gives considerable prominence to Misia. But the publication that will establish her fame is the eagerly anticipated biography by the distinguished gourmet-pianists Robert Fizdale and Arthur Gold.

Although Misia Sert's life is not our subject, some information about her is essential to an understanding of her dual role of advocate for Stravinsky's music vis-à-vis Diaghilev, and mediator during the most bitter of their innumerable quarrels. A granddaughter of the cellist Adrien-François Servais, she was musically precocious and became an accomplished pianist, capable of sight-reading scores for Diaghilev—of such music, at least, as that of *La Boutique Fantasque*. She was a pupil of Fauré, her opinion was respected by Debussy, and Ravel dedicated *La Valse* to her. In 1893, she married Thadée Natanson, co-founder of *La Revue Blanche,* eventually divorcing him to become the third wife of Alfred Edwards, the wealthy publisher of *Le Matin.* Separated from this second husband in 1910, she lived with the painter José-Maria Sert; after they finally married, he divorced her to espouse Princess Roussi Mdivani, then, on becoming a widower, returned to Misia.

Misia Sert's importance derives from the artists with whom she was involved, both as friend (Picasso), and as model (Lautrec, Renoir, Vuillard, and Bonnard in paint, Proust and Cocteau in prose, Mme Verdurin being partly based on her, as well as the Princess in *Thomas l'Imposteur).* It has been said that she never read a book, and her correspondence often seems to support this conclusion, yet she knew Verlaine and was a friend of Mallarmé. Above all, this plain-looking, busy-bodying, insufferably snobbish tyrant of Parisian society had an extraordinary gift of musical perceptiveness.

Misia's name first appears in Igor Stravinsky's letters in a note to Alexander Benois, November 24, 1911:

> I . . . had barely arrived back here [Clarens] from Paris when Diaghilev summoned me by telegram. He had come from London for two days. I went for one day. I was at Mme Edwards's, and I played there what I had composed of *Le Sacre du Printemps.* Everyone liked it very much.

It is probable that Misia accompanied Diaghilev to Bayreuth the following summer, when he and Stravinsky heard *Parsifal* and *Meistersinger.* The composer's memoir of the adventure [14] does not mention her, but this unreliable book also neglects to say that, after Bayreuth, he went with Diaghilev to Lugano, where Nijinsky joined them on August 24 or 25, and that, at Alexander Benois's, Stravinsky played the *Sacre.* A week later, Misia, Diaghilev, Nijinsky, and Stravinsky were together in Venice, as a letter from Misia to the composer the following year (September 6, 1913) confirms.[15]

Since virtually nothing else is known of the association between Stravinsky and Misia before the premiere of the *Sacre,* it is astonishing that on May 30, 1913, the day after the never-to-be-forgotten event, he gave to her the score containing his markings for the choreography.[16] How can this be explained? Disliking autocratic women as he did, it seems improbable that he was especially fond of her personally, while a physical attraction between them is inconceivable. Nor can the gift be construed as a return for financial assistance, since he was not in economic difficulty at the time. The reason for such prodigality becomes evident, however, with a study of the changing relationship between the composer and Diaghilev. Sometime in 1911, Stravinsky realized the extent of Misia's power over Diaghilev and, by the time of the premiere of the *Sacre,* saw that her comprehension of it was more profound than his.

Diaghilev's discovery of Stravinsky's genius is a matter of history, but it is also true that the impresario was unable to keep abreast of his protégé's phenomenal growth. Diaghilev had misunderstood both the unresolved ending of *Petrushka*—going so far as to ask Stravinsky to alter it—and the originality in the conception of the repeated chord in the "*Danses des Adolescentes*" in the *Sacre.* Two recently discovered letters from Misia to Stravinsky reveal that, after the Paris premiere of the *Sacre,* Diaghilev's confidence in the music wavered to the extent that he planned to abridge it for the three London performances.[17]

At the beginning of June 1913, Stravinsky contracted typhus—a result, so he believed, of eating oysters in an R-less month. He was admitted to a *maison de santé* in Neuilly, and, during five weeks there, received many friends, including Misia, who was attentive not only to the patient but also to his family, writing to Stravinsky's wife, and sending "best souvenirs to your mother, if she is still with you." But, though Diaghilev left his calling cards and faithfully inquired about the recovery, he never entered the room of the sick composer.

How and when Stravinsky learned of Diaghilev's intention to make cuts in the *Sacre* in London is not known. Nor is it clear whether Diaghilev decided that Pierre Monteux was to lead only the first of the London performances, but a second conductor, Rhené-Baton, shared the rehearsing. On July 7 or 8, in any case, Stravinsky wrote to Monteux in London entrusting him with the responsibility of giving the *Sacre* complete. The letter crossed in the mail with one written by Monteux on July 7, addressed to the composer in his summer home in Ustilug (Volhynia), where he would receive it a week later:

> Baton [sic] rehearses the strings for Part One while I rehearse the winds for Part Two, and vice versa. . . . Baton will have time for six rehearsals between my performance and his.

Monteux does not mention that the orchestra protested against the music, no doubt calling it ugly and unplayable. Misia was less tactful, but, writing to the composer on the day before the first London performance, she tells a surprising story:

> *Mon cher ami,* I wanted to wait until after the premiere of the *Sacre* to write to you, but I prefer to do it today because of the news I have had from Sert and Cipa.[18] I see that you are tormenting yourself, but unjustly. I think that Delage, if he were the person responsible, might have done better than to trouble you with intentions about which he does not know the truth, and which he attributes to Serge. Nevertheless, I fail to understand how you, who know Serge, could pay attention to Delage. The truth is something that you must keep to yourself: Diaghilev is experiencing a terrible time, with financial difficulties that threaten to end in court or in civil war. He has broken with Bakst, perhaps forever, over *Le Sacre* . . . In spite of the success of *The Firebird* and *Petrushka*, the orchestra made a big scandal at a *Sacre* rehearsal and Monteux lost his temper. . . . Serge always has your best interest at heart, and, in keeping such things from you, simply did not want to worry you. You must understand that he is risking a great deal, and that, at the moment, *Le Sacre* is the justification of his life. I did not tell him of your doubts about him, and I regret that Sert telegraphed to him on this subject. My dear Igor, I am sorry that you cannot come here and quash the gossip and the commentaries of the coteries. . . . Be Russian and stay Russian. . . . Serge has a Russian soul. . . . *Petrushka* was played ravishingly.

Although clearly aware that Diaghilev intended to omit parts of the *Sacre*, Misia had said nothing about this, and, so far from "quashing" gossip, has gratuitously offered an upsetting story that should have been withheld from a convalescent still "feeling like a fly on three legs." [19] Delage's—or Ravel's, or someone else's—meddling was more excusable, since Stravinsky unquestionably had a right to demand that his work be played uncut, the more so in that he had not been consulted. But, as always, Misia's allegiance was to Diaghilev.

After the London performances, Stravinsky's friends, most notably M. D. Calvocoressi, assured him that *Le Sacre* had not provoked any incident there, yet *The Times* of July 27 states that "a section of the audience" participated in "a hostile demonstration" at the premiere. Afterward, Misia cabled to Stravinsky in the Russischer Hof, Berlin:

> Complete success *Sacre* spoiled by your letter Monteux unjustly wounding Serge.

Ignoring her, Stravinsky cabled directly to Diaghilev:

> Sorry to have caused trouble but did not understand your diplomatic position. Cable to me in Ustilug. [Berlin, July 12]

Misia wrote to Stravinsky from Paris, July 15, making no apology for her malicious messages, portraying Diaghilev as the innocent victim, and placing all of the blame on the composer:

> I left Serge overwhelmed with troubles, defeated, exhausted. . . . Nijinsky is intolerable and *mal élevé*, and Bakst no longer speaks to Serge. Only Nouvel remains faithful, though even he left for three days. . . . Keep these details to yourself, for it is useless to have all Paris know about this situation,[20] which friends would enjoy immensely. . . . Diaghilev himself was very imprudent with the French, and naturally everyone was against him, especially those second-rate people who cannot admit that a Diaghilev exists for some purpose other than to perform their trash. Casella, for one, has already started to disparage him. I know that Delage came to see you, tortured you, and almost committed irreparable harm. I must tell you what happened after Monteux's revelation. He said publicly, during a rehearsal, in front of Nijinsky and the whole ballet, on the day of the first performance: "I am Stravinsky's representative and he has written to me: 'Monsieur Diaghilev has the audacity to want to make cuts in my work. You are responsible.'" [Monteux] then said, "Now you can dismiss me and sue me." Serge answered that he really saw the possibility of a suit and trial. . . . But the worst effect of the incident was that it deprived Serge of all authority. The dancers did not want to continue rehearsing, and Nijinsky spoke to Serge as if he were a dog. The unhappy man left the theater alone, and spent the day in a park. . . . I do not want to continue on the subject of the unhappiness that you, dear friend, have caused him.

Stravinsky seems not to have answered this, and Diaghilev did not cable to Ustilug, but, at the end of July, Monteux wrote to Stravinsky, praising the London orchestra, calling the London public

> better behaved than the Parisian. . . . The success was considerable— six or seven curtain calls. I greatly regretted that you were not there . . .

and assuring the composer that "the whole work was heard from beginning to end."

The next communication, Misia's letter from Venice, September 6, 1913, informs Stravinsky that

> Serge is well . . . preparing beautiful things. . . . I hope that he will give your opera [*The Nightingale*], and he hopes so as well.

This is noncommittal, to say the least, and it conveys no greetings, affectionate or otherwise, from Diaghilev. But one of the consequences of Nijinsky's marriage in Buenos Aires, four days later, was that Diaghilev sought consolation from his oldest and closest friends, first among them Stravinsky. Returning to Paris, Diaghilev visited the composer in Lausanne, October 1 and 2,[21] and returned on October 30.[22]

Writing to Benois, October 3, Stravinsky is unable to conceal his shock on discovering that Diaghilev's feelings toward the *Sacre* had indeed changed after the premiere, and the composer now questions the genuineness of Diaghilev's enthusiasm for the piece in the months before. But, though deeply regretting the loss of "the one and truest support in the propagation of my artistic ideas," Stravinsky ends with a characteristic shrug: "But so be it. . . . Enough of *Le Sacre*."

In December, hoping to be reinstated as choreographer and dancer, Nijinsky wrote to Stravinsky—with scarcely believable naïveté: "Ask Diaghilev what is the matter"—entreating him to intercede with the impresario. Stravinsky immediately realized the futility of this, but Misia did not, as the following telegram to him reveals:

> . . . Serge arriving with good news contract signed with Fokine very vexed letter from Nijinsky but I am not without hope of a reconciliation. [December 27, 1913]

Then, in Paris, on January 18, 1914, she and Diaghilev telegraphed together to Stravinsky: "Heard ravishing Chinese songs, *grandes tendresses*." [23] Diaghilev telegraphed again the next day: "Can wait for you in Paris until Tuesday leave Wednesday for Russia."

On January 20, Stravinsky was in Paris, dining with Diaghilev and Misia at her home and playing the first two acts of *The Nightingale* for them. A letter from Stravinsky to his wife the next day says that Misia (not Diaghilev) remarked on the stylistic difference between the earlier and later portions of the opera, though she said that this did not disturb her. The letter continues:

> I talked alone with Diaghilev until 3:00 A.M.[24] and am very pleased with his new, favorable attitude toward *Le Sacre*. . . . He did not actually hear the *Japanese Lyrics* but was told of the brilliance of the work by others.

Since this opinion of the new piece was obviously Misia's, was she not also responsible for Diaghilev's "new, favorable attitude" toward *Le Sacre*? [25] By this time, it was surely apparent to Stravinsky that Misia's critical acumen with regard to his new music outdistanced Diaghilev's, and that, in the future, it would be prudent to approach him through her.

This may seem less than just to Diaghilev, in the light of his continuing flair for the avant-garde.[26] In the following very remarkable letter, for example, he anticipates *musique concrète* and John Cage, but the kind of experimenting that Diaghilev describes had already ceased to interest Stravinsky: [27]

> Dear Igor . . . I believe that we have an idea of genius. After thirty-two rehearsals for Liturgy,[28] I have reached the conclusion that absolute silence in air-space does not and cannot exist. The action must be supported not by music but by sounds . . . the source of which should be unknown. There should be no rhythm at all, since neither the beginning nor the end of the sounds should be perceptible. The instruments that we have in mind are the *guzli*, the aeolian harp, and bells (the tongues of which can be wrapped in felt). All of this has to be worked out, and Marinetti has suggested that we meet in Milan, if only for one day, and listen to the different possibilities of a "noise" orchestra. He promised to bring Pratella [29] and to have him demonstrate his latest creations, which are said to be extraordinary. We can do this between the 15th and 20th of March, so please telegraph to me at the Vesuvius Hotel in Naples that you can come to Milan and see

and hear some Futurist masterpieces. I will go with you to Montreux from there, but I beg you to come: it is very important for the future. I am sending money for the trip immediately. As for Prokofiev's concert in Geneva, he agrees to play . . . on the 20th of November. Embraces, Serge. Compose *Les Noces* quickly. I am in love with it. [March 8, 1915]

At this point, in view of the foregoing suppositions about Misia's musical astuteness, her next letter to Stravinsky comes as a jolt. She had attended a concert at the Barbizon Gallery to hear his Three Pieces for String Quartet:

I detest the second piece—you hear me, I *detest* it, with rage. Yes, yes, why do you do things like that? It is *Boche* music for the poor. . . . The third piece, in which you flagellate yourself, I heard very badly, but under different circumstances I believe that it might have moved me. [1916]

"Flagellate" is a curious word to use here, unless an allusion to the religious character of the music is intended, but the insight into the potential affectiveness of the movement is remarkable. That she does not discuss the first piece may be attributed to its brevity—less than a minute—and to the placement of Stravinsky's opus at the end of a lengthy program of bad new music. As for the reviled second piece, even today a poor performance—in which, for example, the cellist fumbles one of the harmonics—can make an audience feel that the composer was being purposely *outré*, or even trying to parody *Pierrot Lunaire*. Thus Misia's reaction was not as unintelligent and philistine as at first appears. Stravinsky's answer is surprisingly mild:

. . . your fury against the quartet pieces. Really, my dear, you might have taken the trouble to understand, before attacking this unfortunate work, composed in your honor—this is somewhat ironical, isn't it? (to be played in your Chinese room,[30] do you remember?)—that my music is always very difficult and needs my personal supervision before being performed. . . . I can well imagine what they played. . . .

In Naples, early in July 1916, Misia sent a postcard with a portrait of Leoncavallo, signing it, "*avec mon amitié appassionata,*" and a letter:

. . . Diaghilev spoke to me about the *Coq* [*Renard*] with great enthusiasm; he is in despair not to be able to present it.[31]

Returning to Paris, she visited Stravinsky in Geneva, where he played *Les Noces* for her [32]—provoking a response exactly the opposite of that caused by the Three Pieces. She sent a gushing letter (July 22), saying that not only did she love *Les Noces* more than anything else he had written, but also pronouncing it to be his greatest creation. The unpredictable composer exploded, presumably [33] telling the virago to refrain from sending her judgments on his music. She telegraphed:

Your note has made me ill.by its incomprehension of mine which was simply an excess of admiration for you, dear friend. [August 8]

On August 22, Ernest Ansermet wrote to Stravinsky from Madrid:

. . . I journeyed from Paris to San Sebastian with Diaghilev. He talked of the exchanges of letters between you and Mme Edwards, and his version was very different from yours. . . . Turning his back, he said that he thought the Coq [Renard] was a shocking thing. . . .

But the rift was soon healed, as a letter from Diaghilev, in Rome, to Stravinsky, in Morges, shows:

> Ask Misia to tell Erik Satie to send (immediately, by express) his *Piccadilly March* either for piano or in the orchestra manuscript, to ask Ravel to give permission to stage his *Féria*,[34] and to telephone to Bakst and to inform him that Massine and Tommasini have already done more than half of the Scarlatti ballet. [December 1916]

In July 1917, after the Ballets Russes had sailed for South America, Diaghilev visited Stravinsky in Diablerets. Recalling this meeting in a letter to Ansermet, May 26, 1919, the composer wrote:

> In the train in which Diaghilev was going to Italy . . . we reached [an] agreement [concerning *Les Noces* and the money due to me for the performance of my works]. . . . The terms of payment established in this same train are on a piece of paper that I had before me at the moment and on which Diaghilev had already written his name. He had a similar piece of paper containing my signature. . . . We separated at Aigle, Diaghilev leaving for Italy. Returning to Diablerets, I reread the terms and suddenly saw that . . . we had made a mistake in addition. . . .

After the Russian Revolution, Diaghilev had stopped paying author's rights for *The Firebird* and *Petrushka* on grounds that both pieces were now in public domain. He acknowledged a moral obligation to Stravinsky but did nothing to discharge it, and the now-impoverished composer, for whom collections were being raised in New York and Boston, threatened to write to the London newspapers asking why this charity should be necessary at a time when his ballets were being performed every day at the Alhambra Theater. Diaghilev, for his part, went to court, which confirmed the legality of his piracy.

The arguments and imprecations on both sides were relayed through Ansermet, who was conducting the orchestra for Diaghilev's London season, but the dispute was settled by Misia Sert. And although her memoirs accuse Stravinsky of "moneymindedness," and poke fun at his letters to her—the one of October 30, 1919, admittedly reads like that of a tax collector—she alone can be credited for inducing Diaghilev to pay the composer and to make peace with him. This is proven by the dates of Stravinsky's appeals to her,[35] and of Diaghilev's change of policy soon after them. Stravinsky and Mme Sert became good friends thereafter and at one time he even directed that his mail be sent to her care at the Hôtel Meurice:

> Write to me immediately "aux bons soins de Mme Sert" but be sure to make my name very large so that she does not accidentally open a letter in which she could see that you are talking about a concert of which she knows nothing, and of which, at least for the moment, she must not know anything. [Letter to Ansermet, November 1921]

But to have kept a secret from Misia would have been a nearly impossible feat. Chanel, apropos her liaison with Stravinsky in the autumn of 1920, recalled that "Misia began to sense that something was taking place which she did not know about," and, when she found out, "sent a telegram to Stravinsky: 'Coco is a *midinette* who prefers Grand Dukes to artists.' "[36] Yet Stravinsky managed to remain on amicable terms with Misia until his departure for America in September 1939.

The 1919 contract dispute that Misia resolved was the longest and stormiest in Stravinsky-Diaghilev history. Here are three intimate glimpses of Diaghilev at the time, from Ansermet's letters to Stravinsky:

> Diaghilev is impatient to know whether or not you have compromised yourself politically in relation to Russia, and I told him that you are *not* a Bolshevik! He also wants to know whether you are *au courant* and have sailed with the latest boat. When I said that you had written pieces for solo clarinet, he replied: "Good, in Paris they are very interested in the clarinet." But when I . . . explained the general tendency of your recent works, Diaghilev's comment was "Why always these little orchestras? The war is won and there is no longer any need to struggle against Mahler; I want to return to large things." Always this naïve attitude as to the "effect" on Mme Edwards and on the three or four others whom Diaghilev respects. . . . Mme Edwards is under the influence of Cocteau, whose attacks are becoming stronger. It seems that his last work (after the *Cap de Bonne Espérance*) is extremely venomous. . . . When I spoke about the *Soldat*,[37] Diaghilev said: "I would like to give it in Paris, but is it possible to avoid Ramuz? He is not much liked there." Always this hatred of the Swiss around you. . . . I forgot to tell you that Diaghilev has aged greatly, and is much withdrawn, *le pauvre*. . . . [Letter of May 4, 1919]

> On Sunday afternoon I finally trapped Diaghilev alone and read your contract and proposals to him. . . . He tried to protest: . . . "In 1919 Russia was strong and victorious. Then came the Revolution and Bolshevism, and my fortune was gone. . . . Before the War I could lose 120,000 francs in London in a season, knowing that I would be able to find new resources in Russia. One could simply ennoble a merchant then, and with his money make art. Now there are no more Excellencies, no more Grand Dukes. In one year I find myself with a million in debts. London has saved me, but I am not rich and I have all I can do to meet my obligations. . . . These are hardly reasons to . . . forget my friends, and certainly not my ten-year association with Igor. Still, he must understand that my situation is not what it was. . . ." [Letter of June 10]

> Diaghilev is tired and despondent; he wept a great deal. He said that, since he feels out of tune with everybody, "It is time to close my box. In the past, one at least knew where one was going, but no longer, and the very basis of the Ballets Russes is unhealthy. If one is not a Bolshevik and also not an Imperialist, if one loves Russia and can do nothing for her, and if one still wants to work for Russian art, [then why] do a *Boutique Fantasque*? True, Picasso [38] is now with the Ballets Russes, but he would as soon shit on us. Also Derain. And Massine no longer knows where he is going. But, above all, I have lost Stravinsky. . . ." [Letter of July 28]

After *Pulcinella*, Stravinsky composed only two more choreographic works in Diaghilev's lifetime, neither of them for him. The Ballets Russes continued to be the principal performing medium for Stravinsky's music but the two men were never as close after the estrangement of 1919, and Stravinsky's new direction as a composer [39] and new career as a pianist-conductor were only circumstantial factors in this change. Finally, when Diaghilev deprecated parts of *Apollo* and all of *Le Baiser de la Fée*, the relationship came to an end. In the year before Diaghilev's death, the two men met only once and did not correspond at all. On June 19, 1929, Stravinsky wrote to Ansermet in Berlin, asking him to let Diaghilev, or someone in his entourage, know that I will be in London at the same time he is there, and living at Albemarle Court, where he usually stays. Since he has avoided any encounter with me for some time—the reasons for this being known to him alone—I think he should be informed of my plans. . . .

By coincidence, the former friends were on the same Paris-London train, June 23–24, where they passed each other but did not speak or even nod. After conducting a BBC concert, Stravinsky returned to France, not waiting for the Ballets Russes performances of *Le Sacre* and *Renard*.[40] On August 8, Diaghilev was in Venice. On the 15th, Stravinsky wrote to his Paris publisher:

Diaghilev is always the same, never in his life giving a damn about the interests of other people.

Four days later, Diaghilev was dead. Stravinsky did not hear the news until the evening of the 21st, returning to Echarvines after spending the day with Prokofiev at his home in Culoz. By this time, Diaghilev's body had been ferried to San Michele, the island cemetery where, forty-two years later, Stravinsky was to be buried (his grave is the sixth to the right of the Orthodox chapel, as Diaghilev's is the sixth to the left). On the same day, August 21, a Panikheda service was held in the rue Daru Russian Church in Paris. Stravinsky's widow remembers that, at this memorial ceremony, Bronislava Nijinska wept uncontrollably. By the cruelest of ironies, the world sent its condolences to Stravinsky, as if he were the next of kin. "Death of Serge stuns me, want to embrace you, be with you," Cocteau telegraphed. But Manuel de Falla's message is the most typical: "Of all the admirable things that Diaghilev did, the first was his revelation of you."

The Montjoie! *Affair*

In his *Chroniques de Ma Vie* (1935), Stravinsky wrote:

I very willingly granted an interview to Canuedo [sic]. Unfortunately it appeared in the form of a pronouncement on *Le Sacre*, at once grandiloquent and naïve, and, to my great astonishment, signed with my name. I could not recognize myself. . . . But I was too ill at the time to be able to set things right.

The truth concerning the incident is somewhat different. Ricciotto Canudo, poet, author of *Le Livre de l'Evolution* (1908) and *Combats d'Orient* (1917), was a contributor to *The Egoist* during the period of Eliot's assistant editorship, a friend of Picasso (who drew his portrait), of Ravel (who dedicated a five-hand piano piece to him), and of Proust (see the photograph of Canudo in Proust's *Lettres à Madame C.* [Paris: Janin, 1946]).[41] Canudo's name first appears in Stravinsky's correspondence in a letter written in Ustilug, July 1912, to Florent Schmitt.

Stravinsky agreed to contribute an article or interview to *Montjoie!* when he arrived in Paris in May 1913 for *Le Sacre* rehearsals. According to a letter from Canudo to the composer, May 22, 1913, the article had been promised for the next day. A note from Canudo on the 26th says that he and Léger (Alexis St. Léger?) had looked in vain for Stravinsky at the theater, while another note, on the 27th, asks the composer to procure twenty tickets from Diaghilev and to leave them with the concierge at the Crillon, "in order to guarantee a strong avant-garde representation in the hall." Stravinsky had promised to appear at the office of *Montjoie!*, 33 Chaussée d'Antin, between 5:00 and 7:00 P.M., Monday the 26th, to meet a group of artists and writers, but did not come. Still another note from Canudo says that the proofs of the article must be corrected by Tuesday at 4:00 P.M., "otherwise I will be obliged to correct them myself." The article was published on the morning of May 29.

On June 5, 1913, Stravinsky disavowed the interview in a letter to *Montjoie!* (hand-delivered by Maurice Delage, since, by this time, Stravinsky was ill with typhus), published there without Canudo's knowledge. After reading this disclaimer, Canudo wrote to Stravinsky:

> I was shown your refutation of the article that appeared the other day. ... If I had known about this, I would have written to you for an explanation. I was told that M. Delage was acting on your behalf and on that of your friend (as well as mine) Ravel. ... I cannot conceal my surprise concerning your behavior toward me. You should have asked me first. Such a violent and hostile protest will always grieve me. Moreover, it remains inexplicable. I had thought that our relations were cordial, that we had the same ideas, the same noble project of collaboration. Since *Montjoie!* sought to give you support and encouragement, surely I have the right *not* to understand your animosity. Several times I tried to see you, and to have news of your health, but you never answered my letters. I do not deserve this, and I did not expect this from you. *Adieu*, dear Stravinsky.

A Russian version of the interview appeared in *Muzyka*, No. 141, Moscow, August 16, 1913, and, on August 25, Stravinsky, in Ustilug, wrote to the editor, V. V. Derzhanovsky:

> I read an unauthorized translation of my *Montjoie!* article in *Muzyka*. Not only is it extremely inaccurate, but it is also full to overflowing with incorrect information, especially in the part concerning the subject of my work. I have therefore decided to change this translation and to send it in revised form for inclusion in *Muzyka*. The style of the article bothers me a great deal. It was composed practically on the run for *Montjoie!*, which had asked for a few words about *Spring*. But it came out more coherently and properly in French than in that translation which you published in *Muzyka*. In a few days I will send this new version to you, but in the meantime I ask you not to be angry with me about all of this and to believe that I am very upset and even blush when I think about that translation from *Montjoie!*

Stravinsky's copy of *Muzyka*, No. 141, contains numerous changes, in his hand, but they are more verbal than substantive. Nevertheless, the letter establishes his authorship. Derzhanovsky answered on August 29:

> Now I will talk to you about the incident with your *Montjoie!* article. The man who made the translation speaks perfect French and is a professor of philosophy at the Sorbonne as well as a musician. Anything can happen, of course, and probably the translation was not good. I am delighted that you will change it, but how can this be done without embarrassing *Muzyka*? Could it be that the translation from *Montjoie!* was wrong? Is there some new material for it?

A subsequent letter from Derzhanovsky indicates that Stravinsky sent his own translation, but this seems not to have been published. On October 12, Stravinsky wrote to Maximilien Steinberg:

... I'm very angry with *Muzyka* for publishing that terrible and downright incorrect translation of my Paris article in *Montjoie!* (on "Holy Spring").

Letters to Stravinsky from Kussevitzky's secretary in Moscow, November 18 (December 1?), 1913, and January 13 (26?), 1914, indicate that the composer had written an "analysis" of *Le Sacre* for Kussevitzky's programs in Moscow and St. Petersburg in February 1914, and a letter to Stravinsky from the Russisches Musik Verlag in Berlin promises that the new "analysis" will be published in all future scores and programs.

Writing in *The Nation*, June 15, 1970, Professor Simon Karlinsky noted that

> in the Russian text of this [*Montjoie!*] essay . . . there is a curious spillover from the ballet: Stravinsky uses the same archaic, shamanistic bogeyman style he devised for the titles of various sections of the music.

Karlinsky sent his article to Stravinsky on June 17, and, on the 24th, the composer answered (from Evian):

> I did not write that essay. It was concocted by a French journalist, and the Russian version is a translation. I disavowed the essay not only at the time, moreover, but on several later occasions.[42] . . . Nor are the titles of the ballet movements mine, except for a "non-existent Russian word," to which Professor Karlinsky objects but which, no doubt because I coined it, I still like. The other titles were composed by . . . Nikolai Roerich. . . . [*The Nation*, August 3, 1970]

Professor Karlinsky answered Stravinsky directly, in a personal letter (in Russian), and also commented on his reply in a letter to *The Nation*:

> Whoever translated the essay from the French did a clever job of aping the stylistic mannerisms in the Russian titles . . . [which], indeed, resemble the titles Roerich gave his own paintings. . . . [August 3, 1970]

Yet it is clear from Derzhanovsky's letter of August 29, 1913, that Roerich did not translate Stravinsky's article.

Even without Stravinsky's letter to Derzhanovsky, the composer is easily recognizable in such statements as "I have not given the melody to the strings, which are too symbolic and representative of the human voice," since he repeated them on other occasions. The following English translation, by the American critic and composer Edward B. Hill, based on the *Montjoie!* original, was first published in the *Boston Evening Transcript*, Saturday, February 12, 1916:

WHAT I WISHED TO EXPRESS IN "THE CONSECRATION OF SPRING"

> Some years ago the Parisian public was kind enough to receive favorably my *Firebird* and *Petrushka*. My friends have noted the evolution of the underlying idea, which passes from the fantastic fable of one of these works to the purely human generalization of the other. I fear that "The Consecration of Spring," in which I appeal neither to the spirit of fairy tales nor to human joy and grief, but in which I strive toward a somewhat vaster abstraction, may confuse those who have until now manifested a precious sympathy towards me.
>
> In "The Consecration of Spring" I wished to express the sublime uprising of Nature renewing herself—the whole pantheistic uprising of the universal harvest.

In the Prelude, before the curtain rises, I have confided to my orchestra the great fear which weighs on every sensitive soul confronted with potentialities, the "thing in one's self," which may increase and develop infinitely. A feeble flute tone may contain potentiality, spreading throughout the orchestra. It is the obscure and immense sensation of which all things are conscious when Nature renews its forms; it is the vague and profound uneasiness of a universal puberty. Even in my orchestration and my melodic development I have sought to define it.

The whole Prelude is based upon a continuous "mezzo forte." The melody develops in a horizontal line that only masses of instruments (the intense dynamic power of the orchestra and not the melodic line itself) increase or diminish. In consequence, I have not given this melody to the strings, which are too symbolic and representative of the human voice; with the crescendi and diminuendi, I have brought forward the wind instruments which have a drier tone, which are more precise, less endowed with facile expression, and on this account more suitable for my purpose.

In short, I have tried to express in this Prelude the fear of nature before the arising of beauty, a sacred terror at the midday sun, a sort of pagan cry. The musical material itself swells, enlarges, expands. Each instrument is like a bud which grows on the bark of an aged tree; it becomes part of an imposing whole. And the whole orchestra, all this massing of instruments, should have the significance of the Birth of Spring.

In the first scene, some adolescent boys appear with a very old woman, whose age and even whose century is unknown, who knows the secrets of nature, and teaches her sons Prediction. She runs, bent over the earth, half-woman, half-beast. The adolescents at her side are Augurs of Spring, who mark in their steps the rhythm of spring, the pulse-beat of spring.

During this time the adolescent girls come from the river. They form a circle which mingles with the boys' circle. They are not entirely formed beings; their sex is single and double like that of the tree. The groups mingle, but in their rhythms one feels the cataclysm of groups about to form. In fact they divide right and left. It is the realization of form, the synthesis of rhythms, and the thing formed produces a new rhythm.

The groups separate and compete, messengers come from one to the other and they quarrel. It is the defining of forces through struggle, that is to say through games. But a Procession arrives. It is the Saint, the Sage, the Pontifex, the oldest of the clan. All are seized with terror. The Sage gives a benediction to the Earth, stretched flat, his arms and legs stretched out, becoming one with the soil. His benediction is as a signal for an eruption of rhythm. Each, covering his head, runs in spirals, pouring forth in numbers, like the new energies of nature. It is the Dance of the Earth.

The second scene begins with an obscure game of the adolescent girls. At the beginning, a musical picture is based upon a song which accompanies the young girls' dances. The latter mark in their dance the place where the Elect will be confined, and whence she cannot move. The Elect is she whom the Spring is to consecrate, and who will give back to Spring the force that youth has taken from it.

The young girls dance about the Elect, a sort of glorification. Then comes the purification of the soil and the Evocation of the Ancestors. The Ancestors gather around the Elect, who begins the "Dance of Consecration." When she is on the point of falling exhausted, the Ancestors recognize it and glide toward her like rapacious monsters in order that she may not touch the ground; they pick her up and raise her toward heaven. The annual cycle of forces which are born again, and which fall again into the bosom of nature, is accomplished in its essential rhythms.

I am happy to have found in M. Nijinsky the ideal [choreographic] collaborator, and in M. Roerich, the creator of the decorative atmosphere for this work of faith.

The program book for Kussevitzky's concert performance of *Le Sacre du Printemps* in the Salle des Nobles, Moscow, February 18, 1914, contains an "explanatory text of Igor Stravinsky," written at the request of the conductor:

> *Holy Spring* is a musico-choreographic work, without plot. Scenes of pagan Russia are united inwardly by the mystery of the great upsurge of all the creative powers of Spring. The choreographic sequence is as follows. *Part One:* The Kiss of the Earth. The celebrants of Spring are seated on hills. They blow *"dudki."* Youths learn the art of divination from an old woman who knows all of the secrets of Nature. Young maidens, costumed and with painted faces, come from the river in single file. They dance the Spring Dance. After this is the Game of Abduction and the Spring Rounds, for which the youths divide into different tribes that attack each other. An opening is cleared for the Eldest and Wisest, who enters at the head of a religious procession. The games stop and the people wait, trembling, for the blessing of the earth. The Eldest makes a sign to kiss the earth and everyone dances, stomping the earth. *Part Two:* The Great Sacrifice. Night. The maidens perform secret games and group themselves in circles. One of the maidens is chosen for the Sacrifice. Fate points to her twice: twice she is caught in one of the circles without an exit. The maidens dance a martial dance honoring the Chosen One. The Invocation to the Ancestors. The maidens bring the Chosen One to the Elders, and the Sacrificial Dance begins before the Eldest and Wisest.

The discrepancies between this and other versions of the action of *Le Sacre* do not need to be enumerated, but it should be said that in this one Stravinsky's Russian wording seems to identify the "ancestors" with the living elders, perhaps as symbolic of their deceased forefathers.

The Revisions

The 1921 orchestra score of *Le Sacre du Printemps*, the first to be published, differs greatly from the original (1913) version.[43] In a letter to an unidentified French correspondent, January 9, 1918, Stravinsky says that the printing of the first edition was interrupted by the war, and that he possesses only one copy of the proofs.[44] A year later, answering a request by Félix Delgrange [45] to perform the piece, the composer writes that

> The orchestra requires 105 musicians and you have only 80. Above all, you would have to follow my instructions as to how to perform the piece, otherwise this would be nearly impossible, it seems to me. The only orchestra parts of the *Sacre* in existence are here with me,[46] and the price for one performance is 250 francs. [Letter of April 19, 1919]

On February 19, 1916, Stravinsky wrote to his Berlin publishers, Kussevitzky's Russischer Musik Verlag, asking for these parts, but Frau Eric Zingel, wife of the director of the company, replied that, since the set was unique, permission to send it would have to come from a superior—presumably Nicolas Struve, in Moscow,[47] or Kussevitzky himself (letter of February 25). The present writer has not been able to discover exactly when Stravinsky repossessed the parts. He wrote to Gerald Tyrwhitt, in Rome, October 13, 1916, in answer to a request to conduct a concert there:

> The *Sacre:* impossible because it is in Berlin, *capitale des Boches.* ... But the score is here, the *Boches* do not have that, and if San Martino is willing to pay to have the parts extracted . . .

After Monteux's two concert performances of the *Sacre* in Paris, April 5 and 26, 1914, the score and orchestra parts [48] were returned to Berlin, and, on July 11, Herr Zingel informed Stravinsky that the engraving was about to begin. But so did the war, and work proceeded slowly. Nevertheless, the RMV continued to function until some time in 1917, and, on April 16, 1915, Zingel wrote to Stravinsky about the state of the company, remarking that

> Sales of your music are good, but all of our supplies are now exhausted. We must pay cash to the printers in Leipzig, where Breitkopf and Härtel are our agents.

One statement in Zingel's letter might seem puzzling:

> The score [of the ballet] is sold out. In the event that a new edition is made, please send further corrections if you have them. . . .

But the reference is to *Petrushka*, of course, not to the *Sacre*, since Zingel's other correspondence describes the first as a ballet, the second as an orchestra piece.

On December 3, 1914, the manuscript full score and two batches of proofs were sent to Stravinsky in Clarens by registered mail from Berlin. These must have been corrected and returned promptly, since, by the beginning of March 1915, he wrote Zingel asking him to return the manuscript. Zingel answered (March 13) that "Fräulein Eichelberger [49] will bring the score and opera material [*The Nightingale*]," and an RMV bill indicates that the manuscript was returned to Stravinsky on March 30, "through Frl. Eichelberger, by special request." Also, the note from Frau Zingel, February 25, 1916, reminds Stravinsky that "We sent the original manuscript through Frl. Eichelberger, March 30, 1915."

Soon after the end of the war, the score was delivered to the printing firm of C. G. Röder, Leipzig, where this manuscript was to remain until August 1929. In April 1920, Stravinsky asked for a copy, which was sent on May 8, and, in August, his London publisher, Otto Kling of J. & W. Chester, Ltd., on a visit to Leipzig and Berlin, returned with a score and orchestra parts which he sent to the composer in Garches, October 29. ("The Russischer Musik Verlag is a desert," Kling had written from Brussels, September 6.) These parts were used for the revival of the ballet, choreographed by Massine,[50] Théâtre des Champs-Elysées, December 15, 1920, but Ansermet conducted from Stravinsky's copy of the proofs.[51] Before the revival, as well as after it, hearing the work for the first time in seven and a half years, Stravinsky implemented numerous changes,[52] for which reason the first published full score (RMV 197, sent to Stravinsky from Berlin, February 11, 1922, pocket score, RMV 197[b], sent to him on May 21, 1922) should be classified as a revised edition.

In the summer of 1922, studying *Le Sacre* for performances in Berlin, on November 19 and 20,[53] Ansermet compiled a list of errors which he sent to Stravinsky, in Biarritz, August 9. On the 11th, the composer acknowledged this *"Erratumblatt"* and a day or two later wrote:

> I have verified, added, corrected the *errata* and I ask you to copy all of these changes very neatly (since we are dealing with Germans who do not know, or feign not to know, French). . . . Check to see if I have possibly made a new gaffe with the timpani at 57 , 58 , 59 . . . and, since you have the parts, I ask you to coordinate these revisions with them.

Meanwhile, Ansermet conceived the notion of extracting the prelude to the Second Tableau for concert performances, by reducing the number of horns and woodwinds to four in each section, and prevailing upon Stravinsky to compose an ending. Writing to the composer about this on August 29, Ansermet noted that "only a few changes would be necessary in the orchestration," and he undertook to write out the score himself, leaving to Stravinsky the problems whose solutions were not obvious. On September 2, Stravinsky sent "one page of music for the termination of the Prelude," and, on the 10th, Ansermet sent the score, asking the composer to "retouch" as he saw fit:

> I left the flutes at 83 in pencil, hesitating to choose among other possibilities. I believe that this piece can be sold or rented like bread, and I would like to give it myself this winter, in Geneva, in any case, and perhaps in other cities.

In another letter, on the 15th, Ansermet says that he has programmed the Prelude in a concert which he is to conduct in Zürich on October 31, but, whether or not the piece was actually performed then, Ansermet played it on other occasions, including a benefit concert in Victoria Hall, Geneva, February 5, 1923. At least once, too, Ansermet played the first part of the *Sacre* and the Prelude (only) to the second part in the "new version" (his letter to Stravinsky, February 14, 1923).

Stravinsky continued to amend the music, and so extensively in January and February 1926, while preparing to conduct it for the first time,[54] that a new edition was required. It was apparently at this time that he moved the fermata in the opening $\frac{3}{16}$ measure of the *"Danse Sacrale"* from the first to the third 16th rest, thus eliminating the upbeat feeling that the string chord must have had in early performances. On January 26, he wrote to G. Païchadze, director of the Editions Russes de Musique in Paris:

> At the same time as these lines I am sending you the manuscript pages of the reinstrumentation of the *Danse Sacrale*. . . . These are 112, 113, 114, corresponding to those in the printed score, also pages 122 (167), 123, 124, 125 (172 , 173). . . . Tell the copyist that the red broken lines that you find within the measures in my manuscripts should be copied in the same way since they indicate the divisions of the measure within the measure. The measures between 149 and 167 remain in the original instrumentation. . . . I am continuing to work on the reinstrumentation of this *Danse* and will advise you as soon as it is finished.[55]

The new miniature score, which appeared in 1929, bears the same date and publisher's number as the first one, from which it is outwardly distinguishable in only two ways: the cover of the later version includes the publisher's Paris address, and, on the first page of the music, the name of an editor, F. H. Schneider (this in the hope of procuring a copyright in the United States, which was not a party to the Berne Convention).[56]

On January 30, 1926, Stravinsky wrote to Ansermet for reassurance that the new groupings of the measures in the last pages had been copied on the orchestra parts. Stravinsky says that, for the end of the "Danse Sacrale," as for the beginning—and, a little farther on, for the same music a half-step lower in pitch—he has succeeded in rearranging the measures

> in a way that more clearly defines the bass and the dialectical structure of the phrasing, and at the same time determines the accentuation.

In still another letter to Ansermet, Stravinsky accepts the conductor's reasons for restoring the 2/16s and 3/16s after 192, but adds that "in order to play it this way, an orchestra must be as good as yours." What this means is that most conductors had compounded the smaller measures into larger ones (two 3/8s into one 3/4, for example), that these simplifications distort the phrasing and accentuation, and that the return to smaller units is desirable. A year and a half later, restudying the Sacre for a concert in Paris, Ansermet wrote to Stravinsky that

> . . . Païchadze has placed two sets of parts at my disposal, an almost illegible old one and yours. Each of these versions bothers me for different reasons. On the one hand, and in spite of my respect for you, I am not convinced by all of your changes, especially in the music from 148 to 149, where I am also troubled by the rewriting of the bass in order to conform to the new division of measures. At the same time, however, your changes have convinced me that I have been making a very serious error all my life in that the 5 at 148 [1921 version] is not 3 + 2 but 2 + 3. . . . Yet to adapt this 2 + 3 changes many other things as well, and I foresee the need of a more consistent and practical edition. . . . The attached paper will give you an idea of the notation I propose. Please tell me if the 2 + 3 is preferable, in principle, to that of 3 + 2; whether you would like me to prepare a version according to this plan . . . ; if you think that, after all, it might be better to return to the original version (with our now much improved technique); and if it might not also be advisable to re-establish the pizzicati which contributed relief on the accent motive. [November 28, 1929]

Since no letter survives, Stravinsky probably answered this by sending the score with his markings. After the Paris performance, Ansermet wrote:

> . . . I had the impression that the problem is now solved and I believe that I can tell you without deceiving myself that [the "Danse Sacrale"] was as clean and precise as it would have been if played by a Pleyela. Yet I must admit that after 192 I followed my first idea of keeping to 2/16s and 3/16s [in the 5/16 measures], with the one 4/16 [at the measure after 197]] and the 5/16 at the end. Experience convinces me that this is both necessary and the best solution. [January 1, 1929]

Writing to Stravinsky on April 18, 1929, Ansermet expressed regrets that, since the composer was planning to record the Sacre, "the new orchestra parts will not be available for my tour in Russia." Ansermet also warned that the new parts were adjusted in the "Danse Sacrale" to the metrical plan used in his December 1929 Paris concert. "This summer," the conductor added, we absolutely must oblige Païchadze to make a new score of the last pages (if not of the entire work). . . . I enclose a schematic sheet [57] for all conductors who may wish to do the *Sacre*. . . . This sheet shows the meters as inserted into the new orchestra parts. . . . Let me draw your attention especially to the change of the 3/8, nine measures before the end of ⌐142⌐ , and to the 3/16 measures (rather than groupings of 6/16s) from ⌐192⌐ ; the 3/16s are easier, and they produce greater exactitude in performance. . . . Play the second line of the sheet at the piano, left hand, sing the first line, and, at the same time, beat the measures with your right hand. This exercise accustoms one to think the two rhythms at the same time, while habituating the right arm to beat the meter automatically—three functions (two of them rhythmic, one metric) that, together, require both independence and coordination.

On May 12, 1930, writing to the Berlin concert agents H. Wolff and J. Sachs, Stravinsky denied that the regroupings of measures and other alterations constituted a new edition. He also insisted that the *Sacre* conclude any program in which it is performed:

It is evident for all who know *Le Sacre du Printemps* that the great tension generated by this work and the nervous attention that it requires [inevitably put any subsequent work at a disadvantage]. There is no new edition of the *Sacre*. This myth is repeated everywhere simply because I have recently facilitated the performance of the last "*Danse*" by a more exact "cutting" of the measures—but without changing the music or the orchestration.

Yet at least one performance at the time, by Furtwängler in February 1930, was described in the program—and in a review by Dr. Erich Urban, "*Furtwängler Spielt Strawinsky*"—as being of the "*neuer Fassung 1929.*" Also, Stravinsky's letter to Païtchadze, part of which is quoted above, states that the new manuscript pages were intended for a "*nouvelle rédaction.*" Yet Stravinsky also told Wolff and Sachs that he had "not changed anything in the music or in the orchestration," and this despite a letter from Païchadze acknowledging the receipt of the rewritten pages for the "*Danse Sacrale*" and saying that

The new score of the "*Evocation des Ancêtres*" is ready now, and the parts will be ready the day after tomorrow. [January 29, 1926]

Stravinsky did change the orchestration, of course, and rebarred the "*Glorification de l'Elue*," the "*Evocation des Ancêtres*," and the "*Danse Sacrale.*" More important, the score on which he wrote these and other revisions contains many other changes that were not incorporated in later printings. For one example, in the 1921 score he marked (and always wanted) a break (short silence) after the second fermata in the very first measure of the piece, yet this was not included in any later printing. Also, at the first entrance of the two solo muted trumpets in the Introduction to Part Two, he altered the third note of the second trumpet from G to F, a correction that he made in his own performances (when he remembered), though his recordings have now consecrated the wrong note as the right one.

Stravinsky continued to revise the *Sacre*, informing the Paris office of Columbia Records on April 1, 1929, for example, that he had made new corrections in the parts for his forthcoming recording.[58] On August 30, 1929, he wrote to Païchadze apropos the projected new edition of the score:

Only yesterday I received the newly engraved pages of the *Sacre*, together with my original manuscript.[59] This package has taken two weeks and I had to pay 27.75 francs duty, an absurd sum which you owe to me. When will you recover the orchestra parts from the baggage of the Ballets Russes? . . . I leave for Nice this Tuesday at 6 o'clock in the morning. Try to telephone to me there on Wednesday evening. . . . I will send these new, perpetually corrected, proofs [to Berlin]. Through carelessness, one page in the *Danse Sacrale* has been unnecessarily re-engraved—instead of another page, 126 (where I have added horns), which *should* have been re-engraved, and which, accordingly, was marked "N.B." (The page that actually *was* re-engraved contained no such indication.)

Before long, the new "1929" miniature score was also covered with red ink. To cite only two of the emendations, the timpani music at $\boxed{57}$ (and corresponding places) was rewritten, as was the fourth measure before $\boxed{59}$, both in harmonic substance and in instrumentation. Originally scored for eight horns, the lowest part was now reassigned to the second tuba, the uppermost line was doubled an octave below, and an E in the lowest register of two bassoons was added to the sustained chords. Still not satisfied with this solution, Stravinsky rewrote the passage, probably in 1943, canceling the changes of tempo, deleting the E, and reducing the horns to four (as well as confining them to their upper range and rewriting their glissando in the preceding measure as a quintuplet in the time of a quarter). The *Sacre* has not yet (1978) been performed with these alterations.

Stravinsky also continued to change the meters of the "Danse Sacrale," while denying that he had ever grouped the measures of the last pages, or conducted them otherwise than in accordance with the 1929 score. But his correspondence contradicts him. In Chicago, on November 13, 1940, he telegraphed to Eugene Goossens, then rehearsing the piece in Cincinnati, where Stravinsky was to conduct it: "I always beat each measure without reference to the old combinations of measures." Goossens replied that his first experience with the "new version" (the 1929 pocket score) was at the BBC in 1938, and that the performance "required great concentration to get used to the new arrangement of measures in the 'Danse Sacrale.' " Goossens was the fifth conductor to lead the *Sacre*—following Monteux, Rhené-Baton, Kussevitzky, Ansermet—at a concert performance in Queen's Hall, London, June 7, 1921.[60]

In September 1948, Stravinsky was shown part of a letter from Erwin Stein, the chief editor at Boosey & Hawkes:

> There are lots of mistakes in *Le Sacre du Printemps*. . . . It would really be a blessing if Stravinsky would go into this question sometime. Wrong full scores and wrong parts have been used since the work was published. . . .

Stravinsky wrote in the margin:

> Have no time for it. I prefer to compose a new music rather than losing time on this old one.

Not until November 6, 1948,[61] in a letter to Ralph Hawkes, did Stravinsky admit that at least two versions existed, an old one, containing, as he says, "many mistakes and misprints," and "the one with which Païchadze replaced it" (the 1929 miniature score), though this, Stravinsky adds,

> was never completely corrected in the 1920s. Many changes have been

made since then, and I am upset because I was never asked to establish a new edition. . . . The 1943 Associated Music Publishers' version of the *Danse Sacrale*,[62] though requiring the same large orchestra,[63] is much easier to read and to play, as well as definitely superior in balance and sonority.

This and other letters [64] leave no doubt that the new *"Danse Sacrale"* was intended to supersede all other versions.

On March 10, 1944, Stravinsky wrote to Artur Rodzinski, conductor of the New York Philharmonic:

You may be interested to know that recently I have rewritten the last Sacred Dance for my Boston performances. Unfortunately, [these] did not materialize . . . In the entire movement I established monochronical eighths instead of alternate eighths and sixteenths. This facilitates . . . performance. Also, I have . . . fractioned some complex measures into their integral parts. . . . [Original in English]

On October 27, 1944, Stravinsky wrote again to Rodzinski:

As for the finale of *Le Sacre,* I believe that for the moment it is perhaps easier to play the original version. For one thing, you would have to rent the supplementary material, and, for another, the reasons which led me to undertake this work, and the ideas that guided me, demand certain conditions for the performance, in order that people will not come to false conclusions. An appropriate time will come for the clarification of these questions, which interest me as much as they do you. [Original in French]

More than a year later—December 19, 1945—Stravinsky wrote to the manager of the Philharmonic apropos "Rodzinski's planned performance" of the *Sacre,* saying that the representatives of "Kussevitzky's publications have recently expired and [been] transferred to the jurisdiction of Boosey & Hawkes." Stravinsky adds that he will write again, "since Ralph Hawkes is in Los Angeles."

Stravinsky's high claims for the new version of the final movement were challenged by Arthur Cohn of the Philadelphia Free Library, in a letter published in the *New York Times,* December 24, 1950. Referring to the original *Sacre* as a "synoptic orchestrational bible," Mr. Cohn objected that, so far as its final movement is concerned, the *Sacre* must now be regarded as

disowned by its creator. What are teachers of orchestration to do? . . . If Stravinsky believed some of his works required revising because he could improve on them, that would be a motivating cause.

This was the "motivating cause," of course, but the letter rankled Stravinsky, since the new *"Danse Sacrale"* had not yet been performed.[65] Writing in the margin of the newspaper article, he advised Mr. Cohn—for reasons not understood by the present writer—to "read Kafka's *Hunger Artist,"* and, on December 28, drafted an answer for the *Times:*

I have considered revising the *"Danse Sacrale"* for many years. My long experience in conducting it . . . convinced me that . . . changes in orchestration would clarify the harmonies and the design, that much in the original version was simply not heard, and that changes in the re-barring would simplify performance. I also changed the unit of beat from the sixteenth to the eighth and divided the five-beat bars into twos and threes. . . . I wanted to prepare this new version for my recording with the New York Philharmonic [66] in [connection with] a project for *The Rite of Spring*, and I had already finished the revised *"Danse Sacrale"* when this project fell through. . . . The real problems posed in revision are to determine when a change in spelling becomes a change in structure and to show how these changes, affect the form of the original.

Stravinsky added that what Mr. Cohn had referred to as the "bible" of the original (i.e., the 1921 score) was in truth quite unlike the actual original.

Technical problems concerning part of the *"Danse Sacrale"* were raised yet again by Ernest Ansermet, in a letter from Geneva, May 23, 1957:

> *Mon cher Igor* . . . I have just recorded the *Sacre* again. . . . I submit an idea: beginning with the third measure after [198], the basses and timpani, which until this point "accompany" the melodic rhythm, now take a regular binary rhythm which dominates the other and against which the other forms syncopations. Since it is the very devil to obtain the exactitude of the basses in the unequal measures . . . would it not be reasonable to notate the rhythm in this passage according to the rhythm of the basses?

> The same thing occurs in the three measures before [195], but for this section [no change is necessary]. . . . *Je vous embrasse. Mille bonnes choses à Vera et à Bob. Votre E.A.*

The last corrections in the *Sacre* score in Stravinsky's hand, dating from August 1966, confirm that in the oboe part at [9], the quintuplets are always staccato, the sextuplets always slurred, and that the trills in the lower strings at [78] are whole-tones. Stravinsky also eliminated the A-natural in the piccolo clarinet part two measures before [34], mistakenly it seems, since the figure should probably be the same as at [34], as in the original orchestra parts.

Appendix C

RENARD AND OLD POSSUM
(Stravinsky and T. S. Eliot)

T. S. Eliot's first published reference to Stravinsky appeared in a 1921 "London Letter" in the *Dial*:

> Stravinsky was . . . our lion. . . . Stravinsky, Lucifer of the season, brightest in the firmament . . . took the call many times . . . small and correctly neat in pince-nez. . . . [*Le Sacre du Printemps*] was received with wild applause.[1] . . . The music seemed very remarkable . . . but at all events struck me as possessing a quality of modernity which I missed from the ballet which accompanied it. . . . Music accompanying . . . an action must have a drama which has been put through the same process of development as the music itself. . . . The spirit of the music was modern, and the spirit of the ballet was primitive ceremony. . . . Even *The Golden Bough* can be read in two ways: as a collection of entertaining myths, or as a revelation of that vanished mind of which our mind is a continuation. In everything in *Le Sacre du Printemps*, except in the music, one missed the sense of the present. . . . Stravinsky's music . . . seem[ed] to transform . . . the barbaric cries of modern life; and to transform these despairing noises into music.

Stravinsky's first public reference to Eliot, the quotation of a passage from "Tradition and the Individual Talent," occurred in a lecture at the University of Chicago, January 20, 1944. Jacques Maritain, a member of the audience, may have drawn the musician's attention to this essay, but, at a considerably earlier date, he had been aware of the poet from St. John Perse and others. Eliot's name begins to appear in Stravinsky's correspondence and interviews in the 1940s; a letter from John U. Nef, for example, mentions the composer's discussion, during a luncheon, of "The Music of Poetry," and in an interview in *Pour la Victoire* (February 24, 1945), Stravinsky says:

> I use the word "tradition" in the sense that Eliot has given to it. To be in a tradition, one must possess a historical sense, perceive the presence of the past and the simultaneity of the entire universal intellectual inheritance. Only with this sense can a creative artist become aware of his place in the contemporary world.

But the poet and the composer did not meet until December 8, 1956, when they were introduced by Stephen Spender, who wrote:

> I made notes of Eliot's conversation during his first meeting with Igor Stravinsky, which Nicolas Nabokov had asked me to arrange. In them, Stravinsky steals the show, but that he should have done so is also characteristic of Eliot. . . . I drove Eliot to the Savoy. He was in good humor. The conversation was carried on mostly in English, though some of it was in French, which Eliot spoke slowly and meticulously. Stravinsky started talking about his health. He complained that all the doctors told him to do different, sometimes quite [contradictory] things. He suffered from excessive thickness of the blood. Moving his hands as though molding an extremely rich substance, he said: "They say my blood is so thick, so rich, so very rich it might turn into crystals, like rubies, if I didn't drink beer, plenty of beer and an occasional whiskey, all the time." Eliot said that a pint of beer did him less harm in the middle of the day than two glasses of red wine. Stravinsky returned to the subject of the thickness of his blood, and Eliot said meditatively: "I remember that in Heidelberg when I was young I went to a doctor and was examined, and the doctor said: 'Mr. Eliot, you have the thinnest blood I've ever tested.' "
>
> Stravinsky talked about Auden writing the libretto of *The Rake's Progress*. He said it went marvelously. Auden arrived at the Stravinskys' house in Hollywood, ate an enormous dinner and drank much wine, went to bed at exactly half past ten, and then was up at eight the next morning ready to listen to Stravinsky's ideas. No sooner were these divulged than the librettist started writing. He would think of something, write it, then ask himself where it could be fitted in, pulling out lines and phrases and finding places in which to insert them, as though he were fitting the pieces into a puzzle. After consulting with Chester Kallman, within a few days Auden returned the libretto,[2] neatly typed out. Only minor alterations had to be made, and Stravinsky had only to suggest that there was some difficulty somewhere, and the solution to the problem would arrive by return of post.
>
> Then Stravinsky spoke of the annoyance of publicity. A reporter had rung up and suggested coming to his hotel to take down notes of his reactions to the performance of one of his works on the BBC. Vera Stravinsky chipped in here and said, "We explained that we never listen to the radio." Stravinsky added a terse comment on the British conductor. Eliot asked him what he did when people wrote asking for photographs, and Stravinsky said he did not send them because they cost money. He said that when he was in Venice where a choral work of his was performed in St. Mark's, *Time* had created a link between him and Eliot by captioning their review of it: "Murder in the Cathedral." He said that after this performance he waited twenty-five minutes so that the crowds might disperse,[3] and then, accompanied by friends, walked out in the Piazza. There were very few people by this time, but as he walked across the Piazza, people seated at tables saw him and started clapping. He said he was extremely touched. These people, most of them young, had waited in order to applaud.[4]

A year later, Stravinsky sought Eliot's advice as a publisher:

> Dear Mr. Eliot, I would like to send a manuscript of a short (about 40,000 words) book of *Dialogues* of mine. It will be published in Germany, France, and Italy in the fall, but I have not yet arranged for English publication. . . . I think [that the dialogues] are in the order in which they [were] written [and that they are] not categorized, as perhaps they should be. I will greatly value your opinion, especially [about] what to cut. . . . Very sincerely yours, Igor Stravinsky. [Letter of January 30, 1958]

Eliot answered, on February 5, expressing the "keenest interest" in reading the book. Then, on March 19, he wrote to say that Faber and Faber wanted to publish it, but that he wondered whether "you could be persuaded to continue the 'Conversations' in the same vein." Stravinsky replied on March 25:

> Dear Mr. Eliot, I thank you for your kind letter and, of course, I am very pleased with your and your colleagues' interest in the book. . . . I have not seen the manuscript that was sent [to] you. Someone in New York [5] was responsible for the "grouping" according to subject. I might not like this. . . . [Yet] a merely chronological order . . . will not do either; the questions range too widely. Perhaps we should work with the manuscript that you have. . . . I should like to do immediately what work has to be done on it. I finished the composition of my *Threni* a few days ago and have now a little time between musical composition. . . . [6] With best wishes, most sincerely yours, Igor Stravinsky.

Eliot's next letter, dated October 23, is an invitation—"*Cher maître,*" this time—to a reception for Stravinsky by Faber and Faber during the composer's forthcoming stay in London. He answered from the Sacher Hotel, Vienna, November 1:

> Dear Mr. Eliot . . . My time will be more free at the very beginning of my stay in London.[7] In fact, since I arrive on the morning of [December] second, perhaps the party could take place that afternoon, or, even better, the next. . . . With best wishes, I am yours sincerely, I. Str.

At the party, Eliot had hoped to introduce Stravinsky to Jacob Epstein, who wanted to make a bronze head of the composer, but the sculptor was ill and could not attend. A few days later (December 8), the Stravinskys dined with the Eliots in their Kensington Gardens ground-floor flat:

> T.S.E. provides lapidary translations (for his wife) of the French and German expressions that occur with regularity in Stravinsky's talk, but disclaims ever having been a linguist: "I only pretended to be one in order to get a job in a bank." He breathes heavily, harrumphs— "Hm, hmm, hmmm," each additional "m," so it seems, deepening the significance—and he folds and unfolds his fidgety fingers, or touches them tip-to-tip (which makes me aware that Stravinsky's hands, otherwise remarkable for the large spans between the knuckles, are the least nervous I have ever seen). Eliot carves and serves the meat and walks around the table to fill our wine glasses. His manners are formal, reserved, slightly parsonical, and his talk is marked by pauses and deliberations, which, when adjudication is required, is restricted to implications; Stravinsky, in comparison, seems to think with the tip of his tongue. When asked about public readings, Eliot says: "I cannot remember my poetry because it was rewritten so many times that I forget which version was final." Most of his stories are self-deprecating: "One day in a New York taxi with Djuna Barnes, I noticed that the driver had become engrossed in our conversation. Then after Miss Barnes had left, he asked whether 'that woman is a writer.'" When the talk turns to mutual French friends, Eliot is interested above all in Stravinsky's recollections of Jacques Rivière [8] and of *his* brother-in-law, Alain-Fournier. Cocteau's name comes up, too, and Eliot remarks, devastatingly, "He was brilliant when I saw him last, but I had the impression he was rehearsing for a more important occasion." [From R.C.'s diary]

The following day, Eliot sent a copy of *Old Possum's Book of Practical*

Cats,[9] inscribed "To Madame Igor Stravinsky in memory of a very happy evening."

Eliot's next letter, addressed to Stravinsky in Tokyo, discusses a project for an opera. Eliot had been offered a commission to write the libretto, Stravinsky an equal sum [10] to compose the music, but, in the letter, Eliot expatiates on his lack of qualifications, saying that "distinction as a poet" is not necessarily an asset in a librettist, and that the book of *The Rake's Progress* did not succeed in the attempt to combine the very different subjects of Hogarth and the traditional pact with the devil.[11] Yet the letter did not reject the possibility of a collaboration. Stravinsky answered from the Imperial Hotel, Tokyo, April 8, 1959:

> Dear T. S. Eliot, The proposition from Mr. Paul Horgan came at a very bad moment for me, and until your letter I had not thought seriously about it. . . . I myself am not very attracted by the operatic form at present, and I would certainly not undertake to write an opera like *The Rake's Progress* for any fee. . . . $20,000 is not much after the United States Bureau of Internal Revenue has enjoyed *jus primae noctis* with it. . . . Perhaps I [may] . . . propose another kind of work, a cantata, or a static stage piece (genre my *Oedipus Rex*), shorter than an opera and . . . more suitable to my present non-operatic musical thought—perhaps a Greek-subject piece in a contemporary re-interpretation.[12] I will think about this. . . . Of course it would be a pleasure and an honor to work with you, and I [believe] that we might invent something interesting together. Would you give me your thoughts about this suggestion (it is not really a proposition) and let me manage what I can manage? . . . My wife joins in sending most affectionate regards. I. Str.
> P.S. I hope we can talk someday about the *Rake* libretto. . . .
> P.P.S. Do you have a copy of your article about Julien Benda? . . . It must be 20–25 years old [and] I do not remember the magazine, but I wish to say a few words about Benda, whom I met once on a transatlantic crossing.

Eliot replied on May 21, enclosing a copy of his June 1928 essay on Benda but expressing dissatisfaction with it, and surprise at the opinion of Péguy's prose writings set forth therein, since Eliot supposed that he had always admired them, after his first exposure to them by Alain-Fournier.[13]

Stravinsky was in Copenhagen when this letter came, and he did not answer it until August 6:

> Dear T. S. Eliot, I did not write . . . because I was anxious to complete my new composition [14] and could not consider other work. . . . I have received a proposal from NBC television, meanwhile, that has helped me to see my own direction—commissioners always have in mind a work of one's past [that] they want repeated, but the very reference to a past work helps one to realize how unrepeatable it is. Perhaps . . . NBC or even the Arts Council of Great Britain (I have an offer from that organization too) will commission us . . . [and] an ex post facto commission [may] be preferred [since these people] think in the categories that they know—ballets, operas, plays—and I do not propose to write in any of these.
> I have been considering the story of Noah. I can imagine a dramatic work [based on] it [and] involving narration (as in my *Oedipus Rex*), singing—a chorus, the voices of Noah and his sons, and perhaps an angel—and scenic and choreographic elements. It might follow the form of a medieval morality play, for example, with narration used to connect sequences of set pieces, instrumental and vocal numbers, pure, i.e., spoken verse (what delightful animal rhymes . . . you could

do . . .), dances. . . . Here, anyway, is a subject I hope you will consider. . . .

Thank you for your cable. We will fly to London from New York September 2 . . . and telephone . . . as soon as our heads have cleared from the flight. . . . Most cordially, I. Str.

Eliot answered on August 16, saying that he was more certain than ever of his lack of vocation as a librettist. At dinner in Claridge's on September 6, the subject was not discussed:

> T.S.E. looks younger and is livelier and more talkative than last year, but he seems to think of himself as a hoary ancient with little time left. He chats about the weather—"Isn't it unusual? Why last year at this time . . ."—then says that social obligations are the bane of his existence: "I cannot accept lectures because the people who pay for them expect me to attend cocktail parties at which I am caught between someone wanting to know what I think of Existentialism and someone asking what I really meant by such and such a line." Mrs. Eliot asks if we have read "Edmund Wilson's attack" on her husband, and Eliot intercepts to say that Wilson's "only good line must have come from personal experience or have been told to him by someone else. It occurs in one of his stories, where a man, stroking a woman's back, exclaims how soft it is, and she says 'What the hell did you expect, scales?' " Speaking of Aldous Huxley, Eliot says: "I don't read him, of course—I am much too fond of him for that—but he was pretty pessimistic when we saw him last. Too many people in the world and more all the time. So there are indeed, indeed, indeed." The subject changes to Pound's recent Cantos, and Eliot observes that "There are more Chinese characters than ever; Ezra is becoming the best Chinese poet in English." When Stravinsky describes his impressions of the Japanese theater, Eliot says that he once watched a Noh dancer in a play by Yeats and was very moved by the performance: "One really could believe that the dancer had become a bird." Stravinsky mentions Büchner, and Eliot says that "Wozzeck is too simple for a play, just simple enough for an opera." He gazes at each of us in rotation, beaming affection toward his wife each time around. He drinks a gin and tonic before, claret during, and whiskey after dinner, which in his case consists of a partridge; and though he obviously enjoys sniffing the cheese platter, he does not, after a final moment of indecision, actually make a choice. [R.C., op. cit.]

On November 24, Stravinsky wrote from the Gladstone Hotel, East 52nd Street, New York:

> Dear T. S. Eliot, We were obliged to change our plans and sail back rather than fly. We therefore reached New York later than we expected, in fact a day after you sailed. . . . You have probably not had much time to consider our project, nor, frankly, have I, with all of my concerts in the past two months. . . . I am going to read the York Mystery plays. . . . I haven't had time to read "The Deluge" yet.
>
> I expect to see Mr. E. Martin Browne's production of Charles Williams's Cranmer next week; I will report on that later. I was interested in some remarks of yours in . . . The Paris Review—that a poet hears his own voice reading everything he writes. So, too, I think, does a composer write vocal music for his own voice (even if he cannot sing). Kindest regards, Igor Stravinsky.

Eliot answered, on December 8, offering to help with "suggestions for the arrangement of the texts" from "The Deluge," and adding that "Your programme of travel and work while in Europe astounded me." But Stravinsky postponed "The Deluge" [15] (The Flood) to compose A

Sermon, a Narrative, and a Prayer, and he did not see the Eliots again for nearly two years, during which period, however, their Christmas cards became more affectionate ("With love from," even "Our Love"). On January 5, 1961, Eliot read his poetry at the 92nd Street YMHA in New York—introduced by Robert Lowell, who was very droll at the expense of Sandburg—and the Stravinskys were invited to join the Eliots afterward at the home of e. e. cummings; but the composer had a recording session the same evening and could not attend.

Composer and poet dined together at the Savoy Hotel, London, October 16, 1961, ostensibly to consider a proposal from Cambridge University Press that Stravinsky set "two lyrical stanzas," as Eliot described them, from "Little Gidding." On October 11, Mr. P. F. du Sautoy of Faber & Faber wrote to M. A. Black of the Cambridge Press:

> I have asked Mr. Eliot to raise the question [of the setting with Stravinsky, but] whether the two great men will remember to discuss this . . . when they meet, I cannot be sure. . . .

In fact nothing was said about this at the dinner:

> Eliot has aged very noticeably since we last saw him, and his color has changed; his lips and ears are an unhealthy purple. He complains of the nuisance of having to refuse repeated invitations to Tagore Centenary celebrations; "I took something of his from the library the other day, to be certain I had not made a mistake, but could make nothing of it. Difficult to tell that to the Indians, though. Yeats once pretended to like it, but he was making a case for 'The East' at the time. . . ." The composer and poet talk about their favorite *romans policiers.* Both men are Simenon addicts, and Eliot says that "I can read about Maigret when I can read nothing else." Another mutually admired sleuth is Perry Mason. "Gardner knows California law," Eliot remarks, "but Chandler is a better writer." At one point, when Mrs. Stravinsky voices some criticisms of Switzerland, Eliot agrees with her but says that "I like it nevertheless because more than any other country it resembles what it used to be." (R.C., *op. cit.*)

On November 24, Eliot wrote to a representative of the Cambridge Press about the stanzas from "Little Gidding":

> I would be willing to have [them] set to music if the composer was [sic] Stravinsky. Stravinsky could get more out of me that way than any man living.

Shortly before this, Stravinsky had arrived in New Zealand, where, at a press conference,

> Asked why he had never set to music a poem by his friend T. S. Eliot, Stravinsky replied: "I have thought about it. But his words . . . do not need music. I can find notes for Shakespeare because he wrote words for singing.[16] Eliot's are for speaking." [*Wellington Evening Post,* November 16, 1961]

Six weeks later, back in California, Stravinsky wrote:

> Dear T. S. Eliot, First of all I send you and your wife my best wishes for the New Year, though these greetings will probably reach you out-of-season and some time after the event. . . . I have finally seen the correspondence concerning Cambridge. . . . I would like very much to set the two beautiful verses from *East Coker* [sic]. They are certainly "verses to be sung," and the standard, four-part-hymn choral is the

way to present them, I think. Such a piece would be only a minute or a minute-and-a-half long—like my *Epitaphium* (for flute, clarinet and harp)—or twice that because the second verse would repeat the same music. If I undertake to do this, it will be as a tribute to you. . . .

I must continue my series of concerts, but I will inform you of my progress. Cordially as ever, Igor Stravinsky [Hollywood, December 26, 1961]

The anthem, *The Dove Descending*,[17] was completed on January 2, 1962, before Stravinsky's next concert, and his papers contain a memo:

Airmailed manuscript 1-4-62 with a word asking, after printed, to give the MS as an homage to T. S. Eliot.

Eliot was informed of the gift while vacationing in Barbados, but thanked the composer from London, March 28, 1962.

On April 6, 1962, Stravinsky wrote again from Hollywood:

Dear Eliot . . . I have not yet had news of any performance of the *Anthem* in Europe, though I believe it was sung in Venice (Biennale) last week. I will conduct it in Toronto next week myself . . . recording it "commercially" at the same time, and I promise to send the record as soon as it is released. . . . I do not expect to be in London this year . . . but I will be in Paris for a few weeks . . . and in Hamburg conducting my ballets in the latter part of June. Please let me know (Hôtel Berkeley, 7, Avenue Matignon, Paris, 8ième, May 15–17) when and if you expect to be in the United States. . . . With most cordial regards to you and Mrs. Eliot, Igor Stravinsky

P.S. Have you ever considered *Oedipus at Colonus* as a subject for contemporary musico-dramatic treatment?

Stravinsky had not read and had not seen *The Elder Statesman* and was therefore unaware that it was based on this very play. It seems uncanny that Stravinsky thought that the Sophocles might have appealed to Eliot, and this intuition cannot have been founded solely on the awareness that

The Nightingales . . . singing near
The Convent of the Sacred Heart

were present in the sacred wood in which Oedipus died. No wonder Eliot did not mention the proposal in his reply (April 24). The final letter was from Stravinsky:

Dear Eliot, I have seen a quotation from your *Sunday Telegraph* piece concerning mistranslations in the New English Bible. As this is a matter of acute interest to me, could you kindly send a copy of the text? . . . We expect to be in London at the end of May ourselves en route to Ireland and will hope to see you. Best New Year's wishes and kindest regards to both of you. Yours very cordially, Igor Stravinsky (Hollywood, December 26, 1962)

In Paris at the beginning of May 1963, Stravinsky cancelled a concert in Bergen, Norway, with the excuse that he was ill. He immediately received a cable:

Distressed to hear on the wireless of your illness and we send our cordial wishes my dear maestro for your speedy recovery. T. S. Eliot

Stravinsky cabled that he was actually quite well and invited the Eliots to dinner on the 28th—which Eliot accepted by cable. But this date was later changed:

May 29, 1963. London. The Eliots have heard the fiftieth-anniversary performance of the *Sacre* "on the wireless," and they applaud the composer as he enters their apartment.[18] Comparing tonight's ovation with the reception in 1921, Eliot observes that "The English think it is polite to laugh when confronted with something serious that they do not understand." The conversation switches to this afternoon's Derby, and he says: "I used to wager in the Calcutta Sweepstakes but never drew a horse. During a visit to Stockholm in 1948 I put some money on a long shot called Queen Mary—out of loyalty, of course, it was not a hunch—but we came in last." He says that the British Arts Council asked him to receive Yevtushenko, but that the meeting was not a success: "I am unable to speak through a translator unless I know him. . . . Incidentally, Igor, one of your Russian 'r's' reminds me of the variety of 'r' sounds in Sanskrit that Indians do not recognize as differentiations, although they pronounce them." When Stravinsky refers to Eliot's recent pamphlet on George Herbert, Eliot says that "Herbert is one of the very few poets whom I can still read and read again. Mallarmé is another, and, hm, so is Edward Lear. . . ." [R.C., *op. cit.*]

December 11, 1963. New York. Dinner with the Eliots at the Pavilion. We call for them in a car at the River Club on East Fifty-Second, Eliot's favorite New York street, he says, "Because it is a dead end." Glimpsing the United Nations building on the way to the restaurant, he denounces it as "the center of an anti-European conspiracy." He drinks and eats almost nothing but sits upright from time to time, focusing his piercingly intelligent gray eyes on each of us in turn. "I am rereading *Nostromo*," he says. "After I first read Conrad it was a terrible shock to hear him talk. He had a very guttural accent." "Was it like mine?" Stravinsky asks, but the question is deflected with "Yours, Igor, is easier to understand." On the subject of languages, Eliot says: "My Italian was quite fluent when I was at Lloyds, but Dante's Italian is not the most suitable instrument for modern business phraseology.[19] I had a smattering of Rumanian too, and of modern Greek, and for this reason the manager of the bank insisted that I must also know Polish—indeed, that not to know Polish would be illogical." When we leave, Stravinsky and Eliot walk arm in arm to the vestiaire, where the headwaiter remarks to the attendant: "There you see together the greatest living composer and the greatest living poet." But Mrs. Stravinsky saves the day—and the two men from embarrassment—by remarking, in exactly the right tone, "Well, they do their best." [R.C., *op. cit.*]

On January 4, 1965, the day of Eliot's death, Stravinsky was in New York. After returning to California, he composed an *Introitus* (January 14–February 17), "*Requiem eternam dona eis, Lux perpetua luceat eis.*" In a letter to his publisher, February 26, 1965, Stravinsky describes the piece as "A Panikheda chorus in memory of the unforgettable Eliot."

Appendix D

STRAVINSKY'S POLITICS:
Left, Right, Left

In 1901, at the age of nineteen, Igor Stravinsky entered St. Petersburg University to study law. A quarter of a century later, he told the *Journal de Genève* that the choice of this profession was not his:

> My father wanted me to avoid an artist's life, knowing its difficulties.
> ... He sent me to study law and I passed my exams and received my grades. [November 14, 1928]

These were merely passing in seven of the eight branches in which he was enrolled, though in financial law he earned the highest possible mark—as he did in all of his language courses. For most of his university years, he was concurrently studying composition with Rimsky-Korsakov, a leading figure in the liberal movement, who influenced his greatest pupil in the direction of progressive political and social thought.

Stravinsky often contrasted this intellectual atmosphere, so important to his development, with the stultification at home. Little is known about his parents' political affiliations, though on August 9, 1894, Fyodor Stravinsky received a watch from the Tsar, Alexander III, and twice accepted the Order of St. Stanislas from him, an honor that liberals often refused; as a leading singer at the Imperial Opera, however, would he have had such an option? In later life, Igor Stravinsky deplored Rimsky's "leftist, anti-religious mentality," but in the early 1900s the pupil's political views reflected his teacher's. At a 1905 concert in Rimsky's honor in the Komisarzhevsky Theater, it is probable that Stravinsky took part in an anti-government demonstration that had to be quelled by the police, and, in the same year, he may have been arrested with a group of protesting students and even have spent an hour or two in jail. In July 1906, he wrote to his mother explaining his decision not to go to the Crimea:

> We could not live quietly there where the revolutionary ferment is strongest. ... The ship crews strike almost daily, and meetings and clashes are all around. ... One cannot be indifferent to the life surrounding one, and unless one regards the great Russian revolution with hatred, it is impossible to live in such a boiling pot. As you know, we are of the opposite conviction.

Stravinsky's correspondence before World War I, and after he had become a celebrated composer, shows his disgust with the corruption in his native country. He wrote to Alexander Benois, February 15, 1912:

> The word "artistic" must be understood ironically in Russia. Rotten petty tradesmen and crooks, who pay service to rot alone, to pettiness, to baseness, people such as Burenin and Suvorin [extreme rightists] and the rest of the scum from whom there is no getting away in Russia.

Three weeks later, Stravinsky wrote to Andrey Rimsky-Korsakov, one of the composer's sons:

> I am living away from everything that seethes and rumbles, but I follow it intensely. [May 7, 1912]

The war fired Stravinsky's patriotism. Romain Rolland quotes him from a conversation in Vevey, September 26, 1914:

> To Russia belongs the role of a beautiful and mighty country, pregnant with embryos of new ideas, able to engender world thought. . . . At the end of the war a revolution will take place, overturning the Imperial dynasty and creating a Slavonic United States. [Journal des Années des Guerres]

Stravinsky was outspokenly anti-German.[1] He scandalized the Russian Embassy in Rome by remarking, when his exit visa was signed (November 9, 1916) by "Vice Consul B. de Teutern," and when he was introduced to First Secretary Strandtmann, "Don't you have any Russian names here?" Basil Khvoshinsky, one of the composer's friends in the Diplomatic Service, scolded him:

> Your question in the Embassy was utterly tactless. The paper which First Secretary Strandtmann got for you, and which enabled you to leave Italy so easily, carrying a package of paintings and your music, was procured as a special favor. If you require a similar paper in Paris, you will have to go to First Secretary Ungern-Sternberg.[2] When do you think all of the members of our Ambassadorial Service will meet with your approval? Perhaps not until you sever connections with the German nurse who educated you [i.e., taught you your manners]. [Letter of November 16, 1916]

Stravinsky, "flabbergasted at the misunderstanding," answered the reprimand by referring to jokes that he and Diaghilev were in the habit of exchanging on the subject of German names, Ungern-Sternberg's among them (letter from Morges, November 21, 1916). According to one story, the Baron was on a train near Vitebsk when he was asked his name by a fellow passenger, who responded, "And I am Ungern [i.e., reluctantly] Finkelstein." He then asked Ungern-Sternberg his destination. "Baden-Baden. And yours?" "Minsk-Minsk." [3]

Stravinsky was deeply concerned with Russian politics. At the time of Ansermet's performances of Petrushka in Geneva, in January and February 1915, the composer encountered a former deputy of the Petrograd government, G. Alexinsky, who later recalled

> the pleasure of meeting Stravinsky at the beginning of the First World War. He was living in . . . the small town of Morges, and his neighbor was a pianist named Paderewski,[4] who, everyone believed, would become the first President of a liberated Poland. At this time Switzerland was infested with German agents working, in agreement with Lenin, to undermine the morale of the Russian colony, which was

divided into two camps, the defeatists and Germanophiles, and the
"*jusqu'au boutistes*" and pro-Allies. Stravinsky fell in with the latter
group. . . . [*Nation Belge*, Brussels, May 29, 1952]

Alexinsky's pleasure seems not to have been shared, however, to judge
by the inscription on the envelope of a letter from him (March 18, 1916)
in Stravinsky's hand: "An annoying man who is trying to promote his
book *Russia and the War*." Alexinsky had asked the composer to contribute a chapter on European art in Russia.

At one time, Stravinsky was a Ukrainian revanchist, perhaps less
for political reasons than for economic ones: he held mortages and
owned considerable property in "Little Russia." Always a vigilant fol-
lower of contemporary events, Stravinsky clipped newspaper articles
and added comments, in one case in musical form, setting the refrain
of a poem, published in *La Tribune* in June 1917, praising the President
of the Swiss Federation. The composer was also quick to inform editors
of their mistakes, particularly on Russian and Ukrainian affairs:

> *Cher Monsieur*, I have just read a paragraph entitled "Russia and Con-
> stantinople" in the *Gazette de Lausanne*, February 19 [1917]. A
> strange historical detail revealed therein astonished me. In order to
> justify Ukrainian aspirations vis-à-vis Constantinople, the essay refers
> to Prince Oleg as a Ukrainian. But by opening any dictionary (Bouillet,
> for example), one can learn that Prince Oleg was a Russian, and a
> descendant of Rurik. Furthermore, any mention of a "Ukraine" prior
> to the tenth century is anachronistic. The history of the Ukraine, if one
> can speak of it independently of the history of Russia, begins in the
> eighteenth century.

Like many Russians abroad, on receiving word of the abdication of the
Tsar (March 16, 1917), Stravinsky became optimistic for the future of
his homeland, and, indeed, a note from Ansermet in Rome, a few days
later, provokes a thought about what the new country might have become:

> Diaghilev arrived from Paris today [March 16, 1917]. He received a
> request, signed by Gorky, Benois, Chaliapin, Bilibin, and the other
> Russian artists most in view, asking him to return to Russia and to
> take charge of all artistic affairs, becoming, in effect, a commissar of
> the arts. Diaghilev was greatly flattered. . . .

Stravinsky was in Rome himself soon afterward to conduct his *Fireworks*, *Firebird*, and excerpts from *Petrushka*:

> Diaghilev had rented the Palazzo Theodori on the Piazza Colonna, in
> spite of the noise of the crowd and of the fountains. One day at his
> dinner table were Stravinsky, Picasso, and a number of Italian musi-
> cians and painters. Stravinsky was saying that "It takes sixty measures
> to prepare the atmosphere of *Das Rheingold* . . . for German brains,
> but a Scarlatti, for example, can create the proper atmosphere for
> Latins in fewer than ten measures." [Michel Georges-Michel, from an
> article in *La Marche des Temps*, February 11, 1945]

Stravinsky was invited to compose the new Russian national anthem on the theme of *The Song of the Volga Boatmen* (telegram from
Rodzianko, of the Duma, to Diaghilev). On April 8, Stravinsky harmo-
nized and orchestrated his arrangement of the piece, dictating the score
to Ansermet, after which Picasso daubed a red banner at the head
of the manuscript. (See Paul Morand's *Journal d'un Attaché
d'Ambassade*, April 10, 1917.) The "Hymn to the New Russia," as the

composer titled it, was flagrantly inappropriate, a symbol for the eternally downtrodden and serf-like in the Old Russia. Audiences must have felt this, since the arrangement was performed only a few times.

Stravinsky expected that the abdication would be followed by a redoubled Russian war effort:

> For more than two years, M. Stravinsky has had no news from his Russian home in Volhynia. . . . The district is occupied by the Germans. . . . He greatly regrets the resignation of M. Miliukov, with whose foreign policy he was in entire agreement. . . . M. Kerensky he considers thoroughly reliable, as well as a man of great moral strength and intelligence, perhaps the only one now in power who can restrain the extremists. . . . "Russia is a vast country, and it will take time for her people to become accustomed to the new and sudden change of life that the Revolution has brought about; fanatics and extremists will come and go. For many, the Revolution comes first, the war being quite secondary, but . . . the first duty that the Russians owe to their country and to themselves is to beat the Germans." [*New York Herald*, Paris, May 30, 1917]

Stravinsky soon revised his opinion of Kerensky, partly as a result of eyewitness accounts, such as the following from Benois, dated Petrograd, July 5, 1917, and received by the composer in Diablerets on July 30:

> *Plus ça change, plus ce n'est pas la même chose!* Everything is worse! What happened to [the projected performances] of *The Nightingale* is typical—like a Russian history written by Miliukov and Kerensky but corrected by Lloyd George and Ribot. You probably think we are in the Kingdom of Freedom. In fact we live in the Kingdom of Excesses and Stupidities. It is very bad here and we envy you that you are far away and do not see this nightmare.

By this time, Stravinsky began to realize the consequences of a Bolshevik victory. He continued to advocate Russia's re-entry into the war, and, after a concert in Lausanne, in April 1918, discussed this policy with Jacques Rivière with such fervor that, weeks later, Rivière wrote:

> I understand why you so strongly desire the reconstruction of a Russian front. But you are one all by yourself, tackling Germany from the rear. [June 29, 1918]

For Stravinsky, the Russian Revolution proved to be a disaster of incalculable proportions. It separated him from relatives and friends—forever, in some instances—as well as from his entire formative world. He lost homes, citizenship, property, sources of income, manuscripts, libraries, personal possessions, and even the copyright protection for his works. Moreover, it was no longer feasible for him to compose music using his native language, which, for several reasons, was much less frequently sung outside of Russia in the 1920s than is the case today. Now obliged to earn his living by giving concerts, he spent as much as half of his time in travel, which entailed complications for any stateless person, even one with friends in the French and other governments who helped to procure special treatment.

Until the Stalin blackout, the new Russia did not impose interdictions on Stravinsky's music, and, on the contrary, beginning with Meyerhold's staging of *The Nightingale* at the Maryinsky Theater (May 30, 1918), Stravinsky's creations were better received under the new regime than in the pre-Revolutionary one. But, by 1925, hardships and disillusionments had affected Russian musical life, as Stravinsky learned from his friend Stepan Mitussov's letters about the difficulties in organizing performances in Leningrad of *Pribaoutki* and the *Japanese Lyrics*. In the same year, Stravinsky was invited to conduct in the Soviet Union, but, though tempted to accept, he decided to await the reports of Ansermet, Stiedry, and others who performed his music there. They assured him of a triumphant reception, as did his brother and the many Russian musicians, known and unknown, who begged him to come. But, by this time, and despite the comparative freedom—one of the composer's Leningrad nieces was permitted to live with his family in France for a year—his fears of "the Bolsheviks," and of being detained, were already too deep-seated.

In view of the chaos of the last years of Imperial Russia, and of the first ones of the Soviet Union, with the consequent personal catastrophes, Stravinsky's attraction to the strong-armed government of Mussolini, beginning in the mid-1920s, is understandable. It follows, too, that a man with an obsessive, almost pathological need for order would feel comfortable with oligarchies and autocracies. Aside from that, after leaving Switzerland in 1920, Stravinsky had wanted to live in Rome, not Paris; he once told a reporter, "I consider myself to be partly Italian by sympathy and affection." It should also be mentioned that he may have been influenced by his Futurist friends, who were ardent Fascists. Giacomo Balla had created a visual counterpart for *Fireworks*,[5] and Fortunato Depero had designed costumes and sets for *The Song of the Nightingale*. Stravinsky also knew Marinetti, Boccioni, Carrà, Pratella, and Russolo, while that other proto-fascist, D'Annunzio, had been a friend from the time of Debussy's *Le Martyre de Saint-Sébastien*.

In September 1925, Stravinsky played his Sonata in a series of contemporary-music concerts in Venice—"*Sotto Il Patronato di S.E. Benito Mussolini*," this in large letters on the program, as if the dictator were seeking the support of the avant-garde. A Stravinsky festival, free of political auspices, had already taken place in Rome, in April, with two concerts conducted by him, a third in which he played his Concerto, and a production of *Histoire du Soldat* by Pirandello. From then until the Second World War, Stravinsky regularly fulfilled engagements with Italian orchestras, and conducted his stage works at La Scala and the Rome Opera. In 1930, Mussolini invited him to the Palazzo Venezia. Stravinsky talked openly about the meeting at the time, but in later years dismissed it facetiously ("When Mussolini said that he played the violin, I suppressed a remark about Nero"—*Expositions and Developments*, 1962) and gave the impression that his attendance had been not entirely by choice. Documentation contradicts this, as, for instance, in an interview in *Il Piccolo*, May 27, 1935:

> Unless my ears deceive me, the voice of Rome is the voice of Il Duce. I told him that I felt like a fascist myself. Today, fascists are everywhere in Europe. . . .[6] In spite of being extremely busy, Mussolini did me the great honor of conversing with me for three-quarters of an hour. We talked about music, art, and politics.

Three days after this statement, Stravinsky was again summoned to the Palazzo Venezia, and his account of Mussolini on this occasion is found in *Le Gazetta del Popolo*, May 31. Whether or not these newspapers put words into Stravinsky's mouth, the same explanation cannot be used for the following letter to Yury Schleiffer, a Russian refugee living in the Italian capital. The date is July 14, 1936, and the contents are startling:

On leaving Rome in March [7] I delivered . . . the second volume of my *Chronicles* with a dedication to Il Duce, as well as a small gold medal (representing Napoleon and Marie Louise), with the request that Depirro [sic] present them to Il Duce together with the expression of my profound admiration for him and for his work. In presenting this small gold token to the Treasury of the Italian State, I feel the satisfaction of participating in the fine deeds with which Italian patriots have shown allegiance to their party. I had also asked Signor Depirro that there be no publicity. . . . In the past, Il Duce has always acknowledged the receipt of music, books, or messages from me. . . .[8]

By this time, the "fine deeds of Italian patriots" included the bombing of defenseless Ethiopian villages. On October 13, Stravinsky accepted "*avec joie*" a request to begin a concert in Naples the following month with the Fascist Hymn.

Stravinsky was also concerned that "there be no publicity" about his support of Falangist Spain. When interviewed on the French radio (by Charles-Albert Cingria), after conducting concerts in Barcelona, the composer would say only that

As always in a country in which some political upheaval is taking place, one sees nothing and appearances in the street are perfectly normal. [March 23, 1936]

While in Barcelona, however, he had revealed some of his beliefs, and, incidentally, showed that he was familiar with Ramon Lull, as well as with the sixteenth-century Spanish mystics:

I do not work with subjective elements . . . my artistic goal is to make an object. . . . I create the object because God makes me create it, just as he created me. . . . I cannot accept surrealism or communism, despite my conviction that both are right on many points. The bourgeois is the one who is not right. . . . Esthetically I am unable to accept materialism. . . . My religion makes me a dualist. [*La Noche*, March 12, 1936]

Six weeks later, Stravinsky was in Buenos Aires, and in trouble there with the progressivist press. Under the heading "How a True Artistic Genius Thinks," the newspaper *Los Diarios* quoted him saying:

I know very little of the contemporary music of my country [Russia], but I believe that nothing great, or that nothing new, exists there. A nation that has suffered such an upheaval in its social structure cannot, for the moment, produce interesting works of art. Something else is being born, and I suspect that it is not art but simply propaganda. When Bolshevism burst forth, everything was for the Left, and whatever came from the Left was good. . . . But truly great works of art are made with Faith. . . . Materialist philosophy is very remote from me, and it is for this reason that I have not been able to return to my homeland. It is not worthy of man to give his life for a material paradise. . . . I find myself very far removed from the oscillations of politics . . . but I *am* anti-parliamentarian. This I cannot tolerate, as a horse might be unable to tolerate a camel. . . . [April 26]

The reactions to the composer's statements were intemperate, and the mildest was the one in *Los Recortes*, April 25, under the headline "*Stravinsky es enemigo de la democracia*":

The declarations of Stravinsky have made a deplorable impression. They deny any democratic attitude and exalt the efficacy of dictatorships.

El Liberal, May 6, titled its report, *"Concepto deplorable,"* while *Critica*, April 25, remarking that Stravinsky's statements had produced a "seismic shock," went on to deduce that "a genius can be an infant with respect to the profound social problems of the day." On May 6, the Marxist *Senales* published a scurrilous piece, "Stravinsky has come to siphon off the Argentine Treasury."

After returning to France, Stravinsky wrote to his Argentine friend Victoria Ocampo to say that their project of performing *Perséphone* in Madrid could not be carried out because of currency controls (letter of July 10). But a letter from Juan Mestres Calvet, former musical director of Barcelona's Gran Teatro del Liceu, thanks the composer *"pour votre noble geste en nous adhérant au document à la Cause,"* and invites him

> to conduct two concerts in San Sebastián and a third in Burgos, the city of the Generalissimo's palace.

This is dated January 13, 1938, nearly a year after Guernica.

With regard to Germany in the 1930s, Stravinsky attempted to observe impossible distinctions. He loathed the Nazis, and filled scrapbooks with newspaper photographs of Himmler and Goering in ridiculous poses, adding captions such as *"cons"* and *"derrières."* The composer protested, too, when his *Chronicles* was censored for the German edition, but he did not evince any concern for other authors to whom this had happened. In August 1937, he informed his Zürich publisher, Martin Hürlimann:

> I remarked some cuts that unfortunately destroy the meaning, for which reason I insist again, and it is a condition *sine qua non*, that at each change or cut in the German text, the reader be directed to a marginal note [footnote] referring him to the original French edition. . . . Please be advised that the English, American and Spanish editors were not permitted to make any cuts or alterations in my text, nor did these editors question the passage about Bayreuth that is inadmissible for present-day Germany. I can cite another cut made in your edition to appease the Nazi censor or reader. . . . .

Yet, in the same month, Stravinsky wrote to the West German Concert Direction in Cologne,

> . . . I am addressing you directly on the subject of a series of concerts that I would be happy to conduct in Germany this season . . . after the 22nd of October . . . [August 8]

and, on September 7, sent a second letter:

> In the event that I go to America, I will still be able to come to Germany in the autumn of 1938.

When the persecution began, in 1933, Otto Klemperer asked Stravinsky to sign a petition on behalf of musicians being driven from their posts in the Reich. He sought the advice of Gavril Païchadze:

> Cautious, because of Germany, I am hesitant about signing. Also, I do not know the positioning of my name on the list and do not want to be next to such trash as Milhaud. . . . Is it politically wise to join in this common cause? [Letter of September 7, 1933] [9]

If political and financial wisdom were synonymous for Stravinsky in 1933, it was because the largest share of his income came from Germany, and his royalties there had begun to shrink. Also, he had not received any offers for performing engagements in that country for 1934 and 1935. As it happened, his unique concert in the Third Reich took place at the insistence of B. Schott's Söhne, Stravinsky's music publishers in Mainz. In April 1936, he and his younger son played the Concerto for Two Solo Pianos at the Baden-Baden International Festival of Contemporary Music, the National Socialist Party's challenge to the International Society for Contemporary Music. Stravinsky appeared here in the least distinguished company of his career, and, though he managed to avoid hearing a program of pieces by Egk and others acceptable to Dr. Goebbels, the Concerto was played next to a work by the official Nazi composer Paul Graener.

Meanwhile, how did such close friends and associates of Stravinsky as Samuel Dushkin and Arthur Lourié regard the composer's "caution," concerned as they were with the plight of Jewish refugees? [10] And what, for that matter, was Stravinsky's own position on the same question? In Paris, on December 1, 1941, his younger son signed a statement, *"Igor Stravinsky n'est pas Israélite,"* and, the following November 17, obtained police certification of this. But this is certainly no final proof of "Aryanism," since conversions to the Orthodox Church can rarely be traced back as far as the time of Catherine II and the establishment of the Pale of Settlement—within which, it must be noted, both of Stravinsky's parents were born, his father in the Minsk district, his mother in Kiev. When the *Revue de Paris*, October 1, 1931, described Stravinsky as "Jewish—thin, *roux*, wearing a pince-nez," he wrote to the editor: "I am not Jewish . . . do not have red hair, and wear a pince-nez less frequently than spectacles with ear frames." In fact, though it seems irrelevant, Stravinsky *was* "sandy" or "ginger"-haired, and, since the reference is to the early 1920s, he would more likely have been wearing a pince-nez than lunettes. But what does this have to do with being Jewish?

In order not to misunderstand many references to Jews, the reader of the composer's correspondence must be aware of the late-nineteenth-century Russian society in which he was raised, a society that enforced a quota system, encouraged such organizations as the Black Hundreds, and fabricated the "Protocols of the Elders of Zion." This is the Russia that Stravinsky fled. And an expression such as the one that he uses for his concert agent (and Mengelberg's secretary) Salamon Bottenheim, "my dear *Hausjude*" (letter of August 25, 1928), simply betrays Stravinsky's Russian upbringing; whatever the effect produced today by this term, his intention, as the context shows, was affectionate. Finally, the Stravinsky of the American years would not have made a remark of this kind.

In December 1937, passing through Berlin after concerts in Riga and Tallinn, Stravinsky met with representatives of Telefunken to discuss a recording of *Jeu de Cartes* that he was to make with the Berlin Philharmonic in February 1938. Back in Paris, he was asked to join Picasso, Ramuz, and others in sponsoring an exhibition of painters— Klee and Kandinsky among them—whose works had been branded in Munich as *"Entartete Kunst"* ("Degenerate Art"). Stravinsky seems not to have complied with the request. Then, on May 25, 1938, in a huge demonstration at the Düsseldorf Kunstpalast, his own compositions were denounced as *"Entartete Musik."* The *Deutsche Allgemeine Zeitung* of that date explained that

> . . . Stravinsky and Arnold Schoenberg are . . . the leaders of the decadent cultural Bolshevist tendencies in art today . . .

and another German newspaper defined

the Stravinsky problem [as] this: we advocate national art and are opposed to the international, which he represents.

On June 6, the Paris *New York Herald Tribune* reported that

The Nazi leaders have issued a declaration of war against atonality and "modernism" in music and are proceeding, with their customary thoroughness, to stamp out in the Third Reich this phase of "Jewish Culture Bolshevism." . . . The exhibition is arranged in the manner of a partitioned gramophone shop, with the exception that sound-proofing and intervening doors have been omitted. A patron . . . enters a doorless alcove and . . . presses a white button. Immediately a gramophone plays a recorded atonal selection from Stravinsky or Arnold Schoenberg. . . . Often the exhibition hall is filled with a din. . . . The proper contrast was provided by the so-called Reich Symphony Orchestra. . . . Its programs concentrated on Wagner. Its members [wore] Nazi brown dinner jackets, brown bow ties, and brown shoes.

Stravinsky lodged a complaint through his friend and one-time piano teacher, Isidor Philipp, who knew the French Ambassador in Berlin, André François-Ponçet.[11] Stravinsky's letter (May 30) shows that he still had not recognized Nazism for what it was, since he ignored the no-less-vicious abuse of other composers and attributed the attack to a cabal of German musicians acting against him alone. Philipp placed him in communication with Jean Marx,[12] plenipotentiary to the French Minister of Foreign Affairs, and, on May 31, the composer wrote to Marx insisting that the Düsseldorf incident "represents a well-organized campaign by German musicians against my music." François-Ponçet filed a protest, setting in motion some perfunctory correspondence, and, on June 23, Henri Jourdan, of the French Institute in Berlin, informed Stravinsky—surely sarcastically!—that "the Reich is not in the habit of making public amends." Yet, at the beginning of August, Stravinsky did receive an apology, conveyed by Marx (letter of the 4th) and claiming that the assault had been directed against

certain tendencies rather than against any individual; your works are still being performed in Berlin.

That a man of Stravinsky's intellect, powers of perception and imagination, historical knowledge, breadth of experience could have accepted this "change in attitude toward my music" and even "looked forward to improved relations with Germany" (letter to Jourdan, August 6) is incomprehensible. So, also, is his failure to answer a letter from Schoenberg and Leopold Godowsky, asking for help in establishing a conservatory in Palestine for refugees. But neither did Stravinsky anticipate the start of the war—"In spite of the terrible tensions of the moment," as he wrote to Roland-Manuel, August 24, 1939.

In May 1940, in Los Angeles, Stravinsky wrote to Carlos Chávez that

Life has become a constant anxiety because of the tragic news from Europe. . . . The terrible events in Europe have made me ill and unable to work.

Stravinsky listened to the radio several times each day and charted the Allied positions on maps of Europe and North Africa with pinpoint flags that he had made himself. In August, he tried to contribute to the war effort by improving the harmony of the *Star-Spangled Banner*:

> I notice that while Congress passed a law making this piece the national anthem, they failed to specify which harmonization was standardized. . . . [That] of the honorable Dr. Damrosch . . . renders it characterless. . . . [To Leonard Feist]

But Stravinsky's more interesting version met with D.A.R. and other opposition in every city in which he attempted to introduce it.

Stravinsky had three children in France at the beginning of the Occupation. In a letter (to Victoria Ocampo, April 10, 1941) in which he laments the death of Virginia Woolf [13] ("Why not Hitler?" he adds), mention is made of his pianist son's success in a concert in the Salle Gaveau; Stravinsky seems not to have realized that, to most people in England and the Americas, Paris, at the moment, was perhaps not the proper place in which to be succeeding. In the spring of 1942, Darius Milhaud, now a fellow Californian, came to Stravinsky's aid and, it may be, even saved the life of his daughter, then in the Haute Savoie. Milhaud's father had died, in Aix, and, in spite of the large "racial tax" that the Vichy government had subtracted from his widow's inheritance, enough money remained to enable Milhaud to help needy friends. At intervals, he cabled to his mother, "Stravinsky's health unchanged," which was a signal for her to send 30,000 francs to Stravinsky's daughter, after which Stravinsky reimbursed Milhaud at the Algerian rate of dollar-franc exchange. Mme Milhaud continued to make these payments even after seventy German soldiers were billeted in her home, but, in November 1943, the system was discovered and blocked, and, two months later, the brave lady died.

The invasion of Norway inspired the *Four Norwegian Moods*, and, though Stravinsky had written that, between De Gaulle and Pétain, *"Je suis Dégueuliste"* (letter to Nadia Boulanger, July 29, 1941), the composer was pleased when the General attended a performance at Lewisohn Stadium, July 1944. Similarly, the invasion of Russia not only inspired music for the film *North Star*, but also led to benefit concerts, and even to committee work, with Louis B. Mayer, for Russian War Relief. Stravinsky's largest creation of the war years is a programmatic Symphony that contains a parody of German marches, a dramatic structure whose peripeteia suggests the crisis at Stalingrad, and a finale that expresses the jubilation of the victory. Above all, this Symphony reveals Stravinsky's intense pride in Russia. While working on the composition, he remembered the seventieth birthday of the Soviet composer Reinhold Glière, and, on January 4, 1945, cabled a greeting to him that must have astonished anyone who knew Stravinsky in 1939:

> Sincerely wish you strength . . . for the furtherance of our Fatherland's musical culture.

On April 21, 1945, the Russian-American Club of Los Angeles wrote to Stravinsky asking him to contribute to an "American-Russian Friendship Concert," announced for May 16, 1945, in the Shrine Auditorium, and to be performed by "Leopold Stokowski and his orchestra." In fact, the program was jointly conducted by Otto Klemperer (the national anthems, Tchaikovsky's Fifth Symphony, Prokofiev's *Alexander Nevsky* Cantata), and by Stravinsky (the *Firebird* Suite). After intermission, Edward G. Robinson addressed the audience, the Soviet delegates to the San Francisco Conference were presented, and Stravinsky led the *Firebird*. It should be mentioned that he aided the concert as well by attending fund-raising social functions, including a reception given by Olivia de Havilland on May 6.

Finally, Stravinsky's letter to Hanns Eisler, October 5, 1947, was clearly motivated by sympathy for his political plight—Eisler and his wife had been arraigned in Los Angeles on the charge of having concealed their Communist Party membership when applying for U.S. visas—as well as esteem for his music:

> As I do not know when I will see you, I would like to tell you how much I enjoyed your music for *Galileo*, which I heard twice at the Coronet Theater [366 North La Cienega]. I sincerely regret not having [had] the opportunity . . . to express personally my appreciation of your craftsmanship and the high quality of your music. With best regards, Igor Stravinsky

On October 6, *The New Republic* published a report by Martha Gellhorn, "Cry Shame! An Eye-Witness Account of the Hanns Eisler Hearing." On the 10th, Thomas Mann wrote to Agnes Meyer:

> Since the Inquisition has turned [Eisler] over to the "secular area" for deportation, there is danger that he will land in a German camp. I hear that Stravinsky (a White Russian!) means to start a demonstration in his favor. But I have a wife and children and am not inquiring further into the matter.

On October 17, Mrs. Clifford Odets, Larry Adler, and two others sent a letter to Stravinsky, inviting him and his wife to attend a discussion of the Eisler question on October 26, at the home of John Huston. Stravinsky seems not to have gone, but, through the intermediary of John Houseman (the director, actor, and a friend), to have agreed to head a group of composers—Copland, Sessions, Toch, and Harris were the others—in sponsoring a concert of Eisler's music at the Coronet Theater on December 14. Stravinsky and Houseman met again, on November 13, at the composer's home, after a performance at the Coronet of *La Casa de Bernarda Alba*.

On December 6, however, Stravinsky's attorney, Aaron Sapiro, received a reprint of the *New Republic* article, told the composer that his sponsorship was "an attempt of the Communist crowd to . . . use your prestige for the benefit of the Communist Party campaign for the Eislers," and sought to induce him to withdraw his name from the committee. Three days later, *L'Humanité* (Paris) published a letter from Chaplin to Picasso, asking the artist to protest Eisler's deportation, and, on December 12, after the *Los Angeles Times* had printed this story, Stravinsky wrote to the editor:

> My name appears as a sponsor of the Hanns Eisler concert . . . My understanding . . . was that my name would not be used for political purposes . . . In spite of this understanding, politics has entered in the case. Rather than hurt Hanns Eisler's concert, I would not withdraw from the sponsor committee at this late hour. I wish to state, however, that I disavow all political implications; my interest remains purely musical.

The letter was not published. Soon after the concert, Houseman wrote to Stravinsky from New York:

> I was most deeply distressed to learn . . . via Berman, that you felt the Eisler committee's pledge had not been kept . . . the promise I gave

you, and which they *most formally* gave me, was that no kind of political implication would be allowed to intrude on the purely musical nature of the evening . . .

Stravinsky answered Houseman on December 29:

> . . . The truth is that people received the program of Eisler's concert [with the] political leaflet, "Cry Shame!", in the same envelope . . . [Since my] letter [to the *Los Angeles Times*] was not published, the only thing that I could do to protest . . . was not to attend the concert.

Appendix E

*A SELECTED, ANNOTATED BIBLIOGRAPHY
OF
RUSSIAN AND ENGLISH PUBLICATIONS
SINCE 1971*

Books in Russian

1. *Dialogi,* excerpts from volumes 1–4 of the Stravinsky-Craft "Conversation" books, translated and edited by V. A. Lennik, G. A. Orlova, and M. S. Druskin (Leningrad, 1971).

The paralipomena that Soviet musicologists have provided for their anthology of these "Conversation" books is valuable chiefly in the area of Stravinsky's Russian background. Though some of the information is the result of routine research, the legwork has provided important data on the concerts and operas that the composer attended in his youth, on his studies with Rimsky-Korsakov, and on the discrepancies between Stravinsky's and others' accounts of the staging of his Russian theater pieces. Stravinsky's memory of distances and of dates has also required extensive correction.

In a few instances, the Soviet scholars have based their rectifications on dubious premises. Thus Stravinsky recalled that, in his youth, he had admired Tanaev's *Mobile Counterpoint of the Strict School.* But, since this treatise was not published until 1909, the editors argue that, at this late date, the composer would hardly have needed to consult such a textbook. In fact, however, Stravinsky was never above studying even the most elementary theoretical writings, and, for one example, even at seventy he was influenced by Krenek's *Studies in Counterpoint.*

When the Soviet editors chide Stravinsky for his partiality to Kandinsky, Larionov, Malevich, and other émigré artists, and for ignoring the Socialist Realist School, the reader feels that Zhdanovism is not altogether dead. And when the editors identify Lourdes—which Stravinsky mentions in connection with Werfel's *Bernadette*—by means of a reference to Emile Zola's writings on the subject, the effect is bizarre. Nor is the Soviet text reliable on Stravinsky's post-Russia years. Thus the Ugly Duchess, in Auden's first draft of *The Rake's Progress,* was not, as the editors suppose, based on Marguerite, Duchess of Tyrol (1318–69), the protagonist of Feuchtwanger's *The Ugly Duchess;* the concept and name originated with Auden. Stravinsky knew Feuchtwanger in California but had not read this novel.

2. *F. Stravinsky: Stat'i, Pis'ma, Vospominaniya (F. Stravinsky: Essays, Letters, Memoirs)*, compiled and annotated by Larisa Kutateladze, edited by A. Gozenpud (Leningrad, 1972).

To readers only minimally concerned with Igor Stravinsky's family before his appearance in it, his letters to his parent are the chief interest in this biography of his father. When a booklet about Fyodor Stravinsky was published in 1951, the composer read it without comment, probably because it consisted of little more than an outline of the eminent bass's career, a listing of his sixty-six roles at the Maryinsky Theater, and a garland of quotations from Tchaikovsky and others on the elder Stravinsky's remarkable artistic and intellectual qualities. Unlike this earlier publication, the new book looks at Fyodor Stravinsky from the perspective of the father of the composer, though without slighting the achievements of the parent in his own right.

Fyodor Stravinsky was renowned as a gifted graphic artist, as well as a singer and actor, and as a bibliophile and *littérateur*. The new biography reproduces thirty-two of his water-colors, but, unfortunately, only in black and white. Fyodor Stravinsky's library was among the largest privately owned ones in all Russia, and of such importance that, in January 1919, the Ispolkom of the Union of Communes of the Northern Territory passed a resolution placing his widow's apartment under protective guard. Three years later, she bequeathed her husband's collection of music to the Petrograd Conservatory. In 1941–2, during the siege of Leningrad, most of the remaining books were destroyed.

The biography of Fyodor Stravinsky—bookish singer, actor in public, introvert in private—is indispensable to anyone interested in the son, for the composer inherited his father's complex character as well as his musical gifts. Fyodor Stravinsky endowed his son with other talents, too: histrionic (the composer's early letters describe his acting in amateur theatricals), graphic and calligraphic (as a young man, Stravinsky painted in oils, and, throughout his life, did sketches and drawings), literary and bibliophilic (Stravinsky had an almost fanatical respect for learning, and he bound in leather many of the books that had influenced his thinking).

The table of contents is as follows:

3. *I. F. Stravinsky: Stat'i i Materialy (I. F. Stravinsky: Essays and Materials)*, compiled by L. S. Dyachkova, edited by B. M. Yarustovsky, 527 pp. (Sovietsky Kompozitor, Moscow, 1973). First printing, 12,000 copies.

Of this book's four sections, the most valuable is the last, a collection of sixty-two of Stravinsky's letters to Russian addressees. The letters are greatly superior to the composer's correspondence in other languages, partly, perhaps, because he was not yet concerned with posterity, but mainly because, as he grew older, his disputes with publishers, conductors, and critics consumed the time that was formerly spent sharing artistic opinions with friends. It should also be said that his Russian letters are as expansive as those in French are circumspect and stingy with words. His correspondence grew with his fame, of course, and, by the 1920s, when French had superseded Russian as the principal language, had reached unmanageable proportions. Yet his most important letters were often drafted in Russian first.

The letters from the American period present the greatest editorial difficulties, since many of them were written with secretarial assistance and therefore contain a farrago of styles. Stravinsky's chief scribe before 1947 was Mrs. Adolph Bolm, and, after that date, his son-in-law André Marion, an example of whose collaboration is apparent in a letter about Dylan Thomas published in the magazine *Adam* in 1954. Other letters of these years, such as one concerning Artur Schnabel (*The Observer*, 1962), were written with the help of the present writer. Both letters say neither more nor less than what Stravinsky wanted them to say, but the stamp of personality is blurred, which is never the case when he is writing in Russian.

The *Essays and Materials* volume begins with a preface by the late Ekaterina Furtseva, Soviet Minister of Culture, decreeing that a committee be formed in Moscow to coordinate studies of the music of "the outstanding Russian composer Igor Stravinsky." This is followed by eulogies from the late Dmitri Shostakovich, the late David Oistrakh, the late Aram Khatchaturian, and five other, still living, state-owned musicians. The full table of contents is as follows:

4. *Igor Stravinsky, Work, Opinions,* by M. Druskin, 213 pp. (Moscow, 1974).

The importance of Druskin's study is that it includes analyses of *Threni* and other later works heretofore ignored in the U.S.S.R. A German translation of the book was published in 1977.

5. *Letters.* In two parts, edited by Igor Blazhkov (Moscow, 1978).

At the time of writing, this book has been announced but not yet published. Blazhkov, conductor, spokesman, intermediary with musicians in the West, has been one of the most active forces on behalf of Stravinsky's music in the U.S.S.R. Blazhkov first made himself known to Stravinsky in 1959 in a letter that the composer answered on January 26, 1960. Blazhkov wrote again, requesting scores, and, on June 28, Stravinsky sent copies of the piano scores of *Jeu de Cartes* and *Le Baiser de la Fée,* a vocal score of *The Nightingale,* and full scores of *Orpheus,* the Divertimento, and *Agon.* In 1963, Blazhkov sent a book of *lubok* (primitive Russian graphic art of the eighteenth and nineteenth centuries), which Stravinsky acknowledged in a letter on June 20. Blazhkov has reportedly reconstructed the text of *Histoire du Soldat* from the original sources in Afanasiev.

6. *Igor Stravinsky and His Intimates,* by Xenia Yurievna Stravinsky (Leningrad, 1978).

At the time of writing, this book has been announced but not yet published.

Oral Histories and Books in English

1. Two oral histories were compiled shortly after Stravinsky's death. The first, a series of thirteen one-hour documentaries, "The Life and Times of Igor Stravinsky," prepared and produced for the Canadian Broadcasting Corporation by Margaret Ireland, was broadcast on Sunday afternoons between January 4 and March 28, 1976. The participants were Mrs. Igor Stravinsky, George Balanchine, William Brown, Elliott Carter, Aaron Copland, Robert Craft, Lucia Davidova, Richard Hammond, Paul Horgan, Christopher Isherwood, Lincoln Kirstein, Goddard Lieberson, Sylvia Marlowe, Nicolas Nabokov, Vittorio Rieti, Jerome Robbins, Kyriena Siloti, Arnold Weissberger, and Vera Zorina. Recorded comments by Stravinsky and W. H. Auden from the CBS archives were also used.

The second oral history, "Igor Stravinsky: The Man and His Music," consisting of ten ninety-minute programs, was made in 1976 by Frederick Maroth and William Malloch, for Educational Media Associates of America, Berkeley, California, and, in 1977, was released on fifteen stereo records. About two-thirds of each program is made up of live performances of Stravinsky's music, taped by, among others, the Hungarian Radio, Kol Israel, Radio Moscow, the Radiodiffusion-Télévision Belge, the Südwestfunk (Baden-Baden), the Westdeutscher Rundfunk (Cologne), and the Swiss Broadcasting Corporation. The remaining third of each program is filled by interviews with Mrs. Stravinsky, Elliott Carter, Robert Craft, Samuel Dushkin, Lukas Foss, Ernst Krenek, Lawrence Morton, Aladár Rácz, Gregg Smith, Claudio Spies, Virgil Thomson, Jean Villard (who played in the first *Histoire du Sol-*

dat), Charles Wuorinen, Vera Zorina. Stravinsky's own talk is interpolated from lectures (the University of Cincinnati in 1965), recording sessions—he was unaware of this eavesdropping by machines left on when he was *not* conducting—and other sources.

2. *Encounters with Stravinsky,* by Paul Horgan (New York: Farrar, Straus, and Giroux, 1972).

Mr. Horgan's portraits of Stravinsky are accurate, balanced, and affectionate. A few factual errors should be noted: the Stravinskys were not in Santa Fe in 1958; *Oedipus Rex* was not performed in Washington in 1960 (on a double bill with *The Nightingale*), but in January 1962, with *L'Heure Espagnol*; and the Stravinskys returned from Washington to New York on December 31, 1960, not January 1, 1961.

3. *Stravinsky,* by Francis Routh (London: Dent, 1975).

The main shortcoming of this brief survey is a result of its format. Stravinsky's music is more suited to a chronological approach than to one by category. Thus the chapter on the songs makes strange bedfellows of the pre-1920 Russian cycles and the songs from the 1950s and 1960s. *Pribaoutki* and the *Berceuses du Chat,* for example, belong to the context of *Renard* and *Les Noces,* the Shakespeare songs and *The Owl and the Pussy-Cat* to that of the serial music.

Still another criticism of the book's format concerns the questionable utility of a "personalia" which includes people not mentioned in the text (some of whom, moreover, are incorrectly described). Thus, Pierre Suvchinsky cannot be called a "close lifelong friend of Stravinsky," since the two did not meet until the composer was over forty, and they were not in communication at all between 1939 and 1956. Finally, the book contains factual errors. For instance, the statements that "Stravinsky's son Soulima . . . kept seeing his father as often as his professional activities permitted," and that "During the last summer at Evian (1970) [Theodore] saw [his father] daily." Although Soulima and his father lived in France less than one hundred miles apart in the summer of 1970, and, though both were on vacation, Soulima did not visit his father (or telephone to him, or send a letter or postcard). And Theodore saw his father at Evian only one day in four, as the nurses' records confirm.

4. *Igor Fyodorovich Stravinsky: A Practical Guide to Publications of His Music,* by René de Lerma (Kent State University Press, Ohio, 1974).

Almost every page of this most impractical guide is blighted with errors, both original and repeated from other books. A single example must suffice: Schoenberg is identified as a "co-composer" of the *Genesis* Suite in one place and as the "co-composer" of Stravinsky's *Babel* in another. (P. 147)

5. *The Stravinsky Festival of the New York City Ballet,* by Nancy Goldner (New York: Eakins Press, 1974).

The Stravinsky-Balanchine collaboration is the perspective in this attractive photograph album.

6. *Catherine and Igor Stravinsky: A Family Album*, by Theodore Stravinsky (London: Boosey & Hawkes, 1973).

Regrettably, Theodore Stravinsky's memoir does not include a portrait of his mother, a gifted painter and musician, a deeply thoughtful woman ("Life would be horrible if we knew exactly why it has been given to us," she wrote to her husband, November 10, 1937), and a kindly, wholly unselfish person, utterly incapable of meanness or jealousy ("I kiss Vera and hope she gets some rest," in another letter, March 4, 1936). Nor does Theodore's book throw any light on his father's apparent lack of generosity to his wife with money and with himself. Thus, she wrote to him on March 8, 1936, "I am so looking forward to the three days I'll have with you," expecting these days to be the only ones between January and late June. Here are some revealing excerpts from her other letters of the period:

> I've been without money for the last few days. There remain 3 fr. in my purse. (February 12, 1936)

> Dr. Rist came and wanted to see me. I said that I had no means of paying for the consultations. (March 1, 1936)

> Please send money . . . someday I'll free you from payment of all these large bills. (March 13, 1936)

> If you can manage, send 1900 francs, since there is still the bus, the porter, the tips on the train, and it's most unpleasant to travel with an empty purse. (March 21, 1936)

Stravinsky seems to have kept his terminally ill wife fully informed of his own minor ailments. She wrote to him, without sarcasm:

> My poor dear, how terrible that you still have this pharyngitis troubling you, and especially as you are straining your voice during rehearsals. (March 21, 1936)

> . . . Oh, the unpleasant peculiarities from which you are constantly suffering! But better this than something more serious. . . . We must suffer . . . Imagine having full health and also enjoying success in everything! (November 10, 1937)

Theodore Stravinsky's book contains a few inaccuracies. Thus, he writes that:

> Father had brought back from one of his journey's [sic] a collection of unpublished works and unfinished fragments of Pergolesi's things that Diaghilev had picked up in different European libraries,

and that

> a mutual confidence born of mutual admiration united the three great men, Diaghilev, Stravinsky, Picasso.

Stravinsky never had any "fragments of Pergolesi's things," but only manuscript copies of completed pieces, most of them already published.[1] And, so far as the trust and good will are concerned, during some of the composition of *Pulcinella*, Stravinsky was scarcely on speaking terms with Diaghilev, whom he was threatening to sue for performance fees, not paid since 1917, for *The Firebird* [2] and *Petrushka*.

Theodore Stravinsky recalls a journey in 1910 from Ustilug, Russia, to La Baule, Brittany, where, as he says, "we had taken [a dwelling] for the last weeks of summer" (though in fact the Stravinskys had moved to Chardon Jogny, near Vevey, by mid-August). But, to return to the journey, Theodore Stravinsky states that "after several hours jolting we were at Vladimir-Volynsk" (actually a seven-mile trip, always referred to by his father as a very brief excursion). "Then in the evening Kovel. . . . Next morning the little station, cool with an early autumn tang in the air" (but it was July 4) "and then the wheezing train to Warsaw. . . . In Berlin the whole staff of the Edition[s] Russe de Musique came to see Stravinsky off at the station" (even though Stravinsky's publisher at this date was Jurgenson, whose offices were in Moscow and Leipzig?). "Next stage Paris, and a night at the Hôtel d'Egypte. . . ." (In fact the Stravinskys spent three nights in Paris so that the composer and his wife could attend the last performance of *The Firebird*, on July 7, with Lopokova replacing Karsavina.) "At last La Baule," Theodore Stravinsky continues: "I can still hear the cry of the waffle-seller on the beach—'*Arrivez papas, arrivez mamans, faites plaisir à vos enfants*' " (a demonstration of amazing mnemonic powers for a child of three, the more so in that the language involved was foreign).

Theodore Stravinsky says that "Mina Svitalski . . . governess . . . was to stay the rest of her life with one or the other of us." The truth is that Mlle Svitalski, a woman of rare intelligence and a profound understanding of Stravinsky's character, was quickly jettisoned in California, first by Theodore's sister, then by his brother. The composer himself continued to support Mlle Svitalski, to the extent of paying for a room over a garage, rented for her from Jean Renoir, but she was obliged to earn her living as a dressmaker, which she succeeded in doing, thanks, in considerable measure, to the help of Maria Huxley.

Presumably referring to Stravinsky's California period, Theodore remarks that "circumstances later hindered Father from religious practice." Here it must be said that most of those who knew the composer in his last thirty years would be grateful for elucidation. Hollywood had two Russian Orthodox churches, and Stravinsky did not lack means of conveyance to either of them. Yet, during his three decades in California, he rarely attended church services, and never after 1951—for reasons that he confided to no one. When it becomes possible to write a full biography of Stravinsky, this question warrants examination in detail.

> 7. *The Unknown Country: A Life of Igor Stravinsky*, by Neil
> Tierney, 272 pp. (London: Robert Hale, 1977).

The "unknown," for this reviewer, is the rationale for the publication of a book crammed with errors, abominably written, and whose only effect can be to perpetuate an inane impression of the composer and his music. Almost everything in the volume is wrong, from the first sentence

> . . . in the bedroom of a New York hotel, Stravinsky died . . .

to the caption on the last page of illustrations:

> A water hearse carries Stravinsky's coffin across the Canal San Giovanni and Paolo en route to the church for the funeral service. Following it, in a motor boat, are his widow and son.

For the first, Stravinsky died at home and, for the second, the photograph shows the cortège in the lagoon (Venice has no "Canal San Giovanni and Paolo") after, not before, the funeral service. Stravinsky's widow is in a gondola, not a motorboat, and she is not accompanied by either of her husband's *two* sons.

One has to be profoundly unfamiliar with twentieth-century music to say that

> Written at a time when Stravinsky had become Parisian by adoption, *The Soldier's Tale* shows him trying out the vogue of flip, penny-whistle tunes cultivated by the group known as *Les Six.*

At the time of the *Soldat* (1918)—which had to wait six years before being staged in Paris precisely because it was considered to be "too Swiss"—Stravinsky, far from Parisian-minded, was planning to live in Rome. Furthermore, he was unaware of a vogue, if it existed, of "flip" tunes cultivated by *"Les Six,"* a name used for the first time in 1926. But the book's misinformation is too abundant to be compiled here, Mr. Tierney actually referring to *Renard* as a "suite . . . scored for thirteen wind instruments and percussion . . . ," crediting Monteux (confused in one place with Montreux) with introducing an "orchestral suite of *The Rite* . . ." to Boston, and saying that

> [Stravinsky] had begun in the Symphony in C, by imitating the grandiosity of nineteenth-century Russian composers.

Mr. Tierney probably means the Symphony in E-flat, but even then the description of Stravinsky's intentions would be false. Perhaps no more need be said of a book so frequently unintelligible:

> He read many Russian folk poems. Captivated by the sweeping sound of their language, he visualized, for future use, themes involving Russian dancing scenes based on the folk poetry of Pushkin's age. This ethnical rebirth persuaded the composer, in some measure, to reappraise the instrumentation for its realization.

8. *Stravinsky,* by Roger Nichols (The Open University. Milton Keynes, England, 1978).

This "correspondence text "is an excellent syllabus on examples of Stravinsky's early music (to 1926). As an instance of Nichols's originality of approach, he observes that in the first dance in *Le Sacre du Printemps:*

> At first sight there seems to be no pattern in the distribution of accents. . . . Taking the initial [eighth note] of 13–1 as a natural accent, we have . . . the following groups of [eighth notes]: 9, 2, 6, 3, 4, 5, 3. . . . These apparently random numbers make sense when split into two groups

$$
\begin{array}{cccc}
9 & 6 & 4 & 3 \\
\ & 2 & 3 & 5 \\
\end{array}
$$

> . . . the top line is decreasing, the bottom line is increasing, and by respectively decreasing and increasing amounts. The complete table of rhythmic values reads:

$$
\begin{array}{ccccc}
 & & 0 & & \\
 & 1 & & 1 & \\
 & 3 & 2 & & 1 \\
9 & 6 & & 4 & 3 \\
\hline
 & 2 & 3 & 5 & \\
 & 1 & & 2 & \\
 & & 1 & & \\
\end{array}
$$

Whether Stravinsky worked them out like this we shall probably never know. But the way two different rhythmic "orders" interfere with each other to produce apparent chaos is . . . a typically Stravinskyan notion.

It must be said that the "initial . . . natural accent" is not equivalent to the written ones, and that *some* first impressions are not of a chaotic distribution of the accents but of a logical pattern, partly because it is repeated. Two groups of dancers are involved in the ballet at this point, and in some way may have been associated in Stravinsky's mind with the two rhythmic "orders"—except that the choreographic accents, beginning an eighth ahead of the musical ones, form still another pattern, 7, 3, 3, 3.

9. *And Music at the Close: Stravinsky's Last Years*, by Lillian Libman (New York: Norton, 1972).

Miss Libman's memoir is marred by three shortcomings: she relies too heavily on fantasy and hearsay; she gives no indication of having understood anything about Stravinsky; and the majority of her statements are either factually wrong (totally or in part), or misleading in viewpoint and interpretation. For reasons of space, this review must be confined to only a few of the book's more than one thousand errors of fact, and must exclude all examples of the type that anyone even cursorily acquainted with the subject will be able to correct for himself. Thus, when Miss Libman writes that

> Between the time he began [*Les Noces*] in 1914 and the completion of the short score three years later, [Stravinsky] produced at least half a dozen other major pieces, including *Renard* and *The Soldier's Tale* . . . [P. 227]

a reader with even the sketchiest knowledge of twentieth-century music does not need to be told that those "half a dozen other major pieces" ("at least") are non-existent, and that *The Soldier's Tale* was completed a year after the "short score" of *Les Noces*.

Yet the book's legacy of simple misinformation will trouble future students of Stravinsky's life and work less than the concoctions of hearsay and invention, and than the assurance with which Miss Libman pronounces judgments on matters requiring expert opinion, such as music (as Eliot wrote, "The biographer ought to know a great deal about the art of his subject, if the subject is an artist"), the abilities of physicians whom she had never observed, and the "true" thoughts of one of the most subtle minds of the age.

Future readers of Miss Libman will be troubled, too, by the discrepancies between her account and the factual ones of other biographers. Thus, while she says in her book that

> . . . the truth . . . is that every day [in the winter of 1969–70, Stravinsky] withdrew a little more . . . [p. 365]

she wrote to Stravinsky's secretary, Marilyn Stalvey, February 4, 1970, that

> Everything seems to be working out and I do feel that if Maestro continues the way he is doing, there is a good likelihood that they'll go to Paris.

And, again, Miss Libman states that

> ... when I met Stravinsky at the Indianapolis airport [in June 1965],
> for the first time bringing a wheelchair along with the porter, my mind
> was made up that the concerts would be reduced to a minimum so
> long as I was handling them. [p. 185]

In the first place, Stravinsky had been using wheelchairs in airports
since 1962; in fact, she was with him in the Chicago airport, December
4, 1962, on which day he wrote in his diary: "$8 tip to porter for
wheelchair." But the truth is that Miss Libman was proposing more
concerts than ever for 1966 and beyond, and, as the records show,
pocketed handsome commissions for Stravinsky's engagements in
1967. On August 4, 1966, she telegraphed to Robert Paterson, Stravinsky's concert agent in London: "Stravinsky interested in four concerts
you proposed only [after] March 1967. He is now exclusively under
Hurok management. . . ." And, shortly after Indiana—where, in any
case, Stravinsky did not conduct—Miss Libman was in Chicago promoting new concerts for him, as is revealed in the *Chicago Tribune*,
February 10, 1966:

> Silas Edman, manager of the Chicago Symphony Orchestra . . . said
> yesterday he had been approached by Mr. Stravinsky's manager last
> summer "in the middle of the street" and asked to bring up the matter
> [of Stravinsky's engagement] with the Ravinia officials.

Future biographers will wonder, too, at the contradiction between
Miss Libman's asserted posture of deep reverence for Stravinsky and
her continual belittling of him, and of her pretense of affection for Mrs.
Stravinsky versus her actual animosity toward her—though Miss Libman is evidently unaware of this. Thus she told *The New York Times*
that the present reviewer "convinced Stravinsky of the validity of serial
music," as if Stravinsky were incapable of deciding that for himself.
And she wrote that the Stravinskys'

> [New York] apartment [was] impulsively purchased and occupied by
> its owner for one brief week . . . [p. 27]; . . . the apartment with which
> Mrs. Stravinsky had fallen in love after a five-minute tour . . . not hav-
> ing noticed that there wasn't enough electricity . . . that the air-con-
> ditioning was totally inadequate; that a new kitchen was necessary;
> that the plumbing had to be entirely refurbished . . . she signed [the
> check for it] without so much as a glance at its six figures. . . . [Pp.
> 380–1]

In fact Mrs. Stravinsky's purchase of the apartment, three months after
she began her search, was the result of long deliberation following the
careful inspection of more than a score of other residences, and she
visited the chosen apartment several times, had it appraised by her
attorney, and was advised by him as well as by others that it was both
ideal for her husband and a bargain at the price—which was considerably reduced in view of the necessity of certain repairs, greatly exaggerated by Miss Libman. Obviously Mrs. Stravinsky was perfectly
aware of the sum on the check she had written. And the owner was
Mrs., not Mr. Stravinsky, as Miss Libman knew (though she accuses
Mr. Stravinsky of being the impulsive purchaser). Finally, Miss Libman
herself, during most of the apartment-hunting period, was employed
far from New York, by a concert agency.
    Still on the subject of Miss Libman's belittling of Stravinsky, she
actually sides against him and with his son-in-law concerning a "gen-

eral release" that the latter [3] had demanded of Stravinsky, and that, according to Miss Libman (p. 360), he signed. (In fact the release that he signed, December 22, 1969, was a very different one.) Miss Libman describes the release as "the usual legal hodgepodge," and she denigrates Stravinsky for his

> tendency to argue about the minutest accounting details. . . . [But] whatever it was, the release was worded in such an unfortunate way that it made André sound as though he expected to be accused. [Pp. 358–9]

Yet this was a perfectly reasonable expectation, since, in August 1969, Marion and his wife, and Soulima Stravinsky and his wife, signed a contract with Stravinsky's lawyer of the time, William Montapert, to remove approximately $500,000 from Stravinsky's bank in Basle and to divide the sum 50 percent for Montapert, one-third of the remaining 50 percent for each of the children. Moreover, the money actually *was* removed, at least for a time.

> Miss Libman belittles Stravinsky in her statement:

> [At the beginning of 1970] the money I drew each week covered my transportation, cigarettes, and an occasional trip to the hairdresser's. (Mr. Hurok never believed it!) [p. 368]

But why tell Mr. Hurok the Stravinskys' personal business, especially since the story is intended to expose their lack of generosity? Furthermore, this duplicity often added to their burdens. For example, Miss Libman wrote that

> On April 6, 1970, Stravinsky was rushed to the Intensive Care Unit at Lenox Hill. . . . Theodore and Denise flew in from Geneva, and the world—represented by the members of the press with whom I dealt for the greater part of each day—prepared to say *adieu*. [P. 369]

Here Miss Libman's elation at the thought of being a spokesman to "the world" has caused her to forget that Stravinsky was admitted to the hospital under a false name and with strict orders from his wife that no report be given out, this in order to avoid the telegrams, letters, flowers, gifts that had overwhelmed her, and that had to be acknowledged, when he was hospitalized the year before. Now Miss Libman reveals that she spent "the greater part of each day" publicizing the Stravinskys' secret. (It must be said, too, that the wording implies that Stravinsky's son and daughter-in-law flew to New York on April 6, though in fact they came on April 17, by which time Stravinsky had long since been moved from Intensive Care to a private room.)

Miss Libman's largest hallucinations should be dispelled first. She writes:

> [I was Stravinsky's] traveling companion for most of his . . . Latin American engagements. [P. 12]

With rare exceptions during the last fifty years of his life, Stravinsky's traveling companion was his wife. Furthermore, Miss Libman was not with Stravinsky in Brazil at the time of his tours there, and not in Colombia, Peru, Chile, Argentina, or Venezuela on his visits to these countries, which comprised "most of his Latin American engagements."

Miss Libman's estimate as to the amount of time she spent "with Stravinsky" is not confirmed by the documents of his life:

> ... from July 1959 to ... April 6, 1971 ... I ... was, for the most part, close by [p. 11]; ... almost three-quarters of my time over twelve years was spent with Stravinsky or on matters that were his concern.... [P. 13]

"For the most part"? "Three-quarters of my time"? The truth is closer to about one-twentieth of these figures. During those twelve years, Miss Libman was in the vicinity of the composer for no more than 275 days, and never "with Stravinsky" in anything like the sense that the phrase implies (i.e., being in communication with him). Throughout her book, "with Stravinsky" should be translated to "in the employ of the Stravinskys." In 1967 and 1969, moreover, two of the four years concerning which she pretends to be an authority, she saw the composer on only twelve and eleven days respectively.

As for Miss Libman's claim that

> [I was the] writer of most of [Stravinsky's] performing contracts ... [P. 12]

the truth is that, between 1960 and 1967, the period to which she refers, she wrote about half, not "most," of his contracts. From the time that she met Stravinsky until his death, he conducted portions of approximately 131 concerts. Miss Libman was present at only 41 of these, having written the contracts for them and for 27 others which she did not attend.

Miss Libman also claims that

> I came to be ... occasionally his cook, his valet, his seamstress ... and, before his final illness, his "nurse." [P. 12]

But these occupations are entirely imaginary, unless pouring water over a tea bag qualifies one as a cook, and sewing on a button backstage makes one a seamstress. Nor was Miss Libman ever—not for two minutes, not at any time—Stravinsky's "nurse," unless fetching a Kleenex, watering the chrysanthemums, and switching the TV channels so accredits one. From January 1969 until his death, Stravinsky was constantly attended by professional nurses. Their record books, which account for every minute of that period, mention Miss Libman only once, and not as a nurses' aide.

Another of Miss Libman's imaginary occupations is that of having been Stravinsky's chauffeur:

> Stravinsky ... would sit up front with me while his wife caught a nap ... in the back seat. [P. 216]

The word "would" is an insidious device for making a single experience sound like routine procedure. The truth is, in this case, that Miss Libman drove the composer two or three times in this fashion, but against the two or three thousand times that Mrs. Stravinsky drove him, nor was he ever happy when anyone other than his wife was behind the wheel. Yet Miss Libman consistently implies that, during the period of her "association," Mrs. Stravinsky was always in the back seat, or background, or was occupied elsewhere, owing to which Miss Libman filled her place as Stravinsky's principal companion. Another example of this is Miss Libman's recollection that in Hollywood, in the summer of 1968,

... we went to one or two dinner parties, although [Stravinsky] tired quickly and would ask me to take him home in advance of the others. Once there, he would sink into bed and either reach for his book or doze until the sound of the car arriving with his wife and Robert awakened him. [Pp. 340-1]

The facts are that Stravinsky attended only one dinner party in the summer of 1968 (except for small dinners at his daughter's and at Lawrence Morton's); that he left not from fatigue, but, as he told his wife, from boredom; that Mrs. Stravinsky returned with another guest about twenty minutes after her husband; and that "Robert" did not attend at all, as the host, Mr. Jack Quinn, has testified.

Miss Libman's "we" serves the same purpose as her "would." Thus she writes that

[In September 1968, in New York] Mrs. Stravinsky prepared a good many meals ... but otherwise we ordered from room service. [Three friends] came to visit. ... There was no movie-going, although Stravinsky did venture down to dinner once or twice. [P. 348]

But Miss Libman was not living with the Stravinskys; and in fact she seldom saw them, hence her "we" should be read as "they." Also, Stravinsky visited with more than a score of friends in New York in September 1968, he went to the movies and even to the theater (*Plaza Suite*), and he dined out several times at Passy, a restaurant new to him.

The more preposterous of Miss Libman's fantasies, however, are those that are intended to create a picture of intimacy which did not exist. Thus Stravinsky would have been extremely surprised to read that

... what began as a professional relationship between Stravinsky and myself, involving my functions as personal manager and press representative, developed into a privileged position. [P. 12]

In actuality Miss Libman's "relationship" with Stravinsky was always indirect, her only access to him being through his wife or through this reviewer. For a glimpse of the relationship in action, the following story, reported in the *Mexico DF News*, August 7, 1960, is typical of her management of Stravinsky's "public relations"—as Miss Libman frankly admits, saying that the Mexican engagement, "Stravinsky's first return ... after a ten-year absence" (in fact he conducted concerts there in the 1950s) "established a work pattern for the future." [P. 115]

STRAVINSKY A HARD MAN TO SEE

Immediately upon her arrival we contacted Mrs. Liebman [sic] and tried to get an interview with the famous maestro. Mrs. Liebman told us that day (Monday afternoon) we would get an interview immediately after the press conference scheduled for Tuesday at 5 P.M. in his hotel.

"Jamen, please come Wednesday at 5 P.M., maestro is very tired." So we arrived at the hotel and announced our arrival. A gentleman told us we should wait twenty minutes and Stravinsky would receive us. A few minutes later we took the elevator up, rang the doorbell and were met by Mrs. Liebman again.

"Jamen, please come in, sit down. The maestro will not be long. Would you like something to drink—(insisting)—whiskey? brandy?"

"O, well, brandy, please." We warmed the cup in the palm of our hand and Mrs. Liebman made conversation: "Jamen (she kept pronouncing our name wrong [4]), do you remember Rossi-Lemeni . . . ?" Time flies on as we sip our drink. No sign of the maestro. "Well, ma'am, the maestro is not here and you have something to do. Will you give me a formal appointment?"

"Jamen, please come Friday at 9:30 P.M."

Friday came and we were at the hotel. We saw Mrs. Liebman come out of the elevator.

"Jamen, the maestro begs you to excuse him, but he was suddenly called to the auditorium for rehearsals of Sunday's concert.[5] Maestro Stravinsky says will you come Saturday at 12:30?"

Saturday, 12 o'clock. Mrs. Liebman comes in from the street and we hear her tell an employee of the hotel: "In about fifteen minutes please go up to Room 601 with Mr. Farrill." Fifteen minutes later we were taken up to Room 601 and were surprised to see that Stravinsky was not in. Mrs. Liebman explained later:

"Jamen, don't you understand? Maestro Stravinsky never grants an interview to anyone."

Apparently feeling sentimental, Miss Libman describes a night in Stravinsky's home in Los Angeles some five years before his death.

I bent to kiss him good night, and this time I could not keep from holding his small frame close for a moment. . . . Light was beginning to seep into Los Angeles, and I went back into the office and sat there watching it grow brighter for an hour or so. . . . I went downstairs to make some coffee and only then realized that my face was wet. [P. 278]

But is it possible to be unaware of one's tears for as long as "an hour or so," especially if one is at the same time watching a light grow brighter? Miss Libman offers no explanation for this premature Pietà, but uses it to suggest a profound closeness between herself and "the maestro" that did not exist. Other examples are found throughout the volume:

He would look up from his porridge just long enough to give me a kiss [p. 365]; . . . he put his arms around me and kissed me twice. . . . [P. 348]

The point here is simply that Miss Libman has attached undue significance to Stravinsky's most perfunctory embracings, his habitual Russian form of greeting, bestowed on everyone from his gardener to his cook.

Still another of Miss Libman's displays of the depth of her devotion is in her reference to

. . . my own bed, set up seven days before [Stravinsky's death] in the "office" . . . for I wanted to sit with the Master. [P. 19]

The facts are that the bed was the Stravinskys', not Miss Libman's, and that it served other guests as well; that Miss Libman, who was substituting as a secretary at the time, slept on it for only two nights; and, finally, that she was rarely even in the apartment during the week and never sat "with the Master."

But the most preposterous of all of Miss Libman's claims is that

The final threescore days of Stravinsky's life were lived for him by his wife, Robert, and me. [P. 379]

Absolutely nothing would surprise Stravinsky more than to learn that he had lived his last two months to any extent whatever through Miss Libman. At no time did *anyone* live Stravinsky's life "for" him, of course, but, then, Miss Libman does not seem to understand that a man's most profound living may take place on his deathbed, as in the case of Ivan Ilyich.[6] The truth is that Miss Libman rarely even saw Stravinsky during "the final threescore days." She had virtually disappeared from the Stravinskys' world during the seven months before that period, not having been in their employ between June 27, 1970, and February 8, 1971. Then, from February 8 until the end (April 6), practically all of her time was spent in the new apartment—rather than in the Essex House, where, except for two weeks that the composer spent in the hospital, the Stravinskys were still living. It is for this reason that Miss Libman saw the composer only occasionally, dropping in for a moment while he was at lunch, or in the early evening before his music hour. And since he was largely unaware of her functions during this period, it made not the slightest difference to him who performed them.

Miss Libman is misguided regarding every aspect of her subject. She writes:

> ... (What had ... printed quarrels to do with [Stravinsky] after all, who was really concerned only with music?) ... [P. 173]

But all of the closer acquaintances of Stravinsky shared the knowledge of at least one of his idiosyncrasies, which was that, in countless files and volumes of scrapbooks, he carefully documented his numerous and lifelong "printed quarrels." One such folder, for example, is headed: "Hermann Scherchen: His Hypocrisy and His Lies"; another, "*Folie d'E. Ansermet*"; and still another, "Olin Downes's Incompetence."

Then, too, one wonders how Miss Libman can have spent any time in Stravinsky's company and still say that he "placed not a financial but rather a historical value on [his] archives" (p. 330). The truth is that Stravinsky placed an exact financial value on every salable item in them, as autograph and manuscript dealers could have told her. On the other hand, the very thought of "history" might have induced him to destroy them, as he began to do in 1965, while moving them to a new house. At that time, more than one observer saw him dig into this "historic" material, read something, then burn it. If the composer had considered the matter, and if he had had an opportunity, he would, more than likely, have made an *auto-da-fé* of, at least, his personal papers.

Miss Libman goes on to report, however, that, in 1970, Stravinsky's children were

> highly disturbed at the news that the manuscripts had been put on the world market [p. 381]

even though the world market is where they had always been, having been put there by Stravinsky himself. As early as 1915, he had wanted to sell the manuscript of *The Firebird* to Otto Kahn. Misia Sert wrote to

Stravinsky at about the same time, saying: "I will make a cover for your *Firebird* score, since this seems to help with our contemporary Maecenases." He did sell it two years later—for 8,000 Swiss francs, an enormous sum at the time—to an oilionaire. All of his life, Stravinsky disposed of his manuscripts at every opportunity, and the famous gifts to Werner Reinhart of the scores of *Histoire du Soldat* and *Noces* were actually sales, as the Reinhart correspondence reveals. Not only was the majority of Stravinsky's manuscripts sold before his death, moreover, but his elder son had been a commission-earning party to many of these transactions. In a letter of March 1, 1950, the composer instructs this son to send the manuscripts of *Perséphone*, the Piano Concerto, *Capriccio*, the Violin Concerto, and *Mavra* to New York, where it is hoped that purchasers can be found, and, in a letter of June 15, 1950, Stravinsky lists manuscripts, with minimum prices, that he wants this same son to try to sell. In a letter to his younger son, August 15, 1952, Stravinsky enclosed a check marked "commission" for the sale of the manuscript of *Mavra*. Writing on May 20, 1964, to Adriana Panni, in Rome, Stravinsky reminds her that "I gave the manuscripts of *Agon* and *Canticum Sacrum* to my son Theodore, who sold them to you some years ago because he needed money."

How could anyone claiming a twelve-year "association" with Stravinsky fail to know what languages he spoke?, yet the reader is told:

> . . . a "non-American" cook . . . was engaged. . . . Her complete lack of English, French, or German (the Stravinskys made their needs known to her in a mixture of Polish, Russian and Hungarian) . . . [p. 211]

In fact the Stravinskys could not speak any Hungarian or any Polish. (In 1940, before the five-year reign of Lizaveta Alexandrovna, they did have a Polish cook for two months, but they conversed with her in Russian.) The "non-American" cook was a Czech who spoke German with her employers, since she herself did not speak the three languages that Miss Libman mentions last. Also, how can Miss Libman declare that Stravinsky's "brand of English prose [was] enriched and colorful [sic] with his . . . Russian grammatical constructions" (p. 13) when she was unable even to recognize a Russian grammatical construction?

Still assuming the role of linguist, Miss Libman writes that

> [Stravinsky] always sounded better and more literary in languages over whose idiom he had a more complete command than over English. Robert, therefore, created a style that he felt conveyed the quality of Stravinsky's exact expressions. [P. 240]

In truth, "Robert" recognized, as have most others quoting Stravinsky, that no such style could be created.[7] But although his own English in later years was always superior to that of his collaborations with this writer or with anyone else, Stravinsky's writings and conversations could not be published without the assistance, inevitably injurious as it was, of another hand. At the time of Miss Libman's "association," Russian was the only other language over which Stravinsky had a more complete command than English, but since she neither spoke nor understood his other languages, one wonders how she is able to pronounce judgment on his use of them. Stravinsky's German was reportedly more correct than his French (which was never idiomatic), and few of his German interviewers fail to comment on his expert command of that language: *"Er spricht sehr gewandt Deutsch, nur mit dem leichten Akzent des Russen"* (*Telegram-Zeitung*, Munich, November 11, 1930). The *Münchner Neueste Nachrichten*, November 13, 1930, after noting the manuscript on the music rack of the piano in his rooms at the Bayerischen Hof, reported that *"Professor Stravinsky begrüsst uns in bestem deutsch, ungezwungen und selbstverständlich gehen ihm die deutschen Worte vom Mund, fügen sich zu wohlgefaster, scharf pointeierter Rede."* But Stravinsky lived in the English-speaking world longer than he did in the French, and, late in life, he read and wrote in English more regularly and more easily than he did in French. Of the more than seventy Simenon *romans* that he read in his last years, for example, by preference all but five were in English translations. Stravinsky's English, in his later years was inventive, amazingly resourceful in vocabulary, too cosmopolitan in grammar. It is·for the last reason that his writings and conversations could not be published without the assistance, however regrettable, of another hand. But what makes Miss Libman think that to sound "more literary" is to "sound better"?

At one point Miss Libman assures the reader that

> [Stravinsky] regarded his [conductor's] career as a terrible waste of time. There was only one thing *he* wanted to do: stay home and compose. [P. 110]

But here Miss Libman should be allowed to refute herself:

> [Stravinsky] was one of the greatest hams in the history of the theater. . . . Furthermore, he was fond of saying that he *liked* to perform. Some evidence of the enjoyment he derived from treading the boards . . . emerged during every engagement within my recollection. [P. 124]

And the truth is found in countless letters, such as the following from Stravinsky to Ansermet, January 24, 1927: *"Le Bon Dieu ne m'a pas privé de talent d'exécuteur, et je ne voudrais pas me priver de cette joie."*
Miss Libman writes that Stravinsky

> was capable of standing and conducting continuously for . . . forty-five minutes . . . although . . . the music usually involved . . . did not impose the strain on him that his later compositions did. [P. 233]

But Stravinsky *never* conducted his later compositions (*The Flood, Abraham and Isaac, Variations, Requiem Canticles*), which a concert agent dealing with his programs should know.
Miss Libman is very far afield when she writes that

> Stravinsky had long before entered the lists as a touring artist, for purely financial reasons. Between 1922 . . . and 1927 . . . [this] kept him so busy that he produced little more than one work per year, a very small output for this most prolific master. He composed chiefly during the summer months, and during the remainder of the year appeared as piano soloist in his *Sonata, Serenade, Concerto,* and *Capriccio,* although he also began to conduct a certain amount after 1923. . . . He did some concert traveling in the early forties as well . . . and then resumed this activity in the fifties, covering a great deal of insignificant territory. [P. 88]

The truth is that Stravinsky became a touring artist as much for artistic as for financial reasons; that he composed seven works in the five years between 1922 and 1927 (*Mavra,* Octet, Piano Concerto, Sonata, Serenade, *Oedipus Rex, Apollo*), versus only nine works for the next ten years; that he was never prolific (considering his sixty-five-year lifespan as a composer and taking Richard Strauss, for example, as the measure of a prolific one); that he could not have appeared as piano soloist in the as-yet-unwritten *Capriccio;* that he played the Sonata and Serenade only a few times in his entire life; that, despite his forty appearances as piano soloist in the Concerto, his principal concertizing even between 1922 and 1927, was as a conductor; that his concerts in the early 1940s number almost as many as those in the entire Libman period; and that the "insignificant territory" which he "covered" in the 1950s includes six appearances in Paris (versus none there during the Libman period), two in Vienna (versus none, etc.), and many more concerts before Libman than after in London, New York, and Rome. These cities are world music capitals. It was under Miss Libman's aegis that Stravinsky was appearing in Bogotá, Auckland, Pretoria, etc.

Concerning Stravinsky's medical history and his physicians, Miss Libman writes that

> The Los Angeles doctors now seemed to think that the attacks [in the summer of 1969] were due to a flare-up of his old tuberculosis. . . . But after he left the West Coast no such medical proof (at least that I know of) was ever offered when he suffered similar congestion. [P. 353]

The Los Angeles doctors did not "seem to think" but had made tests and found proof positive of tuberculosis. In New York, the same tests showed the same result, as Miss Libman could have learned from the nurses' record books of September 26 and 30, in the Plaza Hotel, New York, when chest X-rays taken by Dr. E. Riley revealed an active tubercular cavity in the upper apex. In fact, the final "negative" result was not obtained until December 1, 1969. But Miss Libman was not in California, and she was rarely near the scene in New York.

Miss Libman writes, too, that

> Dr. Edell [sic] had been treating [Stravinsky] . . . ever since . . . the Aldous Huxleys had first called the Stravinsky's [sic] attention to him in the forties . . . [and] was far and away the best of the doctors who treated Stravinsky, at least during my association with the composer. [P. 312]

The truth is that the connection with Dr. Edel began through Catherine d'Erlanger and not with any suggestion from the Huxleys, Dr. Edel's medical philosophy being at the polar opposite of any that they, with their faith-healing, experimental, and wholly unorthodox approach to medicine, would ever have recommended. The name, furthermore, is "Edel," nor would Miss Libman's error seem to be merely typographical since she repeats it in every reference to him. (She may have confused the spelling with that of Los Angeles's Ebell Theater.) To anyone who knew the Stravinskys, "Edell" seems strange indeed, the doctor having been one of the composer's close friends as well as a time-to-time physician. But how can Miss Libman presume to pass judgment on Stravinsky's doctors? Of the sixty or so who treated him during her "association," she met no more than a few and was not present during medical examinations. Nor did she observe Dr. Edel in his role as physician, at least during any of Stravinsky's serious illnesses, when other observers began to be concerned about the medical treatment Stravinsky was receiving. (The Stravinskys dismissed Dr. Edel in December 1967, for having failed to discover that a thrombosis, and not gout, was the cause of severe pains in the left hand, and for having persisted in the gout prognosis for a month and a half before consulting a specialist.) Among Edel's colleagues who treated Stravinsky during some of the same years are the doctors Aschner, Bernstein, Corday, Disraeli, Dreyfus, Elek, Engelman, Epstein, Garbat, Glass, Goldberg, Grossman, Gunzburg, Ilfeld, Jaffe, Knauer, Joseph, Landowski, Linsman, Mantchik (Thomas Mann's physician at the same time), Marcus, Mauer, Pinkus, Rothenberg, Rubin, Schiff, Seletz, Waitzfelder, and Wallerstein, none of whom is mentioned by Miss Libman. Furthermore, in the only period in Hollywood when Stravinsky was under constant medical care, and when Miss Libman was also somewhere near the scene (July 20 to September 7, 1968), his chief physicians were the doctors Corday, Bernstein, Gold, Gabor, Glass, Ilfeld, Knauer, Marcus, Pincus, Rothenberg, and Weinstein, none of whom appears in her "personal memoir." (Dr. Weinstein is one of the world's leading hematologists, while Dr. Corday was chosen in 1975 as the only doctor from California in a group of physicians representing the United States in a conference in Peking.)

Miss Libman's narrative about

> installing the Stravinskys ... at the Plaza Hotel ... (Nixon's permanent residence had finally driven them out of the Pierre) [p. 353]

is wholly untrue. In fact she was not even in New York when the Stravinskys, accompanied by a nurse, Miriam Pollack, "installed" themselves at the Plaza. Yet, for good measure, Miss Libman says that she met the Stravinskys' airplane. And, so far from being driven out of the Pierre by the Nixon staff, which was in the hotel in 1968, the Stravinskys lived in the Pierre from April to July 1969, the longest period that they had ever spent there.

The dangers of hearsay history are exemplified in Miss Libman's assurance that

> ... nothing much happened in October [1969], either. And when, no longer Stravinsky's attorney, Montapert visited Mrs. Stravinsky at the Essex House on the twentieth. ... [P. 358]

Montapert's *three* visits took place on September 19 and 20, in the Plaza Hotel, Suite 1270–71–73, not in the Essex House. Also, Montapert *was* Stravinsky's attorney at that time (and until October 3), though, clearly, he was representing not Stravinsky but his son-in-law on these visits. Miss Libman's "nothing much happened" is simply a way of saying that she was nowhere around. (She was in Texas during the first part of October, going from there to Los Angeles on the 19th; but elsewhere—page 349—she admits, "I was not with Stravinsky very much in 1969.") Actually, a great deal "happened in October 1969." The Trapezoid Corporation, owner of Stravinsky's manuscripts and archives, was formed at a meeting on October 6, and, on the 14th, the Stravinskys moved to an apartment in the Essex House. Also, he received numerous visitors, including the Archimandrite of San Francisco and the daughter of Joseph Stalin.

Miss Libman incorrectly recalls that

> [At Muncie . . . Stravinsky] . . . sat onstage in an armchair and Robert
> stood at a lectern conducting the discussion. . . . I recall that a student
> who had obviously read some Stravinsky/Craft asked his [sic] opinion
> of Richard Strauss as a composer. Answer: "He was a good conductor.
> . . . I do not like his major works and I do not like his minor works."
> [P. 186]

The problem here is that Miss Libman has confused the occasion with
one that she did not attend in Austin, Texas, three months earlier.
Stravinsky was onstage in Austin, not Muncie, and his onstage companion was his wife, not "Robert." In fact, the most memorable moment of the composer's appearance was when he turned to his wife
and asked her for the English translation of "*znatok*," to which she
replied "*connoisseur*," pronouncing the word in the French rather than
in the English way, so that the students laughed. The Strauss question
was asked in Austin, too, not Muncie, and by a German exchange
student who made it evident that she had not read any Stravinsky/Craft.
But since the entire scene was filmed (April 2) by CBS Television and
shown on prime time, millions of viewers will recall this. The Strauss
incident, moreover, has already been told correctly in numerous books
published long before Miss Libman's. Here, for example, is Oscar Levant, writing in 1967:

> I watched him on television . . . at the University of Texas. A student
> asked for his opinion of Richard Strauss. With his charming, lethal
> smile, the impish octogenarian stated that he disliked all of Strauss's
> works, major and minor.

Miss Libman writes that

> [Stravinsky] conducted [Le Sacre] for the last time in Mexico City in
> April 1961. [P. 197]

In actuality Stravinsky conducted Le Sacre for the last time on September 24, 1961, in Stockholm—though in Warsaw, May 31, 1965, he
conducted parts of Le Sacre for CBS television.

Miss Libman states that

> In June [1964, the Stravinskys] took off for London. . . . A return to
> Ravinia and then another transatlantic flight to Jerusalem were accom-
> plished before they saw Hollywood again at the end of August. [P.
> 197]

In actuality the Stravinskys were in Hollywood twice between London
and Jerusalem, July 5–16 and July 20–August 14.

Miss Libman assures the reader that

> On September 6 [1965, in New York] I put the trio on a Lufthansa
> flight for Berlin. [P. 250]

But Stravinsky visited Berlin for the last time in 1964, by Air France
from Paris, and with Miss Libman nowhere around.

Miss Libman writes:

> ... Boulez, whom [Stravinsky] had met some years before through [Pierre] Suvchinsky.... [P. 104]

Boulez met Stravinsky at Virgil Thomson's in New York during the period of seventeen years when Stravinsky and Suvchinsky were not on speaking terms. The meeting is accurately described by Mr. Thomson in a book published many years before Miss Libman's.

According to Miss Libman

> [In Washington, March 31, 1948] Auden brought the rather startling news that he had a co-librettist, Chester Kallman—an announcement not anticipated by Stravinsky on any occasion, according to Robert. [P. 102]

"Robert's" and Stravinsky's book *Memories and Commentaries* (1960) publishes the letter from Auden to Stravinsky, January 16, 1948, announcing the collaboration of Chester Kallman. But it would seem that Miss Libman did not read Stravinsky's "Conversation" books. It is also apparent, on page after page of her book, that neither did she read his autobiography and *Poetics of Music*. She writes, for example:

> "Music is powerless to express anything at all." This statement, made at Harvard during his delivery of the Charles Eliot Norton Lectures ... [P. 190]

The statement, the most widely quoted that Stravinsky ever uttered, occurs in his autobiography, not in his lectures.

And Music at the Close reveals that Miss Libman is unfamiliar not only with Stravinsky's character, but also with the most elementary facts of his life. She recalls a conversation in which Stravinsky referred to a time

> when he and his younger brother Guri were small boys and living at the Stravinsky summer residence in Ustilug.... [P. 216]

But Stravinsky was not in Ustilug as a small boy and no Stravinsky residence existed there. And she assures the reader that Stravinsky

> fled communism, and later the world the Nazis tried to create ... [and] chose [to live in] the United States.... [P. 33]

But Stravinsky did not flee communism, which was not yet available to flee from when he left Russia in 1910. To those who made the same mistake, he used to say: "I am an émigré from the Tsars, not the Soviets." (*Time*, July 26, 1948) Also, and regrettably, he did not flee "the world the Nazis tried to create" but was welcome in the Axis countries. When he came to the United States in September 1939 to lecture and give concerts, it was with every intention of returning to France. The events of May 1940 caused him to change his mind.

Miss Libman frequently neglects to tell the reader that she has not seen the contents of documents that she pretends to be revealing. Thus she writes that

the [new will] [8] differed from the one of a month earlier only in . . .
the omission of André's name (although this could in no way affect
him—he was Milène's husband and what was hers was his . . .) . . . .
[P. 356]

Here Miss Libman misses the point of the change in wills, which is
that if Milène were to die before her husband, he would receive nothing. Miss Libman goes on to report that

> in every will from 1967 on, Robert had a status comparable to that of
> each of Stravinsky's children. . . . [P. 356]

The wills bequeath one-ninth to "Robert," two-ninths to each of the
children. But, of the differences among the several wills, Miss Libman
never had an inkling. She was not a witness to Stravinsky's first will,
as she claims (p. 355), nor even of the first within the period of her
"association," that one having been signed on April 26, 1960.[9] She did
witness a will in 1966, about which she wrongly states that "it had
been a new experience for [Mrs. Stravinsky] as well" (p. 355).

Miss Libman does not even observe Stravinsky's culinary habits
correctly:

> . . . When I knew him [Stravinsky] did not take any unusual interest
> in exotic dishes. . . . He had already arrived at the stage where he
> chose broiled or poached seafoods or lamb. . . . [P. 210]

The truth is that Stravinsky was enjoying tours gastronomiques as late
as 1965. (The testimony of David Oppenheim, the New York University
Dean who dined with Stravinsky in Saulieu in May of that year, would
destroy Miss Libman's "poached seafoods or lamb" theory.) The composer's favorite restaurant during the time of the Libman "association,"
and the last one he was to visit in Los Angeles (1969), was the Luau,
which specialized in the "exotic." Moreover, one of his favorite dishes
was a fiery couscous, prepared by his daughter. At home, Stravinsky
ate Russian cutlets much more frequently than lamb, while the only
seafoods that he ever savored—besides saumon fumé—were crusta-
ceans and bivalves,[10] which Mrs. Stravinsky procured at the Santa
Monica pier twice weekly during the season.

From Libman's description of the Stravinsky California household,
many of the composer's friends have wondered if she had ever even
been there. For example, she says that one of the sofas in Stravinsky's
house had

> a rare Coptic textile . . . with strange hieratic-looking figures in black
> and ochre decorat[ing] the back of [it], antimacassar-fashion. [P. 204]

The "rare Coptic textile" was an inexpensive linen purchased in a store
on La Cienega Boulevard in Los Angeles, and the "hieratic-looking
figures" are brass rubbings of knights in black armor of the popular
"Sir Sampson Meverill" design. Stravinsky was fond of Coptic art, and
he carefully framed the three tiny swatches of cloth that he had. (Would
anybody use a Coptic textile—all of them are "rare," of course—as an
antimacassar?) Her description of his workroom is also inaccurate:

> On top of [a cabinet containing his portfolios of sketches] stood his
> bust in bronze. . . . [the room also contained] photographs of Weber,
> Schubert, Mendelssohn . . . an Italian carved-wood hand, holding an
> electric bulb in the form of a torch. . . . [Pp. 205–6]

The cabinet was reserved exclusively for *published* scores, as can be
seen from a photograph of it in Arnold Newman's *Bravo Stravinsky* (p.
49). The "photographs" of Weber and Schubert are drawings, these
composers having died even before the discovery of the daguerreotype.
And the "Italian carved-wood hand" is the well-known prop from Cocteau's *La Belle et la Bête*, made by him in France (not Italy) and immediately identified by his trademark star—from which an arm, as well
as the "hand," protrudes.

But the following remark is the most revealing of her *faux pas* in
this domain:

> [In August 1968, for] a friend's birthday that was traditionally cele-
> brated at 1218 North Wetherly . . . a substitute "chef" had been sum-
> moned . . . and she turned out to be a lady. . . . [P. 346]

The "chef" who "turned out to be a lady" had been working for the
Stravinskys sporadically since 1963, when they borrowed her from Dr.
Edel. She worked for the Stravinskys more regularly after 1964, the
year of the death of her former employer, Cole Porter, and it would
have been impossible to "frequent" the Stravinsky household, as Miss
Libman implies she had, and not have known that perfect lady, Sarah
Robin.

On the same subject, Miss Libman informs the reader that

> [Stravinsky] knew little about vintage wines. . . . [P. 210] André [Mar-
> ion] appeared to have more reliable knowledge of . . . wine than the
> Stravinskys. Mrs. Stravinsky was the only member of the trio who
> knew anything about wines at all. . . . [P. 281]

These incorrect statements apparently irritated Stravinsky's daughter
more than any others in the book, since she wrote to Miss Libman,
October 10, 1972:

> On the contrary my father was a connoisseur of wines . . . and André
> had always been impressed by his father-in-law's knowledge. . . .
> André did not know more than father did. . . .

(Miss Libman, who could barely tell white wine from red, answered,
characteristically: "I have to stand on my impression here.") But why
did Miss Libman not consult those friends of Stravinsky who knew
wines—the Marquis Lur-Saluces of Château Yquem, for one, or, closer
to home, Louis, the Monégasque vintner on Santa Monica Boulevard
from whom Stravinsky purchased not only his *grandes années* château
wines but also his *piquettes*? Or why did she not consult some of the
written material on the subject, such as Janet Flanner's *New Yorker*
profile ("Stravinsky is a connoisseur of claret, which he buys in the
barrel at Bordeaux and has bottled for his special use . . ."); or Nicolas
Nabokov's description (in *Old Friends and New Music*) of Stravinsky
the host ("What would you like to drink for lunch? What about a
Mouton Rothschild 1937?"); or any of the countless reports in newspapers written by those who had observed that Stravinsky always traveled with his own Château Latour or Haut-Brion (see, for example, the
Cleveland Press, February 20, 1937, which pictures him "hastily gulp-

ing [from the] private stock of wine that he carries with him"). In 1971 and 1972, *Esquire* posthumously designated Stravinsky and Cole Porter as outstanding connoisseurs of wine, partly on the testimony of cooks, headwaiters, and friends who dined with them. (Not only was Stravinsky a keen wine-taster, but he was also knowledgeable about wine-making—chaptalization and so forth—he had an eye for ullage, and, in addition to collecting the great years of the great clarets, he kept a shelf of *marc*.)

That Miss Libman did not witness most of the scenes she describes is of no importance in the case of a tale such as the following (though writers are expected to verify statements even of this sort):

> [The Stravinskys' Cadillac] loaded down to the ground ... [was] driven East at ... an average speed of a hundred miles per hour.... Later Ed Allen drove it back, similarly loaded. [P. 339]

The Stravinskys' car (driven by Mr. Ronnie Knox) left Hollywood on September 2, 1968, and met the composer's flight at the Newark Airport on the night of September 8. (It is self-evidently impossible to drive a car "loaded to the ground" at an average speed of a hundred miles an hour.) In October, the Cadillac was driven from New York to Florida, and, in November, totally empty, from there to California, not by Mr. Allen but by Hideki Takami.

Miss Libman's fabricating seems to grow in relation to her distance from the scene. For example, even though she was far from Princeton during the premiere there of the *Requiem Canticles*, she does not scruple to report that, on this occasion

> Dr. Robert Oppenheimer ... expressed the wish that the *Requiem Canticles* be performed as part of the memorial service that would be held when his own death occurred. [Pp. 296–7]

It scarcely needs to be said that Dr. Oppenheimer was not so tactless as to express any such wish at that time. (At some date after the concert, he did express this wish in a letter, with the instruction that it be opened only after his death; the day following this sad event, which occurred on February 18, 1967, Mrs. Oppenheimer opened the envelope and gave it to Nicolas Nabokov, who informed Stravinsky of the contents.)

The Princeton concert, according to Miss Libman, was

> arranged by Robert, who applied himself, immediately after Louisville, to securing the sponsorship. [P. 296]

"Robert" had nothing to do with "securing the sponsorship," which had been established more than a year before in a contract drawn up by Stravinsky's lawyer, Montapert. But surely Miss Libman, as a booking agent, must realize that such concerts are not arranged on three weeks' notice (Louisville having taken place on September 17, Princeton on October 8)!

Yet Miss Libman freely describes and judges incidents that took place when she was in other parts of the country:

> On the day of the recording [New York, October 11, Stravinsky] re-

mained in bed in the morning, and Robert departed to begin the sessions, reporting, on his arrival at the studio, that the composer would be there "later." ... Mrs. Stravinsky [telephoned] that her husband was not well enough to come. ... Robert himself telephoned [to her], had a rapid and intense conversation in French, and around five o'clock a grim and silent Stravinsky appeared, escorted by his wife and Ed Allen ... He [sic] remained only for a brief period. ... One of the engineers, and a musician with whom I spoke later were unanimous in their impression that Stravinsky's attitude clearly showed he was there against his will. ... And I am sure ... that the "forcing" on Robert's part was entirely motivated by the knowledge that if the composer were *not* present, there would be no more Stravinsky records, and consequently no Craft records either. [Pp. 298–9]

To base a story, such as this one, solely on the "unanimous" impressions of two bystanders seems somewhat dubious. But the report is entirely wrong. Stravinsky did not remain in bed on the morning of the recording session, but went to Dr. Lewithin (at 11:00) and to Dr. Temple (at 12:00), both of whom pronounced him fit and able to fly to California the next morning. At 1:30, the Stravinskys received a visit from the Isaiah Berlins, with whom, but for the recording session, Stravinsky would have spent part of the afternoon. Moreover, it was Mrs. Stravinsky who objected to her husband's attendance at the session, the composer himself having anticipated the recording of his new work with great interest, as the large letters with which he entered the event in his calendar-diary suggest. Nor was her husband's *health* the reason for Mrs. Stravinsky's objection, or she would certainly not have allowed him to fly to California only twelve hours later. Her quarrel was with the Artists and Repertory Department of Columbia Records, which, she felt, had humiliated the composer by "forcing" him to record his Mass as a condition to the recording of the *Canticles* by "Robert" (Stravinsky being technically unable to conduct this new work). When Mrs. Stravinsky informed Columbia's John McClure that her husband would not record the Mass, McClure requested that the composer merely listen from the control room while "Robert" recorded it, so that the performance could be advertised as "supervised by the composer." McClure dispatched a limousine to fetch the Stravinskys.

"Robert," of course, was well aware that if he had *not* urged Stravinsky to come, then he, "Robert," would have been criticized for keeping the composer away in order to do all of the recording himself. But, fortunately, the incident had a happy conclusion, which, for some reason, Miss Libman omits. Suffering no ill effects from his attendance at the session, Stravinsky acquired a recording of the *Canticles* that was to remain one of his most cherished possessions to the end of his life. But one final rectification of Miss Libman's account is necessary. "Craft's records"—meaning Columbia's Schoenberg series—had been terminated by the company's sales department more than a year before this incident.

It is strange, too, that Miss Libman chooses to describe another incident that she did not witness at still another recording session. She begins:

When Stravinsky recorded in Hollywood, the sessions were usually held in a wooden building on Highland Avenue. ... [P. 219]

The sessions were rarely held there, most of them taking place in Columbia's own studio on Sunset Boulevard, and, before that, at Radio Recorders on Melrose. She continues:

> [During the *Pulcinella*] . . . a wind player made an error, which Stravinsky corrected sharply. Robert said something in an undertone; Stravinsky threw him an ominous glance and began to conduct the passage again. The player made the same error. Stravinsky lost his temper and dealt with the offender briefly but pointedly, with a generalization about stupidity. I had moved closer to him by that time, although not quite close enough to hear exactly what Robert said, but the expression on his face clearly indicated that he was taking Stravinsky to task. . . . [P. 230]

In the first place, the work recorded was not *Pulcinella* but *Le Baiser de la Fée*. (That "Robert" did not attend the *Pulcinella* session Miss Libman can still verify by consulting singers, orchestra players, engineers, but the damage to Stravinsky is already irreparable.[11]) In the second place, Stravinsky's "loss of temper" was not the first of the morning, for he had already spoken so harshly to a young clarinetist that an orchestra delegate complained to the composer after the session. The "wind player [who] made an error, which Stravinsky corrected sharply," refers to a later outburst, when the first hornist "flubbed" some notes of the difficult solo in the "Valse." Seeming not to understand that the player was aware of this, Stravinsky did criticize him "sharply"—as well as needlessly and with deleterious effect, for the second and third attempts to record the passage were even less successful. (The orchestra was tense not only because of this, however, but also because of a previous incident, still fresh in the minds of some of the musicians, when a similar reprimand by Stravinsky during a rehearsal of the Los Angeles Philharmonic caused the first hornist there to lose his job.) "Robert" expostulated with Stravinsky, saying that the "flubs" ("*couacs*") were not the same as wrong notes, and that the player was already very conscious of them. An altercation ensued, but in French, which neither Miss Libman, "moving closer," nor anyone else within earshot, understood. Stravinsky told "Robert" that he was "*très impertinent*," whereupon "Robert," less contrite than he might have been, departed. But, whatever Miss Libman's motive in choosing to tell two stories that might seem to indicate dissension—rather than one of the hundreds of harmonious and more interesting anecdotes— such incidents as the above make little sense divorced from their background and described by someone with extremely limited knowledge of music in general and of the characteristics of horn-playing in particular.

Concerning the resolution of the quarrel, Miss Libman fills still more space with speculations. The truth is that Stravinsky settled it by sending a note to "Robert," one that made him feel more despicable than at any other time in his life, but that also changed it forever by restoring the relationship to which the composer refers:

> Dear Bob, whom I love, with my ardent longing for our former relations that gave me so much happiness. Maybe my age is spoiling everything? Excuse me this feeling never leaving my heart. Love, I. Str.

Miss Libman continually distorts her accounts of events involving Stravinsky by failing to mention other people who were present. Thus, describing the Stravinsky's sojourn in Chicago at Christmas 1966 (pp. 307–10), she neglects to say that he received a visit from his son and daughter-in-law, does not mention a dinner in Stravinsky's honor given by officials of United Airlines, fails to note that Professor Watkins, the composer's friend from Ann Arbor, spent three days with him, and that an acquaintance came from Portland. On the other hand, Miss Libman *does* mention the presence of someone who was *not* there—herself. "The second performance on New Year's Day was even better than the first," she says. But she did not hear the second performance, having left Chicago before the beginning of the concert. Elsewhere she writes that

> in the midst of a snowstorm that left New York looking like a map of the prehistoric South Pole, I met this hale and hearty trio at the S.S. *Rotterdam* pier and installed them in the St. Regis. [P. 107]

In fact the "trio" was met in Weehawken by Paul Horgan, as well, and by Deborah Ishlon, in whose limousine (provided by Columbia Records) the Stravinskys rode to the St. Regis Hotel. (A map of the prehistoric South Pole would be quite an archeological discovery!)

Miss Libman never managed to learn even the most abbreviated catalogue of Stravinsky's works, knew almost nothing about their history—she actually states (p. 189) that the premiere of the *Rite of Spring* took place at the Paris Opéra—and could not distinguish one of his compositions from another. For an example of the last, she writes that

> the final . . . score [of the film *Discover America*] (. . . *Symphony in C* for Manhattan) was assembled and edited by Robert. . . .[12] [P. 177]

But the piece in question was the Symphony in Three Movements, which she had heard countless times in concerts as well as in the recording session for the film.

Yet these limitations do not stop Miss Libman from retailing a mass of totally false information about the composer's musical habits and opinions. She assures the reader that

> Normally it was not in [Stravinsky's] nature to look back. The final manuscript page that went to the photostater was, in every sense, final—and the mark of an erasure could never be detected. [P. 227]

Actually, few composers in the whole of music history can have been more constant rewriters than Stravinsky, who changed, emended, corrected his scores practically every time he heard or performed them. In truth, no page was *ever* "final," while few were without erasures, deletions, inked-in revisions. Rolf Liebermann's memoirs quote the eighty-year-old Stravinsky saying, "One must revise endlessly," and what most seemed to have impressed the newsmen who observed him at his first rehearsal in Sydney, Australia, in 1961, was that "not even his own scores are sacred to Stravinsky" (caption to a photograph in *Pix*, December 9, 1961, showing Stravinsky rewriting some measures and quoting him: "I think we'll change this passage slightly"). Furthermore, if "it was not in his nature to look back," he certainly did so with remarkable frequency, rewriting every measure of *Petrushka,* for example, as well as the *Firebird* Suite and the *Symphonies of Wind Instruments.* As Robert Rudolf, who made a reduced-orchestra version of the *Sacre,* wrote to Stravinsky, May 18, 1954:

> In both the *Firebird* and *Petrushka* you have in certain places taken a radical departure from the original score by adding altogether new music or at least new passages.

And Stravinsky did not "photostat" his manuscripts after the mid-1940s.

Miss Libman writes, no less wrongly, that

> As far as I know, Stravinsky did *not* listen to playbacks, at least not during any of the sessions I attended. As for editing, this was a task in which he had never involved himself. . . . But there is no question in my own mind that if Stravinsky *had* listened, he would have been able to determine immediately which takes were his and which were Robert's. . . . [P. 224]

The truth is that Stravinsky always listened to playbacks, both after his recording sessions and in rest periods during them; but since Miss Libman can be seen in a few of the photographs that were taken at the latter times, it would seem that she must not have understood what he was doing. Also, Stravinsky usually did "involve himself" in the editing. Neither Stravinsky nor anyone else, however, was able to tell whether a section might have come from one of his "takes" or from one of "Robert's"—or from those of others, for that matter, since some measures from Klemperer's recording of the *Pulcinella* Suite were dubbed into Stravinsky's because Columbia Records's director, without "Robert's" help at the session, had neglected to record them.

Miss Libman not only assigns her own opinions to Stravinsky, but also, as in the following example, denies that he *had* any when *she* did not:

> [In Phoenix in 1968] he watched [*The Rake*] in a "mod" decor: hippie clothes . . . discotheques . . . I have . . . no idea . . . what Stravinsky *really* thought about it; nor, do I think, has anyone else. [P. 333]

But who else did Miss Libman ask? Here is Donald Gramm on Stravinsky's thoughts about the "mod" production. Mr. Gramm sang a leading role in Phoenix, as well as in other productions that Stravinsky supervised:

> Stravinsky was always happy when people brought new ideas to his opera. . . . It was decided to set the Mother Goose scene in a disco . . . [and in Los Angeles] Stravinsky was disappointed that it wasn't as loud as his Arizona experience. But he was content to have my Nick [Shadow] dressed up in a black turtleneck sweater and for Baba the Turk to be played by a hermaphrodite and sung by a counter-tenor. [Interview in the London *Times*, June 16, 1975]

Another example:

> [Schoenberg was] a composer to whom [Stravinsky] was far from dedicated. . . . [P. 221]

But Stravinsky's obviously very complex feelings about Schoenberg were as unknown to Miss Libman as to everyone else.[13] The remark, which does Stravinsky a great injustice, would have to be contradicted by the numerous musicians in Los Angeles who were present with Stravinsky at dozens of rehearsals of Schoenberg's chamber music. And the remark *is* contradicted by a manuscript copy that Stravinsky made of a Schoenberg work, as well as by numerous documents, such as this note to Mrs. Schoenberg on her late husband's birthday:

> Hollywood, Sept[ember] 12, 1954: Dear Mrs. Schoenberg, this day of September 13 must be kept high in every musician's mind, and I am deeply regretful not to be able to attend your noble musical gathering

to commemorate the great Arnold Schoenberg. Most sincerely, Igor Stravinsky

(In later years, Mrs. Schoenberg gave scores of her husband's music to Stravinsky.) In the spring of 1955, when *Tempo* was preparing to publish an analysis of "Stravinsky's Schoenbergian Technique," the magazine's editor wrote to Stravinsky to ask whether he objected to the title, and he answered that he was, on the contrary, very proud. Here, too, is an anecdote by the violinist Zvi Zeitlin, published in the New York Philharmonic program book, January 5, 1967:

> In September 1962, at the Galei Kinnereth restaurant in Tiberias . . . Stravinsky, with glass raised, turned to me and said, "I would strongly urge you to play the Schoenberg Concerto."

But Miss Libman's remoteness from the artistic life of her subject is less surprising than her ignorance of the elementary realities of his business dealings.

> Boosey & Hawkes had been talking for some time about publishing the *Rite* sketches (since they held the right of first refusal, as with all other Stravinsky materials in their possession). . . . [P. 253]

The *Rite* sketches had never been in the possession of Boosey & Hawkes but were the property of a well-known Parisian collector, the late André Meyer. Since these sketches belonged to a work which is in the public domain in America, they could have been published there without anyone's permission. In 1965, the year to which Miss Libman is referring, Boosey & Hawkes did not hold the rights to publishing "all other Stravinsky materials in their possession."

Miss Libman also wrongly assures the reader that

> Stravinsky's ready acquiescence [in granting the publication rights to his archives to Boosey & Hawkes] was partly due to the composer's complete faith in the late Dr. Ernst Roth, director of the London office. [P. 330]

Stravinsky gave these rights for one reason only, to create a job for his friend Pierre Suvchinsky. Whatever Stravinsky's "faith" in Roth, it had nothing to do with music. Roth was a conservative who rejected every one of Stravinsky's recommendations to publish new works by new composers and even objected to his affiliations with younger musicians, as the following exchange shows:

> Dr. Roth thinks that the Donaueschingen Music Festival has become . . . a sort of "curiosity shop" performing *musique concrète* and specializing in similar sensational experiments and therefore does not think it is an outstanding event for the performance of a new work of yours. [R. Ampenoff of Boosey & Hawkes to Stravinsky, August 1954]

> Whether the Donaueschingen Festival is a "curiosity shop" is not in my view as important as the fact that Hans Rosbaud will be the conductor. . . . [Stravinsky to Ampenoff, August 13, 1954]

A final garland of quotations is offered in tribute to the diversity of Miss Libman's errors.

Item:

> Save for one or two brief interruptions, I remained with the Stravin-

skys during the . . . winter months and through the spring of 1962.
. . . As I had discerned in Mexico [in December 1961], minds were
already made up [to go to Russia in 1962]. . . . The works in question
[for the concerts there] were, of course, the post-1914 compositions,
which were not copyrighted in Russia. [Pp. 152–3]

In the entire year from July 1961 to July 1962, Miss Libman saw Stravinsky on only nineteen days, and she was not "with the Stravinskys"
at all during the "winter months" of 1962, when the composer and his
wife were in California (February 3–April 18), as is shown in Miss
Libman's letter from New York, February 16, to this reviewer, in California. As for Stravinsky's mind being made up about Russia, Miss
Libman's "discernment" proves to be hindsight: letters to his friends
show that he had not yet made up his mind a week before the trip.
None of Stravinsky's music was copyrighted in the U.S.S.R. at the time,
and, in any case, the program staples were pre-1914 compositions
(Fireworks, Firebird, Petrushka, Le Sacre du Printemps).

Item:

> Reports [in October and November of 1968] reaching me from Europe
> on [Stravinsky's] general weakness . . . [P. 350]

The truth is that during this period only two people, Nicolas Nabokov
and Lawrence Morton, knew Miss Libman and also saw Stravinsky
more than once, and neither of them communicated with her. Actually
Stravinsky was in better health in Europe in October-November 1968
than he had been during his trip there two years before. While in
Zürich, the composer was able to dispense with nurses entirely, and,
in Paris, he took only a part-time one, this versus the round-the-clock
nursing in Los Angeles at various times in the year before. Miss Libman
might have had news of Stravinsky's health from his doctor in New
York, Leon Lewithin, who wrote to the composer's son-in-law on October 16: "I am very happy that we succeeded in improving the condition of [the] maestro . . . during [his] stay here in New York, and I'm
glad that [he is] feeling well in Switzerland."

Item:

> Venice, that water-bound place where so earthy and vital a stream of
> life contradicts the celestial stones of its surroundings. Such contrasts
> were the very soul of [Stravinsky's] music, and . . . the works he began
> or completed during the many years he lived in Venice, on and off,
> are witness to the inspiration he found there. . . . [He was] the only
> non-Italian granted the privilege of conducting [in St. Mark's]. . . . He
> was borne [to] the Ducal Palace, as was customary, on a litter. And
> Venice was where so much music he admired began, the spontaneity
> of whose forms he loved. [P. 32]

The truth is that, "on and off" and altogether, Stravinsky spent considerably less than one year in "water-bound" Venice; that countless
non-Italians, from Adrian Willaert in the sixteenth century to Robert
Craft in the twentieth, have conducted in St. Mark's; that it was not
"customary" to be borne to the Great Council Hall on a litter, none of
the other conductors having reached the room this way, and Stravinsky
being jeered at by the press for resorting to the expedient; that Stravinsky was never inspired by any place ("Stravinsky, having lived in
many places, does not believe that geography or external influences

have any effect on his composition"—*San Francisco Chronicle*, March 20, 1946); that he did not complete any of his works there but only two motets by Gesualdo; that the forms of the polyphonic Venetian music which interested Stravinsky are anything but "spontaneous"; and that, because of the wilting weather, he found it more difficult to work in Venice than in any other city.

Item:

> In point of fact Stravinsky had wanted only one concert [in New York in December-January 1959–60], and this was the most interesting revelation of all, since it now became clear that the idea of the series had been Robert's alone. . . . [P. 63]

The truth is that Stravinsky had counted on at least two concerts from the very first, for the obvious reason that the *Movements* and *Le Sacre du Printemps*—the recording of these two works being the *raison d'être* for the concerts—could hardly be played on the same program and in the same hall. Stravinsky's correspondence with Columbia Records and with Margrit Weber (the pianist in the *Movements*), particularly his letter to Miss Weber of August 15, 1959, makes this clear. Miss Libman dates her "revelation" from September 1959, when Stravinsky was in Europe, but his handwritten notes concerning the contents of the *two* programs are dated "August 25, 1959."

Item:

> One of the exercises devised to keep Stravinsky close to everyone else's life [in 1971] was the signing of correspondence. . . . It was a practice I hated (although it may have been good for him), and I would have nothing to do with it. [P. 370]

Miss Libman should have consulted the letters, in the Stravinsky archives, that she typed in his name, that he signed, and to which she affixed both his and her initials. One of the last of these, dated March 11, 1971, is a reply to a letter in Russian from Dr. Gerald Seaman, Conservatorium of Music, Auckland.

Item:

> At Stravinsky's request, I listened to a proposal from a major film studio which offered one million dollars, plus other benefits . . . for a "few minutes" of new music to be used as a theme in a projected Biblical epic, Dino di [sic] Laurentis's [sic] *The Bible*. The tax bite would have left Stravinsky with very minor compensation . . . Some such project would be placed before me once a year on an average. . . . [Pp. 177–8]

The truth is that Miss Libman was not involved with the *Bible* project, which was proposed by the Hollywood agents Kohner and Guggenheim, and which greatly interested Stravinsky because he would pay no taxes and because the music would consist entirely of his old compositions. For these reasons, his attorney William Montapert drew up a contract, which Stravinsky actually did sign and which was then presented to an astonished De Laurentiis, since he had never made any proposal at all. Miss Libman's statement that film projects were "placed before her" every year is without foundation.

Item:

> ... after a few moments, when it became so apparent that the [To-
> ronto] orchestra could not follow his beat and that all was confusion,
> I rushed out and ran for several blocks. . . . [P. 319]

The truth is to be found in the Toronto newspapers, and in a CBC film
of the performance, which was of the *Pulcinella* Suite. Some trouble
was encountered in the "Tarantella," owing to an ambiguous gesture
that Stravinsky often made in starting that movement. But if Miss Libman left "after a few moments," she did not hear this. As for Stravinsky's mental and physical vigor that evening, Miss Libman can still
interview Tikhon Khulokovsky, nephew of the Tsar and a resident of
Toronto, with whom the composer talked at length after the concert.

Item:

> I remained outside the door of Stravinsky's room [at Mount Sinai, in
> November 1967] . . . while [Mrs. Stravinsky and Robert] went in. I saw
> him lying there like a tiny, aged doll in a huge bed. . . . [P. 324]

> For me, who had last glimpsed him . . . at Mount Sinai, [seeing Stra-
> vinsky on February 16, 1968] was a pleasant surprise. He had regained
> some of his lost weight. . . . (P. 327)

Miss Libman did not glimpse Stravinsky at Mount Sinai, but even if
she had, could not have told anything about his weight. It was nearly
11:00 P.M. when she followed Mrs. Stravinsky and this writer to Stravinsky's room, where the lights had been extinguished and Stravinsky
was asleep. He was invisible to anyone outside the door, owing to the
raised sideboards of his bed. Miss Libman's last glimpse of him had
been in May 1967, six months before he was hospitalized, at which
time he was eleven pounds *heavier* than on February 16, 1968.

Item:

> [After Stravinsky s death] I wakened Mrs. Stravinsky. . . . She sat up
> and whispered, "Yes? He is gone?" I said, "Yes." "Call Bob," she said.
> . . . I ran to Robert's room. He thrust out his hand as though to stop me
> and said, "No.". . . At her door Mrs. Stravinsky stood waiting. . . . one
> of the most influential forces in the history of music had gone from
> us. [Pp. 20–1]

In actuality "Robert" was asleep when Miss Libman came to his room,
woke him, and said, "He is slipping," which is the reason that "Robert"
believed Stravinsky was still alive. Furthermore, Mrs. Stravinsky was
in bed and not waiting by the door (waiting for what?) when "Robert"
went to her, woke her, and told her that her husband was dead. But
neither Mrs. Stravinsky nor "Robert" could have spoken the words
which Miss Libman has put into their mouths, for the reason that neither was expecting Stravinsky's death. If Mrs. Stravinsky had been
expecting it, she would never have gone to bed, nor would Stravinsky's
chief nurse, who knew him more closely than his doctors, have gone
home for the night (not being present at Stravinsky's death, as Miss
Libman falsely informed *The New York Times*, while omitting the
names of the nurses and doctors who actually were there). Stravinsky
had rallied so remarkably in the late evening that, given his history of
similar recoveries, the people closest to him were optimistic. Apart
from these inventions of Miss Libman, however, is it conceivable that,

at such a time, anyone with any feelings for Stravinsky could have entertained that platitudinous bit of press-agentry about "the history of music"? A beloved human being had gone from us, not an "influential force."

> There is little evidence in support of statements in the dispatches of the French, Prussian and Saxon ambassadors claiming that Biron entrusted his secrets only to Libman, that [Libman] was present at all interviews, that "Libman is the true ruler of Russia." Were there any basic truth in these reports, surely Rondeau . . . would have mentioned Libman's presence. But the name never appears in the . . . dispatches. [*A Forgotten Empress: Anna Ivanovna and Her Era*, by Mina Curtiss (New York: Frederick Ungar, 1974), p. 86]

10. *The Harmonic Organization of "The Rite of Spring,"* by Allen Forte (New Haven: Yale University Press, 1978).

The sixty-fifth birthday of *The Rite of Spring*, May 29, 1978, was marked by the publication of the most valuable study of this, or perhaps any other, representative twentieth-century masterpiece. Allen Forte has revealed the music's harmonic construction, identified its characteristic chordal formations, and mapped their relationships. His book is of capital importance because it provides the long-awaited analytical means with which Stravinsky's harmonic system can be understood and at the same time throws new light on his mind, showing, for instance, that what seemed to be most immediate was often most reflective. Everyone with an interest in contemporary music is indebted to the author for one of a very few permanent studies of the subject.

I

Professor Forte's presentation is technical and directed to a small audience—which is even worse than addressing a large one, as Eliot wrote, adding that "The only better thing is to address the one hypothetical Intelligent Man who does not exist and who is the audience of the Artist." Yet the book's arguments and conclusions should be made available to a larger readership than that of Forte's fellow theorists. Commentators between the segregated worlds of the layman and the scholar-specialist, however, are more often barriers than bridges. The present reviewer's primary goal, therefore, is simply to attract readers to the book, and, secondarily, to raise questions about it. No attempt will be made at explication.

The principal shortcoming of Professor Forte's study is a consequence of that notorious problem of scholarship, the over-narrowing of focus; but this does not affect the achievement, the codification of the harmony. Thus he postulates that the unity of *The Rite of Spring* is obtained

> not so much by . . . thematic relations of a traditional kind, as by the underlying harmonic units. . . . A family of sets . . . serve [sic] to unify [the music] in the general harmonic sense.

But can the harmonic function be circumscribed to this extent, and can it be proved that the harmonic relationships are stronger than the thematic ones? In "Phonogénie d'un 'Sacre' " (1978), Alain Clavier was convinced, so he writes, that the borrowing could no longer be detected as "an original phrase from the *Rite*," yet its identity remains evident.

And obviously neither melody nor harmony is always pre-eminent. As Stravinsky said a day or two before the first performance, "[at times] the dynamic power of the orchestra is more important than the melodic line itself." [14] Forte also declares that he will not

> ... cover such features of the music as tonality, large scale linear connections, register,[15] or orchestration.[16]

He might have added "rhythm," which to most listeners is the most prominent feature of *The Rite of Spring*. Thus augmentation is a rhythmic as well as a harmonic event, and the two elements are inseparable. Forte himself demonstrates the interlocking of rhythm and harmony in places where rhythmic variation introduces unfamiliar chords (cf. $\boxed{99}$). Moreover, he shows that the essential sets, or chords, those defining the music's harmonic character, tend to coincide with the first, or accented, beat of the measure:

> ... metrically accented verticals are usually significant sets. [P. 48]
> ... metrically accented chords are now familiar sets. ... [P. 56]

This reviewer must also question whether the subject of tonality can be avoided in a harmonic analysis of a piece that is "characterized [by] the juxtaposition [of] diatonic and atonal components," without, at any rate, drastically limiting the perspectives. Furthermore, Forte avoids the by no means unimportant question of "the function of ... emphasized individual pitches," while acknowledging that, for example, "the sustained [E-flat at $\boxed{97}$] affects the harmonies." Indeed. It changes them.

Forte rightly warns the reader that Stravinsky's reminder, on one sketch, to "transpose this to C# major" does not imply

> a traditional tonal orientation but [is] merely the only way [Stravinsky] would have to express the transpositional relation.

Yet the same cannot be said for other transpositions, such as that of the Khorovod tune in the "Augurs of Spring." Moreover, the obsolescence of a terminology designating tonal relationships does not mean that they do not exist. Forte's descriptions are superior to such conventional ones as, for the beginning of the "Introduction to Part II," "a D# minor and a C# minor triad oscillating above a sustained D minor triad." In his words and symbols, the music in this passage consists of "two successive forms" of a set (6-Z19), a statement that contains more information ("Z" indicates a relationship) as well as a means, inaccessible to the older jargon, of associating the harmony with other constructions.

Finally, Forte does not keep his resolve not to "cover" orchestration; his musical examples include the instrumentation, but superfluously, for the reader cannot follow the analysis without a full score, and sometimes erroneously (as when he marks the uppermost line in Ex. 76b as played by a flute). And he *does* mention the influence of orchestration on harmonic structure in, for instance, a reference to "the instrumentally determined component" of a set (6-Z48), though in what ways this component was determined is not explained—and cannot be, since the instrumentation is different in the earliest draft.

II

Professor Forte's approach to Stravinsky's creative processes is purely empirical, leaving no room for speculation about intuitive phenomena or unconscious perception. Forte's emphasis is entirely on the logic of the harmonic construction. He views each "compositional operation" as a reasoned step, and plainly does not believe in the single exception that he himself allows:

> The association of [two harmonies] may well be accidental, but nevertheless it is a demonstrable relation in the music. [P. 56]

At one point he examines an "ad hoc explanation," but quickly dismisses it as "not convincing" (p. 110).

The book begins at the simplest level, with the chromatic scale and definitions of various ways in which its pitches are combined. The examples in music type, the diagrams, the charts and tables are admirably clear, far more so than the verbal explanations. In common with other academics, jealous, perhaps, of an "in-group" membership, accustomed to writing only for each other, and possibly inspired by such examples as Jacques Lacan, who has successfully promoted his work by boasting of its unreadability, Forte does not seem to recognize that the more difficult the material to be communicated, the more imperative the obligation to present it clearly. The reader must find correct forms of words for himself and even provide missing ones—"a set type may be multiply represented . . ." ("a multiple"?); "The accompaniment . . . is not the dyad B♭ -D but the trichord A-B♭ -D, which the melodic note D♭ creates the set . . ." ("which, with the melodic note D♭ ,"?). Furthermore, subjects and verbs disagree ("all occur elsewhere . . . though none are . . ."), the misplacement of pronouns doubles the reading time, the diction is hideous (we read of "the belongedness of a set," and that "the asterisk designates which of the larger sets is a superset of the main set in the set complex . . ."), and the word order is indirect, as well as, at times, hopelessly confusing:

> Several harmonies are found that do not relate to the basic structure of the work and that do not occur elsewhere in the music. The more familiar ones include . . .

But how can a harmony be familiar if it is heard in only one place?

Finally, in an essay that depends on precision of language, the vocabulary is remarkably vague. Thus "harmonies" is used interchangeably with "sonorities" (which refers primarily to resonance), "sonically" is suddenly introduced without explanation ("the hexachord . . . clearly refers sonically to the two variants"), and "trilled" describes a figure of two slowly repeated eighth-notes separately phrased on each beat. No sooner does the reader learn the new locutions, moreover, than he is jolted by solecisms from the conventional ones. Forte writes that

> The interval between two notated pitches is measured by counting the number of half steps that separate them.

But "half steps" is an anachronism in the context, none of the twelve equal divisions of the chromatic scale being the "half" of any other. The theorist should define the measurement in his own tongue.

III

The main part of the book, a "Chronological Survey of the Work" (a "Survey of the Chronology . . ."?), starts unpromisingly:

> [The opening melody] . . . is the source of the diatonic melodic figures
> that characterize certain parts of the music. . . . (Clearly what Stravin-
> sky wished to express with these different diatonic formations is the
> folk mysticism of the ballet. . . .)

But do "diatonic formations" express folk mysticism? And how could anyone know what the composer wished to express? "It seems plausible," Forte continues, that the "Introduction to Part I"

> was written at a very early stage, perhaps even before Stravinsky had
> the outlines of the entire work clearly in mind. Two surface features
> render this convincing: nowhere else in the piece is there an obvious
> use of familiar diatonic formations together with primitive chromatic
> progressions. . . .

That Stravinsky did not have the outlines of the entire work in mind until he began the last movement is obvious, but why is it not plausible for the "Introduction" to have been written after the "Augurs of Spring" and "Spring Rounds," and in calculated contrast to them, just as the diatonic second section ([149]) of the "Sacrificial Dance" was written after the chromatic first? Stravinsky told one of his early biographers [17] that this was the order of composition, and the composer's correspondence of the time does not contradict him. On September 26, 1911, he wrote to Nicolas Roerich, co-author of the scenario: "I have sketched the beginning for *dudki* [reed pipes] and the 'Augurs of Spring.'" The Soviet musicologist Vershinina accepts the Russian word as referring to the first bassoon solo,[18] but the libretto that Stravinsky and Roerich had devised two months before the date of the composer's letter states that *dudki* are played in the "Augurs of Spring" by "the young men" (at [14] in the score). It might be mentioned that Stravinsky rarely began a composition at the actual beginning, because "one has to know what one is introducing," and "to find the entrance to a work is the most difficult task of all." Thus the Second Tableau of *Petrushka* was written before the First, and the Prelude to the next-to-last scene in *The Rake's Progress* before anything else in the opera. These and a hundred other examples do not rule out the *Rite* as an exception, but they do make Forte's conclusion somewhat less foregone.

What can be said with certainty concerning the extant notations for *The Rite of Spring* is that the first ones were not intended for the "Introduction" but for the "Augurs," "Spring Rounds," and possibly later movements. Yet even if the "Introduction" had been written first, this would not have been "at a very early stage" but in the same three-week period as the "Augurs," September 2–26, 1911; except for a few sketches, the composition had not been started before Stravinsky's return to Russia on the former date from a trip to Lugano and Berlin. A year earlier, three weeks before shelving the *Rite* to compose *Petrushka*, Stravinsky had written to Roerich:

> I have started work (sketches for *The Great Sacrifice*). Have you done
> anything for it? [August 9; 1910; the original of the letter is in the
> Tretyakov Museum, Moscow.]

Roerich did make some drawings, at least two of which are known, but the composer's 1910 sketches, whatever they may have been, are apparently lost, and the one that follows seems to be the first to have survived. The so-called "Augurs of Spring" chord, which Stravinsky said he had discovered in July 1911,[19] is a combination of the dominant sevenths in the treble part in the first two measures (pitch class set 7–

32 in Forte's nomenclature [20]); the single dominant seventh chord (4–27) belongs to five principal harmonies in the *Rite*. The complete first chord (*with* the bass) is an important harmony (both in this form—cf. [40]—and as the source of 6-Z43), especially in the "Sacrificial Dance," while the chord at the beginning of the bottom line of the manuscript (a subset of 7–31) is no less crucial in the work as a whole. Also, the rhythmic and melodic designs of the sketch anticipate parts of the "Ritual of Two Rival Tribes" and the "Sacrificial Dance." Thus this earliest known notation for the *Rite* contains the motto chord of the entire work, together with other basic harmonies:

Still another notation used in the *Rite*, though not originally intended for it, dates from July 1911, when Stravinsky copied a poem by Sergei Klychkov [21] into a small, lined exercise book, attached rhythmic values to the words, and fitted them to a metrically irregular melody, lengthening the stressed syllables. The composer had just set three texts by Konstantin Balmont, and was evidently planning to write another song to words by this symbolist poet's young colleague. A few weeks later, Stravinsky inserted a much simplified form of the melody at the top of a page of notations for "Spring Rounds" (Sketchbook, p. 8).[22] The melody as it appears in the Klychkov notebook is clearly the source of the one in the "Augurs of Spring" at the fifth measure of [28] (though Forte says that the "derivation is in an obvious way from 4–10 as a subset of 5–32 in the Khorovod tune").

IV

Forte expresses a doubt whether

one can assume that [the Sketchbook] contains a major portion of the sketches [and whether] the sketch pages (as, is the case with many of the Beethoven sketchbooks) may not be correctly collated.

But one can be more definite on both questions simply by counting the passages in the *Rite* not covered in the Sketchbook, and by estimating the number of entries that must have been followed by others representing more developed stages. In addition, to judge by Stravinsky's drafts for instrumentation in other works, it seems safe to conclude that he made orchestral sketches for every section of the *Rite* before beginning the full score—of which he also finished a preliminary version for the whole of Part I. The Sketchbook contains only a few such drafts, none of them as complete as that for the "Introduction to Part I." [23] As for chronology, the volume was neither compiled nor paginated by Stravinsky, and the presence of sketches for the *Berceuses du Chat* (1915) before those for the orchestration of passages from Part I is hardly reassuring. A letter to Stravinsky from the Paris representative of the publisher of the book, February 3, 1967, suggests the possibility that some of the pages might have been assembled in the wrong order after photographing.

In addition to the Sketchbook, Forte's texts are the four-hand reduction (1913),[24] which, he wrongly says, was "prepared for the ballet rehearsals" (a two-hand score was used, as a letter from Monteux to Stravinsky, February 22, 1913, confirms) and "the 1921 orchestra score," even though, as he adds, "one can assume that Stravinsky approved all changes [in subsequent editions]." Then why not consult these later editions, since this would have spared the reader much bewilderment? Instead, Forte treats seriously, as variant readings, the most obvious proofreaders' oversights, calling attention to "an apparent [mistake] in clarinet 2," and devoting most of a paragraph to a note that is different in the piano and orchestra scores, despite the correction of both "errors" in the 1947 edition. In one instance (Ex. B, p. 24), Forte actually discusses the harmony resulting from two typographical errors in the piano score that have been corrected in every edition of the orchestra score including the 1921, then acknowledges in a footnote that these "differences" might be misprints.[25]

Then, with deliberate inconsistency, it seems, Forte refers to the 1943 version of the final movement on some matters but not on others. Affecting to be puzzled as to whether a note in the climactic chord is a misprint, and genuinely baffled in the previous measure as to "what the main upper voice is intended to be," he nevertheless refrains from peeking at the 1943 score, which answers both questions. Finally, when he concedes "little doubt that" a certain trombone note should be changed—as it has been in all later editions—yet goes on to give the formula for the chord including the wrong note, the reader suspects that the Professor's interest in analysis exceeds his interest in music.

Where pedantry is really needed, however, it is missing. Thus Forte writes that the final section of "The Ritual of Abduction" "presents no new music but repeats the introduction to the movement," though, in actuality, the music from measure 3 of "the final section" is transposed above the corresponding passage (at $\boxed{48}$), in preparation for the following movement. And he writes that at two measures before $\boxed{22}$, "the violas should have an E-natural and F-sharp, not E-flat and F-sharp"; but the wrong note is in the second violins, not the violas. And, though he indicates near the beginning of the book (Ex. 13) that the second note of a trill is of equal importance with the first (and, in conventional language, a whole tone higher unless marked otherwise), he later defines the upper note of a trill as "embellishing and hence secondary" (p. 60). In Example 30, he does not include the "secondary notes" of any of the trilling parts, though some of these pitches are not in the sets.

V

The analysis of Part II of the *Rite* is more intricate than that of Part I, in correspondence to the more "sophisticated . . . compositional procedures," in which, for example, "transposition and inversion" are more typical. The "Introduction to Part II" exhibits "greater diversity" with respect to the chords used than any other movements except the "Sacrificial Dance" and the "Mystic Circle," and this "Introduction" is especially interesting with regard to the control of vertical succession. The verticals consist almost exclusively of sets that are significant throughout the work.

The section on the "Sacrificial Dance" is the most absorbing in the book, showing to what extent the mixture of new harmonies with familiar ones charges the music with its colossal energy. But, for a notion of the complexity of the structure here, the reader must turn to Forte's summary.

At one level, Forte's achievement consists in having codified the harmonies of the *Rite* and traced the connections among them (by means of, for example, similarity relationships [26] such as the linking of sets through subsets). At another level, his analysis exposes a few minor faults in the composition. For example, he shows that "Two sets, 4-14 and 5-27, neither relate well at all to the other sets in the passage"; that, at one place, "two thematic components do not fit well into the over-all harmonic sense"; and that an unimportant chord on the strongest beat (at ⟨92⟩) raises a doubt about the metrical structure. Readers who turn to the music will no doubt find themselves in agreement, as well as pleased to have concrete explanations for felt but heretofore-not-understood weaknesses. This is the most valuable kind of music criticism.

More generally, Forte has provided the basis for a re-evaluation of the schematic side of Stravinsky's mind, which can now be seen to have resembled Schoenberg's more closely than has been supposed.[27] Forte writes, in connection with a point that supports his thesis of Stravinsky's attraction, natural or logical, to certain basic vertical constructions:

> [This] is significant insofar as it substantiates the extent to which Stravinsky worked out his sonorities within a specific scheme.

The harmonic changes in the 1943 "Sacrificial Dance" strengthen this interpretation—as well as reveal the continuity of Stravinsky's musical thought at a time remote from the *Rite* in artistic philosophy—and so do two sketches from the Klychkov notebook. Forte reproduces a chord sequence from the Sketchbook, first conceived for the "Sacrificial Dance" (at ⟨161⟩), and observes that "Stravinsky's predilection for this progression"—he re-employed it in the "Introduction to Part II"— "very likely is based on the fact that it contains many, if not all, of the basic harmonies of the work." The two early sketches show the evolution of the harmonic content, with only three of the seven chords of the ultimate version appearing in the first one. The "Klychkov sketches" also reveal that the contrary motion and diatonic scales of the frame were not part of the original idea. Stravinsky did indeed gravitate, instinctively and consciously, toward the music's fundamental combinations.

A synoptic study of *The Rite of Spring*, one that would consider all of its elements, remains to be undertaken. But Forte's book is the first that substantially helps to accomplish this goal. And, finally, his dissection does not reduce, but, on the contrary, greatly increases the mystery of the masterpiece.

Notes

PART ONE

1. Catherine Gavrilovna Nossenko (1881–1939), Stravinsky's first cousin and later his wife.

2. Nossenko (1872–1953), cousin of Catherine, whose married name was Schwarz. Writing to C. F. Ramuz, October 25, 1928, Stravinsky asks this friend to fetch him at the station in Lausanne, "only do not tell anyone that I am coming. I am afraid of being caught by my wife's relatives, Mr. [sic] and Mme Schwarz, and I have not enough time to share it . . . above all with such uninteresting people. . . . I will be hungry and will not refuse if you offer me a good or even a bad dinner."

3. The composer's younger brother (1884–1917).

4. Nossenko (1882–1969), cousin of Catherine and sister of Olga, became a medical doctor and lived in Leysin, Switzerland until her death. "Tell Mademoiselle Vera of the pleasure we have had in hearing about her medical successes," Maurice Delage wrote to Stravinsky, November 11, 1913. In his youth, Stravinsky was not fond of Vera Nossenko, at least to judge by a remark in a letter to his parents: "Vera Dmitrievna not only puts on airs but is insolent. . . . The behavior of this coquette really embarrasses me, and, in my view, the older she becomes the more her bad qualities increase. To anger such a sweet and gentle person as Safonov is difficult, but she managed to do even that. Yesterday we were going into the forest to sketch, and just before we left she was so rude to Safonov that he nearly stayed at home. He was terribly angry." (Letter of July 7, 1901) When Stravinsky conducted in Geneva in October 1951, Vera Dmitrievna wrote to him from Leysin, but he seems not to have answered.

5. Velsovskaya (d. 1917). She was related to the Nossenkos and became the nurse of Stravinsky's children.

6. Nossenko (1849–1942), mother of Olga and Vera Nossenko.

7. Jean-Marie Guyau (1854–1883). See *Jean-Marie Guyau*, by F. J. W. Hardings (Geneva: Drot, 1974).

8. Now renamed Khmel'nitsky.

9. Zhmerinka is about thirty miles west of Voronovitsa and the Sayn-Wittgenstein estate, where Liszt lived for a year.

10. On June 26, 1901, at the end of term in his Gymnasium, Stravinsky went with his parents for a holiday to Pechisky, and from there to Ustilug (though in *Expositions and Developments* he states that he was not in Pechisky as late as 1901). Pechisky, 150 kilometers south of Ustilug, was the name of the Stravinsky estate, and it was there that Roman, the composer's elder brother, died and was buried.

11. Catherine Nossenko.

12. Liudmilla Gavrilovna Nossenko (by marriage, Beliankina), also known as Miliusia and Milochka (1878–1937), sister of Catherine Nossenko.

13. Now Lomonosov.

14. Under this name, Alexei Tolstoy and the brothers Zhemchuzhnikov wrote a book of humorous and nonsensical verse popular in Tsarist Russia. See B. H. Monter's *Koz'ma Prutkov: The Art of Parody* (The Hague: Mouton, 1972).

15. This was published in the U.S.S.R., in 1973, and in England, edited by Eric Walter White (London: Faber and Faber), in 1975.

16. Stravinsky does not mention that this piece was dedicated to Rimsky-Korsakov's daughter Nadyezhda, and, since she did not acknowledge it, Stravinsky omitted her name from later publications and arrangements of the music. Writing a program note for the piece at the time that he recorded it with violin and four woodwinds (Paris, May 6, 1933), he says—mistakenly, as the letter to Timofeyev shows—that the music was composed in the winter of 1906–7. In the program note, too, Stravinsky claims that he had always had the intention.of giving "*un charactère essentiellement champêtre*" to the music and had always wanted to arrange the piano accompaniment for a small wind instrument ensemble, which he achieved in 1923.

17. Stravinsky does not mention *Fireworks* here, and his Autobiography seems to indicate that he did not begin work on the piece until the early summer. "I finished it in six weeks and sent it off to the country place where [Rimsky-Korsakov] was staying," Stravinsky writes in the book, but in London, in October 1927, closer in time to the circumstances, he remembered "putting *The Fireworks* aside in order to compose a homage to Rimsky-Korsakov's memory, a short symphonic poem, or *Chant Funèbre*." In both the *Chroniques de Ma Vie* and these earlier reminiscences, Stravinsky says that the *Chant Funèbre* was performed in the autumn of 1908, but the correct date is February 13, 1909.

18. 1881–1942. Editor of the magazine *Muzyka*, published in Moscow from 1910 to 1916.

19. *Scherzo Fantastique* (op. 3).

20. Alexander Siloti (born near Kharkov, October 10, 1863, died in New York, December 8, 1945), pianist and conductor, pupil of Liszt. In October 1909, Siloti wrote three letters to Schott, the German music publisher, recommending Stravinsky's *Fireworks* as "*nicht schwer und sehr effektvolles*." (Letter of October 9, from Wiborg, Finland)

21. Grigory Petrovich Jurgenson, son of Piotr Ivanovich Jurgenson (1839–1904), who, in 1851, founded the St. Petersburg music-publishing company.

22. See p. 63.

23. Scott's inclusion in this company may be attributed to his role as principal organizer of the concert, which was to have taken place in London. He visited Stravinsky in Clarens to discuss the program with him.

24. November 5, 1910, conducted by Siloti. Serge Kussevitzky was in the audience, and he determined forthwith to become Stravinsky's publisher. Kussevitzky had founded the Russischer Musik Verlag in Berlin in 1909. Its first director was Nicolas Struve, who, during World War I, had to return to Moscow, where he directed the Russian branch of the company. His place in Berlin was taken first by Herr Vogel, then by Eric Zingel, and finally by Herr F. V. Weber. After the war, Stravinsky's business with the company was conducted mainly through the Paris branch, Editions Russes de Musique—sometimes spelled in the singular by Stravinsky—whose directors were Ernest Oeberg (d. December 1925) and Gavril Grigorievich Païchadze (1881–1976). In 1946, the Editions was purchased by Boosey & Hawkes, with whom, on January 1, 1947, Stravinsky signed an exclusive contract with a $25,000-per-annum guarantee. Struve, Oeberg, and Païchadze play important roles in Stravinsky's biography, and numerous references to them occur throughout this book. Stravinsky was greatly shocked by the bizarre death of Struve (decapitation in an accident in a Paris elevator), and by the sudden one of Oeberg, who was taken ill while dining with the composer and rushed to a hospital, where he died of peritonitis a few days later.

25. Andrey Rimsky-Korsakov (1878–1940), to whom the score is dedi-

cated, did come to the final performance, July 7, together with Stravinsky's friend, the pianist Nikolai Richter.

26. From a Turin newspaper (not identified), August 30, 1933.

27. Nadyezhda Nikolayevna Rimsky-Korsakov, née Purgold (1859–1919).

28. (1893–1943). His ballet *Midas*, performed in London in June 1914 on a program with Stravinsky's *Nightingale*, was a fiasco.

29. Caracas, 1875–Paris, 1947. A pupil of Massenet, Hahn, aged fourteen, composed the popular song "Si mes vers avaient des ailes," which was recorded by Melba in 1904. He wrote operas, operettas, and much other music, conducted *Don Giovanni* at Salzburg in 1906, and, as a tenor, enjoyed a great reputation as a salon artist, his voice being small and suitable only for drawing rooms and recording studios. A recent disc (Rococo Records, Toronto) containing his performances of twenty pieces by himself and other composers can be recommended to anyone interested in the musical world of Marcel Proust, who was one of Hahn's closest friends.

30. "Sans grimaces," a phrase frequently used by Stravinsky in both English and French, "grimace," in his mind, being synonymous with "insincerity."

31. Hahn's review of the *Sacre* accused Stravinsky of exaggeration.

32. 1882–1970. Another son of the composer.

33. Eduard Frantsyevich Napravnik (1839–1916), conductor and composer. He lived next door to the Stravinsky family on the Krukov Canal.

34. Albert Coates (1882–1953), English conductor, born in St. Petersburg. On May 30, 1918, he directed *The Nightingale* at the Maryinsky Theater, in the Meyerhold-and-Golovine staging, the first performance of any work by Stravinsky in his native city after the Revolution. Coates befriended Stravinsky's mother during these years and, on leaving Petrograd in 1919, brought news of her to the composer. "Coates . . . who came one evening to hear *The Firebird*, told me that your mother was in good health when he left her [in Petrograd], but that she was anxious because of the lack of money." (Letter from Ansermet in London to Stravinsky in Morges, May 6, 1919)

35. On February 15, 1912, Stravinsky wrote to Alexander Benois: "I have just received the news from Mama that Diaghilev will not be playing in Petersburg. So does our motherland treat us. It is obvious how necessary we are to her. The Theater of the Literary-Artistic Society, as (it seems) the Maly Theater is called, charged such an incredible price that Diaghilev with all his resourcefulness could not do a thing about it!"

36. Stravinsky first visited the Vatican in April 1911, while in Rome to finish the composition of *Petrushka*.

37. Alexander Nikolayevich Benois (1870–1960).

38. Pseudonym of Lev Samoilovich Rosenberg (1866–1924). In the 1960s and 1970s, Bakst's artistic reputation soared, as Benois's declined. Bakst was one of the few with whom Stravinsky used the intimate "tu," the others including Diaghilev, Nijinsky, Nouvel, Goncharova, Larionov, Mitussov, Stelletsky, Andrey and Vladimir Rimsky-Korsakov, Baron Osten-Sachen, Artur Rubinstein, Picasso, Cocteau, and, in later years, José-Maria and Misia Sert.

39. Prince Vladimir Nikolayevich Argutinsky-Dolgurokov (1874–1941), an official of the Russian Foreign Ministry in Paris, was an intimate friend of Diaghilev. After the Revolution, as before it, Argutinsky remained one of the few who may be described as a close friend of the composer. Argutinsky became famous for a moment in 1922 when he discovered a Rembrandt drawing in a flea market in a small town outside of Paris, and sold it to Oscar Reinhart of Winterthur. According to Mrs. Stravinsky's diary, her husband was greatly disturbed when the news of Argutinsky's death reached him in Hollywood, February 12, 1942. John Warrack's *Tchaikovsky* (London: Hamish Hamilton, 1973) contains a striking photograph of the young Argutinsky with the composer of the *Symphonie Pathétique*.

40. On June 16, 1914, Stravinsky's wife wrote to him in London to the effect that a letter had come from Benois hinting that the composer was being overly persistent in seeking the painter's advice and opinions.

41. See Benois's letter to Stravinsky on pages 133-134.

42. In 1931, Bartók wrote: "It may be that . . . Stravinsky . . . did not go on

journeys of collection, and mainly drew [his] material from the collections of others, but [he] too, I feel sure, must have studied not only books and museums but the living music of [his country]." (*Béla Bartók Essays* [London: Faber and Faber, 1976])

43. *Podblyudnya*, songs of Yuletide divination, on texts from Afanasiev's *The Slav's Poetic Attitudes Toward Nature* (Vol. II, Moscow, 1869, p. 194). In the same sketchbook in which Stravinsky first drafted these choruses, he also entered notations, in piano score and without words, for a "Flagellants' Song"; the date is 1915 or 1916. As for the Yuletide songs, the first of them, "The Pike," was completed in Clarens on December 16, 1914. "Master Portly" (or "Mr. Gross-belly"), the second in order of composition, was written in Château d'Oex, January 16, 1915. The third, "Saints' Day in Chigisakh" (or "Christ in Chigisakh," or "Chigisakh Across Yauza"), was completed in Morges, December 22, 1916. (Stravinsky believed that this text was North Russian, but the editor of the Soviet edition of Stravinsky's "Conversation" books identifies it as Central Russian.) "Autumn," the final piece of the group, was also written in Morges, on January 14, 1917. Thus all four choruses are contemporaneous with *Les Noces*. In the summer of 1954, Stravinsky added an accompaniment of four horns to the pieces, which were performed in this new version at the Monday Evening Concerts, Los Angeles, October 11, 1954, the present writer conducting, Marilyn Horne, soprano soloist. The original *a cappella* choruses were sung in Geneva, probably in 1917, by the Russian Choir of Vassily Kibalchich, who had irritated Stravinsky at first by putting his name on the program as conductor, without the composer's permission. Kibalchich moved to Paris, after the war and his chorus sang the first performances of *Les Noces*. He then migrated to America and formed the Kibalchich Russian Symphonic Choir. He wrote to Stravinsky and saw him on his American tours. In a letter to his elder son, April 19, 1951, Stravinsky says that "Kibalchich visited me in Hollywood several years ago. Last December I heard that he was gravely ill in Philadelphia."

44. "Together with Mussorgsky, Stravinsky is perhaps the only one who wrote essentially Russian music." (Otto Klemperer, *Die Tat*, Zürich, October 14, 1961)

45. The "*Chant Dissident*" from the *Quatre Chants Russes*, on a text from Kireyevsky (No. 351, p. 445). Stravinsky's first idea for this song is found in a notebook after a sketch for the end of Kastchei's dance in the 1919 *Firebird* Suite. The words are very similar, the music utterly different:

Nous en est ve - nu vers loi

But this diatonic style is less remote from the music for the second and final verses, which was composed before the music to the first verse. The passage from ⑥ to the end (instrumental score) was probably written after a sketch for the *Song of the Nightingale* and a sketch for the fourth tableau of *Les Noces*. Stravinsky rewrote the "*Chant Dissident*" at least three times, and the flute and cimbalom parts are radically different from one version to another. It should also be mentioned that, in 1922, when arranging the piece for player piano, he omitted the music of the flute obbligato (printed in small notes in the piano edition of the piece). Béla Bartók played the piano part in a performance in Budapest in April 1921 and wrote afterward: "Stravinsky's songs, despite their originality and innovative movements, had a decided success with the audience—to the extent that one of them, the 'Chanson pour Compter,' was encored. Here the public was not a good judge: in my opinion . . . the 'Chant Dissident' is undoubtedly the best. This song is a veritable gem among small, modern lyrics; it is full of moving intimacy, lacking all those jests and extravagances that we meet so often in Stravinsky's works." (*Op. cit.*) The *Quatre Chants Russes* consist of "*Le Canard*," composed January 28, 1918; "*Chanson pour Compter*," completed February 16, 1918; "*Le Moineau Est Assis*," completed January 23, 1919; and the "*Chant Dissident*," completed in February 1919. The first performance took place in the Salle Gaveau, Paris, Saturday,

February 7, 1920, on a program of Stravinsky's chamber music that included both the first and second performances in the French capital of the Suite from *Histoire du Soldat* for violin, clarinet, and piano. The singer was Mme Koubitzky.

46. 1865–1943.

47. Throughout the book, the numbers in boxes refer to rehearsal numbers.

48. Karl Kerényi to Thomas Mann, February 1934: "Your inclusion of irony as an Apollonian concept is certainly correct." That the artist must detach himself from his creation is part of the concept of irony developed by Fichte and Friedrich Schlegel, and it is a profound part of Stravinsky's philosophy.

49. On April 4, 1913, Stravinsky wrote to his publisher, Jurgenson, asking for a copy of Scriabin's Three Etudes (Op. 65). Also, Scriabin's First Symphony, arranged for piano four-hands, was included in a packet of music (along with Dargomizhsky's *Collection of Romances* and Debussy's *Images* and *Des Pas sur la Neige*) sent to Stravinsky by his Moscow publisher, February 18, 1914. Yet only a year after Scriabin's death, in a sketchbook for *Renard* and *Podblyudnya*, Stravinsky wrote: "I sometimes think that taste does not matter, but then I listen to Scriabin." On March 5, 1938, Stravinsky wrote in the margin of an article by Charles-Albert Cingria, next to the name "Scriabin," that he was a "pseudo-esoteric symbolist"—and next to the name "Rimsky-Korsakov," that he was an "irritating folklorist," and next to the names "Berlioz" and "Wagner," that they were "romantic orgiasts."

50. Compare this with Stravinsky's outburst against *Ein Heldenleben* ("quel horreur de musique") in a letter to Ansermet, April 20, 1928, and with the composer's total silence after hearing Strauss's *Ariadne* in Mannheim in December 1930.

51. From Warsaw, to be precise, where Stravinsky had spent two days with his friend, and the librettist for *The Nightingale*, S. S. Mitussov. The Stravinskys and Scriabin left Russia at Alexandrov, the border station, on September 22, and, the next day, in Berlin, Stravinsky purchased copies of Scriabin's Sixth and Seventh Sonatas, and of Brahms's Opus 121. The Stravinsky family was accompanied by Sofiya Dmitrievna Velisovskaya, then employed as a nurse for the composer's children.

52. V. G. Karatygin (1875–1925) was a composer and critic. Five days after hearing *Pierrot Lunaire* in Berlin, December 8, 1912, Stravinsky wrote to him: "In *Pierrot Lunaire*, the whole unusual stamp of [Schoenberg's] creative genius comes to light at its most intensive." (Clarens, December 13, 1912)

53. On January 23, 1963, Stravinsky wrote to Henry Kissinger, Director of the Harvard International Seminar, recommending Marina Scriabin, the composer's daughter, as a candidate, because of her "double training in esthetics and linguistics."

54. George Balanchine has stated that these adjectives exactly describe Fokine as he knew him.

55. C. F. Ramuz (1878–1947). Swiss writer.

56. Swiss writer of Dalmatian origin (1883–1954). Of Stravinsky's friends in Switzerland during World War I, Cingria is the one—in the opinion of the present writer, who observed him with Stravinsky in Venice in 1951 and in Paris in 1952—for whom the composer felt the most affection. Stravinsky had known Cingria before May 1914; a note from Ansermet to Stravinsky, June 22, 1914, says: "Cingria told me how cordially you received him in Paris [after *The Nightingale*]." On July 3, 1928, René Auberjonois wrote to Stravinsky: "If you are very nice (about which I am not at all sure), you will subscribe for a small book by Cingria, to appear in August. The success of the volume is not assured because there are many mistakes in the Latin and much disorder. I am looking for subscribers because Ch. Albert merits them." See Stravinsky's obituary ("Hommage") in *La Nouvelle Revue Française*, March 1, 1955.

57. Swiss conductor (1883–1969). One of Stravinsky's closest associates.

58. Painter (1872–1957). He designed the sets and costumes for *Histoire du Soldat* in 1918 and was one of Stravinsky's closest friends during the Swiss years.

59. By this time Otto Kahn, Chairman of the Metropolitan Opera, had asked Henry Russell, Director of the Boston Opera, to escort Nijinsky to New York. Russell's letter to Stravinsky from Monte Carlo, March 29, 1916, seems to accuse the composer of having advised against Nijinsky's departure, Nijinsky himself apparently having cited Stravinsky's opposition as the principal reason for not leaving Switzerland. On April 4, Stravinsky answered Russell, who had gone to Paris, saying that what Russell had written about Nijinsky was not surprising: "I know this boy all too well, and he never remembers what he says or what he has done, though to repeat this tragi-comic story here would be too long and too boring." Stravinsky asks if Nijinsky has cabled a different explanation to Otto Kahn for the lateness of the trip. As for the gossip about detaining the dancer, this was too ridiculous even to bother to deny, and Russell would have to see Diaghilev's cables to understand the worthlessness of the allegations. Stravinsky supposed that Golovague, the military attaché at the Russian Legation in Berne, was the General whom Nijinsky mentioned, but the composer says that he does not know Golovague, has never seen him, and has heard about him only from Nijinsky.

After leaving Stravinsky in Morges, c. February 15, Nijinsky and his family returned to Berne. They were in Paris on March 24 and in Bordeaux on the 25th, from whence they sailed for New York. By the end of 1916, Nijinsky was remote from both Stravinsky and Diaghilev. On December 3, Diaghilev wrote to Stravinsky from Rome: "I received three cables signed 'Watza'—Nijinsky begging me to come immediately to America. He is convinced that the only salvation for *me* (!!!) is to work together with him, and he says that 'it is better late than never.' Even to send such cables as these is proof that he feels 'a knife at his throat.' . . . I have not received a penny from America these last three months." "Watza" was Nijinsky's nickname. Referring to him in telegrams, Stravinsky and Diaghilev also used the name "Vestris," after Gaëton Apolline Balthasar Vestris (1729–1808), who had danced in Mozart's *Les Petits Riens*.

60. Here is an excerpt from the written testimony of Mrs. Dorrance Stalvey, Stravinsky's secretary during his last four years in California, in a lawsuit which the Stravinsky children brought against their stepmother in February 1974: "In the years when I was in the house, the children avoided all responsibility—in sickness, in health, and in general—except for Milène [Marion, Stravinsky's younger daughter], who 'did her duty,' and often complained about that. Milène and I had a conversation once, in my office. She remarked on how time-consuming it was to come to the house practically every day, and that the visits made her late in getting dinner for [her husband], which put him in a very bad humor. She also said, 'I think my father killed my mother with all of his demands.' " (Marilyn Stalvey, June 20, 1974)

61. Later Mrs. Igor Markevich. The present writer made her acquaintance in Rome in November 1951, but Stravinsky saw her only once again, in San Francisco, December 11, 1954, after conducting a performance of *Petrushka* with Anton Dolin in the title role.

62. Stravinsky continued to receive letters from the U.S.S.R., however. Thus Alexander Efimov wrote to him from Kiev, August 16, 1932, referring to the many years since they had seen each other, and begging for a package of coffee and sugar.

63. On May 2, 1922, Stravinsky's publisher, J. & W. Chester, wrote to the composer asking for an article on Mussorgsky similar to the one on Tchaikovsky, and Stravinsky refused.

64. "Rimsky civilized out of *Boris* its real value," Stravinsky told an interviewer in New York in January 1937. But Stravinsky, who was quite regularly questioned about Mussorgsky and *Boris*, sometimes gave different answers, as in the case of some further remarks in this same interview: "Dargomizhsky's *Stone Guest* is an essay, an attempt rather than a complete achievement. . . . [But as for] *Boris*, the original is too heavy for me. It is very interesting, like a problem, but too long. I should like to see it refashioned. . . . It has a remarkable monolithic quality, but after a while it becomes monotonous. . . . Mussorgsky has a remarkable freshness of ear." The interviewer then asked Stravinsky what he thought of Mussorgsky "being called the Dostoevsky of music," and was rebuffed with "I do not like facile analogies." (*New York World-Telegram*,

January 23, 1937) In a letter to Maximilien Steinberg, March 2, 1913, Stravinsky said that "It behooves us all to wage an energetic battle against the 'Balyayevski Committee,' which did not consider it necessary to commemorate the 100th birthday of Dargomizhsky in its concerts . . . but even almost deliberately puts in the programs Zolotarev's *Little Russian Sketches* instead of Dargomizhsky's *Little Russian Kazachok*."

65. The simplicity of this instrumentation bears out Stravinsky's criticisms of Rimsky-Korsakov's versions of Mussorgsky. The Shostakovich edition of *Khovanshchina* being at present the most accessible, the reader is invited to compare it at [307] in Act III with the following descriptions of Stravinsky's still unpublished score: in the first five measures, Stravinsky mutes the strings and accents each bass note; in the second measure of [308], he doubles the voice with a solo cello (not muted), and, in the third measure, he gives the bass line to the bass clarinet; in the measure before [309], the sustained chord is scored for horns and bassoon alone (and this measure, like the three before it, is marked *piano* and *pianissimo*); from [309] to [310], Stravinsky uses bassoons, horn, and string bass, switching to four horns at [310]; in the fourth measure of [310], the horns are relieved by three trombones and tuba; at [312], a single clarinet plays the line that Shostakovich gives to all of the violas. In both the Stravinsky and Shostakovich scores, the music is transposed a half-step higher than Mussorgsky's original. It may be worth mentioning that when asked his opinion of Shostakovich's arrangement of *Boris*, Stravinsky answered: "Stokowski, Shostakowski—*je ne vois pas de différence*." (*Le Quartier Latin*, Montreal, March 23, 1945)

66. In a letter to H. Bessel, St. Petersburg, the publisher of the final chorus, Stravinsky describes his work as an "original composition on Mussorgsky's theme" (letter of October 22, 1913). On November 24, 1913, Bessel paid 600 rubles to Stravinsky for the *Khovanshchina* pieces and the orchestration of Mussorgsky's "Flea," but the publisher had still not received the score and parts for the final chorus from Diaghilev, and Bessel asked Stravinsky to retrieve them. Stravinsky seems never to have received a copy of his full score, but only copies of the vocal score (which contains indications for the instrumentation).

67. Maurice Delage wrote to Stravinsky, January 23, 1920: "Didn't you begin [the *Marriage*] before, and what are the rights of the publisher Bessel? Do you still intend to work on this score?"

68. Some months after hearing *Boris Godunov* in Moscow in September 1962, Stravinsky wrote to Pierre Suvchinsky: "The problem of *Boris* is and always will be very complex. It is right to speak of chamber music, and even the chorus does not require an opera orchestra. . . . But how could Mussorgsky's new treatment of intervals be understood by a composer such as Rimsky, who never mentioned the great Verdi or the brilliant Puccini; and what can be expected from people for whom Glazunov was an object of enthusiasm?" (Letter of January 19, 1963)

69. French composer and critic (1871–1958).

70. Thomas Mann: *The Story of a Novel* (New York: Knopf, 1961).

71. *Ibid.*

72. The Curzon Line was east of Rovno. After Versailles, therefore, the settlement of the mortgage was subject to Polish law. Yarotsky sold the land in 1921, after paying Stravinsky 652 zlotys in May of that year (letter to Stravinsky from Alexander Gliklich, attorney, Warsaw, November 2, 1924). Yarotsky died on August 11, 1931. Catherine Stravinsky wrote to her husband, December 31, 1934: "Grisha [Beliankin] is going to Warsaw, Gliklich having informed him that money has been received from Rovno."

73. Ghima and Guimochka were Igor's nicknames. At the time, he was painting as well as composing, but it is clear from this and the next letter that Frau Wilhelm has confused him with his brother.

74. Camillo Everardi (1825–99), singer and teacher, born in Belgium, died in Moscow.

75. *Cf.* Stravinsky's letter to G. H. Timofeyev, pp. 21–22.

76. On January 4, 1946, Stravinsky wrote to Dmitri Borodin, explaining that "Julia Lazarevna was not my late brother's widow but the widow of Mi-

khailayevich Rimsky-Korsakov's brother Andrey, who had died two years earlier." Apparently Mikhail Mikhailayevich had written about his brother's widow, not Stravinsky's.

77. Sofiya Kirillovna Kholodovskaya died in Leningrad in July 1929, while Stravinsky was in Echarvines-les-Bains.

78. Catherine's sister Liudmilla (1878–1937).

79. Yury was in the Caucasus with his wife.

80. 1879–1944. A cable from Diaghilev in London to Stravinsky in Morges, December 3, 1919, reveals that Grovlez was being considered as a replacement for Ansermet as the chief conductor of the Ballets Russes.

81. An acquaintance of Stravinsky's who had lived near him at Salvan in the summer of 1914.

82. Son of Heinrich Julius Zimmerman (1851–1922), music publisher and manufacturer of wind instruments.

83. The Symphony in E-flat. The autograph score, with corrections in Rimsky-Korsakov's hand, is in the Bibliothèque Nationale, Paris. The published score that Stravinsky used in his own performances incorporated many revisions, but he made further changes in the American years (such as the reduction in the slow movement of the six measures before 7 to four measures) that have not yet been published.

84. The Faun and the Shepherdess.

85. "Spring" ("The Cloister").

86. Serge Gorodyetsky. (1884–1967). He became a friend of Vera Sudeikina's in the Crimea during the Revolution.

87. Rimsky-Korsakov had advised Stravinsky to "forget about Zimmerman, and, instead, to publish, when possible, with Belaiev." (Stravinsky to his mother, August 19, 1907)

88. Nikolai Vassilievich Artsybashev (1859–1937), a pupil of Rimsky-Korsakov. On July 31, 1907, Rimsky-Korsakov wrote to Artsybashev from Lyubensk, giving Stravinsky's Ustilug address.

89. Count Alexander Dimitrievich Sheremetyev (1859–1919), composer and conductor, had his own orchestra.

90. Vladimir Rimsky-Korsakov, Andrey's brother.

91. Mikhail Vladimirovich Isaacson (1870–1932).

92. "Looking ahead" for a reference to himself in the last pages? In July 1937, answering a publisher who had asked him to write an introduction to a new French edition of the volume, Stravinsky said that he lacked both the time and the inclination, not having a great deal of sympathy with the book.

93. Mikhail Mikhailovich Ivanov (1849–1927), a music critic and composer.

94. Victor Grigoriev Valter (1865–1927), concertmaster of the Maryinsky Theater orchestra. In later years, he harshly attacked Stravinsky, who, already in 1910, called him "insufferable and disgusting," and referred to the "vulgarity and condescension of this ignorant, flippant boor. . . . We do not have a single newspaper free of such filth"—which sounds remarkably like the Stravinsky of a later date.

95. The premiere took place on June 2, 1909, in the Théâtre du Châtelet.

96. Alphonse Jean Hasselmans (1845–1912).

97. As late as 1921, Béla Bartók described Fireworks as "stupefying in its instrumentation." (Op. cit.)

98. The use of folk songs in Petrushka is not a neglected subject, but Irina Vershinina's Stravinsky's Early Ballets (Moscow 1967) is the first study to identify the derivation of the flute and cello themes at the beginning of the score from the cries of the vendors of coal, marinated apples, and herring. Other writers have noted that the melody of the Dance of the Coachmen is known in Russian collections as "O, snow now thaws" (Ulichnaya), that it comes from the county of Tombosk, and that it is a variant of the popular theme "Umorilas" ("Ia na gorkku shla"). Still another folk melody is the Easter song at 2 and 3 and in the two measures after 123. This tune, also known as the "Song of the Volochebniki," comes from the province of Smolyensk. In the music from 311 to 358, Stravinsky anticipates the use of "Song of St. John's Eve" (the June Solstice) from the village of Bashevskaya in the county of

Totemsk. Another popular song that should be mentioned is "Down in the Petersky," which is found in the Fourth Tableau as well as in Balakirev's *Overture on Three Russian Themes*. (In *War and Peace*, Tolstoy describes a troop of soldiers on the march singing the same tune.) Still another folk melody, used in counterpoint with the "Petersky," is *"Akh vy sieni, moi sieni"*:

As is well known, the waltzes at five measures after 71 and at 72 were adapted from Joseph Lanner's *Steyrische Tänze* (Op. 165) and *Die Schönbrunner* (Op. 200), respectively.

Stravinsky heard the melody *"Elle avait une jambe en bois,"* at two measures after 13, played by a hand organ under his window in Beaulieu-sur-Mer, and his use of the theme proved to be an expensive plagiarism, since the music, by Emile Spencer (d. May 24, 1921), had been copyrighted in 1909. As Stravinsky recalled in a letter to his publishers, October 23, 1952, Diaghilev was obliged to pay ten francs to Spencer at each performance of *Petrushka* in 1911, and, by 1932, this had become 220 francs for concert as well as ballet performances. In short, the publisher of the tune was receiving about ten percent of Stravinsky's *Petrushka* royalties, though, as Stravinsky objected, this music did not comprise ten percent of the piece but only twenty-six measures lasting less than forty seconds. Worse still, Spencer's melody is not in the *Petrushka* Suite, but since no separate "Suite" was ever published, the non-performance of the twenty-six measures could not be proved. Boosey & Hawkes's Dr. E. Roth actually suggested to Stravinsky that he "replace these few bars by something which . . . equally serves the purpose." (Letter of February 19, 1951) Stravinsky answered that "One piece of wit cannot be replaced by another in a work already well known to the public, nor can the passage be removed from music that is already in print throughout the world." Even today (1978), one twelfth of *Petrushka*'s royalties in Berne-copyright countries goes to the publisher of Spencer's tune and to the authors of its words.

99. Stravinsky's brother Gury.

100. Gurevich (1844–1906), director of the Gurevich School.

101. Mikhail Fabianovich Gnessen (1883–1957), composer, pupil of Rimsky-Korsakov.

102. Nicolas Roerich—Nikolai Konstantinovich Rerikh (1874–1947)—painter, writer, archeologist, co-author of the scenario of *Le Sacre du Printemps* and designer of the costumes and decors for its first production.

103. Ivan Jakovlevich Bilibin (1876–1942), painter, employed by Diaghilev to work on his production of *Boris Godunov* (1908). He was a friend of Vera Sudeikina in the Crimea in 1917.

104. Dmitri S. Stelletsky (1875–1947), painter and sculptor, made a bust of Stravinsky's brother Yury that was included in the *Art in the Crimea* exhibition in Yalta, in 1918. Diaghilev employed Stelletsky to work with Golovine on *Ivan the Terrible* and *Pskovityanka*. Stelletsky wrote to Stravinsky from Paris, February 15, 1913: "Dear Igor, I think very often about you, and I know everything that has happened to you lately, including the news that you were ill. I am not very happy and, having no heat in my apartment, am living in Argutinsky's, 7, rue François 1er. How all this will finish I do not know. Write a few words. It's always nice to know you have friends. Greetings to your wife. I embrace you. Your Stelletsky."

105. Ilya Efimovich Repin (1844–1930), the greatest Russian painter.

106. Vassili Grigorievich Perov (1833–1882), painter.

107. Pryanishnikov (1840–1894), painter.

108. A. P. Ryabushkin (1861–1904), painter.

109. Stravinsky already seems half aware that this prediction would come true. But, as early as August 19, 1907, in a letter to his mother, he had referred to the Rimsky-Korsakov children as "those nasty Korsaki."

110. The writer E. Anichkov (1866–1937). The book that Andrey sent was *Forerunners and Contemporary Men in Russia and the West*.

111. Theodore and Liudmilla.

112. So far as the observation about "feelings" is concerned, the "we" would seem to be limited to Stravinsky and his correspondent.

113. The thumb between the first two fingers, meaning "to hell with him."

114. Diaghilev's monograph on Levitsky, a copy of which is in the Yale University Library. Dmitri Grigorevich Levitsky (1735–1822) was a portrait painter.

115. On July 8, 1913, Derzhanovsky wrote to Stravinsky in Ustilug: "I somehow feel that Andrey Rimsky-Korsakov is against you personally in his criticisms of Le Sacre. Nikolai Jacovlevich Miaskovsky [1881–1950] wrote to me about A. R.-Korsakov: 'Stravinsky is a much bigger musical event than R.-K. suspects.' "

116. The novelty of the use of the piano as an orchestral instrument in Petrushka is mentioned in most reviews of the time.

117. The friendliness of Stravinsky's letter to Steinberg in Paris (Poste Restante) is suspect, and the following evasion, for example, definitely protests too much: "Dear Max, I would be very happy to see you and to embrace you most warmly. But though I am ready to give my time, I cannot come to see you because of my financial situation. 'Nonsense,' you will say, but sometimes it happens to me, though thank God not often. . . . Also, I must go to Monte Carlo in a week. I kiss you and wait for you impatiently. . . ." (Clarens, March 25, 1912) In later years, Stravinsky avoided Steinberg, as this note from him indicates: "Dear Igor Fyodorovich, I am in Paris and sad that you cannot find time to see me. I want to go to Pulcinella and The Song of the Nightingale but cannot afford tickets. I hope that you can get them for me." (June 16, 1925)

118. Stravinsky was never satisfied with his original scoring of Petrushka, and he spent much time revising it. Writing to Léonide Massine, August 27, 1946, the composer remarks that the original Petrushka requires 100 musicians, whereas the new version reduces the size of the orchestra to 68 "without distortion of combination and balance. This was very difficult work, which is the reason why I am puzzled that anyone can consider doing it with 45 players." Stravinsky adds that he cannot approve of the way it is done by "such enterprises as that of Hurok."

119. In May 1914, Rimsky-Korsakov's widow had published an interview in the St. Petersburg Gazette criticizing Diaghilev's staging of the Coq d'Or. In August, she telegraphed to Stravinsky asking for news of her son Vladimir, who had been cut off in Italy by the war. She knew that Vladimir had planned to meet Stravinsky's brother in Milan; in fact, Vladimir had written to Stravinsky from Venice on July 23. On August 19, she wrote to say that Vladimir was returning by way of Constantinople and asked Stravinsky when he was coming back to Russia.

120. Otto Marius Kling (d. May 6, 1924), director of the London branch of Breitkopf & Härtel until 1915, at which time he became the director of J. & W. Chester. In the latter position, Kling was succeeded by his son Henry, on whose death, in 1936, Stravinsky wrote: "It is sad but necessary to say that Henry Kling died in order that justice could triumph." (Letter to Willy Strecker, October 22, 1936)

121. See Appendix A.

122. Months earlier, in the summer of 1915, Stravinsky had agreed to contribute a manuscript for a book to be edited by Edith Wharton and sold for the benefit of homeless Belgian children. The novelist wrote to Stravinsky on August 12, 1915: "Monsieur Bakst has led me to hope that you would give a page of music for 'Le Livre des Sans Foyer.' Your manuscript will be part of a large collection in a volume that I am preparing for the benefit of the refugees, and I will be personally very proud to have you on my list of writers and musicians who have shown their concern. I am enclosing our little circular, et vous prie, Monsieur, de croire à mes sentiments très distingués, Edith Wharton." Stravinsky composed the Souvenir d'une Marche Boche, September 1, 1915, for this anthology.

123. Writing to Stravinsky apropos this performance, Léon Bakst said that he had been inspired with a new conception of The Firebird, and that he hoped to realize it at the Maryinsky Theater with Siloti. Bakst knew that Stravinsky

had been dissatisfied by Golovine's decors. (The letter also asks Stravinsky to make excuses on Bakst's behalf to Misia Sert.)

124. Stravinsky entrusted the English translation of this text to Edwin Evans, though he had long ago described him as "naïve and not very intelligent." (Letter to Ansermet, June 6, 1919) It should be mentioned that Stravinsky rejected Aeolian's first contract on the grounds that neither *The Firebird* nor *Petrushka* could be "characterized by excerpts." (Letter of July 18, 1927) Prokofiev wrote to Stravinsky, November 22, 1927, asking for information about the Aeolian project, then, after a stay in London, wrote again: "Saerchinger annoyed me in London with the question of a book of biographies of dead composers written—or at any rate signed—by living ones. He said that you had done one of Mussorgsky on which Evans had supposedly worked with you. Before I agree to participate, I would like to know if Evans is lying. . . ." Stravinsky wrote in the margin: "Of course he lies."

125. Mrs. Stravinsky's diary, August 14, 1955, describes her husband's fury on reading, in Heinrich Strobel's *Stravinsky: Classical Humanist*, that he was introduced to Debussy's music by Diaghilev: "Igor says that he remembers playing *The Afternoon of a Faun* to Rimsky-Korsakov years before meeting Diaghilev."

126. The beginning of *Le Sacre du Printemps* was once thought to have been suggested by the beginning of *The Afternoon of a Faun* (see, for example, the *Mercure de France*, October 1, 1913, p. 629). But the melody much more closely resembles the bassoon-solo introduction to Gritsko's aria, *"Zachem ty, serdtse,"* in *The Fair at Sorochinsk,* and No. 157 of A. Yushkenich's *Melodu Lundowe Litewskie,* Part I (Cracow, 1900).

127. This is not the same concert mentioned on page 23.

128. Désiré-Emile Inghelbrecht, the conductor (1880–1965). Stravinsky thought enough of him to paste his obituary from the London *Times* in the sketchbook for the *Requiem Canticles*.

129. Swiss musicologist (1866–1950). Ansermet's correspondence reveals that Godet was hostile to Stravinsky's music.

130. This was during Stravinsky's visit to Paris to conduct *The Firebird* and to discuss the contract for *Renard* with the Princesse Edmond de Polignac.

131. That Stravinsky was a dandy is shown by the bills of his Paris tailor, James Pile. On July 20, 1923, for example, the composer ordered a "black cashmere smoking suit," on September 27, "a green jacket and gray flannel pants," and, every few days, it seems, he bought neckties, scarves, hats. "He has such elegance," *Lidové Noviny,* the Prague newspaper, said, February 25, 1930, "that one would attribute twenty other professions to him before that of a composer of music. A pink shirt, silk tie, perfectly cut brown suit . . ." Many of his letters mention clothes, as, for example, when writing to his publisher, Willy Strecker, October 6, 1932, Stravinsky asks him, while in London, to fetch some *tricotées* linen shirts that had been ordered from Hilditch and Key. Scarcely an interview throughout Stravinsky's life fails to describe his apparel. "A bowler worn to protect the neck, a yellow tie hidden by a dark blue pullover . . . and beneath that a light linen vest. . . ." (*Le Soir,* Brussels, January 15, 1924) "He was dressed in a brown and rose sweater, which replaced the colorful orange shirt and scarf and black ulster in which he landed from the liner *Paris* on Sunday" (*New York Times,* January 6, 1925). "He wore a grey jacket, violet shirt, green tie, golden bracelet, and a monocle on a black tether" (*Die Stunde,* Vienna, March 17, 1926). "[He was] clad in a dark, double-breasted suit, with gray spats peeping beneath perfectly pressed trousers, and a white handkerchief dazzling in his pocket" (*Washington Post,* March 24, 1935). "Igor Stravinsky entered the room without my hearing him. I turned at the sound of his voice. He was dressed in a white linen suit with a sport shirt open at the neck" (*Excelsior,* Paris, September 11, 1935). At Harvard, in 1939, on one occasion, "Stravinsky's clothes [were] collegiate: a brown suit-coat, contrasting gray trousers, black shirt, grayish sweater." Even in the American Midwest and South his garments were always considered to be worthy of notice: "He wore plain dark trousers, with a matching V-neck, slip-over sweater of soft wool, a checkered black and white coat, yellow socks and black oxfords" (*Urbana News-Gazette,* March 3, 1949); "doffing a small black Homburg and a white

muffler ... smoking a Turkish cigarette" (*Atlanta Journal*, January 27, 1955); "This little man who has just bustled in wears a comfortable wind-breaker jacket and unpressed khaki trousers" (*Downbeat*, September 9, 1946, describing the Hollywood recording session of the *Ebony Concerto*). The wardrobe of Stravinsky's first wife provides a striking contrast to that of the composer: "I am very ashamed to admit that I've ordered myself a skirt, as I've only one summer skirt ..." (November 4, 1937); "My telegram gives you an account of money needs ... because I have little left and want to buy a woolen shirt and sweater" (October 12, 1937); "I am going to ask you for a present when you come in November. Bring some boots of the same kind that you gave me before. ... We can dispense with considerations of elegance. I write about this now because perhaps it's better to buy such things in London than in Paris" (October 16, 1937). Catherine Stravinsky once wrote to her husband: "The prices at Pile's are frightful, but it's difficult to find another tailor after having dressed yourself there for so many years. Perhaps you could buy yourself a ready-made traveling coat, though, of course, they are never so good ..."

132. These remarks may have been provoked by such comments in the press as the following by, first, Florent Schmitt: "... Igor Stravinsky is, I believe, the Messiah for whom we have been waiting since Wagner, and for whom Mussorgsky and Claude Debussy, Richard Strauss and Arnold Schoenberg seem to have prepared the path ..." (*La France*, June 4, 1913); and, second, by Stravinsky himself: "I want to suggest neither situations nor emotions, but simply to manifest, to express them. I think there is in what are called 'impressionist' methods a certain amount of hypocrisy, of, at least, a tendency toward vagueness and ambiguity. That I shun above all things, and that, perhaps, is the reason why my methods differ as much from those of the impressionists as they differ from conventional academic methods. I always aim at straightforward expression in its simplest form. ... The one essential thing is to feel and to convey one's feelings" (Interview from Carl Van Vechten's "Igor Stravinsky: A New Composer," in *Music After the Great War and Other Studies* [New York: Schirmer, 1915], pp. 92–3).

133. Stravinsky's letters to Debussy, one of them in the possession of a New York collector, the others owned by Serge Lifar, have not been made available.

134. Louis Laloy (1874–1944), Debussy's friend.

135. Mikhail Dmitri Calvocoressi (1877–1944) translated into French the libretto of Stravinsky's *Nightingale*, and the texts of his Gorodyetzky and Balmont songs.

136. In November 1951, in an interview on the Geneva Radio with Franz Walter, Stravinsky confirmed that he had begun the composition of *Petrushka* in Lausanne, but a sketchbook in the possession of Mrs. Arthur Wilhelm of Basel is signed and dated September 1910, Clarens.

137. Writing from Ustilug, June 18, 1912, to V. V. Derzhanovsky, Stravinsky says that: "In the event that one of the organizers of the concerts is bothered by the pantomimic nature of the last pages, there is a special ending ... which is attached to the score and the parts for a concert production of the work. But if you want my frank opinion, *Petrushka* should be performed from beginning to end without a single cut, change, or this special ending."

138. American composer (1877–1933). As the patron of the violinist Samuel Dushkin (1891–1976)—or "adopted father," as Stravinsky says in his letters—Fairchild played a significant role in Stravinsky's life in the early 1930s. As late as the summer of 1932, Dushkin's letters to Stravinsky begin "*Cher Monsieur Stravinsky*," while those of Fairchild begin "*Mon cher ami.*"

139. *Diaghilev* (New York: Putnam, 1940).

140. For a discussion of Stravinsky's changing attitudes concerning Nijinsky's choreography, see Appendix B.

141. *Igra Umykaniya*, or mock abduction of the bride, a ritual common to exogamous societies.

142. Nikolai Fyodorovich Findeizen (1868–1928), editor of *The Russian Newspaper*.

143. Diaghilev had already suggested Poe's *The Masque of the Red Death* to Stravinsky as a possible subject for his next ballet.

144. Vladimir Arkadylovich Telyakovsky (1861–1924), director of the Imperial Russian Theater.

145. *Expositions and Developments* (New York: Doubleday, 1962). In 1929, Stravinsky told his biographer André Schaffner that the incident with the bull occurred on the return trip to Volhynia.

146. A year later, Stravinsky noted the receipt of 100 kronen in his *Copie des Lettres*. This book, so valuable for the study of Stravinsky's hurried, run-on Russian prose style, is regrettably illegible in places, like a volume of blotters. Also, the contents and index are not in perfect agreement. But the mystery of the *Copie* is the reason why some years between the first and last entries, 1912 and 1927, are not represented at all.

147. Reed pipes. The statement seems to contradict one by Stravinsky to the effect that he composed the Introduction after finishing "Spring Rounds." The sketches in the collection of the late André Meyer include only two notations for the Introduction, and the only manuscript for the movement known to the present writer is the abbreviated full score (six pages) in the possession of Serge Lifar. This contains indications for instrumentation, but they are not detailed, and numerous other differences are found between this draft and the final score. Other stages in the composition obviously preceded this one.

148. "The old woman" enters at ⎿15⏌, according to Stravinsky's notation in the score that he prepared for Nijinsky.

149. Misia Godebska Edwards Sert (1872–1950). See Appendix B.

150. According to *The Rite of Spring Sketches* (London: Boosey & Hawkes, 1969), this was "after the London performances of *Petrushka*," but these took place in February 1913.

151. 1875–1964.

152. Pierre Monteux, *Dance Index*, New York, 1948.

153. Laloy's recollections were written fifteen years after the event (*La Musique Retrouvée*, 1928), but he mentions *Le Sacre* in *La Grande Revue*, June 25, 1912, and makes clear that he has just heard the music. Also, Debussy recalls the occasion in an undated letter postmarked "Clarens, November 8, 1912."

154. Of Part One only, at this date.

155. Gabriel Astruc (1884–1938), impresario.

156. Actually the home of Maurice Delage.

157. *Quicksilver*, by Dame Marie Rambert (London: Macmillan, 1972). See Appendix B.

158. Manager of Diaghilev's Ballets Russes (1883–1968).

159. See Part I, note 52.

160. *Op. cit.*

161. Louis François Aubert (1877–1968), composer, pupil of Fauré.

162. Alfredo Casella (1883–1947), composer.

163. Emile Vuillermoz (1878–1960), critic.

164. The Société Musicale Indépendante, founded by Ravel, Koechlin, and others in 1910, disbanded in the 1930s. Stravinsky was a member, having been proposed by Debussy.

165. Stravinsky had recommended the Bartók and Schoenberg works for performance.

166. "Lazare-Lévy": Lazare Lévy (1882–1964), pianist and composer.

167. René Dumesnil (1879–?), librettist and critic.

168. *The Correspondence of S. S. Prokofiev and N. Y. Miaskovsky*, introduction by Dmitri Kabalevsky (published by *Soviet Composer*, Moscow, 1977).

169. Evans wrote to Stravinsky, then in the Savoy Hotel, February 4, 1913: "*Je serais très heureux de faire votre connaissance*," mentioning "*mon ami*" Delage as a reference. Later that month, Evans introduced the composer to a London dealer from whom Stravinsky purchased a copy of a German edition of Aubrey Beardsley's *Lysistratus*—which may have established the association, made famous in Stravinsky's Autobiography, between *Pierrot Lunaire*, heard in Berlin only two months before, and the esthetics of "the Beardsley cult."

170. On December 30, 1913 (January 12, 1914?), Kussevitzky, in Moscow, wrote to Stravinsky in the Hôtel Châtelard, Clarens, requesting permission to

have the piccolo tromba part played by a standard (B♭ or C) instrument, since "The D trumpet does not exist in Moscow." Kussevitzky adds that if the instrument is available in Paris, he would like to buy it.

171. This refers to a lawsuit that Stravinsky brought against Mme Miquel Alzieu, who had borrowed 3,000 rubles from him with which to make a concert tour in India; she had not repaid the loan. On February 5, 1914, Maurice Delage, in Paris, wrote to Stravinsky in Clarens: "Fanet. Il paraît que la vente . . . produit bien peu de choses. Je me viens au courant de leur agisse et veux bien finir avec le père Alzieu. Voilà, mais comment?" During the entire period of the first Sacre performances, Stravinsky was involved in this litigation.

172. See Appendix B.

173. Only a few reviews of the first performance contain any factual information about the choreography, nor can many details be gleaned from the mountains of rhetoric and opinion published in the days, weeks, and months after the event. Apart from Jacques Rivière's well-known essay, perhaps only one other review deserves mention, that by Jean Marnold in the Mercure de France, October 1, 1913. On October 24, 1924, Robert Lyon, Stravinsky's friend and the proprietor of Pleyel, sent a collection of twenty-six extracts from the press of both the premiere and Monteux's concert performance a year later. The contents of Lyon's booklet would comprise a volume in itself, valuable especially for psychologists studying audience behavior—including that of reviewers, not one of whom acknowledged that the music was difficult to digest and to comprehend, comparing it, instead, to noises, and dismissing it as nonsense. As for the scandal, two writers invoke the first night of Ubu Roi, others the first nights of Hernani and Tannhäuser.

174. According to Janet Flanner (op. cit.): "Maurice Ravel cried on hearing [that Stravinsky] was ill."

175. 1879–1940. Monteux's letters to Stravinsky spell the name this way—without a hyphen, as if the conductor were a character in a Restoration comedy. Stravinsky also addressed him as "Mon cher Baton" (letter of July 25, 1931). Rhené-Baton was the conductor of the Concerts Pasdeloup from 1916 to 1925. In a letter to Schmitt, July 1912, Stravinsky comments on a performance of The Firebird conducted by Rhené-Baton. Shortly after that, Stravinsky loaned the Scherzo Fantastique score to him; a card from Rhené-Baton to Stravinsky in Ustilug (forwarded from there to Clarens October 5, 1912) indicates that the conductor hoped to play the Scherzo that winter.

176. Cf. Sokolova: "I remember a group of Ancients with long beards and hair, who stood huddled together, shaking and trembling as if they were dying of fear."

177. Diaghilev.

178. The Baroness d'Erlanger, who was the Stravinskys' neighbor in Hollywood for two decades. Four years after her death (1960), they purchased her house, extensively remodeled it, and spent their last years in California there. Stravinsky had known her in Paris and London in the Diaghilev period: "Private performances and suppers were given by Mlle Gabrielle Chanel in her superb [Faubourg] St.-Honoré mansion, with Diaghilev, Picasso, Cocteau, Stravinsky, Baroness d'Erlanger, Mme Sert, Comte de Beaumont, and other international personalities as guests. In London, the Ballet was fêted by the late Mrs. Samuel Courtauld . . . in Madrid, by the Duque de Tovar; in Rome, by the British diplomatic staff." (Janet Flanner, op. cit.)

179. "Cela ne la gêne point," Stravinsky quotes Misia in a card to his wife, January 22: "Seriozha is delighted, and he has completely changed his opinion about my music." Percy Scholes wrote in Everyman, May 1, 1914: "In five years Stravinsky's style has completely changed. . . . He says that he has tried to continue the work in the older style, and that where differences are found they must be taken as the result of unconscious forces which are too strong for him."

180. Stravinsky next heard from Diaghilev in a telegram from Cologne, February 14: "Petrushka two performances great success Fokine very good. I am leaving for London, Savoy." Then, on April 21, Diaghilev sent an Easter telegram from Monte Carlo: "Christ is Risen. Will we be risen in Paris? Dying of fear? Count on hearing Sacre Paris Sunday." The fear refers to the forthcom-

ing season and the new productions, including that of *The Nightingale.* Diaghilev telegraphed on April 24: "Will be at the Crillon Sunday morning have tickets from Monteux. Delighted to see you." But Stravinsky did not attend Monteux's second concert performance of *Le Sacre,* April 26.

181. Stravinsky first played the complete opera for his friends in April: "I have been one of a party of friends, to whom the composer played the whole work, partly from proof and partly from manuscript. . . . Stravinsky, with whom I recently had the pleasure of spending several hours . . . displays a frankness and fulness of expression that, to the interviewer, are very welcome." (Scholes, *op. cit.*)

182. Swiss painter, Dalcrozian eurhythmicist and pianist (1891–1921). While in Leysin, Thévenaz played the *Sacre* four-hands with a lady patient. On September 21, 1916, Diaghilev, in San Sebastián, telegraphed to Stravinsky: "Get an answer from Thévenaz." Stravinsky telegraphed: "Thévenaz to return to Paris three days pretends everything arranged for his departure for America beginning November. . . . Will nevertheless try to see him in Paris." Thévenaz wrote to Stravinsky from America and again later, after returning to Europe.

Radiguet and Barbette were two other Cocteau protégés who became friends of Stravinsky. On December 4, 1923, Paul Collaer wrote to Stravinsky: "Cocteau wrote to me that you were very enthusiastic about Barbette. What perfection! What beauty!" A note to Stravinsky, December 18, 1923, from Georges Auric, announcing the death of Radiguet, greatly shocked Stravinsky.

183. Eugenia Errazuriz was an intimate friend of both John Singer Sargent and Pablo Picasso (!). From 1916 to the end of the war, she sent a stipend of a thousand francs a month to Stravinsky. He described her death in an automobile accident—in Chile in 1951, under bizarre circumstances—in a letter to his elder son, April 27, 1951.

184. Three Pieces for String Quartet.

185. Alexander Akimovich Sanine (1868–1956).

186. Telegram, April 27.

187. Rimsky-Korsakov.

188. Stepan Stepanovich Mitussov (1878–1942), co-librettist of *The Nightingale,* was one of Stravinsky's closest friends. In 1913, Mitussov gave the manuscript of two songs to Stravinsky that he later used in, respectively, *Renard* and *Les Noces.* Mitussov was related to the wife of Nicolas Roerich, and it was Mitussov who had introduced Stravinsky to his future co-scenarist of *Le Sacre du Printemps.* A trained musician, after the Revolution Mitussov became the conductor of the chorus at the Marzhdanov Theater and also organized concerts of new music. On May 4, 1925, he wrote to Stravinsky "from the same apartment in which you started to be pregnant with *The Nightingale.* . . . We are studying *Pribaoutki* and will perform it in a concert on May 10. Is the $\downarrow$ = 66, con moto, correct? Shouldn't it be faster? . . . I spend the whole day at the piano." The letter is affectionate and nostalgic, but well written, with a superior vocabulary. Stravinsky replied, and Mitussov wrote describing the concert: "Your brother [Yury] came, and Karatygin, who especially liked the *Japanese Lyrics.* . . . Finally I have received the *Berceuses du Chat.* . . ."

189. "Walter" (Vladimir Fyodorovich) Nouvel.

190. A dramatization of Dostoevsky's novel.

191. As late as November 27, 1913, Sanine telegraphed to Stravinsky that Roerich, not Benois, was to make the decors.

192. This contradicts Stravinsky's statement "I was with Diaghilev in the Montreux Palace Hotel when he heard the news of Nijinsky's marriage, and I watched him turn into a madman who begged me and my wife not to leave him alone." (Cf. *Memories and Commentaries* [New York: Doubleday, 1960]) But since the marriage had taken place less than three weeks earlier (September 10, Buenos Aires), Diaghilev was undoubtedly still in a very disturbed state of mind. The meeting took place in the Hôtel Beau Rivage, Lausanne. Diaghilev came to Switzerland October 30 to discuss *The Nightingale* with Stravinsky, and it was apparently at this time that the two decided that Messager should be asked to conduct it. On November 2, 1913, Diaghilev telegraphed to Stravinsky asking him to send the letter for Messager in care of Misia, and, on January

6, 1914, Diaghilev telegraphed to Stravinsky asking him to thank Messager for having accepted.

193. Valerian I. Svetlov (1860–1934), a well-known balletomane.

194. Benois believed that Nijinsky had married an heiress.

195. Konstantin Alexandrovich Marzhdanov (1872–1933), Director of the Moscow Art Theater. Ilya Ehrenburg described him in *First Years of Revolution, 1918–21* as "a man of gentle but uncompromising spirit."

196. Stravinsky's idea was to have the Emperor fixed on his throne like a doll.

197. Milène Stravinsky.

198. Benois's wife.

199. In one of his "Conversation" books, Stravinsky describes a ride with Colette on the Paris-Marseille train, saying that she "got drunk and sang Wagner." This evidently took place in December 1924, since she wrote to Stravinsky from Marseille telling him that she looked forward to hearing his Marseille concert on the 21st of that month.

200. *Op. cit.*

201. Diaghilev had cabled to Salvan on June 13: "Where is Igor? His immediate presence in London is very important." Stravinsky arrived on the 14th or 15th, at the Hotel Cecil, and, on the latter date, went to the Coliseum to hear a "Grand Futurist Concert of Noises," during which Marinetti discoursed on "The Art of Noises" and Luigi Russolo conducted his Two Noise Spirals. The orchestra of "23 Noise Tuners" included "Buzzers, Whistlers, Rattlers, Exploders, Murmurers, Cracklers, Thunderers, Gurglers, and Roarers." The new electric instruments were "invented and constructed by Russolo and Ugo Piatti." Stravinsky's wife wrote on the 16th, "Finally I received a telegram from you; why didn't you stay in the Savoy?"; again on the 17th, asking for some postcards; and, on the 18th: "What interests me is your conversation with Andrey [Rimsky-Korsakov]. Since you do not write about Nadyezhda Nikolayevna, probably she did not come and they could not prevent the performance of *Le Coq d'Or*. What does Diaghilev think of your request to be paid for the London performances of *The Nightingale*?" On the 18th, Stravinsky's daughter wrote asking for a box of paints. On the 19th, his wife wrote: "I forgot your birthday because of the Russian calendar. Then today I received a telegram from your mother and I telegraphed to you. I remember how last year in Neuilly I bought a watch for you. You were so ill then, but I think that your birthday was the turning point."

202. The actual date of the letter is July 14, but this must be Old Style, Diaghilev's telegram being dated July 16. *The Nightingale* was performed on June 29, July 14, and July 23.

203. Stravinsky's wife wrote to him on the 20th: "Yesterday I received your letter and telegram. Diaghilev is always the same [literally, "always true to himself"]. Because of the timing, you could not have *The Nightingale* as you wanted it and your whole hope was that it would finally be good in London, as it was not in Paris. What did Andrey [Rimsky-Korsakov] say about *The Nightingale*?"

204. Either Rubinstein's chronology is mistaken, since *Petrushka* was not given until after Strauss's ballet, or, more likely, the work was *The Nightingale*.

205. Paul Kochanski (1887–1934), violinist, and his wife, Zosia. The first of Stravinsky's arrangements of excerpts from his ballets for violin and piano—the *Suite Italienne* from *Pulcinella*, completed August 24, 1925—is dedicated to Kochanski, who wrote to "Igor Igorushka" on September 14, 1925, thanking him, and remarking that "the fingerings are very good." The first performance, at Frankfurt, November 25, 1925, under the title "Suite for Violin and Piano," was by the violinist Alma Moodie, accompanied by the composer. The following year, Stravinsky arranged the "*Berceuse*" and "*Ronde des Princesses*" from *The Firebird* for violin and piano, and he also gave these to Kochanski; a letter from Stravinsky to H. Kling, December 23, 1926, refers to these *Firebird* arrangements as having been completed "*dernièrement*."

206. Karol Szymanowski. He and Stravinsky were good friends in later years, though the Polish master was a closer friend of Vera Sudeikina, who used to visit him in his sanatorium at Davos. When Stravinsky played his Piano

Concerto in Warsaw in 1924, Szymanowski telegraphed from Lwow: *"Désolé de ne pas pouvoir venir . . . Amitiés pour Strawinski."*

207. Stravinsky was one of Dada's innumerable vice-presidents, and Tristan Tzara persuaded him to donate the manuscript of the *"Chanson pour Compter"* to a Dada magazine. The newspaper *La Suisse* classified another Stravinsky song, *"Le Moineau Est Assis,"* as an example of Dada, and, on February 19, 1920, printed the French text (erroneously attributing this translation to Stravinsky), together with some mocking remarks and a parody version. In Paris two years later, Tzara, Marcel Duchamp, and Francis Picabia became closer friends of Stravinsky through Vera Sudeikina, and Picabia was constantly sending scenarios to Stravinsky as subjects for possible collaboration. One of these, a twelve-minute spectacle, *Les Yeux Chauds,* required several light projectors, cinematography, a monkey and other animals, a parrot, five nude women, and some acrobats. Picabia delivered this to the composer in room 327, the Hôtel Continental, Paris, September 26, 1921, with a note: *"J'espère à mercredi soir pour dîner. Très sympathiquement à vous."*

208. Ansermet quoted Carl Maria von Weber on Beethoven's Fourth Symphony, and the statement impressed Stravinsky to the extent that he framed it and kept it on the walls of his studios for the remainder of his life.

209. Russian artist (1881–1962), granddaughter of Pushkin. She designed the first production of *Les Noces.*

210. Russian painter (1881–1964), husband of Goncharova. He designed the first production of *Renard,* drew one solo portrait of the composer, in 1924, and seven others of him in groups: with Diaghilev and Goncharova, Paris, May 1914; with "Diaghilev, Massine, Katia" *("La Ronde Célèbre"),* 1915; with Cocteau, Ansermet, Massine, Diaghilev, 1915; with Cocteau, Ansermet, Massine, Diaghilev, and "B.F." (?), 1915; with Picasso, Misia Sert, Olga Kokhlova, 1917; with Satie, Prokofiev, Misia Sert, Massine, 1921; with Picasso, Misia Sert, Apollinaire, Massine, Lifar, Cocteau, Ansermet, January 20, 1924.

211. At this stage, Diaghilev praised Massine's choreography: "Nightingale: Massine works marvels. Sending 4,000 francs." (Telegram, Diaghilev to Stravinsky, December 3, 1919)

212. Second violinist of the Flonzaley Quartet (1878–1959).

213. The pieces were played in Paris, probably on that date. A letter from Pochon to Stravinsky, May 19, asks for information about the Paris performance. Casella, in a note dated March 17, 1915, requests permission to present the Pieces at the Salle des Agriculteurs, Paris, on April 13, but this performance may have been postponed until May 19. When the Pieces were performed in Paris in November 1916, Léon Bakst wrote to Stravinsky (on the 17th): "Violette Murat is fantastically excited about your Quartet and wants to buy the manuscript." Francis Poulenc was present at this performance, as his letter to Stravinsky, March 5, 1917, indicates. (Poulenc had written to Stravinsky through his close friend Dmitri Stelletsky.) On Tuesday, July 18, 1917, the Three Pieces were given at the Salle d'Antin, which was then exhibiting Picasso's *Les Demoiselles d'Avignon,* as well as paintings by Chirico, Matisse, Rouault, Derain, Dufy, Léger, and Modigliani. The quartet players were Mlle Yvonne Astruc, Darius Milhaud, Arthur Honegger, and Félix Delgrange. A letter from Delgrange to Stravinsky, November 2, 1916, explains that Milhaud had borrowed the parts, or score, from the Princesse de Polignac. On January 12 and 24, 1916, Stravinsky's friend Mme Khvoshinsky, wife of the attaché to the Russian Embassy in Rome, wrote to ask for the parts, but a performance in the Italian city evidently did not take place at that time. (Stravinsky preserved a photograph of himself with Mme Khvoshinsky in Belle Rive, 1915.)

214. *Op. cit.*

215. In later years, Vera Janacopoulos sang in several concerts with Stravinsky. A letter from Marya Freund, October 18, 1915, indicates that Stravinsky had given two of the *Pribaoutki* manuscripts to her in the spring of 1915. Stravinsky wanted her to return them, and she replied that she had left them in Breslau but hoped that her mother could send them.

216. Georges Barrère (1878–1944).

217. Stravinsky's wife wrote to him in London, June 20, 1914: "Yesterday I had a letter from Liudmilla. Grisha [Grigory, her husband] advises you to

come to Kiev in June because later he cannot be with you there. . . . She received *The Firebird* (score). Today mother will come [from Milan]. Rubakin arrived. . . ." But Stravinsky had been planning to go to Kiev since April, and, in Paris, at the beginning of that month, told his friends that he would go in a week or two. Cocteau telegraphed from Paris on April 27 expressing the hope that Stravinsky's business affairs had been successful, and Delage wrote, on April 30: "Have you returned from Kiev? I suppose so," adding, "I am still very moved by your great triumph in Paris."

218. This great Slavophile, who died in 1856, compiled some twelve volumes of Russian folk songs, drawing on the work of other collectors, including Pushkin.

219. On January 19, 1924, Stravinsky wrote to Harry Kling: "I have just finished an orchestration of the song *Tilimbom (Trois Histoires pour Enfants)* [composed May 22, 1917], which had such a great success in my last concert in Antwerp on January 7. . . . Since the piece is too short for a separate concert number, I enlarged it and wrote the verses myself. . . ."

220. See Part I, note 14.

221. See Part I, note 222.

222. Benois's letter is dated July 23, but this must be Old Style.

223. Russian humorous magazine.

224. See Part I, note 14.

225. 1869–1940.

226. Stravinsky had met the Marchioness of Ripon the year before. He wrote to Benois, from Clarens, November 21, 1911: "Diaghilev has finally made up with Astruc and in the evening of the day I was in Paris we all got together at Astruc's home and put on *The Firebird* and *Petrushka* for the Marquise Ripon . . . who would like to have them in London."

227. Polignac telegraphed from Paris on January 31, 1916: "*Espère arriver Beau Rivage Ouchy samedi.*" (February 5 was a Saturday.) A vintner's bills reveal that Stravinsky purchased a dozen bottles of champagne in January. He was in Italy in the last week of that month.

228. Lydia Lopokova was born in St. Petersburg in 1891. Stravinsky kept several photographs of her from the Madrid period, and he went to Bordeaux to see her in September 1916, shortly before the Ballets Russes sailed from there to New York; a photograph has survived of the two together at that time. In September 1965, in Festival Hall, London, Lopokova, then Lady Keynes (the widow of John Maynard Keynes), saw Stravinsky backstage after he had conducted the *Fireworks* and *Firebird* Suite, and wept.

229. Falla later inscribed a photograph of his portrait by Picasso: "*A Igor Stravinsky, l'élu. . . .*"

230. On March 23, 1918, Stravinsky sent a telegram to Mme Errazuriz: "*. . . vous enverrai prochainement un ragtime récemment composé pour vous . . . ,*" but this refers to the *Ragtime* for eleven instruments, not to the *Piano-Rag-Music.*

231. In London, in 1921, Stravinsky had a brief romance with Juanita Gandarillas, the wife of Mme Errazuriz's nephew, Tony Gandarillas. Mme Gandarillas gave a pair of sapphire-and-diamond cufflinks to Stravinsky, one of which he lost, while the other he made into a brooch for his second wife.

232. Stravinsky received his Spanish visa in Paris, March 12, 1921, and left France at La Hendaye on the 16th, after looking for a residence for his family at Anglet (Bayonne). He then went to Seville with Diaghilev and Boris Kochno, returning in April to Madrid for the ballet season. Back in Madrid, Robert Delaunay painted the composer's portrait.

233. It should be mentioned that although Stravinsky totally rejected Victor Belayev's book about *Les Noces*, the composer took the trouble to correct specific points of Belayev's analysis. For example, the latter gives the tonality at ⟦50⟧ as C major, and Stravinsky writes over this "A minor"; Belayev identifies ⟦58⟧ as A major and ⟦59⟧ as C major, which Stravinsky changes to, respectively, "A minor" and "Aeolian." Also, Stravinsky questions the attribution of the tonality B at ⟦87⟧, ⟦98⟧, and ⟦130⟧, of C at ⟦106⟧, and of E at ⟦114⟧, and he writes that there are three codas, at ⟦127⟧, ⟦130⟧, and ⟦133⟧. Finally, when

Belayev refers to a "development," Stravinsky denies this and writes "rather dialogue."

234. Jerome Robbins wrote to Stravinsky, November 11, 1953: "I notice that sometimes you fit and reshift the words to accommodate them within a set metric pattern and at other times you change the time signature to fit the rhythm of the words. . . . I have talked with Dubrovska, who danced the bride originally, and who . . . informed me that, instead of learning counts, the corps de ballet knew and danced to the Russian words . . . [and] that Nijinska followed the oral patterns and accents."

235. Stravinsky's sketches include a note: "Among the songs collected by Pushkin, see pages 54–60 [Kireyevsky]." These pages contain references to "dancing in the bath." Another note reminds the composer to "See Customs, Songs, Rituals, etc. in the Province of Pskov, pages 48–54 [Kireyevsky]," which refers to the same thing. Stravinsky's sketches contain several reminders to himself to look up words in Vladimir Dal's *Explanatory Dictionary of the Living Great Russian Language*, and in a letter to Païchadze, March 25, 1929, Stravinsky lists Dal's dictionary as one of the "sources" of *Svadebka (Les Noces)*. Professor William Harkins of Columbia University has written that at [52] "Stravinsky has retained the Pskov dialect use of *ch* for the standard Russian *ts* in *cherkov* for *tsérkov* ('church') but he corrects it elsewhere in the same quotation (*potselovát*, for *pochelovát*, 'to kiss'). The apparent inconsistency is probably to be explained by the fact that the non-standard form *chér-kov* is relatively more comprehensible, particularly in combination with *sobor*, 'cathedral,' than is *pochelovát*." See the chapter on "Wedding Ceremonials and Chants" in Sokolov's *Russian Folklore* (New York: Macmillan, 1950, for the American Council of Learned Societies), pp. 203–23, also Birkan's "On the Poetic Text of *Les Noces*," in *Muzyka*, Moscow, 1966, and *Russian Folk Poetic Creativity* (Moscow: Uchpedgiz, 1956), p. 239.

236. Casella, in his monograph on Stravinsky (1926), likened *Les Noces* to Vecchi's *Amfiparnasso* (1594), a farfetched comparison, but one that may have been suggested by Stravinsky himself, who was fond of throwing out false scents of this kind. It may be regretted that Stravinsky never explained the anthropological background of the piece, the rituals and cultural traditions of which Western audiences are largely unaware. Some knowledge of the customs of exogamous marriage, of the mock abduction of the bride—such as Mandelstam saw in a 1930 Abkhazian wedding ceremony (and recalled in a poem)—makes *Les Noces* more meaningful. The listener should realize that the *druzhka*'s music resembles that of Russian village street criers. An awareness of the background of the element of lamentation is also vital to an understanding of the mixture of irony and religion, and of the pagan underground of *Les Noces*.

237. Plaited hair is "a fetish which Freud places at the origins of weaning (institutionally assigned to women). The braid replaces the missing penis . . . so that cutting off the braid, whether on the level of play . . . or whether as social aggression among the ancient Chinese, for whom the pigtail was the phallic perquisite of the masters and the Manchu invaders, is an act of castration." (From *Erté*, by Roland Barthes [New York: Rizzoli International, 1975])

238. "Darling, my little wife, Natasha, we will live together very happily, and everybody will envy us."

239. *Op. cit.*

240. From the *Oktoëchos* or "Book of Eight Tones." Russian ecclesiastical chant, which derives from the Byzantine, is based on a system of eight *echoi*. These are the Byzantine modes—as distinguished from *tonoi*, the Greek modes—each of which possesses different melodic formulas. Thus the Sticheron (Psalm tropes), Troparion (hymns sung between the verses of the Psalms), and Irmos (a Byzantine strophic chant) are sung to eight different "tones" (same sense as in Gregorian Chant), each of which includes three versions for the Sticheron, three for the Troparion, and three for the Irmos. The chant that Stravinsky chose, the Fifth Tone of Sticheron, sung after the matin Psalm "Lord, I cried unto Thee," occurs during the part of the service in which typological parallels are drawn between Old and New Testament prophecies. Stravinsky no longer possessed his copy of the *Oktoëchos* in America, but in

the early 1950s the Byzantine monastery at Grottaferrata presented an Italian translation *(Ottoeco)* to him.

241. "Les Noces . . . is written for a polyphonic, contrapuntal chorus. I go back to Bach and to Palestrina and to old Russian church music. You in the western world do not know this, but in Russia any chorus can sing this music, because for years they sang it in the churches. There were no instruments. . . . I did not want anything so human as violins. The voices give the music of the wind instruments, and there is an intransigent quality about it that you cannot get from the strings. Four pianos give the percussion effect. You would be surprised at what can be done with such a combination." *(Musical America,* New York, January 10, 1925)

242. On March 6, 1915, Stravinsky arranged the Polka for four hands, a combination used the previous summer in *Valse des Fleurs.* Misia Sert seems to have seen the Polka before Diaghilev (to whom it is dedicated), at least to judge from the following telegram, Diaghilev to Stravinsky: *"Misia 29 envoie moi polka cable combien sans blague voudrais recevoir?"* (Rome, February 24, 1915). Casella wrote to Stravinsky from Rome, March 3, 1917: "The concert in which I want to play your four-hand pieces has been advanced to March 23. Diaghilev tells me that he has the Polka. . . . Send me [the other] pieces by diplomatic courier, in other words by friend Khvoshinsky, or else the music will arrive too late."

243. These telegrams are dated January 1, 3, 13, 14, 15, 16, and February 6. Stravinsky had promised to come on the 15th of January, but canceled because of the Avezzano earthquake. Finally, he traveled to Rome February 11, after hearing Ansermet conduct *Petrushka* in Geneva on the 10th.

244. A letter from Arthur Lourié to Stravinsky, July 24, 1925, contains the statement "I remember what you once said about Tcherepnine and the *guzli,*" but does not repeat Stravinsky's story.

245. A trapezoidal zither whose metal strings are struck with a light hammer. According to Plutarch, Homer's verses were sung at the public games accompanied by a zither, the music having been composed by Terpander of Lesbos.

246. Aladár Rácz (1886–1958). His account of the meeting, published in *Feuilles Musicales,* Lausanne, March-April 1962, and, later, together with a memoir by his widow, Yvonne Rácz-Barblan, in The *Hungarian Book Review,* May-August 1972, contains chronological and other inaccuracies, as is shown by a letter to Stravinsky from his friend Adrien Bovy, January 29, 1915. The reliable parts of Rácz's story are that he performed a Serbian kolo *("J'ai l'honneur de vous envoyer les danses serbes que vous m'avez demandées");* that Stravinsky wore a monocle, a red tie, a green waistcoat; that, after purchasing a cimbalom, Stravinsky "prepared the flour paste, and cleaned the rusty strings himself"; and that Stravinsky took lessons from Rácz. On March 4, 1916, Rácz sent an invoice to him for two pairs of cimbalom baguettes, for pieces of gray and white felt, and for railroad tickets from Geneva to Morges, Stravinsky having employed Rácz to repair the pedals on the instrument. As the composer's correspondence with Ansermet reveals, Stravinsky later wanted to engage Rácz as a musical secretary in Paris.

247. Bartók describes the compass as "fifty tones," refers to the invention of a pedal by Josef Schunda—Stravinsky's instrument was a Schunda—and mentions the use of the cimbalom in *Renard. (Op. cit.)*

248. When Paul Sacher, conductor of the Basler Kammerorchester, included the *Ragtime* in a program in 1930, but was at first unable to find a cimbalomist, Stravinsky advised him to replace the instrument by a piano with the head of a nail or tack attached to each hammer: "Not long ago—last May—Alfred Cortot conducted the piece in Paris and Pleyel provided an instrument prepared in this manner that did produce a comparable effect." (Letter of July 9, 1930)

249. Léon Bakst heard the performance and wrote to Stravinsky the next day: "I would not have believed that such a success was possible in this hole, Geneva. . . . I hope to see you in Rome. Tell that fat spider Diaghilev. . . ."

250. On March 3, 1915, Diaghilev telegraphed from Rome: "Try to arrange for Prokofiev to play his second concerto. . . ." On March 22, by which date

Stravinsky was back in Clarens, Diaghilev telegraphed: "Hope to see you at the end of this week in Milan," and, on the 27th, telegraphed money for the trip. On the 28th, he asked Stravinsky "to be at the Hotel Continentale Wednesday morning with all of your music," but on the 29th telegraphed that due to a delay in Rome he himself could not be in Milan before Thursday morning. On April 3, Prokofiev wrote to Miaskovsky from Milan: "In Milan I have been with Stravinsky and Diaghilev and have become very friendly with Stravinsky, both of us having the same musical sympathies. His *Pribaoutki*, orchestrated, are excellent." Stravinsky wrote to Prokofiev, May 12, 1915: "Someone told me that a note, rather well done, about my *Noces* appeared in the [Russian] *Stock Exchange News*. Was it from you? I would be grateful if you would send the note; it appeared, so I am informed, at the end of March or the beginning of April, our style."

251. Diaghilev telegraphed to Stravinsky from Rome, April 18, 1915, "Will be in Montreux end of this week," and from Milan on the 25th, "Will be in Montreux tonight at nine."

252. Stravinsky entered France on December 24 and returned to Switzerland on January 6.

253. Stravinsky had to go to Berne to get permission from the Russian authorities to leave Switzerland, as well as, on the same day, April 2, an Italian visa. He returned to Morges, completed *The Song of the Nightingale* on the 4th, then left for Rome via Iselle on the 5th, entrusting his wife to make a copy of the full score of the new work.

254. August 3, in Iasi, Rumania. A telegram from Stravinsky's mother in Petrograd, July 4, 1915, had informed him that Gury had been transferred to Bessarabia. Gury was posthumously awarded the Order of St. George, a medal with a low-relief of the Tsar. This was given to Igor Stravinsky by his mother, and the composer kept it near him for the rest of his life.

255. Letter to Kling, September 4, 1923.

256. Stravinsky's December 1918 arrangement of fragments of the Fourth Tableau of *Petrushka* for pianola is scored for four pianos, eight hands, the combination of the final version of *Les Noces*.

257. " 'You tell me that Igor has an extraordinary new idea for the orchestra. . . . Three or four men. But perhaps the instruments cannot be found anywhere. And, above all, can't he do without the chorus? No director will provide a chorus except Rouché, and *what* a chorus.' " (Letter from Ansermet to Stravinsky, June 10, 1919, quoting Diaghilev) Jacques Rouché (1862–1957) was director of the Paris Opéra from 1914 to 1945.

258. One unemployed Russian, taking the name Prince Serge de Temmenoff, printed some calling cards with the name "Igor Stravinsky," wrote a message on them recommending himself and forging Stravinsky's signature, then solicited the Princesse de Polignac for money. (Her letter and enclosures, June 14, 1924)

259. Laloy gives the names of the vocal soloists in the premiere, but libraries and collectors possessing either the original program or this issue of *Comoedia* should be advised that Smirov did not sing the bass part as scheduled, having been replaced by D'Arial.

260. *Living Well Is the Best Revenge,* by Calvin Tomkins (New York: Viking, 1971) gives the date as June 17, but Stravinsky kept his hand-delivered invitation—"Sunday July 1, 8 P.M., *The Maréchal Joffre,* docked near the Chambres des Députés, Rive Gauche (*téléphone:* Fleurus 31–74)"—and Vera Sudeikina described the event in her diary for July 1.

261. The Villa Rogivue, but it has never had more than one turret.

262. The Maison Bornand.

263. The dancer and patroness (d. 1960) who was later to commission both *Le Baiser de la Fée* and *Perséphone.* Stravinsky planned to discuss the *Anthony and Cleopatra* project with her in Paris, but, on October 13, 1917, he telegraphed to Bakst: "*Examen médical consular russe m'a délivré passeport avec interdiction tout déplacement raison santé.*"

264. Goncharova had copied actual Russian peasant costumes, the "sparkling clothes" (bangles) mentioned by Stravinsky in his first drafts of the scenario; then the composer decided to abandon colors completely and to dress

everyone in brown. This uniformity now seems regrettable, though it is in keeping with Nijinska's choreography, which cannot have corresponded to Stravinsky's wishes, at least if the current (1977) Royal Ballet reconstruction is faithful to the original. In the first place, the choreography, with its endless arc-shaped arm positions, jumps, and platoon-like groupings, lacks invention. In the second place, the Fourth Tableau should be an orgy, not a rigid confrontation of two phalanxes, like a scene from Riefenstahl's Nuremberg rally. The bas-relief poses are attractive but not when repeated *ad infinitum*. Among the other absurdities are the raising of the curtain several moments after the music begins, and the limitation to one lamenting mother in the interlude between the third and fourth tableaux.

265. The death of Stravinsky's younger brother.

266. The *Three Easy Pieces* and the *Five Easy Pieces*. Stravinsky's account book for 1917 shows that he sent copies of the *Three Easy Pieces* to Casella, Fausto Torrefranco (the musicologist), Mme Bischoff, René Morax, Mme Auberjonois, Mme Odeschalchi, Lord Berners, and the Princesse Murat, as well as four other copies to unidentified friends in Italy.

267. According to a letter to Païchadze, October 26, 1928, Stravinsky had completed about half of this in the spring of that year. On July 15, 1928, in Talloires, where he had resumed the instrumentation, he wrote to Félix Delgrange referring to the opus as a "short overture." In a letter to Païchadze, October 18, 1928, apropos a pair of concerts with the Orchestre Symphonique de Paris on the 16th and 17th of November, Stravinsky explains that "the *Etude* for Orchestra listed in the program is the unpublished *Etude* for Pianola, of which I have orchestrated about half and which I will bring with me completed to Paris—or, rather, since you will not have time to copy it in eight days, I will send it to you by the first of November. You must do the impossible and extract the parts because it is impossible to withdraw the piece (a premiere) from the program. The work is very short and the orchestra is normal." Stravinsky conducted the premiere on November 16 but changed the program the next day. A year later, he added the opus to his orchestrations of the "Three Pieces for String Quartet," baptized the new suite "Four Etudes for Orchestra," and gave the former pianola study the name *Madrid*.

268. The still unpublished full score of the music on the pianola roll, R967B, Aeolian Company, Ltd., is written on six staves.

269. Proust also seems to have been fascinated by the pianola, to judge by the scene in which Albertine chooses new pieces for Marcel to play on the instrument. Stravinsky once remarked in an interview that "Bach wrote for the clavier because that was the instrument of his time. I live according to my time. Why, then, should I not write for the mechanical piano?" (*La Revue Musicale*, December 1923) But could Stravinsky really have believed that the pianola was the instrument of his time? (See also his letter to Ramuz, on the subject, in Gilbert Guisan, *C. F. Ramuz: Ses Amis, Son Temps*, Vol. V [La Bibliothèque des Arts, 1970, Lausanne-Paris].) *Fireworks* and *Scherzo Fantastique*, the first of Stravinsky's works to appear in pianola arrangements, were performed by Peter Warlock and Alvin Langdon Coburn in Aeolian Hall, London, in May 1915.

270. See p. 93.

271. In a letter to his publisher, October 28, 1917, Stravinsky doubts that time can be found to arrange *Petrushka* and the *Sacre* for pianola. But he did make both transcriptions and "perforated" the pianola roll of the *Etude* himself, for a second time, at Morges. (Letter of November 5, 1918)

272. *Op. cit.*

273. Stravinsky heeded this observation, as can be seen in his arrangement of the *Chant Dissident* for pianola, in which he octave-doubles much of the bass part of the cimbalom, or piano, part.

274. The interviewer misunderstood Stravinsky, who had already made forty-four rolls (not pieces) for Pleyel, but who signed a seven-year contract with the Aeolian Company of Connecticut, beginning October 29, 1924, to make twenty-eight records for the Duo-Art Reproducing Piano. For this, Stravinsky was to receive between $2,000 and $4,000 a year. He began in New York in 1925, recording the first movement of his Piano Concerto for the Duo-Art

Reproducing Piano, and the "Berceuse" and "Finale" from *The Firebird* for the Duo-Art organ. The contract was dissolved in 1930 by mutual agreement.

275. Jacques Dalcroze attended the dress rehearsal and wrote an enthusiastic letter to the composer. So did the singer Marya Freund, whose letter conveys some of the excitement of the event.

276. Though it is scarcely credible, neither Ansermet nor Ramuz seems to have read Afanasiev. Ramuz wrote to Stravinsky, June 7, 1929: "What is the name of the Russian folklorist, the author of the two large tomes that you had in Morges in which you found the *Histoire du Soldat?*"

277. This was Elie Gagnebin, who became a good friend of Stravinsky's: "... *Stravinsky, pendant longtemps, fut presque notre compatriote—tant il savait goûter le petit vin vaudois,*" Gagnebin wrote to Cocteau, November 22, 1921; "*J'entretiens avec lui des relations amicales.*" Gagnebin died in July 1949, aged fifty-eight.

278. Stravinsky remained on close terms with the Pitoëffs and, at about the time of the *Soldat,* witnessed the baptism of their daughter Svetlana in the rue Lefort Russian church in Geneva. On August 2, Auberjonois wrote to Stravinsky that Mme Pitoëff was unable to find dance slippers in Switzerland and asked him to write to Tyrwhitt in Rome for help.

279. Stravinsky's telephone number was Morges No. 3, according to a telegram that he sent to Jacques Rivière.

280. The borrowing from popular songs in the *Soldat* would make a subject for a thesis. The violin melody from the second measure of ⟨10⟩ in "The Music to Scene I," for example, is the Russian street song, very slightly transformed, "I am pretty, I am pretty, but badly dressed," and this tune, as well as the one at two measures before ⟨5⟩ in "The Music to Scene II," is found in Stravinsky's 1916 sketchbook.

281. In a letter in the *Gazette de Lausanne,* dated October 6, 1918, Ramuz wrote: "I read in your *Chronique-zurichoise* of the 25th: 'M. Ramuz will read excerpts from his new work, *Histoire du Soldat,* with incidental music by Igor Stravinsky. . . .' First, the Zürich representation had to be canceled because of the grippe. Second, there is no question of reading excerpts, but of the entire work. . . . Finally, and above all, M. Stravinsky is not merely the author of the 'incidental music' but of the work in general, and *au même titre que moi. . . .*"

282. Nevertheless, the sketches also contain notations for larger instrumental complements. Thus the music at ⟨11⟩ in "The Soldier's March" originally required three trumpets, and one of the first notations for the "Triumphal March" employed four horns.

283. Of Stravinsky's use of ragtime, one of the reviews of the first performance remarked: "Sociologists are predicting that this American dance step will soon be abandoned, but M. Stravinsky's answer is, 'It is sufficient to be true in 1918.'"

284. A letter from Michel Larionov, in Paris, undated but probably from the end of 1917 or the beginning of 1918, tells Stravinsky about an American jazz orchestra that has been performing in Paris, and of how much he would like the music. Larionov says that Stravinsky must acquire the "Negro instruments"—presumably percussion—and that he, Larionov, knows where they can be bought. A note from Ansermet, in Zürich, to Stravinsky, September 25, 1918, asks him to "bring your bass drum and cymbal to Lausanne because the instruments here are inferior."

285. Jules Piotton, Stravinsky's copyist. A receipt dated September 9, 1918, shows that he received 20 francs from Stravinsky on August 2 and 50 francs on August 6.

286. Fernand Closset, violinist, who played in the first performance.

287. Stravinsky spent the afternoon of August 12 coaching Gagnebin, for whom the composer notated the rhythm of the Narrator's part.

288. Jean Bartholoni, oil millionaire (Ural, Caspian, Taganrog, etc.). In 1835, his family founded the Geneva Conservatory of Music, and they continued to support it. In 1917, he purchased the full-score manuscript of *The Firebird* from Stravinsky for 8,000 francs. Bartholoni wrote to a friend: "I have the greatest admiration for the orchestral genius, the unique and extraordinary color of Mr. Stravinsky, and the idea that he is suffering [monetary] anxieties

fills me with anxiety myself."

289. August Brandenbourg was the director of the Lausanne branch of the Union of Swiss Banks. On April 18, 1918, Stravinsky had written to M. Aurèle Sandoz, in Ouchy: "Through M. Brandenbourg I have learned about your interest in our project, and I would like to thank you personally. If it would interest you to dine with me one evening, I will invite M. Ramuz and M. Brandenbourg. . . ."

290. Edmond Allegra, clarinetist, played in the first *Histoire* and also gave the first performances of Stravinsky's Three Pieces for Clarinet.

291. Stravinsky might have mentioned that Ramuz's memory of their first meeting was erroneous. This took place not in the autumn of 1915 but in midsummer. Ramuz's first letter to the composer is dated August 9, 1915.

292. Born in Kiev, December 8, 1853, died in Biarritz in the 1920s. She was a fashion couturière in Kiev.

293. 1893–1958.

294. Susan Bradshaw, *Tempo*, London, 1971.

295. *Ibid.*

296. *Avant d'Oublier* (Paris: Fayard, 1976). Hugo does not give a date, but it may have been December 1918, when Stravinsky played the piece in Paris for other friends as well. On January 9, 1919, Lord Berners wrote from Rome: "I have word of you from Carlo Placci, whom I saw in Paris. He was very enthusiastic about the *Ragtime* you played for him."

297. In a letter to Stravinsky in 1922, Ansermet says that in a performance of the *Firebird* Suite that he conducted in Winterthur, Reinhart played the bass clarinet.

298. Jean Hugo, *op. cit.*

299. Satie to Stravinsky, Saturday, September 15, 1923: "I have finished the second act of *Le Médecin Malgré Lui.* I compose Gounod, which is not more stupid than composing Ravel. . . . You, I adore you. Are you not the great Stravinsky? I am only the little E.S."

300. Jean Hugo, *op. cit.*

OBITER DICTA: SOURCES

1. Unidentified newspaper, Brussels, January 1924 (French).
2. To Jacques Rivière, April 1919 (French).
3. *Neues Wiener Journal*, March 17, 1926.
4. *La Nación*, Buenos Aires, April 25, 1936.
5. *Beaux Arts*, Paris, February 28, 1936.
6. Same as 4.
7. *L'Etoile Belge*, May 22, 1930.
8. *Le Vingtième Siècle*, May 27, 1930.
9. *Ibid.*
10. *New York World-Telegram*, January 23, 1937.
11. To Edwin Evans, December 13, 1929 (French).
12. *Journal de Genève*, November 14, 1928.
13. *Ibid.*, December 1928.
14. *Seattle Post-Intelligencer*, March 2, 1967.
15. *La Veu de Catalunya*, Barcelona, March 1925 (Catalonian).
16. Same as 3.
17. Same as 1.
18. Same as 3.
19. *Time*, July 26, 1948.
20. Same as 8.
21. *La Noche*, Barcelona, May 12, 1936 (Spanish).
22. Same as 8.
23. *Radio-Paris*, March 23, 1936.
24. Same as 1.
25. Same as 3.
26. Same as 5.

27. *Musical America,* January 10, 1937.
28. *Esquire,* December 1953.
29. Unidentified Boston newspaper.
30. Same as 8.
31. Same as 3.
32. *Modern Music,* Summer 1946.
33. Unpublished MS., December 1928 (French).
34. Brussels, January 15, 1924.
35. Paris, 1923.
36. *Musical America,* January 10, 1925.
37. *Praguer Presse,* February 23, 1930.
38. *New York World-Telegram,* November 23, 1937.
39. Same as 3.
40. *Lidové Noviny,* February 25, 1930 (Czech).
41. *Journal des Années des Guerres,* by Romain Rolland, quoting Stravinsky in a conversation of September 24, 1914.
42. Same as 40.
43. *Christian Science Monitor,* January 7, 1925.
44. *El Debate,* Montevideo, April 30, 1936.
45. To Erwin Stein, October 16, 1950 (English).
46. *The Observer,* London, July 3, 1921.
47. To Ernest Ansermet, December 14 and 19, 1937 (French).
48. To Léon Bakst, July 14, 1917 (Russian).
49. Same as 19.
50. Same as 13.
51. Same as 4.
52. *Les Nouvelles Littéraires,* December 8, 1928.
53. *Candide,* Paris, June 6, 1935.
54. To Gavril Grigorievich Païchadze, director of Editions Russes de Musique, March 13, 1928 (Russian).
55. *Moi et Mes Amis,* by Francis Poulenc (Paris: Editions la Palatine, 1963).
56. *Comoedia,* Paris, January 31, 1920.
57. To the President of the Société des Auteurs, March 19, 1935 (French).
58. *Neue Badische Landes-Zeitung,* Mannheim, 1930.
59. *Le Figaro,* May 1922.
60. To Païchadze, August 2, 1928 (Russian).
61. To Païchadze, October 26, 1928 (Russian).
62. Same as 34.
63. To his mother, March 29, 1912.
64. *Washington Post,* December 24, 1960.
65. To Ansermet, April 4, 1935.
66. To Willy Strecker, December 29, 1930 (German).
67. To Pierre Suvchinsky, June 12, 1961 (Russian).
68. To Suvchinsky, August 18, 1961 (Russian).
69. To Suvchinsky, January 27, 1960 (Russian).
70. Same as 7.
71. Unpublished MS., December 4, 1934 (French).
72. Radio broadcast, WQXR, New York, November 1, 1949.
73. *Le Jour,* Paris, March 4, 1938.
74. *Times-Picayune,* New Orleans, January 30, 1954.
75. Same as 7.
76. Same as 8.
77. *Excelsior,* Paris, December 21, 1933.
78. From a music sketchbook, 1968.
79. Same as 28.
80. Same as 52.
81. To Païchadze, July 23, 1927 (Russian).
82. Same as 64.
83. *Excelsior,* Paris, September 11, 1935.
84. *Etude,* New York, January 1925.
85. Quoted by Strecker in a magazine article, 1930s (German).
86. *Boston Herald,* October 22, 1939.

87. *Dresdener Neuesten Nachrichten*, February 1, 1929.
88. *Börsencourrier*, Berlin, September 1931.
89. *Il Resto di Carlino*, Bologna, May 1935 (Italian).
90. To Boosey & Hawkes, January 8, 1952 (English).
91. Same as 15.
92. Nicole Hirsch, in the *Paris Express*, September 6, 1964 (French).
93. Same as 64.

PART TWO

1. This same day was probably also the first time that Stravinsky had seen Diaghilev since his quarrel with Massine. Stravinsky had written to Ansermet from Garches, February 11, 1921: "I see that you never received my card in which I told you that Diaghilev and Massine separated in Rome. Diaghilev comes to Paris in a few days and I will have all of the details. . . ." On February 17, Otto Kling wrote to Stravinsky from London: "I understand that there has been a fight in the Diaghilev ménage and that Massine has been dismissed, a calamity that I am scarcely able to believe."

2. Stravinsky had appeared in public in both capacities before this date, of course, but only as an occasional performer.

3. *Mavra* (1922) was the turning point in this regard. As Cocteau wrote to Elie Gagnebin, June 21, 1922: *"Igor ne peut se consoler de ses unsuccès . . . Renard-Mavra. Comment ne comprend-il pas qu'il est impossible de se renouveler de changer la peau sans déplaire. 'Mavra' est, d'après les lettres et les articles, un véritable hommage à Satie. . . ."* In another letter to Gagnebin, on June 28, Cocteau characterizes the failure of the one-act opera as the *"affaire Dreyfus-Mavra."* For the rest of Stravinsky's life, he would accept no criticism of the maligned *opéra-bouffe*, which he seems to have enjoyed composing almost more than any other piece, even writing to friends to say how well his work on it was progressing: *"L'Opéra se compose bien, même très bien—vous aurez du plaisir—c'est très différent de ce que je faisais"* (to Ansermet, September 10, 1921); *"Je compose déjà deux mois sans relâche et je crois avoir fait de la bonne besogne"* (to Ansermet, no date); "I do not budge and I work without let-up on my opera, which has all the signs of becoming a 'masterpiece.' " (To Ansermet, Friday, December 2, 1921) The sketches contain only two dates, February 4, 1922, at 140, and March 6, 1922, at the end.

4. Prokofiev wrote to Miaskovsky, June 1, 1924: "Stravinsky's Piano Concerto is like Bach and Handel and I do not like it very much, but it is very strongly sewn together, very lively, and very austere in sound, because of the wind orchestra. Syncopated dance rhythms in a concerto make the old Bach sound new." Prokofiev wrote to Miaskovsky again on March 25, 1925: "Stravinsky's concerto mixes two different styles, but he manifests a constancy and perseverance. The Bach similarity you feel already in the Octet and now, after the concerto, he composes a sonata in the same way. For me, *Le Sacre* and *Les Noces* are more precious."

5. Writing to G. F. Malipiero, March 3, 1920, Stravinsky expressed regrets that a certain apartment had been leased only one day before his telegram arrived. Still, on March 9, he obtained a visa, valid until May 30, to go to Rome. A letter from Otto Kling, April 30, 1920, acknowledges the receipt from Stravinsky of a piano score of the *Sacre* which was to be forwarded to Malipiero, and a visit from M. Sauvin, a long-distance mover from Geneva, ". . . who informed me of your plans to move and asked me to do certain things for you in Rome; not having received any news from there, however, I see no possibility of leaving for Italy before the 12th of May." On May 31, Count Henri Valperga di San Martino, President of the Accademia di Santa Cecilia—of which Stravinsky was a member—wrote to say that no residence had been found. By this time, as a letter to Stravinsky from the violinist Alfred Pochon reveals, the composer was planning to spend the summer in Positano. On June 20, 1920, the Paris critic Henri Prunières wrote to Stravinsky in Carantec: "I am glad that you have abandoned the plan to go to Rome. Tommasini, in Paris

at the moment, says that life in Italy is more difficult now than ever."

6. Stravinsky was especially concerned as to the fate of his bicycle, which was not listed in Sauvin's inventory. (Letter of August 17, 1920)

7. See Appendix D.

8. According to one of Stravinsky's notebooks, where Chanel's name and telephone number (Garches 214) appear shortly after a reference to his decision to move from Morges to Paris, he must have met her, through Misia Sert, in May 1920. Chanel underwrote the December 1920 revival of the *Sacre*, but, in 1922, Stravinsky had a row with her.

9. Stravinsky revealed his project for a concert of his music in Paris to Misia in May 1919. He wanted Monteux to conduct, but she suggested Rhené-Baton, then decided that the concert, *"une grande manifestation musicale Stravinsky,"* should be given by "the orchestra of Diaghilev."

10. *L'Allure de Chanel* (Paris: Hermann, 1976). Stravinsky entered Spain at La Hendaye, March 16, 1921, and spent the Semana Santa, Easter (March 27), and some of the Feria, in Seville with Diaghilev and Boris Kochno. It was in Seville that Stravinsky played the score of *La Belle au Bois Dormant*, and rediscovered his enthusiasm for Tchaikovsky.

11. 1921 and 1922 were Stravinsky's years of *"chercher la femme."* Still the companion of Chanel in January 1921, he met Mme Sudeikina in February and saw her, with her husband, two or three times in early March. In March, too, Stravinsky met the Chauve-Souris dancer Katinka (pseudonym of Zhenia Nikitina) through the Sudeikins, the Chauve-Souris having been founded by a friend of theirs, Baliev, who had been the proprietor of a nightclub in Moscow. Baliev asked the Sudeikins to invite Diaghilev and Stravinsky, who became infatuated with Katinka and asked her, through and with the Sudeikins, to a dinner at Fouquet. She soon begged him to compose something for her, and, since he was orchestrating the "Polka" (*Three Easy Pieces*) at the time, he added her theme-song to the piece (measures 7, 6, 5, and 4 before the end, trombone and flute). The next year, he preserved a photograph of himself at a corrida in Bayonne sitting next to "Geneviève Via (*cantatrice aux yeux verts*) . . ."

12. *Op. cit.* But Stravinsky already wore a monocle in 1915 and, from all evidence, could never have been accurately described as timid. Morand's hostile tone toward Stravinsky here is puzzling in that the novelist, to the end of his life, sent his books to the composer with cordial inscriptions ending *"son vieil ami."*

13. Later, after the Stravinskys had resettled in Nice, the composer once instructed a Paris journalist to introduce him with the statement: "Before his departure for Nice where he vacations [!] every year, Monsieur Igor Stravinsky has agreed to grant us an interview. . . ." (René Duhamel, *L'Intransigeant*, 1926)

14. The Paris director from 1926 to 1946 of Kussevitzky's Editions Russes de Musique.

15. This selective, rather than comprehensive, biography cannot enter into the relationships between Stravinsky and his first wife and children, but, in the opinion of the present writer, Vaslav Nijinsky's observations of the family (see p. 31) are the most insightful that have ever been published. Regrettably, it must be admitted that, by present standards of child-rearing, Stravinsky would hardly qualify as an adequate parent, having not only treated his children despotically, but also abandoned them emotionally. He was generous to them materially, at least under pressure, but this was the easiest way of salving his conscience, as he himself said when, for example, sending a check for 3,000 francs to his elder son: *"Avec cela je me sentirai la conscience soulagée."* (Letter of November 17, 1952) Gifts such as these were almost always effected through the intervention of Stravinsky's second wife. In a typical letter to his publisher, July 9, 1964, the composer asks that $2,000 be sent to the wife of his younger son for the reconstruction of her house in La Clidelle, France: "Being ashamed to ask me directly, she spoke about it to Vera, breaking down in tears. But give the money to the poor girl, since taxes will not allow me to take it to my grave."

16. This is not to say that he was an agnostic before that, but, to judge by his reading during the Swiss years, religious literature was far less important

to him. True, in August 1915, he subscribed to Maurice Baud's *Pius X*, but the payment for the book had to be collected by a lawyer in January 1917.

17. Stravinsky captioned a photograph: "Our chapel in the apartment of Father Nicolas, Nice, 1927." To judge by Padasseroff's letters to the composer, this Archimandrite had a "poetic nature." In a letter describing his place of retreat in the Basses Alpes, August 26, 1926 (O.S.), he regrets that "the stars, God's eyes, are not looking down on Russian soil, and that there is no real Russian village nearby. . . ." Padasseroff was Stravinsky's confessor in Nice as Abbé Touya' had been in Biarritz. Some of Stravinsky's wife's letters, on most of which she drew the sign of the cross at the top, would seem to indicate that by the late 1930s his sacerdotalism was less fervent than hers: "Mama writes that today you were going to take communion, and I am so happy. . . . You do not mention Fedya's painting of the image of St. Peter of Panteleimon" (November 6, 1937).

18. Writing to Païchadze, October 17, 1926, Stravinsky says: "I am waiting to send my *Pater Noster* in order to make a piano reduction, which it lacks." He first conducted the *Pater Noster*—and its companion pieces, the *Credo* (1932) and *Ave Maria* (1934)—in the Salle Gaveau, May 18, 1934, as part of a memorial concert for the American composer Blair Fairchild (d. April 23, 1933). Sixteen years later, Stravinsky answered an ASCAP questionnaire about "the author of the lyrics" of *Pater Noster* and *Ave Maria*: "The text of the former is by Jesus Christ, of the latter, the Archangel Gabriel." (August 30, 1950) Stravinsky began a fourth *a cappella* chorus, also in Old Slavonic, *Of the Cherubim* (ИЖЕ ХЕРУВИМЫ), in Paris, in the mid-1930s, but completed only a few measures.

19. He lived from July 1921 in the Cottage l'Argenté, Anglet (near Bayonne), moving, in October 1921, to the Châlet des Rochers, rue la Frégate, Biarritz.

20. After the birth of her second daughter, January 15, 1914, Stravinsky's wife was almost constantly in poor health. For example, in a letter to Ernest Oeberg, director of the Editions Russes de Musique in Paris, May 7, 1925, Stravinsky explains that she had been gravely ill in Rome, having caught pleurisy. If the illness follows a normal course, and if he has no other fears for his wife, the composer says, he will come to Paris soon. Again, in a letter to Robert Lyon, July 18, 1927, Stravinsky writes: "*Je suis triste, mon vieux Robert, ma femme que j'ai trouvée en rentrant souffrante, a, comme le docteur l'a constaté hier, une pleurisie. . . . Si tout marche normalement ce n'est que dans un mois la convalescence.*" Writing to Païchadze, April 1, 1929, Stravinsky says: "Ekaterina Gavrilovna has a throat boil and she's been sick three days already. The throat doctor comes twice a day. . . . Tomorrow the question of whether or not to lance it is to be settled." In a letter, June 2, 1935, Paris, Dr. Rist informs the composer that the pneumothorax on his wife's left lung has not been beneficial, and proposes to perform the operation on the right side in about fifteen days. Rist says that he hesitates to do a phrenisectomy "which will, in any case, block the respiration in an area that is healthy." Rist refers to a newly infected passage on an old oleothorax in the right side, and, though he tries to be hopeful, is obviously hinting that the case is fatal.

21. In a letter to the Director of the Royal Theater, Copenhagen, February 25, 1966, explaining the impossibility of reducing the size of the orchestra of *Le Sacre*, Stravinsky recalled that "for the performances of *Le Sacre* with Diaghilev in London in 1921, the orchestra pit was smaller than it was in Paris, and therefore the orchestra space had to be increased by two boxes taken from the public, to the right and to the left, over the orchestra pit."

22. See Appendix B.

23. Writing to his publisher on February 19, 1921, Stravinsky complains that it is literally impossible for him to continue working on *Les Noces* until he finds an atelier in Paris. Concerning the participation of mechanical instruments, he explains that he must verify at Pleyel what he has already written.

24. From *Paris Sketches*, in Vladimir Mayakovsky, *The Complete Collected Works* (Moscow: Sobranie Polnoe Sochinenii, 1955–61). Mayakovsky was in Paris during Proust's funeral, which Diaghilev attended.

25. Stravinsky's pens at this time were the "Waverly" and the "Marly,"

which, from about September 1920, he purchased from London in large quantities.

26. *Gringoire*, Paris, October 27, 1937.

27. In a letter to Werner Reinhart, July 25, 1925, Stravinsky explains that, in order to earn a living, he sees himself obliged to spend part of each year concertizing.

28. Stravinsky told an interviewer for *L'Etoile Belge*, May 22, 1930: "I like to conduct my works, and I experience the greatest joy in making the players in an orchestra understand my music. I have the impression that only in conducting his works does a composer feel the fullest blossoming of his temperament. To realize the composition that one has conceived gives an incomparable pleasure."

29. "When, a few years ago, Stravinsky found the European public wished to pay to see him play and direct his own works, he thought them mistaken, but by labor and will he became a concert pianist. . . ." (Janet Flanner, *op. cit.*) Otto Klemperer recalled that "At a mature age [Stravinsky] took piano lessons from [Isadore] Philipp in Paris. . . ." (*Die Tat*, Zürich, October 14, 1961) In fact Stravinsky took lessons from Philipp in 1924 before playing the Piano Concerto, and during the next twenty-two years practiced exercises from Philipp's *Complete School of Technic for the Pianoforte* (Philadelphia: Theodore Presser, 1908).

30. *The Writings of Elliott Carter* (Bloomington: University of Indiana, 1977).

31. When he played the first of these pieces in Boston, in January 1925, Stravinsky told a reporter for the *Post*: "No one else has played this Concerto. Only I can play it. That is, I won't *let* anyone else play it until I no longer want to." Exclusivity to perform the Sonata, as well, is set forth in a letter to Ernest Oeberg, September 17, 1924, but this could hardly be enforced, the music being for sale.

32. Bartók, in his Harvard lectures, wrote that ". . . the new Hungarian art music is always based on a single fundamental tone. . . . And the same is the case with Stravinsky's music. He lays stress on this circumstance even in the titles of some of his works. He says, for instance, 'Concerto in *A*.'" (*Op. cit.*)

33. On November 17, 1926, Stravinsky wrote a blurb for the Pleyel piano that the company published in its advertisements. The composer says that he likes the Pleyel instrument because of its "clear bass notes" and because its "lightness and strength are exactly what is required in our anti-romantic era." On April 12, 1929, Stravinsky wrote to F. W. Weber in Berlin: "I have agreed to play my Concerto with Klemperer on the 8th of June. . . . Ask Steinway to reserve a large concert instrument with a light fingering and a bright (not velvety) sound." Shortly before recording the *Capriccio*, he wrote to Columbia Records, Paris, asking for "a piano with a very light, clear sound, above all, not velvety." (Letter of April 26, 1930)

34. Writing to Païchadze, August 14, 1927, on the question of permitting other pianists to play the Concerto, Stravinsky says: "Evidently this must be decided, for the piece risks being forgotten if it is not played. Yet the Concerto also risks being compromised if incompetent or romantic hands begin to 'interpret' it before undiscriminating audiences. Try, above all, to place it in the hands of honest pianists of the genre Borovsky, Orlov, Marcelle Meyer. . . ."

35. In 1915, the Indian composer Sorabji wrote to Stravinsky from London imploring him to compose for the piano since "your Etudes Op. 7 and the piano scores that you have made from your orchestral works show a technical mastery of the piano equaled only by that which you possess over the orchestra."

36. On the first page of his copy of this piece—dated November 1922 on the cover—Stravinsky wrote: "On July 8, 1924, I began to learn to play it." Stravinsky's fingerings are on every page, as well as many changes and rewritings.

37. Stravinsky wrote to Ansermet, September 10, 1921: "I finished *Petrushka* for Rubinstein." The pianist was staying in the Hôtel du Palais, Biarritz, at the time. A month later, on his way to New York aboard the S.S. *Caronia*, he wrote to Stravinsky: "I never write, but I have a great need to tell

you how much happiness I owe to you during these last months. . . . It is beautiful to live near a human being such as you are." (Letter of October 8, 1921)

38. Stravinsky always played the second piano part. On August 8, 1939, he wrote from Sancellemoz (Haute-Savoie) to Alexis Kall saying that it would be impossible to give piano recitals in the United States because of insufficient repertory, the Sonata and Serenade being difficult for audiences but at the same time too short to comprise a program. Stravinsky therefore asked Kall to find "a good young pianist" who could learn the first piano part of the Concerto for Two Solo Pianos, saying that "I am accustomed to playing the second part myself," that "the two parts are equally important," and that before each performance he would "give a talk of about ten minutes." The first pianist to play the Concerto with him in America was Beveridge Webster, the second was Adele Marcus, and the third (and last), Willard MacGregor.

39. A celebrated passage in Marx's *Eighteenth Brumaire* describes the phenomenon which applies to Stravinsky's development at this stage: "Just when they seem to be engaged in revolutionizing themselves and things, in creating ·something that has never yet existed, precisely in such periods of revolutionary crisis they anxiously conjure up the spirits of the past to their service and take from them names . . . costumes . . . borrowed language. . . ."

40. In a letter to Henri Prunières, April 21, 1925, Stravinsky says: "You are making a grave fault in appreciation to prefer Wiéner to Marcelle Meyer. . . . Last year I spoke to Wiéner myself, advising him not to play the *Three Movements from Petrushka;* I find that his technique and his strength are not equal to this score."

41. The *Dialogue* was abandoned in favor of *Oedipus Rex.* Two entries for the latter, the ostinato in B-flat and D-flat triplets, scored for piano, harp and timpani, and the motive in dotted quarter-notes, D-flat, B-flat, and E-natural, in descending sequence and scored for trombones, appear in Stravinsky's sketchbook next to the *Dialogue.*

42. The embryo of the third piece is found in a 1917 sketchbook. "The Five Fingers," as Stravinsky called the opus, was inspired by a request from America, transmitted by Alfred Pochon of the Flonzaley Quartet, for ten pieces for children, five for piano, the others for piano and voice. Stravinsky answered Pochon on November 15, 1920, saying that it was impossible to guarantee that the piano pieces would be based on Russian folklore, as requested, because that could not be done to order. Stravinsky added that he would prefer to compose for flute or violin, or two violins, which he had wanted to do for a long time. He was especially fond of Mozart's Duo for violin and viola, K. 423.

43. An interview about Wagner—"*Igor Stravinsky n'est pas Wagnérien*" (*Paris-Midi,* January 13, 1921)—may shed some light on this: "Wagner had a marvelous understanding of wind and brass instruments, but his vanity required something sublime, and for this reason he put the wind instruments, the brass, and the strings together. But he deprives the strings of their natural sonority. The greatest of all musicians, Mozart, was also the greatest master of instrumental harmony, and he never fell into error . . . but I try not to talk about the composition of Wagner, since his inspiration escapes my modern spirit. Nor am I competent to judge the philosopher in him, who all too often dominated the musician. My opinion is exactly the same as Nietzsche's, who had the courage to oppose Bizet to the idol of Bayreuth." When C. F. Ramuz chided Stravinsky on his condemnation of Wagner in the *Chroniques de Ma Vie,* Stravinsky answered that what he did not like about Wagner was "his tomb and his theater, both of them in Bayreuth." (Letter of June 29, 1935)

But some of Stravinsky's ethnic notions were as eccentric as Wagner's, and no amount of reading and discussion later in life could change them: "Wagner's origins shocked Nietzsche, with his Slavic affinities," he told the same *Paris-Midi* reporter—it was still the time when Nietzsche was believed to have been descended from Polish aristocracy—"and for this reason the two geniuses could never understand each other." In an interview in the *Journal de Genève* (November 14, 1928), Stravinsky remarked that "I·don't consider myself especially Russian. Though naturally I owe some of my qualities to my Russian nationality, I am a cosmopolitan. I love music as all Russians love it. There are two really musical peoples, the Slavs and the Italians. The musical culture in

Germany is great, and it is progressing in America, but musical talent and the love of music are innate only in the Slavs."

44. From "Some Ideas About My Octet," January 1924, a mistranslation of "*Quelques Idées à Propos de Mon Octuor*" (1923). In letters at the time, Stravinsky objected to the English version of this important article, which was not even published complete.

45. Sketches for the *Symphonies* and the Concertino antedate *Pulcinella* (1919–20), those for the *Symphonies* being the earlier of the two. But the Concertino was completed first. In a letter to Ansermet, September 20, 1920, Stravinsky says that he is just finishing a concerto [sic] for string quartet, and that "the Debussy will come later."

46. Stravinsky's affirmation of "tonality" (and declaration of war on "atonality") was stated for the first time by Francis Poulenc in an article on *Mavra*: "In this work, Stravinsky has confined himself to the system of modulation. *C'est par juxtaposition horizontale de tons éloignés qu'il a obtenu une musique précise, bondissante et éminemment tonale (qualité rare aujourd'hui). . . .*"

47. The subject of the fugato grows out of, is in fact the fifteenth entry in, the sketches for the abandoned "*Cinq Pièces Monométriques,*" though the theme is already implicit in the first sketch for this earlier piece, and this sketch, in turn, clearly derives from the Concertino. After a dozen more notations for the "*Cinq Pièces,*" Stravinsky wrote the fugato in a four-stave open score, but soon began to add indications for trumpets, trombones, bassoons, clarinet. The sketches also contain a fast tempo ($\downarrow$ = 160) variation on the subject. He did not finish the full score of the fugato until a year and a half later, August 18, 1922. The complete draft of the first movement is dated August 8, Biarritz, but he may have begun the first movement allegro as early as the summer of 1919, planning the piece for piano and a wind ensemble with timpani (one version specifies oboe, two flutes, and piano). The waltz variation in the second movement, first conceived for harmonium, clearly belongs to the spring of 1919, though the theme of the second movement, originally titled "*Thème avec Variations Monométriques,*" was not completed until August 23, 1922, and the remainder of that movement not until November 18. The finale is dated May 20, 1923.

48. The chronology is not entirely in agreement with this. Immediately after completing the *Ragtime* (February 5, 1918), Stravinsky began the Piano-Rag-Music, but, after six pages of sketches, he entered two notations for the opening "bell motive" of the *Symphonies of Wind Instruments*. The Piano-Rag-Music was probably resumed in March 1919, but again, about halfway through the new draft, Stravinsky composed the first motive for the chorale eventually used in the *Symphonies*—and entered a figure marked for harmonium. These sketches probably date from May 1919. Then, after finishing the Rag-Music, Stravinsky filled ten pages with sketches for what was to become the *Symphonies*, the last of them mixed with notations for the Concertino and for the Octet. Stravinsky's first ideas for the latter were in the form of music for two bassoons bearing affinities to the passage in the second bassoon after $\boxed{14}$, and immediately before $\boxed{17}$ and $\boxed{21}$; but the music in these sketches is more chromatic than that in the final version of the piece. Another idea, of approximately the same date, was for the music at $\boxed{33}$ in the Octet, but this sketch is remarkably similar to the final version of that piece—though this fragment was used in the *Symphonies of Wind Instruments* first, a whole year before he discovered that it did not belong there. (The "Octet" excerpt, too, is scored for harmonium.) In sum, Stravinsky was working on three pieces at the same time, and at an earlier date than has been assumed.

49. *Op. cit.*

50. *Journal de Genève*, November 14, 1928. A few weeks later Stravinsky received an invitation to address the Cambridge University Slavonic Club, but declined. In the Introduction to his *Chroniques de Ma Vie*, Stravinsky states that "In the numerous interviews that I have given, my thoughts, my words, and even facts, have often been disfigured." Certainly this is true, but only to some extent, as a comparison of the composer's letters contemporary with those interviews reveals. The *Chroniques*, on the other hand, consistently contradicts what Stravinsky thought, felt, and said at early periods of his life.

Then, too, many statements attributed to Stravinsky were not written by him. For example, in a letter, December 13, 1929, to Edwin Evans, who had asked the composer to contribute some remarks to the *Musical Courier*, Stravinsky says: "Send the text, which you will surely do better than I could, and I will sign it and send it."

51. Arthur Vincent Lourié (1892–1966). See Benedikt Livshit's memoir *The One and A Half-Eyed Archer* (*Polutoraglazyi strelets*, Leningrad, 1933) (Newtonville, Massachusetts, 1977).

52. Later in life, Stravinsky interpreted *Apollo* very differently, regarding it, partly because of its "melos uncontaminated by folk music," and its polyphony, as his most "revolutionary" work. But a more traditional "revolutionary" feature is the music's audacity, for *Apollo* is arguably a more daring score, in the sense of being a lonely swimmer against the flood, than *Le Sacre du Printemps*, which is the tidal wave itself.

See also Lourié's booklet on *Oedipus Rex* (Editions Russe de Musique) and his study, with its incidental disquisition on Pascal, of Stravinsky's piano Sonata (*La Revue Musicale*). Stravinsky's feelings about Maritain were complex. (The two men met for the first time after a concert, June 10, 1926, as a letter from Maritain to Stravinsky reveals.) On July 10, 1936, Stravinsky wrote to Victoria Ocampo: "I will try to see Maritain for you even though his *entourage me donne de légers nausées*." On November 5, 1936, the composer wrote to her again that he was not surprised by the "good impression Maritain has made on you," and reminding her that "I had recommended Maritain very highly." But Stravinsky goes on to classify Maritain as "one of those people of superior intelligence who are lacking in humanity, and if Maritain himself does not deserve this judgment, certainly it applies to a great deal of his work. Maritain is still attached to the nihilism of his youth, and this can be sensed in all of his books, despite the great value of his work in Christian and Thomist thought."

53. Concerning Olga Sudeikina, see Chapter 33 of Nadyezhda Mandelstam's *Hope Abandoned* (New York: Atheneum, 1974), and Arthur Lourié's memoir in *Vozdushnye Puti* ("Aerial Ways"), No. 5, New York, 1967.

54. Anatoly Vasilievich Lunacharsky (1875–1933) was Minister of Education from 1917 to 1929.

55. "Many profound thanks for your help to my mother. She is absolutely alone now, after the death of my brother, and, except for your kindness and aid, I do not think that she would still be alive. She must sell everything belonging to me in order to pay for the voyage. Please help her. I am also writing to Arthur Lourié, who can help. But it must be done before the winter. I am very worried about her health and cannot come to escort her myself because my own health has been poor for more than a year. I hope that with energy you will accomplish everything possible. I am eager to have an answer from you. Write to me at Garches (S. et O.), France, Villa Bel Respiro, Avenue Alphonse de Neuville." (September 2, 1920)

Stravinsky wrote to Lourié on the same day, addressing him as "Tovarich" and "Cher ami": "I was touched by your kind help to my poor mother, and I thank you very much for it. Now I want to ask you: Can you assist me in selling everything in my apartment in order to raise money to pay for her voyage to France? I am unable to do it myself, since I live abroad for reasons of health. She is without money, and it is impossible now to send any to Russia. I think that only you are able to obtain a passport and visa for her. Now something else. My mother has told me that you are interested in my music, and that I should send to you everything I have composed since 1914. Only let me know the best address and how to send it."

Stravinsky's letters to his mother were not entrusted to the mails but to travelers to Petrograd. Thus, on August 31, 1920, a Mr. Desbaillets from J. & W. Chester, Ltd., wrote to him: "I have received the letter, addressed to your mother, which you asked me to send to Mr. Zingel in Berlin for him to deliver in Petrograd."

56. Stravinsky to Païchadze, October 28, 1926, concerning the piano score of the Octet: "I have found numerous mistakes, but for the moment I will point out only the most disagreeable and dangerous, p. 8, measure 3, third line for

the right hand: It should be the bass and not the treble clef. How could Lourié fail to remark this? It leaps at the eye."

57. "It appears that you told M. Lourié that he could keep the orchestra score of the *Soldat* . . . in compensation for all the work that he had to do with the corrections of *Les Noces*. But don't you think that you should have informed us of your intentions to make a gift of this score?" (Letter from Kling, May 28, 1925; the score could be claimed as the property of J. & W. Chester.)

58. Fyodor Kuzmich Sologub (1863–1927), author of *The Little Demon*, was a friend of Vera Sudeikina's.

59. Leo Theremin (b. 1896) was the inventor of the electric instrument named for him and often employed in performances of Varèse's *Equatorial* (1934).

60. These three words are in French in the original; the remainder of the letter is in Russian.

61. Stravinsky's associates seem to have promoted a sense of rivalry between him and the Schoenberg school. Thus Ansermet wrote, April 5, 1922, that *"On parle trop de Schoenberg à Paris et on vous oublie un peu."* And George Auric, in an article, *"L'Apothéose d'Igor Stravinsky,"* inspired by two performances of *Le Sacre* that Stravinsky had conducted in Paris in February 1928, was not content to acclaim the composer, but went on to contrast him with Alban Berg, the approximately contemporaneous performance of whose Chamber Concerto had been interrupted and even terminated by the Parisian audience. "Berg's Concerto," Auric wrote, "is a scholastic bore masking under a lugubrious esthetic at the furthest extreme from the strong and great art of Stravinsky. Mr. Alban Berg multiplies zeros on a blackboard. . . . We rejoice at the triumph of Stravinsky." On January 24, 1934, when the series of concerts of contemporary music called "Triton" (rue de la Boétie, Paris) invited Stravinsky to the double bill of *Histoire du Soldat* and *Pierrot Lunaire*, both conducted by Scherchen, on January 27, Stravinsky seems not to have answered. On January 28, 1934, the *Neue Zürcher Zeitung* featured an imaginary dialogue between a Stravinsky and a Schoenberg disciple, written by Jacques Handschin.

62. See p. 65. Stravinsky used to refer to Sabaneyev as *"Sabaka"* (dog).

63. J. & W. Chester, Ltd. In a letter to Willy Strecker, February 20, 1932, Stravinsky says that he is ill because of Chester and would like "never to think of this ignoble bandit whose martyr I have been for twenty years."

64. After the publication of Adorno's *Philosophy of Modern Music*, Schoenberg wrote to his biographer H. H. Stuckenschmidt, December 5, 1949: "It is disgusting, by the way, how he treats Stravinsky. I am certainly no admirer of Stravinsky, although I like a piece of his here and there very much— but one should not write like that." A year and a half before, on March 15, 1948, Schoenberg had written to René Leibowitz: "I find Stravinsky's present-day attitude a dignified one." In 1947, Stravinsky drew up a list of questions for a visitor from Paris, beginning with: "What are the relations between Messiaen and his group and the Schoenberg system?"

65. " 'Why do they blame me for my music?' Stravinsky would rage. 'Why don't they blame God? He gave me my gifts!' " (*First Person Plural*, by Dagmar Godowsky [New York: Viking, 1958])

66. For an example of his talks to audiences, see page 327.

67. Stravinsky was fond of Spanish wines and of Madeira. In Lisbon, May 30, 1966, he gave a manuscript to a woman, her name set to eleven pitches, in appreciation for the gift of a bottle of Madeira:

Ma-ri-a An-ton-ia De Bri-to Gomez_

68. In 1937, Stravinsky began to dictate a continuation of these memoirs, but he completed notes only for the year from the autumn of 1933 to the end of 1934, and these have not been translated from the Russian.

69. Stravinsky would have agreed with Malraux that "the Byzantines had

grasped that you could not paint a portrait of Christ. . . . The icon can represent Christ because it is not the representation of a man, but is a symbol. . . . As soon as human genius deserted symbolic means and turned to a direct representation, or emotional means in music, the sacred vanished from art." (Interview with Guy Suarès, 1973)

70. Whether Stravinsky is referring to this or to another habitation, he wrote underneath a photo of his children sitting on a doorstep: "*Notre très misérable demeure à Carantec.*"

71. Not all of the notices were hostile, *The Spectator*, for example, finding that Stravinsky had "achieved remarkable results with his 23 instruments [sic; 25 are required]. The naked directness of the opening bars provoked an audible protest from all parts of the hall. . . . We may still worship at the shrine of Beethoven, but it is not possible to appreciate Stravinsky if we persist in thinking that music must be limited to the idiom in which Beethoven wrote."

72. Stravinsky procured a visa in Paris on June 6, and his passport is stamped "Dover, June 7. Permitted to land at the Port of Dover on condition that holder reports at once to Police"—which he did at the Bow Street Station, London— "and leaves United Kingdom at expiration of two months." But Stravinsky returned to France and came back to England on June 21.

73. "The public was generally respectful, but disconcerted," Ansermet wrote to Stravinsky on December 5. "A few people vaguely protested, but without whistling."

74. Otto Kling wrote to Stravinsky, January 9, 1922: "Haven't you had news of the concert? It went very well, even though the unhappy part of the audience outnumbered the happy part."

75. The draft of a telegram to Ansermet, May 11, 1919, contains, on the back of the paper, a list of "remarks for the harmonium."

76. None of the sketches for this score is dated, but one of them contains a copy of Stravinsky's letter to Schoenberg, May 27, 1919, and the music and words were obviously written at the same time. In a letter of April 1919, to Struve, Stravinsky refers to the new ensemble for *Les Noces*, and he lists the instruments in a letter to Ansermet on July 23. On August 8, 1919, Stravinsky wrote to thank the cimbalomist, Aladár Rácz, for a pair of baguettes.

77. Changes and corrections in this movement delayed the publication of the score for several years. As late as August 7, 1924, Harry Kling wrote to Stravinsky: "I wait anxiously from day to day for the *Histoire du Soldat* proofs. . . ." On April 22, 1925, Kling wrote: "It is disagreeable to hear that the printed orchestra score is still full of errors."

78. For his first performance, Ansermet had the full, original ensemble. He wrote to Stravinsky after the first rehearsal: "How I love the cry of the clarinet, the tranquil flow of the low flute and the basset horn, the brilliant bursts of the brass." (Letter of October 13, 1921)

79. Ansermet is referring to the third proof score, but the question is not based on a very intelligent analysis of the harmony.

80. Writing to Ernest Oeberg from Nice, September 23, 1925, Stravinsky says: "I spoke with Toscanini about his wish to purchase the manuscript of the *Nightingale* and promised him to try to arrange it with you. . . . He said the price does not matter. Make a price, but not extremely low. . . ." In 1930, Stravinsky told an interviewer for *L'Etoile Belge* (May 22) that "Toscanini is the greatest among living conductors." Then, in the late 1930s, Stravinsky and Toscanini became enemies partly because of the conductor's opposition to contemporary music, partly because of his political views. In September 1939, the two men sailed to America on the same ship but avoided each other. After Ansermet's performance of the *Symphonies*, however, Stravinsky believed that Toscanini might permit other guest conductors to play even Stravinsky, whose music was so neglected at that time, and who was so eager to have it performed that he wrote to Toscanini asking him to arrange for the present writer to conduct the Symphony in C with the NBC orchestra. Toscanini did not acknowledge Stravinsky's letter.

81. *Pulcinella* antedates this statement by only a year and a half.

82. Stravinsky's correspondence with Strasser, Intendant of the State Opera in Kiel, contains detailed directions for staging the piece, especially in a letter from the composer dated October 5, 1925.

83. On the 18th of August, 1921, Stravinsky's publishers in Berlin wrote to him: "The Glinka music that you want is unobtainable here, and we do not think that it can be had anywhere."

84. This would seem to indicate that the visit took place in April 1913. Mrs. Stravinsky recalls that the younger Nelidova had returned from Paris with photographs of Nijinsky in the *Faune*.

85. She later danced in *Les Biches*. Kashuba was another dancer in the Nelidova School at the same time as Mme Stravinsky.

86. In contrast, Artur, as a young man, had run away and joined the navy in Riga, where he acquired a tattoo.

87. 1874–1946.

88. 1875–1937.

89. See Blok's *Diary*, May 31, 1914.

90. See page 43, caption to the painting by Stravinsky's sister-in-law.

91. The marriage was dissolved by a Boston court, March 5, 1940, by which date the Sudeikins had not seen each other for more than fifteen years. But on April 15, 1945, to satisfy a Los Angeles court ruling on the Stravinskys' application for citizenship, the composer was obliged to fabricate a statement saying that his wife's marriage to Sudeikin had been terminated on February 20, 1920, in Tiflis. In truth, however, Vera Shilling and Serge Sudeikin were never married at all, since neither of them, in the havoc of the Russian Revolution, was able to obtain a divorce.

92. Osip Mandelstam, *Selected Poems*, translated by Clarence Brown and W. S. Merwin (New York: Atheneum, 1974).

93. Cambridge University Press, 1973.

94. Lydia Sokolova used the same word to describe Stravinsky: "...I went off to the supper party at Diaghilev's hotel, the Continental [after the performance of *Le Sacre du Printemps*, December 15, 1920]. Diaghilev sat at one end of the table and Stravinsky at the other. ...I should have liked to sit quietly listening to Stravinsky who could be very amusing...." (*Op. cit.*) "Stephen Spender and Natasha Spender ... on one occasion brought down Stravinsky [to Saltwood]. ...I think he enjoyed himself and [he] wrote a perfectly incomprehensible bar of music in our book. He was one of the most entertaining men I have ever met...." (Kenneth Clark, *The Other Half* [London: John Murray, 1977])

95. A note in Mrs. Stravinsky's diary says that she finished the work on November 18. On January 20, 1927, Ansermet wrote to Stravinsky: "Diaghilev is more capricious and stubborn than ever. He wanted to change certain movements of *The Firebird*, using the pretext that the piece needs to be rejuvenated."

96. *De Meyer*, by Philippe Jullian (New York: Knopf, 1976).

97. This production of *Petrushka* was imported by the Teatro Colón, Buenos Aires, the following year, and Ansermet, returning to Europe from that city, described it in a letter to Stravinsky dated October 1, 1926: "Sudeikin's decors struck me as execrable, and, as for the choreography, I did not have the courage to felicitate [Adolph] Bolm. The Petrushka dies with a lot of *chichi* and the Magician weeps and laments over the death of his puppet.... It was a *Petrushka* by Ibsen. The crowd was a museum, with Goyas, Daumiers, and everyone a 'personality.'"

98. *"Besser ein schlechter Interpret als eine ideale Maschine,"* Stravinsky told Dr. Eric Simon, in an interview in *Phono*, April 1956. Simon had played one of the clarinets in Schoenberg's Septet-Suite when Stravinsky heard the work in Venice in September 1937. In an interview in *La Razón*, Buenos Aires, August 28, 1960, Stravinsky says: "I cannot discuss the subject of electronic music, because I do not think there *is* electronic music but only electronic noises."

99. *Souvenirs, op. cit.*

100. 1898–1957.

101. American composer (1909–59). Stravinsky wrote to Ansermet, March 15, 1923: "I receive letter after letter from Antheil, who always demands that I inform him by telegram where I am or will be so that he can come to see me. But he never gives his address and the telegrams do not follow him; I've just had my telegram to Budapest returned with a note saying that Antheil has

left." Stravinsky wrote again on May 22: "A letter has come from G. Antheil, as idiotic as are all the others from him." Stravinsky did not hear Antheil's *Ballet Mécanique* until 1952, when the present writer recorded it in Los Angeles, and, at that time, Stravinsky dismissed the piece as an arrant plagiarism from *Les Noces.*

102. *Bad Boy of Music* (New York: Doubleday, 1945).

103. Following Diaghilev's instructions, Ansermet had cut the "Variation of Terpsichore" in performances of *Apollo* that Stravinsky did not attend.

104. Ansermet wrote to Stravinsky, February 2, 1926: "There are always the ten or twenty who like the *Chant du Rossignol*, but the others understand it no better after five years, with the difference that they are accustomed to it now and no longer protest out loud. I play it here [Geneva] for a public of intellectuals ... who scorn the eloquence of Hugo, preferring Mallarmé and Valéry, in whom everything depends on the quality of the words. ... These people like rhetoric in music."

105. Literally, buckwheat, or millet, but, figuratively, a popular Russian expression meaning "boasting."

106. Stravinsky had conducted *Jeu de Cartes* there a month before.

107. Ansermet's telegram to Stravinsky in December 1938, after the death of his daughter, is official in tone and contrasts strangely with the letters of condolence from other Swiss friends, such as Ramuz, Oliveri, René Morax, Cingria.

108. In two volumes (Neuchâtel: A la Baconnière, 1961).

109. Stravinsky had underscored and questioned a statement about the "science" and "talent" of the young French musicians in an article on Cocteau and "Les Six" in *Comoedia*, January 16, 1920. What is most troubling to the student of Stravinsky's relationships to these composers is his contempt for Milhaud, later his close personal friend. On October 1, 1928, Stravinsky wrote to Ansermet: "I have read with satisfaction your program in which the Free Masonic music of Darius Milhaud is happily absent."

110. Stravinsky had gone to Weimar with Vera Sudeikina on the 16th of August. The concert was on the 19th. They returned to Paris via Wiesbaden. On August 26, they went with Benois to Magny-sur-Vexins to visit Argutinsky, and stayed until the 28th. They arrived in Paris on the 29th, Stravinsky taking the night train to Biarritz on the 30th.

111. Scherchen wrote to Stravinsky in July 1923 asking permission to perform *Les Noces* in German. Werner Reinhart had already written from Copenhagen in June: "What do you think of Scherchen's proposition to produce the *Noces* in German, at Frankfurt, with his small chorus? I heard them in an enormously difficult work by Schoenberg and it was perfect."

112. Interview in the *Dresdner Neuesten Nachrichten*, February 1, 1929.

113. Mme Torpadie lived in Göteborg and came to see Stravinsky when he gave a concert with Dushkin in that city, October 11, 1935.

114. A harpsichord was substituted for the cimbalom in *Ragtime.*

115. To judge by the questions of the interviewers in every American city in which Stravinsky appeared, quarter-tones were the principal concern of the "modernists." Stravinsky was not interested.

116. Stravinsky had played his Piano Concerto in Boston with Kussevitzky the previous evening and returned to New York on the night train.

117. The musicians are described on the program as "An ensemble from the [N.Y.] Philharmonic Orchestra."

118. This was Sablin, Stravinsky's valet, a former member of the Russian merchant marine. He accompanied the composer from Paris and translated for him, but after the tour the employment ended in litigation.

119. This is puzzling. Rosenfeld does not suggest that *he* speaks Russian, but Stravinsky's English was not fluent enough at that time to carry on the ensuing conversation. Very likely Stravinsky did use English mixed with French and German, which Rosenfeld rewrote.

120. Paul Rosenfeld, *Musical Impressions* (reprinted by Hill and Wang, New York, 1969).

121. The S.S. *Aquitania* left New York March 14 and docked in France on the 20th.

122. Stravinsky's photograph albums contain several pictures of the car and driver.

123. Schoenberg wrote to Stravinsky on April 24, 1919, asking for a new work to be played in Schoenberg's "Society for Private Musical Performances" and Stravinsky answered on May 27: "Honored Master, I thank you for your letter of 24.4.19. I am sending to you a copy of my '3 Pièces pour quatuor à cordes' by my brother-in-law [Grigory Beliankin]. I ask you to send this work back to me immediately after its performance. . . ." Apparently Stravinsky did not receive the manuscript and in 1922 he complained to Otto Kling that Schoenberg had not returned it. Kling answered on April 19, 1922: "Edwin Evans . . . tells us that there is a misunderstanding on the subject of your Quatuor. Dr. Wellesz wrote to him that the manuscript in question was returned to you two years ago, and that the secretary of the Schoenberg Verein advised you of the return at the time."

124. In New York, more than thirty years later, Schoenberg's son-in-law, Felix Greissle, told Stravinsky that, in the 1920s, Schoenberg had heard and liked Histoire du Soldat.

125. On October 22, Stravinsky wrote to Ansermet: "I have finished my thing (Sonata) and am practicing hard at the piano. Perhaps I will play the piece on my tours if I feel that I can do it well."

126. Stravinsky returned to Nice from Italy on September 21.

127. From Passport to Paris, by Vernon Duke (Boston: Little, Brown, 1955).

128. In Dialogues and a Diary, Stravinsky questioned the word "Oedipoda" in the Messenger's part and suggested changing it. Years later, George Seferis wrote to him citing the instance of this form of the word in Seneca's version of the play. On October 25, 1969, Stravinsky answered, saying that it had never occurred to him to compare Daniélou's Latin with Seneca's, but that Daniélou (Cocteau's translator) might well have borrowed the "Oedipoda" form from the Latin play. (The spellings Oidipus, Oidipous—the correct pronunciation of the word in Stravinsky's score—and Oidipodia are common in Greek literature.)

129. Oedipus Rex was composed for the twentieth anniversary of Diaghilev's company, but his only recorded comment on the anniversary present is "C'est ennuyeux," a remark that did not appear in print until October 1, 1929, in the Musical Times, London.

130. Stravinsky marked his copy of the vocal score here, "sordamente" (deafly).

131. Style and Idea (London: Faber and Faber, 1975).

132. Mr. Bernstein surely means "that tool for ambiguity," since the tool itself is not ambiguous.

133. Leonard Bernstein, The Unanswered Question (Cambridge, Mass.: Harvard University Press, 1976).

134. Cf. Part II footnote 43.

135. Writing to Stravinsky for biographical information, June 22, 1929, Schaeffner identifies himself as "one of those who carried you from the hall after Monteux's triumphant performance of Le Sacre du Printemps in 1914." Stravinsky accorded several interviews to Schaeffner in Paris in the autumn of 1929, and invited him to Nice to inspect documents in the first days of January 1930, and again at Easter 1930. A letter from Schaeffner to Stravinsky, September 1929, reveals that the composer had already induced his biographer to read the ultra-reactionary Rozanov.

136. The mention of "three or four dancers" suggests that Stravinsky had discussed the commission while in America in 1925. In a letter to Païchadze, April 11, 1927, Stravinsky says that he intends to compose "a pantomime of about twenty minutes' duration." He later told an interviewer in the Hotel Ritz in Barcelona (while posing for the painter Callico): "Apollo is the protagonist. The concept of the ballet is very simple . . . and the dances will be traditional. This new ballet will be universal and personal at the same time." (La Veu de Catalunya, March 25, 1925)

137. The goddess of childbirth. The Greek version is "Eileithyia" and the Roman "Ilithyia."

138. Stravinsky was especially gratified by a review which said that his

recording of the *Sacre* "respects the text in a way that no other conductor has done." (*Rhythmes et Arts Phoniques*, January 1930) The recording, at least of Part One, seemed to please Vera Sudeikina's fox terrier, "Pilu," who always fled to the bathroom, however, during the crescendo before the "*Elue.*"

139. One exception was Fritz Busch. Stravinsky wrote to Ansermet from Paris, November 16, 1929: "[Busch] is an excellent musician and a good conductor—a very good performance of *La Dame de Pique* [in Dresden]—but he has a rather hostile mentality for all new tendencies, which is something rare these days in a man of 38. I would be the first to receive this kind of spirit with open arms, but on condition that it has passed through the ideas of our time, by which I do not mean that it is sufficient to hear and condemn Darius Milhaud or Alfredo Casella. . . ."

140. On December 4, 1940, in the Barbizon Plaza Hotel, New York, Stravinsky wrote to Nadia Boulanger in Cambridge, asking her to intervene on his behalf to persuade Kussevitzky to pay for a rental of the orchestra materials of the Symphony in C, which the conductor had expected the composer to furnish.

141. In a letter to Païchadze, October 26, 1928, Stravinsky claims that "no hint of Andersen has survived. . . ."

142. "What bad luck not to have seen you," Stravinsky wrote to Ramuz, August 11, 1928. "I arrived at this triste casino of Thonon at noon, and no one was there except Auberjonois . . . who told me about the projected trip in Mermod's Buick. . . . Let's do it, all of us together. . . . If you come toward six in the evenings, I will spend time after that with you, but the whole of the mornings and afternoons I must devote to work. . . ." Stravinsky visited Thonon again in the summer of 1929 and in July 1935. And while staying in Evian in the summer of 1970, he went to the hospital in Thonon seven times (June 27, July 6 and 28, August 4, 8, 12, 19) for transfusions of "*globules rouges lavées*," in amounts that started at 500 c.c.'s and were reduced to 300 c.c.'s and 250 c.c.'s.

143. For a full account of the trial, see *Le Journal de Paris*, July 6, 1928.

144. Diaghilev never made the trip to Athos, but Stravinsky sent money there regularly, to a Father Gerasim, as well as lists of the names of those who were to be remembered in prayers. See Stravinsky's letter to Gerasim, October 18, 1932. A photograph of Gerasim was always on Stravinsky's night table.

145. In London. Stravinsky typed all of his Russian letters on it thereafter and until the end of his life.

146. Stravinsky's relations with Serge Lifar were much less cordial after Diaghilev's death, and when Lifar last wrote to the composer, in May 1959, to inform him that he had been awarded the Diaghilev Prize by the Université de la Danse, of which Lifar was the director, Stravinsky did not answer, but scrawled on the envelope, "Oh, the megalomania!" Benois's copy of Lifar's book on Diaghilev, with hundreds of annotations in the painter's hand, is now in the collection of Edwin Allen.

147. Diaghilev had cut the Variation of Terpsichore.

148. Two years later, in August 1931, the music critic Guido Gatti, after a visit to Stravinsky in La Vironnière (Grenoble), described the composer attending a Panikheda service on the day of Diaghilev's death, at the Russian Orthodox chapel in Rives. (*L'Ambrosiana*, Milan, August 26, 1931)

149. Stravinsky never met Blok, but was an admirer and faithful reader of his poetry. On January 23, 1963, Stravinsky received a letter from the Oxford University Club requesting permission to use excerpts from *Petrushka* as the musical setting for a performance of Blok's one-act play *Balaganchik*. The idea pleased Stravinsky, and, five days later, he sent his permission.

150. When the present writer first saw Lourié, in Tanglewood in the summer of 1946, the former commissar had recordings of Anna Akhmatova reading her poems.

151. See pp. 214–30 in *The One and a Half-Eyed Archer*, op. cit.

152. Sudeikin's work in "The Cellar of Fallen Angels" in New York (1924) was similar.

153. "I am Orthodox, but our two churches support each other on more than one point. I particularly admire Léon Bloy, who was so unheeded, and scoffed at. . . ." (Interview: *Le Vingtième Siècle*, Brussels, May 22, 1930) Reviewing a book by Maritain in the *Times Literary Supplement*, November 8, 1928, T. S. Eliot refers to "the violent and rhapsodical novelist Léon Bloy . . ."

154. *Bagázh*, by Nicolas Nabokov (New York: Atheneum, 1975).

155. In *With Strings Attached* (New York: Knopf, 1967), Joseph Szigeti recalls "That memorable session at Blüthner's piano store in Leipzig in 1923 with Stravinsky playing his Piano Sonata to an audience of three—a friend [Vera Sudeikina], the representative of the Kussevitzky Publishing House, and myself—after a very prolonged and very Russian midday meal that followed the Furtwängler rehearsal for the Gewandhaus premiere of [Stravinsky's] Piano Concerto. . . . I had my violin along, as I had been asked by Stravinsky to play Bach's Solo Sonata in A minor for him afterwards. He played his Sonata twice in succession, then turned around and said simply to us . . . 'Tchistaya rabota!' ('Clean work!')." Actually the first performance of the Concerto in Leipzig took place on December 4, 1924, under Furtwängler; neither the Sonata nor the Concerto was finished in 1923. The 1924 Leipzig concert contained a program essay by Rudolf Kastner comparing Stravinsky and Schoenberg as the two "ways" of new music.

156. *Op. cit.*

157. As Oscar Levant reported it—he had heard the story from Goddard Lieberson via Mrs. Stravinsky—Stravinsky "was informed that one of the requisites to becoming a patient was the total abstinence from alcoholic beverages. 'Good-bye, Doctor,' was his reply, as he hastily took his departure." (*The Unimportance of Being Oscar* [New York: Putnam, 1968])

158. Abbé Sébastien Kneipp (1821–97). Stravinsky's copy of *Das Grosse Kneippbuch* was given to him by Willy Strecker.

159. Janet Flanner, *op. cit.*

160. In January 1926, Stravinsky acquired a copy of Weber's death mask.

161. Contrast these rehearsal manners with those of Stravinsky, the pianist, in a concert: ". . . Stravinsky sat before the piano . . . in a dignified, scholarly fashion . . . the most vigorous and interesting musical personality of today . . . nothing showy or dramatic or spectacular in his piano manner; it was just sound playing by a sound musician." (Leon Edel, in the *Montreal Star*, March 13, 1929, reviewing a concert in Paris)

162. *Op. cit.*

163. Szigeti, *op. cit.* The performance was in Carnegie Hall, February 8, 1946, the recording in Hollywood, October 11 and 13, 1945.

164. Stravinsky seems *never* to have spoken very favorably about Prokofiev's music, the first Violin Concerto excepted. On April 15, 1916, Mme Basil Khvoshinsky wrote to Stravinsky calling his attention to a review in the January *Apollo* of *Alla and Lolly*, "the ballet that Diaghilev did not like." But neither did Stravinsky like the music, and he said so.

165. Stravinsky had a concert in Milan, February 11, 1933, and another one in Rome on February 20.

166. The part should be sung by a *tenore di forza*, Stravinsky noted in a letter to a CBS program director, March 28, 1945, and the chorus should contain twenty-five each of sopranos, altos, tenors, and basses. (The same letter describes the voices for *Oedipus Rex* as a *tenore di grazia* for the Shepherd, a *basso cantante* for Creon, and a *basso profundo* for Tiresias.)

167. *Alban Berg*, by Mosco Carner (London: Duckworth, 1975).

168. Ansermet had conducted *Perséphone* in the New York Philharmonic's Stravinsky Festival, July 1966.

169. *Op. cit.*

170. In Dagmar Godowsky's *First Person Plural* (*op. cit.*), Stravinsky underlined the statement "Born Count Strava—the Strava River flowed through his family estates" and filled the margin with protesting exclamation points. Yet on May 31, 1938, Stravinsky wrote to M. Marx of the French Foreign Office apropos the "*Entartete Kunst*" exhibition in Düsseldorf: ". . . On a essayé de me faire passer pour un juif. . . . Mon origine de la noblesse polonaise—et depuis 150 ans de la noblesse héréditaire—prouvant le contraire. . . ." Perhaps Monsieur Marx's sympathies were not deeply stirred by this argument. (See Appendix D.) Stravinsky commissioned a Parisian genealogist to trace a coat of arms and thereafter wore an armigerous ring.

171. Fyodor Stravinsky first sang the roles of Rangoni, January 2, 1877, and of Varlaam, December 1, 1878, three and four years *after* the first performance of *Boris* (1874).

172. This is one of Miss Flanner's most acute observations. In fact, Stravinsky set himself to master anything that attracted his interest.

173. On a stage, in a classroom, or at a press conference, Stravinsky would usually talk longer than he had promised: "He greeted the newspaper representatives with the salutation, 'I have ten minutes,' but long after the ten minutes, he was graciously discussing . . ." (News Gazette, Urbana, Illinois, March 3, 1949).

174. Janet Flanner, op. cit.

175. In New York, in 1941, Mme Maritain sent a copy of her volume of memoirs, Les Grandes Amitiés, to Stravinsky, inscribing it "Sincère et amicale hommage d'admiration."

176. Actually, November 21.

177. Raïssa's Journal (Albany, N.Y.: Magi, 1974).

178. From the Journal de l'Université des Annales, December 15, 1935. In a lecture given in Paris, January 24, 1936, Mme Dmitri Riabouchinsky discussed this categorization of the concerto by the composer. Stravinsky and his son recorded the work for French Columbia, Paris, February 14 and 16, 1938, and Stravinsky recorded the complete lecture in Los Angeles, April 7, 1949.

179. Gian-Carlo Menotti.

180. New York, April 27, 1937.

181. Actually A Bullet in the Ballet. The ballet in this film was to have been Petrushka, and Stravinsky was to have conducted the sound-track recording. Negotiations continued for more than a year and a half.

182. Two months later, in New York, Hemingway wrote to Stravinsky: "To Igor Stravinsky from his great admirer who wishes to meet him. Ernest Hemingway."

183. The program in Princeton, as on the previous day in Allentown, Pennsylvania, included Tchaikovsky's Symphonie Pathétique.

184. Stravinsky seems to have had the Chicago Symphony in mind from the beginning, but no mutual agreement had been reached until he was completing the third movement and broached the matter of a commission with Mrs. Elizabeth Sprague Coolidge at a dinner in Cambridge in the spring of 1940.

185. Stravinsky had several recordings of lyrebirds and in the 1950s he corresponded with Australians who increased his collection of tapes. In an interview in the Sydney Sun, November 21, 1961, he said of the birds: "They are wonderful. I have three recordings of them. But I must admit I would not like to conduct an orchestra of lyrebirds." The 1938 Australian tour that did not take place is referred to almost as a certainty in numerous letters of the time. It was being organized by a London concert agency.

186. Sir Kenneth Clark describes Mrs. Bliss as "the queen of Georgetown. . . . We had gladly accepted an invitation to stay with her in Dumbarton Oaks. . . . After the war Dumbarton Oaks became famous as the site of an economic conference and the title of one of Stravinsky's [concertos]." (Op. cit.)

187. After the death, her husband, Yuri Mandelstamm, sent a poem about her and a touching letter to Stravinsky, who kept both in his wallet. On the evidence of these writings, it is clear that Mandelstamm was deeply in love with his wife, and grief-stricken ("Mika is no longer there . . . at night I start to reach for her hand. . . . She was so pure. . . . But she looked happy in her death . . ."). Stravinsky's wife first met her future son-in-law in May 1935 and wrote to her husband on the 21st: "I immediately felt in him not just the niceness, but the complete goodness of the man. He is obviously intelligent and kind and loves Mika earnestly, with a genuine love."

188. As early as 1927, however, Stravinsky wrote to Païchadze concerning a proposal by the Philharmonic of Paris: "How pathetic all of this! And to say that this Paris which lifted me in triumph seventeen years ago can offer me nothing better now than a public appearance in a chamber-music concert of this kind. One would think that one was in Zagreb." (August 16, 1927)

189. "The idea for this ballet entered my head one evening in a fiacre while I was on my way to visit some friends. I was so delighted that I stopped the driver and invited him to have a drink with me." (Le Jour, Paris, February 3, 1938)

190. The first concert performance in Paris, which came long after those

in many other European cities, was no more than a *succès d'estime*. Darius Milhaud had written a perhaps overenthusiastic review of the piece when Stravinsky conducted it three months before in Venice: "The Princess of Piedmont attended the last concert of *The Firebird*, in which Stravinsky triumphed, with much brilliance. . . . *Jeu de Cartes* enchanted everyone. In exploiting extremely simple elements, Stravinsky achieves unforgettable effects of sonority, fantasy, tenderness, mixed with the most perfect humor. What a musician, and what a lesson for us all!" (*Le Figaro*, September 19, 1937)

191. June 8, 1937, at the Théâtre des Champs-Elysées, as part of the Exposition Internationale de Paris 1937. On the same program, Nadia Boulanger conducted works by her sister, by Léo Preger, and by Bach; Maurice Jaubert conducted his *Jeanne d'Arc*.

192. Stravinsky seems not to have heard of the Rudolf von Laban and the Raoul Ager Feuillet systems of choreographic notation, to name only two. Yet the composer was certainly aware of Laban, who, in 1921, had proposed to choreograph *Petrushka* and *Pulcinella* in Mannheim, with Stravinsky's knowledge.

193. In later years, Stravinsky used to say that he had "stood" because his friends had convinced him that Academicians were accorded civilities particularly useful to an extensive traveler.

194. Stravinsky is referring to Gabriel Pierné and Jacques-Emile Blanche. When questioned about the affair by a reporter for *L'Intransigeant*, October 13, 1937, Stravinsky said: "I have been told that I became a French citizen too recently. . . . I was in Rome, however, when Paul Dukas died"—Stravinsky was to have taken Dukas's place—"and I conducted a piece by him in one of my concerts, for which I am still waiting for a word of thanks from a representative of France."

195. Florent Schmitt received the remaining twenty-seven. When a vacancy occurred in 1938, Schmitt asked André Schaeffner to try to persuade Stravinsky to become a candidate, but the composer refused.

PART THREE

1. Stravinsky was unusually concerned with his mental processes. In a letter to Nicolas Nabokov, January 1948, criticizing "Sartre's Kierkegaard" and asking for the score of Handel's *Caesar*, Stravinsky says that each day he reads three or four pages of Shestov's Kierkegaard before going to bed, "putting what I read in my unprepared brain with great care in order to make it readily accessible to my memory."

Stravinsky's brain, or, rather, the medical documents relating to it in the last fifteen years of his life, deserve the attention of neurophysiologists. However superior the development of the right hemisphere (artistic ability, the simultaneous—versus the sequential—processing of information), the left hemisphere (logical thought, the analytical use of language) must have evolved to an almost equal degree in his case, but perhaps, in some artistic geniuses, both sides possess the same potential. In his seventy-fifth year, at any rate, Stravinsky suffered an "ischaemic episode in the basilar artery" that left him with a permanent partial paralysis on the left side of his body, and impairment in various right-hemisphere functions, such as orientation in space. Yet, in the months that followed, he composed *Agon*. (See Julian Jaynes's *The Origin of Consciousness in the Breakdown of the Bicameral Mind* [Boston: Houghton Mifflin, 1978].)

2. *Musical Digest*, Hollywood, September 1946.

3. Otto Kahn was apparently the chief contributor to one of the sustentation funds.

4. In a letter to Nadia Boulanger, November 4, 1945, Stravinsky refers to "inevitable repairs on our Dodge which is becoming old and a little tired after five years of continual work." But the Dodge was not exchanged for a new car until January 1950.

5. Stravinsky had heard Shostakovich's *Lady Macbeth of Mzensk* in New

York, February 4, 1935, conducted by Artur Rodzinski. On the 14th of that month, the *Novaya Zarya* (*Russian Daily*) of San Francisco quoted Stravinsky as saying that he had been "deeply disappointed by the opera and its tragic realism." In the same interview, Stravinsky says that he had heard a symphony (No. 1) by the Soviet composer and found it "rather better." On April 4, Stravinsky wrote to Ansermet: "It is formless, monotonous music—a system of recitatives and entr'actes—with formless and extremely noisy marches, genre Prokofiev. . . . This premiere (and, I hope, *dernier*) reminded me of the spectacles of Kurt Weill two years ago in Paris, with all the *conneries* of the Prunières and the snobs of my dear new country. Happily, there is more than this in the United States, which, this time, has made a rather good impression on me."

6. Stravinsky was in Washington to conduct two performances of his opera, but he is mistaken about the date of the Russian premiere. *The Nightingale* was given in Petrograd in 1918, after the Soviets had come to power, and when his younger brother was dead. Also, Stravinsky was not invited to Russia under Lenin, but shortly after Lenin's death.

7. Stravinsky used to quote Dickens to justify his own preference for financial rather than artistic discussions with a certain mealy-mouthed type of patron: "Apropos Charles Dickens's visit to America, the people who had invited him to lecture here were astonished about his interest in fees and contracts. 'Money is not a shocking thing to an artist,' Dickens insisted." (*Musical Digest*, Hollywood, September 1946)

8. *Washington Post*, March 24, 1935.

9. On April 26, 1956, Stravinsky wrote to Boosey & Hawkes in London asking them to check the postal rates, since, each time he received a package from this firm, he had to pay a special postal duty of fifteen cents. He also complained to Boosey & Hawkes, May 22, 1950, that, going through their statements, he noticed they had charged to him a $4.38 telephone call which he had been obliged to make since their office had not answered him by mail. The call, Stravinsky adds, was necessary because of the carelessness of their staff. In still another letter to the publisher, answering a request for a reproduction of a page of the manuscript of *Agon*, he says that, rather than bring the page to his reproduction service, wait a few hours, and then miss the post, he preferred to make a new page, which has taken him forty-five minutes. (But a messenger service would have performed the errand he describes for about ten dollars, while his forty-five minutes were worth at least ten thousand.)

10. Alexis Remisov (the writer), Zika Kamenetzky, Ira Belline, Pierre Suvchinsky, the daughter of Bachnitzky, Felix von Lebel, Olga Sallard were only a few of this company.

11. Stravinsky's "open letter" to Guy de Pourtales concerning his *Berlioz et l'Europe Romantique* was entirely written by Roland-Manuel but signed and sent by Stravinsky (from Florence, May 18, 1939).

12. Stravinsky first lectured in English during his recital tours with Samuel Dushkin in 1935 and 1937, reading brief commentaries about his programs; some of his concert contracts, including one for the Brooklyn Academy of Music in 1937, required that he lecture as well. His first extemporaneous talk in English took place in Beverly Hills, August 11, 1940, for a women's organization. Beginning in December 1939, his press conferences were exclusively in English. "English—pretty pure and extensively articulate—was the only language Stravinsky would talk at all," Alfred Frankenstein wrote of one of these, in San Francisco, January 6, 1942. As for the style, the same critic observed of a Stravinsky lecture in English at Mills College two years later: "In essence it was another exposition of the principles of definiteness, specificity, clarity, and scientific self-consciousness that run all through Stravinsky's writings." Stravinsky repeated the Mills College lecture for the Art Alliance, in the Barclay Hotel in Philadelphia, February 21, 1945, and afterward played his Sonata for two pianos with Vincent Persichetti. In the correspondence concerning this event, Stravinsky estimated that the lecture would last fifty minutes.

13. After the October 18 lecture, Stravinsky attended a reception fortified with scraps of paper containing the names of several "*élèves de Nadia*," Walter Piston, Tillman Merritt, and Alexei Haieff among them. These papers also included warnings, such as a note to "beware of Hugo Leichtentritt [the musi-

cologist], who is dangerous and argumentative about Monteverdi." (Had Professor Leichtentritt criticized Mlle Boulanger's Monteverdi recordings?) It should be recalled that Stravinsky's only teaching experience before Harvard had been in Mlle Boulanger's classes in Paris and Fontainebleau, in the 1930s. Thanks to Nadia Boulanger, on September 17, 1935, he was appointed "Inspector of the Composition Course" at the Ecole Normale de Musique de Paris, replacing Paul Dukas.

In December 1942, Stravinsky, as a judge for the Lili Boulanger Prize, awarded the $500 to Haieff (letter from Nadia Boulanger to Stravinsky, November 28, 1942). Haieff remained a faithful friend of Stravinsky's until the end, moreover, making a special trip to see him in Hollywood in March 1969, and a trip to see him in the New York Hospital in June 1969.

14. "When he walks . . . he is not considered the best-dressed man in Cambridge, perhaps, but certainly he is one of the *most*-dressed. Often he wears a sweater and two coats, one of them a fur coat. Spats, a stick, and a scarf well up to his ears complete the picture." (*Philadelphia Enquirer*)

15. The *Poetics of Music*. This was one of the last books that Hermann Hesse read, and he discusses Stravinsky on Beethoven in a letter of July 1962. (See H. Hesse, *Ausgewälte Briefe* [Frankfurt-am-Main: Suhrkamp, 1974]). On May 19, 1962, Hesse had written to Dr. Wayne Andrews thanking him for "the beautiful Gesualdo record," the reference probably being to the Columbia album containing Stravinsky's *Monumentum*.

16. "The futurists no longer interest me, nor the past-ists, and I never eat leftovers. I live in the present. St. Augustine wrote a masterpiece about [the importance of doing just] that." (Interview in an unidentified Paris newspaper, 1938)

17. The names Stravinsky and Schoenberg continued to be placed together, or in opposition, as the leaders of modern music ("Can you send me critical articles to be used in a radio broadcast to demonstrate that Beethoven had the same bad press as Stravinsky and Schoenberg?" Peter Gradenwitz wrote to Stravinsky from Tel Aviv, November 22, 1936). But the one composer's actual exposure to the music of the other had been minimal and accidental. Thus, Stravinsky first heard Schoenberg's Chamber Symphony, Op. 9, because Ansermet played it, January 8, 1928, on a broadcast with the Stravinsky Octet, and first heard Schoenberg's Septet-Suite in Venice, September 9, 1937, because of adjoining rehearsals.

Yet, as late as 1946, when Schoenberg's influence had become widespread, Stravinsky answered a request to write program notes for the first performance of his Concerto in D, saying that, although the music is "the least atonal that can be imagined," the audience "ought to have the pleasure of discovering this for itself." (Letter to Paul Sacher, October 25, 1946) Two years later, Mrs. William Kiskadden, a Los Angeles friend of Stravinsky's, asked him to listen to a composition by her son, now President Derek Bok of Harvard University. Mr. Bok's piece, which he played on a wire recorder, was written in a twelve-tone idiom, and after the audition he told his mother (who told this writer) that Stravinsky had absolutely no idea of how the music was constructed. On October 23, 1949, Stravinsky attended the Los Angeles concert in which Schoenberg read his speech accepting the honorary citizenship of Vienna, yet Stravinsky's correspondence does not mention the event. The change of attitude toward Schoenberg occurred during 1950 and may be explained to some extent by a phrase in a letter from Schoenberg to the conductor Fritz Stiedry, January 2, 1951: ". . . my young friend, Mr. Craft . . . is slowly working himself into my music by performing my music a lot. And finally he will succeed."

18. Stravinsky first heard music by Sauguet in 1924 and, after that, frequently mentioned him as *the* outstanding contemporary French composer. In Prague, in 1930, Stravinsky made a point of recommending Sauguet (in an interview that alludes to the Schoenberg school with the statement: "Mahler has had many descendants"). In interviews in South America in 1936, Stravinsky named Rieti, Petrassi, and Conrad Beck as promising composers.

19. In fact Haydn was the composer whom, at the time, Stravinsky most revered. (It was to be Mozart during the composition of *The Rake's Progress*, Bach during the serial period, and Beethoven when Stravinsky had ceased to

compose.) "My new symphony is severe in form, like Haydn yet not so good as Haydn," Stravinsky told the *New York Post* (April 13, 1940), and the *Montreal Gazette,* March 3, 1945, noted that "after drawing a comparison between Haydn and Mozart in favor of Haydn, Stravinsky hastily added: 'I would not for a single moment criticize a measure of Mozart's music. That is something beyond my capacity.... [But] Haydn was the great inventor. He possessed in the highest degree two indispensable constituents, invention and method.' "

Haydn, for Stravinsky, was a buffer against "German" music. Writing to Ansermet in August 1922, Stravinsky was pleased to quote a passage from Michel Brennet's *Haydn,* to the effect that "the revolution of the *Lied* was parallel to that of German lyric poetry, but there is absolutely no indication that Haydn was interested in either." Stravinsky's anti-"German" bias became more pronounced after Brest-Litovsk, and, by July 1921, he was telling the London *Observer* that "Beethoven's works are never purely musical in their construction; his form is always dialectic, influenced by the philosophical constructions of Hegel. Wagner commits the same sin, influenced for his part by Schopenhauer. And so with all Germans!"

20. Stravinsky's taste for Gounod began in 1923: "I heard a marvel of music, *Philémon et Baucis* by Gounod, in the Trianon Lyrique theater." (Letter to Ansermet, February 11, 1923)

21. In January 1944, Stravinsky told a Boston newspaperman that it was impossible to compose film music "if you want to be responsible for your own work"—a remark that also explains his opposition to the 1960s fad involving improvisation by the performer.

22. Princess Mestchersky, who was so homesick in South Carolina that she kept the clocks in her home there on Paris time. She was the wife of Dr. Pearce Baily (1903–76), the president of the American Academy of Neurology, who had studied with Freud, Jung, and Adler, and, together with Otto Rank, founded the Psychological Center in Paris.

23. On the application, in answer to the question concerning his occupation, Stravinsky wrote: "I am striving to be a creative artist...."

24. Stravinsky to Nadia Boulanger, from the Chateau Marmont, Hollywood, March 3, 1941: "We are having great difficulty in finding a house for a permanent residence, everything except horrors already being taken.... *Il y a beaucoup de monde ici.*" On April 10, he wrote to Victoria Ocampo: "We have installed ourselves here in Hollywood and have bought a ravishing little house." But, before long, Mrs. Stravinsky was writing to Olga Sallard in Paris: "I do not like the 'residential districts' of Hollywood with their endless houses and gardens and green lawns (which must be perfect, not to offend the neighbors) but without a single store, café, delicatessen, kiosk (for cigarettes or a newspaper), or even any life. Children do not play on the grass, and even the dogs do not chase each other.... Everything has to be done by telephone or by car, and friends do not come unexpectedly but have to call two weeks before...."

25. *Here Lies the Heart,* by Mercedes de Acosta (New York: Reynal, 1960). Vera Stravinsky's diary for May 1, 1941, reads: "I like Mercedes, a very ladylike lesbian." Mercedes de Acosta made the French and English translations of Stravinsky's article on Diaghilev, originally written in Russian in March 1937.

26. Among the other good Hollywood friends of the war years were the painters Corrado Cagli (1910–76) and Rico Le Brun, the photographer Baron Gayne de Meyer, the actor Mischa Auer. But, during this period, the Stravinskys' social life centered in Santa Barbara, where they spent one or two weekends each month in the home of Mr. and Mrs. Arthur Sachs. The other guests there often included Nadia Boulanger, Marcelle de Manziarly, Marc Chadourne, Mayette Mayneng. Since the last two were writers, it is disappointing that neither has left a memoir of the composer at this time.

27. Mrs. Stravinsky and Vladimir Sokoloff had known each other before the Russian Revolution when they were both employed at the Kamerny Theater in Moscow.

28. In December 1940, the *New York World-Telegram* reported that Stravinsky frequently visited the Savoy Ballroom in Harlem, where he especially relished the solo licks ("when the players go by themselves"). Three months

earlier, he had composed a *Tango*—Stravinsky's "last tango," mercifully—his second composition both begun and completed in the United States.

29. Stravinsky acquired manuals and method books, as well as music, for both instruments, although he had scored for them previously, guitar in *The Nightingale*, saxophones in *Preludium*. He consulted *The Thompson Progressive Method for Saxophone* (Southern California Music Company) and Nick Manoloff's *Complete Chord and Harmony Manual for Guitar*, the latter a gift from Sol Babitz. The sheet music on Stravinsky's shelves included "Feelin' My Way," "Moonlight Cocktail," etc., etc. He even studied the *Eureka Method for the Banjo* (Boston: Oliver Ditson). Later, at the time of *Agon* and the arrangement of the piano part of the Four Russian Songs for flute, harp, and guitar, Stravinsky familiarized himself with John Dowland's lute gailliards in versions for guitar. Stravinsky's first experience with saxophones dates from 1930, when he permitted Jack Hylton to arrange part of *Mavra* for his jazz band—one of the strangest incidents in Stravinsky's career, since, in a letter to Arthur Brooks of Columbia Records, London, in 1931, the composer claims that the arrangement was authorized not by him but by the Editions Russes de Musique, and that he was unaware that a recording of the Hylton version had been made. Yet Stravinsky was photographed at the recording session.

30. "Stravinsky is in Hollywood, but we can't see him often, Hollywood and San Francisco being about the same distance apart as Paris and Marseille. He came here with Vera for three days, gave a lecture at the College and played with Nadia at two pianos his new and admirable Sonata and *Scherzo à la Russe* (very *Petrushka* 1944). . . ." (Darius Milhaud to Francis Poulenc, February 17, 1945). During this visit, Manfred Bukofzer played some recordings of medieval music that he had made with his students at the University of California in Berkeley. The music had a powerful effect on Stravinsky. Later, Bukofzer sent an essay on the isorhythmic motet, which also influenced the composer. (Letter to Stravinsky, April 8, 1947)

31. When driving through Spain with Stravinsky in 1955, the present writer deeply offended him by reading impiously from a guidebook the list of relics in the Cathedral of Oviedo: ". . . hair of Mary Magdalene, five thorns from the crown of the Savior, one of Judas' pieces of silver, St. Peter's right sandal, a piece of the rod of Moses. . . ."

32. The first movement was completed on April 17, 1939. Ten days later, Stravinsky began the second movement but interrupted work for concerts in Milan and Florence. He resumed the composition on May 27 (at 76) and completed it on July 19.

33. In interviews at the time, however, Stravinsky said that he had had Toulouse-Lautrec in mind and had not intended "a contribution to the American scene." (*Montreal Gazette, op. cit.*)

34. The "Eclogue," completed on February 12, 1943. Stravinsky's manuscript says "Song for Bessie" at what later became rehearsal number 20 .

35. At one time, Stravinsky planned to compose music for the entire film and he made verbal notations for other scenes, such as "First Party (Thornfield Hall—Jane Eyre, sitting down on the top step of the stairs to listen—lady's solo over, a duet follows)" and "Second Party, a brilliant Prelude." He made a Russian-English dictionary as he read the book, some of its vocabulary being unfamiliar to him.

36. On May 18, Stravinsky wrote to Nadia Boulanger: "A hot wind is blowing from the desert, this after 40 days in New York with its *giboulées de printemps*. It makes one meditate on the imperfection of human physiology, and it also makes the recommencing of work extremely difficult."

37. Stravinsky wrote to Kussevitzky on April 9, 1943, accepting the commission for the *Ode*, and the conductor acknowledged the receipt of the manuscript in Lenox, July 21. A letter from Stravinsky, September 27, 1943 to John Burk, the Boston Symphony program annotator, contains an analysis of the opus that, unfortunately, is too long to be included here. But the true story of the *Ode* premiere is manifestly different from Stravinsky's published reminiscences of the event. After hearing Kussevitzky's broadcast of the piece, October 8, 1943, Stravinsky sent a telegram: "Just heard the *Ode* in your most penetrating performance. Profoundly touched. My thoughts with you and your orches-

tral family." (According to Mrs. Stravinsky's diary, her husband's private comment on the performance was "very bad"; furthermore, he spent an hour weighing acceptable phrases before settling for "penetrating.") On October 11, Stravinsky wrote to Kussevitzky diplomatically pointing out that page 23 of the "Epitaph" contains three score systems, not two, but saying that the two systems which Kussevitzky had played together "are [after all] almost integrated in the same mode. Also, at $\boxed{139}$ the trumpet is in C, not B-flat."

38. The music for this opus for orchestra begins at measure $\boxed{17}$ in the Sonata and is nearly identical with that work for eleven measures, continuing with eight measures that occur in the piano piece, but transposed, at sixteen measures from the end of the first movement. The orchestra piece then takes a different form from the Sonata. Completed on August 12, 1943, before Stravinsky began the Sonata, the score of the unpublished work requires strings, flute, oboe, English horn, two clarinets, two bassoons, trombone.

39. In the original agreement, and in the publicity of the Janssen Symphony, which was to give the premiere of the "Genesis Suite Based on Biblical Scenes, for Orchestra, Choir, and Narrator," the Prelude is announced as being by Hindemith. In August 1945, he withdrew and was replaced by Schoenberg, who signed his contract on August 14. Apparently he and Stravinsky asked to see each other's contracts, to be certain that they were both receiving the same fee.

40. Alphonse Onnou (d. 1940). According to a letter from him to Stravinsky, August 27, 1923, the composer had coached Onnou's "Pro Arte" Quartet in the Concertino and Three Pieces before the ensemble played these works in the 1923 Salzburg Festival. After the Salzburg performance, letters to Stravinsky from Poulenc and others praise the group's playing, and W. Reinhart wrote that "There was no comparison with the way the Flonzaley Quartet used to play this music." Twice, in 1936 and again in 1937, Elizabeth Sprague Coolidge asked Stravinsky to compose a string quartet for the "Pro Arte." Writing on August 15, 1936, he accepted her commission but warned that "every minute of my composing time is already heavily committed."

The Elegy appears to have been composed in November 1941, immediately after Danses Concertantes. The sketches are found in the same notebook, following those for the "Pas de Deux," the last part of Danses Concertantes to be composed, and the handwriting and pencil are the same. Moreover, the idea of the Elegy fugue derives from the sixteenth-note figures in the final section of the "Pas de Deux," Stravinsky's second sketch for the fugue being entirely in sixteenth notes (and too fast to be played by a single viola). In the brief first sketch, the second statement of the "subject" is varied, indicating that Stravinsky did not yet envisage a fugue, and the music suggests a lively character as well. The third sketch is in the viola range and contains a fingering for the instrument. In all likelihood, the prelude, originally in C minor, was composed after the fugue. A separate sketch exists for the entire Elegy—written at a different date, to judge by the change in handwriting—correcting the version in the Danses Concertantes notebook.

41. In a letter to Stravinsky from Lake Arrowhead, California, August 22, 1944.

42. Writer and close friend of Stravinsky's in the 1920s (1887–1961). In Blaise Cendrars Vous Parle (Paris: Denoël, 1952), Cendrars praises "the composer's great knowledge of Catholic symbolism." Cendrars spoke some Russian, and parts of his letters to Stravinsky are in that language. In April 1918, Stravinsky was approached by the Editions de la Sirène, Paris, with an offer to publish his new works and "a new edition of Le Sacre." An extensive correspondence followed between the composer and Cendrars, as spokesman for the publisher, and finally, on December 19, 1918, Stravinsky signed a contract with the Sirène for an edition of 1,000 copies of his piano reduction of Ragtime. In a telegram to Cocteau, February 5, 1919, thanking him for his new book, Stravinsky asked him whether this contract had been received by the Sirène. Then, on May 24, Laffitte, the director of the Editions, wrote to Stravinsky: "I saw Picasso this morning, and he promised his drawing for the cover by this evening." On August 29, Laffitte wrote again saying that Picasso "is not satisfied with his drawing and wants to do another one." When Stravinsky finally

received the printed copy of the *Ragtime*, he telegraphed to Laffitte: ". . . Must immediately correct appalling mistake in dedication to Mme Errazuriz. To avoid such surprises, I expressly asked to see the final proofs, which you did not send." (December 22, 1919)

43. Meaning that the Cervantes is not a proper subject for the cinema? The context is unclear.

44. *Musical Digest*, Hollywood, September 1946.

45. In the early years, these often record Stravinsky's remarks. Thus, in returning from a rehearsal in Pittsburgh, January 25, 1940: "I cleaned the orchestra like with toothbrushes."

46. The bulk of Stravinsky's own correspondence is concerned with business matters. The largest exchanges of personal letters in the decade, apart from family round-robins, are with Nicolas Nabokov and this writer. In fact, Stravinsky wrote to the former (November 24, 1947) for information about the latter—and received the reply that the subject of the inquiry was reported to be "a very serious person."

47. Mrs. Stravinsky wrote to Olga Sallard, a Russian friend in France: "During the war we were permitted to have a vegetable garden in the front yard and chickens in the back. I bought a dozen of them and, the first night, put them in the bathtub with newspapers and hot water bottles. But the heat did not last and in the morning one was dead. Then we bought two dozen hens and built a coop behind the garage. The hens wanted to hatch, so we bought two roosters. Soon we had forty chicks—as well as many complaints from the neighbors, for the roosters crowed at 4 A.M. One of them, big, white, red-crested, I called the general, but his crowing was so loud that I went in my nightgown to find him in the dark. He squawked and, like a baby taken from its warm bed, made a lot of noise. But I grabbed him, held tight, and put him in the closet in the den. We decided to give him to a poor Russian family. When I opened the closet door in the morning, however, he flew out and ran through the house, chased by four of us with brooms and towels. We caught him and put him in the car, but two days later he was poisoned by some neighbors of the Russian family."

48. Gershwin is said to have asked Stravinsky for lessons in composition and been answered with a question about the younger composer's income. When Gershwin supposedly named a sum in six figures, Stravinsky is reported to have said: "In that case, it is I who should take lessons from you." Stravinsky repeatedly denied the truth of this story, which Warner Brothers hoped to recreate on film, and a letter from Stravinsky, July 17, 1959, replying to an inquiry concerning Boris Morros's supposed role in the affair, seems conclusive. Yet Stravinsky did know Gershwin, and the American composer Richard Hammond, a close friend of Stravinsky's, has testified that the incident occurred in the Paris apartment of the violinist Paul Kochanski. Furthermore, when the story appeared in Gershwin's obituary in the *New York Herald Tribune*, Stravinsky did not add the question marks that he always attached to apocryphal anecdotes.

Countless stories have been told about Stravinsky and money. Thus, he wrote to Alexander Benois apropos the division of *Petrushka* royalties: "The author of the music usually receives three-fourths, but since you and I are splitting the authorship of the whole work, each of us will receive a half of this quarter." (Letter of November 12, 1911; four days later, Benois signed an agreement for one-sixth, with another sixth to go to Fokine, four-sixths to Stravinsky.) Similarly, Gregor Piatigorsky, recalling his "work with Stravinsky in Paris on the cello arrangement of the *Suite Italienne*," wrote that when "Stravinsky [came] to see me in New York [in 1935], he produced a paper and said, 'Here is the contract for you to sign. But . . . I want to explain the conditions.' 'Conditions? But, dear Igor Fyodorovich, I did not count on anything. I was happy to collaborate. . . .' 'No, my friend, you are entitled to royalties. I insist. The question is if you would agree to the proposition, which is fifty-fifty . . . half for you, half for me. . . . You see, I am the composer of the music, of which we are both the transcribers. As a composer I get ninety percent, and as the arrangers we divide the remaining ten percent into equal parts. In *toto*, ninety-five percent for me, five percent for you, which makes fifty-fifty." (*Cell-*

ist, by Gregor Piatigorsky [New York: Doubleday, 1965])

49. Stravinsky's attorney in 1948, Aaron Sapiro (d. 1959), urged him not to compose the opera, on the grounds that it would make him an accessory to the "homosexual joke of Baba the Turk." But Stravinsky had understood Baba from the beginning, as well as the libretto's other problems, which he defended against every criticism.

50. "Stravinsky spoke of Walt Disney's treatment of his music in *Fantasia* as terrible. 'I saw part of it in the studio and walked out.' " (*Champaign-Urbana Courier*, March 3, 1949)

51. Stravinsky wrote to Ansermet, from the Ansonia Hotel, New York, February 2, 1935: "I think that Stokowski detests me, knowing by many accommodating tongues what I think of him."

52. Ira Belline, Stravinsky's niece. The two women were to see each other only once again, shortly after Stravinsky's death, thirty-two years later. Mlle Belline survived her uncle by only four months.

53. Daughter of Adolph and Beatrice Bolm. Stravinsky had known Adolph Bolm, the Diaghilev dancer, since 1910, Beatrice—Beata Alexandrovna—Bolm since 1916. In the spring of that year, she sailed with the Nijinskys from Bordeaux to New York on the S.S. *Rochambeau*, carrying the manuscript of Stravinsky's *Trois Pièces Faciles* to Ansermet. She died in Hollywood a few days after the composer's eighty-fifth birthday.

54. On May 19, 1941, he had written to Nadia Boulanger that "*Les nouvelles troublantes de Vichy m'effrayent.*"

55. A draft of this variation is found on the same page as a sketch for one of the harmonizations of "The Star-Spangled Banner," a more radically improving one than that which Stravinsky eventually published:

56. Like Prévost, the late Michael Mann, the violist son of the novelist, was an early champion of the *Elegy*. On November 10, 1949, he wrote to Stravinsky from Dufourstrasse, Zollikon, recalling "the unforgettable hour you permitted me to spend with you discussing [the *Elegy*]," and promising fidelity to "exactly every dynamic and agogic detail as you have demonstrated [them] to me. . . ."

57. The late Goddard Lieberson told the present writer that when he dined with Stravinsky on the day after Bartók's death, Stravinsky's only reaction was "I never liked his music anyway"—a remark that, regrettably, rings true; also, others have testified to hearing the same words at a later date. Actually, however, Stravinsky did not know Bartók's music, and after their first encounter, at Henri Prunière's, in Paris, April 8, 1922, the two composers seldom met. On December 31, 1925, the Budapest agency Rozsavölgyi wrote to Stravinsky apropos his forthcoming concert in the Hungarian capital: "In the event that *Les Noces* is included in the program, our friend Béla Bartók would be pleased to play one of the piano parts." But Stravinsky did not acknowledge this offer.

58. From a letter of Nadia Boulanger to Stravinsky, August 22, 1944, it seems that she had read through the *Scherzo* with an ensemble in Montreal shortly before, but perhaps without saxophones, since the Abbé Fortrier, who had organized the audition and extracted the parts could not understand the transposition systems of these instruments. This Abbé was so impressed by the 1944 Sonata, as performed by Mlle Boulanger and a pupil, that he gave Stravinsky a copy of Bossuet's *Elévations sur les Mystères*.

59. "Marilyn begins to talk of a special record . . . Woody Herman playing Stravinsky. Arthur wishes to share this pleasure and Strasberg puts it on. A marvelous record, says Arthur." (Norman Mailer, *Marilyn* [New York: Grosset and Dunlap, 1973])

60. Died in Barcelona, September 1976, aged sixty-one.

61. Five months later, in September 1948, Stravinsky sold the full score, for more than half the price of the commission, to the University of California (Berkeley).

62. Cf. *La Correspondencia,* Madrid, March 29, 1924: "There was a great applause after *The Firebird* . . . and Stravinsky returned to the podium three or four times and saluted with bows from the waist, at a perfect right angle, and repeated rhythmically, like a Swedish gymnastic exercise."

63. Four months later, Miss Tallchief, the daughter of an Osage Indian chief, danced the role of Eurydice in *Orpheus.*

64. Actually hibiscus.

65. Actually a white piqué robe.

66. Charles Olson, the poet, was a friend of Stravinsky's and dedicated a poem to him.

67. Nabokov does not mention that Popka was silent, and readers of Stravinsky's letters to René Auberjonois, published in *Adam* (1967), may wonder at the presence of a parrot in the composer's home. He wrote to Auberjonois from Biarritz, August 14, 1922: "A parrot across the street prevents me from working, because of his idiot squawk and imitations of all kinds. All day long a child teaches stupidities to the bird—including a very foul curse-word—which the miserable creature repeats incessantly."

68. Actually more than forty, including several cockatoos. Otherwise, this description of the Stravinsky aviary is correct, yet the composer was more interested in hummingbirds than in his parrots and canary. "During those war years I felt [that the Stravinskys] were my family. I used to go to their house continually, and often we would sit up late into the night drinking tea and discussing the news. Igor was like a child. He was excited to see how quickly everything grew in Southern California. He is a great lover of birds and he was always pointing out to me the different ones that flew into the garden or perched on the trees. His favorite was the hummingbird. Lots of them came for the honeysuckle that grew on his porch." (Mercedes de Acosta, *op. cit.*)

69. The Stravinskys had another cat, Pancho, but Vasska's jealousy was so great that Pancho had to be evicted; he found his way back to the Stravinsky house several times, nevertheless, and over distances of more than twenty miles.

70. The actual size was much smaller.

71. The entrance to the studio was its most important feature. "A cork lining and a double door keep the studio hermetically insulated from the outside world. They also keep the outer world from overhearing the pounding and tinkling process. . . . Stravinsky cannot compose if he thinks anyone is listening to him. The double door . . . is the subject of a special rule. If one of the doors is left open, his wife may enter; if both doors are closed, no one may enter." (*Life,* March 23, 1953)

72. The Bach-Webern *Ricercar* is an example, and Purcell's *Funeral Music for Queen Mary.* Stravinsky's manuscripts of Lasso and Gesualdo madrigals are extraordinarily beautiful.

73. "I do my gymnastics every morning and sunbathe from twelve to one o'clock." (Letter to Ansermet, September 9, 1923)

74. "After the concert we had a dinner with Stravinsky who told a great many very indecent stories." (Prokofiev to Miaskovsky, January 29, 1938)

75. "I ask you not to *mandeet* [waste time masturbating] with [Ida Rubinstein], and thus shit up the broadcast. . . ." (Letter to Païchadze, March 25, 1929)

76. Like Freud, Stravinsky was an ardent admirer of Busch.

77. Stravinsky's housekeeper.

78. With Gene Shalit, March 3, 1949, in the Urbana Lincoln Hotel, the University of Illinois.

79. "As he suffered from diabetes, Diaghilev always had a little box (gift of Stravinsky) containing saccharine." (*Diaghilev et les Ballets Russes,* by Michel Larionov [Paris: Bibliothèque des Arts, 1970])

80. Victoria Ocampo, the writer and editor of *Sur,* was a very close friend of Stravinsky's. He gave the original piano score of the manuscript of *Perséphone* to her.

81. This judgment was reversed in 1967 and 1968, when Stravinsky re-

read Tolstoy, but he did not reread Proust.

82. From the *Paris Review Interviews* (New York: Viking, 1976).

83. The present writer remembers the scene differently: Stravinsky was greatly impressed by the acting of Julie Harris, whom Isherwood later brought to dinner at the Stravinskys' in Hollywood. As for Dietrich, she was an old friend of the composer and used to send roses to him in hotel rooms in cities in which he was conducting.

84. The Stravinskys' cat.

85. Yvgenia Petrovna, the Stravinskys' housekeeper and cook, was a Frau, not a Fräulein.

86. Wife of the actor Vladimir Sokoloff, and co-director, with Vera Stravinsky, of the art gallery La Boutique.

87. Catherine d'Erlanger, but she had only two cats.

88. This refers to Stravinsky's lawyer's objections to Baba, and to the composer's own annoyance with Auden for having taken a co-librettist.

89. When the present writer first heard Auden lecture, at Barnard College in the spring of 1946, the poet was continually interrupted by requests to spell out on the blackboard what he had said, which provoked *sotto voce* but clearly enunciated derogations on the intelligence of the audience.

90. The extent of Chester Kallman's contribution to *The Rake's Progress* is revealed in the following letter: "77 St. Mark's Place, New York City 3, N.Y., February 10, 1959. Dear Bob: Many thanks for your letter. By all means make use of any correspondence that you have. (I agree that Ebert should be omitted.) As there is a double question of interest about collaboration: a) composer-librettist b) librettist-librettist, it might be worthwhile introducing some of the discussions between Chester and myself. For instance, though of course two librettists are not two people but a composite personality, I have been amused at the way in which critics, trying to decide who wrote what, have guessed wrong. The actual facts are: *Act I:* Scene I. Down to end of Tom's aria . . . "This beggar should ride." W.H.A. From there to end of scene. C.K. Scene 2. W.H.A. Scene 3. C.K. *Act II:* Scene 1. Down to end of Tom's aria . . ."in my heart the dark." C.K. From there to end of scene. W.H.A. Scene 2. C.K. Scene 3. W.H.A. *Act III:* Scene 1. C.K. (except for the lyrics sung offstage by Tom and Shadow). Scene 2. Baba's verses at beginning and end of scene. W.H.A. Middle (card-guessing game). C.K. Scene 3 and Epilogue. W.H.A. Do you have a copy of the original draft scenario at which we had arrived when I left Hollywood in November 1947? If you do, we would very much like a copy to refresh our memories and the exact stages by which we arrived at a final version. Love to all, Wystan."

91. "One day [in the Gotham Book Mart] Vera Stravinsky was browsing attentively through the books by Edith Sitwell and I beckoned to Robert Craft, who was with her, to say that I could get them inscribed to her if she wished. After speaking to Madame Stravinsky, he said that she would rather meet her. When Dame Edith called the next morning, it was arranged that the Sitwells would sit with the Stravinskys in their box at Town Hall where Robert Craft was conducting. Auden was reading . . . and they all met after the performance." (Frances Steloff, *The Harvard Advocate*, 1976)

92. Auden wrote to the present writer from there, saying, "[I] heard *L'Assedio di Corinto* in Florence and thought it was wonderful."

93. Stein had written: "I do not think there is any work of yours which has so wide a scope."

94. Stravinsky first set English in *Babel* (1944).

95. Betty Bean, of Boosey & Hawkes.

96. A letter from Stravinsky to his younger son, dated April 17, 1951, contradicts this, saying that, while nothing precise was discovered during Bolm's medical examinations, he was "declining before my eyes."

97. Even on his fiftieth birthday, in June 1932, Stravinsky received press cuttings about the event in which the name of Schoenberg was invoked, the *Ostdeutsche Illustrierte Funkwoche*, for instance, informing its readers that "Stravinsky was influenced by Schoenberg."

98. 1879–1964.

99. In Mascot airport, Sydney, asked by reporters whether she had been

inspired by anything in Australia, Mrs. Stravinsky answered: "What is inspiring about hotels?" Asked if she had done any painting in Australia, she said, "I am too busy getting up on chairs to stuff paper in the air-conditioning." (*Herald*, November 30, 1961)

100. Orphaned during World War II, Catherine Mandelstamm was adopted by Mr. and Mrs. Theodore Stravinsky in 1952. The Naples meeting with her grandfather was the first since she was taken to Leysin, after the death of her mother, November 30, 1938. There, suffering from tuberculosis, she lived in the Clinique Les Oiselets from January 1939 to August 1946, under the care of Dr. Vera Nossenko, Stravinsky's first wife's cousin. A medical certificate signed by Dr. Maurice Gilbert on August 10, 1950, describes the young woman's tuberculosis and says that she has been his patient since August 1946. In January 1967, Catherine gave birth to a daughter, Svetlana. The father, Pierre Théus, from Geneva but living in Fribourg, had married at age twenty-three, but had abandoned his wife for Catherine Stravinsky. She had written to her aunt, Milène Marion, and Stravinsky asked his friend M. Monnet, Conseil Constitutionnel of France, to investigate the matter, sending $6,000 for Catherine. Monnet wrote to Stravinsky from Lausanne on January 8: "Obliged, so she believed, to earn her livelihood from the age of eighteen, she preferred to work independently in Geneva rather than performing more or less servile tasks for Theodore (or, rather, for his wife)." Briefly, Théus did not divorce his wife and marry Catherine: but as the adopted daughter of Theodore Stravinsky, and as an heir on a equal basis with him, her inheritance will be double that of Stravinsky's children. She was brought up by Mina Svitalski.

101. Stravinsky did not have an exceptionally acute ear for pitch, nor, by comparison with most full-time conductors, an exceptionally keen ear in detecting wrong notes; tempo, rhythm, and character received his uppermost attention at rehearsals. Other observers may testify differently about this, but the bulk of the documentary evidence—in recordings made under optimum conditions but still containing very conspicuous errors—supports this statement. Thus, in the composer's first recording of his Symphony in Three Movements, the solo cellist at 130 plays in the bass clef, instead of, as written, in the tenor. Stravinsky had rehearsed this exceptionally transparent passage several times and conducted it in concerts without noticing the mistake—which, in fact, he never discovered by himself.

102. Here, for comparison, is a view of Stravinsky written by one of the players, the cellist Janos Starker: "At a rehearsal of *The Rake's Progress* at the Metropolitan Opera House . . . I can still remember being taken aback by [Stravinsky's] small and fragile figure, . . . having imagined him, on the basis of his music, to be a giant. His head was huge, or seemed to be, as he read the score, or turned the pages, with his legendary spectacles on his brow. He jumped up nervously from time to time, came to the orchestra pit, and, speaking in a thick accent in English, asked for some correction. To proposals coming from the stage director, or the conductor, he sometimes gave an appreciative nod, but generally reacted with a 'no.'

"Some weeks later Stravinsky took the baton himself and conducted the first recording of his opera in a studio. Then, as on many more instances during consecutive years, I was surprised by his unconventional manner of conducting an orchestra. Whether standing or sitting, his head was buried in the score, and he almost completely failed to fulfill the traditional duties of a conductor. He gave entrances in a sloppy way, and his corrective signals seldom if ever had reference to actual problems in, or faults of, performance. He seemed not to be concerned with the performance at all, but to be totally enveloped in his creative inner hearing. And yet, these performances which had nothing of the high precision which characterizes some of the brilliant Stravinsky interpretations of our days, still remained memorable events. It was as if we musicians were not participating in a performance of Stravinsky's music, but in a rare session of spiritual communication with him. Entrances, dynamic nuances, and all the customary paraphernalia of conductors we simply had to imagine for ourselves. But we started together, we breathed together. When the performance came to an end, a smile more like a grin appeared on the maestro's face. Perhaps he was not even there, perhaps only his spirit, or his image, appeared."

(Hungarian Book Review, 1972)

103. Stravinsky also received countless tapes of music that people thought he should hear: for example, on September 8, 1959, a Mr. Wood, in Lund, Sweden, sent a recording of Janáček's *Rikadla*, with a note: "You have never mentioned Janáček . . . but I think you must respect him. . . ."

104. The score is dated April 26, but Stravinsky continued to make changes—adding the mandolin to the first piece, for example (letter to Roth, May 8)—even at the recording session, June 18.

105. The piece was first performed in concert, June 17, 1957, conducted by the present writer.

106. Later Pope John XXIII.

107. "In 1900," writes Philippe Jullian (*op. cit.*) the Baroness d'Erlanger "was a sort of forerunner of the Bright Young Things of the twenties. She had a great talent for interior decoration and redecorated her house from top to bottom every time she took a new lover. Her portrait by Romaine Brooks shows her to be tall and majestic. She had been born in the Faubourg Saint-Germain in Paris and had married a banker. . . . Catherine d'Erlanger owned houses in a number of places: a Moorish palace near Tunis, a Palladian mansion on the Brenta. Strangely enough, she spent the end of her life in Hollywood, where she had become manageress of a bar. She enjoyed extravagant living, and in the 1940s this was more possible in California than in Europe." Catherine d'Erlanger played a considerable role in the lives of the Stravinskys, and this account should be amended to say that she was never the manageress of a bar, but rather the owner of three successive restaurant-nightclubs, and that she was far from wealthy during the 1940s, when her assets were frozen in England. Hamilton House, where Byron had lived, on Green Park, London, belonged to her, and she had another home in Falconwood. Her "Palladian mansion" was the Villa Malcontenta.

108. This is quickly revealed by a comparison of Stravinsky's foreign-language correspondence and the "Conversation" books. Thus a Los Angeles journalist once took exception to the "obscure" word "tergiversation" in one of Stravinsky's volumes of talk, but here is the composer in a 1951 letter to his elder son: *"Cette décision vient d'être après beaucoup de tergiversations avec des théâtres américains."*

109. *Op. cit.*

110. Marion was not working as his father-in-law's secretary at this time, but, from the middle 1950s until after Stravinsky's death, was employed in a travel agency. This led to friction of another kind, as, for example, when Stravinsky, in England, reserved rooms in a Venice hotel directly and without arranging for them through his son-in-law's agency in California, thereby depriving the agency of a commission and provoking an insulting note from Marion. Stravinsky responded in a letter to his daughter, September 11, 1957, demanding "a word from André regretting his ill-considered reaction and rudeness toward me. . . ." It was Vera Stravinsky's idea to bring the Marions to California, to take care of Stravinsky in the event that something should happen to her. On April 19, 1947, Stravinsky wrote to Nadia Boulanger: *"Quel bonheur d'avoir enfin Milène ici."*

111. Rolf Liebermann, *Actes et Entr'actes* (Paris: Stock, 1976).

112. *Ibid.*

113. Alexis St. Léger to Stravinsky, March 2: "The performance of the *Symphony of Psalms* was particularly moving."

114. This characteristic gesture of Stravinsky seemed to ruffle English people. Once, at a dinner party at Stephen Spender's, Mrs. Stravinsky was seated next to Sir Kenneth Clark, and, illustrating a point in an anecdote that she was relating, she touched Sir Kenneth's sleeve, after which he involuntarily smoothed with his hand the place of contact.

115. Stravinsky rarely attended concerts of his own music, partly because he knew that he was not likely to approve of what he heard. The following two sentences are accurate: "When Stravinsky attends concerts and opera performances . . . he often takes a score and reads it with a flashlight during the entire performance. . . . At ballet performances he has been known to rise from his seat, spluttering 'but they're doing it wrong.' " (*Life*, March 23, 1953)

116. 1884–1969. His *Stravinsky* (Editions Claude Aveline, Paris, 1929) was translated into English by Ezra Pound and published serially in *The Dial.* Stravinsky detested the book and underlined and commented on passages in his copy of it. *"L'opéra de Mozart n'est pas un spectacle,"* Schloezer writes, and Stravinsky remarks that "the truth is exactly the contrary." And when Schloezer reproaches Stravinsky with *"Toujours vers le passé,"* the composer replies: "Inevitably, since it is impossible to turn toward the future, which is unknown."

117. *Op. cit.*

118. After 1948, Stravinsky's religious affiliations are not entirely clear. In March 1953, *Life* reported: "He loves to read theologians like St. Thomas Aquinas and Kierkegaard and is fairly regular in his attendance at Los Angeles's Russian Orthodox Church." But, next to the statement about church attendance, Stravinsky wrote in his copy of the magazine "not true." In earlier years, he talked freely about his devotional attitudes. Thus, in an interview in Barcelona in March 1928, he revealed his intense interest in philosophies of religion and in such mystics as John of the Cross and Teresa of Avila.

119. The money was placed in Stravinsky's numbered account (43656-III) on September 19, 1959, but the letter reveals his mistaken belief that the account was a joint one with his wife, which was not to be the case until October 1968, when he visited the bank and made a new contract. His sole beneficiary before that date was his son-in-law, André Marion, though William Montapert had a power-of-attorney over Stravinsky (from February 12, 1962), recognized by the bank. Stravinsky's numbered accounts in Basel go back to 1933. On July 7 of that year, he wrote to Païchadze thanking him for forwarding "a letter from B"—Basel—and warning him that "the B bank does not use my name but only my number." Before 1933, the composer used his own name—in the Union des Banques Suisses at Lausanne. He was banking in Kiev as late as 1917.

120. Lawrence Moss, *The Score,* January 1960.

121. The note from Aldous Huxley to Stravinsky, May 3, 1955 (see page 392), seems to indicate that the composer had been inquiring about the same text.

122. Mrs. Kennedy had written to Stravinsky on November 21, 1961: "Dear Mr. Stravinsky, the President and I would so like to have you here for a dinner in your honor on or around your 80th birthday next June 5th. It would give us great pleasure to have you with us on such an important occasion. We send our very best wishes and will await your answer." Stravinsky replied on December 9 to the effect that he had just returned from a concert tour and only just received her thoughtful invitation, but he regretted that he could not come owing to some concert engagements in June. Arthur Schlesinger, Jr., then wrote to Nicolas Nabokov: "This is not a very satisfactory exchange. He might at least have said that his concert engagements were out of the country. Can you get him to amplify his response by mail and raise the possibility of his coming to the White House on some other occasion than June 5? Yours ever, signed: Arthur Schlesinger, Jr., Special Assistant to the President."

123. From *Bergman on Bergman* (New York: Simon and Schuster, 1974).

124. Stravinsky's most incisive comment on Berg's opera was made in a conversation with Nicolas Nabokov in Venice, September 20, 1959: "Berg's music is like a woman about whom one says, 'How beautiful she must have been when she was young.' "

125. *Op. cit.*

126. *Ibid.*

127. Stravinsky preferred this division to the published version. In a letter to Chester Kallman, January 31, 1952, the composer reminds the co-librettist that the solution of four scenes in the Second Act was agreed upon in New York by Auden, Armistead, Balanchine, and himself. He adds, emphatically, that he will not accept any stops between scenes, as was the case in Venice.

128. Liebermann's account states that the present writer accompanied Mrs. Stravinsky, but this is a slip of memory.

129. *Op. cit.*

130. *Ibid.*

131. When Suvchinsky wrote to Stravinsky about Yastrebzev again in 1963, the composer decided that he had confounded this chronicler with Belsky, one of Rimsky-Korsakov's librettists for whom Stravinsky had once arranged for the payment of some royalties. Stravinsky says that he had taken Yastrebzev to be "one of those stupid [musical] reactionaries typical of Rimsky's surroundings."

132. Maria Yudina, pianist, Doctor of Philosophy, and the U.S.S.R.'s most ardent Stravinskyan. (She once inscribed a volume of Pasternak for the present writer: *"Dem lieben Freunde welcher im Lux* [sic] *von Stravinsky lebt und wirkt."*) She died a few months before the composer.

133. *Op. cit.*

134. The story is true, but Mr. Liebermann is confused about the location.

135. *op. cit.*

136. Auden dined with Stravinsky again at the Essex House in 1970, and the poet was his first visitor in the new apartment at Fifth Avenue and 73rd Street, just a week before his death. Mrs. Stravinsky saw Auden twice after that: "New York, Auden and Kallman for dinner, the first time we have seen them together since Kallman moved to Europe, or either of them since Stravinsky's death. Conversation is like old times: Wagner, life in Niederösterreich, fellow poets. The librettists disagree on the merits of *Crow,* Auden defending the language of the book and insisting that it contains 'quite good things.' Some of the talk is *from* old times, Auden repeating his hoary anecdote about dinner at the Eliots' in the early 1930s, when the guest told Mrs. T.S.E. that he was glad to be there and she said: 'Well, Tom's not glad.' When Auden announces that his bedtime hour has struck, Kallman admonishes him, saying that *he* is not ready to leave, whereupon the reproved one becomes petulant." (From R.C.'s diary, January 11, 1972)

"February 21, 1972. We go to Auden's birthday party and combination farewell dinner and last supper, at the Coffee House on West Forty-Fifth Street. It is a mob scene during cocktails, but at the actual cenacle the host is seated at a table that is slightly elevated and no less appropriately, Arthurianly round. Glasses are tapped for silence, telegrams are read in a not-very-pious hush, and a toast is proposed. But no sooner has the speaker begun, with "I don't know what genius is . . . ,' than he is interrupted by an indignant 'Well, who does?'— from, of all people, Auden himself." (From R.C.'s diary)

137. *Kniga o Stravinskom* (Leningrad: Triton, 1929). "Glebov" was the nom-de-plume of Boris Asafiev (1884–1949). The book was reprinted in 1977 with an introduction by Boris Yarustovsky. Stravinsky wrote to Ansermet from Amsterdam, April 20, 1928: "I am astonished by your enthusiasm for Boris Asafiev. I do not know him personally, but have often had occasion to read his writings on music, and if you were to do the same you would change your opinion. I have read his books on Rimsky and on Tchaikovsky and am surprised to see that he is closer to Andrey Rimsky and Steinberg than to those who are opposed to this nest of old wasps. . . ."

138. [Interviewer to Poulenc:] "You say that Stravinsky had a huge culture, and that even his daily conversation employed a very superior dialectic. I ask to what extent did this enormous culture contribute to the proteoform aspect of his work?" [Poulenc:] "Stravinsky's culture was always directly related to what he was doing. For example, he decided to write an opera. So he steeped himself not merely in operas, but also in libretti; and suddenly he became interested in Da Ponte." (Poulenc: *Moi et Mes Amis,* Paris, 1963)

139. Alexis St. Léger once inscribed a book to the composer: *"Stravinsky, qui sait ce qu'il y a d'action et de solitude secrète dans la création."*

140. *La Tribune Musicale,* June 16, 1914.

141. Debussy's word for Stravinsky in 1916, commenting, in this case, on his taste for "tumultuous cravats."

142. Lucia Davidova, a close friend of the Stravinskys since Paris, 1921, when she was employed by the Chauve-Souris. She accompanied them on their trip to Egypt in 1961.

143. Natasha Nabokov, first wife of Nicolas Nabokov, and onetime employee of the Voice of America, for which Stravinsky had made several broadcasts.

144. Carter, *op. cit.*

145. Nabokov, in his *Bagázh*, gives this date for a different incident.

APPENDIX A

1. Dated March 22, 1920.

APPENDIX B

1. *Nijinsky Dancing*, by Lincoln Kirstein (New York: Knopf, 1975).

2. *Diaghilev Observed by Critics in England and the United States, 1911–1929*, by Nesta Macdonald (New York: Dance Horizons, 1975).

3. *The Times*, July 27, 1913.

4. *Mercure de France*, October 1, 1913.

5. "You know, without doubt, that *Petrúshka* and *The Firebird* have had a great success here. . . . Yesterday I had lunch with M. Ansermet, who gave me a great deal of information about *Les Noces*. . . ." (Letter to Stravinsky from Carl Van Vechten, in New York, January 29, 1916)

6. Massine's *My Life in Ballet* (New York: St. Martin's, 1969) contains only scraps of information about his choreography for *Le Sacre* (which was revived in the Théâtre des Champs-Elysées on June 13, 25, and 28, 1924, and again in New York in 1930, with Martha Graham as the Chosen Virgin, and, finally, for the Royal Swedish Ballet in 1956). Thus he claims to have based his production "on the simple movements of the Russian peasants' round dances," and says that the part of the Chosen Virgin "involved repetitions of complex *jetés* and other *terre à terre* twisted steps."

Nor does Lydia Sokolova's *Dancing for Diaghilev* give a full account, though she was a member of the *corps de ballet* at the premiere of the Nijinsky version and danced the Chosen Virgin in the Massine. The former, she says, "was a vague work, far less complicated and accurate than Massine's." On the contrary, Stravinsky's score containing his markings for Nijinsky shows that this version was far more complex. Sokolova is doubtless more reliable concerning her own fears and triumphs: ". . . the most terrifying experience of my life in the theater was the first orchestra rehearsal of *Le Sacre*. Igor Stravinsky, wearing an expression which would have frightened a hundred Chosen Virgins, pranced up and down the center aisle of the Champs-Elysées, while Ansermet practiced difficult passages of music with the orchestra. . . . I became so scared that I nearly ran away. [But at the performance] the applause was deafening . . . and Stravinsky had kissed my hand before the audience."

7. Stravinsky continued to criticize the Nijinsky version in later years. In an interview in *Candide*, Paris, June 6, 1935, Stravinsky said: "Why bring up the question of the admirable Nijinsky here? Because of the name of truth, of which there is very little in Mme Romola Nijinsky's biography of her unfortunate husband." In *Memories and Commentaries*, the composer remarked that in the *"Danses des Adolescentes"* he had "imagined a row of almost motionless dancers; Nijinsky made of this piece a big jumping match." But Stravinsky himself had marked the jumps, most of which are in counterpoint to the musical accents. Without the jumps, in fact, the music between 18 and 22 is scarcely more than an accompaniment.

8. From *The Tragedy of Nijinsky*, by Anatole Bourman, one of the five who danced in both the Nijinsky and Massine versions (New York and London: Whittlesey House, 1936).

9. Letter from Lincoln Kirstein to Robert Craft, October 21, 1973.

10. Dame Marie Rambert. Some months after the first performance, she asked Stravinsky for a score, saying that she remembered everything that Nijinsky had said during the rehearsals and wanted to write it down. According to her memoirs (*Quicksilver*, 1972), she was living in London at that time, but an invoice from Stravinsky's Berlin publisher shows that the score was sent, De-

cember 8, 1913, to "Mlle Myriam Ramberg, 2, rue des Handriettes, Paris." Dame Marie only recently discovered this fully annotated score; in 1920, she had forgotten about its existence.

11. The two men did not know each other at this date, but Dalcroze's letters to Stravinsky a year later address him as *"cher ami"* and *"cher collègue."* A letter from Diaghilev to Stravinsky (March 3, 1915) implies that Stravinsky had recommended Dalcroze. Romain Rolland, who apparently had attended the stage premiere of the *Sacre*, reported that the composer was critical of Dalcroze: "[Stravinsky] agrees that a . . . theatrical representation of such a work must diminish the appeal of the music and also narrow its emotional content. Nevertheless, he is in favor of stage movement, though of a more artistic variety than the rhythmic gymnastics of Dalcroze. . . ." (*Op. cit.*)

12. Since this was written (March 1976), the American Ballet Theater has given (June 21, 1976) a *Sacre* by Glen Tetley (first produced in Munich and later in Stuttgart) that had no connection either to the original scenarios or to the music, which, in any case, as played by a half-size orchestra, was in places scarcely recognizable.

13. Paris: Hermann, 1976.

14. *Chroniques de Ma Vie* (1935).

15. Sert and Stravinsky photographed each other in a gondola. The Stravinsky archives contain a photograph that he took of Sert and Misia with Benois's three children at the Paris Fair, May 1914.

16. In 1920, she presented this to Diaghilev, apparently expecting him to sell it to raise money for the revival of *Le Sacre*, but he did not do so.

17. July 11, 18, 24. Diaghilev may also have canceled two of the six performances that he scheduled for Paris (telegram to Astruc, April 28, 1913).

18. Cipa Godebski, Misia's brother. Sert had written of Stravinsky's distrust of Diaghilev.

19. Stravinsky to Maximilien Steinberg, July 3, 1913.

20. *Sic.* Misia, one of the most celebrated gossips of the day, is writing from Paris to a hard-working composer in a remote Ukrainian village.

21. These dates are correct despite Diaghilev's telegrams, first, from Venice, September 29: *"Arrive demain,"* and, second, from Sion at 9:00 A.M. on the 30th, *"Passe par Montreux à 10:15."*

22. On October 20, Diaghilev telegraphed from Paris, *"Viens bientôt,"* and, on October 29: *"Arrive demain matin."* The well-known photograph of Diaghilev on a tree-lined walk was taken by Stravinsky during this visit.

23. The reference is to the first performance of Stravinsky's *Three Japanese Lyrics*.

24. Diaghilev left for Russia a few hours later. He and Stravinsky were to have dined with Debussy that evening, but Stravinsky was alone with the French master, who "looked very pale and seemed to be agonized in spirit."

25. Misia wrote to Stravinsky, at a slightly later date: "Cher ami . . . no one . . . has absorbed your work with more passion than I have, and, with *Boris, Le Sacre du Printemps* is what I love most in the world." In a 1966 issue of *Soviet Music*, next to a statement that "the Comtesse Greffuhle and Misia Sert were extraordinarily intelligent musically," Stravinsky wrote "what nonsense" and circled the name of Greffuhle.

26. Diaghilev's concern about Stravinsky's music of the later Swiss years, quoted in a 1919 letter on page 521, is revealing in this sense: "Is Stravinsky *au courant?*" and has he "Sailed with the latest boat?" In 1920, Stravinsky told an interviewer, "What I like above all in M. Diaghilev is that he is a man of the avant-garde." (*Comoedia*, January 31, 1920)

27. Nevertheless, in a sketchbook for 1917, Stravinsky entered some notations for the rhythm and pitch of "an automobile horn."

28. In October 1914, Diaghilev asked Stravinsky to compose music for Liturgy, but he postponed and eventually rejected the project.

29. Francesco Pratella (1880–1955), Futurist composer. The Neapolitan Futurist sculptor, painter, and poet Francesco Cangiullo describes this meeting in his autobiography, but incorrectly attributes it to April 1914: "Pratella arrived in Milan hoping to find that none of the guests had turned up, and that he would not have to play a note. But he was dragged to the piano and forced

to play and sing his music. . . . Somehow the piece was finished and [Luigi] Russolo [1885–1947] approached one of the eight or nine Noise Intoners. A Crackler crackled and sent up a thousand sparks. . . . Stravinsky leaped from the divan like an exploding bedspring, with a whistle of overjoyed excitement. At the same time, a Rustler rustled. . . . The frenetic composer hurled himself on the piano in an attempt to find that . . . sound. Meanwhile Massine swung his legs, and Diaghilev went 'Uh, Ah.' . . . Marinetti was happy . . . and Boccioni whispered to Carrà that the guests were won over. . . . Stravinsky and the Slav pianist [Prokofiev] played a four-hand version of *The Firebird*."

30. In 1922, Cocteau wrote on a color postcard of a garish Chinese pavilion restaurant near Nice: "*Cher Igor, aimes-tu le salon de Misia ci-contre, peint par Sert?*" (September 23)

31. *Renard* was commissioned by the Princesse de Polignac but was eventually staged by Diaghilev's company.

32. J. E. Blanche, in *Cahiers d'un Artiste*, describes an earlier piano audition of *Les Noces* in Misia's Quai Voltaire apartment, Christmas 1915, with Massine turning the pages for Stravinsky.

33. The letter has not survived.

34. "*Féria*" is the fourth movement of *Rapsodie Espagnol*, and Stravinsky, after hearing it in Paris in November 1916, had praised the piece to Diaghilev.

35. Stravinsky first explained his grievances to Misia in a letter of June 18, 1919.

36. Morand, *op. cit.* He quotes Chanel: "Stravinsky courted me. 'But you are married, Igor. When Catherine your wife finds out . . .' 'She already knows,' he said. 'To whom, if not to one's wife, does one confide something so important?' "

37. Ansermet to Stravinsky, July 18, 1919: "Diaghilev sent for me in the theater to ask about the details for the *Soldat*. When I described the work in general, Massine objected to its 'literary' character. Diaghilev told him: 'You forget that Stravinsky is a man who knows what he is doing, and that if we take his work, we must take it as it is.' There I recognize Misia's influence. . . ."

38. Stravinsky to Ansermet, September 9, 1923: "Diaghilev is at Antibes with Picasso, for whom Benois seems to have little enthusiasm, which upsets me very much. I attribute Benois's feelings to jealousy, an understandable jealousy, though Diaghilev, who has a jealous nature himself, will interpret everything quite differently. Diaghilev arrives the 12th, and when these two 'old friends' see each other, I am convinced that there will be trouble."

39. "Diaghilev wanted to make me say that you are emptied out. . . . I told him, 'Not at all; Igor is in other ideas, from which he will return to you, but let him have time. . . .' " (Ansermet to Stravinsky, January 23, 1923)

40. On July 17, Serge Lifar cabled to Stravinsky that *Renard* had been a triumph.

41. In November 1977, a "Congresso Internazionale Ricciotto Canudo" was held in Bari to celebrate the centenary of the writer's birth.

42. In spite of this statement, the *Montjoie!* notes were often reprinted. Excerpts from them appear in a program conducted by Ansermet in Geneva, February 5, 1923, and it is difficult to believe that this conductor was unaware of Stravinsky's feelings about the article, or, if aware, would not have respected them.

43. The reduction for piano four-hands (RMV 196) was printed several weeks before the first performance of the ballet.

44. "If you have the proofs of *Le Sacre* to be corrected, I am at your service," Ansermet wrote to Stravinsky, July 27, 1914.

45. French conductor and cellist. In a letter of November 2, 1916, Delgrange inquires about a cello sonata that Stravinsky had promised to compose.

46. The problem of the parts did not seem to concern Stravinsky when he wrote to Ansermet, March 14, 1916: "After the colossal success of *Petrushka* in Rome, conducted by Toscanini, he has said that he will play *Le Sacre* next year." Nor does the composer mention the parts when instructing his representative in London, Otto Kling, to "charge 125 francs or 50 rubles for each concert performance of *Le Sacre du Printemps*" (letters of August 18 and September 18, 1916), or when answering a request from the Netherlands Opera, Amster-

dam, March 23, 1917, to give ten performances (but, then, Stravinsky's reply, March 24, is largely confined to explaining that Le Sacre "is not an opera but a ballet"). In another instance, too, when Blaise Cendrars wrote to Stravinsky proposing that he negotiate with Abel Gance for a film of Le Sacre (letter of August 17, 1918), the fact of the single set of parts seems not to have entered into Stravinsky's negative decision.

47. On July 14, 1916, Stravinsky telegraphed to Diaghilev in San Sebastián, giving the RMV's Russian address: "Editions Russes de Musique, Pont des Marichaux, 6, Moscow."

48. Some of these still exist and bear the publisher's number "RMV 198," as well as countless directions in red ink for the printer, and such graffiti as, on page one of the first-violin part, the prefix "Mas" before the title ("Sacre"), an infinitely repeated joke of the time. The parts do not contain metronomic indications, and changes of tempo have been written in by the players. Some words in English suggest that these parts were used in London in July 1913.

49. Maria Adolphovna Eichelberger, as Stravinsky addressed her, was apparently related to his nanya, Bertha Essert, and must have lived with her in the Stravinsky family in St. Petersburg some time before World War I. Both women came from Königsberg, and on the day of Bertha's death, April 28, 1917, Stravinsky sent a next-of-kin telegram informing Fräulein Eichelberger, who wrote from Königsberg the next day, expressing the wish to see the grave. The letter also says that Bertha had kept her informed of events in the Stravinsky household in Clarens and Morges 1915–17, letters that could be of considerable interest to biographers, particularly concerning the story of Soulima's governess, Fräulein Wys-Staub. Fräulein Eichelberger wrote to Stravinsky (in Russian) in October 1931, after seeing his photograph in a newspaper in connection with the forthcoming premiere of the Violin Concerto in Berlin. Describing her miseries—she was sixty-two and impoverished—she asks for a loan of 400 or 500 marks. Stravinsky, in Wiesbaden, refused, saying that he had been obliged to move from Nice to Voreppe to reduce expenses, but his mother seems to have intervened, and he made the loan, albeit neglecting to sign the first check. One of Fräulein Eichelberger's letters to him in 1932 refers to "a very nice Christmas letter from your mother," and to the trip to Clarens in April 1915.

50. Massine's name replaced Nijinsky's in the contract of the Société des Auteurs on January 20, 1962, when, at Massine's request, Stravinsky signed two copies of a "Bulletin de Déclaration" which classifies Massine's version as an "adaptation."

51. "Do not forget to give me your proofs of the Sacre score," Ansermet wrote to Stravinsky on October 1.

52. A letter from the RMV, in Berlin, December 8, 1921, informed Stravinsky that all of his corrections for the Sacre had been included.

53. On November 21, 1922, Pierre Suvchinsky wrote to Stravinsky from Berlin: "I have just come from Ansermet's concert of the Sacre. The poor man had worked very hard struggling against the stupid Germans, and after the dress rehearsal he received an ovation. But at the performance, the Germans blew little whistles which provoked part of the audience to applaud until, finally, the applause was louder than the noise of the opposition. . . . I want to ask one question, but please do not be angry with me. It seems to me that the very end is not strong enough, and that the strings weaken it. Would it not be preferable to have the winds and percussion alone? The strings are not rhythmic enough, and there are too many violins at ⟦196⟧ . . . . D'Albert applauded Le Sacre vociferously. . . . I remember so well your sojourn in Berlin and the knowledge that you live on this earth helps me to go on. . . . The compositions of your American friend [Antheil] will be performed . . . and there was a concert of horrible music by Busoni. . . . I kiss the hand of Anna Karlovna."

54. In Amsterdam, February 28, 1926. Le Sacre was to have been given in Stravinsky's original programs with the New York Philharmonic in January 1925, but, after part of a rehearsal, he withdrew the piece for lack of time. Clarence Mackay wrote to him, asking him to reconsider and offering an extra rehearsal, but Stravinsky answered that this would not be sufficient. Rumors

circulated to the effect that Stravinsky's conducting technique had not been adequate for the difficulties of *Le Sacre*—which Wilhelm Furtwängler presented with the orchestra later in the month.

55. Stravinsky was concurrently composing the opening chorus and first aria of *Oedipus Rex*.

56. In 1923, the Copyright Office of the Library of Congress, Washington, D.C., ruled that Stravinsky's Pleyela rolls could be protected in America only if they were listed as having been "transcribed for pianola by Robert Lyon," the Paris director of Pleyel. Stravinsky could hardly agree to this, since the value of the transcriptions was that he had made them. Then, in the spring of 1926, the Copyright Office informed him that a number of American publishers had protested against the protection by an intermediary of the revision of works by composers who were not citizens of countries subject to the Berne Convention. Stravinsky's Copenhagen publisher, Wilhelm Hansen, wrote to the composer on this subject on May 1, 1926, explaining that his arrangement of his Concertino for piano four-hands would be considered to be in the public domain in the United States.

57. This is a two-stave skeleton score, upper treble line and bass, from ⬚192⬚ to the end.

58. With the Orchestre Straram, May 7, 8, 9 (two sessions), and 10.

59. According to a letter from Röder, in Leipzig, to Païchadze, in Paris, November 7, 1929, the manuscript was sent to Stravinsky in Talloires, August 15, 1929, together with a corrected proof score. Röder's letter also says that the composer returned the proofs with more corrections and demanded second proofs. Writing to Païchadze, October 29, 1929, Stravinsky says: "It is already about two weeks ago, when I was still in Paris, that I sent the second proofs of *Le Sacre* to [Fyodor Vladimirovich] Weber [the then director of the Berlin branch of the Russischer Musik Verlag]."

The manuscript full score was in the possession of the Editions Russes de Musique until 1947, when Boosey & Hawkes acquired it from Kussevitzky. In the spring of 1962, it was loaned to the New York Public Library for an exhibition, then given by the publisher to the composer for his eightieth birthday. (Letter from E. Roth to Stravinsky in Hamburg, June 14, 1962) The composer then had it placed in a bank vault in Geneva, from which it was removed on at least one occasion in order to make a photocopy. In Zürich, on October 11, 1968, Stravinsky made a gift of the score to his wife.

60. "Goossens is quite ready to come to Paris for two or three days to see you and to discuss various questions about [*Le Sacre*]. Are the score and parts in your hands at present?" (Letter from H. Kling, London, January 12, 1921, to Stravinsky, Hôtel Continental, Paris) Goossens himself wrote soon after, saying that he had attended all of the rehearsals for *Le Sacre* in London in 1913.

61. On November 20, 1948, Ansermet, in Geneva, wrote to Stravinsky, in Hollywood. "I have just given *Le Sacre* with the new Boosey & Hawkes score, in which I have found numerous errors that were in the old one as well. Would you like me to send my *errata*—which I am taking with me for my performance in Cleveland?" Stravinsky answered on November 27, thanking Ansermet but asking him to send the list of errors directly to Boosey & Hawkes in New York, "In the name of my young friend, Robert Craft, who will be in charge of reviewing the materials with other correctors and with myself when I will be in New York." Then on February 8, 1949, when Ansermet wrote to ask "whether the motive

is ever intended to be

"

Stravinsky realized that the conductor had never understood the idea of the dialogue, which is that one form of the figure occurs in the trombones and horns, the other in the upper winds. Early in January 1950, Stravinsky compiled and sent to Boosey & Hawkes an errata sheet.

62. Completed December 1, 1943, and published in December 1945. According to Stravinsky's contract, September 21, 1944, AMP commissioned this version in 1941 for $500. Stravinsky prepared a page of revisions and corrections, never published, for a performance that he conducted in Stockholm in September 1961. On November 9, 1966, Stravinsky sent a list of errors to Boosey & Hawkes, intended for the completely reset 1967 edition of the score.

63. Stravinsky repeatedly denied that the orchestra could be reduced, though on April 20, 1945, in an effort to persuade him to rewrite the piece using fewer instruments, the Leeds Music Company went so far as to draft an agreement offering him a tempting sum. On December 26, 1948, he answered a letter from Eugene Ormandy: "I never found it possible to arrange Le Sacre for a smaller orchestra." And in a letter to Robert Rudolf, June 14, 1954, Stravinsky says: ". . . I am not interested in furthering the career of the Rite. . . . It is already played out of all proportion to my other works, and I do not believe that the large orchestra is an obstacle. . . ." Yet Stravinsky permitted Rudolf to attempt the reduction in fulfillment of a Master of Arts Degree. Ironically, Rudolf's standard-orchestra version, which would have horrified Stravinsky, is now widely played in the United States, where Le Sacre is not protected by copyright.

64. Stravinsky wrote to Dr. Julius Alf of the Düsseldorf Opera, July 10, 1953, that the 1943 version "improved the sonority and vigor of some chords." And to E. Roth, of Boosey & Hawkes, Stravinsky wrote on July 16, 1955: ". . . I would like to say frankly that, even outside of any question of copyright, I do prefer to have [the 1943] 'Danse Sacrale' performed with my Sacre instead of the old version. It is better, in my opinion, and it is also easier to perform. . . . If you have a chance to take it over and to promote it, I shall be delighted."

65. Stravinsky first heard the Sacre with the 1943 "Danse Sacrale" at a rehearsal of the North German Radio Orchestra conducted by this writer, in Venice, September 1958.

66. Made in a single session, 1:30 to 6:00 P.M., April 4, 1940, under the supervision of Goddard Lieberson. An anecdote told by the late Dagmar Godowsky concerning the events of that afternoon was confirmed by Stravinsky when Miss Godowsky's memoirs appeared. She wrote that "[Bruno] Zirato called me. There was already a crisis. 'Miss Godowsky, Stravinsky has locked himself in the bathroom. You have got to come down and get him out.' " (First Person Plural). Stravinsky's third and final recording of the Sacre was made with a pick-up orchestra in a ballroom of the St. George Hotel, Brooklyn, January 4, 1960.

APPENDIX C

1. London, June 27, 1921. On June 28, The Times reported that "M. Stravinsky got a laurel wreath . . . and the whole house roared itself hoarse." According to Robert Sencourt, "After the performance Eliot stood up and cheered." (T. S. Eliot: A Memoir [New York: Dodd, Mead, 1971]) Three years later, Eliot recalled his "efforts, several years ago, to restrain (with the point of an umbrella) the mirth of my neighbors in a 'family house' which seemed united to deride . . . the music of one of the greatest musicians, Stravinsky." (The Criterion, October 1924)

2. Actually five months later.

3. ". . . 3,000 special guests . . . followed purple-robed Cardinal Roncalli [later Pope John XXIII] into the Byzantine basilica of St. Mark's for one of the strangest events in its 1,000-year history. Outside, thousands more were gathered around loudspeakers to hear Igor Stravinsky's latest work. . . ." (Time, September 24, 1956) "The Patriarch of Venice wanted the concert to be broadcast for those who could not afford to pay. . . ." (Vera Stravinsky to Catherine d'Erlanger, September 15, 1956)

4. Encounter, April 1965.

5. Ms. Deborah Ishlon of Columbia Records.

6. Here Stravinsky enters into detail with respect to the title of the book,

but in a letter to Faber & Faber, August 21, he states the same arguments more succinctly: "I objected to 'Dialogues' for the reason that [the exchanges] do not amount to enough of a consequential thesis to satisfy that word (which I respect so much). However, they are not 'Conversations' either. Answers to questions is what they more nearly are. . . ."

7. Because of a rehearsal for a BBC concert later.

8. It was on Eliot's recommendation that Stravinsky included some of Rivière's letters in the "Conversation" book.

9. Stravinsky, an aelourophile and admirer of Eliot's onomastic genius, had memorized passages from these poems.

10. The money had been pledged by Mr. André Senutovich of New Mexico.

11. Auden had shown the completed libretto to Eliot before giving it to Stravinsky, and the typescript has penciled corrections in Eliot's hand.

12. In 1938, a commission from Ida Rubinstein to Stravinsky and Claudel came to nothing when the would-be collaborators failed to agree on a subject, the composer insisting that it be Greek, the poet demanding something biblical. Claudel wrote to Stravinsky, June 21, 1938: "There can be no question of *Prométhée* but only of *Tobit*, of which I have just finished the first part. For nothing on earth would I stick my nose in that antique, pagan, threadbare frippery which even Offenbach could not revive. . . ."

13. Eliot's obituary for Rivière in *La Nouvelle Revue Française*, April 1, 1925, states that the two men met in 1911, and it is possible that Eliot heard one of the first performances of *Petrushka*, which Rivière was acclaiming. Also, the expression "the trick of the passe-passe" occurs in one of Eliot's early pieces of criticism. Eliot probably saw Nijinsky in *Le Spectre de la Rose* at this time.

14. *Movements* for piano and orchestra.

15. In Venice during the inundation of October 14–15, 1960, Stravinsky wrote the word "DELUGE" across these two pages of his diary, and, shortly afterward, made some musical notations.

16. This refers to the songs in the plays. In 1953, Stravinsky had composed music for "Full Fadom five" and "When Dasies pied."

17. Next to the word "redeem," Stravinsky wrote *"spasat' zvlyecat."*

18. "Last summer a special pleasure for [the Eliots] was the visit of the Igor Stravinskys at the end of an evening in which Stravinsky managed to hear half of the performance of *Figaro* at Covent Garden, and the second half of a gala performance, conducted by Pierre Monteux, of his own work, at the Albert Hall." (Stephen Spender, *New York Times*, October 7, 1963)

19. But Eliot did read books in contemporary Italian, and in fact he first mentions "Little Gidding"—referring to Crashaw's connection with the retreat—in a review of Mario Praz's *Secentismo e Marinismo in Inghilterra* (*Times Literary Supplement*, December 17, 1925). Praz's book may even have influenced Eliot to withdraw his own essay on Crashaw, which is a pity since its incidental comments on Shelley's "The Skylark" contain some of Eliot's most amusing criticism: "The line 'that from heaven or near it' merely . . . provide[s] an imperfect rhyme for spirit. . . . I am still ignorant [of] what the devil [Shelley] means by an intense lamp narrowing in the white dawn."

APPENDIX D

1. "My hatred of Germans grows not by the day but by the hour," Stravinsky wrote to Léon Bakst, September 20, 1914, and, in a music sketchbook, the composer confided that "Germans are the caricatures of mankind: they seek to avoid youth by being *wunderkinds* and to avoid old age by being *überwunderkinds.*"

2. Baron Roman Fyodorovich Ungern Von Sternberg. See *The Russian Fascists, 1925-1945*, by John Stephan, Harper & Row, 1978.

3. Khvoshinsky tried to repair the break with Stravinsky, as a letter from the composer, in Diablerets, to Khvoshinsky at the Grand Hotel, Leysin, re-

veals: "Dear Vassily Bogdanovich, In yesterday's letter you express the desire to renew our former relations. But you continue to justify your acts as a member of the Embassy and to express your assuredness that I will understand your actions as an official of the Embassy and not as a private person. But I cannot negotiate with someone who retreats behind a double nature. I believe that our former relations can be restored only by a sincere admission on your part that the charges in your letter to me were baseless and inappropriate." (August 5, 1917)

4. At the beginning of the war, Stravinsky was living in Clarens, and, in Morges, not next to Paderewski until 1917.

5. This was presented in Rome by Diaghilev, at the Teatro Costanzi, April 12, 1917, Stravinsky conducting. "Balla built a complex of prismatic wooden shapes covered with canvas and painted. These were topped with smaller forms of translucent fabric which could be illuminated from inside, and all these shapes were illuminated against a black background. Ballet dancers were replaced by the movement of colored light over these geometric surfaces. . . . During the five minutes it took to perform, some forty-nine different sequences and combinations of light were projected onto the shapes from a keyboard devised by Balla in the prompter's box." (From *Futurism* by Tisdale and Bozzolla, London: Thames and Hudson, 1977)

6. So far as French politics were concerned—Stravinsky had been a French citizen since 1934—he told the *San Francisco Chronicle*, "I am opposed to the right, abhor the left, and am out of sympathy with the center" (March 22, 1937). Some months before, he had written to a friend that "the flame of the unknown soldier is France's new religion." Two years later, he wrote in the margin of a speech by Herriot published in a Paris newspaper (November 5, 1938): "What an address! This is how one placates the Right in order to become a candidate for President."

7. Stravinsky had conducted a chamber-music concert in the Sala della Quirinetta, March 3. The next day his wife wrote to him: "I've just seen in *Paris-Soir* that crowd in Rome during the victory celebration, that sea of people which you probably saw."

8. Schleiffer answered, July 21, that the Ministry of Propaganda had moved, and that Depero was absent. On August 4, Schleiffer wrote that Mussolini's secretary, Colonel Nani, had confirmed the receipt of the objects. Schleiffer adds that he hopes "to be able to transmit the Duce's homage to you directly." The Duce had thanked Stravinsky directly on October 4, 1933, for birthday greetings, and, on February 27, 1934, for the score of *Duo Concertante*.

9. At Klemperer's request, Stravinsky became an advisor of UNIO in November 1933. In February 1935, when Richard Strauss asked Stefan Zweig to withdraw his name from this organization, the writer replied that it did not "have anything to do with politics." [Letter of February 18] Strauss, meanwhile, in an interview published in the *Frankischer Kurier*, November 28, 1934, had remarked that: "It is mistaken to say that Stravinsky is a Jew when in fact he is a pure Aryan from the Baltic aristocracy . . . The Russian Igor Stravinsky *begeistert zu den Ideen Adolf Hitler*."

10. Dushkin wrote that one of his brothers was preparing to move, with his family, to Palestine. [Letter to Stravinsky from Chicago, September 8, 1934]

11. 1887–1978.

12. The following year, appealing indirectly to Marx to facilitate the procuring of travel documents for a voyage to New York, Stravinsky wrote to Rolland-Manuel: "I know Mr. Marx, who is a mixture of Jean Zey and Larmanjat. Marx is rather a nice man, deeply disturbed by the international situation. I think he was a member of the *front populaire*, but, in any case, he was a disciple of Léon Blum, which is not a very excellent thing!" (Sancellemoz, June 24, 1939)

13. A photograph of Mrs. Woolf was in Stravinsky's studio during all of the years that the present writer knew him.

1. The Trio Sonatas and String Concertinos from which Stravinsky borrowed were published in the eighteenth century, but this music is almost certainly not by Pergolesi. See, however, Katherine Hoover's *Pulcinella: Stravinsky's Homage to Pergolesi* (1972), a thesis on file at the Manhattan School of Music. Ms. Hoover fails to identify only one section, the *"più vivo"* between [20] and [23] . This music was taken from Pergolesi's canzona for bass, *"Benedetto Maledetto,"* except that Pergolesi's melody is in the key of G and begins on the tonic. In this instance, Stravinsky worked from a photostat of a manuscript copy.

2. In a letter to Willy Strecker, April 25, 1929, Stravinsky explains that Diaghilev had never rented the orchestra parts for *The Firebird*, since he had owned a set of them before the work had a publisher, but that Diaghilev had paid Stravinsky's "author's rights" for each "spectacle."

3. André Marion, husband of Stravinsky's younger daughter. Before World War II, he had worked in the commissary of a French shipping company.

4. The author's name is Jaime O'Farrill.

5. Needless to say, orchestra rehearsals cannot be "suddenly called" in Mexico City at night.

6. The recorded testimony of Dr. Henry Lax, Stravinsky's physician during the last fifteen months of the composer's life, is that Stravinsky's mental acuteness was unimpaired to the end.

7. See Paul Horgan's discussion of this problem in his *Encounters with Stravinsky*. In fact, no one was ever successful in the attempt to convey Stravinsky's Russian accent in English. Here is a typical example: "When Igor Stravinsky appeared . . . to guide the orchestra in his *Baiser de la Fée*, Alexandra Danilova . . . made a sweeping curtsy, the kind you make to royalty. Mr. Stravinsky bowed low in return. . . . 'Maestro Stravinsky!' announced the Ballets Russes's musical director, Emmanuel Balaban . . . and the musicians dropped their instruments to applaud. . . . Stravinsky was using [English] calmly and effectively on the awe-inspired orchestra. 'No, no, no,' he said quite gently to the bassoons. 'You are not short enough.' . . . His calm patience didn't leave him when he went over the same passage with the harpist for the fourth time. 'I don't like very motch your D,' he said. . . . The harpist retuned her D. 'Wance more,' and he moved the tempo as she played it again. 'Yes—now I like it very motch.' " (PM, New York, February 17, 1946. The rehearsal took place on February 14, and Stravinsky conducted his ballet on the 17th.)

8. Describing the will-signing ceremony, Miss Libman assures the reader that Stravinsky was " 'of sound mind,' . . . for when we greeted each other he whispered . . . 'I would like a Scotch' " (pp. 356–7). But the desire for alcohol is not generally considered to be evidence of mental competency, and, to some readers, the whole procedure might sound more like bamboozling.

9. This, the first of the Montapert wills, did not provide for Stravinsky's granddaughter, but made her the heir to the childless Theodore Stravinskys. The composer changed his will in order to give his granddaughter an equal share with his three surviving children.

10. Edwin Evans, in London, to Stravinsky, February 27, 1913: "Are the oysters good in Clarens?" Catherine Stravinsky to her husband, October 28, 1937: "I forgot to ask you not to eat oysters, as they made you vomit on two occasions last year. But I fear that you will eat them all the same."

"If it were up to Igor, he would have lived on oysters," Dagmar Godowsky wrote, correctly, in *First Person Plural*, a book with similarities to *And Music at the Close*, and whose chronological and other errors—in the latter part, concerning Stravinsky—are comparable. But, unlike Miss Libman, Miss Godowsky was actually close to Stravinsky (they both lived in New York's Navarro Hotel for a time in the autumn of 1939), as well as being his "personal manager" during a period—the late 1930s—when he actually needed one. Miss Godowsky's book has at least some value, too, since it contains the unique personal account of Stravinsky in South America in 1936. Reading her memoirs in 1959, Stravinsky expressed his horror by underscoring lines and by adding exclamation marks, most vehemently in connection with the statement:

"M. D'Anjou was not as generous as God." ("Monsieur D'Anjou" was an alias used by the composer in his communications with Miss Godowsky, 22 rue d'Anjou being the address of his Paris music-publishers.) What Stravinsky would have written in Miss Libman's book defies imagination—except that he might have died of apoplexy before finishing the introduction, which she concludes characteristically assuring the reader that Stravinsky "would have approved" the "proper mood of objectivity" (!!!) which she establishes.

11. For example, in an article on *Pulcinella* (*Tempo*, June 1973), Hans Keller remarks of Stravinsky's CBS recording of the work: "if indeed it is Stravinsky's own."

12. The score was assembled and edited by William Bernal, a screenwriter with a flair for this work.

13. Stravinsky tended to hide his acquisitions of Schoenberg's music. For example, instead of writing directly to Schoenberg's publishers, Stravinsky asked David Adams of Boosey & Hawkes to procure the orchestral and piano scores of the Piano Concerto. And a note, postmarked May 9, 1962, from John Roberts in Toronto, informs Stravinsky that Schoenberg's *Prelude* was photographed as requested before the score was returned to its publisher—Stravinsky having attended a recording session of the piece but evidently not wanting anyone to know of his great interest in it. Stravinsky's archives contain numerous letters to his publishers in London asking them to obtain tapes of works by Schoenberg from German radio stations and even the BBC. On September 23, 1963, Stravinsky wrote to E. Roth with instructions for the printing of *Abraham and Isaac*: "This vocal score should be sent to Israel and the adding of the Hebrew letters and the spelling of the English phonetics should be done according to the State rules or uses in the University. . . . This, incidentally, is how Schoenberg's *De Profundis* was published, Hebrew on top, Latin underneath, English in the flyleaf."

14. *Montjoie!* Paris, May 29, 1913.

15. Considerations of register are not essential to a discussion of harmonic organization, and, in any case, can hardly be separated from those of timbre, yet the "feature" of, for example, the first melody is as much the intensity of the high register of the bassoon as it is the "contour" or the "set." In another instrument, in normal register, the music could seem insignificant, inconceivable as the beginning of *The Rite of Spring*.

16. Among other features not covered is that of the relationship between harmony and tempo, or the rate of harmonic change in differing degrees of fixity and of flux. But the *reductio ad absurdum* of Forte's self-imposed limits is exemplified in his discussion of the "enigmatic" bass-clarinet figure three measures before the "Sacrificial Dance." Though at a loss to explain the harmonic implications of the music, he nevertheless does not mention the connection with the similar figure in the "Introduction" (at ⑥), which laymen listeners are quick to recognize for the reasons that the instrument and range are the same in both places, that the rhythm corresponds (five-note and eight-note groups), that the eight-note configurations resemble each other, and that both could hardly be more exposed.

17. See *Stravinsky*, by André Schaeffner (Paris, 1931).

18. Stravinsky adapted this melody from No. 157 in Juskiewicz's *Litauische Volksweisen* (Cracow, 1900).

19. Schaeffner, *op cit.*

20. The information in parentheses may be disregarded without jeopardizing comprehension of the present review, but the references are included for those who may wish to follow them. A "pitch class" is simply a note of the chromatic scale from C (numbered 0) to B (numbered 11). A "set" is a harmonic structure (formed linearly as well as vertically), and "32" is a further classification of the harmony.

21. 1889–1937. In *Hope Against Hope*, Nadyezhda Mandelstam describes Klychkov as "an outlandish but most gentle creature. . . . He was our neighbor for many years in Herzen House and then in Furmanov Street, and we were always very friendly with him. . . . Mandelstam very much admired Klychkov's cycle of poems on the theme of being an outcast, and often read passages from them." The verse chosen by Stravinsky is from *Songs*, published in January

1911. The book was reviewed by Serge Gorodyetsky, two of whose poems Stravinsky had set while still a pupil of Rimsky-Korsakov.

22. The Rite of Spring: *Sketches: 1911–1913* (London: Boosey & Hawkes, 1969). The title misleadingly implies that the sketches are complete.

23. The property of Serge Lifar, this score was on display in the Diaghilev Exhibition, Paris, 1972. The music differs substantially from the final version.

24. Forte calls this the "Piano Duet" and seems to think of it as an arrangement for two pianos. "In the duet score [in the second measure of 155] there is no change of harmony," he writes. But the harmony does change; the G-sharp is not doubled in the Seconda because it is being played in the Prima.

25. Errors abound in Forte's musical examples. To mention only a few, the last subset in Ex. L should have an E♭, not an E natural; the fermata in Ex. 8 should not be on B, but on G# (not given); in Ex. 9, the A should have the tie, not the D#; in Ex. 29, the hexachord contains a gratuitous seventh note; set 4-18 in Ex. 74 has, in the actual score, either six or seven notes, depending on the execution of the trill.

26. In one instance, the cello solo at the end of the "Introduction to Part II," Forte does not see that a set which neither fits nor follows, and which is insignificant in the work as a whole, was chosen for precisely these reasons—i.e., relief.

27. Forte's statement is misleading, that in the *Rite* "Stravinsky employed extensively for the first time the new harmonies that first emerged in the works of Schoenberg and Webern around 1907–08." Stravinsky did not find his harmonies in these works, which he had not yet heard or seen, but created his harmonic system independently. In 1924, questioned by an interviewer for a Prague music magazine as to which pieces by Schoenberg Stravinsky had heard, Stravinsky answered, "Only *Pierrot Lunaire*."

Index

Foss, Lukas, 476
Fountain, The (Morgan), 321
Four Etudes for Orchestra, 438
Four Norwegian Moods (S.), 370
Fox Strangways, A. H., 126–127
Fraggi, Hector, 214
France, La, 53, 90, 94, 101, 376
Frances, Esteban, 379
François-Poncet, Ambassador André, 555
Frankenstein, Alfred, 642, Plate 1
Frankfurter Zeitung, 123
French Academy, 82, 342
Freud, Sigmund, 350, 649
Freund, Marya, 617, 623
Fromm, Paul, 449
Fuchs, George, 55
Fuller, Loïe, 53
Furman, Roman (great-grandfather), Plate 1
Furtwängler, Wilhelm, 310, 530, 639, 659

Gagnebin, Elie, 261, 623, 626
Gallié, Louis, 503
Gallimard, Gaston, 110
Gandarillas, Juanita, 618
Gandarillas, Tony, 476, 618
Gatti, Guido, 281
Gatti-Casazza, Giulio, 134
Gaudichon, Dr. F., 300
Gazette de Lausanne, 169
Gazette des Lettres, La, 350
Geddes, Norman Bel, 369
Gellhorn, Martha, 557
Gémier, Firmin, 283
Genealogical table, 188–189
Genet, Jean, 473
Georges-Michel, Michel, 277, 549
Gerasim, Father, 638
Gerisovsky, Valerian Bogdanovich, 469
Gershwin, George, 360, 647
Gesualdo di Venosa, Carlo, 456–457, 643
Gide, André, 36, 111, 161–163, 199, 313–319, 372
Gieseking, Walter, 436
Gil Blas (magazine), 100–101, 119
Gilliard, Edmond, 162
Gilot, Françoise, 183
Giordano, Umberto, 413
Glazunov, Alexander, 19, 22, 52, 142, 201, 607
Glebov, Igor (pseud. of Boris Asafiev), 494
Glière, Reinhold, 556

Gliklich, Alexander, 607
Glinka, Mikhail, 232, 233, 635
Glock, Sir William, 440, 442
Gnessen, M. F., 54, 67, 609
Godebski, Cipa, 656
Godet, Robert, 64, 66, 611
Godowsky, Dagmar, 330, 331, 633, 639, 660, 663–664
Godowsky, Leopold, 331, 555
Gold, Arthur, 514
Goldfarb, Herman, 377
Goldman, Milton, 494
Goldmark, Aaron, 377
Goldner, Nancy, 565
Goldoni, Carlo, 118
Goldstein, Sylvia, 403
Goldwyn, Sam, 325–326
Gollancz, Victor, 319
Golovine, A. J. (1863–1930), 58, 611
Goncharov, I. A., 235
Goncharova, Nathalie, 135, 162, 179, 235, 603, 617, 621–622
Goodman, Benny, 368
Goossens, Eugene, 224, 287, 531, 659
Gorky, Maxim, 239, 549
Gorodyetsky, Serge, 608, 665, Plate 10
Gosling, Nigel, 67, 440, 447
Gounod, Charles, 42, 302, 303, 353, 624, 644
Gozenpud, A., 562
Graener, Paul, 554
Graff, Robert, 453, 463, 467
Graham, Martha, 655
Grammar of Assent (Newman), 400
Gramophone, 494
Grande Revue, La, 87
Great Morning (Osbert Sitwell), 120
Great Russian Songs and Folk Harmonizations (Linevaya), 28
Green, Henry (pseud. of Henry Yorke), 447
Greffuhle, Comtesse, 31
Greissle, Felix, 637
Grigoriev, Serge, 93, 105
Gringoire (Paris newspaper), 299
Grove, Edith, 122
Grovlez, Gabriel, 47, 171
Guard, William, 134–135
Gueden, Hilde, 418
Guggenheim Foundation, The, 398
Gulbenkian Foundation, The, 418, 480
Günther, Dr. Felix, 368
Gurevich, J. G. (1844–1906), 54, 609
Gustave VI Adolphe, King of Sweden, 462
Guyau, Marie-Jean, 20